Psychology of Race & Ethnic Relations

EDITED BY LISA HARRISON AND HUGH VILLALTA

City College of San Francisco

Taken from:

Strangers to These Shores, Seventh Edition
by Vincent N. Parrillo

Understanding Race and Ethnic Relations, Second Edition
by Vincent N. Parrillo

The Psychology of Prejudice
by Todd D. Nelson

Cover Art: *Simultaneous Formation*, by Robin MacDonald-Foley

Taken from:

Strangers to These Shores: Race and Ethnic Relations in the United States, Seventh Edition
by Vincent N. Parrillo
Copyright © 2003, 2000, 1997, 1994, 1990, 1985 by Pearson Education, Inc.
Published by Allyn and Bacon
Boston, Massachusetts 02116

Understanding Race and Ethnic Relations, Second Edition
by Vincent N. Parillo
Copyright © 2005, 2002 by Pearson Education, Inc.
Published by Allyn and Bacon

The Psychology of Prejudice
by Todd D. Nelson
Copyright © 2002 by Allyn and Bacon

Copyright © 2004 by Pearson Custom Publishing
All rights reserved.

Printed in the United States of America

10 9 8 7 6 5

ISBN 0-536-83509-8

2004500073

SR/JM

Please visit our web site at *www.pearsoncustom.com*

PEARSON CUSTOM PUBLISHING
75 Arlington Street, Suite 300, Boston, MA 02116
A Pearson Education Company

Brief Contents

1 The Study of Minorities

We pride ourselves on being a nation of immigrants. Many still call the United States a great melting pot where people of all races, religions, and nationalities come to be free and to improve their lives. Certainly, a great number of immigrants offer living testimony to that ideal; their enthusiasm for their adopted country is evident in countless interviews found in oral histories at Ellis Island and elsewhere. As college students, regardless of how long ago your family emigrated to the United States, most of you also provide evidence of the American Dream of freedom of choice, economic opportunity, and upward mobility.

Yet beneath the Fourth of July speeches, the nation's absorption of diverse peoples over the years, and the numerous success stories lies a disquieting truth. Native-born Americans have not always welcomed newcomers with open arms; indeed, they have often responded with overt acts of discrimination, ranging from avoidance to violence and murder. The dominant group's treatment of native-born Blacks and Native Americans disturbingly illustrates the persistence of subjugation and entrenched inequality. Today, we continue to face serious problems in attitudes toward and treatment of Native Americans on reservations, poor Blacks in urban ghettos, and large concentrations of recent Asian and Hispanic immigrants. For some, the American Dream becomes a reality; for others, blocked opportunities create an American nightmare.

Interethnic tensions and hostilities within a nation's borders are a worldwide phenomenon dating from thousands of years ago to the present. In 2001, we witnessed the horror of the terrorist attacks in New York and Washington, D.C. Car bombings and suicide bombers continue throughout the world. In the 1990s, we saw the tragedy of Orthodox Christian Serbs expelling and killing Bosnian Muslims in the name of "ethnic cleansing," and then, in 1999, the tragedy in Kosovo where Serb killing and expulsion of ethnic Albanians prompted NATO military action. In Rwanda in 1994, tribal warfare between the Tutsi and Hutu led to the massacre of hundreds of thousands. Religious factions in the Middle East and Northern Ireland still harbor animosity toward one another. Animosity also persists among the Hausa, Ibo, and Yoruba tribes of Nigeria, among whom a bloody war raged in the 1980s. A few years earlier, appalling bloodbaths among Kampucheans (Cambodians), Chinese,

Laotians, and Vietnamese horrified the world. In 1988, Iraq killed thousands of Kurds, including infants and children, with poison gas. Elsewhere, other minorities, such as West Indians in Britain, Algerians in France, Turks in Germany, Romany (Gypsies) in the Czech Republic, and Palestinians in Israel, have encountered prejudice, discrimination, and physical attacks. Within any society, groupings of people by race, religion, tribe, culture, or lifestyle can generate prejudices, tensions, and sporadic outbursts of violence.

Individuals of the dominant group usually absolve themselves of blame for a minority group's low status and problems, ascribing these instead to specific flaws they perceive within the group itself (e.g., slowness in learning the main language of the country or supposed lack of the work ethic). Sociologists, however, note among different groups distinct patterns of interaction that transcend national boundaries, specific periods, or idiosyncrasies of particular groups. Opinions may vary as to the causes of these patterns of behavior, but a consensus does exist about their presence.

The Stranger as a Social Phenomenon

To understand intergroup relations, we must recognize that differences among various peoples cause each group to look on other groups as strangers. Among isolated peoples, the arrival of a stranger has always been a momentous occasion, often eliciting strong emotional responses. Reactions might range from warm hospitality to conciliatory or protective ceremonies to hostile acts. In an urbanized and mobile society, the stranger still evokes similar responses. From the Tiwi of northern Australia, who consistently killed intruders, to the nativists of any country or time, who continually strive to keep out "undesirable elements," the underlying premise is the same: The outsiders are not good enough to share the land and resources with the "chosen people" already there.

Similarity and Attraction

At least since Aristotle (384–322 BCE) commented, "We like those who resemble us, and are engaged in the same pursuits," social observers have been aware of the similarity-attraction relationship.[1] Numerous studies have explored the extent to which a person likes others because of similar attitudes, values, beliefs, social status, or physical appearance. Examining the development of attraction among people who are initially strangers to one another, an impressive number of these studies have found a positive relationship between the similarity of two people and their liking for each other. Most significantly, the findings show that people's perception of similarity between themselves is a more powerful determinant than actual similarity.[2] Cross-cultural studies also support this conclusion.[3] Considerable evidence exists showing greater human receptivity to strangers who are perceived as similar than to those who are perceived as different.

Social Distance

One excellent technique for evaluating how perceptions of similarity attract closer interaction patterns consists of ranking **social distance**. Devised by Emory Bogardus in 1926, this measurement device has been used repeatedly since then.[4] In five comparable studies spanning 50 years, researchers obtained responses from a fairly evenly divided group of undergraduate and graduate students aged 18 to 35, about 10 percent of whom were Black. The students selected the degree of social closeness or distance personally acceptable to members of a particular group.

These five national surveys measured the students' preferences among thirty groups, most of them Europeans but also including Native Americans, Canadians, Black Americans, and six Asian groups (Asian Indians, Chinese, Filipinos, Japanese, Japanese Americans, and Koreans). Some fluctuation occurred over the 50-year span of these surveys, most notably Blacks moving upward from near the bottom to the middle. Generally, the distribution showed White Americans, Canadians, northern and western Europeans in the top third, with southern, central, and eastern Europeans in the middle third, and racial minorities in the bottom third.

With a few exceptions, the relatively consistent positioning of response patterns illustrates the similarity-attraction relationship. Italians have moved up steadily, becoming the first group not from northwest Europe to break into the top ten. The leap upward by Blacks was even more dramatic, from near the bottom to the midpoint. International politics or war usually causes groups to drop: Germans, Italians, and Japanese in 1946 and Russians after 1946 (Cold War, McCarthyism, Vietnam).[5] However, the political changes Russia underwent in the 1990s enabled Russians to rise to fourteenth place in a smaller 1993 study.[6]

In 2001, this author updated both the wording of the choices and the list of groups.[7] I eliminated mostly homogenized groups (e.g., Armenians, Czechs, Finns, Norwegians, Scots, and Swedes) and added various Asian, Hispanic, and West Indian groups. In this new national study, the available choices were:

1. Would accept marrying into my family (1 point).
2. Would accept as a personal friend in my social circle (2 points).
3. Would accept as a neighbor on my street (3 points).
4. Would work in the same office (4 points).
5. Would only have as speaking acquaintances (5 points).
6. Would only have as visitors to my country (6 points).
7. Would bar from entering my country (7 points).

As expected, nonethnic Whites remained in the top position as the most accepted group, with other top-ten slots filled by Canadians, British, Irish, French, Germans, and Dutch, essentially continuing a 70-year pattern. What is particularly striking about the new listing, however, is the dramatic rise of African Americans. In placing ninth, they broke the racial barrier in entering the top sector and placing ahead of other White ethnic groups. The rise of Italians into the second position ahead of the previously dominating English, Canadians, and French, as well as the movement of Greeks into the seventh position, were other significant changes. However, only one-hundredth of a point separates a group from the next ranked group in positions 13 through 25. Therefore, in the middle part of the list in Table 1.1, the exact placement of a group in relation to those near it should not be given much importance, in view of the close scores, because these rankings may be the result of sampling variability.

Although this analysis is not directly comparable with the 1977 data in Table 1.1 because of changes in the list of groups, some comparisons are still possible and the findings are encouraging in many ways. The spread in social distance—despite (1) increased diversity in society, (2) a revised list reflecting that demographic reality, and (3) increased diversity among respondents—continues to shrink. The 2001 overall mean score of 1.44 is significantly lower than the 1977 overall mean score of 1.93, as is the spread in social distance of 0.87 compared with 1.38. Despite the removal of more assimilated groups and the addition of less assimilated groups to the list, the downward trend in both indicators of social distance has continued. These results suggest a growing level of acceptance of diverse groups, even though many are recent arrivals, racial minorities, and/or from non-Western lands.

Remarkably, despite media reports of sporadic instances in the 9/11 aftermath of group blame and hate crimes against those identified (sometimes erroneously) as Arabs or Muslims, that mindset did not extend to most respondents in this survey. Although relegating Muslims and Arabs to the bottom, respondents nevertheless gave them lower (i.e., more socially acceptable) mean scores than those received by seventeen of the thirty groups in the 1977 study. Their distinction between the ethnicity of the terrorists and others who were Arabs and/or Muslims resulted in even lower scores than given to past low-ranked groups, which is indeed an impressive finding.

The ranking of Muslims and Arabs in the last two places is hardly surprising as a repercussion of the terrorist attacks, but how do we explain their comparatively low social distance nonetheless? Perhaps the answer is the same as for the strong findings for African Americans and other groups as well. This study may bear witness to a "unity syndrome," the coalescing of various groups against a common enemy who attacked us. Only time will tell how lasting this new spirit is, both in the bottom rankings of Muslims and Arabs and in the low social distance scores for all groups. This study only captures social acceptance of groups at a given moment in time, on the heels of 9/11. It is neither conclusive nor yet indicative of new patterns. Future social distance studies incorporating the new groups will ideally give a clearer picture of how tolerant Americans are in their ever-growing multiracial, multicultural society.

Sometimes the social distance maintained between minority groups is greater than that preserved between each minority and the dominant group. For example, a 1989 study of 708 Anglos, 249 Blacks, and 256 Mexican Americans in Texas found Blacks and Mexican Americans more accepting of Anglos than of each other. However, higher-status members (those having more education and

TABLE 1.1 U.S. Social Distance Changes, 1977 and 2001

1977		2001	
1. Americans (U.S. Whites)	1.25	1. Americans (U.S. Whites)	1.07
2. English	1.39	2. Italians	1.15
3. Canadians	1.42	3. Canadians	1.20
4. French	1.58	4. British	1.23
5. Italians	1.65	5. Irish	1.24
6. Swedish	1.68	6. French	1.28
7. Irish	1.69	7. Greeks	1.32
8. Hollanders	1.83	8. Germans	1.33
9. Scots	1.83	9. African Americans	1.34
10. Indians (American)	1.84	10. Dutch	1.35
11. Germans	1.87	11. Jews	1.38
12. Norwegians	1.93	12. Indians (American)	1.40
13. Spanish	1.98	13. Africans	1.43
14. Finns	2.00	14. Polish	1.44
15. Jews	2.01	15. Other Hispanic/Latino	1.45
16. Greeks	2.02	16. Filipinos	1.46
17. Negroes	2.03	17. Chinese	1.47
18. Poles	2.11	18. Puerto Ricans	1.48
19. Mexican Americans	2.17	19. Jamaicans	1.49
20. Japanese Americans	2.18	20. Russians	1.50
21. Armenians	2.20	21. Dominicans	1.51
22. Czechs	2.23	22. Japanese	1.52
23. Chinese	2.29	23. Cubans	1.53
24. Filipinos	2.31	24. Koreans	1.54
25. Japanese	2.38	25. Mexicans	1.55
26. Mexicans	2.40	26. Indians (from India)	1.60
27. Turks	2.55	27. Haitians	1.63
28. Indians (from India)	2.55	28. Vietnamese	1.69
29. Russians	2.57	29. Muslims	1.88
30. Koreans	2.63	30. Arabs	1.94
Arithmetic mean of 44,640		Arithmetic mean of 126,053	
racial reactions	1.93	racial reactions	1.44
Spread in distance	1.38	Spread in distance	0.87

Sources: Carolyn A. Owen, Howard C. Eisner, and Thomas R. McFaul, "A Half-Century of Social Distance Research: National Replication of the Bogardus Studies," *Sociology and Social Research* 66 (October 1981): 89; and Vincent N. Parrillo and Christopher Donoghue, "Updating the Bogardus Social Distance Studies: A New National Survey," *The Social Science Journal,* forthcoming.

higher incomes) and youths of all three groups were generally more accepting of contact with the outgroup minority than were lower-status group members.[8]

Another interesting aspect of social distance appears to be its relationship to the rates at which immigrants become citizens. A 1990 study found that immigrants belonging to ethnic groups less accepted by Americans were five times more likely to become American citizens than immigrants of low social distance who were otherwise similarly situated.[9] Perhaps the relatively low level of social acceptance impels these immigrants to seek citizenship to gain at least a legal acknowledgment that they belong.

Perceptions

By definition, the stranger is not only an outsider but also someone different and personally unknown. People perceive strangers primarily through **categoric knowing**—the classification of others on the basis of limited information obtained visually and perhaps verbally.[10] People make judgments and generalizations on the basis of scanty information, confusing an individual's characteristics with typical group-member characteristics. For instance, if a visiting Swede asks for tea rather than coffee, the host may incorrectly conclude that all Swedes dislike coffee.

Native-born Americans have in the past perceived immigrants—first-generation Americans of different racial and ethnic groups—as a particular kind of stranger: one who intends to stay. Eventually, the presence of immigrants became less of a novelty; then fear, suspicion, and distrust often replaced the natives' initial curiosity. The strangers remained strangers as each group sought its own kind for personal interaction.

The role of a stranger can be analyzed regardless of the particular period in history: Georg Simmel (1858–1918) theorized that strangers represent both *nearness*, because they are physically close, and *remoteness*, because they react differently to the immediate situation and have different values and ways of doing things.[11] The stranger is both inside and outside: physically present and participating but also outside the situation as a result of being from another place.

The natives perceive the stranger in an abstract, typified way. That is, the individual becomes the *totality*, or stereotype, of the group. The stranger, however, perceives the natives in concrete, individual terms. Simmel suggested that strangers have a higher degree of objectivity about the natives because the strangers' geographical mobility reflects mobility in their minds as well. The stranger is free from indigenous habit, piety, and precedent. Furthermore, because strangers do not participate fully in society, they have a certain mental detachment, causing them to see things more objectively.

Interactions

Simmel approached the role of the stranger through an analysis of the formal structures of life. In contrast, Alfred Schutz (1899–1959)—himself an immigrant to the United States—analyzed the stranger as lacking "intersubjective understanding."[12] By this he meant that people from the same social world mutually "know" the language (including slang), customs, beliefs, symbols, and everyday behavior patterns that the stranger usually does not.

For the native, then, every social situation is a coming together not only of roles and identities but also of shared realities—the intersubjective structure of consciousness. What is taken for granted by the native is problematic to the stranger. In a familiar world, people live through the day by responding to daily routines without questions or reflection. To strangers, however, every situation is new and is therefore experienced as a crisis.

Strangers experience a "lack of historicity"—a lack of the shared memories of those with whom they live. Human beings who interact together over a period of time "grow old together"; strangers, however, are "young" because they are newcomers, and they experience at least an approximation of the freshness of childhood. They are aware of things that go unnoticed by the natives, such as the natives' customs, social institutions, appearance, and lifestyle.

Sometimes the stranger may be made the comical butt of jokes because of unfamiliarity with the everyday routine of life in the new setting. In time, however, strangers take on the natives' perspective; the strangers' consciousness lessens because the freshness of their perceptions is lost. Concurrently, the natives' **abstract typifications** about the strangers become more concrete through social interaction. As Schutz said, "The vacant frames become occupied by vivid experiences." As acculturation takes place, the native begins to view the stranger more concretely, and the stranger becomes less questioning about daily activities. Use of the term *naturalized citizen* takes on a curious connotation when examined from this perspective because it implies that people are in some way odd or unnatural until they have acquired the characteristics of the natives.

Many strangers have come—and are still coming—to the United States in search of a better life. Through an examination of sociological theory and the experiences of these many racial and ethnic groups, the story of how the stranger perceives the society and is received by it will continually be retold. The adjustment from stranger to neighbor may be viewed as movement along a continuum, but this continuum is not frictionless, and assimilation is not inevitable. Rather, it is the process of social interaction among different groups of people.

A Sociological Perspective

Sociology is the study of human relationships and patterns of behavior. Through scientific investigation, sociologists seek to determine the social forces that influence behavior as well as to identify recurring patterns that help them and others better understand that behavior.

Using historical documents, reports, surveys, ethnographies, journalistic materials, and direct observation, sociologists systematically gather empirical evidence about intergroup relations. The sociologist then analyzes these data in an effort to discover and describe the causes, functions, relationships, meanings, and consequences of intergroup harmony or tension. Ascertaining reasons for the beginning, continuance, intensification, or alleviation of readily observable patterns of behavior among different peoples is complex and difficult, and not all sociologists concur when interpreting the data. Different theories, ideas, concepts, and even ideologies and prejudices may influence a sociologist's conclusions too.

Disagreement among sociologists is no more unusual than in other areas of scientific investigation, where such matters as how the universe was created, what constitutes a mental disorder, or whether heredity or environment is more important in shaping behavior are discussed. Nonetheless, differing sociological theories have played an important role in influencing the pattern of relations and are grounded in the social scientists' values regarding those relations. In sociological investigation, three major perspectives shape analysis of the study of minorities: functional theory, conflict theory, and interactionist theory. Each has a contribution to make, for each acts as a different lens providing a distinct focus on the subject.

Functional Theory

Proponents of **functional theory,** such as Talcott Parsons (1902–1979) and Robert Merton (1910–2003), believe that a stable, cooperative social system is the basis of society. All the elements of a society function together to maintain order and stability. Under ideal conditions, a society would be in a state of balance, with all its parts interacting harmoniously. Problems arise when parts of the social system become dysfunctional and upset the society's equilibrium. This system disorganization can occur for many reasons, but the most frequent cause is rapid social change. Changes in one part of the system necessitate compensatory adjustments elsewhere, but these usually do not occur fast enough, resulting in tensions and conflict.

Functionalists view dysfunctions as temporary maladjustments to an otherwise interdependent and relatively harmonious society. Because this perspective focuses on societal stability, the key issue in this analysis of social disorganization is whether to restore the equilibrium to its predisturbance state or to seek a new and different equilibrium. For example, how do we overcome the problem of undocumented aliens? Do we expel them to eliminate their exploitation, their alleged depression of regional wage scales, and their high costs to taxpayers in the form of health, education, and welfare benefits? Or do we grant them amnesty, help them enter the economic mainstream, and seal our borders against further undocumented entries? Whatever the solution—and these two suggestions do not exhaust the possibilities—functionalists emphasize that all problems regarding minorities can be resolved through adjustments to the social system that restore it to a state of equilibrium.

Conflict Theory

Proponents of **conflict theory,** influenced by Karl Marx's socioeconomic view of an elite exploiting the masses, see society as continually engaged in a series of disagreements, tensions, and clashes as different groups compete for limited resources. Rejecting the functionalist model of societal parts that usually work harmoniously, conflict theorists see disequilibrium and change as the norm. Their focus is on the inequalities that generate racial and ethnic antagonisms between groups. To explain why discrimination persists, conflict theorists ask this question: Who benefits? Those already in power—employers and holders of wealth and property—exploit the powerless, seeking additional profits at the expense of unassimilated minorities. Because lower wages allow higher profits, ethnic discrimination serves the interests of investors and owners by weakening workers' bargaining power.

By putting economics into perspective, Marxist analysis offers penetrating insight into intergroup relations, but John Solomos and Les Back argue that this methodology does not provide a substantial explanation for contemporary racism and its associated problems.[13] Conflict theorists counter that racism has much to do with maintaining power and controlling resources. Racism is an **ideology**—a set of generalized beliefs used to explain and justify the interests of those who hold them.

In this sense, **false consciousness**—holding attitudes that do not accurately reflect the objective facts of the situation—exists, impelling workers to adopt attitudes that run counter to their own real interests. If workers believe that the economic gains by workers of other groups would adversely affect their own living standards, they will not support actions to end discriminatory practices. If workers struggling to improve their situation believe other groups entrenched in better job positions are holding them back, they will view their own gains as possible only at the expense of the better-established groups. In both cases, the wealthy and powerful benefit by pitting exploited workers of different racial and ethnic groups against each other, causing each to have strong negative feelings about the others. This distorted view foments conflict and occasional outbursts of violence between groups, preventing workers from recognizing their common bond of joint oppression and uniting to overcome it.[14]

Interactionist Theory

A third theoretical approach, **interactionist theory,** examines the microsocial world of personal interaction patterns in everyday life (e.g., social distance when talking, individual use of commonly understood terms) rather than the macrosocial aspects of social institutions and their harmony or conflict. **Symbolic interaction**—the shared symbols and definitions people use when communicating with one another—provides the focus for understanding how individuals create and interpret the life situations they experience. Symbols— such as our spoken language, expressions, body language, tone of voice, appearance, and images on television and other mass media—are what constitute our social worlds.[15] By means of these symbols, we communicate, create impressions, and develop understandings of the surrounding world. Symbolic interaction theories are useful in understanding race and ethnic relations because they assume that minority groups are responsive and creative rather than passive.[16]

Essential to this perspective, according to Peter L. Berger and Thomas Luckmann, is how people define their reality through a process they called the **social construction of reality**.[17] Individuals create a background against which to understand their separate actions and interactions with others. In a continuing social situation, the participants' interactions create a shared history resulting in **reciprocal typifications**—mutual categorizations—of one another. Taken-for-granted routines emerge on the basis of shared expectations. Participants see this socially constructed world as legitimate by virtue of its "objective" existence. When problems arise, specific "universe-maintenance" procedures become necessary to preserve stability; such conceptual machineries as mythology, theology, philosophy, and science may be used for this purpose. In short, people create cultural products: material artifacts, social institutions, ideologies, and so on (externalization). Over time, they lose awareness of having created their own social and cultural environment (objectification); and subsequently, they learn these supposedly objective facts of reality through the socialization process (internalization).

Figure 1.1 summarizes the three sociological perspectives discussed here.

FIGURE 1.1   Sociological Perspectives

Functional Theory
- A stable, cooperative social system in which everything has a function and provides the basis of a harmonious society.
- Societal elements function together to maintain order, stability, and equilibrium.
- Social problems, or dysfunctions, result from temporary disorganization or maladjustment.
- Rapid social change is the most frequent cause of loss of societal equilibrium.
- Necessary adjustments will restore the social system to a state of equilibrium.

Conflict Theory
- Society is continually engaged in a series of disagreements, tensions, and clashes.
- Conflict is inevitable because new elites form, even after the previously oppressed group "wins."
- Disequilibrium and change are the norm because of societal inequalities.
- If we know who benefits from exploitation, we understand why discrimination persists.
- False consciousness is a technique by which a ruling elite maintains power and control of resources.
- Group cohesiveness and struggle against oppression are necessary to effect social change.

Interactionist Theory
- This theory focuses on the microsocial world of personal interaction patterns in everyday life.
- Shared symbols and definitions provide the basis for interpreting life experiences.
- A social construction of reality becomes internalized, making it seem to those who adopt it as if it were objective fact.
- Shared expectations and understandings, or the absence of these, explain intergroup relations.
- Better communication and intercultural awareness improve majority–minority interaction patterns.

Minority Groups

Sociologists use the term *group* to refer to collectivities of different sizes. Often, a **group** connotes a small, closely interacting set of persons. A **secondary group** consists of people who interact on an impersonal or limited emotional basis for some practical or specific purpose. Larger still, a group such as a *minority* can refer to an aggregate of millions of people. Throughout this book, I will use the term *group* in this broad sense when referring to minorities because groups and group identity are important components of racial and ethnic relations.

Development of a Definition

Sociologists use the term **minority group** to indicate a group's relative power and status in a society, not to designate its numerical representation. The term was first used in the World War I peace treaties to protect approximately 22 million of 110 million people in east central Europe, but it was most frequently used as a description of biological features or national traits. Donald Young in 1932 thus observed that Americans make distinctions among people according to race and national origin.[18]

Louis Wirth expanded Young's original conception of minority groups to include the consequences of those distinctions: group consciousness and differential treatment.[19] Wirth's contribution marked two important turning points in sociological inquiry. First, by broadening the definition of minority group to encompass any physical or cultural trait instead of just race or national origin, Wirth enlarged the range of variables to include also the aged, people with disabilities, members of various religions or sects, and groups with unconventional lifestyles. Second, his emphasis on the social consequences of minority status leads to a focus on prejudice, discrimination, and oppression. Not everyone agrees with this approach. Richard Schermerhorn, for example, notes that this "victimological" approach does not adequately explain the similarities and differences among groups or analyze relationships between majority and minority groups.[20]

A third attempt to define minority groups rests on examining relationships between groups in terms of each group's position in the social hierarchy.[21] This approach stresses a group's social power, which may vary from one country to another as, for example, does that of the Jews in Russia and in Israel. The emphasis on stratification instead of population size explains situations in which a relatively small group subjugates a larger number of people (e.g., the European colonization of African and Asian populations). Schermerhorn adopts a variation on this viewpoint. He also viewed social power as an important variable in determining a group's position in the hierarchy, but he believes that other factors are equally important. Size (a minority group must be less than one half the population), ethnicity (as defined by Wirth's physical and cultural traits), and group consciousness also help define a minority group.[22]

Minority-Group Characteristics

As social scientists reached some consensus on a definition of minority groups, anthropologists Charles Wagley and Marvin Harris identified five characteristics shared by minorities worldwide:

1. The group receives unequal treatment as a group.
2. The group is easily identifiable because of distinguishing physical or cultural characteristics that are held in low esteem.
3. The group feels a sense of peoplehood—that each of them shares something in common with other members.
4. Membership in the minority group has **ascribed status:** One is born into it.
5. Group members practice **endogamy:** They tend to marry within their group, either by choice or by necessity because of their social isolation.[23]

In our discussion of racial and ethnic minorities, these five features provide helpful guidelines. However, we should also understand that the last two characteristics do not apply to certain other types of minority groups: Women constitute a minority group, whether married or not, as do the aged or people with disabilities. One is not born old, and people with disabilities are not always born that way.

Because our discussion of various minority groups rests on their subordination to a more powerful, although not necessarily larger group, we will use the term **dominant group** when referring to a minority group's relationships with the rest of society. Another consideration is that a person may be a member of both dominant and minority groups in different categories. For example, an American Roman Catholic who is White belongs to a prominent religious minority group but also is a member of the racially dominant group.

Racial and Ethnic Groups

Race may seem at first glance an easy way to group people, but it is not. The more than 6 billion humans inhabiting this planet exhibit a wide range of physical differences in body build, hair texture, facial features, and skin color. Centuries of migration, conquest, intermarriage, and evolutionary physical adaptation to the environment have caused these varieties. Anthropologists have attempted racial categorizations, ranging from three to more than a hundred. Some, such as Ashley Montagu, even argue that only one race exists—the human race.[24] Just as anthropologists apply different interpretations to biological groupings, so do most people. It is by examining these social interpretations that sociologists attempt to analyze and explain racial prejudice.

Racial classification is a sociopolitical construct, not a biological absolute. In Latin America, various gradations of race exist, reflecting the multiracial heritage of the people. More than 3 million people of mixed racial parentage live in the United States, where there is a more rigid racial categorization. Some social scientists have recently called for the "deconstruction of race," arguing against the artificial boundaries that promote racial prejudice.[25]

Racism may be defined as linking the biological conditions of a human organism with alleged sociocultural capabilities and behavior to assert the superiority of one race. When people believe that one race is superior to another because of economic advantages or specific achievements, racist thinking prevails. The subordinate group experiences prejudice and discrimination, which the dominant group justifies by reference to such invidious perceptions. In addition to Blacks and Native Americans, Asians, Hispanics, and even White southern Europeans have encountered hostility because of social categorizations of their abilities based simply on their physical appearance.

Members of an ethnic group (which may or may not be racially different from the dominant group in a society) have a common cultural heritage. As Max Weber observed, they share a sense of belonging based on national origin, language, religion, and other cultural attributes.

The word *race* often is incorrectly used as a social rather than a biological concept. Thus, the British and Japanese are frequently classified as races, as are Hindus, Latins, Aryans, Gypsies, Arabs, Native Americans, Basques, and Jews.[26] Many people—even sociologists, anthropologists, and psychologists—use race in a general sense that includes racial and ethnic groups, thereby giving the term both a biological and a social meaning. *Ethnic group* is now commonly used to include the three elements of race, religion, and national origin.[27] Such varied use of these terms results in endless confusion because racial distinctions are socially defined categories based on physical distinctions. Some groups, such as African Americans, were once defined on racial grounds but emerged as ethnocultural groups. Various ethnic groups often get lumped together in much broader racial categories—for example, Asians and Native Americans.

In this book, the word *race* will refer to the common social distinctions made on the basis of physical appearance. The term *ethnic group* will refer only to social groupings that the dominant group considers unique because of religious, linguistic, or cultural characteristics. Both terms will be used in discussing groups whose racial and ethnic characteristics overlap.

Ethnocentrism

Understanding the concept of the stranger is important to understanding **ethnocentrism**—a "view of things in which one's own group is the center of everything, and all others are scaled and rated with reference to it."[28] Ethnocentrism thus refers to people's tendency to identify with their own ethnic or national group as a means of fulfilling their needs for group belongingness and security. (The word is derived from two Greek words: *ethnos*, meaning "nation," and *kentron*, meaning "center.") As a result of ethnocentrism, people usually view their own cultural values as somehow more real than, and therefore superior to, those of other groups, and they prefer their own way of doing things. Unfortunately for human relations, such ethnocentric thought is often extended until it negatively affects attitudes toward and emotions about those who are perceived as different.

Sociologists define an **ingroup** as a group to which individuals belong and feel loyal; thus, everyone—whether a member of a majority group or a minority group—is part of an ingroup. An **outgroup** is defined, in relation to ingroups, as groups consisting of all people who are not members of one's ingroup. Studying majority groups as ingroups helps us understand their reactions to strangers of another race or culture entering their society. Conversely, considering minority groups as ingroups enables us to understand their efforts to maintain their ethnic identity and solidarity in the midst of the dominant culture.

From European social psychologists comes one of the more promising explanations for ingroup favoritism. **Social identity theory** holds that ingroup members almost automatically think of their group as being better than outgroups because doing so enhances their own social status or social identity and thus raises the value of their personal identity or self-image.[29]

There is ample evidence about people from past civilizations who have regarded other cultures as inferior, incorrect, or immoral. This assumption that *we* are better than *they* are generally results in outgroups becoming objects of ridicule, contempt, or hatred. Such attitudes may lead to stereotyping, prejudice, discrimination, and even violence. What actually occurs depends on many factors, including structural and economic conditions; these factors will be discussed in subsequent chapters.

Despite its ethnocentric beliefs, the ingroup does not always view the outgroup as inferior. In numerous documented cases, groups have retained their values and standards while recognizing the superiority of another group in specific areas.[30] Moreover, countless people reject their own ingroup by becoming "voluntary exiles, expatriates, outgroup emulators, social climbers, renegades, and traitors."[31] An outgroup may become a positive **reference group**—that is, it may serve as an exemplary model—if members of the ingroup perceive it as having a conspicuous advantage over them in terms of survival or adaptation to the environment, success in warfare, a stronger political structure, greater wealth, or a higher occupational status.[32]

Ethnocentrism is an important factor in determining minority-group status in society, but because of many variations in intergroup relations, it alone cannot explain the causes of prejudice. For example, majority-group members may view minority groups with suspicion, but not all minority groups become the targets of extreme prejudice and discrimination.

Some social-conflict theorists argue that when the ingroup perceives the outgroup as a serious threat competing for scarce resources, the ingroup reacts with increased solidarity and ethnocentrism—and concomitant prejudice, discrimination, and hostility toward the outgroup.[33] According to this view, the degree of this hostility depends on several economic and geographic

"Free Trade Lunch"

The immigrant laborer often was seen as an economic threat. Here English, Italian, Mexican, Russian, and German immigrants are shown devouring meat, symbolizing American workingmen's wages, and bread, symbolizing prosperity. In the background, immigrants are shown preventing the American laborer from entering the restaurant to get his share of the free lunch. This cartoon appeared in *Judge* on July 28, 1888.

(*Source:* The Distorted Image, courtesy John and Selma Appel Collection)

considerations. It would thus appear that ethnocentrism leads to negative consequences when the ingroup feels threatened. One counterargument to this view is that ethnocentric attitudes—thinking that because others are different, they are thus a threat—initially caused the problem. The primary difficulty with this approach, however, is that it does not explain variations in the frequency, type, or intensity of intergroup conflict from one society to the next or between different immigrant groups and the ingroup.

In the United States

Often, an ethnocentric attitude is not deliberate but rather an outgrowth of growing up and living within a familiar environment. Even so, if recognized for the bias it is, it can be overcome. Consider, for example, that Americans have labeled their Major League Baseball championship games a *World Series,* although until recently not even Canadian teams were included in an otherwise exclusively U.S. professional sports program. *American* is another word we use—even in this book—to identify ourselves to the exclusion of people in other parts of North, Central, and South America. The Organization of American States (OAS), which consists of countries in North, Central, and South America, should remind us that others are equally entitled to call themselves Americans.

At one point in this country's history, many state and national leaders identified their expansionist goals as Manifest Destiny, as if divine providence had ordained specific boundaries for the United States. Indeed, many members of the clergy over the years preached fiery sermons regarding God's special plans for this country, and all presidents have invoked the deity in their inaugural addresses for special assistance to this country.

In Other Times and Lands

Throughout history, people of many cultures have demonstrated an ethnocentric view of the world. For example, British Victorians, believing their way of life superior to all others, felt obliged to carry the "white man's burden" of cultural and intellectual superiority in colonizing and "civilizing" the non-Western world. Yet 2,000 years earlier, the Romans had thought natives of Britain were an especially inferior people, as indicated in this excerpt from a letter written by the orator Cicero to his friend Atticus: "Do not obtain your slaves from Britain because they are so stupid and so utterly incapable of being taught that they are not fit to form a part of the household of Athens."

The Greeks, whose civilization predated the Roman Empire, considered all those around them—Persians, Egyptians, Macedonians, and others—distinctly inferior and called them barbarians. (*Barbarikos*, a Greek word, described those who did not speak Greek as making noises that sounded like *bar-bar*.)

Religious chauvinism blended with ethnocentrism in the Middle Ages when the Crusaders, spurred on by their beliefs, considered it their duty to free the Holy Land from the control of the "infidels." They traveled a great distance by land and sea, taking with them horses, armor, and armaments, to wrest control from the native inhabitants because the "infidels" had the audacity to follow the teachings of Muhammad rather than Jesus. On their journey across Europe, the Crusaders slaughtered Jews (whom they falsely labeled "Christ killers"), regardless of whether they were men, women, or children, all in the name of the Prince of Peace. The Crusaders saw both Muslims and Jews not only as inferior peoples but also as enemies.

In the following passage, Brewton Berry offers several other examples of ethnocentric thinking in past times:

> Some writers have attributed the superiority of their people to favorable geographical influences, but others incline to a biological explanation. The Roman, Vitruvius, maintained that those who live in southern climates have the keener

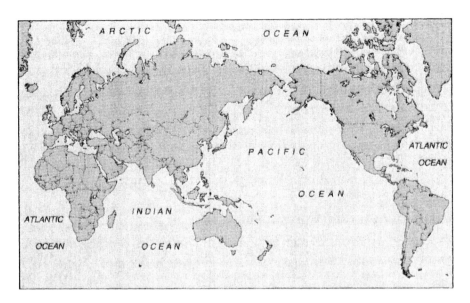

Unlike most U.S. maps of the world showing the American continents on the left side, this map—a common one in many Asian countries—puts the Americas on the right. The effect is to place these countries (such as Japan) in the center and not the edge, thus emphasizing the Pacific Rim rather than the Atlantic. Such repositioning is a form of ethnocentrism, shaping perceptions of the rest of the world.

intelligence, due to the rarity of the atmosphere, whereas "northern nations, being enveloped in a dense atmosphere, and chilled by moisture from the obstructing air, have a sluggish intelligence." . . . Ibn Khaldun argued that the Arabians were the superior people, because their country, although in a warm zone, was surrounded by water, which exerted a cooling effect. Bodin, in the sixteenth century, found an astrological explanation for ethnic group differences. The planets, he thought, exerted their combined and best influence upon that section of the globe occupied by France, and the French, accordingly, were destined by nature to be the masters of the world. Needless to say, Ibn Khaldun was an Arab, and Bodin a Frenchman. The Italian, Sergi, regarded the Mediterranean peoples as the true bearers of civilization and insisted that Germans and Asiatics only destroy what the Mediterraneans create. In like manner, the superiority of Nordics, Alpines, Teutons, Aryans, and others has been asserted by those who were members of each of these groups, or thought they were.[34]

Anthropologists examining the cultures of other peoples have identified countless instances of ethnocentric attitudes. One frequent practice has been in geographic reference and mapmaking. For example, some commercially prepared Australian world maps depicted that continent in the center in relation to the rest of the world.

There is nothing unusual about this type of thinking: the Chinese, who called their country the Middle Kingdom, were convinced that China was the center of the world, and similar beliefs were held by other nations—and are still held. The British drew the Prime Meridian of longitude to run through Greenwich, near London. Europeans drew maps of the world with Europe at the center, Americans with the New World at the center.[35]

But beyond providing a group-centered approach to living, ethnocentrism is of utmost significance in understanding motivation, attitudes, and behavior when members of racially or ethnically distinct groups interact, for it often helps explain misunderstandings, prejudice, and discrimination.

Eurocentrism and Afrocentrism

In recent years, many scholars and minority leaders have criticized the underrepresentation of non-European curriculum materials in the schools and colleges, calling this approach Eurocentric. **Eurocentrism** is a variation of ethnocentrism in which the content, emphasis, or both in history, literature, and other humanities primarily, if not exclusively, concern Western culture. Critics argue that this focus, ranging from the ancient civilizations of Greece and Rome to the writings of Shakespeare, Dickens, and other English poets and authors, ignores the accomplishments and importance of other peoples.

One counterforce to Eurocentrism is **Afrocentrism,** a viewpoint emphasizing African culture and its influence on Western civilization and the behavior of American Blacks. In its moderate form, Afrocentrism is an effort to counterbalance Eurocentrism and the suppression of the African influence in American culture by teaching African heritage as well.[36] In its bolder form, Afrocentrism becomes another variation of ethnocentrism. For example, a New York professor of African American Studies, Leon Jeffries, became embroiled in controversy when he asserted the superiority of African "sun people" over European "ice people." Others who argue that Western civilization merely reflects the Black African influence on Egyptian civilization find critics who charge them with excessively distorting history.[37]

For most advocates of pluralism, however, ethnocentrism in any form produces erroneous views. What is needed is a balanced approach that is inclusive, not exclusive, of the cultures, civilizations, and contributions of all peoples, both in our curriculum and in our thinking (see the accompanying International Scene box for an example from abroad).

Objectivity

When we are talking about people, usually those who differ from us, we commonly offer our own assumptions and opinions more readily than when we are discussing some other area, such as statistics or biology. But if we

Afrocentrist schools, such as this one in Roxbury, Massachusetts, have emerged as an alternative to the nation's troubled urban public schools. Their advocates maintain that, by providing pride in students' cultural heritage and enhancing self-esteem, such schools enhance student motivation and academic performance and encourage completion of school.

(*Source:* © Akso Szilvasi/Stock, Boston)

are to undertake a sociological study of ethnicity, we must question our assumptions and opinions—everything we have always believed without question. How can we scientifically investigate a problem if we have already reached a conclusion?

Sociologists attempt to examine group relationships objectively, but it is impossible to exclude their own subjectivity altogether. All human beings have **values**—socially shared conceptions of what is good, desirable, and proper, or bad, undesirable, and improper. Because we are human, we cannot be completely objective because these values influence our orientations, actions, reactions, and interpretations. For example, selecting intergroup relations as an area of interest and concern, emphasizing the sociological perspective of this subject, and organizing the material in this book thematically all represent value judgments regarding priorities.

The International Scene
Overcoming German Ethnocentrism

CDS International, an organization that runs exchange programs, distributed a pamphlet, "An Information Guide for Germans on American Culture," to Germans working as interns in U.S. companies during the 1990s. The pamphlet was based on previous German interns' experiences and on their interviews with other colleagues; its intent was to provide insights into U.S. culture and to overcome ethnocentric reactions.

- Americans say "Hello" or "How are you?" when they see each other. "How are you?" is like "Hello." A long answer is not expected; just answer "Thank you, fine. How are you?"
- Using deodorant is a must.
- American women usually shave their legs and under their arms. Women who don't like to do this should consider wearing clothes that cover these areas.
- Expect to be treated like all other Americans. You won't receive special treatment because you are a German. Try not to talk with other Germans in German if Americans are around; this could make them feel uncomfortable.
- Please consider the differences in verbal communication styles between Americans and Germans. The typical German speaking style sounds abrupt and rude to Americans. Keep this in mind when talking to Americans.
- Be polite. Use words like "please" and "thank you." It is better to use these too often than not enough. Also, be conscious of your voice and the expression on your face. Your voice should be friendly, and you should wear a smile. Don't be confused by the friendliness and easygoing, nonexcitable nature of the people. They are deliberate, think independently, and do things their own way. Americans are proud of their independence.
- Keep yourself out of any discussions at work about race, sex, religion, or politics. Be open-minded; don't make judgments based on past experiences in Germany.
- Be aware that there are a lot of different cultures in the United States. There are also many different churches, which mean a great deal to their members. Don't be quick to judge these cultures; this could hurt people's feelings.
- Do it the American way and try to intermingle with the Americans. Think positive.

Critical thinking question: What guidelines for avoiding ethnocentrism should Americans follow when traveling to or working in other countries?

In fact, **value neutrality** may be impossible to attain because we are all members of groups and have been influenced by many others in our perceptions and experiences. It is nevertheless important to try conscientiously to maintain an open mind to examine this subject as objectively as possible. You must be aware of your own strong feelings about these matters and be willing to examine new concepts, even if they challenge previously held beliefs. To study this subject properly, you should attempt to be a stranger in your familiar world. Look at everything as if you were seeing it for the first time, trying to understand how and why it is rather than just taking it for granted. In addition, you should recognize that all of us are members of groups; consequently, the debate about and study of intergroup relations are themselves part of what we are studying. As part of an ingroup, we find all other outgroup members unlike our reference group; for this reason, our judgments about these "outsiders" are not as fully informed as the ones we make about known "insiders."

Trying to be *objective* about race and ethnic relations presents a strong challenge. People tend to use selective perception, accepting only information that agrees with their values or interpreting data in a way that confirms their attitudes about other groups. Many variables in life influence people's subjectivity about minority relations. Some views may be based on personal or emotional considerations or even on false premises. Sometimes, however, reasonable and responsible people disagree on the matter in an unemotional way. Whatever the situation, the study of minority-group relations poses a challenge for objective examination.

The subject of race and ethnic relations is complex and touches our lives in many ways. As members of the groups we are studying, all readers of this book come to this subject with preconceived notions. Because many individuals have a strong tendency to tune out disagreeable information, you must make a continual effort to remain open-minded and receptive to new data.

The Dillingham Flaw

Part of the problem with complaints about today's foreign-born presence in the United States lies in the critics' mistaken belief that they are reaching their judgments objectively. In comparing the supposedly nonassimilating newcomers to past immigrants, many detractors fall victim to a fallacy of thinking that I call the **Dillingham Flaw**.[38]

Senator William P. Dillingham chaired a congressional commission on immigration that conducted extensive hearings between 1907 and 1911 on the massive immigration then occurring. In issuing its forty-one-volume report, the commission erred in its interpretation of the data by using simplistic categories and unfair comparisons of past and present immigrants by ignoring three important factors: (1) differences of technological evolution in the immigrants' countries of origin; (2) the longer interval during which past immigrants had time to acculturate; and (3) changed structural conditions in the United States wrought by industrialization and urbanization.[39]

The Dillingham Flaw thus refers to any inaccurate comparison based on simplistic categorizations and anachronistic judgments. This also occurs any time we apply modern classifications or sensibilities to an earlier time, when either they did not exist or, if they did, they had a different form or meaning. To avoid the Dillingham Flaw, we must resist the temptation to use modern perceptions to explain a past that contemporaneous people viewed quite differently.

Here is an illustration of this concept. Anyone who criticizes today's immigrants as being slower to Americanize, learn English, and become a cohesive part of American society than past immigrants is overlooking the reality of the past. Previous immigrant groups went through the same gradual acculturation process and encountered the same complaints. Ethnic groups that are now held up as role models and as studies in contrast to today's immigrants were themselves once the objects of scorn and condemnation.

To understand what is happening today, we need to view the present in a larger context—from a sociohistorical perspective. That is in part the approach taken in this book. By understanding past patterns in intergroup relations, we will better comprehend what is occurring in our times, and we will avoid becoming judgmental victims of the Dillingham Flaw.

Personal Troubles and Public Issues

Both ethnocentrism and subjectivity are commonplace in problems involving intergroup relations. In *The Sociological Imagination,* C. Wright Mills explained that an intricate connection exists between the patterns of individual lives and the larger historical context of society. Ordinary people do not realize this, however, and so view their personal troubles as private matters. Their awareness is limited to their "immediate relations with others" and "the social setting that is directly open to personal experience and to some extent [their] willful activity." Personal troubles occur when individuals believe their values are threatened.

However, said Mills, what we experience in diverse and distinct social settings is often traceable to structural changes and institutional contradictions. The public issues of the social structure transcend these local environments of the individual; many local settings "overlap and interpenetrate to form the larger structure of social and historical life." An issue is a public matter concerning segments of the public who believe that one of their cherished values is being threatened.[40]

To illustrate, if a handful of undocumented aliens are smuggled into the United States and placed in a sweatshop in virtual slavery, that is their personal trouble, and we look for a resolution of that particular problem. But if large-scale smuggling of undocumented aliens into the country occurs, resulting in an underground economy of illegal sweatshops in many locales (as indeed happens), we need "to consider the economic and political institutions of the society, not just the personal situation and character of a scatter of individuals."[41]

Similarly, if a few urban African American or Hispanic American youths drop out of school, the personal problems leading to their quitting and the means by which they secure economic stability in their lives become the focus of our attention. But if their dropout rate in most U.S. cities is consistently far greater than the national average (and it is), we must examine the economic, educational, and political issues that confront our urban institutions. These are larger issues, and we cannot resolve them by improving motivation, discipline, and opportunities for a few individuals.

Throughout this book, and particularly in chapters 2 and 3, we will examine this interplay of culture and social structure, ethnicity and social class. What often passes for assigned or assumed group characteristics—or for individual character flaws or troubles—needs to be understood within the larger context of public issues involving the social structure and interaction patterns.

Mills also wrote, "All sociology worthy of the name is 'historical' sociology."[42] Therefore, we should place all groups we study within a sociohistorical perspective so we can understand both historical and contemporary social structures that affect intergroup relations.

The Dynamics of Intergroup Relations

The study of intergroup relations is both fascinating and challenging because relationships continually change. The patterns of relating may change for many reasons: industrialization, urbanization, shifts in migration patterns, social movements, upward or downward economic trends, and so on. However, sometimes the changing relationships also reflect changing attitudes as, for example, in the interaction between Whites and Native Americans. Whites continually changed the emphasis: exploitation; extermination; isolation; segregation; paternalism; forced assimilation; and more recently, tolerance for pluralism and restoration of certain (but not all) Native American ways. Similarly, African Americans, Asian Americans, Jews, Catholics, and other minority groups have all had varying relations with the host society.

Some recent world events also illustrate changing dominant-group orientations toward minority groups, such as Arabs and Muslims after 9/11. The large migrations of diverse peoples into Belgium, Denmark, France, Germany, the Netherlands, Sweden, and the United Kingdom triggered a backlash in each of those countries. Strict new laws enacted in most of these nations in 1993 and 1994 resulted in a marked increase in deportations. **Ethnoviolence**—hostile behavior against people solely because of their race, religion, ethnicity, or sexual orientation—also flared up, particularly in Germany and Italy, where neo-Nazi youths assaulted foreigners and firebombed their residences.

Elsewhere, intergroup relations fluctuate, as between Blacks and Whites in South Africa, Hindus and Muslims in India, Muslims and Christians in Lebanon, Arabs and Jews in the Middle East, Catholics and Protestants in Northern Ireland, and many other groups. All go through varying periods of tumult and calm in their dealings with one another.

The field of race and ethnic relations is rife with theoreticians and investigators examining changing events and migration patterns. Each year, a vast outpouring of information from papers presented at meetings and from articles, books, and other sources adds to our knowledge. New insights, new concepts, and new interpretations of old knowledge inundate the interested observer. What both the sociologist and the student must attempt to understand, therefore, is not a fixed and static phenomenon but a dynamic, ever-changing one, about which more is being learned all the time.

Retrospect

Human beings follow certain patterns when responding to strangers. Their perceptions of newcomers reflect categoric knowing; if they perceive that the newcomers are similar, people are more receptive to their presence. What makes interaction with strangers difficult is the varying perceptions of each to the other, occasioned by a lack of shared understandings and perceptions of reality.

In sociological investigation of minorities, three perspectives shape analysis: Functional theory stresses the orderly interdependence of a society and the adjustments needed to restore equilibrium when dysfunctions occur. Conflict theory emphasizes the tensions and conflicts that result from exploitation and competition for limited resources. Interactionist theory concentrates on everyday interaction patterns operating within a socially constructed perception of reality.

By definition, minority groups—regardless of their size—receive unequal treatment, possess identifying physical or cultural characteristics held in low esteem, are conscious of their shared ascribed status, and tend to practice endogamy. Racial groups are biologically similar groups, and ethnic groups are groups that share a learned cultural heritage. Intergroup relations are dynamic and continually changing.

Ethnocentrism—the tendency to identify with one's own group—is a universal human condition that contributes to potential problems in relating to outgroups. Examples of ethnocentric thinking and actions can be found in all countries throughout history. Eurocentrism and Afrocentrism are views emphasizing one culture or civilization over others.

The study of minorities presents a difficult challenge because our value orientations and life experiences can impair our objectivity. Even trained sociologists, being human, encounter difficulty in maintaining value neutrality. Indeed, some people argue that sociologists should take sides and not attempt a sterile approach to the subject. The Dillingham Flaw—using an inaccurate comparison based on simplistic categorizations and anachronistic judgments—seriously undermines the scientific worth of supposedly objective evaluations. Both ethnocentrism and subjectivity are commonplace in problems involving intergroup relations.

KEY TERMS

Abstract typifications
Afrocentrism
Ascribed status
Categoric knowing
Conflict theory
Dillingham Flaw
Dominant group
Endogamy
Ethnocentrism
Ethnoviolence
Eurocentrism
False consciousness
Functional theory
Group
Ideology

Ingroup
Interactionist theory
Minority group
Outgroup
Race
Racism
Reciprocal typifications
Reference group
Secondary group
Social construction of reality
Social distance
Social identity theory
Symbolic interaction
Value neutrality
Values

REVIEW QUESTIONS

1. What is ethnocentrism? Why is it important in relations between dominant and minority groups?

2. Why is objective study of racial and ethnic minorities difficult?

3. Explain the Dillingham Flaw and offer some examples.

4. What are the focal points of the functional, conflict, and interactionist theories?

5. How does a minority group differ from an ethnic group? How does a race differ from an ethnic group?

SUGGESTED READINGS

Asante, Molefi K. *The Afrocentric Idea,* rev. ed. Philadelphia: Temple University Press, 1998.
   Presents the provocative thesis that African culture permeates Western civilization and American Black behavior.

Berger, Peter L., and Thomas Luckmann. *The Social Construction of Reality.* Garden City, N.Y.: Doubleday, 1967.
   Highly influential work discussing how people define their reality and interact on the basis of shared expectations.

Doob, Christopher B. *Racism: An American Caldron.* New York: HarperCollins, 1993.
   Examination of the economic, political, and social forces that create racism and their functions and consequences today.

Gilroy, Paul. *Against Race: Imagining Political Culture Beyond the Color Line.* Cambridge, Mass.: Harvard University Press, 2000.
> A provocative book that is both factual and utopian in its premise that humanity should not be divided into groups based on skin color.

Parrillo, Vincent N. *Diversity in America.* Thousand Oaks, Calif.: Pine Forge Press, 1996.
> Explains the Dillingham Flaw and examines multiculturalism throughout U.S. history.

Schutz, Alfred. "The Stranger," *American Sociological Review* 69 (May 1944): 449–507.
> Early, influential essay, still highly pertinent today, explaining the interaction problems of a stranger.

Simmel, Georg. "The Stranger," in Kurt H. Wolff (ed.), *The Sociology of Georg Simmel.* New York: Free Press, 1950.
> Classic analysis of the role of the stranger made through an analysis of the formal structures of life.

Waters, Mary. *Ethnic Options: Choosing Identity in America.* Berkeley: University of California Press, 1990.
> Informative discussion of the role ethnicity plays in the pluralistic society of the United States and the evolution of group identity politics.

2

Defense Mechanisms

Defense mechanisms are unconsciously applied techniques that protect the self, or ego, against strong feelings or anxiety. There are three types of anxiety: The basic type, realistic anxiety, represents the individual's fears of tangible dangers in the external world. Neurotic anxiety, which results from a conflict between the id (the instinctive aspect of personality that seeks immediate gratification of impulses) and reality, represents a fear of punishment. Moral anxiety is due to conflict between the id and the superego (the aspect of personality that refers to ethical or moral considerations) and represents the individual's fear of his/her own consciousness. The defense mechanisms are mental structures used by the ego (the aspect of personality that encompasses the sense of "self" in contact with the real world and operates on the reality principle) to reduce anxiety. Defense mechanisms vary with regard to their processes and manifestations. They share two basic similarities: (1) all defense mechanisms represent a distortion or denial of reality, and (2) all defense mechanisms operate unconsciously. Remember, defense mechanisms are unconsciously applied techniques that protect the self against strong feelings of anxiety. Defense mechanisms are normal, even common, reactions.

A. Repression

The most basic of defense mechanisms in which anxiety-producing events are forced from awareness into the unconscious and cannot be remembered. Repression involves an involuntary removal of unacceptable impulses, desires and thoughts from consciousness in order to suppress or divert the development of affect (to avoid painful feelings). Repression can affect a variety of processes, including memory, perception of the present and even physiological functioning. Repression can be viewed as the goal of all other defense mechanisms. The task is to bring in consciousness that which has been repressed into unconsciousness.

B. Regression

Regression occurs when an individual, in response to threatening thoughts and feelings, returns to an earlier period of life that was more pleasurable, secure, and free from anxiety. Healthy, well-adjusted people make regressions from time to time. In order to reduce anxiety (blow off steam), they destroy property, break laws, lose their tempers, and rebel against or submit to authority. These are some forms of regression used by adults.

C. Fixation

Fixation occurs when the individual's energy remains invested in an unresolved conflict. Fixation is another defense against anxiety. A fixated person is afraid to take the next step due to the hazards and hardships that he sees lying ahead. The chief dangers are insecurity, failure, and punishment.

D. Reaction Formation

Reaction formations are employed against external threats as well as internal ones. A person who is afraid of another person may bend over backward to be friendly. Or a fear of society may take the form of strict obedience to the conventions of society. Whenever there is exaggerated and rigid conformity to any set of rules, one can be fairly certain that the conformity is a reaction formation, and that behind the mask of conformity the person is really driven by rebellion and antagonism. A good example of a reaction formation is one displayed by men who are afraid to demonstrate any sign of softness, which they equate with femininity, in their make-up. Remember this defense mechanism involves defending against a disturbing impulse by actively expressing its opposite.

E. Denial

When using denial, the individual admits that an anxiety-evoking impulse, thought, etc. exists, but denies that it is personally relevant.

F. Projection

Projection involves attributing undesirable impulses to the external world. This provides the individual with greater control over his/her negative effect and impulses.

G. Introjection

This involves ascribing the thoughts and behaviors of others to oneself in order to better control one's effective responses to those behaviors and thoughts.

H. Rationalization

Rationalization is the intellectualization which occurs when an individual interprets his or her behavior in a way which makes it seem more rational, logical, and/or socially acceptable, e.g., generating excuses for one's behavior rather than facing the real reasons. A good example is when a student blames the instructor or blames society instead of facing the truth about his shortcomings.

I. Displacement

This defense mechanism involves a transfer of unacceptable feelings associated with one object to a more acceptable or safe object. In essence the person is directing one's motives at some substitute person or object rather than expressing them directly.

J. Sublimation

Sublimation occurs when an unacceptable impulse is displaced or transferred into a socially desirable activity or behavior. Sublimation is the basis for all intellectual and creative pursuits as well as social organization and civilization. Sublimation does not result in complete satisfaction; there is always some residual tension, which cannot be discharged by sublimated object-choice.

K. Transference

Transference is the result of developing feelings, attitudes and defenses toward others based on past experiences. Usually it represents a displacement of past feelings. A good example would be the development of an unexplained negative relationship between a student and instructor.

Retaining Benefits—
Avoiding Responsibility

WE HAVE SEEN how people of color experience acts of violence such as rape, battery, economic discrimination, lack of police protection/police brutality and poor health care. There is no time that a person of color is immune to harassment, discrimination or the possibility that she or he will be attacked. Money and other accoutrements of power afford some protection, but not completely, and not always.

During the first few years that I worked with men who are violent I was continually perplexed by their inability to see the effects of their actions and by their ability to deny the violence they had done to their partners or children. I only slowly became aware of the complex set of tactics that men use to make violence against women invisible and to avoid taking responsibility for their actions. These tactics are listed below in the rough order that men employ them.

Tactic	Typical Statement
Denial	"I didn't hit her."
Minimization	"It was only a slap."
Blame	"She asked for it."
Redefinition	"It was mutual combat."
Unintentionality	"Things got out of hand."
It's over now	"I'll never do it again."
It's only a few men	"Most men wouldn't hurt a woman."
Counterattack	"She controls everything."
Competing victimization	"Everybody is against men."

Reprinted from *Uprooting Racism: How White People Can Work for Racial Justice*, (1996), by permission of New Society Publishers, www.newsociety.com.

These tactics are part of a cycle in which these claims, particularly those of blame, counterattack, and competing victimization, lead to a justification of further violence.

As the battered women's movement tried to bring the prevalence and destructiveness of male violence to national attention it became clear that these tactics were used not only by individual men, but were also in general use in our society to avoid naming and responding to male violence.

As more of us began to interconnect issues of gender, race, class and sexual orientation, we could see how these tactics are used, consciously and unconsciously, by those in power to cover over the violence that is directed toward groups of people with less power. These are not gender specific tactics. They are the tactics of those who seek to retain their power and the privileges they have accrued.

Although these tactics follow a logical progression from outright denial to competing victimization, they are often used in combinations that make them confusing to argue against. It is important to remember that, although they appear as logical reasoning, all of the tactics are part of a strategy for explaining or justifying *already existing* injustice and violence.

We can learn to recognize and counter these tactics. I am going to use the history of the relationship between white Europeans and Native Americans to illustrate how these tactics have been (and still are) used to cover up the violence that white people commit toward people of color. There is more detailed information about that history in Part IV in the section on Native Americans. A brief summary here will have to suffice.

Denial

Denial is usually the first tactic employed and works very simply. The batterer says, "I didn't hit her."

European Americans say that Columbus was just looking for a trade route, the Pilgrims found a vast wilderness, and that the early colonists befriended the Indians and exchanged presents with them. At this level there is absolute denial that violence occurred and therefore of any responsibility for it.

Today we are using the tactic of denial when we say, "It's a level playing field," "Discrimination is a thing of the past," or "This is a land of equal opportunity."

Minimization

If the denial doesn't hold up because of the evidence—she has a broken arm—then the violence is minimized. The batterer says, "I didn't hit her, well, it was only a slap."

Native Americans were killed and their land taken. In response we say, "A few Indians died because they didn't have immunity to European diseases." We try to minimize the presence of the 12–15 million Native Americans in North America prior to 1492 and to minimize the violence we committed toward them.

Today we continue to minimize racism by saying, "Personal achievement mostly depends on personal ability," "Racism isn't prevalent anymore," or (about slavery) "There were a lot of kind slaveowners."

Blame

If the minimization doesn't hold up because the victim is in the hospital, then the batterer's effort shifts to a combination of justifying the violence and blaming the victim. "She asked for it." "She should have known not to say that to me." If the discussion is more general then men might make statements like, "Women are too emotional/manipulative/backstabbing."

Similarly, we know that millions of Native Americans died, not only from intentional transmission of diseases, but from being shot, tortured and enslaved. Since the blame has to fall on entire societies, we make statements like, "Indians were primitive." "They had not developed the technology to compete." "They were not physically able to resist the diseases, hold up under slavery [they didn't make good slaves!], they were naive, simple, heathens."

These justifications rely on a series of biological and psychological justifications for the abuse. Historically there have been continual attempts to "explain" away white violence against people of color as the inevitable result of genetic, biological, chemical, physiological or psychological differences. These differences often do not exist. Where they do, they are seldom related to real differences in behavior. In any case they never justify injustice and violence. What they do is shift the focus from the perpetrators of violence to the victims, subtly blaming them for being inferior or vulnerable to violence.

When we describe what happened in terms of the agency of the person or people with power the uses of these explanations becomes clearer. He hit her. He broke her arm. He put her in the hospital. Columbus invaded, killed, enslaved and tortured the Taino/Arawak peoples. The U.S. Army at Fort Clark deliberately distributed small pox infected blankets to the Mandan in order to kill them (Churchill 1994 p. 35).

Today we blame people of color for racism by saying, "Look at the way they act." "If they weren't so angry..." Or, "They are immoral, lazy, dumb or unambitious."

Redefinition

We want to hold adults responsible for what they do. Therefore we must carefully and accurately investigate what happened so that we can stop violence. If we don't look at the overall context and take differentials of power into account, we can be susceptible to the tactic of redefinition. For example, he says, "It was mutual combat." "She hit me first." "It takes two to fight."

If we can no longer claim that Columbus simply and innocently discovered America, we try to redefine that event too. The 1992 Quincentennial museum exhibit in New York was called "Encounter," a word implying some level of mutuality, equality and neutrality. In the same vein we say, "The settlers had to protect themselves from Indian attacks."

Today we redefine racism as a mutual problem by saying, "This country is just a big melting pot." "Anybody can be prejudiced." Or, "People of color attack white people too."

It Was Unintentional

At this point in the battle the group or individual with more power, who has clearly done something that resulted in some kind of devastation, might claim that the damage was unintentional and therefore their responsibility was minimal. The batterer says things such as, "I didn't intend to hit her." "I didn't mean to hit her so hard." "Things got out of hand."

First of all, claims of innocence by someone who has hurt you are always suspect. Adults are responsible for their actions and for the results of those actions. "I didn't mean to" is not an acceptable legal or moral excuse for being violent toward another person. Secondly, actual intent is often discernible from the pattern of action of the perpetrators of violence. When a man systematically tries to control a woman and then says, "I didn't mean to hit her," he is saying that he hoped to control her by non-physical means. When all else failed he resorted to hitting. The issue is power and control. Intent is clearly evident in the entire pattern of behavior.

We have said that the near-eradication of Native Americans and their food supplies, hunting areas and natural resources was the unintended result of European immigration. We know that the complete elimination of Native Americans from the United States was government policy as well as part of the general, everyday discourse of white Americans (see Section IV for details). It was stated government policy to kill Indians. Smallpox-infected blankets were intentionally distributed to Indians by government representatives.

Today we continue to claim racism is unintentional by saying, "Discrimination may happen, but most people are well intentioned." "She probably didn't mean it like that." Or, "It was only a joke."

It's All Over Now

Another way to defuse responsibility is by claiming that the violence happened in the past and is no longer an issue. The batterer says, "It's over with," or "I'll never do it again." He may finally claim responsibility (often indirectly), but he asserts that things have changed. Part of his claim is that the effects of the violence are similarly in the past and shouldn't influence us anymore. The trauma, pain, mistrust, fear, disrespect and vulnerability should just be forgotten. This discounts the seriousness of the violence, blames the survivor for not being able to let go of it and move on, and focuses on the perpetrator's words, not his actions. All we have is his promise that it won't happen again.

White people often claim that genocide, land grabbing and exploitation are things of the past. Most of our images of Indians reinforce that belief by focusing on Native Americans who lived one to three hundred years ago. The reality is that the effects of colonial violence are still readily apparent today. The small number of remaining Native Americans, the poor economic conditions, the alcoholism, the shattered traditions and devastated communities are the direct result of five hundred years of systematic oppression.

Furthermore, the same policies are in play today as they were hundreds of years ago. The violence did not magically stop at some point. White civilization did not back off and allow the Native nations to heal and recover. Across the country, land is still being taken, treaties are still being broken, Native culture, religion and artifacts are still being stolen and/or exploited, Native American nations are still denied sovereignty, Native Americans are still being killed by whites with some degree of impunity, and their land is still being exploited and laid to waste on a massive scale. Some of the violence takes different forms than it did a hundred years ago. It is important that we not use those differences to claim that we are not responsible for the violence that occurs today, or to blame Native Americans for the results of violence that white people committed in the past and continue to commit today. When we are dealing with structural violence, the proof of change is structural change, not claims of innocence.

Today we claim racism is all over by saying, "Slavery was over a long time ago." "The days of land grabbing are long gone." "That was before the Civil Rights Era." Or, "There aren't any Indians left."

It's Only a Few People

If we are unable to maintain that the violence was all in the past, we may switch to another tactic to make a current situation seem isolated. We might say that it's really only a few people who are like that—it is not systemic or institutionalized. In the case of domestic violence we contend that only a few men are batterers, most men treat women well. However, if 25–33 percent of all heterosexual relationships have an incident of the man hitting the woman—three to five million such incidents a year—then we are clearly talking about a social issue, not the isolated anger of a few men (Women's Action Coalition, pps 55–57).

Similarly, it wasn't just rogue officers like Custer disobeying orders, or cruel, greedy men like Columbus, or a few cowboys who killed Native Americans. Slavery, genocide and racism were built into the structure of all the institutions of our society and were everyday occurrences. We have inherited, perpetuated and benefitted from these actions. All of us are implicated.

Today we continue to use this tactic when we say, "Housing and job discrimination are the result of a few bigoted people." "The Far Right is behind the scapegoating of immigrants." "It's only neo-Nazis and Skinheads who do that sort of thing."

Counterattack and Competing Victimization

When all else fails and responsibility for the violence is inexorably falling on the shoulders of those who committed the acts themselves, there is a counterattack, an attempt to claim a reversal of the power relationships. This approach is usually combined with the final tactic, competing victimization. An individual batterer might say, "She really has all the power in our family." "If I didn't hit her she would run all over me." On a national level there are more and more claims that men are battered by women too, that women win custody and men don't, and that there is too much male-bashing.

To counter this tactic we must go back to what happened, who has power, and what violence is being done. Who ended up in the hospital, and who remained in control of the family resources? In the claims above we find that in about 95 percent of domestic violence cases the woman is the victim of a pattern of abuse, and in 5 percent of the cases the man is the victim (Women's

Action Coalition, pps 55–57). In 80 percent of custody cases the man does not even contest custody. In the remaining 20 percent, where the man wants custody, men get custody 63 percent of the time (*The Divorce Revolution: The Unexpected Social and Economic Consequences for Women and Children in America*, L. J. Weitzman, Free Press, New York 1985). The reality is not what the men would claim, nor what media reporting would have us believe.

We now have a national debate about multiculturalism which claims that people of color and women have so much power that American society itself is threatened. We are told that Native Americans and other people of color are a danger and a threat to our national unity and to our "American" way of life. White people are filing a competing claim of victimization, claiming to be the victims of multiculturalism.

We need to ask ourselves who was killed and who ended up with the land base of this country? Today, who has the jobs, who gets into the universities, who earns more pay, and who gets more media attention for their concerns, white people or people of color?

White people are counterattacking today by saying, "Political correctness rules the universities." "We just want our rights too." "They want special status." "They're taking away our jobs." Some of the ways we claim to be victims include saying, "White males have rights too." "I have it just as bad as anybody." And, "White people are under attack."

Those with power have many resources for having their view of reality prevail, and they have a lot at stake in maintaining the status quo. They will employ the above tactics to defend their interests. We must be aware of these tactics and able to counter them. When unchallenged, they can be used to justify further inequality and violence. If we keep our eyes clearly on the power and the violence we can see that these tactics are transparent for what they are, attempts to prevent placing responsibility on those who commit and benefit from acts of injustice. Our strongest tools are a critical analysis of who has power and an understanding of the patterns and consequences of present actions and policies.

Fear and Danger

*M*ANY OF US in the United States today are afraid. We worry about crime, drugs, our children's future and our own security. Our fear is a result of many economic, social, political and personal factors. It is also linked to violence in news media, TV and the movies.

In a society where we are constantly presented with tales of danger and violence and told how vulnerable we are, it is not surprising that most of us are fearful. Racism produces a fear based society in which no one feels safe. However *being afraid is not the same as being in danger.*

For example, white people often fear people of color, and most people of color fear white people. White people are not usually in danger from people of color. People of color are in danger from individual acts of discrimination, hate crimes and police brutality from white people, as well as institutional practices which kill people through lack of health care, lack of police protection and unequal legal prosecution. White people are rarely killed, harassed or discriminated against by people of color.

To understand whiteness we need to look at how fear of people of color is manufactured and used to justify repression and exploitation of communities of color.

Have you ever been in your car when a person of color drove past, and you reached over to lock your car door? Have you ever had a man of color walk by and you touched your wallet or purse or held it tighter? Have you ever seen a person of color in your neighborhood and you closed a window, pulled a blind or locked a door? Have you ever had an adult or young person of color in your house and wondered, ever so briefly, if valuables were out? Have you ever seen a person of color with quality clothes, an expensive car or other item and wondered how they got the money?

Reprinted from *Uprooting Racism: How White People Can Work for Racial Justice,* (1996), by permission of New Society Publishers, www.newsociety.com.

I have done all of these things. I was taught to fear people of color. I was told that they were dangerous and that they would steal, cheat or otherwise grab whatever I had.

Many of these motions were practically involuntary. My hand was on my wallet before I realized it. Of course, I tried to turn the gesture into a casual motion so it wouldn't be apparent what I had done. For many years I did not realize I was doing this. Then I listened to people of color, particularly African American men (who we have been trained to fear the most), describe how white people were always afraid of them. I began to notice my own and other people's gestures—the tensing, the guardedness, the suspicion, the watchfulness.

White fear is primarily fear of men of color. (We also have fears about women of color, but they are not as visceral or pervasive.) For example, I grew up playing cowboys and Indians, always wanting to be the brave cowboy who protected the innocent homesteaders and settlers from the vicious (male) Indians ready to sweep down and destroy white outposts. I was learning that as a man I would have to protect (white) womanhood and (white) civilization.

Growing up in Los Angeles in the 1950s and early 1960s, I heard repeated stories about the masses of Mexican and Central American people pushing against our borders, pressing to get in, to overwhelm us. I remember a discussion with my parents in which I said I didn't think I ever wanted to have children because there were already so many people in the world. My parents tried to convince me that it was important that I have children because I was smart and educated and we needed more of our kind. I understood "our kind" to be white.* Again I was getting the message that we had to defend ourselves, reproduce ourselves, protect what was ours because we were under attack.

Many of the racial images that we hear today such as "illegal alien," "border patrol," "drug wars," and "the invasion of Japanese capital" are based on images of protection, defense, borders and danger. Many of us feel besieged. We talk as if we are under attack in many areas of our lives where we use to feel safe. We complain that we can't say what we want with impunity, we can't go where we want. We notice that people of color in the United States and abroad are demanding a more equitable distribution of the world's wealth. To counter these attacks on white power and to divert attention from the benefits we have accrued, we have created a fear of potential, retaliatory violence from people of color.

This pattern has a long history. Individual white settlers who took Native American lands feared retaliation. But many white people lived in cities and were not worried about Indian attack. White settlers, in conjunction with the

---

* Because we were Jewish and this was after the Holocaust, I also received messages about the importance of having children so that Hitler will not have succeeded in eliminating us.

U.S. government which wanted to "open up" Native American land, had to convince the public that Native Americans were dangerous and needed to be exterminated. A campaign, using books, pictures and the media, created images of Indians as primitive, cruel savages who wanted to kill white men and rape white women. This campaign made it easier to justify the appropriation of Native American lands, and the death and removal of Native Americans themselves. In the process, generations of us learned to fear Indians. Many children growing up today still do, even though there are only about three million Native Americans in all of the United States and Canada.* They are the ones who have suffered the effects of racial violence.

Over the course of 240 years of slavery, white slaveowners created the illusion of danger from African Americans to justify the harshness of their treatment, and to scare other white people into supporting their subjugation. White people feared African Americans even though they were so thoroughly dominated and brutalized as to offer little threat to whites. Slaves were brutalized publicly and routinely. Some fought back, but most were more interested in escaping than in retaliation.

This pattern of white fear and violence continues today. We are still presented with selected news coverage conveying African American men as the embodiment of danger itself. It is difficult for any white American not to have an immediate feeling of fear in the presence of an African American male. This fear, in turn, has justified massive and continuous control of the African American community through the schools, police, legal system, jails, prisons and the military. This control starts in pre-school or elementary school. It limits educational opportunities, jobs, skills and access to health care. It is enforced by police brutality and various forms of discrimination. These conditions produce stress, despair and desperation for African American young men, leading to their killing each other and themselves at high rates, living six years less than white men on the average. White violence leads to fear which is used to justify further white violence. African American men, not white people, are the victims of this cycle of violence.

Many times we use stories to justify the fear that we feel toward people of color. We might introduce them by such phrases as "I was attacked once by..." "I don't want to sound prejudiced, but I know someone who had a bad experience with..." or "It's unfortunate, but my one negative experience was..." We then use these single examples to reinforce a stereotype about a whole category of people and to prove the legitimacy of our fear of them.

---

* This number is from government figures. Racially motivated governmental policies exclude Hispanics and African Americans with Native American ancestry from current estimates. All current demographic figures are highly contested.

Is there a story that you use to justify your fears of people of color? What are stories that you've heard other white people use?

These shared stories can be a way to strengthen white solidarity by implying that we share a common danger. They reinforce our desire to be with white people and to avoid people of color. They also raise the stakes if we challenge racism because to do so seems to threaten our own security. How can we challenge other whites when we may need them in case of an attack?

Sometimes, when I realize the extent of the stereotypes I have learned and act from, I want to disavow the fear altogether and convince myself that there is nothing to be afraid of. Or, to counter the stereotype, I try to assume that all men of color are safe and all white men are dangerous. Yet I know that I am foolish if I simply reverse the stereotypes. In a society in which many people are dangerous and violence is a threat, we need to evaluate the danger from each person we're with. Any preconceived notions of danger or safety based on skin color are dysfunctional—they can actually increase our danger and make us less able to protect ourselves. For example, even as white women have moved to the suburbs, put locks on their doors and windows, and avoided urban streets at night, they have remained vulnerable to robbery and assault from white male friends, lovers, neighbors and co-workers.

Was there ever a time when you heard about violence that a white man committed and you said to yourself, "I never would have imagined that so-and-so could have done something like that"? We are often awarded a presumption of innocence if we are white. This works to our benefit when we are stopped by the police, shopping in a store, walking down the street, or renting equipment such as cars, tools or movies. Other white people assume we are safe until we are proven dangerous.

Have you ever been surprised that an African American or Latino man could commit a particular act of violence? We expect men of color to be dangerous. When Susan Smith killed her two children, she claimed that an African American man had kidnapped them. When Charles Stuart killed his pregnant wife in New York City, he stabbed himself and claimed an African American man had attacked them. When the federal building in Oklahoma City was bombed, most people immediately suspected Arab men as the culprits. Many of us accepted these statements without question because they fit with our expectations. In each situation search for the guilty white person was temporarily diverted toward men of color.

We fear people of color in great disproportion to any danger they may have for us. We trust white men in spite of the danger some of them pose. These fears become expectations which influence who we trust and how we evaluate danger. Even our personal vigilance is often increased when people of color are present and relaxed when only white people are around.

These expectations translate into feeling uneasy whenever there are significant numbers of people of color around us. It has been found that whites are most comfortable in interracial situations where people of color constitute a small percentage of the population. When the percentage rises to 15–20, white people often begin to feel that "they" are dominating or are unfairly represented. When people of color constitute 20–25 percent of the population, white people begin to describe people of color as the majority, or as having taken over.

As white people we must start by acknowledging the violence we have done to people of color throughout our history. We must understand how we have demonized them to justify that violence. Our fear of violence to ourselves is related to the violence we have done and continue to do to people of color. Therefore one way to lower our fear is to acknowledge and reduce our violence.

Jewish people have likewise been portrayed as dangerous—economically dangerous. Stereotypes that Jews own the banks and are crafty, unscrupulous and untrustworthy contribute to such anti-Semitic fears. Age-old Christian teachings that Jews killed Christ, and false documents like the "Protocols of the Elders of Zion,"* are additional currents in this river of fear.

Jewish people in the United States have been subject to verbal and physical attack, bombings, desecration of cemeteries, intimidation and murder by white Christians. Christians have not been attacked by Jews for being Christian. Again we can see that although the fear is mutual, Jewish people are in some danger from Christians whereas Christians are in no danger from being attacked by Jews.

Economically, most banks, major corporations and other institutions that make the financial decisions about jobs, pensions and health care are owned by Christians. They make the decisions to rob our Savings & Loans, steal from the government, move jobs overseas, create unsafe working conditions and bust unions. Christian fear works, like all racial fear, to divert people from the source of danger—people inside the mainstream who hold political, economic and social power. Jews are blamed for economic problems for which they are not responsible, and become the targets of further anti-Semitic violence.

All Jews experience the stereotypes and fear that white Christians and other non-Jews have of them. Jewish people know what it's like to be attacked because others have been trained to fear you. Jews who are white are feared

* The "Protocols" is a forged document purporting to be a plan by Jews to control the world. It was first published in Russia by Tsarist officials in the beginning of this century to direct Russian peasant's wrath for harsh economic conditions onto Jews. It was widely distributed by Henry Ford and other industrialists in the United States during the Depression and still circulates throughout the world.

and are taught to fear people of color. Many white Jewish concerns about violence focus on danger from African Americans, even though most anti-Semitic violence is committed by white Christians. Anti-Semitism should be challenged wherever it occurs, but primary energy should always go to defend against those with most power to do harm. Meanwhile, Jews of color* are attacked from all sides, by white Christians and Jews, and by Christian people of color.

The focus by white Jews on external danger from people of color also helps conceal the significant levels of domestic violence, sexual assault and child abuse within the Jewish community. When Jewish family violence is denied and minimized, and Jewish family values are held up as better than African Americans,' then racism is perpetuated. This racism justifies violence against African Americans while obscuring violence against Jewish women and children.

All of us who are white need to recognize just how deeply we have been trained to fear and distrust people of color and how much that fear guides our behavior, because that fear is easily manipulated by politicians, the media or corporate leaders. Christians need to acknowledge their fear and distrust of Jews for the same reasons. Our fear often leads us to misconstrue our own best political interests because our racial fear overrides our best thinking.

Our fear of African Americans is such that a single person can come to represent the danger we feel from an entire community. Many different individuals have been held up by politicians and the media to represent the "danger" of African Americans to white people in the last few decades since the beginning of the Civil Rights Movement. Such people as Malcolm X, Huey Newton, Eldridge Cleaver, Martin Luther King, Jr., Angela Davis, "Willie" Horton, Ice Cube, Jesse Jackson and Sister Souljah have all been used to symbolize danger and to manipulate white people's fears. As our fears of people of color increase we are more easily deceived by white leaders who have an aura of trustworthiness simply because they are white.

---

* A distinction between Jews who are white and Jews of color is only useful within the framework of a discussion of racism.

3

Social Psychology

Why We Care: A Topic Preview

Social psychology is the field of psychology concerned with how others influence the thoughts, feelings, and behaviors of the individual. We care about the material in this chapter because, in a real sense, social psychology deals with us as we live: in a social world, interacting with, influencing, and being influenced by others. Social psychologists focus on the person or individual, not on the group per se (which is more likely to be the concern of sociologists).

As we have seen many times, other areas of psychology are interested in reactions that are social in nature also. Developmental psychologists, for example, are interested in how styles of cooperative and competitive play change and develop through the early years of life. Personality psychologists are interested in individual characteristics that affect interpersonal behavior, such as friendliness and aggression. Learning theorists are interested in how the perception of someone else being rewarded (vicarious reinforcement) affects behavior change. Clinical psychologists recognize that social relationships can play an important role in the development of psychological disorders and their treatment.

In this chapter, we'll consider two major content areas in social psychology: (1) social cognition, or the perception and evaluation of oneself and other people in social situations, and (2) in Topic 14B, social influence, or how other people affect the psychological reactions of the individual.

A basic premise of this topic is that we do not view our social environment solely on the basis of the stimulus information that it presents to us (Higgins & Bargh, 1987). Instead, the argument goes, we have developed a number of cognitive structures and processes (attitudes, schemas, prejudices, and the like) that shape and influence our interpretation of the world around us. Put another way, a focus on social cognition involves two related questions: What information about the social

From: *Psychology: An Introduction*, (1992), by permission of Pearson Education, Inc.

nature of our world do we have stored in memory, and how does that stored information influence future social judgments, choices, and behaviors (Sherman, Judd, & Park, 1989)?

To provide the proper context, we begin with a discussion of the perspective from which social psychologists study behavior and mental processes. Then, we'll spend the bulk of this topic dealing with attitudes. We'll see how social psychologists define attitudes, and we'll study how attitudes are formed and how they may be changed. We'll look at some of the factors that determine how we process information about ourselves and others in social situations, which is to say, how we attribute behaviors to different causes. We'll close this topic with a review of interpersonal (or social) attraction and consider some of the factors that influence how and why people are attracted to others.

The Social-Psychological Perspective

Since we are all social organisms, we are familiar, each in our own way, with many of the concerns of social psychology. Getting along with other people is considered to be an asset, and those of us who are able to do so easily may be demonstrating an appreciation of social psychology in the sense that we are skilled in predicting the behaviors of others and understanding how they affect us. All of us seem to put a great deal of effort into trying to understand social behavior.

To claim that we are familiar with the concerns of social psychology has certain implications. On the one hand, it means that social psychology tends to be perceived as interesting and relevant because it deals with everyday situations that affect us all. On the other hand, it means that often we are willing to accept common sense, personal experience, and even folklore as the basis for our explanations and assumptions about social behavior. Although common sense often may be valid, it is not an acceptable basis for a scientific approach to understanding social behavior. Social psychology relies on experimentation and other scientific methods as sources of knowledge about social behavior, even if the results of applying these methods are contrary to intuition. As we shall see in this chapter, some of the most influential discoveries in social psychology have been unexpected and counterintuitive. During the last 20 years, social psychology has, like many other areas of psychology, taken on a clearly *cognitive* flavor. That is, social psychologists are attempting more and more to understand social behavior by examining the mental structures and processes that are reflected in such behavior.

To give you an appreciation for this approach, and to provide an example we can return to later, let's review a classic classroom project undertaken more than 20 years ago. In the late 1960s, a third-grade teacher in a small elementary school in Riceville, Iowa, wanted to give her pupils a firsthand experience of prejudice. Jane Elliott announced to her students that she had evidence that blue-eyed children clearly were superior in all regards to children with brown eyes. As a result, children with brown eyes were declared second-class citizens. They were forced to sit in the back of the classroom. They had to stand at the end of the lunch line, allowing the blue-eyed children first choice; they were not allowed second helpings of food. They were not allowed to use the drinking fountain. The "superior" blue-eyed children were given special privileges, including extra recess time. To make them more visible, brown-eyed children were forced to wear paper collars that identified their lowly status form a distance.

It wasn't long before students in Ms. Elliott's third-grade class became active participants in her demonstration. The classroom behaviors of the brown-eyed children deteriorated; they performed below their usual levels on a number of academic tasks. The blue-eyed children did better than usual. They voluntarily avoided contact with their "inferior" brown-eyed classmates. Fights and arguments broke out. The behavior of the blue-eyed children became aggressive, contemptuous, and occasionally vicious—all in one day.

The next school day, Ms. Elliott informed the class that she had made a terrible mistake: She had gotten the evidence reversed. It was blue-eyed children who were inferior; the best people were those with brown-eyes! With displays of great joy and enthusiasm, the brown-eyed children tore off their offensive collars and helped fit the blue-eyed pupils with paper collars that identified *them* as inadequate and inferior. Even after their experience of the previous day, the behaviors of the children in the class were exactly the same, only the roles were reversed. Those who just the day before were the objects of prejudice now sat in the front of the class, performed well on classroom tests, rushed to be the first in the line at lunch time, and treated their blue-eyed classmates very badly.

On the third day, Ms. Elliott shared her original intent with her pupils and told them that none of what she had said the last two days was, in fact, true. The effects of this classroom demonstration were not long-lived. The children soon returned to their normal classroom routine. The artificially induced prejudice disappeared almost as quickly as it had been created. This exercise was not a carefully controlled experiment, and given current concern about the ethics involved in such manipulations, it is unlikely to be replicated. Nonetheless, the experience was a meaningful one for those Iowa third-graders and a significant one for us, too. It tells us a great deal about the irrationality of prejudice based solely on physical characteristics (Elliott, 1977; Leonard, 1970; Peters, 1971).

Now let's review this demonstration as a social psychologist might. On the first day, children with blue eyes developed unfavorable ideas about brown-eyed classmates. Pupils with brown eyes were thought of as inferior, lazy, and irresponsible. These cognitions developed without any real test. On the basis of very little actual evidence or data, blue-eyed children were willing to think of all brown-eyed children as inferior. They were willing to ignore their previous experiences with their brown-eyed classmates. They formed a **stereotype**—a generalized set of cognitions about members of a group that is based on limited experience and that does not allow for individual differences.

Although this particular example of a stereotype had negative implications because it is based on erroneous information, stereotypes are not necessarily bad. When they are based on accurate information they are useful tools that help us

stereotype a generalized mental (cognitive) representation of someone that minimizes individual differences and is based on limited experience

simplify and deal more efficiently with a complex world (Jussim et al., 1987). All of us have formed many stereotypes. Some of those stereotypes are based on accurate, reliable appraisals; some are based on false information. For instance, assume that you have a stereotype of law enforcement officers that includes the belief (cognition) that they will arrest you for speeding. If you are out on the highway and see a law enforcement vehicle in your rear-view mirror, you'll make sure that you are not exceeding the posted speed limit, regardless of whether you see that vehicle as belonging to a state trooper, a city police officer, or a county sheriff. You won't pause to wonder what that officer is doing out there on the highway until after you have checked your speed. Because you have formed a stereotype, your behavior has become predictable and virtually automatic.

Notice also that once the pupils in Jane Elliott's class developed the idea of superiority and inferiority on the basis of eye color, their behaviors changed accordingly. The students had rather strong notions about how one deals with or reacts to classmates who are "inferior." They are to sit at the back of the class, they are to stand at the end of lunch lines, and they are not to be spoken to in a friendly manner, *because* they are inferior.

We all develop a complex set of rules or expectations about how to behave that guides and directs our social actions. In other words, we have come to know what we are supposed to do in different social situations. Perhaps you recall our discussion of discrimination learning back in Topic 5B, where we found that we often learn to make discriminations about which behaviors are acceptable in a given social situation and which behaviors are unacceptable. Shared expectations about how the members of a group *ought to behave* are called social **norms** (Levine & Moreland, 1990). Clearly, norms have a cognitive basis if we are to use them consistently. Like stereotypes, they are cognitions that we may use to help simplify our social world. Because we have developed social norms, we know how we are to act in a wide variety of social situations. Note how uncomfortable you feel when you find yourself in a new and different situation—perhaps a foreign country, a strange religious ceremony, a country club, or a ghetto. Our feelings of discomfort reflect the fact that we do not know what is expected of us; we don't know the rules of behavior; we have not learned the appropriate norms. Now that we have a sense of what we mean by social cognition, let's explore some areas of social psychology in which this concept has been useful.

norms rules or expectations that guide our behavior in certain social situaitons by prescribing how we ought to behave

Social Psychology

*O*ver 30 years ago, a New York City cocktail waitress named Kitty Genovese was brutally murdered in front of her apartment building as she returned from work about 3:30 in the morning. What made this particular murder noteworthy was that so many of Kitty Genovese's neighbors watched as she was bludgeoned and stabbed to death. Here is the account of the incident:

> For more than half an hour, 38 respectable law-abiding citizens in Queens watched a killer stalk and stab a woman in three separate attacks in Kew Gardens.
>
> Twice the sound of their voices and the sudden glow of their bedroom lights interrupted him and frightened him off. Each time he returned, sought her out, stabbed her again. Not one person telephoned the police during the assault; one witness called after the woman was dead. (*New York Times*, March 27, 1964)

This story has become a classic example in the social psychology of violence and bystander behaviors. Still, could it be that because the incident took place so many years ago, it might have lost some of its relevance? Then, there was another newspaper story:

> **Cheering bystanders spur on woman's killer.** Oakland, Calif. (AP): A dozen people who chanted "Kill her, kill her," as a 32-year-old woman was stabbed to death could face murder charges, authorities say. Police said Friday they were looking for members of the crowd who egged on the woman's attacker. The people could be charged with aiding and abetting a killing. "Usually, you hear of people who stand by, watch, and do nothing," police Sergeant John McKenna said, "but this is the other end of things, where the people watched and participated, apparently for a thrill, to watch the kill" (*The Toronto Times*, August 15, 1993).

Yes, the murder of Kitty Genovese occurred over 30 years ago. No, sadly, the story is not dated; nor is it irrelevant.

And, then there is the case of Vanessa Moretti. Vanessa and her father were driving to a beach in Italy. After they entered a tunnel, Vanessa's father began to feel ill so he pulled over. He was having a heart attack. His last words to his daughter were to get out of the tunnel and get help. Vanessa did what her father said. She got out of the car and walked the remaining length of the tunnel. Once outside, she tried to flag down a passing motorist for help. But, nobody would stop. Cars sped by so fast that they actually knocked Vanessa down. Finally, the exhausted Vanessa, now dirty and bleeding, got someone to stop. The police were called. Unfortunately, Vanessa's father did not survive.

The stories of Kitty Genovese, the 32-year-old woman, and Vanessa Moretti are strikingly similar and show that what happened to Kitty Genovese over 30 years ago was not a fluke, nor is it something that only happened in the past. The behavior of the "bystanders" in these three incidents raises some fundamental questions about what controls behavior. Were the bystanders simply uncaring, cold people who allowed these events to happen? Or, was it something about the social environment that had a chilling effect on one's desire to help?

One perspective on behavior is that we are motivated by internal factors. So, we could conclude from this perspective that the bystanders in the three incidents were, in fact, cold and uncaring. However, as we will see in this chapter, we also need to take into account the situational forces that affect behavior. Social psychology deals with people as they live and as they die: in a social world, influencing and being influenced by others.

In this chapter, we will consider two major content areas in social psychology: (1) in Topic 14A, social cognition, or the perception and evaluation of oneself and others in social situations, and (2) in Topic 14B, social influence, or how others affect the reactions of the individual.

social psychology
the field of
psychology con-
cerned with how
others influence the
thoughts, feelings,
and behaviors of
the individual

Social psychology is the field of psychology concerned with how others influence the thoughts, feelings, and behaviors of the individual. Social psychologists focus on the person or the individual in a group setting and not on the group *per se*, which is more likely to be the focus of sociologists. Because we are social organisms, we are each in our own way familiar with many of the concerns of social psychology. However, social psychologists do not ignore the role of internal factors, such as personality. The model that dominates social psychology is one put forth by Kurt Lewin back in 1936. According to Lewin's model, social behavior is a function (related to) of the interaction between two factors: the internal characteristics of the person (personality, attitudes, etc.) and the social situation (the physical setting, presence of others, etc.).

To claim that we are familiar with the concerns of social psychology has certain implications. On the one hand, it means that social psychology is perceived as relevant because it deals with everyday situations that affect us all. On the other hand, it means that we are often willing to accept common sense and our personal experiences as the basis for our explanations about social behavior. Although common sense and personal experience may sometimes be valid, they are not acceptable for a scientific approach to understanding social behavior. Social psychology relies on experimentation and other scientific methods as sources of knowledge about social behavior.

Social Cognitions: Attitudes, Attributions, and Attraction

Over the last 25 years, much of social psychology has taken on a cognitive flavor. That is, social psychologists are attempting to understand social behavior by examining the mental structures and processes reflected in such behavior. A basic premise of this approach, and of this Topic, is that we do not view our social environment solely on the basis of the stimulus information it presents us (Baldwin, 1992; Berscheid, 1994; Higgins & Bargh, 1987). Instead, the argument goes, we have developed cognitive structures or processes (for example, attitudes and schemas) that influence our interpretation of the world around us. "Discovering how people mentally organize and represent information about themselves and others has been a central task of social cognition research" (Berscheid, 1994, p. 84). Social cognition involves two related questions: What information about the social nature of the world do we have stored in memory? How does that information influence social judgments, choices, attractions, and behaviors (Sherman et al., 1989)?

Key Questions to Answer   As you read Topic 14A, find the answers to the following questions:

1. What is the definition of social psychology?
2. How did Lewin explain social behavior?
3. What is the basic premise of the cognitive approach to social psychology?
4. What is an attitude?
5. What are the three components of an attitude?
6. What is the fourth component of an attitude?
7. What are the three ways in which attitudes might be acquired?
8. What is cognitive dissonance theory?
9. What is the insufficient justification effect?
10. Under what conditions will disconfirmation of a belief increase the strength of that belief?
11. What is postdecisional dissonance, and how is it resolved?
12. What is self-perception theory?
13. What is persuasion, and what is the most widely accepted model of persuasion?
14. What are the three factors in the Yale Communication Model that influence persuasion?
15. What is the credibility of a communicator?
16. Other than credibility, what other source factors affect persuasion?

17. When should a one-sided or two-sided message be used?

18. What is discrepancy and how does it relate to persuasion?

19. What are rational and emotional appeals?

20. What is the elaboration likelihood model?

21. What are attributions?

22. What errors are made in the attribution process?

23. What are the four approaches that account for interpersonal attraction?

24. What are four determinants of interpersonal attraction?

Attitudes

attitude a relatively stable evaluative disposition directed toward some object or event; it consists of feelings, behaviors, and beliefs

Since the 1920s, a central concern in social psychology has been the nature of attitudes. An **attitude** is a relatively stable disposition to evaluate an object or event. An attitude has consequences for influencing one's beliefs, feelings, and behaviors toward that object or event (Olson & Zanna, 1993).

The concept of *evaluation* in this definition refers to a dimension of attitudes that includes such notions as being for or against, or positive or negative (Eagly & Chaiken; 1992). By *disposition* we mean a tendency, or a preparedness, to respond to the object of an attitude (actual responding isn't necessary). Note that, by definition, attitudes have *objects*. We do not have attitudes in general; we have attitudes about some object or event. We recognize that the word *attitude* is occasionally used differently in common speech. We may hear that someone has a "bad attitude" or "an attitude" in general as in "Boy, does he have an attitude!" In psychology, however an attitude requires an object, that is, a specific object or event attached to the attitude.

Anything can be the object of an attitude, whether it be a person, an object, or an idea (Fazio, 1990; Petty & Cacioppo, 1986). You may have attitudes about this course, the car you drive, your father, the president, or the corner fast-food restaurant where you eat lunch. Some of our attitudes are more important than others, of course, but the fact that we have attitudes about so many things is precisely why the study of attitudes is so central in social psychology.

The Components of Attitudes

Although many definitions of attitude have been proposed over the years, most of them suggest that an attitude consists of three components (Chaiken & Stangor, 1987). When we use the term in everyday conversation, we are most likely referring to the *affective component,* which consists of our feelings about the attitudinal object (Zanna & Rempel, 1988). It is the affective component that makes attitudes special and sets them apart from other cognitive schemas. The *behavioral component* consists of our response tendencies toward the object of our attitude. This component includes our behaviors and our intentions to act should the opportunity arise. The *cognitive component* includes our beliefs about the attitudinal object. Any of these three may be primary. Essentially, the cognitive component is the information storage component of an attitude, making an attitude similar to other information processing cognitive schemes. We form a positive attitude toward a particular beverage because we know it is good for us (cognitive), because it is very convenient to buy (behavioral), or because we like the way it tastes (affective). By now, these three components of affect, behavior, and cognition, or ABCs, ought to be familiar.

Most of the time, the cognitive, affective, and behavioral components of attitudes are consistent. We think that classical music is relaxing and like to listen to it, so we buy classical music recordings. You believe that knowledge of psychology will be an asset in your career, you are enjoying your introductory psychology class, and you plan to take more psychology classes in the future. There are occasions, however, when behaviors are not consistent with beliefs and feelings (Ajzen & Fishbein, 1980). For example, we may have very strong, unfavorable beliefs and very negative feelings about someone, yet when we encounter that person at a social gathering, we smile, extend our hand, and say something pleasant. The social situation may "overpower" the cognitive and affective components of our attitudes. In other words, the components of an attitude may lack consistency, and it is the behavioral component that is most often inconsistent with the other two.

Because our actual behaviors may not reflect our true feelings or beliefs, some social psychologists (for example, Fazio, 1989) exclude the behavioral component from their definition, reserving the term *attitude* to refer only to the basic like or dislike for the attitudinal object. Others argue that *attitude* is a two-dimensional concept involving affect and cognition, but not behavior (Bagozzi & Burnkrant, 1979; Zajonc & Markus, 1982). Still others (Fishbein & Ajzen, 1975) add a fourth component: a **behavior intention.** Just as its name implies, a behavior intention is a specific intention to perform a given behavior. For example, you may have a positive attitude toward a particular candidate yet not vote because you do not form an intention to vote. A behavior intention is affected by three things (Ajzen, 1991): one's attitude toward a behavior (for example, your attitude toward voting), normative pressures (are your friends voting?), and the degree to which you perceive that the behavior will matter (will your vote count?). So, if you think that voting is important, all of your friends are going to vote, and you think your vote will count, you will form an intention to vote. Such behavior intentions are better predictors of specific behaviors like voting than one's general political attitudes.

behavior intention
a specific intention to perform a given behavior that relates to behavior better than general attitudes

Attitude Formation

As it happens, we have formed many attitudes about a wide range of objects and events. Where did they came from? Most experts agree that attitudes are learned, and that simple conditioning processes go a long way toward explaining attitude formation.

Some attitudes are acquired through the associative process of *classical conditioning.* As shown in Figure 14A.1, pleasant events (unconditioned stimuli) can be paired with an attitudinal object (conditioned stimulus). As a result of this association, the attitudinal object comes to elicit the same good feeling (a positive evaluation) originally produced by the unconditioned stimulus. The good feeling, originally an unconditioned response elicited by a pleasant event, now becomes a

F I G U R E   1 4 A . 1   A schematic diagram of how attitudes may be formed through classical conditioning. At first, the attitudinal object is a neutral stimulus (NS), eliciting no particular response or interest. When it is paired with a stimulus (the unconditional stimulus, or UCS) that naturally produces an evaluative response (the unconditioned response, or (UCR), the attitudinal object becomes a conditioned stimulus (CS) that elicits a learned, or conditioned, response (CR).

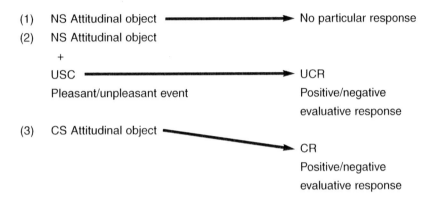

conditioned response elicited by the attitudinal object. Of course, negative attitudes can be acquired in the same way (for example, Cacioppo et al., 1992).

Some advertising uses conditioning techniques to change attitudes about a product by taking an originally neutral object (the product) and trying to create positive associations for it. For instance, a soft drink advertisement may depict attractive young people having a great time playing volleyball, dancing, or enjoying a concert while drinking a particular soft drink. The obvious intent is that we will associate the product with good times and having fun. That sports figures often wear brand name logos or trademarks on their uniforms also suggests that manufacturers want us to learn to associate their product with the skills of the athlete we are watching. Advertisements with sexual themes operate along the same lines.

Attitudes can also be formed as a result of the direct reinforcement of behaviors consistent with an attitudinal position, a matter of *operant conditioning*. Several studies have shown that verbal reinforcement (saying "good" or "that's right") when people agree with attitudinal statements leads to the development of attitudes consistent with the position expressed in those statements (Insko, 1965).

People often imitate behaviors that they have seen reinforced in others (called vicarious reinforcement). To the extent we perceive others gaining reinforcers for having and expressing some attitude, we are likely to adopt that attitude ourselves. Advertising that relies on the testimonials of satisfied customers is appealing to this sort of *observational learning*. The consumer is shown that someone has used a certain product with success (received reinforcement), and the advertiser hopes that this will lead the observer to develop a favorable evaluation of the product. Obviously, the advertiser is going to show us only those people who are happy with their product or service. We seldom stop to think about how many people may have used the product or service and are unhappy with it.

Before You Go On

What is social psychology?

What is an attitude, and what are its components?

Describe how attitudes are formed.

Attitude Change and Persuasion

Once attitudes have been formed, can they be changed? Experience tells us that they can. Political polls regularly track changes in attitudes about politicians. Based on poll numbers, political strategists develop political advertisements designed to change your attitudes and behaviors about the candidates. What psychological mechanisms account for attitude change? In this section, we will explore social psychological models of attitude change, beginning with cognitive dissonance theory.

Cognitive Dissonance Theory

It seems reasonable that one's attitudes will affect one's behaviors and that attitude change will lead to behavior change. In 1957, Leon Festinger proposed just the reverse: that attitudes follow behavior. Festinger's theory involves a concept he called **cognitive dissonance**, which is a negative motivational state that arises when our attitudes, thoughts and behaviors are out of balance or inconsistent. Cognitive dissonance often arises when we realize (a cognition) we have behaved in a manner inconsistent (dissonant) with other cognitions. Once dissonance is aroused, we are motivated to reduce or eliminate it. After all, like hunger, cognitive dissonance is a negative motivational state that we want to eliminate.

cognitive dissonance a state of tension or distress that occurs when there is a lack of balance, or equilibrium, between or among one's cognitions

An excellent example of how cognitive dissonance works is found in one of the original demonstrations of the phenomenon (Festinger & Carlsmith, 1959). Participants in the research were asked to perform an extremely boring task of rotating row after row of small wooden knobs. Following a lengthy knob-turning session, the experimenter explained that the research really had to do with the effects of motivation on such a task. Further, the participant was told that the person in the waiting area was to be the next participant in the project. This person was to be led to believe that the knob-turning task was interesting, fun, and educational. The experimenter explained that his assistant, who usually told these "lies" to the waiting participant, was absent. Would the participant do this "selling" job? The participant would be paid for his or her help. Participants invariably agreed and worked very hard to convince the next participant the project was fun and educational. Weeks later, at the end of the semester, all participants filled out a questionnaire that asked about their reactions to the knob-turning experiment.

The experimental manipulation was simple: some of the participants were paid $20 for trying to convince the waiting person (who was really not a participant, but was in on the experiment) that the obviously boring task was fun and interesting, whereas others were paid only $1. In all other respects, everyone was treated in the same way. Remember that this was the late 1950s, and for college students, $20 was a lot of money. The purpose of the experiment was to determine whether participants changed their attitudes toward the boring task.

At the end of the semester, which participants do you suppose expressed more positive attitudes about the project, the ones paid $20 or those paid $1? Doesn't it seem logical that those college students paid $20 would remember the task as being fun and enjoyable and indicate a willingness to participate in similar projects? Festinger and Carlsmith predicted just the opposite. They reasoned that students paid only $1 would feel that their behavior had not been sufficiently justified. They had told a "lie" and had been given only a trivial amount of money for doing so. They would experience a great deal of tension or discomfort—cognitive dissonance would be created. The dollar that a participant was paid does not provide sufficient justification for the lie. In essence, one comes to the conclusion that "I lied for a lousy dollar." This is known as the insufficient justification effect. Because the participants could not undo the lie, they resolved the dissonance by changing their attitude about the project (to a more positive one) so that it fit better with their behavior—a sort of, "Well, I didn't really lie, because the experiment wasn't all that bad; in fact, it was kinda fun at that."

Participants paid $20, on the other hand, had plenty of justification for their actions. Sure, they lied, but they had good reason to do so and would experience little cognitive dissonance. They should not be expected to change their attitude about the experiment. "Yeah, I lied, but I got paid twenty bucks." The results of this experiment are presented in Figure 14A.2. Seldom do we find differences in an experiment as clear-cut as these.

The results of this experiment (and numerous others) suggest that one way to change people's attitudes is to get them to change their behaviors first. Additionally, there is a clear advantage in offering as little incentive as possible to bring about that change in behavior. Simply "buying one off" to change his or her behavior may get you compliance, but it will not produce the cognitive dissonance needed to bring about lasting attitude change.

You should be able to generate other examples of cognitive dissonance bringing about attitude change. Consider those students who have changed their attitude about a course, or a discipline, because they were required to take a class in it. For example, as a chemistry major, your (quite negative) attitudes about psychology might change because of the dissonance created when you are required to take a (very enjoyable and informative) course in introductory psychology.

Cognitive dissonance theory can help us understand behaviors that are seemingly incomprehensible. For example, why would members of a cult (for example, members of the People's Temple and Heaven's Gate) commit mass suicide? Strange behavior, but it did happen. We can interpret such behavior from a cognitive dissonance perspective.

Festinger, Riecken, & Schachter (1982) found that members of a group that adhere to a belief strongly actually increase their strength in the belief after it is disconfirmed. Festinger and his colleagues joined a "doomsday" group that predicted the earth would end on a particular day. When the earth did not end, Festinger noticed that members increased their commitment to the belief and the group. Festinger reports that five conditions must be met for this effect to occur:

- The belief must be held with deep conviction and must be reflected in the believer's overt behavior,
- The believer must be strongly committed to the beliefs and taken steps toward commitment that are difficult to undo,
- The belief must be specific and relate to real-world events so that the belief can be disconfirmed,
- There must be undeniable evidence that the belief is false,
- The individual believer must have social support after disconfirmation.

Dissonance is created when one's previous behavior (for example, a strong commitment to the group) is dissonant with the disconfirming evidence (the world is still here). One cannot undo all of the commitments made to the group—to

FIGURE 14A.2 After being paid either $1 or $20 to "lie" about their participation in a boring task, subjects were later asked to rate the task in terms of enjoyment, interest, and educational value. As can be seen in the graph above, those paid $1 (those with cognitive dissonance) gave the task much higher ratings than did subjects paid $20. (From Festinger & Carlsmith, 1959.)

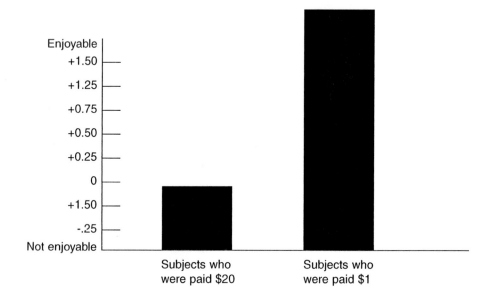

admit that the belief was wrong would generate more dissonance. To reduce dissonance the belief actually becomes stronger, and the believer rationalizes that the group's actions helped stave off the end of the earth. In the ultimate expression of this effect, individuals may be willing to go to their deaths (as in the People's Temple and the Branch Davidians) rather than face the prospect that they were wrong and all of the dissonance that would accrue.

There are many other situations that arouse dissonance. For example, situations that produce negative consequences are more likely to arouse dissonance than ones that produce positive consequences (Cooper & Scher, 1992). In such situations most of the negative affect is produced by feelings of personal responsibility for the negative event (Cooper & Fazio, 1984).

Dissonance is also aroused after you have made a choice between two mutually exclusive, equally attractive, but different alternatives. For example, imagine that you have to choose between two jobs. You can only have one of the jobs. Both are equally attractive, but they are different (one is near your favorite city, whereas the other is nearer to your family). After you make your decision, say you choose the job near the city, all of the positive cognitions associated with that job are consistent with your decision. However, all of the positive cognitions associated with the unchosen job are inconsistent with your decision. This inconsistency gives rise to **postdecisional dissonance.** How could you reduce the dissonance? Well, changing your decision won't help. That would just shift the source of the dissonance. What people tend to do is to think of negative things about the unchosen alternative. For example, one might begin to see being close to one's family as a drawback (for example, remaining dependent on the family, having to go to every family gathering).

postdecisional dissonance the cognitive dissonance experienced after making a decision between to mutually exclusive, equally attractive, different alternatives

Self-Perception Theory: An Alternative to Cognitive Dissonance Theory

The key assumption of cognitive dissonance theory is that attitude change is tied to the arousal of a negative motivational state (cognitive dissonance). Not everyone agrees with this position. Daryl Bern (1972) proposed an alternative to dissonance theory that eliminates the need for an internal negative motivational state. According to **self-perception theory** we keenly observe behavior, including our own, and then look for an explanation for that behavior. For example, when you eat you probably tell yourself that you are hungry. In Festinger and Carlsmith's classic experiment discussed above, dissonance theory presumes that attitude change about the experiment occurred because participants experienced dissonance relating to the inconsistency between their original cognitions ("I hated the experiment") and their later behavior (telling others that they liked the experiment) and when they were paid only $1. Self-perception theory takes a different approach. For those participants paid $1, they ask themselves: "Why did I tell this other person that the experiment was interesting when it wasn't?" The answer they come up with after analyzing the situation is: "I must have liked the experiment better than I thought." This response occurs without the experience of cognitive dissonance.

self-perception theory an alternative to cognitive dissonance theory that says we keenly observe behavior, including our own, and look for an explanation for that behavior

Attitude Change Through Persuasion

persuasion the application of rational and/or emotional arguments to change an individual's attitudes and behavior

A wholly different approach to attitude change focuses on the process of **persuasion** which is the application of rational and/or emotional arguments to convince others to change their attitudes or behavior (Horowitz & Bordens, 1995). The most widely accepted model of persuasion is the **Yale Communication Model** (Hovland, Janis, & Kelley, 1953). According to the Yale model (named after Yale University where the founders of the model did their research), the ability to persuade someone depends on three factors: the source of a message (who delivers the message), the characteristics of the message (what is said), and the nature of the audience (to whom the message is directed). According to the model these three factors affect internal processes such as attention to, comprehension of, and acceptance of a persuasive message. Change is measured in a person's attitudes, opinions (verbal expression and attitude) and overt behavior. In the sections that follow, we will explore how the source, message, and audience affect persuasion.

Yale Communication Model the most widely accepted model of persuasion that considers the influence of the sources of a message, the structure of a message, and the audience for a message

The Source of Persuasive Communication

credibility the believability of the communicator involving the expertise and trustworthiness of the communicator

The most important characteristic of the source of a persuasive message is the communicator's **credibility**, or the believability of the communicator. All other things being equal, a high credibility communicator will be more persuasive than a low credibility communicator (Hovland, Janis, & Kelley, 1953). There are two components comprising credibility: *expertise* and *trustworthiness*. Expertise refers to the qualifications, skills, and credentials of the communicator. For example, retired General Colin Powell (the former Chairman of the Joint Chiefs of Staff for the U.S. military) has a high level of expertise on military matters. You would be more impressed by a message coming from him about military matters than, say, a Private pulled from the ranks. Trustworthiness refers to the motivations behind the communicator's attempt to persuade you. Trustworthiness goes to the question of "why is this person trying to convince me?" For example, you would probably trust an automotive review you read in *Consumer Reports* because they have no vested interest in convincing you to buy one car or another. On the other hand, you might have less trust of a review in a magazine that accepts large sums of money from a particular car maker. In this case, you might question the motives of the reviewer (honest review or help sell cars made by the benefactor). A communicator who argues against his or her own best interests (for example, a Senator representing a tobacco-growing state arguing for strict control of cigarettes) is likely to be perceived as trustworthy. Although credibility is the most important source characteristic in persuasion, there are others. For example, vocal pleasantness and facial expressiveness affect persuasiveness (Burgoon, Birk, & Pfau, 1990). Additionally, the attractiveness of the communicator (more persuasion with greater attractiveness), the similarity of the communicator to the target of the message, and the rate of speech (moderately fast delivery enhances persuasion) affect persuasion.

The Message and the Audience

There are several things about how a persuasive message is constructed that can affect persuasion. Many of these message factors interact with the nature of the audience to affect persuasion. One factor is whether the message is one-sided (presenting only one side of an argument) or two-sided (providing both sides). A one-sided message is best if your audience is not well-informed or is on your side to begin with (Hovland et al., 1953), whereas a two-sided message is best for an educated audience (Hovland et al., 1953). Another message factor is the amount of discrepancy between the position taken in a persuasive message and the initial attitude of the audience. Too little or too much discrepancy does not lead to much persuasion. When there is too little discrepancy, you are simply restating the position of your audience, so little persuasion is possible. With too much discrepancy, your audience is likely to reject your message because it is so different from their position. A moderate amount of discrepancy leads to the most persuasion.

An important message characteristic is the nature of the appeal made. In a *rational appeal* one uses facts and figures to persuade the audience. For example, if we wanted to persuade people not to drink and drive we could present statistics on the number of alcohol-related traffic deaths that occur each year. Although rational appeals can be effective, emotional appeals can be even more effective. This is especially true of the *fear appeal* which attempts to persuade through the arousal of the negative emotion of fear. A fear appeal for a campaign against drinking and driving might show the aftermath of an alcohol-related accident. Generally, fear appeals are very effective. However, if they are to be effective three conditions must be met:

First, the appeal must arouse a significant amount of fear. Second, the target of the appeal must be convinced that the dire consequences can happen to him or her. Finally, the appeal must include instructions on how to avoid the dire consequences (for example, appoint a designated driver). Without this third factor a fear appeal does not work even if the first two criteria are met.

elaboration likelihood model
a model of persuasion stating that there are two routes to persuasion: the central route and the peripheral route

The Elaboration Likelihood Model

The Yale model makes a key assumption about the persuasion process: a person carefully attends to a message, carefully processes the content of the message, and changes attitudes and behavior when the message is accepted. There are situations, however, where persuasion is obtained even when a person doesn't pay careful attention to the content of the message. The **elaboration likelihood model** proposed by

Petty and Cacioppo (1986) takes up where the Yale model leaves off. According to this model, there are two routes to persuasion: the *central route* and the *peripheral route*. When a message is processed along the central route, the nature and quality of the persuasive message itself is the deciding factor. Here what matters most is a strong message—who delivers it, or how it is delivered is not terribly important. For example, a juror who carefully listens to the evidence during a trial and makes her decision based on the quality of the evidence has been persuaded along the central route. Persuasion along the peripheral route involves issues above and beyond the content of the message, such as the source of the message. For example, there was a trial in which a police officer was accused of murdering his wife. There were no witnesses (other than the defendant), and the jury had to rely on conflicting, ambiguous, and technically difficult evidence. The jury found the defendant not guilty. Some jurors noted after the trial that they found the defendant not guilty because they did not like "the way the prosecutor ran the show."

Central route processing is likely to occur when the audience is motivated to pay attention to the message and can comprehend the message. If the audience cares little about the topic of a persuasive message, or if the message is too difficult to comprehend, peripheral route processing is used. Generally, attitude change brought about along the central route is more resistant to further change than attitude change brought about along the peripheral route.

Before You Go On

What is persuasion, and what is the most widely accepted model of persuasion?

Describe what comprises credibility and how it affects persuasion.

When is it best to use a one-sided or a two-sided persuasive message?

Describe what makes a fear appeal work.

What is the relationship between discrepancy and persuasion?

Describe the elaboration likelihood model.

Attribution Processes

Another facet of the cognitive orientation we find in social psychology is a focus on *attribution processes*. Social psychologists working with attributions are interested in understanding the cognitions we use when we try to explain the causes or sources of behavior (our own and the behavior of others) (Jones, 1990). We might ask, "Do we tend to attribute behaviors or events we observe in the world around us to internal or external sources, personal dispositions, or environmental factors?

Internal and External Attributions

internal attribution an explanation of behavior in terms of something (a trait) within the person; a dispositional attribution

external attribution an explanation of behavior in terms of something outside the person; a situational attribution

An **internal attribution** explains the source of a person's behavior in terms of some characteristic of the person, often a personality trait or disposition (for this reason they are sometimes called dispositional attributions). For example, if you have a friend who is chronically late, you might conclude that this is a personality characteristic. You would have made an external attribution. An **external attribution** explains the source of a person's behavior in terms of the situation or context outside the individual and are referred to as situational attributions. For example, if you have a friend who is hardly ever late, you will probably make an external attribution if he is late once or twice (an alarm clock failed to go off, heavy traffic, etc.).

We tend to rely on different types of information when making judgments about the sources of behavior. Imagine, for example, that your friend is late only when he is supposed to be at work. He is not late any other time. That information is useful because of its *distinctiveness* (lateness shows up only when he's dealing with work). As a result, you may take it as a signal of a troubled relationship. A second source of information is *consistency,* or how regular is the behavior pattern you observe. For example, if your friend is always late for work, this is a consistent pattern of behavior. Compare this with a person who is late occasionally. This is a less consistent pattern of behavior. The final source of information is *consensus,* which is a question of what other people do in the same situation. If nobody else is consistently late for work, then consensus is low. If everyone is late for work, consensus is high. Compared to the other two types of information, consensus information tends to be underused.

Using information about distinctiveness, consensus, and consistency is important in determining the kinds of attributions we make about our own behaviors and about the behaviors of others (Kelley, 1967, 1973, 1992; Kelley & Michela, 1980). The manner in which the three sources of information mix determines the type of attribution you make. *High consensus* (everyone else is late for work), *high consistency* (my friend is always late), and *high distinctiveness* (my friend is only late for work) leads to an external attribution. That is, it must be something about the job situation causing lateness (perhaps a boss who doesn't care if people are late for work). On the other hand, *low consensus* (nobody else is late for work), *high consistency* (my friend is always late for work), and *low distinctiveness* (my friend is late for just about anything: golf games, dates, etc.) leads to an internal attribution. It must be something about your friend that causes his lateness.

One focus of research is how people make inferences about the behaviors of others. Current thinking is that there are two basic processes involved, the *trait inference process* and the *situational inference process* (Krull & Erickson, 1995). In some cases, we want know about a particular person ("Just what kind of a guy is he, really?"). We might (1) note the person's behavior, (2) draw an inference about the presence of some trait the person has that led to that behavior, and (3) revise or modify that inference or attribution as we consider the situation more fully. In other cases, we want to know about a particular situation ("Just what kind of a party is this, really?"). In this case, we may reverse steps (2) and (3). First, we (1) note a person's behaviors, then we (2) infer that the situation has caused these behaviors, and then we (3) revise or modify our inferences on the basis of what we know or dis-

fundamental attribution error the tendency to overuse internal attributions when explaining behavior

cover about the person we observed. In brief: Using internal or external attributions will depend on whether one is interested in the person or the situation.

Another area of research deals with the errors we make in our social thinking. In general terms we make attribution errors because preexisting cognitive biases influence our judgments of causality. An example of such a bias is the **fundamental attribution error**—the tendency to favor internal or personal attributions for behaviors rather than external situational explanations (Jones, 1979; Ross, 1977). We see a man pick up a wallet that has been dropped on the pavement and race half a block to return it to its owner. We say to ourselves, "Now there's an honest man." (And we predict that he will act honestly in a variety of situations.) The truth is, however that the fellow returned the wallet only because he knew that we saw him pick it up. If no one else was around, the wallet may not have been returned. The fundamental attribution error is the tendency to disregard, or discount, situational factors in favor of internal, dispositional factors when we make inferences about the causes of behaviors. There is evidence that biases such as the fundamental attribution error are more common in Western cultures. People from India, for example, make fewer dispositional attributions than Americans (Miller, 1984). Indians are more likely than Americans to explain behavior in terms of the situation or the environment than in terms of personality traits, abilities, or inabilities. That is, they are more likely to use a situational inference process than Americans.

just world hypothesis the belief that the world is just and that people get what they deserve

There are other biases that lead us to make incorrect attributions about ourselves or others. One is called the **just world hypothesis**, in which people believe that we live in a world where good things happen only to good people and bad things happen only to bad people (Lerner. 1965, 1980). It's a sort of "everybody gets what they deserve" mentality. We see this bias (or fallacy) when we hear people claim that victims of rape often "ask for it by the way they dress and act." In fact, even the victims of rape sometimes engage in self-blame in an attempt to grasp the random nature of the crime in which they were the victim (Janoff-Bulman, 1979; McCaul et al., 1990).

self-serving bias the tendency to attribute our successes to our own effort and abilities, and our failures to situational, external sources

Another bias that affects our attributions is the **self-serving bias**. It occurs when we attribute successes or positive outcomes to personal, internal sources and failures or negative outcomes to situational, external sources (Harvey & Weary, 1984; Miller & Ross, 1975). We tend to think that we do well because we're able, talented, and work hard. Whereas when we do poorly it is the fault of someone or something else. "Boy, I did a great job of painting that room" versus "The room looks so shoddy because the paint was cheap and the brush was old" is an example. The same process is at work even in the social groups of which we feel a part. If someone in *our group* (be it an ethnic group, cultural group, social group, or gender) succeeds, we're likely to attribute that success to internal, personal effort or an ability. If someone *outside our group* succeeds, we're likely to attribute that success to the situation (Finchilescu, 1994).

actor-observer bias the overuse of internal attributions to explain the behaviors of others and external attributions to explain our own behaviors

Some cognitive theorists argue that depression can be explained as a failure to apply the self-serving bias. That is, some people may get into the habit of blaming themselves for failures and negative outcomes regardless of where the real blame resides or regardless of whether there even is any blame to attribute.

Yet another attribution error is the **actor-observer bias** (Jones & Nisbett, 1971; Monson & Snyder. 1977). This is a discrepancy between the way we explain our behavior (as actor) and the way we explain someone else's (as observer). Generally, we use external attributions when we talk about why we do things. When we explain someone else's behaviors, we are more likely to use internal attributions and refer to characteristics of the person. "I took that class because the instructor is excellent," versus "He took that class because he's so lazy." "I am dating Bill because he's so caring and considerate," versus "She's dating him only because she wants to be seen with an athlete." "I went there because the rates were lower than anyplace else," versus "He went there because he wanted to show off."

That we explain our own behaviors in ways that are different from the ways we explain the behaviors of others is not surprising. For one thing, we have more information about ourselves and our own past experiences than we do about anyone else. In fact, the more information we have about someone else, the less likely we are to use internal attributions to explain his or her behaviors. Also, in any situation, the actor gets a different view of what is happening than does the observer; that is, actors and observers attempt to attribute the causes of behavior on the basis of different information.

Before You Go On

What is an internal attribution and an external attribution?

Describe the three sources of information used to make attributions.

What mix of information leads to an internal or external attribution?

Describe the various attribution errors.

Interpersonal Attraction

interpersonal attraction a powerful, favorable attitude toward another person

Interpersonal attraction is an attitude toward another person—a favorable and powerful attitude at that. Interpersonal attraction reflects the extent to which a person has formed positive feelings and beliefs about another person and is prepared to act on those affects and cognitions.

Theories of Interpersonal Attraction

Social psychologists have put forth several theoretical models to explain the basis of interpersonal attraction. Let's briefly review four such theories.

The simplest theory is the *reinforcement-affect model* (Clore & Byrne, 1974; Lott & Lott, 1974) which states that we are attracted to (have positive attitudes toward) people that we associate with rewarding experiences. It also follows that we tend not to be attracted to those we associate with punishment. One implication of this point of view is that you're going to like your instructor more, and seek him or her out for other classes in the future, if you get (or earn) a high grade in his or her class than you will if you get a low grade.

Another popular theory of interpersonal attraction is *social exchange theory* (Kelley & Thibault, 1978; Thibault & Kelley, 1959). According to this theory, what matters most is a comparison of the costs and benefits of establishing or maintaining a relationship. For example. Leslie may judge that John is attractive but that entering into a relationship with him is not worth the grief she would get from friends and family, who believe John to be lazy and untrustworthy. On the other hand, if Leslie has recently gone through a series of failed relationships with other men who were not physically attractive, she might take a chance on John, judging (in her frustration) that he is "worth it." This theory takes into account a series of comparative judgments made in social situations. Being attracted to someone else is not just a matter of "Is this a good thing?" It's a matter of, "Is the reward I might get from this relationship worth the cost, and what other alternatives exist at the moment?"

A third approach to interpersonal attraction is *equity theory*, which is more of an extension of social exchange theory than a departure from it (Greenberg & Cohen, 1982; Walster et al., 1978). Equity theory adds the appraisal of rewards and costs for *both* parties of a social relationship. That is, you may feel a relationship is worth the effort you have been putting into it, but if your partner in that relationship does not feel likewise, the relationship is in danger. What matters, then, is that both (or all) members of a relationship feel they are getting a fair deal (equity). Notice two things about this model: (1) Both members of a relationship do not have to share rewards equally. What matters is that the ratio of costs to rewards be equitable for both members. (2) If one person were to feel that he or she is getting more from a relationship than is deserved (on the basis of costs and compared to the other's rewards), the relationship would not be equitable and would be jeopardized. The best relationships are those in which all members receive an equal ratio of rewards to costs.

A more recent approach to understanding interpersonal relationships is one based on feelings or affect more than on cognitions. This model is referred to as *attachment theory* (Berscheid, 1994; Feeney & Noller, 1990; Hazan & Shaver, 1987). It suggests that interpersonal relationships can be classified into one of three types depending on the attitudes one has about such relationships (from Shaver, Hazan, & Bradshaw, 1988, p. 80):

Secure: "I find it relatively easy to get close to others and am comfortable depending on them and having them depend on me. I don't often worry about being abandoned or about someone getting too close to me."

Avoidant: "I am somewhat uncomfortable being close to others; I find it difficult to trust them completely, difficult to allow myself to depend on them. I get nervous when anyone gets too close, and partners often want me to be more intimate than I feel comfortable being."

Anxious/ambivalent: "I find that others are reluctant to get as close as I would like. I often worry that my partner doesn't really love me or won't stay with me. I want to merge completely with another person, and this desire sometimes scares people away."

One of the things that makes attachment theory appealing is the evidence that suggests that one's "style" of forming attachments with others is remarkably stable throughout the life span. It may be that the types of interpersonal relationships we form as adults are influenced by the types of attachments we developed as very young children.

Finally, we should remind you of a point we first discussed in the context of mate selection: few people enter into relationships having carefully considered all of the factors these models imply. That is, assessments of reinforcement, exchange, or equity value are seldom made at a conscious level; nor do we purposively seek out relationships that mirror those we had in childhood (Bargh, 1993).

Factors Affecting Interpersonal Attraction

Having reviewed four general models of interpersonal attraction, let's now look at some empirical evidence related to attraction. What determines who you will be attracted to? What factors tend to provide the rewards, or the positive reward/cost ratios, that serve as the basis for strong relationships? We'll consider four common determinants of attraction.

Reciprocity, our first principle, is perhaps the most obvious: we tend to value and like people who like and value us (Backman & Secord, 1959; Curtis & Miller, 1986). We noted when discussing operant conditioning that the attention of others can be a powerful reinforcer. This is particularly true if the attention is positive, supportive, or affectionate. The value of someone else caring for us is particularly strong when that someone else initially seemed to have neutral or negative attitudes toward us (Aronson & Linder, 1965). In other words, we are most attracted to people who like us now, but who didn't originally.

Our second principle, *proximity*, suggests that physical closeness yields attraction. Sociologists, as well as your own experience, will tell you that people tend to establish friendships (and romances) with others with whom they have grown up, worked, or gone to school. Residents of apartments or dormitories, for example, tend to become friends with those other residents living closest to them (Festinger et al., 1950). Being around others gives us the opportunity to discover just who provides those interpersonal rewards we seek in friendship. Of course, with the advent of the internet we have to redefine the definition of proximity. *Physical* closeness is becoming less and less important. One's ability to communicate with someone halfway around the world as if he or she were right next door brings people close together interpersonally and psychologically, if not physically.

mere exposure phenomenon the tendency to increase our liking of people and things as a result of recurring contact

There may be a social-psychological phenomenon at work here called the **mere exposure phenomenon.** Research, pioneered by Robert Zajonc (1968), has shown with a variety of stimuli that liking tends to increase with repeated exposure. Examples of this phenomenon are abundant in everyday life. Have you ever bought a CD you had not heard previously, assuming you would like it because you have liked all the other CDs made by the performer? The first time you listen to your new CD, however, your reaction is lukewarm at best, and you are disappointed with your purchase. Not wanting to feel you've wasted your money, you play the CD a few more times. More often than not you soon realize you like this CD. The mere exposure effect has occurred. This also commonly happens in our formation of attitudes about other people. Familiarity is apt to breed attraction, not contempt. Although there is ample evidence that the mere exposure phenomenon is real, there remains considerable disagreement about *why* familiarity and repeated interactions breed attraction (Birnbaum & Mellers, 1979; Kunst-Wilson & Zajonc, 1980). However, there are limits. Too much exposure may lead to boredom and to devaluation (Bornstein, 1989; Bornstein, Kale, & Cornell, 1990).

Physical attractiveness is related to interpersonal attraction. The power of physical attractiveness in the context of dating has been demonstrated experimentally in a classic study directed by Elaine Walster (Walster et al., 1966). University of Minnesota freshmen completed several psychological tests as part of an orientation program. Students were then randomly matched for dates to an orientation dance, during which they took a break and evaluated their assigned partners. The researchers hoped to uncover intricate, complex, and subtle facts about interpersonal attraction, such as which personality traits might mesh in such a way as to produce attraction. As it turned out, none of these factors were important. The impact of physical attractiveness was so powerful that it wiped out all other effects. For both men and women, the more physically attractive their date, the more they liked that date and the more they wanted to date her or him again. Numerous studies of physical attractiveness followed this one. Some of these studies gave participants a chance to pick a date from a group of several potential partners (using descriptions or pictures). Not surprisingly, participants almost invariably selected the most attractive person to be their date (Reis et al., 1980).

We seldom have the luxury of asking for a date without the possibility of being turned down. When experiments added the possibility of rejection, an interesting effect emerged: people no longer chose the most attractive candidate, but selected partners whose level of physical attractiveness was more similar to their own. This behavior is called the **matching phenomenon** and occurs for physical attractiveness and social status (Schoen & Wooldredge, 1989). Even when we consider relationships between or among friends of the same sex, we find that such friends tend to be similar when rated for physical attractiveness (Cash & Derlega, 1978).

Our fourth determinant of interpersonal attraction is *similarity*. There is a large body of research on similarity and attraction, but the findings are consistent, and we can summarize them briefly. Much of this research has been done by Donn Byrne and his colleagues (Byrne, 1971; Smeaton et al., 1989). Simply put, the more similar another person is to you, the more you will tend to like that person and the more you are likely to believe that person likes you (Buss, 1985; Davis, 1985; Gonzales et al., 1983; Rubin, 1973). We also tend to be repelled, or put off, by persons we believe to be dissimilar to us (Rosenbaum, 1986). Opposites may occasionally attract, but similarity is probably the glue that over the long haul holds together romances and friendships. It is this principle that makes it unusual, or difficult, for people to form significant interpersonal relationships with persons of other cultures or other ethnic groups (Stephan, 1985).

matching phenomenon the tendency to select partners whose level of physical attractiveness matches our own

4

Social Influence

So far, we have reviewed some of the ways in which our social nature has an impact on our cognitions—our perceptions and beliefs about ourselves and others. Now it is time to consider more direct influences of the social world on our everyday behaviors. We'll deal with the processes of conformity and obedience, and consider bystander apathy and intervention. We'll end by reviewing a few other situations in which social influence is a potent force in our lives.

Key Questions to Answer   As you read Topic 14B, look for the answers to the following questions:

1. What is conformity?
2. What were the methods and findings of Asch's conformity studies?
3. What were the different reasons given by Asch's participants for conforming?
4. What were the different reasons given by Asch's participants for not conforming?
5. What is the true partner effect?
6. What factors have been found to influence the rate of conformity?
7. Can a minority in a group influence the majority?
8. How did Milgram study obedience?
9. What did Milgram find about factors that affect obedience?
10. What steps are involved in the decision to help in an emergency situation?
11. What effect does the presence of others have on a person's willingness to help in an emergency?
12. What explanations have been given for the bystander effect?
13. What is the relationship between empathy and altruism?
14. What are social loafing, social interference, and social facilitation?
15. What factors influence group decision-making?
16. What is group polarization?

Reprinted from *Psychology: An Introduction*, Sixth Edition, (2000), Thomson Learning, by permission of the authors.

17. What is groupthink and what are its "symptoms"?

18. What does research suggest about the validity of groupthink?

Conformity

One of the most direct forms of social influence occurs when we modify our behavior, under perceived pressure to do so, so that it is consistent with the behavior of others, a process referred to as **conformity**. Although we often think of conformity in a negative way, it is natural and often desirable. Conformity helps make social behaviors efficient and, at least to some degree, predictable.

conformity the changing of one's behavior, under perceived pressure, so that it is consistent with the behavior of others

When he began his research on conformity, Solomon Asch believed people are not that susceptible to social pressure when the situation in which they find themselves is clear-cut and unambiguous. Asch thought people would behave independently of group pressure when there was little doubt their own judgments were accurate. He developed an interesting technique for testing his hypothesis (Asch, 1951, 1956).

A participant in Asch's experiment joined a group seated around a table. In his original study, the group consisted of seven people. Unknown to the participant, six of the people in the group were confederates of the experimenter; they were "in on" the experiment. The real participant was told that the study dealt with the ability to make perceptual judgments. The participant had to do nothing more than decide which of three lines was the same length as a standard line (Figure 14A.3). The experimenter showed each set of lines to the group and collected responses, one by one, from each member of the group. There were 18 sets of lines to judge, and the real participant was always the last one to respond.

Each judgment involved unambiguous stimuli: the correct answer was obvious. On 12 of the 18 trials, however, the confederates gave a unanimous but *incorrect* answer. What would the participants do? How would they resolve this conflict? Their eyes were telling them what the right answer was, but the group was saying something else.

The results of his initial study surprised Asch, because they did not confirm his hypothesis. When confederates gave "wrong" answers, conformity occurred 37 percent of the time. Participants responded with an incorrect answer that agreed with the majority on more than one-third of the trials. Moreover, three-quarters of Asch's participants conformed to the group pressure at least once.

Based on postexperimental interviews, Asch determined that participants conformed or remained independent for a variety of reasons. He categorized participants as yielding or independent. He found that some participants, although very few, yielded because they had come to accept the majority's judgments as correct. Most participants yielded because they did not have confidence in their own judgments. Another group of participants yielded because they did not want to appear to be defective in the eyes of the confederates. These individuals knew the majority was wrong but went along anyway. Independent participants also fell into three categories. Some participants remained independent because they knew the majority was wrong and had confidence in their own judgments. Other participants remained independent because they felt a strong personal need to do so. These

F I G U R E   1 4 A . 3 **The type of stimuli used in Asch's conformity experiments.**
Subjects are to say which of the three lines on the right (A, B, or C) equals the line on the left.
Associates of the experimenter will occasionally make incorrect choices, even though the correct
choice is always as obvious as this one.

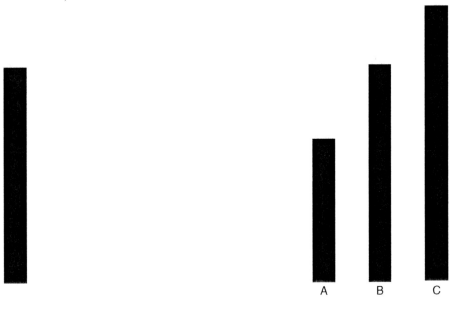

individuals might be called nonconformists or even anticonformists. The final
group of independent participants remained independent because they wanted to
perform well on the task.

In subsequent studies, Asch tried several variations of his original procedure. In
one experiment, he varied the size of the unanimous, incorrect majority. As you
might expect, the level of conformity increased as the size of the majority increased,
leveling off at three or four people (Asch, 1956; Knowles, 1983). Participants gave
incorrect judgments only 4 percent of the time when just one other incorrect judgment preceded their own. In another study, Asch found that participants gave an
erroneous judgment only 10 percent of the time when there was but one dissenter
among the six confederates who voiced an accurate judgment before the participants gave theirs. In other words, when the participants had any social support for
what their eyes had told them, they tended to trust their own judgment. This is
known as the **true partner effect**. If the true partner withdrew his support, conformity returned to its previous rate.

true partner effect
the effect occurring
when a person
emerges to support
the judgment of
the minority in a
conformity experi-
ment leading to a

Experiencing Psychology

Norms and Compliance

We live in a social world in which we have all formed expectations about the acceptability of behaviors in given situations. That is, we have learned how one is expected to act, or "supposed to act," in a social context. These expectations are called norms. This exercise asks that you see what happens when you violate those social norms. Can you get anyone else to change his or her behaviors just by violating a few common social norms? Please be very careful here. Some people become very upset when social norms are violated. Try these activities in good humor and be sensitive to the feelings of others, quickly explaining what you are doing at any sign of discomfort.

1. While others can watch you, try eating a banana by peeling back only part of the peel, and eat it as you would an ear of corn. Or, eat a chocolate bar with a knife and fork, cutting the chocolate into small, bite-sized pieces. (This violation of social norms became a running gag in the *Seinfeld* television program for weeks.)

2. Dress in a manner that is radically different from how you usually do when going to classes. How long does it take for your friends and acquaintances to comment on your choice of clothes?

3. Note the reactions you get if you simply walk across campus holding hands with a friend of the same sex.

4. Here's a classic (from the old television program *Candid Camera)*. Enter an elevator and ride up and down for a while facing the rear. Does anyone enter and join in facing the rear? Now try the same thing with some friends. What is the reaction of someone entering an elevator to find four of you facing the rear?

5. As you stand at a pay phone with a one dollar bill in your hand, see how many people will respond. to your request for change.

6. You should get the permission of your instructor for this one. Enter a class a bit early, go to a seat, but simply stand there— do not sit down, even as the class begins. Try the same thing with the aid of five or six classmates—and the permission of the instructor. How do people react when they come into a classroom and find six of you standing?

7. Here's another situation that requires the help of some friends—five or six will do. In the library or in a hallway, approach a student and ask if you can borrow a sheet of notebook paper. Then, a minute or so later, have a friend make the same request of the same student. Then a second friend, and a third, and so on, make the same request. Be sure to explain what you were up to, and ask the student how he or she felt as more and more people asked for a sheet of paper.

reduction in
conformity

Years of research on conformity show that the following factors influence the amount of conformity observed:

- The more competent the majority is perceived to be, the greater the conformity,
- The more competent the minority perceives itself, the lower the levels of conformity,
- As the ambiguity of the stimulus increases, conformity increases,
- There is a small gender difference, with women conforming more than men under certain circumstances (for example, a male experimenter or a group-pressure situation),
- Conformity varies across cultures with some cultures showing more conformity than others. There is also a relationship between the sociopolitical climate of the times and conformity rates.

Other researchers have demonstrated that the minority opinion (say, even one dissenter) can have significant effects on conformity, especially if the minority position is stated forcefully, held consistently (but not rigidly), and if the minority adopts a flexible. negotiating style (Moscovici et al., 1969, 1985; Nemeth, 1986). Moscovici suggests that majority and minority influence operate through two separate processes. According to Moscovici, majority influence comes about via group pressure, whereas minority influence comes about by the minority changing the attitudes of the majority. Other social psychologists disagree. Latané (1981) suggests that there is a single process that accounts for both majority and minority influence. Although both positions may be partially correct, the evidence seems to support the single-process approach more than the two-process approach.

Conformity involves yielding to the perceived pressure of a group. In most cases, it is assumed, group members are peers, or at least similar to the conformer. When one yields to the pressure of a perceived authority, the result is obedience. It is to the issue of obedience we turn next.

Before You Go On

What is the definition of conformity?

Describe the experiment conducted by Asch on conformity and his results.

Describe the reasons why participants yielded or remained independent in Asch's experiment.

What is the true partner effect?

What factors affect conformity?

Describe the conditions under which minority influence takes place.

Obedience to Authority

Adolph Eichmann, arguably the "architect" of the holocaust was captured by Israeli agents. He was brought to Israel where he was placed on trial for the crimes he committed against humanity. During his trial, Eichmann's principle defense was that he was a mid-level officer who was just "following orders." His contention was that his actions were taken at the behest of individuals who had the power to inflict punishment if he did not obey their orders.

Is "just following orders" a legitimate excuse? As we saw in the section on attributions, our predisposition is to attribute such behaviors internally. So, Eichmann becomes an inhuman monster and not a human being caught up in a highly unusual social situation. Which is it? Was Eichmann a monster, or was he a victim of circumstances?

This question preyed on the mind of the late social psychologist Stanley Milgram (1933–1984). Milgram was a student of Solomon Asch, so Milgram was interested in the conditions that lead to conformity. The participants in Asch's studies took the procedures seriously, but the consequences of either conforming or maintaining independence were rather trivial. At worst, participants might have experienced some discomfort as a result of voicing independent judgments. There were no external rewards or punishments for their behavior, and there was no one telling them how to respond. Milgram went beyond Asch's procedure. He wanted to see if an "ordinary" person placed in an "extraordinary" situation would obey an authority figure and inflict pain on an innocent victim. Milgram's research, conducted in the early 1960s, has become among the most famous and controversial in all of psychology. His experiments pressured participants to comply with the demand of an authority figure. The demand was both unreasonable and troubling (Milgram, 1963, 1965, 1974).

All of Milgram's studies involved the same basic procedure. Participants arrived at the laboratory to find that they would be participating with a second person (a confederate of the experimenter). The experimenter explained that the research dealt with the effects of punishment on learning and that one participant would serve as a "teacher," while the other would act as a "learner." The roles were assigned by a rigged drawing in which the actual participant was always assigned the role of teacher, while the confederate was always the learner. The participant watched as the learner was taken into a room and wired to electrodes to be used for delivering punishment in the form of electric shocks.

After receiving a sample shock of 45 volts, the teacher received his instructions. First, he was to read to the learner a list of four pairs of words. The teacher was then to read the first word of one of the pairs, and the learner was to supply the second word. The teacher sat in front of a rather imposing electric "shock generator" that had 30 switches. From left to right, the switches increased by increments of 15 volts, ranging from 15 volts to 450 volts. Labels were printed under the switches on the generator, ranging from "Slight" to "Moderate" to "Extreme Intensity" to "Danger: Severe Shock." The label at the 450-volt end read "XXX."

As the task proceeded, the learner periodically made errors according to a prearranged schedule. The teacher had been instructed to deliver an electric shock for every incorrect answer. With each error, the teacher was to move up the scale of shocks, giving the learner a more potent shock with each new mistake. (The learner, remember, was part of the act, and no one was actually receiving any shocks.)

Whenever the teacher hesitated or questioned whether he should continue, the experimenter was ready with a verbal prod, "Please continue," or "The experiment requires that you continue." If the participant protested, the experimenter became more assertive and offered an alternative prod, such as, "You have no choice; you must go on." Milgram was astonished by the results of his own study, and the results still amaze us. Twenty-six of Milgram's 40 participants—65 percent—obeyed the demands of the experimenter and went all the way to the highest shock and closed all of the switches. In fact, no participant stopped prior to the 300-volt level, the point at which the learner pounded on the wall in protest. One later variation of this study added vocal responses from the learner (voice feedback), who delivered an increasingly stronger series of demands to be let out of the experiment. The level of obedience in this study was still unbelievably high, as 25 of 40 participants—62.5 percent—continued to administer shocks to the 450-volt level. As shown in Figure 14A.4, the level of obedience decreased as the distance between the "teacher" and "learner" decreased. Obedience dropped when the teacher and learner were in the same room (proximity). The lowest levels of obedience were observed when the "teacher" was required to force the "learner's" hand onto a shock plate (touch proximity).

The behavior of Milgram's participants indicated that they *were* concerned about the learner. All participants claimed that they experienced genuine and extreme stress in this situation. Some fidgeted, some trembled, many perspired profusely. Several giggled nervously. In short, the people caught up in this situation showed obvious signs of conflict and anxiety. Nonetheless, they continued to obey

FIGURE 14A.4 Results from Milgram's experiments on the distance between the teacher and the learner.

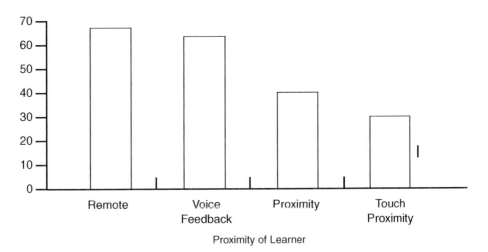

the orders of the experimenter even though they had good reason to believe they might be harming the learner.

Milgram's first study was performed with male participants ranging in age from 20 to 50. A later replication with adult women produced precisely the same results: 65 percent obeyed fully. Other variations of the procedure, however, uncovered several factors that could reduce the amount of obedience. Putting the learner and teacher in the same room, or having the experimenter deliver his orders over the telephone, reduced levels of obedience markedly. When the shocks were delivered by a team consisting of the participant and two confederates who refused to give the shocks, full-scale obedience dropped to only 10 percent. If the experimenter left the room and gave orders by telephone obedience also dropped. Obedience was also extremely low if there were conflicting authority figures; one urging the participant to continue delivering shocks and the other urging the participant to stop. When given a choice, participants obey the authority figure who said stop.

Attribution Errors and a Word of Caution

Upon first hearing about these distressing results, many people tend to think of Milgram's obedient participants as unfeeling, unusual, or even downright cruel and sadistic people (Safer, 1980). Nothing could be further from the truth. The participants were truly troubled by what was happening. If you thought Milgram's participants must be strange or different, perhaps you were a victim of what we identified in our last Topic as an *attribution error*. You were willing to attribute the participants' behavior to internal personality characteristics instead of recognizing the powerful situational forces at work.

Attributing negative personality characteristics to the "teachers" is particularly understandable in light of the unexpected nature of the results. In commenting on this research, many psychologists have suggested, in fact, that the most significant aspect of Milgram's findings is that they are so surprising. As part of his research, Milgram asked people, including a group of psychiatrists and a group of ministers, to predict what they would do under these circumstances, and asked them to predict how far others would go before refusing the authority. Respondents predicted very little obedience, expecting practically no one to proceed all the way to the final switch on the shock generator.

A Reminder About Ethics in Research

In reading about Milgram's research, it should have occurred to you that putting people in such a stressful situation could be considered ethically objectionable. Milgram himself was concerned with the welfare of his participants. He took great care to debrief them fully after each session. He informed them that they had not really administered any shocks and explained why deception had been used. It is, of course, standard practice in psychological experiments to conclude the session by disclosing the true purpose of the study and alleviating any anxiety that might have arisen.

Milgram reported that, after debriefing, the people in his studies were not upset at having been deceived. Their principal reaction was one of relief when they learned that no electric shock had been used. Milgram indicated that a follow-up study performed a year later with some of the same participants showed that no long-term adverse effects had been created by his procedure. Despite his precautions, Milgram was severely criticized for placing people in such an extremely stressful situation. One of the effects of his research was to establish in the scientific community a higher level of awareness of the need to protect the well-being of human research participants.

Before You Go On

Describe the experiments conducted by Milgram on obedience, and what he found.

What happened when Milgram moved the teacher and learner closer together?

What factors did Milgram explore that could affect obedience, and what was found?

How could attribution errors affect how Milgram's participants are perceived?

Bystander Intervention

Remember the story of Kitty Genovese that opened this chapter? Here was a young woman brutally slain in full view of at least 38 witnesses, none of whom came to her aid. This tragic event stimulated public concern and sparked much commentary in the media. People wondered how all those witnesses could have shown such a lack of concern for another human being. *Apathy* and *alienation* were terms used to describe what had happened.

Bibb Latané and John Darley, two social psychologists who at the time were at universities in New York City, were not satisfied that terms such as *bystander apathy* or *alienation* adequately explained what happened in the Genovese case. They were not willing to attribute people's failure to help to internal, dispositional, or personality factors. They were convinced that situational factors make such events possible. Latané and Darley (1970) pointed out that there are logical reasons people should not be expected to offer help in an emergency. Emergencies tend to happen quickly and without advance warning. Except for medical technicians, firefighters, and a few other select categories of individuals, people are not prepared to deal with emergencies when they arise. In fact, one good predictor of who will intervene in an emergency turns out to be previous experience with similar emergency situations (Cramer et al., 1988; Huston et al., 1981).

A Cognitive Model of Bystander Intervention

Latané and Darley (1968) suggest that a series of cognitive events must occur before a bystander can intervene in an emergency (Figure 14A.5). First, the bystander must *notice* what is going on. A person who is window shopping and fails to see someone collapse on the opposite side of the street cannot be expected to rush over and offer assistance. Second, if the bystander does notice something happen, he or she still must *label* the situation as an emergency; perhaps the person who has collapsed is simply drunk or tired and not really having a stroke or a heart attack. The third step involves the decision that it is the bystander's (and not someone else's) *responsibility* to do something.

Even if the bystander has noticed something happening, has labeled the situation as one calling for action, and has assumed responsibility for helping, he or she still faces the decision of what form of assistance to offer. Should he or she try to

FIGURE 14A.5 Some of the decisions and outcomes involved as a bystander considers intervening in an emergency situation. (Latané & Darley, 1968.)

give first aid? Should he or she try to find the nearest telephone, or simply start shouting for help? As a final step, the person must decide how to *implement* his or her decision to act. What is the best first aid under these circumstances? Just where can a phone be found? Thus, we can see that intervening on behalf of someone else in a social situation involves a series of cognitive choices.

A negative outcome at any of these steps will lead to a decision to not offer assistance. When one considers the cognitive events necessary for helping, it becomes apparent that the deck is stacked against the victim in an emergency. Ironically. it is the very presence of others that leads to this social-psychological phenomenon (Cunningham, 1984; Shotland, 1985). Perhaps we should be surprised that bystanders ever *do* offer help. There seem to be several psychological processes that account for what is called the **bystander effect** or *social inhibition of helping*. Let's review just three (Latané & Darley, 1970; Latané & Nida, 1981).

Audience Inhibition

Audience inhibition refers to our tendency to be hesitant to do things in front of others, especially strangers. We tend to be concerned about how others will evaluate us. In public, no one wants to do anything that might appear to be improper, incompetent, or silly. The bystander who intervenes risks embarrassment if he or she blunders, and that risk increases as the number of people present increases. People who are particularly sensitive to becoming embarrassed in public are most likely to be inhibited (Tice & Baumeister, 1985).

Pluralistic Ignorance

Emergencies tend to be ambiguous: is the man who has collapsed on the street ill or drunk? Is the commotion in a neighboring apartment an assault or a family quarrel that's just a little out of hand? When social reality is not clear, we often turn to others for clues. While someone is in the process of getting information from others, he or she will probably try to remain calm, cool, and collected, behaving as if there is no emergency. Everyone else, of course, is doing the very same thing, showing no outward sign of concern. The result is that each person is led by the others to think that the situation is really not an emergency after all, a phenomenon called **pluralistic ignorance (Miller & McFarland,** 1987). Pluralistic ignorance is the belief on the part of the individual that only she or he is confused and doesn't know what to do in an emergency, whereas everyone else is standing around doing nothing for a good reason. The group becomes paralyzed by a type of conformity—conformity to the inaction of others.

This process was demonstrated in a classic experiment by Latané and Darley (1968, 1970). Columbia University students reported to a campus building to participate in an interview. They were sent to a waiting room where they were to fill out some forms. While they did so, smoke began to billow through a vent in the wall. After six minutes (the point at which the procedure was terminated if the "emergency" had not been reported), there was enough smoke in the room to interfere with breathing and prevent seeing across the room.

bystander effect the phenomenon that a person is less likely to receive help when there are many bystanders as opposed to few or one

audience inhibition reluctance to intervene and offer assistance in front of others

pluralistic ignorance a condition in which the inaction of others leads each individual in a group to interpret a situation as a non-emergency, thus leading to general inactivity

When participants were alone in the waiting room, 75 percent of them came out to report the smoke. However, when two passive confederates were in the room with the participant. only 10 percent responded. Those people who reported the smoke did so quickly. Those from the groups who failed to do so generated all sorts of explanations for the smoke: steam, vapors from the air conditioner, smog introduced to simulate an urban environment, even "truth gas." In short, participants who remained unresponsive had been led by the inaction of others to conclude almost anything but the obvious—that something was very wrong.

Diffusion of Responsibility

In the Kitty Genovese murder, it was terribly clear that an emergency was in progress. There was little ambiguity about what was going on. Further, the 38 witnesses in the Genovese case were not in a face-to-face group that would allow social influence processes such as pluralistic ignorance to operate. Latané and Darley suggested that a third process is necessary to complete the explanation of bystander behavior.

A single bystander in an emergency situation must bear the full responsibility for offering assistance, but the witness who is part of a group shares that responsibility with other onlookers. The greater the number of other people present, the smaller is each individual's perceived obligation to intervene, a process referred to as **diffusion of responsibility**.

diffusion of responsibility the tendency to allow others to share in the obligation to intervene

Latané and Darley devised a clever demonstration of this phenomenon. College students arrived at a laboratory to take part in a group discussion on some of the personal problems they experienced as students attending an urban campus. To reduce embarrassment of talking about such matters in public, each group member was isolated in his or her own cubicle and could communicate with the others only through an intercom system. Actually, there were no other group members, only tape-recorded voices. Thus, there really was only one student in each group, and the perceived size of the group could be manipulated to see if diffusion of responsibility would occur.

The first person to "speak" mentioned that he was prone to seizures when under stress, such as when studying for an exam. The others, including the actual participant, then took turns talking about their problems. A second round of discussion began again with the seizure-prone student who, as he started talking, began to suffer one of his seizures. Clearly, something was wrong. As the "victim" began stammering, choking, and pleading for help, the typical participant became nervous—some trembled. The study had another feature in common with the Genovese episode: participants could not be sure if any other bystanders (members of the group) had taken any action. (In fact, remember, there were no others.)

As expected, the likelihood of helping decreased as the perceived size of the group increased. Eighty-five percent of those in two-person groups (just the participant and victim) left the cubicle to report the emergency. When the participant thought he or she was in a three-person group, 62 percent responded. Only 31 percent of the students who believed they were in a six-person group took any step to intervene. Additionally, help was given slower with more bystanders. So, a person is less likely to get help when there are many bystanders around and the help that is forthcoming takes longer to receive. The responsibility for reporting the seizure was divided (diffused) among those thought to be present.

Incidentally, diffusion of responsibility does come in forms less serious in their implications. Those of you with a few siblings can probably recall times at home when the telephone rang five or six times before anyone made a move to answer it, even though the entire family was home at the time. Some of you probably have been at parties where the doorbell went unanswered with everyone thinking that "someone else" would get it.

The Empathy-Altruism Connection

Traditionally, the focus of social psychologists interested in altruism has been the impact of the social environment on helping. However, other social psychologists point out that situational factors might interact with characteristics of the individual helper to affect helping. For example, true caring for a victim may motivate us to provide help (Batson 1987 1990a,b). This caring is rooted in an emotional state called **empathy,** which is compassionate understanding of how the person in need feels. If someone needs our help, feelings of empathy would include sympathy, pity, and sorrow (Eisenberg & Miller, 1987). For example, if you read about the victims of an airplane crash and feel the anguish of those who suffered, you are feeling empathy. Batson suggests that empathy may lead to altruistic acts. According to this **empathy-altruism hypothesis**, empathy is one reason for helping those in need. However, it is not the only reason.

empathy a compassionate understanding of how a person in need feels

empathy-altruism hypothesis a hypothesis stating that empathy is one reason for helping those in need

egoism helping someone in need to avoid personal distress for not helping

You might be motivated to help a person in need to relieve your *personal distress* associated with not helping. This motive for helping is called **egoism**. For example, if you saw a motorist stranded on the side of the road and said to yourself, "I better do something or I'll feel terrible all day," your helping is designed to relieve your own distress and not the distress of the victim. So, empathy is focused on the distress and suffering of the *victim,* whereas egoism is focused on *your own* distress and suffering. This indicates that there are at least two paths to helping: empathy and egoism. Generally, research by Batson (1990a,b) and others (Dovidio, Allen, & Schroeder, 1990) supports the empathy-altruism hypothesis. Empathy is one important motivator for altruistic acts (Dovidio et al., 1990).

The Bystander Effect: A Conclusion

The situational determinants of helping behavior continued to be a popular research topic for social psychologists throughout the 1970s. Many of these studies manipulated the size of the group witnessing the event that created the need for help in the first place. Latané and Nida (1981) reviewed nearly 50 studies involving almost 100 helping-not-helping situations. Although they involved a wide range of settings, procedures, and participants, the social inhibition of helping (the bystander effect) occurred in almost every instance. Latané and Nida combined the data from all of these studies in a meta-analysis. Their conclusion: A person is more likely to help when he or she is alone rather than in a group. The bystander effect is a remarkably consistent phenomenon, perhaps as predictable as any phenomenon in social psychology.

Before You Go On

Describe the five steps a person goes through before giving help.

What is the bystander effect?

What explanations have been offered for the bystander effect?

What are empathy and egoism?

Describe the empathy-altruism hypothesis.

Social Loafing and Facilitation

Latané, Williams, and Harkins (1979) have identified a process of social influence they call **social loafing:** the tendency to work less (to decrease individual effort) as the size of the group in which one is working becomes larger. Their studies had participants shout or clap as loud as possible, either in groups or alone. If people were led to believe their performance could not be identified, they invested less effort in the task as group size increased. Other studies (Harkins & Petty, 1983; Karou & Williams, 1993; Weldon & Gargano, 1988; Williams & Karou, 1991) have used different, more cognitive tasks, such as evaluating poetry. The results tend to be consistent: when people can hide in the crowd, their effort (and hence their productivity) declines.

Although social loafing is a widespread phenomenon, it is not always predicted when one works in a group setting. Remember our earlier discussions of cultures that can be described in terms of the extent to which they exhibit collectivist or individualist characteristics? As you might predict, social loafing is significantly less likely in those (collectivist) cultures—such as in Japan, China, and other Asian countries—which place a high value on participation in group activities (Early, 1989; Gabrena et al., 1985). In individualist cultures, such as in the United States and most Western countries, social loafing can be virtually eliminated if group members believe their effort is special and required for the group's success, or if group members believe that their performance can be identified and evaluated individually (Harkins, 1987; Harkins & Syzmanski, 1989; Williams et al., 1981, 1989).

Indeed, there are situations in which social influence actually facilitates behavior. Many years ago, psychologist Norman Triplett observed that bicycle riders competing against other cyclists outperformed those racing against a clock. He then performed what is considered the first laboratory experiment in social psychology (Triplett, 1898). Triplett had children wind a fishing reel as rapidly as they could. They engaged in this task either alone or with another child alongside doing the same thing. Just as he had noticed in his records of bicycle races, Triplett found that the children worked faster when another child was present. We now know that such an effect sometimes occurs not only with coactors (others engaged in the same task)

social loafing the tendency to decrease one's individual work effort as the size of the group in which one is working increases

but if a person performs before an audience. For example, joggers, both male and female, pick up the pace and run faster when going past a woman sitting on a park bench (Worringham & Messick, 1983). When the presence of others improves an individual's performance on some task, it is called **social facilitation**.

Numerous studies of these phenomena were performed early in the 20th century with a puzzling inconsistency in results. Sometimes social facilitation would occur, but on other occasions, the opposite would happen. Sometimes people performed more poorly in the presence of others than they did alone, an effect social psychologists called **social interference** The inconsistency in these findings was so bewildering that most social psychologists eventually gave up investigating social facilitation.

In 1965, Robert Zajonc resurrected the topic of social facilitation by providing a plausible interpretation for the lack of consistency in social facilitation effects. In his examination of the research, Zajonc noticed that social facilitation occurred whenever the behavior under study was simple, routine, or very well-learned (for example, bicycle riding, or winding a fishing reel). Social interference, on the other hand, tended to occur whenever the behavior involved was complex or not well-learned. Zajonc's insight was that the presence of others creates increased arousal which in turn energizes the dominant (most likely) response under the circumstances. When the dominant response is correct, as with a simple, well-practiced task, facilitation occurs. When the dominant response is incorrect, as with a complex task or one with which we have had little practice, the result is interference (Levine et al., 1993).

You may have experienced this effect yourself if you have ever tried to acquire a skill at a sport totally new to you. Whereas skilled athletes often perform better in front of audiences, the novice tends to do better when alone. (Even skilled athletes don't always perform better in front of audiences, sometimes "choking" in front of home crowds during important games [Baumeister, 1985].) You may have experienced—as a novice, that is—the frustration of making contact with a golf ball or tennis ball when there are others standing nearby, watching you.

In conclusion, we may safely assume that social interference and social loafing are more common phenomena than is social facilitation. Although there are occasions in which coworkers or an audience may enhance an individual's performance, the presence of others is more likely to inhibit it.

social facilitation improved performance due to the presence of others on a simple, well-learned task

social interference impaired performance due to the presence of others, especially on a complex task

Decision-making in Groups

Many of the decisions we face in our daily lives are the sort that are made in group settings. Committees, boards, family groups, and group projects for a class are only a few examples. There is logic in the belief that group efforts to solve problems should be superior to the efforts of individuals. Having more people available should mean having more talent and knowledge available. It also seems logical that the cohesiveness of the group might contribute to a more productive effort (for some groups and some problems, this is exactly the case). But, we know better than to assume that just because a conclusion is logical it is necessarily true.

Group Decision-making

Decades of research show us that groups can, and often do, outperform individuals. Here is a partial list of what we know about group decision-making:

- Groups outperform the average individual in the group mainly because groups recognize a correct answer to a problem faster, reject an incorrect answer, and have better memory systems than the average individual.
- Groups comprising high-quality members perform better than groups with low-quality members.
- As you increase the size of the group, you increase the resources available to the group. However, you also increase *process loss* (loss of productivity due to faulty group interaction). Additionally, in larger groups you get even less member participation than in smaller groups.
- When the problem a group must solve involves a great deal of interaction, *interpersonal cohesiveness* (how much members like each other) and *task-based cohesiveness* (mutual respect for skills and abilities) increase productivity. When a problem does not require much interaction task-based cohesiveness increases productivity, but interpersonal cohesiveness does not.

Before You Go On

What are social loafing, social facilitation, and social inhibition?

When does each occur?

Describe Zajonc's theory of social facilitation.

What factors affect group decision-making?

Group Polarization and Groupthink

Although it is generally true that groups outperform individuals, there are some liabilities attached to using groups to make decisions. In this section, we consider two aspects of group decision-making that can lead, in some cases, to low-quality decisions.

Group Polarization

When he was an MIT graduate student in industrial management, James Stoner gave participants in his study a series of dilemmas to grapple with (Stoner, 1961). The result of each decision was to be a statement of how much risk the fictitious character in the dilemma should take. Much to his surprise, Stoner found that the decisions rendered by groups were much riskier than those individual group members made prior to the group decision. Stoner called this move away from conservative solutions a *risky shift*. For example, doctors, if asked individually, might claim that a patient's problem (whatever it might be) could be handled with medication and a change in diet. If these same doctors were to jointly discuss the patient's situation, they might conclude that a new and potentially dangerous (risky) surgical procedure was necessary.

Several hundred experimental studies later, we now know that this effect also occurs in the opposite direction (Levine & Moreland. 1990; Moscovici et al., 1985). In other words, the risky shift is simply a specific case of a more general **group polarization** effect—that group participation will make an individual's reactions more extreme, or polarized. Group discussion usually leads to an enhancement of the beliefs and attitudes of the group members that existed before the discussion began. One explanation for group polarization is that open discussion gives group members an opportunity to hear persuasive arguments they have not previously considered, leading to a strengthening of their original attitudes (Isenberg, 1986). Another possibility is that after comparing attitudinal positions with one another. some group members feel pressure to catch up with other group members who have more extreme attitudes (Hinsz & Davis, 1984).

group polarization the tendency for members of a group to give more extreme judgments following a difficult discussion than they gave initially

Groupthink

Irving Janis (1972, 1983a) has described a related phenomenon of influence he calls **groupthink**, an excessive concern for reaching a consensus in group decision-making to the extent that critical evaluations are withheld. Janis maintains that this style of thinking emerges when group members are so interested in maintaining harmony in the group that differences of opinion or alternative courses of action are suppressed. Janis also maintained that groupthink is most likely to occur in cohesive groups.

Janis (1972) saw some common threads running through bad group decisions that led to "historical fiascoes." He identified eight "symptoms" of groupthink:

groupthink an excessive concern for reaching a consensus in group decision-making to the extent that critical evaluations of input are withheld

1. An illusion of invulnerability: The group members believe that nothing can harm them, which leads to excessive optimism,

2. Rationalization: Rather than realistically evaluating information, group members collectively rationalize away damaging information,

3. Unquestioned belief in the group's inherent morality: The group sees itself on the side of what is right and just. This leads group members to ignore the moral implications and consequences of their actions,

4. Stereotyped views of the enemy: The "enemy" is characterized as too weak or stupid to put up any meaningful resistance to the group's planned course of action,

5. Conformity pressures: Direct pressure is placed on any member of the group who dissents from what the group wants to do,

6. Self-censorship: Because of the conformity pressure, individual members of the group who may want to say something keep silent because of the potential consequences,

7. An illusion of unanimity: Because of self-censorship. the group suffers the illusion that everyone agrees with the course of action planned by the group,

8. Emergence of self-appointed mindguards: Self-appointed mindguards emerge to protect the group from damaging outside information. These people intercept potentially damaging information and don't pass it along to the group.

By analyzing several key historical events such as responding to the bombing of Pearl Harbor, the Bay of Pigs invasion, and the Challenger explosion, in terms of groupthink, Janis found that such situations involved a cohesive decision-making group that was relatively isolated from outside judgments, a directive leader who supplied pressure to conform to his position, and an illusion of unanimity (see also, McCauley, 1989). When, for example, decisions about women or minorities are made by a group of white males, we might suspect that groupthink could be at work.

Groupthink can be found in John F. Kennedy's decision to invade Cuba at the Bay of Pigs in 1961 (Janis, 1972). During the presidential campaign of 1960, Kennedy promised Cubans living in the United States that he would do something about Fidel Castro, Cuba's communist leader. After the election he and his national security staff inherited a plan for around 1,500 Cuban refugees to invade Cuba and overthrow Castro. Kennedy's policymaking group (made up of some of the brightest people in the country) went to work on the plan.

All of the antecedent conditions were present: the group worked in isolation, Kennedy was a highly directive leader, and there was a high degree of cohesiveness. The group decided to go ahead with the planned invasion. On April 17, 1961 the invasion began, and it was a disaster. Most of the 1,500 man brigade was captured and held for ransom, which was paid for their release. More ominously, the invasion sealed a mutual defense and security pact between Cuba and the Soviet Union. Shortly thereafter, the Soviets began installing land-based offensive nuclear missiles in Cuba, a mere 90 miles from the shores of Florida.

Janis' analysis of the Bay of Pigs invasion showed many of the symptoms of groupthink. Kennedy's group had an illusion of invulnerability. They had just won a close election and came into office on an emotional high. Several members of the group censored themselves, which led to an illusion of unanimity. The Cuban military was stereotyped as weak and disorganized. (In fact, the 1,500 Cuban refugees were met by a well-trained and well-equipped force of nearly 200,000 supported by an air force flying state-of-the-art Soviet Mig jet fighters.) Finally, Robert Kennedy emerged as a self-appointed mindguard, keeping potentially damaging information from the group.

History afforded Janis a unique opportunity. A few months after the Bay of Pigs debacle, Kennedy and the same group of advisors were faced with another crucial decision concerning the Cuban Missile Crisis. Kennedy and his group handled this crisis much differently (Janis, 1972). Kennedy abandoned the directive leadership style that permeated the Bay of Pigs decision. In fact, he did not let other group members know what he wanted to do about the missiles. The group considered several options (ranging from an all-out military strike to dropping leaflets), not only one (as was the case in the Bay of Pigs decision). Kennedy also took steps so that the group would not become isolated from outside influence. He invited experts in from the Pentagon and the State Department to address the group. Each member was told to play the role of "Devil's Advocate," questioning everything the group proposed. The group met without Kennedy, and after a decision was made the group was sent back to talk about the options again in a "second chance" meeting. The result was a more positive outcome. The Soviets removed the missiles from Cuba, averting a nuclear war.

Generally, Janis' groupthink hypothesis has weathered the test of time. However, some research suggests that group cohesiveness may not be as crucial to the emergence of groupthink as Janis originally believed (Courtwright, 1978). Directive leadership and consensus seeking, which makes groups more concerned with morale and getting members to agree than with the quality of the decision are important precursors of groupthink (Flowers, 1977; Tetlock, Peterson, McGuire, Chang, & Feld, 1992). Finally, Gerald Whyte (1989) has proposed that group polarization, risk taking, and the potential for a fiasco occur when a group frames its decision in terms of potential failure. Whyte suggests that if a group frames possible outcomes in terms of potential failure the group is more likely to make a risky decision. Working in an environment that favors risky decisions enhances the likelihood of a disastrous group decision (Whyte. 1989).

Before You Go On

What is group polarization?

What is groupthink?

What are the eight symptoms of groupthink?

How did John F. Kennedy's Bay of Pigs and Cuban Missile Crisis group differ?

What are the important factors underlying groupthink?

CHAPTER REVIEW

1 What is the definition of social psychology?

Social psychology is the field of psychology concerned with how others influence the thoughts, feelings, and behaviors of the individual. Social psychologists focus on the person or the individual in a group setting, and not on the group per se. Sociologists are more likely to focus on the behavior of larger groups.

2 How did Lewin explain social behavior?

Lewin developed a mode of social behavior that proposed that social behavior is determined by the interaction between the internal characteristics of the individual (for example, attitudes and personality characteristics) and the social environment (for example, the presence of others or the physical setting). Lewin's model is widely accepted by social psychologists.

3 What is the basic premise of the cognitive approach to social psychology?

The cognitive approach to social psychology suggests that we don't simply respond to the information provided by social stimuli. Instead, we have a set of cognitive processes that help us make sense out of information from the social environment. Cognitive social psychologists try to discover how individuals organize and represent information about themselves and others.

4 What is an attitude?

An attitude is a relatively stable evaluative disposition (positive or negative) directed toward some object or event.

5 What are the three components of an attitude?

An attitude consists of feelings (affects), behaviors (action tendencies), and beliefs (cognitions). Although the affective and cognitive components of attitudes are often consistent with each other, they may be inconsistent with behavior because behavior is influenced by many situational variables.

6 What is the fourth component of an attitude?

Fishbein and Ajzen (1975) suggest a model for attitudes that includes a fourth component: a behavior intention, which is a specific intention to perform a given behavior. Behavior intentions are formed based on three factors: one's attitude toward the target behavior, normative pressures, and the perceived consequences of behavior. Behavior intentions are better predictors of behavior than are general attitudes.

7 What are the three ways in which attitudes might be acquired?

Attitudes may be acquired through classical conditioning: after positive or negative experiences are associated with an attitudinal object, the object by itself comes to produce a positive or negative evaluation. Attitudes may develop as a result of direct reinforcement (operant conditioning), or they may be formed when they are vicariously reinforced (observational learning).

8 What is cognitive dissonance theory?

Cognitive dissonance theory is a theory of attitude change that proposes that attitude change occurs to reduce a negative motivational state called cognitive dissonance. Cognitive dissonance emerges whenever there is inconsistency between our cognitions (thoughts), attitudes, and behavior. Once dissonance is aroused, we are motivated to reduce or eliminate it.

9 What is the insufficient justification effect?

The insufficient justification effect occurs when we behave in an attitude inconsistent way and do not have sufficient reason for the behavior. For example, the participants paid only $1 to lie about an experiment changed their attitude toward the experiment more than participants paid $20 because the $1 was not sufficient to justify the lie. The inconsistency between the participants attitude toward the experiment (boring) and their behavior (tell someone it was interesting) created cognitive dissonance which was resolved by changing the attitude toward the experiment.

10 Under what conditions will disconfirmation of a belief increase the strength of that belief?

Festinger and his colleagues noted that under certain circumstances a disconfirmed belief is strengthened rather than abandoned. Festinger points out that five conditions must be met for this effect to occur: The belief must be held with deep conviction and relate to overt behavior, the believer must have taken steps toward commitment to the belief that cannot be easily undone, the belief must be specific and relate to real-world events, there must be undeniable evidence that the belief is false, and social support is needed after the belief has been disconfirmed.

11 What is postdecisional dissonance and how is it resolved?

Dissonance is aroused when you are forced to make a choice between two mutually exclusive, equally attractive, but different alternatives. It is resolved by developing negative cognitions concerning the unchosen alternative.

12 What is self-perception theory?

Self-perception theory was developed to account for dissonance-related attitude change. The theory proposes that dissonance is not needed for attitude change to occur. The theory says that we observe our behavior and then look for reasons why we might have behaved in the manner we did.

13 What is persuasion, and what is the most widely accepted model of persuasion?

Persuasion is the application of rational and/or emotional arguments to convince others to change their attitudes or behavior. The Yale Communication Model is the most widely accepted model of persuasion.

14 What are the three factors in the Yale Communication Model that influence persuasion?

The three factors outlined by the Yale Communication Model that affect persuasion are the source of a persuasive message (who delivers the message), the characteristics of the message, and the nature of the audience.

15 What is the credibility of a communicator?

A communicator's credibility refers to his or her believability. Credibility comprises two components: expertise (the qualifications of the source) and trustworthiness (the motivation of the source). All other things being equal, a communicator with high credibility is more persuasive than one with low credibility.

16 Other than credibility what other source factors affect persuasion?

In addition to credibility, the attractiveness of the communicator, the similarity of the communicator to the audience, and the rate of speech of the communicator affect persuasion.

17 When should a one-sided or two-sided message be used?

A one-sided message is best if the audience is not well-informed on the topic or is on your side to begin with. A two-sided message is best for an educated audience.

18 What is discrepancy and how does it relate to persuasion?

Discrepancy refers to the difference between the initial position of the audience and the content of a persuasive message. Too much or too little discrepancy leads to little or no attitude change. A moderate amount of discrepancy leads to the most persuasion.

19 What are rational and emotional appeals?

Rational appeals are persuasive messages that attempt to persuade by providing facts and figures. Emotional appeals try to persuade by arousing emotion, especially fear. Fear appeals are effective in producing attitude and behavior change when three conditions are met. First, the fear aroused must be quite high. Second, the target of the message must believe that the dire consequences depicted in the appeal could happen. Third, specific instructions must be given on how to avoid the dire consequences. The third factor is crucial. Without it, a fear appeal will not work, even if the first two conditions are met.

20 What is the elaboration likelihood model?

The elaboration likelihood model was proposed to account for situations in which persuasion occurs even in the absence of careful processing of a persuasive message. According to the model, messages can be processed along either a central route (involving careful processing of the content of the message) or a peripheral route (where the content of the message is not carefully considered. Rather, peripheral cues like the attractiveness of the communicator become important). A message will be processed along the central route if the audience can understand the message and is motivated to process it. Otherwise, the message will be processed along the peripheral route. Attitude change brought about by central processing is more enduring than change brought about by peripheral processing.

21 What are attributions?

Attributions are cognitions we use to explain the sources of the behaviors we see in our social worlds. Internal attributions identify the source of behavior as within the person and are also called dispositional attributions. External attributions find the source of behaviors to be outside the person and are also called situational attributions.

22 What errors are made in the attribution process?

The fundamental attribution error leads us to overuse internal, or personal, attributions when explaining behaviors. Those persons who hold to the just world hypothesis are likely to believe that good things happen only to good people and that bad things happen only to bad people, who in some way deserve their misfortune. With self-serving bias, we attribute our successes to our own efforts and actions and our failures to other, external factors. The actor-observer bias is the tendency to use external attributions to explain our own (as actor) behaviors, and internal attributions to explain the behaviors of others (as observer).

23 What are the four approaches that account for interpersonal attraction?

The reinforcement model claims that we are attracted to those persons we associate with rewards or reinforcers. The social exchange model adds cost to the equation, claiming that what matters in interpersonal relationships is the ratio of the benefits received to the costs invested in that relationship. The equity model suggests that both or all members of a relationship assess a benefit/cost ratio, and the best, most stable relationships are those in which the ratio is nearly the same (equitable) for both or all parties, no matter what the value of the benefits for any one member of the relationship. Attachment theory tells us that there are only a few relationship styles, and that each individual is consistent over his or her lifetime in the style used when relating to others.

24 What are four determinants of interpersonal attraction?

The principle of reciprocity states that we tend to like people who like us back. This is the most straightforward example of interpersonal attraction being based on a system of rewards. Proximity promotes attraction, in part, by means of the mere exposure effect: being near another person on a frequent basis gives us the opportunity to see what that other person has to offer. We also tend to be attracted to people we judge physically attractive. Finally, the principle of similarity suggests that we tend to be attracted to those we believe similar to ourselves.

25 What is conformity?

Conformity is a social influence process in which behavior is modified in response to perceived pressure from others so that the behavior is consistent with that of others. Conformity is often thought of in negative terms. However, conformity helps make social behavior efficient and predictable.

26 What were the methods and findings of Asch's conformity studies?

In Asch's studies, people made judgments about unambiguous perceptual stimuli: the length of lines. During some trials, confederates gave judgments that were clearly incorrect before the actual participant had a chance to respond. Although there were situations in which yielding to perceived group pressure could be lessened, many of Asch's participants followed suit and conformed.

27 What were the different reasons given by Asch's participants for conforming?

Based on post-experimental interviews, Asch categorized participants who conformed as "yielding" participants. Some, but very few, participants conformed because they accepted that the majority was correct in its judgments. A second group, making up the largest group of yielding participants, conformed because they had little confidence in their own judgments. The final group of yielding participants conformed because they didn't want to appear defective to others.

28 What were the different reasons given by Asch's participants for not conforming?

Asch's "independent" participants fell into one of three categories. First, some participants remained independent because they trusted their own senses and judgments. Others remained independent because they felt a great personal need to do so. Finally, other participants remained independent because they wanted to perform well on the task.

29 What is the true partner effect?

Asch found that if a member of the incorrect majority started to agree with the real participant in his experiment, the conformity rate dropped drastically. If the true partner withdraws his support, the conformity rate went back to its original rate.

30 What factors have been found to influence the rate of conformity?

Several factors affect conformity rates. The size of the majority is one factor. Conformity increases as the size of the majority increases up to a point and then levels off. The more competent the majority is perceived to be, the greater the conformity. If the minority perceives him or herself to be competent, conformity decreases. Conformity increases if an ambiguous task is used. There is a small gender difference, with women conforming more than men when a male is the experimenter or if group pressure is involved. There are also cultural and sociopolitical climate relationships with conformity.

31 Can a minority in a group influence the majority?

Minority influence has been demonstrated when the minority states his or her position forcefully, remains consistent (but not rigid), and adopts a flexible style. A two-process model was proposed to account for minority and majority influence situations. According to this view, majority influence occurs through group pressure and minority influence occurs through persuasion. A single process model called social impact theory proposes one process for both types of influence. There is more support for the single-process model.

32 How did Milgram study obedience?

Participants in Milgram's experiments were led to believe they were administering more and more potent shocks to another person in a learning task. Whenever they hesitated to deliver shocks, an authority figure, the experimenter, prodded them to continue. All participants obeyed to some degree, and nearly two-thirds delivered what they thought was the most intense shock, even over the protests of the learner. Those who obeyed in Milgram's experiments were neither cruel nor inhumane. Rather, the experimenter created a powerful social situation that made it difficult to refuse the authority figure's orders.

33 What did Milgram find about factors that affect obedience?

Milgram found that a participant's gender did not relate to obedience rates. However, as Milgram moved the teacher and learner closer together (in the same room), obedience dropped. The lowest rate of obedience was observed when the teacher actually had to touch the learner to give him a shock. When a group administered the shocks and two group members refused to continue, obedience was reduced. Having the experimenter leave the room and deliver orders by telephone and adding an authority figure who tells the participant to stop the experiment also reduced obedience.

34 What steps are involved in the decision to help in an emergency situation?

Darley and Latané proposed that a person must pass through a series of cognitive events before he or she will help. First, a bystander must notice the emergency. Second, the bystander must label the situation. Third, the bystander must assume responsibility for helping. Fourth, the bystander must decide how to help. Finally, the bystander must implement the decision to help. A negative decision at any point will result in no help being offered.

35 What effect does the presence of others have on a person's willingness to help in an emergency?

The likelihood that someone will intervene on behalf of another in an emergency is lessened as a function of how many others (bystanders) are present at the time. The greater the number of bystanders present, the less likely a person in need will receive help. This is known as the bystander effect.

36 What explanations have been given for the bystander effect?

Several factors have been proposed to account for this phenomenon. Audience inhibition is the term used to describe the hesitancy to intervene in front of others, perhaps for fear of embarrassing oneself. Pluralistic ignorance occurs when others lead one to think (by their inactivity) that nothing is wrong in an ambiguous emergency situation. Diffusion of responsibility causes a member of a group to feel less obligated to intervene (less responsible) than if he or she were alone. Each of these processes tends to discourage helping and is more likely to operate as the number of persons present Increases.

37 What is the relationship between empathy and altruism?

There are two forces that can motivate altruism: empathy and egoism. Empathy is an emotional state in which a person feels the suffering of a victim in need. Helping based on empathy is focused on relieving the suffering of the victim. Egosim motivates a person to help to avoid personal displeasure. The empathy-altruism hypothesis suggests that empathy is one important factor motivating altruism.

38 What are social loafing, social interference, and social facilitation?

Social loafing occurs when one is less likely to invest full effort and energy in the task at hand as a member of a group than he or she would if working alone (at least in Western, individualist cultures). Data suggest that as group size increases, social loafing increases. It is also the case that the quality of one's performance tends to suffer when one works in a group, a phenomenon called social interference. On the other hand, when tasks are simple or well-rehearsed, performance may be enhanced, a process called social facilitation.

39 What factors influence group decision-making?

Groups outperform the average individual because groups recognize a correct answer faster, reject an incorrect answer faster, and have better memory systems than the average person. Groups with high quality members perform better than groups with low quality members. Increasing group size increases resources available to the group, but also increases process loss. In larger groups member participation is less even than in smaller groups. Interpersonal cohesiveness and task-based cohesiveness enhance group performance when a problem requires a great deal of interaction. When a great deal of interaction is not required, only task-based cohesiveness increases productivity.

40 What is group polarization?

Although there are advantages to problem solving in a group setting, there are also liabilities. Group polarization (originally known as the risky shift) is the tendency for group discussion to solidify and enhance preexisting attitudes.

41 What is groupthink, and what are its "symptoms"?

Groupthink is an excessive concern for reaching a consensus at the expense of carefully considering alternative courses of action. Groupthink has been found to contribute to bad group decisions. Irving Janis identified eight symptoms of groupthink: An illusion of invulnerability, rationalization, an unquestioned belief in the group's morality, stereotyped views of the enemy, conformity pressures, self-censorship, an illusion of unanimity, and the emergence of self-appointed mindguards.

42 What does research suggest about the validity of groupthink?

Generally, the groupthink hypothesis has withstood the test of time. However, research shows that cohesiveness may not be as important as Janis originally thought. Directive leadership and consensus seeking are important factors in groupthink. Framing a problem in terms of potential failure may lead to excessive risk taking in groups, leading to bad decisions.

5   The Role of Culture

Understanding what makes people receptive to some, but not all, strangers requires knowledge of how culture affects perceptions and response patterns. Culture provides the guidelines for people's interpretations of situations they encounter and for the responses they consider appropriate. The distinctions and interplay between cultures are important to the assimilation process as well. For example, cultural orientations of both minority and dominant groups shape expectations about how a minority group should fit into the society.

This chapter first examines the various aspects of culture that affect dominant–minority relations, followed by an examination of varying cultural expectations about minority integration.

The Concept of Culture

Human beings both create and grow out of their own social worlds. Adapting to the environment, to new knowledge, and to technology, we learn a way of life within our society. We invent and share rules and patterns of behavior that shape our lives and the way we experience the world about us. The shared products of society that we call *culture,* whether material or immaterial, make social life possible and give our lives meaning. **Material culture** consists of all physical objects created by members of a society and the meanings/significance attached to them (e.g., cars, cell phones, VCRs, high-top sneakers, or clothing). **Nonmaterial culture** consists of abstract human creations and their meanings/significance in life (e.g., beliefs, customs, ideas, languages, norms, social institutions, and values). **Culture,** then, consists of physical or material objects as well as the nonmaterial attitudes, beliefs, customs, lifestyle, and values shared by members of a society and transmitted to the next generation.

These cultural attributes provide a sense of peoplehood and common bonds through which members of a society can relate (see Figure 2.1). Most sociologists therefore emphasize the impact of culture in shaping behavior.[1] Through language and other forms of symbolic interaction, the members of a society learn the thought and behavior patterns that constitute their

FIGURE 2.1   Basic U.S. Values

Within the United States' diverse society of racial, ethnic, and religious groups, each with a distinctive set of values, exists a common core of values. Sociologist Robin Williams, after decades of study, identified fifteen value orientations—the foundation of our beliefs, behaviors, definitions of social goals, and life expectations. Some are contradictory—freedom and individualism but external conformity; democracy and equality but racism and group superiority; nationalism but individualism—and these may spark divisions among people. Although other societies may subscribe to many of these values as well, this particular combination of values—virtually present from the nation's founding—have had and continue to have enormous impact in shaping our society.

1. **Achievement and success.** Competition-oriented, our society places much value on gaining power, prestige, and wealth.
2. **Activity and work.** We firmly believe that everyone should work, and we condemn as lazy those who do not work.
3. **Moral orientation.** We tend to moralize, seeing the world in absolutes of right and wrong.
4. **Humanitarian mores.** Through charitable and crisis aid, we lean toward helping the less fortunate and the underdog.
5. **Efficiency and practicality.** We try to solve problems by the quickest, least costly means.
6. **Progress.** We think technology can solve all problems, and we hold an optimistic outlook toward the future.
7. **Material comfort.** We share the American Dream of a high standard of living and owning many material goods.
8. **Equality.** We believe in the abstract ideal of equality, relating to one another informally as equals.
9. **Freedom.** We cherish individual freedom from domination by others.
10. **External conformity.** Despite our professed belief in individualism, we tend to join, conform, and go along; and we are suspicious of those who do not.
11. **Science and rationality.** We believe that through science we can gain mastery over our environment and secure a better lifestyle.
12. **Nationalism.** We think the American way of life is the best and distrust "un-American" behavior.
13. **Democracy.** We believe that everyone has the right of political participation, that our government is highly democratic.
14. **Individualism.** We emphasize personal rights and responsibilities, giving the individual priority over the group.
15. **Racism and group superiority themes.** Through our attitudes and actions, we favor some racial, religious, and ethnic groups over others.

Source: Robin M. Williams, Jr., *American Society: A Sociological Interpretation,* 3d ed. (New York: Knopf, 1970).

commonality as a people.[2] In this sense, culture is the social cement that binds a society together.

Shared cultural norms encourage solidarity and orient the behavior of members of the ingroup. **Norms** are a culture's rules of conduct—internalized by the members—embodying the society's fundamental expectations. Through norms, ingroup members (majority or minority) know how to react toward the acts of outgroup members that surprise, shock, or annoy them or in any way go against their shared expectations. Anything contrary to this "normal" state is seen as negative or deviant. When minority-group members "act uppity" or "don't know their place," majority-group members often get upset and sometimes act out their anger. Violations of norms usually trigger strong reactions because they appear to threaten the social fabric of a community or society. Eventually, most minority groups adapt their distinctive cultural traits to those of the host society through a process called **acculturation.** Intragroup variations remain, though, because ethnic-group members use different reference groups as role models.

An important component of intragroup cultural variations, one seldom part of the acculturation process, is religion. Indeed, not only does religion have strong links to the immigrant experience in the United States, as well as to African American slavery and pacification efforts toward Native Americans, but it also has many other connections to prejudice and social conflict. Indeed, the Catholic and Jewish faiths of past European immigrants provoked many manifestations (some quite violent and vicious) of Protestant nativism. Similarly, recent immigrants who are believers of such religions as Hinduism, Islam, Rastafarianism, or Santería often experience prejudice and conflict of their faith, as have the Amish, Mormons, Quakers, and many others in the United States in past years. Religious conflict is a sad reality in many parts of the world—the Balkans, India, the Middle East, and Northern Ireland, to mention just a few.

Professional sports are another part of culture, which also provide an area for the study of prejudice and racism. Historically, sports have favored males, a practice fostered by the mistaken belief that females lacked the strength and stamina to be athletes or would be "less feminine" if they were. Long excluded from major league sports, people of color now are prominent participants in baseball, basketball, boxing, football, and track. In fact, African Americans (13 percent of the U.S. population) account for 65 percent of National Football League (NFL) players and 77 percent of National Basketball Association (NBA) players. Nevertheless, the vast majority of owners, managers, and head coaches in all sports are White, and in some sports, such as football, one's race and position on the field are closely linked: Whites dominate in offensive slots and Blacks dominate defensive positions, with Whites more likely to play leadership roles on both sides of the line.[3] Still, many Blacks and Hispanics, and an increasing number of Asians, excel in athletics, serving as a source of racial and/or ethnic pride for many of their fellow group members.

The Reality Construct

Our perception of reality is related to our culture: Through our culture, we learn how to perceive the world about us. Cultural definitions help us interpret the sensory stimuli from our environment and tell us how to respond to them. Thus, "culture is something that intervenes between the human organism and its environment to produce actions."[4] It is the screen through which we "see," and we cannot get rid of it (Figure 2.2).

Language and Other Symbols.   Culture is learned behavior, acquired chiefly through verbal communication, or language. A word is nothing more than a symbol—something that stands for something else. Whether it is tangible (*chair*) or intangible (*honesty*), the word represents a mental concept that is based on empirical reality. Words reflect culture, however, and one word may have different meanings in different cultures. If you are *carrying the torch* in England, you are holding a flashlight, not yearning for a lost love; if you could use a *lift*, you want an elevator, not a ride or a boost to your spirits. Because words symbolically interpret the world to us, the **linguistic relativity** of language may connote both intended and unintended prejudicial meanings. For example, *black* is the symbol for darkness (in the sense of lightlessness) or evil, and *white* symbolizes cleanliness or goodness, and a society may subtly (or not so subtly) transfer these meanings to Black and White people.

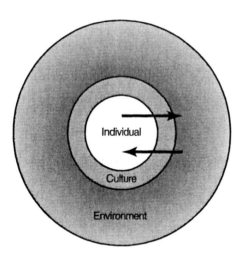

FIGURE 2.2   Cultural Reality
Each *individual* observes the world through
sense perceptions, which are evaluated
in terms of *culture*—values, attitudes,
customs, and beliefs.

Walter Lippmann, a prominent political columnist, once remarked, "First we look, then we name, and only then do we see." He meant that until we learn the symbols of our world, we cannot understand the world. A popular pastime in the early 1950s, called "Droodles," illustrates Lippmann's point. The object was to interpret drawings such as those in Figure 2.3. Many people were unable to see the meaning of the drawings until it was explained. They looked but did not see until they knew the "names." Can you guess what these drawings depict?[5]

Interpreting symbols is not merely an amusing game; it is significant in real life. Human beings do not respond to stimuli but to their definitions of those stimuli as mediated by their culture.[6] The definition of beauty is one example. Beyond the realm of personal taste, definitions of beauty have cultural variations. For instance, in different times and places, societies have based their appraisal of a woman's beauty on her having distended lips, scar markings, tattoos, or beauty marks or on how plump or thin she was.

Nonverbal communication—or body language—is highly important too. Body movements, gestures, physical proximity, facial expressions (there are between 100 and 136 facial expressions, each of which conveys a distinct meaning[7]), and **paralinguistic signals** (sounds but not words, such as a sigh, a kiss-puckering sound, or the *m-m-m* sound of tasting something good) all convey information to the observer-listener. Body language is important in intergroup relations too, whether in conversation, interaction, or perception. Body language may support or belie one's words; it may suggest friendliness, aloofness, or deference.

Although some forms of body language are fairly universal (e.g., most facial expressions), many cultural variations exist in body language itself and in the interpretation of its meanings. Body movements such as posture, bearing, and gait vary from culture to culture. The degree of formality in a person's environment (both past and present) and other cultural factors influence such forms of nonverbal communication. Consider the different meanings one could attach to a student's being unwilling to look directly into the eyes of a teacher. The teacher may assume that this behavior reflects embarrassment, guilt, shyness, inattention, or even disrespect. Yet, if the student is Asian or Hispanic, such demeanor is a mark of respect. The symbol's definition, in

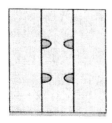 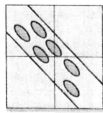  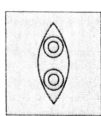

FIGURE 2.3   "Droodles"

this case the teacher's interpretation of what the student's body language means, determines the meaning the observer ascribes to it.

A person who is foreign to a culture must learn both its language and the rest of its symbol system, as the members of the culture did through socialization. Certain gestures may be signs of friendliness in one culture but obscene or vengeful symbols in another. For example, in the United States, placing thumb and forefinger in a circle with the other fingers upraised indicates that everything is fine, but in Japan, this sign refers to money, and in Greece, it is an insulting anal expression.[8] Kisses, tears, dances, emblems, silence, open displays of emotions, and thousands of other symbols can and often do have divergent meanings in different cultures. Symbols, including language, help an ingroup construct a reality that may be unknown to or altogether different for an outgroup. Members of one group may then select, reject, ignore, or distort their sensory input regarding the other group because of cultural definitions.

The Thomas Theorem. William I. Thomas once observed that, if people define situations as real, those situations become real in their consequences.[9] His statement, known as the **Thomas theorem,** is further testimony to the truth of reality constructs: Human beings respond to their definitions of stimuli rather than to the stimuli themselves. People often associate images (e.g., "Yellow peril," "Indian menace," or "illegal aliens") with specific minority groups. They then behave according to the meaning they assign to the situation, and the consequences of their behavior serve to reaffirm the meaning; the definition becomes a self-fulfilling prophecy. For example, when Whites define Blacks as inferior and then offer them fewer opportunities because of that alleged inferiority, Blacks are disadvantaged, which in turn supports the initial definition.

Several variables contribute to the initial definition, but culture is one of the most important of these. Culture establishes the framework through which an individual perceives others, classifies them into groups, and assigns certain general characteristics to them. Because ethnocentrism leads people to consider their way of life as the best and most natural, their culturally defined perceptions of others often lead to suspicion and differential treatment of other groups. In effect, each group constructs myths about other groups and supports those myths through ingroup solidarity and outgroup hostility. As each group's attitudes and actions toward other groups continue, the **vicious-circle phenomenon** plays out.[10] In such instances, people create a culturally determined world of reality, and their actions reinforce their beliefs. Social interaction or social change may counteract such situations, however, leading to their redefinition.

Gregory Razran conducted a study illustrating how cultural definitions can influence perception.[11] Twice within a 2-month interval, he showed the same set of thirty pictures of unknown young women to the same group of one hundred male college students and fifty noncollege men. Using a five-point scale, the subjects rated each woman's beauty, character, intelligence, ambition, and general likableness. At the first presentation, the pictures had no ethnic identification, but at the second presentation, they were labeled with Irish, Italian, Jewish, and old American (English) surnames. All women were rated equally on the first presentation, but when the names were given, the ratings changed. The "Jewish" women received higher ratings in ambition and intelligence. Both "Jewish" and "Italian" women suffered a large decline in general likableness and a slight decline in beauty and character evaluations. This study is one of many illustrating how cultural definitions affect judgments about others.

Through **cultural transmission,** each generation transmits its culture to the next generation, which learns those cultural definitions at an early age. This fact is dramatically expressed in the Rodgers and Hammerstein musical *South Pacific.* The tragic subplot is the touching romance between Lieutenant Cable and the young Tonkinese woman Liat. Although Cable and Liat are sincerely in love, Cable's friends remind him that the couple's life would not be the same in the United States. Their differences in race and culture would work against a happy marriage for them and his own acceptance in Philadelphia high society. Miserable because of the choice his cultural values force him to make, he sings "Carefully Taught," a poignant song about how prejudice is taught to children. The lyrics tell how one must be continually taught to hate and fear people whose eyes are "oddly made" or "whose skin is a different shade." Other lines tell how this teaching must occur before it's too late, that before a child turns eight, he or she must learn to hate all the people one's relatives hate.

These lyrics reinforce the reality construct discussed earlier and illustrated in Figure 2.2. From family, friends, school, mass media, and all other sources of informational input, we learn our values, attitudes, and beliefs. Some of our learning reflects the prejudices of others, which we may incorporate in our own attitudes and actions.

Cultural Change

Culture continually changes. Discoveries, inventions, technological advances, innovations, and natural disasters alter the customs, values, attitudes, and beliefs of a society. This section focuses on two common processes of cultural change: cultural diffusion within a whole society and changes within a particular subculture of that society.

Cultural Diffusion

Paradoxically, although the members of a dominant culture wish to keep their society untainted by contact with foreign elements, cultures are inevitably influenced by other cultures—a phenomenon termed **cultural diffusion.** Ideas, inventions, and practices spread from one culture to another, albeit at different rates of diffusion. Negative attitudes and a large distance between groups can pose formidable barriers, and sometimes cultural diffusion occurs only under temporarily favorable conditions. Sometimes ideas are modified or reinterpreted before being accepted, such as when some Latin Native American tribes of the early twentieth century showed a fondness for automobile tires: They used them to make sandals, for they neither owned nor drove cars.[12]

Borrowed Elements. U.S. anthropologist Ralph Linton calculated that any given culture contains about 90 percent borrowed elements. To demonstrate both the enormity and the subtlety of cultural diffusion, he offered a classic portrait of the "100 percent American" male:

> Our solid American citizen awakens in a bed built on a pattern which originated in the Near East but which was modified in Northern Europe before it was transmitted to America. He throws back covers made from cotton, domesticated in India, or linen, domesticated in the Near East, or wool, from sheep, also domesticated in the Near East, or silk, the use of which was discovered in China. All of these materials have been spun or woven by processes invented in the Near East. He slips into his moccasins, invented by the Indians of the Eastern woodlands, and goes to the bathroom, whose fixtures are a mixture of European and American inventions, both of recent date. He takes off his pajamas, a garment invented in India, and washes with soap, invented by the ancient Gauls. He then shaves, a masochistic rite which seems to have been derived from either Sumer or ancient Egypt.
>
> Returning to the bedroom, he removes his clothes from a chair of southern European type and proceeds to dress. He puts on garments whose form originally derived from the skin clothing of the nomads of the Asiatic steppes, puts on shoes made from skins tanned by a process invented in ancient Egypt and cut to a pattern derived from the classical civilizations of the Mediterranean, and ties around his neck a strip of bright-colored cloth which is a vestigial survival of the shoulder shawls worn by the seventeenth-century Croatians. Before going out for breakfast he glances through the window, made of glass invented in Egypt, and if it is raining puts on overshoes made of rubber discovered by the Central American Indians and takes an umbrella, invented in southeastern Asia. Upon his head he puts a hat made of felt, a material invented in the Asiatic steppes.
>
> On his way to breakfast he stops to buy a paper, paying for it with coins, an ancient Lydian invention. At the restaurant a whole new series of borrowed elements confronts him. His plate is made of a form of pottery invented in China. His knife is of steel, an alloy first made in southern India, his fork a medieval Italian invention, and his spoon a derivative of a Roman original. He begins breakfast with an orange, from the eastern Mediterranean, a cantaloupe from Persia, or perhaps a piece of African watermelon. With this he has coffee, an Abyssinian plant, with cream and sugar. Both the domestication of cows and the idea of milking them originated in the Near East, while sugar was first made in India. After his fruit and first coffee, he goes on to waffles, cakes made by a

Scandinavian technique from wheat domesticated in Asia Minor. Over these he pours maple syrup, invented by the Indians of the Eastern woodlands. As a side dish he may have the egg of a species of bird domesticated in Indo-China, or thin strips of the flesh of an animal domesticated in Eastern Asia which have been salted and smoked by a process developed in northern Europe.

When our friend has finished eating he settles back to smoke, an American Indian habit, consuming a plant domesticated in Brazil in either a pipe, derived from the Indians of Virginia, or a cigarette, derived from Mexico. If he is hardy enough he may even attempt a cigar, transmitted to us from the Antilles by way of Spain. While smoking he reads the news of the day, imprinted in characters invented by the ancient Semites upon a material invented in China by a process invented in Germany. As he absorbs the accounts of foreign troubles he will, if he is a good conservative citizen, thank a Hebrew deity in an Indo-European language that he is 100 percent American.*

Cultural diffusion is also an important element in ethnic relations within our pluralistic society. It can take many forms, including widened food preferences such as tacos or burritos, or use within U.S. corporations of Japanese management techniques such as employee participation in setting work goals. Whatever the form, cultural diffusion is an ongoing process, influencing various aspects of our culture and sometimes altering our views of the cultures of other peoples.

Cultural Contact.   Culture can also undergo change through people of different cultures coming into contact with one another. Because people tend to take their own culture for granted, it operates at a subconscious level in forming their expectations. When people's assumptions are jolted through contact with an unfamiliar culture that supports different expectations, they often experience **culture shock,** which is characterized by feelings of disorientation and anxiety and a sense of being threatened.

Culture shock does not always occur. When people of two different cultures interact, many possible patterns can emerge. The two groups may peacefully coexist, with a gradual cultural diffusion occurring. History offers some excellent examples of connections between migrations and innovations, wherein geographical conditions and native attitudes have determined the extent to which a group has resisted cultural innovations, despite invasions, settlements, or missionary work. The persistent pastoralism of Bedouin tribes and the long-sustained resistance to industrialization of Native Americans are two examples.[13] Stanley Lieberson, however, suggests that power alone determines the outcome, causing one group to become dominant and the other subservient.[14] If the subordinate group proves to be the nonmigratory group, the changes to its social organization can be devastating. No longer possessing the

*Ralph Linton, *The Study of Man* (1936), 326–327. Reprinted by permission of Prentice Hall Inc., Upper Saddle River, N.J.

flexibility and autonomy it once enjoyed, it may suffer material deprivation and find its institutions undermined.

If the migratory group finds itself in the subordinate position, it must adapt to its new environment to survive. Most commonly, the minority group draws from its familiar world as it attempts to cope with the prevailing conditions. Group members form a subculture with unique behavior and interests—neither those of the larger society nor those of their old culture. For example, both Catholicism and Judaism have undergone significant changes in form and expression since taking root in the United States. U.S. ethnic subcultures blend elements of homeland and dominant U.S. cultures once group members adapt to their new environment.

Subcultures

Usually, immigrants follow a pattern of **chain migration,** settling in an area already containing family, friends, or compatriots who located there earlier. An ethnic community evolves, providing an emotional support system to these strangers in a strange land as they strive to forge a better life for themselves. Part of this process of cultural insulation among others like themselves is the re-creation in miniature of the world they left behind. Thus, **parallel social institutions**—their own clubs, organizations, newspapers, stores, churches, and schools duplicating those of the host society—appear, creating cohesiveness within the minority subculture, whether it is an immigrant or native-born grouping.

As **ethnic subcultures** among immigrants in the United States evolve in response to conditions within the host society, the immigrants sometimes develop a group consciousness unknown in their old countries. Many first-generation Americans possess a village orientation toward their homeland rather than a national identity. They may speak different dialects, feud with other regions, and have different values. But their common experience in the United States causes them to coalesce into a national grouping. One example is Italian Americans, who initially identified with their cities of origin: Calabria, Palermo, Naples, Genoa, Salerno, and so on. Within a generation, many came to view themselves as Italians, partly because the host society classified them as such.

Yet, even as a newly arrived group forges its community and subculture, a process called **ethnogenesis** occurs.[15] Shaped partly by the core culture in selectively absorbing some elements and modifying others, the group also retains, modifies, or drops elements from its cultural heritage as it adapts to its new country. The result is a distinctive new ethnic group unlike others in the host country, dominant or minority, but also somewhat different from the people who still live in the group's homeland. For example, first-generation German Americans differ from other ethnic groups and from native-born U.S. citizens, but they also possess cultural traits and values that distinguish them from nonmigrating Germans.

Immigrant groups commonly attempt to preserve their special identity and cultural heritage within the minds of their children. As the assimilation process among the young takes its usual course, adults seek to instill in their children an awareness and appreciation of who and what they are, fearful that otherwise they will lose their sense of peoplehood and simply be absorbed into the dominant society.

(*Source:* Katrina Thomas)

Convergent Subcultures.   Some ethnic subcultures are **convergent subcultures;** that is, they tend toward assimilation with the dominant society. Although recognizable by residential clustering and adherence to the language, dress, and cultural norms of their native land, these ethnic groups are nonetheless becoming assimilated. As the years pass—possibly across several generations—the distinctions between the dominant culture and the convergent subculture gradually lessen. Eventually, this form of subculture becomes completely integrated into the dominant culture.

Because the subculture is undergoing change, its members may experience problems of **marginality**—living under stress in two cultures simultaneously. The older generation may seek to preserve its traditions and heritage while the younger generation may be impatient to achieve full acceptance within the dominant society. Because of the impetus toward assimilation, time obviously favors the younger generation. The Dutch, German, and Irish subcultures are examples of once-prevalent ethnic subcultures that are barely visible today. Italian, Polish, and Slovak subcultures have also begun to converge more fully. These nationality groups still exhibit ethnic pride in many ways, but for the most part, they are no longer set apart by place of residence or

The International Scene
Attempts to Eliminate a Persistent Subculture

The 20 million Kurds are an ethnic group with their own language. They live mostly in the bordering lands of Iran, Iraq, and Turkey—a region known as Kurdistan, or "Land of the Kurds." After World War I, this territory was partitioned among Turkey, Syria, and Iraq. Once a nomadic people who followed the seasonal migrations of their sheep and goat herds, the Kurds were thus compelled to abandon their traditional ways for village life and settled farming.

In the Kurdistan region, the Kurds remain a persistent subculture, whereas those living in urban areas are at least nominally assimilated. Marriages are typically endogamous, with a strong extended family network. The Kurds were once a tribal people under the firm leadership of a sheikh or an aga; however, that aspect of societal life is now felt (to a much smaller degree) only in the villages.

In 1924, the Turkish government engaged in cultural repression by renaming Kurds "Mountain Turks," outlawing their language, and forbidding their wearing the distinctive Kurdish costume in or near major cities. The government also encouraged many to migrate to the urbanized portion of western Turkey to dilute their population concentration. Uprisings in 1925, 1927–30, and 1937–38 were crushed; hundreds of thousands of Kurds were killed or expelled from the area.

Saddam Hussein's killing of thousands of Iraqi Kurds in 1988 with chemical weapons brought these relatively unknown people to the attention of Western cultures. Then came the Kurds' dramatic flight from Hussein's military forces in the spring of 1991 across snowclad mountains. Encouraged by the UN coalition's Gulf War victory, the Kurds rebelled against the repressive Baghdad regime, only to have Hussein's remaining forces drive them out. Iran let 1 million refugees cross its border to safety, but Turkey closed its border to about 500,000, trapping the Kurds in the mountains under harsh weather conditions. After two months, the coalition enticed the Kurds back into Iraq into an area designated as a "safe haven."

In 2003, these Kurds fought with U.S. troops against the Iraq government and hope for a better life under the new government. Today, Kurds remain divided between assimilationist and nationalist goals. Facing varying degrees of government repression and tolerance, they continue to face an uncertain future.

Critical thinking questions: What other persistent subcultures have faced harsh repressive actions? Are there common reasons for these government-endorsed actions?

---

subcultural behavior. Because of their multigenerational length of residence, these nationality groups are less likely to live in clustered housing arrangements or to display behavior patterns such as conflict, deviance, or endogamy to any greater degree than the rest of the majority group.

Persistent Subcultures. Not all subcultures assimilate. Some do not even desire to do so, and others, particularly non-White groups, face difficulties in assimilating. These unassimilated subcultures are known as **persistent subcultures.** Some adhere as much as possible to their own way of life and resist absorption into the dominant culture. Religious groups such as the Amish, some Hutterites, and Hasidic Jews reject modernity and insist on maintaining their traditional ways of life; they may represent the purest form of a persistent subculture in U.S. society. Other ethnic groups adopt a few aspects of the dominant culture but adamantly preserve their own way of life; examples are most Native Americans who live on reservations and many *Hispanos* (Spanish Americans) in the Southwest. Chinatowns also support preservation of the Chinese way of life in many ways.

A minority group's insistence on the right to be different has not usually been well received among dominant-group members. This clash of wills sometimes leads to conflict; at the very least, it invites stereotyping and prejudice on both sides (see the accompanying International Scene example).

Just as convergent subcultures illustrate assimilation, persistent subcultures illustrate pluralism. We next examine these two forms of minority integration, as well as a third.

Theories of Minority Integration

More than 65 million immigrants have come to the United States since its founding as a nation. Over the course of this extensive migration, three different theories have emerged regarding how these ethnically different peoples either should or did fit into U.S. society. These theories are (1) assimilation, or majority-conformity, theory; (2) amalgamation, or melting-pot, theory; and (3) accommodation, or pluralistic, theory.

The type of interaction between minority peoples and those of the dominant culture has depended partly on which ideology was then accepted by those already established in the community and partly on the ideology of the minority groups. People formulate attitudes and expectations based on the values they hold. If those values include a clear image of how an "American" should look, talk, and act, people who differ from that model will find their adjustment to and acceptance by others more difficult. Conversely, if those values allow for diversity, a greater possibility exists that harmonious relationships will evolve.

Assimilation (Majority-Conformity) Theory

Generally speaking, **assimilation (majority-conformity) theory** refers to the functioning within a society of racial or ethnic minority-group members who lack any marked cultural, social, or personal differences from the people of the majority group. Physical or racial differences may persist, but they do not serve as the basis for group prejudice or discrimination. In effect, members of the minority groups no longer appear to be strangers because they have abandoned their own cultural traditions and successfully imitated the dominant group. Assimilation may thus be described as $A + B + C = A$.[16]

Anglo-Conformity. Because most of the people in power in the United States during the eighteenth century were of English descent, English influence on the new nation's culture was enormous—in language, institutional forms, values, and attitudes. By the first quarter of the nineteenth century, a distinct national consciousness had emerged, and many U.S. citizens wanted to deemphasize their English origins and influences. However, when migration patterns changed the composition of the U.S. population in the 1880s, the "Yankees" reestablished the Anglo-Saxon as the superior archetype.[17] Anglo-Saxonism remained dominant well into the twentieth century as the mold into which newcomers must fit.

To preserve their Anglo-Saxon heritage, people in the United States have often attempted, sometimes with success, to curtail the large numbers of non–Anglo-Saxon immigrants. Social pressures demanded that new arrivals shed their native culture and attachments as quickly as possible and be remade into "Americans" along cherished Anglo-Saxon lines. The schools served as an important socializing agent in promoting the shedding of cultural differences.

Sometimes insistence on assimilation reached feverish heights, as evidenced by the **Americanization movement** during World War I. The arrival of a large number of "inferior" people in the preceding 30 years and the participation of the United States in a European conflict raised questions about nationals who were not "100 percent American." Government agencies at all levels, together with many private organizations, acted to encourage more immediate adoption by foreigners of U.S. practices: citizenship, reverence for U.S. institutions, and use of the English language.[18] Because this policy required that all minority groups divest themselves of their distinctive ethnic characteristics and adopt those of the dominant group, George R. Stewart suggested (some decades later) that assimilation be called the "transmuting pot" theory.[19]

Other assimilation efforts have not been very successful—for example, with people whose ancestral history in an area predates the nation's expansion into that territory. Most Native American tribes throughout the United States as well as the Hispanos of the Southwest have resisted this cultural hegemony.

Types of Assimilation. Milton Gordon suggested assimilation has several phases.[20] One important phase is **cultural assimilation (acculturation)**—the change of cultural patterns to match those of the host society. **Marital assimilation (amalgamation)**—large-scale intermarriage with members of the majority society—and **structural assimilation**—large-scale entrance into the cliques, clubs, and institutions of the host society on a primary-group level—best reveal the extent of acceptance of minority groups in the larger society.

Other types of assimilation are *identificational assimilation*, the development of a sense of peoplehood or ethnicity based exclusively on the host society and not on one's homeland; *attitude-receptional assimilation*, reaching the point of encountering no prejudiced attitudes; *behavior-receptional assimilation*, reaching the point of encountering no discriminatory behavior; and *civic assimilation*, the absence of value and power conflicts with the native-born population.

Gordon states, "Once structural assimilation has occurred, either simultaneously with or subsequent to acculturation, all other types of assimilation will naturally follow."[21] Other sociologists disagree, claiming that cultural assimilation does not necessarily result from structural assimilation. Some studies have shown that in the United States no significant structural assimilation has yet occurred for racial and ethnic groups other than those of northern and western European origin.[22]

Louis Wirth maintained that situational variables are important in the assimilation of minority groups.[23] Wirth distinguished among pluralism, assimilation, secession, and militancy as successive orientations by minorities in response to majority-group prejudice and discrimination. As groups begin to gain some power, they generally attempt to gain social tolerance of the group's differences (*pluralism*) and then become absorbed by the dominant society (*assimilation*). Those groups who are prevented from assimilating eventually withdraw from the societal mainstream (*secession*), but if conflict then ensues, they seek more extreme remedies (*militancy*).

Assimilation may be both a majority-group and a minority-group goal, but one or both may view assimilation as undesirable in some cases. Accordingly, the preceding typologies are not always helpful when examining dominant–minority relationships. Gordon shows the complexity of the assimilation process; Wirth suggests that the dynamics of the situation shape the evolution of dominant–minority relations throughout the assimilation process. The larger question of whether the assimilation process is linear remains in all cases. Not all groups seek assimilation, and not all groups who seek assimilation attain it.

Assimilation as a belief, goal, or pattern helps explain many aspects of dominant–minority relations, particularly acceptance and adjustment. For many members of the dominant society, assimilation of minorities has meant their absorption into the mold, reflecting what Barbara Solomon calls "the Anglo Saxon complex."[24] For physically or culturally distinct groups (e.g., Blacks, Native Americans, Asians, or Muslims), this concept has raised a seemingly insurmountable barrier. Even without the Anglo-Saxon role model, assimilation is preceded by a transitional period in which the newcomer gradually blends in with majority-group members. In doing so, the individual acquires a new behavioral identity, perhaps at some personal cost.

Amalgamation (Melting-Pot) Theory

The democratic experiment in the United States fired many an imagination. A new society was being shaped, peopled by immigrants from different European nations and not slavishly dependent on the customs and traditions of the past. This set of circumstances generated a romantic notion of the United States as a melting pot. The **amalgamation (melting-pot) theory** states that all the diverse peoples blend their biological and cultural differences into an altogether new breed—the American. This concept may be expressed as $A + B + C = D.$[25]

Advocates. J. Hector St. John de Crèvecoeur, a French settler in New York, first popularized the idea of a melting pot. Envisioning the United States as more than just a land of opportunity, Crèvecoeur in 1782 spoke of a new breed of humanity emerging from the new society. That he included only White Europeans partly explains the weakness of this approach to minority integration:

> What is an American? He is either a European, or the descendant of a European; hence that strange mixture of blood which you will find in no other country. I could point out to you a man whose grandfather was an Englishman, whose wife was Dutch, whose son married a French woman, and whose present four sons have now four wives of different nations. He is an American, who, leaving behind him all his ancient prejudices and manners, receives new ones from the new mode of life he has embraced, the new government he obeys and the new rank he holds. . . . Here individuals of all nations are melted into a new race of men, whose labors and posterity will one day cause great changes in the world.[26]

This idealistic concept found many advocates over the years. In 1893, Frederick Jackson Turner updated it with his frontier thesis, a notion that greatly influenced historical scholarship for half a century. Turner believed that the challenge of frontier life was the catalyst that fused immigrants into a composite new national stock within an evolving social order:

> Thus the Middle West was teaching the lesson of national cross-fertilization instead of national enmities, the possibility of a newer and richer civilization, not by preserving unmodified or isolated the old component elements, but by breaking down the line-fences, by merging the individual life in the common product—a new product, which held the promise of world brotherhood.[27]

In 1908, the play *The Melting-Pot* by English author Israel Zangwill enthusiastically etched a permanent symbol on the assimilationist ideal:

> There she lies, the great melting pot. Listen! Can't you hear the roaring and the bubbling? There gapes her mouth—the harbor where a thousand mammoth feeders come from the ends of the world to pour in their human freight. Ah, what a stirring and a seething—Celt and Latin, Slav and Teuton, Greek and Syrian. America is God's Crucible, the great Melting Pot where all the races of Europe are melting and reforming!—Here you stand good folk, think I, when I see you at Ellis Island, here you stand, in your fifty groups, with your fifty languages and histories, and your fifty hatreds and rivalries. But you won't be long like that, brothers, for these are the fires of God you come to—these are the fires of

God! . . . Germans and Frenchmen, Irishmen and English, Jews and Russians, into the Crucible with you all! God is making the American! . . . the real American has not yet arrived . . . He will be the fusion of all races, perhaps the coming superman. . . . Ah, Vera, what is the glory of Rome and Jerusalem, where all races and nations come to worship and look back, compared with the glory of America, where all races and nations come to labor and look forward.[28]

Both the frontier thesis and the melting-pot concept have since come under heavy criticism. Although many commentators still pay homage to the melting-pot concept, few social scientists accept this explanation of minority integration into society. Nevertheless, many people in the United States hold this view. The "English-only" movement, arguments against bilingual education, and exclusive emphasis on Western heritage are examples of some U.S. citizens' rejecting multiple cultures and wanting others to "blend in," although they really mean that they want people of ethnic subgroups to assimilate.

Did We Melt?   Over several generations, intermarriages have occurred frequently between people of different nationalities, less frequently between people of different religions, and still less frequently between people of different races. One could thus argue that a biological merging of previously distinct ethnic stocks, and to a lesser extent of different races, has taken place.[29] However, the melting-pot theory spoke not only of intermarriages among the different groups but also of a distinct new national culture evolving from elements of all other cultures. Here the theory has proved to be unrealistic. From its founding, the United States has been dominated by an Anglo-Saxon population and thus by the English language and Anglo-Saxon institutional forms. Rather than various cultural patterns melting into a new U.S. culture, elements of minority cultures have metamorphosed into the Anglo-Saxon mold.

Milton Gordon suggests that only in the institution of religion have minority groups altered the national culture.[30] From a mostly Protestant nation in its early history, the United States has become a land of four major faiths: Protestant, Catholic, Jewish, and Muslim. In the mid-twentieth century, some social observers viewed the United States as a **triple melting pot.** From her studies in New Haven, Connecticut, Ruby Jo Reeves Kennedy reported on extensive intermarriage between various nationalities but only within the then three major religious groupings (Protestant, Catholic, Jew).[31] Will Herberg echoed this analysis, arguing that ethnic differences were disappearing as religious groupings became the primary foci of identity and interaction.[32] Today, the high religious intermarriage rate and the increasing numbers of U.S. believers in Islam, Hinduism, and other non-Western religions render the concept of a triple melting pot obsolete.

In other areas, the entry of diverse minority groups into U.S. society has not produced new social structures or institutional forms in the larger society. Instead, subcultural social structures and institutions have evolved to meet

"Uncle Sam's Troublesome Bedfellows"
This cartoon pictures Uncle Sam annoyed by groups that were seen as unassimilable. Both racial differences (Blacks, Chinese, and Native Americans) and religious differences (Catholics and Mormons) were cause for being kicked out of the symbolic bed. This cartoon appeared in a San Francisco illustrated weekly, *The Wasp*, on February 8, 1879.

(*Source:* The Distorted Image, courtesy John and Selma Appel Collection)

group needs, and the dominant culture has benefited from the labors and certain cultural aspects of minority groups within the already existing dominant culture. For example, minority influences are found in word usage, place names, cuisine, architecture, art, recreational activities, and music.

Sociologist Henry Pratt Fairchild offered a physiological analogy to describe how the absorption of various cultural components or peoples produces assimilation and not amalgamation. An organism consumes food and is somewhat affected (nourished) by it; the food, though, is assimilated in the sense that it becomes an integral part of the organism, retaining none of its original characteristics. This is a one-way process. In a similar manner, U.S. culture has remained basically unchanged, though strengthened, despite the influx of many minority groups.[33]

Most social scientists now believe that the melting-pot theory is a myth. Its idealistic rhetoric continues to attract many followers, however. In reality, the melting meant **Anglo-conformity**—being remade according to the idealized Anglo-Saxon mold, as Herberg so eloquently observed:

But it would be a mistake to infer from this that the American's image of himself—and that means the ethnic group member's image of himself as he becomes American—is a composite or synthesis of the ethnic elements that have gone into the making of the American. It is nothing of the kind; the American's image of himself is still the Anglo-American ideal it was at the beginning of our independent existence. The "national type" as ideal has always been, and remains, pretty well fixed. It is the *Mayflower,* John Smith, Davy Crockett, George Washington, and Abraham Lincoln that define the American's self-image, and this is true whether the American in question is a descendant of the Pilgrims or the grandson of an immigrant from southeastern Europe.[34]

The rejection of the melting-pot theory by many people, coupled with an ethnic consciousness, spawned a third ideology: the accommodation (pluralistic) theory.

Accommodation (Pluralistic) Theory

The **accommodation (pluralistic) theory** recognizes the persistence of racial and ethnic diversity, as in Canada, where the government has adopted multiculturalism as official policy. Pluralist theorists argue that minorities can maintain their distinctive subcultures and simultaneously interact with relative equality in the larger society. In countries such as Switzerland and the United States, this combination of diversity and togetherness is possible to varying degrees because the people agree on certain basic values (refer to Figure 2.1). At the same time, minorities may interact mostly among themselves, live within well-defined communities, have their own forms of organizations, work in similar occupations, and marry within their own group. Applying our descriptive equation, pluralism would be $A + B + C = A + B + C$.[35]

Early Analysis.   Horace Kallen is generally recognized as the first exponent of cultural pluralism. In 1915, he published "Democracy Versus the Melting Pot," in which he rejected the assimilation and amalgamation theories.[36] Not only did each group tend to preserve its own language, institutions, and cultural heritage, he maintained, but democracy gave each group the right to do so. To be sure, minority groups learned the English language and participated in U.S. institutions, but what the United States really had become was a "cooperation of cultural diversities." Seeing Americanization movements as a threat to minority groups and the melting-pot notion as unrealistic, Kallen believed that cultural pluralism could be the basis for a great democratic commonwealth. A philosopher, not a sociologist, Kallen nonetheless directed sociological attention to a longstanding U.S. pattern.

Pluralistic Reality.   From its colonial beginnings, the United States has been a pluralistic country. Early settlements were small ethnic enclaves, each peopled by different nationalities or religious groups. New Amsterdam and

Philadelphia were exceptions; both were heavily pluralistic within their boundaries. Chain-migration patterns resulted in immigrants settling in clusters. Germans and Scandinavians in the Midwest, Poles in Chicago, Irish in New York and Boston, French in Louisiana, Asians in California, Cubans in Miami, and many others illustrate how groups ease their adjustment to a new country by re-creating in miniature the world they left behind. Current immigrant groups and remnants of past immigrant groups are testimony to the pluralism in U.S. society.

Cultural pluralism—two or more culturally distinct groups living in the same society in relative harmony—has been the more noticeable form of pluralism. **Structural pluralism**—the coexistence of racial and ethnic groups in subsocieties within social-class and regional boundaries—is less noticeable.

As Gordon observes, "Cultural pluralism was a fact in American society before it became a theory—at least a theory with explicit relevance for the nation as a whole and articulated and discussed in the general English-speaking circles of American intellectual life."[37] Many minority groups lose their visibility when they acculturate. They may, however, identify with and take pride in their heritage and maintain primary relationships mostly with members of their ethnic group. Despite this pluralistic reality, intolerance of such diversity remains a problem within U.S. society.

Dual Realities.   Although Americans give lip service to the concept of a melting pot, they typically expect foreigners to assimilate as quickly as possible. Mainstream Americans often tolerate pluralism only as a short-term phenomenon, for many believe sustained pluralism is the enemy of assimilation, a threat to the cohesiveness of U.S. society.

Assimilation and pluralism are not mutually exclusive however; nor are they necessarily enemies. In fact, they have always existed simultaneously among different groups, at different levels. Whether as persistent subcultures or as convergent ones that gradually merge into the dominant culture over several generations, culturally distinct groups have always existed. And even when their numbers have been great, they have never threatened the core cultures, as we will see. Assimilation remains a powerful force affecting most minority groups, despite the assertions of anti-immigration fearmongers and radical multiculturalists. Although proponents of one position may decry the other, pluralism and assimilation have always been dual realities within U.S. society.

As Richard D. Alba reminds us, assimilation occurs in different ways and to different degrees, and it does not necessarily mean the obliteration of all traces of ethnic origins. It can occur even as ethnic communities continue to exist in numerous cities and as many individuals continue to identify with their ethnic ancestry.

> [*Assimilation*] refers, above all, to long-term processes that have whittled away at the social foundations for ethnic distinctions. These processes have brought

about a rough parity of opportunities to attain such socioeconomic goods as educational credentials and prestigious jobs, loosened the ties between ethnicity and specific economic niches, diminished cultural differences that serve to signal ethnic membership to others and to sustain ethnic solidarity, shifted residence away from central-city ethnic neighborhoods to ethnically intermixed suburbs, and finally, fostered relatively easy social intermixing across ethnic lines, resulting ultimately in high rates of ethnic intermarriage and ethnically mixed ancestry.[38]

In a 1997 special issue of the *International Migration Review* on "Immigrant Adaptation and Native-Born Responses in the Making of Americans," several leading sociologists addressed the unnecessary intellectual conflict over the dual realities. Herbert Gans suggests that a reconciliation between assimilation and pluralism may be found by recalling the distinction between acculturation and assimilation. Acculturation has always proceeded more quickly than assimilation, providing evidence in support of both traditional assimilationist theory and recent pluralist—or ethnic retention—theory. Moreover, researchers of past and present immigrations have studied different generations of newcomers and have approached their research with "outsider" and "insider" values, respectively.[39] Richard D. Alba and Victor Nee add that the evidence shows that assimilation is occurring among recent arrivals, albeit unevenly, and suggest that some fine-tuning of assimilationist theory to address these variances in settlement, language acquisition, and mobility patterns may improve our understanding of the contemporary ethnic and racial scene.[40]

Is There a White Culture?

In the mid-1990s, interest in White studies rose significantly. White studies essentially focuses on how whiteness has led to racial domination and hegemony, in which White American culture is simply called "American," thereby presuming that Black, Native American, Asian, or Hispanic cultures are not "American" but instead racial and/or ethnic subcultures. The idea that a White culture also exists is difficult for many people to grasp, say the White studies advocates, much like a fish is unaware of water until out of it, because of its environmental universality.

The premise for a White culture existing independent of an "American" culture is that all racial groups have large social/cultural characteristics that change over time. These White values, attitudes, shared understandings, and behavior patterns—like many aspects of culture—are often unrealized by group members because they are part of a taken-for-granted world. Yet even though White culture may not be identifiable among its members, it is nonetheless real and easily recognizable by non-Whites. For example, says Jeff Hitchcock in *Unraveling the White Cocoon*, in Black culture feelings are given precedence over sensibilities. He explains that when a feeling comes upon a person, Black culture says it is appropriate to express it, but White culture

> works hard to keep the volume down, least we all go crazy from the demands we place on each other's capacity for self-control. Experience in the culture helps. We learn how not to step on toes, hurt other people's "feelings," to not make a scene, and all the other little social rules and practices of a lifetime. We rein it in, and trade spontaneity . . . for an orderly demeanor and generally predictable and controlled everyday existence.[41]

Lacking an understanding of the existence of White culture, say its proponents, results in the dominant group misinterpreting alternative cultural experiences as racial or else as the personal failings of someone of color. Recognizing its existence could be a first step toward building a truly multiracial society.

Retrospect

Culture provides the normative definitions by which members of a society perceive and interpret the world about them. Language and other forms of symbolic interaction provide the means by which this accumulated knowledge is transmitted. Becoming acculturated requires learning both the language and the symbol system of the new society. Sometimes, though, situations become real in their consequences because people earlier defined them as real (the Thomas theorem). Unless it is isolated from the rest of the world, a society undergoes change through culture contact and the diffusion of ideas, inventions, and practices. Within large societies, subcultures usually exist. They may gradually be assimilated (convergent subcultures), or they may remain distinct (persistent subcultures).

Three theories of minority integration have emerged. Assimilation, or majority-conformity, became a goal of many, both native-born and foreign-born; yet not all sought this goal or were able to achieve it. The romantic notion of amalgamation, or a melting pot, in which a new breed of people with a distinct culture would emerge, proved unrealistic. Finally, accommodation, or pluralism, arose as a school of thought recognizing the persistence of ethnic diversity in a society with a commonly shared core culture. Assimilation and pluralism are not mutually exclusive; both have always existed simultaneously, with assimilation exerting a constant, powerful force.

KEY TERMS

Accommodation (pluralistic) theory
Acculturation

Amalgamation (melting-pot) theory
Americanization movement

Anglo-conformity
Assimilation (majority-conformity)
   theory
Chain migration
Convergent subcultures
Cultural assimilation (acculturation)
Cultural diffusion
Cultural pluralism
Cultural transmission
Culture
Culture shock
Ethnic subcultures
Ethnogenesis
Linguistic relativity

Marginality
Marital assimilation (amalgamation)
Material culture
Nonmaterial culture
Norms
Paralinguistic signals
Parallel social institutions
Persistent subcultures
Structural assimilation
Structural pluralism
Thomas theorem
Triple melting pot
Vicious-circle phenomenon

REVIEW QUESTIONS

1. What is the relationship among culture, reality, and intergroup relations?

2. How does language affect our perception of reality?

3. How does the Thomas theorem help us understand problems in intergroup relations?

4. How would you answer someone who claims foreigners are changing American culture?

5. What are subcultures? What forms do they take? What significance do these forms have for intergroup relations?

6. Discuss the major theories of minority integration.

SUGGESTED READINGS

Gordon, Milton M. *Assimilation in American Life*. New York: Oxford University Press, 1964.
   A highly influential and still pertinent book offering an analysis of the role of race and ethnicity in American life.

Griswold, Wendy. *Cultures and Societies in a Changing World*. Thousand Oaks, Calif.: Pine Forge Press, 1994.
   A thorough examination of the elements and dynamics of culture and the cultural diffusion spread by technology and the global economy.

Hall, Edward T. *Understanding Cultural Differences*. Yarmouth, Me.: Intercultural Press, 1990.
   Focuses on national cultural contrasts between France, Germany, and the United States through an examination of business and management practices.

Harrison, Lawrence E., and Samuel P. Huntington (eds.). *Culture Matters: How Values Shape Human Progress*. New York: Basic Books, 2001.
   A collection of essays by leading social scientists that examine how culture affects prosperity, democracy, and social justice among both countries and immigrants.

116

Hitchcock, Jeff. *Lifting the White Veil: An Exploration of White Culture in a Multiracial Context.* Roselle, N.J.: Crandall Dostie & Douglass Books, 2003.

An overview of the history of Whiteness in U.S. society, with a personal, provocative argument on the need to recognize the existence of White culture and to "decenter" it.

Ritzer, George. *The McDonaldization of Society,* 3d ed. Thousand Oaks, Calif.: Pine Forge Press, 2000.

Fine use of sociological imagination to show cultural diffusion in the organization of work throughout the world.

CHAPTER

6 Ethnic Stratification

Social structure—the organized patterns of behavior among the basic components of a social system—establishes relatively predictable social relationships among the different peoples in a society.

Structural Conditions

Relations between dominant and minority groups are influenced as much by structural conditions as by differences in culture. The nature of the social structure influences not only the distribution of power resources (economic, political, and social) but also the accessibility of those resources to groups who seek upward mobility. An expanding economy and an open social system create increased opportunities for minority-group members, thereby reducing the likelihood that tensions will arise. In contrast, a stagnant or contracting economy thwarts many efforts to improve status and antagonizes those who feel most threatened by another group's competition for scarce resources. Such a situation may serve as a breeding ground for conflicts among minority groups even more than between majority and minority groups because the group next highest on the socioeconomic ladder may perceive a threat from below more quickly and react negatively.

The state of the economy is just one important structural factor influencing the opportunities for upward mobility. Another is the degree of change between a minority group's old society and the new one. A traditional or agrarian society typically has a much more stable social structure than a society undergoing transformation through industrialization. The latter society offers dramatic changes in opportunities and lifestyles, not all of them for the better. A migrating minority group's compatibility with the social structure of the new land depends on the degree of similarity between the new country's structural conditions and those of its homeland. A person who leaves an agrarian society for an industrial one is poorly prepared to enter any but the lowest social stratum in a low-paying position. Opportunities for upward mobility may exist, however, if the new land's economy is growing rapidly. In this sense, the structural conditions in the United States during the period from 1880 to 1920 were better for unskilled immigrants than are conditions today. Low-skill jobs are less plentiful today, and an unskilled worker's desire to support a family through hard work may not be matched by the opportunity to do so.

Meanwhile, technological advances have made the world smaller. Rapid transportation and communications (radios, televisions, telephones, computers, the Internet, fax machines, and overnight deliveries) permit ties to other parts of the world to remain stronger than in the past.[1] Accessibility to their homeland, friends, or relatives may make people less interested in becoming fully assimilated in a new land. Befriending strangers in the new country becomes less necessary. In addition, people's greater knowledge of the world, the rising social consciousness of a society, and structural opportunities for mobility all help to create a more hospitable environment for minority-group members.

Stratification

Social stratification is the hierarchical classification of the members of society based on the unequal distribution of resources, power, and prestige. The word *resources* refers to such factors as income, property, and borrowing capacity. *Power,* usually reflected by the stratified layers, represents the ability to influence or control others. *Prestige* relates to status, either *ascribed* (based on age, sex, race, or family background) or *achieved* (based on individual accomplishments).

The process of stratification may either moderate or exacerbate any strains or conflicts between groups depending on the form that the stratification takes. The form can range from rigid and explicit to flexible and subtle; from the overt rigidity of slavery, caste, and forced labor to implicit class distinctions and discrimination based on race or ethnic group. Whether racial and ethnic groups face insurmountable barriers or minor obstacles in achieving upward mobility depends on the form of stratification. The more rigid the stratification, the more likely is the emergence of racial, religious, or other ideologies justifying the existing arrangements—as happened with the rise of racism during slavery in the United States.

The form of stratification affects how groups within the various strata of society view one another. Some people confuse structural differentiation with cultural differentiation. For example, they may believe that a group's low socioeconomic status is due to its values and attitudes rather than to such structural conditions as racism, economic stagnation, and high urban unemployment. The form of stratification is an important determinant of the potential for intergroup conflict. In the United States, both the possibility of upward mobility and structural obstacles to that possibility have existed. When the disparity between the perception of the American Dream and the reality of the difficulty of achieving it grows too great, the possibility of conflict increases.

Social Class

Social class is one categorization sociologists use to designate people's place
in the stratification hierarchy; people in a particular social class have a similar level of income, amount of property, degree of power, status, and type of
lifestyle. Many factors help determine a person's social class, including the individual's membership in particular racial, religious, and status groups. Although no clearly defined boundaries exist between class groupings in the
United States, people have a tendency to cluster together according to certain
socioeconomic similarities. The concept or image of social-class reality can be
traced to sociopsychological distinctions people make about one another on
the basis of such variables as where they live and what they own as well as to
interactions that occur because of those distinctions.

In the 1930s, W. Lloyd Warner headed a classic study of social-class differentiation in the United States.[2] Using the **reputational method**—asking
people how they thought others compared to them—Warner found a well-
formulated class system in place. In Newburyport, Massachusetts, a small
town of about 17,000 that he called "Yankee City," Warner identified six classes:
upper-upper, lower-upper, upper-middle, lower-middle, upper-lower, and
lower-lower. When he and his associates examined the distribution of ethnic
groups among the various classes, certain factors emerged. First, a significant
relationship existed between an ethnic group's length of residence and class
status; the more recent arrivals tended to be in the lower classes. In addition,
an ethnic group tended to be less assimilated and less upwardly mobile if its
population in the community was relatively large, if its homeland was close
(e.g., in the case of immigrant French Canadians), if its members had a sojourner rather than a permanent-settler orientation, and if limited opportunities for advancement existed in the community.[3]

Social class becomes important in intergroup relations because it provides a basis for expectations. As Alan Kerckhoff states, social class provides
a particular setting for the interplay between the formative experiences of a
child, others' expectations of the child, and what kind of adult the child becomes.[4] Beyond this significant aspect, social class also serves as a point of reference in others' responses and in one's self-perception. As a result, social
class helps shape an individual's world of reality and influences group interactions. Attitudes and behavior formed within a social-class framework are
not immutable, however; they can change if circumstances change.

Class Consciousness

Just how important are the ethnic factors that Warner and others reported in
shaping an awareness of social class? The significance of ethnic factors depends on numerous variables, including economic conditions, mobility patterns, and prevailing attitudes. John Leggett found that class consciousness

depends on the ethnic factor: The lower a group's ethnic status in the society, the higher the level of class consciousness.[5] Other studies have shown that working-class ethnic groups tend to view their class as hostile to, and under the political control of, the higher-status classes.[6]

Because ethnic minorities are disproportionately represented among the lower classes and because middle-class values dominate in the United States, it seems reasonable to suppose that at least some of the attitudes of each group result from people's value judgments about social class. That is to say, the dominant group's criticism and stereotyping of the minority group probably rests in part on class distinctions.

Social-class status plays an important role in determining a minority group's adjustment to and acceptance by society. For example, because the first waves of Cuban (1960s) and Vietnamese (1970s) refugees who arrived in the United States possessed the education and occupational experience of the middle class, they succeeded in overcoming early native concerns and did not encounter the same degree of negativism as had earlier groups. On the other hand, when unskilled and often illiterate peasants enter the lower-class positions in U.S. society, many U.S. citizens belittle, avoid, and discriminate against them because of their supposedly inferior ways. Frequently, these attitudes and actions reflect an awareness of class differences as well as cultural differences. Because the dominant group usually occupies a higher stratum in the social-class hierarchy, differences in social-class values and lifestyles—in addition to ethnic cultural differences—can be sources of friction.

Ethnicity and Social Class

Differences in stratification among various groups cannot be explained by a single cause, although many observers have tried to do so. For example, in his influential book *The Ethnic Myth*, Stephen Steinberg stressed the importance of social structure and minimized cultural factors.[7] For him, the success of Jews in the United States resulted more from their occupational skills in the urbanized country than from their values. Conversely, Thomas Sowell wrote in *Ethnic America* that the compatibility of a group's cultural characteristics with those of the dominant culture determines the level of a group's economic success.[8] Actually, structural and cultural elements intertwine. Emphasizing only social structure ignores such important cultural variables as values about education. Emphasizing only culture can lead to blaming people who do not succeed.

Colin Greer criticized those who overemphasize ethnic-centered analyses and ignore the larger question of class:

> This kind of ethnic reductionism forces us to accept as predetermined what society defines as truth. Only through ethnicity can identity be securely achieved. The result is that ethnic questions which could, in fact, further our understanding of the relationship of individuals to social structures are always raised in a way that serves to reconcile us to a common heritage of miserable inequities. Instead of realizing that the lack of a well-defined stratification structure, linked

to a legitimated aristocratic tradition, led Americans to employ the language of
ethnic pluralism in exchange for direct divisions by social class, we continue to
ignore the real factors of class in our society. . . . What we must ultimately talk
about is class. The cues of felt ethnicity turn out to be the recognizable characteristics of class position in this society: to feel black, Irish, Italian, Jewish has
meant to learn to live in accommodation with that part of your heritage that is
compatible with the needs and opportunities in America upon arrival and soon
thereafter.[9]

In 1964, 10 years before Greer's observations, Milton Gordon first suggested that dominant–minority relations be examined within the larger context of the social structure.[10] This proposition marked an important turning
point in racial and ethnic studies.[11] Although he believed that all groups
would eventually become assimilated, Gordon offered an explanation of the
present pluralistic society. His central thesis was that four factors, or social
categories, play a part in forming subsocieties within the nation: ethnicity (by
which Gordon also meant race), social class, rural or urban residence, and re-
gionalism.[12] These factors unite in various combinations to create a number
of **ethclasses**—subsocieties resulting from the intersection of stratifications of
race and ethnic group with stratifications of social class. Additional determinants are the rural or urban setting and the particular region of the country in
which a group lives. Examples of ethclasses are lower-middle-class White
Catholics in a northeastern city, lower-class Black Baptists in the rural South,
and upper-class White Jews in a western urban area.

Numerous studies support the concept that race and ethnicity, together
with social class, are important in social structures and intergroup conflicts.[13]
For example, social scientists such as Thomas Pettigrew and Charles Willie
argue that recognizing the intersection of race and class is a key element in understanding the continued existence of Black poverty.[14] Not only do ethclass
groupings exist, but people tend to interact within them for their intimate primary relationships. To the extent that this is true, multiple allegiances and conflicts are inevitable. According to this view, both cultural and structural
pluralism currently exist; numerous groups presently coexist in separate subsocieties based on social class and cultural distinctions. Even people whose
families have been in the United States for several generations are affiliated
with, and participate in, subsocieties. Nonetheless, Gordon views assimilation
as a linear process in which even structural assimilation will eventually occur.

Blaming the Poor or Society?

In 1932, E. Franklin Frazier formulated his conception of a disorganized and
pathological lower-class culture. This thesis served as the inspiration for the
controversial **culture of poverty** viewpoint that emerged in the 1960s.[15] The
writings of two men—Daniel P. Moynihan and Oscar Lewis—sparked an intense debate that continues to resonate today. In his 1965 government report,
"The Negro Family: The Case for National Action," Moynihan used Frazier's

observations as a springboard for arguing that a "tangle of pathology" so pervaded the Black community that it perpetuated a cycle of poverty and deprivation that only outside (government) intervention could overcome.[16]

Family Disintegration.   Moynihan argued that family deterioration was a core cause of the problems of high unemployment, welfare dependence, illegitimacy, low achievement, juvenile delinquency, and adult crime:

> At the heart of the deterioration of the fabric of Negro society is the deterioration of the Negro family. It is the fundamental source of weakness of the Negro community at the present time. . . . The white family has achieved a high degree of stability and is maintaining that stability. By contrast, the family structure of the lower class Negroes is highly unstable, and in many urban centers is approaching complete breakdown.[17]

Moynihan described Black males as occupying an unstable place in the economy, which prevented them from functioning as strong fathers and husbands. This environment, he said, served as a breeding ground for a continuing vicious circle: The women often not only raised the children but also earned the family income. Consequently, the children grew up in a poorly supervised, unstable environment; they often performed poorly or dropped out of school; they could secure only low-paying jobs—and so the cycle began anew.[18] The Moynihan Report called for federal action to create, among other things, jobs for Black male heads of household in the inner city:

> At the center of the tangle of pathology is the weakness of the family structure. Once or twice removed, it will be found to be the principal source of most of the aberrant, inadequate, or anti-social behavior that did not establish but now serves to perpetuate the cycle of poverty and deprivation. . . .
>
> What then is the problem? We feel that the answer is clear enough. Three centuries of injustice have brought about deep-seated structural distortions in the life of the Negro American. At this point, the present tangle of pathology is capable of perpetuating itself without assistance from the white world. The cycle can be broken only if these distortions are set right.[19]

In a highly discussed 1986 television documentary, Bill Moyers echoed Moynihan's view that a link existed between specific cultural values and deteriorating conditions in lower-class Black family life.[20] Then, in 1990, Moynihan reaffirmed his position, citing further social deterioration since the 1960s and noting in particular the startling rise in out-of-wedlock births from 3 percent of White births and 24 percent of Black births in 1963 to 16 percent and 63 percent, respectively, in 1987.[21] These distressing statistics led Moynihan to repeat a statement from his 1965 report:

> From the wild Irish slums of the nineteenth-century Eastern seaboard, to the riot-torn suburbs of Los Angeles, there is one unmistakable lesson in American his-

tory: a community that allows a large number of young men to grow up in broken families, dominated by women, never acquiring a stable relationship to male authority, never acquiring any set of rational expectations about the future—that community asks for and gets chaos. Crime, violence, unrest, disorder—most particularly the furious, unrestrained lashing out at the whole social structure—that is not only to be expected; it is very near to inevitable.[22]

Perpetuation of Poverty. Moynihan's position shares the same premises as Oscar Lewis's theory about a subculture of poverty, detailed in *The Children of Sanchez* (1961) and *La Vida* (1966):[23]

> The culture of poverty, however, is not only an adaptation to a set of objective conditions of the larger society. Once it comes into existence it tends to perpetuate itself from generation to generation because of its effect on the children. By the time slum children are age six or seven they have usually absorbed the basic values and attitudes of their subculture and are not psychologically geared to take full advantage of changing conditions or increased opportunities which may occur in their lifetime.[24]

Politically, Lewis was a leftist, and he did not blame the poor as some critics misinterpreted. Rather, he emphasized the institutionalized tenacity of their poverty, arguing that the system damaged them.[25] Edward Banfield, a conservative, recast Lewis's position to assert that poverty continues because of subcultural patterns. Whereas Lewis held that the mechanics of capitalist production for profit caused poverty, Banfield found its cause in the folkways of its victims. Banfield argued that good jobs, good housing, tripled welfare payments, new schools, quality education, and armies of police officers would not stop the problem. He added:

> If, however, the lower classes were to disappear—if, say, their members were overnight to acquire the attitudes, motivations, and habits of the working class—the most serious and intractable problems of the city would all disappear. . . . The lower-class forms of all problems are at bottom a single problem: the existence of an outlook and style of life which is radically present-oriented and which therefore attaches no value to work, sacrifice, self-improvement, or service to family, friends, or community.[26]

Most people in the United States think the poor are responsible for their own poverty. For example, Joe R. Feagin reported in 1972 that in a poll of a national cross section of adults, 53 percent said that the poor were at fault for their dilemma, and 22 percent said that the social structure was at fault.[27] In another national study, James R. Kluegel and Eliot R. Smith in 1986 reported two prevailing perceptions in the United States: first, that economic opportunity exists for all who work hard; and second, that individuals are causally responsible for their own positions in society. Also, Kluegel and Smith reported, most Americans believe that individuals deserve the income they get, and these beliefs about economic inequality typically orient them to a conservative view of social welfare policy.[28]

Criticism. Although they were not saying the same thing, Moynihan, Lewis, and Banfield all came under heavy criticism during the 1960s and 1970s—the height of the civil-rights movement—from commentators who felt that they were blaming the victim. Critics argued that intergenerational poverty results from discrimination, structural conditions, or stratification rigidity. Fatalism, apathy, low aspiration, and other similar orientations found in lower-class culture are thus situational responses within each generation and not the result of cultural deficiencies transmitted from parents to children.

To William Ryan, blaming the victim results in misdirected social programs. If we rationalize away the socially acquired stigma of poverty as being the expression of a subcultural trait, we ignore the continuing effect of current victimizing social forces. As a result, we focus on helping the "disorganized" Black family instead of on overcoming racism, or we strive to develop "better" attitudes and skills in low-income children rather than revamping the poor-quality schools they attend.[29]

Charles A. Valentine led an emotional attack on the culture of poverty thesis and on Lewis himself.[30] He argued that many of Lewis's "class distinctive traits" of the poor are either "externally imposed conditions" (unemployment, crowded and deteriorated housing, and lack of education) or "unavoidable matters of situational expediency" (hostility toward social institutions and low expectations and self-image).[31] Only by changing the total social structure and the resources available to the poor can we alter any subcultural traits of survival.

Yet Lewis was also saying this.[32] Michael Harrington, whose *The Other America* (1963) helped spark the federal government's "War on Poverty" program, defended Lewis.[33] Harrington—like Lewis—said that society was to blame for the culture of poverty: "The real explanation of why the poor are where they are is that they made the mistake of being born to the wrong parents, in the wrong section of the country, in the wrong industry, or in the wrong racial or ethnic group."[34]

Like Lewis, Valentine, and Harrington, others argued that all people would desire the same things and cherish the same values if they were in an economic position to do so. Because they are not, they adopt an alternative set of values to survive.[35] Eliot Liebow, in a participant-observer study of lower-class Black males, concluded that they try to achieve many of the goals of the larger society but fail for many of the same reasons their fathers did: discrimination, unpreparedness, lack of job skills, and self-doubt.[36] The similarities between generations are due not to cultural transmission but to the sons' independent experience of the same failures. What appears to be a self-sustaining cultural process is actually a secondary adaptation to an adult inability to overcome structural constraints.

Street urchins sleep in New York's Lower East Side, circa 1890. Homeless children, usually orphaned though occasionally runaways, were not uncommon in the immigrant communities. Fending for themselves through hawking newspapers, doing odd jobs, or stealing, they would usually band together in small groups and sleep wherever they could.

(*Source:* Jacob Riis)

In a similar vein, Hyman Rodman suggested that all social classes share the general values of a society but that the lower class, while not rejecting those values, adopts additional values representing realistic levels of attainment. The lower class does not reject the less attainable values of the majority society but adopts a **value-stretch approach,** which encompasses a wider range of values:

> Lower-class persons . . . do not maintain a strong commitment to middle-class values that they cannot attain, and they do not continue to respond to others in a rewarding or punishing way simply on the basis of whether these others are living up to the middle-class values. A change takes place. They come to tolerate and eventually to evaluate favorably certain deviations from the middle-class values. In this way they need not be continually frustrated by their failure to live up to unattainable values. The resultant is a stretched value system.[37]

L. Richard Della Fave adds that the poor adopt this value-stretch approach when the gap between ideal value preference and achievement expectations becomes too great.[38] In other words, the poor do not have different values but have different behaviors that reflect pragmatic coping mechanisms. Since they expect less, they learn to be satisfied with less.

The debate over whether the culture of poverty results from **economic determinism** (structural barriers and discrimination) or from **cultural determinism** (transmission of cultural inadequacies) continues. Studies conducted during the 1970s found considerable intergenerational mobility and little evidence of a vicious circle of poverty.[39] However, research on new longitudinal data sets during the 1980s showed that intragenerational and intergenerational poverty were more persistent than previous analyses of cross-sectional data had indicated.[40] Whatever the cause, most people's attitudes toward welfare and the urban poor (who are predominantly racial and ethnic minorities) reflect a belief in one position or the other. Interestingly, both viewpoints share a belief that determinism of some kind decides the fate of the poor, thereby reflecting the "free-will" thesis popular in Western thought—the notion that every individual "makes" his or her own luck. The two sociological viewpoints also support increased employment and educational opportunities to overcome the persistence of poverty.

Intergroup Conflict

Is conflict inevitable when culturally distinct groups interact? Do structural conditions encourage or reduce the probability of conflict? Robert E. Park argued that a universal, irreversible, possibly slowly evolving cycle of events made conflict and subsequent resolution by assimilation inevitable. This "race relations cycle" had four stages: (1) contact between the groups; (2) competition; (3) adjustment or accommodation; and (4) assimilation and amalgamation. (In Park's day, the term *race* referred to racial and ethnic groups, and his comments should be understood in this broader sense.) According to Park:

> The race relations cycle which takes the form, to state it abstractly, of contact, competition, accommodation, and eventual assimilation, is apparently progressive and irreversible. Customs regulations, immigration restrictions, and racial barriers may slacken the tempo of the movement; may perhaps halt it altogether for a time; but cannot change its direction, cannot, at any rate, reverse it. . . . It does not follow that because the tendencies to the assimilation and eventual amalgamation of races exist, they should not be resisted and, if possible, altogether inhibited . . . . Rising tides of color and oriental exclusion laws are merely incidental evidences of this diminishing distance. . . . In the Hawaiian Islands, where all the races of the Pacific meet and mingle . . . , the native races are disappearing and new peoples are coming into existence. Races and cultures die—it has always been so—but civilization lives on.[41]

Park's theory fit nicely into the prevailing assimilationist thinking of his time, but his race relations cycle has several problems. By its very nature, the claim that all instances of interaction between subgroups in a society must end in assimilation is not testable because any instance of nonassimilation can be explained away as a case in which the cycle is not yet complete.[42] Indeed, Park never cited any example where his cycle had reached completion; but instead of seeing such negative data as refuting the theory, Park and other cyclical theorists attributed the lack of assimilation to temporary obstacles or interference. Such tautological reasoning, argues Stanford M. Lyman, leaves this theory deficient in an essential element of empirical science: It cannot be proved or disproved.[43] Perhaps, though, we might consider one example to be the interaction between Anglo-Saxon residents and Norman-French invaders, both of whom gradually disappeared as the "English" emerged.

Meanwhile, the supposed universality of the stages identified in Park's cyclical theory is refuted by counterexamples in which conflict and competition did not occur when different groups came into contact. Brazil and Hawaii are just two places where relatively peaceful and harmonious interactions have existed among different, unassimilated peoples. In many other instances of intergroup relations, however, some form of stress, tension, or conflict does occur. In this chapter, we will examine the major factors that may underlie such conflict: cultural differentiation and structural differentiation.

Cultural Differentiation

When similarities between the arriving minority group and the indigenous group exist, the relationship tends to be relatively harmonious and assimilation is likely to occur eventually.[44] Conversely, the greater and more visible the **cultural differentiation,** the greater the likelihood that conflict will occur. When large numbers of German and Irish Catholics came to the United States in the mid-nineteenth century, Protestants grew uneasy. As priests and nuns arrived and Catholics built churches, convents, and schools, Protestants became alarmed at what they feared was a papal conspiracy to gain control of the country. Emotions ran high, resulting in civil unrest and violence.

Religion has often been a basis for cultural conflict in the United States as is demonstrated by the history of discriminatory treatment suffered by Mormons, Jews, and Quakers. Yet many other aspects of cultural visibility also can serve as sources of contention. Cultural differences may range from clothing (e.g., Sikh turbans and Hindu saris) to leisure activities (e.g., Hispanic cockfights). Americans once condemned the Chinese as opium smokers, even though the British had introduced opium smoking into China, promoted it among the lower-class Chinese population, and even fought wars against the Chinese government to maintain the lucrative trade.

Cultural differentiation does not necessarily cause intergroup conflict. A partial explanation of variances in relations between culturally distinct groups comes from interactionist theory, which holds that the extent of shared symbols and definitions between intercommunicating groups determines the nature of their interaction patterns. Although actual differences may support conflict, interactionists state the key to harmonious or disharmonious relations lies in the definitions or interpretations of those differences. Tolerance or intolerance—acceptance or rejection of others—thus depends on whether others are perceived as threatening or nonthreatening, assimilable or nonassimilable, worthy or unworthy.

Structural Differentiation

Because they offer macrosocial analyses of a society, both functionalist theory and conflict theory provide bases for understanding how structural conditions (**structural differentiation**) affect intergroup relations. Functionalists seek explanations in the adjustments needed in the social system to compensate for other changes. Conflict theorists emphasize the conscious, purposeful actions of dominant groups to maintain systems of inequality.

Functional Theory. Sometimes economic and technological conditions facilitate minority integration. When the economy is healthy and jobs are plentiful, newcomers find it easier to get established and work their way up the socioeconomic ladder. In the United States today, however, technological progress has reduced the number of low-status, blue-collar jobs and increased the number of high-status, white-collar jobs, which require more highly skilled and educated workers. As a result, fewer jobs are available for unskilled, foreign, marginal, or unassimilated people.

Perhaps because of the importance of a job as a source of economic security and status, **occupational mobility**—the ability of individuals to improve their job position—seems to be an important factor in determining whether prejudice will increase or decrease. A number of studies have shown that downward social mobility increases ethnic hostility.[45] Bruno Bettelheim and Morris Janowitz report from seven studies that persons moving downward in status not only are more prejudiced than the group they left but also are more prejudiced than the lower-status group they enter. Additionally, upwardly mobile people are generally more tolerant than nonmobile individuals.[46] It would appear that loss of status and prestige increases hostility toward outgroups, whereas upward gains enable people to feel more benevolent toward others.

Ethnic Stratification

If one group becomes dominant and another becomes subservient, obviously one group has more power than the other. Social-class status partly reflects this unequal distribution of power, which also may fall along racial or ethnic lines.

Ethnic stratification is the structured inequality of different groups with different access to social rewards as a result of their status in the social hierarchy. Because most Americans associate ethnicity with anything different from the mainstream, they don't realize that ethnicity also exists at the top. Ashley W. Doane, Jr., reminds us that dominant group ethnicity lies "hidden" because its status results in the taken-for-granted nature of dominant group identity.[47]

Stratification is a normal component of all societies, but it typically falls along racial and ethnic lines in diverse societies. How does ethnic stratification continue in a democracy where supposedly all have an equal opportunity for upward mobility? Functionalists suggest that the ethnocentrism of those in the societal mainstream leads to discrimination against those in outgroups, as determined by their racial or cultural differences. Conflict analysts instead stress the subordination of minorities by the dominant group because they benefit from such ethnic stratification. Two middle-range conflict theories offer helpful insights into this perspective. The power-differential theory helps explain the initial phases of domination and conflict, whereas the internal-colonialism theory examines the continuation of such subordination.

The Power-Differential Theory

Stanley Lieberson suggested a **power-differential theory** in which intergroup relations depend on the relative power of the migrant group and the indigenous group.[48] Because the two groups usually do not share the same culture, each strives to maintain its own institutions. Which group becomes *superordinate* (superior in rank, class, or status) and which becomes *subordinate* (inferior in rank, class, or status) govern subsequent relations.

If the newcomers possess superior technology (particularly weapons) and social organization, conflict may occur at an early stage, with a consequent population decline due to warfare, disease, or disruption of sustenance activities. Finding their institutions undermined or co-opted, the local inhabitants may eventually participate in the institutions of the dominant group. In time, a group consciousness may arise, and sometimes the indigenous group even succeeds in ousting the superordinate migrant group. When this happened in many former African colonies and in Southeast Asia, interethnic fighting among the many indigenous groups led to new forms of superordination and subordination within countries (as was the case with the Hutu and Tutsi peoples in Burundi and Rwanda).

Lieberson maintained that neither conflict nor assimilation is an inevitable outcome of racial and ethnic contact. Instead, the particular relationship between the two groups involved determines which alternative will occur. Conflict between a superordinate migrant group and a subordinate indigenous group can be immediate and violent. If the relationship is the reverse, and the indigenous group is superordinate, conflict will be limited and sporadic, and the host society will exert a great deal of pressure on the subordinate migrant group to assimilate, acquiesce, or leave.

In addition, a superordinate indigenous group can limit the numbers and groups entering to reduce the threat of demographic or institutional imbalance. Restrictive U.S. immigration laws against the Chinese in 1882 and against all but northern and western Europeans in 1921 and 1924 illustrate this process. Violent union attempts to remove Asian workers, labor union hostility toward African Americans, and efforts to expel foreigners (e.g., Indians, Japanese, and Filipinos) or to revolutionize the social order (Native American boarding schools and the Americanization movement) illustrate the use of institutional power against minority groups.

Another sociologist, William J. Wilson, has suggested that power relations between superordinate and subordinate groups differ in paternalistic and competitive systems.[49] With **paternalism** (the system that once governed South Africa and the Old South), the dominant group exercises almost absolute control over the subordinate group and can direct virtually unlimited coercion to maintain societal order. In a competitive system (e.g., the United States today), some degree of power reciprocity exists, so the dominant group in society is somewhat vulnerable to political pressures and economic boycotts.

Rapid social change—industrialization, unionization, urbanization, migration, and political change—usually loosens the social structure, leading to new tensions as both groups seek new power resources. If the minority group increases its power resources, through protective laws and improved economic opportunities, it may foresee even greater improvement in its condition. This heightened awareness is likely to lead to conflict unless additional gains are forthcoming. For example, the civil-rights movement of the mid-1960s brought about legislation ensuring minority rights and opportunities in jobs, housing, education, and other aspects of life, but this led to new tensions. The 1960s were marked by urban riots and burnings, protest demonstrations and human barricades to stop construction of low-income housing sites, school-busing controversies, and challenges to labor discrimination.

The Internal-Colonialism Theory

In analyzing the Black militancy of the late 1960s, Robert Blauner attempted to integrate the factors of caste and racism, ethnicity, culture, and economic exploitation.[50] His major point was that U.S. treatment of its Black population resembled past European subjugation and exploitation of non-Western peoples in their own lands. Although he focused on Black–White relations in the United States, he suggested that Mexican Americans might also fit his **internal-colonialism theory** and that Native Americans could be added as another suitable example:

> Of course many ethnic groups in America have lived in ghettoes. What makes the Black ghettoes an expression of colonized status are three special features. First, the ethnic ghettoes arose more from voluntary choice, both in the sense of the choice to immigrate to America and the decision to live among one's fellow

ethnics. Second, the immigrant ghettoes tended to be a one- and two-generation phenomenon; they were actually way-stations in the process of acculturation and assimilation. When they continue to persist as in the case of San Francisco's Chinatown, it is because they are big business for the ethnics themselves and there is a new stream of immigrants. The Black ghetto on the other hand has been a more permanent phenomenon, although some individuals do escape it. But most relevant is the third point. European ethnic groups like the Poles, Italians and Jews generally only experienced a brief period, often less than a generation, during which their residential buildings, commercial stores, and other enterprises were owned by outsiders. The Chinese and Japanese faced handicaps of color prejudice that were almost as strong as the Blacks faced, but very soon gained control of their internal communities, because their traditional ethnic culture and social organization had not been destroyed by slavery and internal colonization. But Afro-Americans are distinct in the extent to which their segregated communities have remained controlled economically, politically, and administratively from the outside.[51]

Several of these statements need to be modified. Chinatowns long persisted not because of any business advantage but because of racial discrimination. In proportion to the Chinatown population, only a few Chinese benefit from the tourist trade. Also, the Chinese and Japanese *always* had "control of their internal communities," although they differ greatly from each other in their structure and cohesiveness.

Blauner considers the exploitation phase that was temporary for other groups to be more nearly permanent for Blacks and possibly Chicanos. He believes that conflict and confrontation, as well as real or apparent chaos and disorder, will continue because this may be the only way an internally colonized group can deal with the dominant society. This conflict orientation suggests that the multigenerational exploitation of certain groups creates a unique situation and a basis for the often violent conflict that sporadically flares up in our cities.

Origins of Ethnic Stratification

For ethnicity to become a basis for stratification, several factors seem necessary:

> Ethnic stratification will emerge when distinct ethnic groups are brought into sustained contact only if the groups are characterized by a high degree of ethnocentrism, competition, *and* differential power. Competition provides the motivation for stratification; ethnocentrism channels the competition along ethnic lines; and the power differential determines whether either group will be able to subordinate the other.[52]

This **power differential** is of enormous importance in race and ethnic relations. If the stratification system is rigid, as in a slave or caste system, so that people have no hope or means of improving their status, intergroup relations

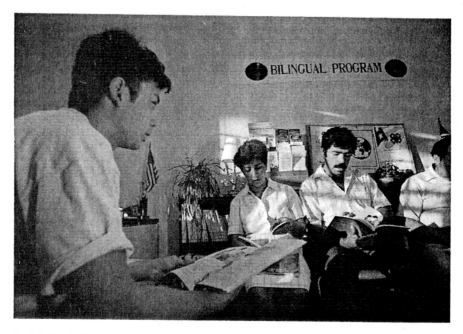

In this English as a Second Language class, these Latino immigrants, like many other newcomers from different countries, seek to bolster their English proficiency to ease their entry into the societal mainstream. Ability to understand and speak English is an important step in the acculturation process that helps reduce cultural differentiation and enhance opportunities for occupational mobility.

(*Source:* © David H. Wells/The Image Works)

may remain stable despite perhaps being far from mutually satisfactory. Dominant power, whether expressed in legalized ways or through structural discrimination, intimidation, or coercion, maintains the social system.

Even if the stratification system allows for upward mobility, some members of the dominant group may believe that the lower-class racial and ethnic groups are challenging the social order as they strive for their share of the "good life." If the dominant group does not feel threatened, the change will be peaceful. If the minority group meets resistance but retains hope and a sense of belonging to the larger society, the struggle for more power will occur within the system (e.g., by means of demonstrations, boycotts, voter-registration drives, or lobbying) rather than through violence.[53] The late-nineteenth-century race-baiting riots on the West Coast against Chinese and Japanese workers and the 1919 Chicago race riots against Blacks attempting to enter the meat-packing industry illustrate violent responses of a dominant group against a minority group over power resources. Similarly, the Black–Korean violence in several urban neighborhoods during the past decade, as well as the 1992 Los Angeles riots and the violence between Blacks and Cubans in Miami in 1988, typify minority-group clashes over limited resources.

Social-Class Antagonisms. Conflict theorists, such as Ralf Dahrendorf, argue that social class is an important variable affecting conflict. Dahrendorf sees a correlation between a group's economic position and the intensity of its conflict with the dominant society. The greater the deprivation in economic resources, social status, and social power, the likelier the weaker group is to resort to intense and violent conflict to achieve gains in any of these three areas. As the social-class position of a group increases, intergroup conflict becomes less intense and less violent.[54]

Years earlier, Max Weber argued that, when economic resources become more evenly distributed among classes, relative status will become the issue of conflict, if conflict occurs at all.[55] Conflict occurs not only because a lower-class group seeks an end to deprivation but also because the group next higher on the socioeconomic ladder feels threatened. Often, the working-class group displays the greatest hostility and prejudice of all established groups in the society toward the upward-striving minority group. Other factors may be at work as well, but status competition is a significant source of conflict.

Social-class antagonisms influence people's perceptions of racial and ethnic groups too.[56] Some social scientists maintain that the problem of Black–White relations is more a problem of social class than of racism. James M. O'Kane illustrates this view:

> The gap exists between the classes, not the races; it is between the white and black middle classes on the one hand, and the white and black lower classes on the other. Skin color and the history of servitude do little to explain the present polarization of the classes. . . . Class differentials, not racial differentials, explain the presence and persistence of poverty in the ranks of the urban Negro.[57]

O'Kane suggests several parallels between Irish, Italian, and Polish immigrants and southern Blacks who migrated to northern cities (the Chinese, some of the Japanese, and others also fit this model). All emigrated from agrarian poverty to urban industrial slums. Encountering prejudice and discrimination, some sought alternative routes to material success: crime, ethnic politics, or stable but unskilled employment.[58] Other social scientists, however, argue that the Black experience does not equate with that of European immigrants. They hold, as did the Kerner Commission investigating the urban riots of the late 1960s, that the dominant society's practice of internal colonialism toward Blacks deprived them of the strong social organizations that other groups had. Moreover, they believe that today's labor market offers fewer unskilled jobs for Blacks than it offered other immigrant groups in earlier times, thereby depriving Blacks of a means to begin moving upward.[59]

This debate over whether race or social class is the primary factor in assessing full integration of Blacks in the United States continues to rage, particularly among Black social scientists.

Retrospect

Structural conditions influence people's perceptions of the world whether they live in an industrialized or agrarian society, a closed or open social system, a growing or contracting economy, a friendly or unfriendly environment, and whether their homeland, friends, and relatives are accessible or remote. Distribution of power resources and compatibility with the existing social structure greatly influence majority–minority relations as well. Interactionists concentrate on perceptions of cultural differences as they affect intergroup relations. Functionalists and conflict theorists emphasize structural conditions.

The interplay between the variables of race, ethnic group, and social class is important for understanding how some problems and conflicts arise. A feature interpreted as an attribute of a race or ethnic group may in fact be a broader aspect of social class. Because many attitudes and values are situational responses to socioeconomic status, a change in status or opportunities will bring about a change in those attitudes and values. Investigative studies have not supported the culture-of-poverty hypothesis of family disintegration and a self-perpetuating poverty value orientation.

KEY TERMS

Cultural determinism	Paternalism
Cultural differentiation	Power differential
Culture of poverty	Power-differential theory
Economic determinism	Reputational method
Ethclasses	Social class
Ethnic stratification	Social stratification
Internal-colonialism theory	Structural differentiation
Occupational mobility	Value-stretch approach

REVIEW QUESTIONS

1. What economic factors can affect intergroup relations?

2. Does social class awareness affect ethnic self-consciousness?

3. What is the relationship between ethnicity and social class?

4. What is meant by the *culture of poverty*? What criticisms exist about this thinking?

5. What is the difference between cultural differentiation and structural differentiation?

6. How do the functional and conflict perspectives approach the factors likely to contribute to intergroup conflict?

SUGGESTED READINGS

Anderson, Elijah, and Massey, Douglas S. (eds.). *Problem of the Century: Racial Stratification in the United States.* New York: Russell Sage Foundation, 2001.
  Offers sixteen essays on racial differentiation as measured by various demographic, economic, and educational indicators.

hooks, bell. *Where We Stand: Class Matters.* New York: Routledge, 2000.
  An incisive examination of how the dilemmas of race and class are intertwined and how everyday interactions reproduce class hierarchy while simultaneously denying its existence.

Reitz, Jeffrey G. *Warmth of the Welcome: The Social Causes of Economic Success for Immigrants in Different Nations and Cities.* Boulder, Colo.: Westview Press, 1998.
  Compares trends in immigrant inequality in Australia, Canada, and the United States through a social institutional approach and analysis of social structure.

Russell, James W. *After the Fifth Sun: Class and Race in North America.* Upper Saddle River, N.J.: Prentice Hall, 1994.
  Explores how different patterns of class and racial inequality developed in Canada, Mexico, and the United States, leading to different definitions of the significance of race.

Steinberg, Stephen. *The Ethnic Myth: Race, Ethnicity, and Class in America.* New York: Scribner, 1981.
  Argues that traits considered as "ethnic" may be more directly related to class, locality, and other social conditions.

CHAPTER

7 Prejudice

When strangers from different groups come into contact with one another, their interaction patterns may take many forms. So far, we have discussed the roles that ethnocentrism, social distance, culture, and social structure play in shaping perceptions of any outgroup. Prejudice and discrimination also emerge as major considerations in understanding intergroup relations. Why do they exist? Why do they persist? Why do certain groups become targets more frequently? How can we eliminate prejudicial attitudes?

The word *prejudice* is derived from the Latin word *praejudicium* and originally meant "prejudgment." Thus, some scholars defined a prejudiced person as one who hastily reached a conclusion before examining the facts.[1] This definition proved inadequate, however, because social scientists discovered that prejudice often arose *after* groups came into contact and had at least some knowledge of one another. For that reason, Louis Wirth described prejudice as "an attitude with an emotional bias."[2]

Because feelings shape our attitudes, they reduce our receptivity to additional information that may alter those attitudes. Ralph Rosnow had this fact in mind when he broadened the definition of prejudice to encompass "any unreasonable attitude that is unusually resistant to rational influence."[3] In fact, a deeply prejudiced person is almost totally immune to information. Gordon Allport offers a classic example of such an individual in the following dialogue:

MR. X: The trouble with the Jews is that they only take care of their own group.

MR. Y: But the record of the Community Chest campaign shows that they gave more generously, in proportion to their numbers, to the general charities of the community, than did non-Jews.

MR. X: That shows they are always trying to buy favor and intrude into Christian affairs. They think of nothing but money; that is why there are so many Jewish bankers.

MR. Y: But a recent study shows that the percentage of Jews in the banking business is negligible, far smaller than the percentage of non-Jews.

MR. X: That's just it; they don't go in for respectable business; they are only in the movie business or run night clubs.*

It is almost as if Mr. X is saying, "My mind is made up; don't confuse me with the facts." He does not refute the argument; rather, he ignores each bit of new and contradictory information and moves on to a new area in which he distorts other facts to support his prejudice against Jews.

Prejudicial attitudes may be either positive or negative. Sociologists primarily study the latter, however, because only negative attitudes can lead to turbulent social relations between dominant and minority groups. Numerous writers, therefore, have defined prejudice as an attitudinal "system of negative beliefs, feelings, and action-orientations regarding a certain group or groups of people."[4] The status of the strangers is an important factor in the development of a negative attitude. Prejudicial attitudes exist among members of both dominant and minority groups. Thus, in the relations between dominant and minority groups, the antipathy felt by one group for another is quite often reciprocated.

Psychological perspectives on prejudice—whether behaviorist, cognitive, or psychoanalytic—focus on the subjective states of mind of individuals. In these perspectives, a person's prejudicial attitudes may result from imitation or conditioning (behaviorist), perceived similarity–dissimilarity of beliefs (cognitive), or specific personality characteristics (psychoanalytic). In contrast, sociological perspectives focus on the objective conditions of society as the social forces behind prejudicial attitudes and behind racial and ethnic relations. Individuals do not live in a vacuum; social reality affects their states of mind.

Both perspectives are necessary to understand prejudice. As psychologist Gordon Allport argued, besides needing a close study of habits, perceptions, motivation, and personality, we need an analysis of social settings, situational forces, demographic and ecological variables, and legal and economic trends.[5] Psychological and sociological perspectives complement each other in providing a fuller explanation of intergroup relations.

The Psychology of Prejudice

We can understand more about prejudice among individuals by focusing on four areas of study: levels of prejudice, self-justification, personality, and frustration.

Levels of Prejudice

Bernard Kramer suggests that prejudice exists on three levels: cognitive, emotional, and action orientation.[6] The **cognitive level of prejudice** encompasses

---

*Gordon W. Allport, *The Nature of Prejudice* (Reading, Mass.: Addison-Wesley, 1954), pp. 13–14.

a person's beliefs and perceptions of a group as threatening or nonthreatening, inferior or equal (e.g., in terms of intellect, status, or biological composition), seclusive or intrusive, impulse-gratifying, acquisitive, or possessing other positive or negative characteristics. Mr. X's cognitive beliefs are that Jews are intrusive and acquisitive. Other illustrations of cognitive beliefs are that the Irish are heavy drinkers and fighters, African Americans are rhythmic and lazy, and the Poles are thick-headed and unintelligent. Generalizations shape both ethnocentric and prejudicial attitudes, but there is a difference. *Ethnocentrism* is a generalized rejection of all outgroups on the basis of an in-group focus, whereas **prejudice** is a rejection of certain people solely on the basis of their membership in a particular group.

In many societies, members of the majority group may believe that a particular low-status minority group is dirty, immoral, violent, or law-breaking. In the United States, the Irish, Italians, African Americans, Mexicans, Chinese, Puerto Ricans, and others have at one time or another been labeled with most, if not all, of these adjectives. In most European countries and in the United States, the group lowest on the socioeconomic ladder has often been depicted in caricature as also lowest on the evolutionary ladder. The Irish and African Americans in the United States and the peasants and various ethnic groups in Europe have all been depicted in the past as apelike:

> The Victorian images of the Irish as "white Negro" and simian Celt, or a combination of the two, derived much of its force and inspiration from physiognomical beliefs . . . [but] every country in Europe had its equivalent of "white Negroes" and simianized men, whether or not they happened to be stereotypes of criminals, assassins, political radicals, revolutionaries, Slavs, gypsies, Jews or peasants.[7]

The **emotional level of prejudice** refers to the feelings that a minority group arouses in an individual. Although these feelings may be based on stereotypes from the cognitive level, they represent a more intense stage of personal involvement. The emotional attitudes may be negative or positive, such as fear/envy, distrust/trust, disgust/admiration, or contempt/empathy. These feelings, based on beliefs about the group, may be triggered by social interaction or by the possibility of interaction. For example, Whites might react with fear or anger to the integration of their schools or neighborhoods, or Protestants might be jealous of the lifestyle of a highly successful Catholic business executive.

An **action-orientation level of prejudice** is the positive or negative predisposition to engage in discriminatory behavior. A person who harbors strong feelings about members of a certain racial or ethnic group may have a tendency to act for or against them—being aggressive or nonaggressive, offering assistance or withholding it. Such an individual would also be likely to want to exclude or include members of that group both in close, personal social relations and in peripheral social relations. For example, some people would want to exclude members of the disliked group from doing business with them or living in their neighborhood. Another manifestation of the action-orientation level of prejudice is the desire to change or maintain the status differential or inequality between the two groups, whether the area is economic, political, educational, social, or a combination. Note that an action orientation is a predisposition to act, not the action itself.

Self-Justification

The act of **self-justification** involves denigrating a person or group to justify maltreatment of them. In this situation, self-justification leads to prejudice and discrimination against members of another group.

Some philosophers argue that we are not so much rational creatures as we are rationalizing creatures. We require reassurance that the things we do and the lives we live are proper—that good reasons for our actions exist. If we can convince ourselves that another group is inferior, immoral, or dangerous, we may feel justified in discriminating against its members, enslaving them, or even killing them.

History is filled with examples of people who thought their maltreatment of others was just and necessary: As defenders of the "true faith," the Crusaders killed "Christ killers" (Jews) and "infidels" (Muslims). Participants in the Spanish Inquisition imprisoned, tortured, and executed "heretics," "the disciples of the Devil." Similarly, the Puritans burned witches, whose refusal to confess "proved they were evil"; pioneers exploited or killed Native Americans who were "heathen savages"; and Whites mistreated, enslaved, or killed African Americans, who were "an inferior species." According to U.S. Army officers, the civilians in the Vietnamese village of My Lai were "probably" aiding the Vietcong; so in 1968, U.S. soldiers fighting in the Vietnam War felt justified in slaughtering more than 300 unarmed people there, including women, children, and the elderly.

Some sociologists believe that self-justification works the other way around. That is, instead of self-justification serving as a basis for subjugating others, the subjugation occurs first and the self-justification follows, resulting in prejudice and continued discrimination.[8] The evolution of racism as a concept after the establishment of the African slave trade would seem to support this idea. Philip Mason offers an insight into this view:

> A specialized society is likely to defeat a simpler society and provide a lower tier still of enslaved and conquered peoples. The rulers and organizers sought security for themselves and their children; to perpetuate the power, the esteem, and the comfort they had achieved, it was necessary not only that the artisans and labourers should work contentedly but that the rulers should sleep without bad dreams. No one can say with certainty how the myths originated, but it is surely relevant that when one of the founders of Western thought set himself to frame an ideal state that would embody social justice, he—like the earliest city dwellers—not only devised a society stratified in tiers but believed it would be necessary to

persuade the traders and work-people that, by divine decree, they were made from brass and iron, while the warriors were made of silver and the rulers of gold.[9]

Another example of self-justification serving as a source of prejudice is the dominant group's assumption of an attitude of superiority over other groups. In this respect, establishing a prestige hierarchy—ranking the status of various ethnic groups—results in differential association. To enhance or maintain self-esteem, a person may avoid social contact with groups deemed inferior and associate only with those identified as being of high status. Through such behavior, self-justification may come to intensify the social distance between groups. As discussed in Chapter 1, *social distance* refers to the degree to which ingroup members do not engage in social or primary relationships with members of various outgroups.

Personality

In *The Authoritarian Personality*, T. W. Adorno and his colleagues reported a correlation between individuals' early childhood experiences of harsh parental discipline and their development of an **authoritarian personality** as adults.[10] If parents assume an excessively domineering posture in their relations with a child, exercising stern measures and threatening to withdraw love if the child does not respond with weakness and submission, the child tends to be insecure and to nurture much latent hostility against the parents. When these children become adults, they may demonstrate **displaced aggression,** directing their hostility against a powerless group to compensate for their feelings of insecurity and fear. Highly prejudiced individuals tend to come from families that emphasize obedience.

The authors identified authoritarianism by the use of a measuring instrument called an F scale (the *F* stands for potential fascism). Other tests included the A-S (anti-Semitism) and E (ethnocentrism) scales, the latter measuring attitudes toward various minorities. One of their major findings was that people who scored high on authoritarianism also consistently showed a high degree of prejudice against all minority groups. These highly prejudiced persons were characterized by rigidity of viewpoint, dislike of ambiguity, strict obedience to leaders, and intolerance of weakness in themselves and others.

No sooner did *The Authoritarian Personality* appear than controversy began. H. H. Hyman and P. B. Sheatsley challenged the methodology and analysis.[11] Solomon Asch questioned the assumptions that the F scale responses represented a belief system and that structural variables (e.g., ideologies, stratification, and mobility) do not play a role in shaping personality.[12] E. A. Shils argued that the authors were interested only in measuring authoritarianism of the political right while ignoring such tendencies in those at the other end of the political spectrum.[13] Other investigators sought alternative explanations for the authoritarian personality. D. Stewart and T. Hoult extended the framework beyond family childhood experiences to include other social factors.[14] H. C. Kelman and Janet Barclay pointed out that substantial evidence exists showing that lower intelligence and less education also correlate with high authoritarianism scores on the F scale.[15]

Despite the critical attacks, the underlying conceptions of *The Authoritarian Personality* were important, and research into personality as a factor in prejudice has continued. Subsequent investigators refined and modified the original study. Correcting scores for response bias, they conducted cross-cultural studies. Respondents in Germany and Near East countries, where more authoritarian social structures exist, scored higher on authoritarianism and social distance between groups. In Japan, Germany, and the United States, authoritarianism and social distance were moderately related. Other studies suggested that an inverse relationship exists between social class and F scale scores: the higher the social class, the lower the authoritarianism.[16]

Although studies of authoritarian personality have helped us understand some aspects of prejudice, they have not provided a causal explanation. Most of the findings in this area show a correlation, but the findings do not prove, for example, that harsh discipline of children causes them to become prejudiced adults. Perhaps the strict parents were themselves prejudiced, and the child learned those attitudes from them. Or as George Simpson and J. Milton Yinger state:

> One must be careful not to assume too quickly that a certain tendency—rigidity of mind, for example—that is correlated with prejudice necessarily causes that prejudice. . . . The sequence may be the other way around. . . . It is more likely that both are related to more basic factors.[17]

For some people, prejudice may indeed be rooted in subconscious childhood tensions, but we do not know whether these tensions directly cause a high degree of prejudice in the adult or whether other powerful social forces are the determinants. Whatever the explanation, authoritarianism is a significant phenomenon worthy of continued investigation. Research, however, stresses social and situational factors, rather than personality, as primary causes of prejudice and discrimination.[18]

Yet another dimension of the personality component is that people with low self-esteem are more prejudiced than those who feel good about themselves. Some researchers have argued that individuals with low self-esteem deprecate others to improve their feelings about themselves.[19] One study asserts that "low self-esteem individuals seem to have a generally negative view of themselves, their ingroup, outgroups, and perhaps the world," and thus, their tendency to be more prejudiced is not due to rating the outgroup negatively in comparison to their ingroup.[20]

Frustration

Frustration is the result of relative deprivation in which expectations remain unsatisfied. **Relative deprivation** is a lack of resources, or rewards, in one's standard of living in comparison with those of others in the society. A number of investigators have suggested that frustrations tend to increase aggression toward others.[21] Frustrated people may easily strike out against the perceived cause of their frustration. However, this reaction may not be possible because the true source of the frustration is often too nebulous to be identified or too powerful to act against. In such instances, the result may be displaced aggression; in this situation, the frustrated individual or group usually redirects anger against a more visible, vulnerable, and socially sanctioned target that is unable to strike back. Minorities meet these criteria and are thus frequently the recipients of displaced aggression by the dominant group.

Blaming others for something that is not their fault is known as **scapegoating.** The term comes from the ancient Hebrew custom of using a goat during the Day of Atonement as a symbol of the sins of the people. In an annual ceremony, a priest placed his hands on the head of a goat and listed the people's sins in a symbolic transference of guilt; he then chased the goat out of the community, thereby freeing the people of sin.[22] Since those times, the powerful group has usually punished the scapegoat group rather than allowing it to escape.

There have been many instances throughout world history of minority groups serving as scapegoats, including the Christians in ancient Rome, the Huguenots in France, the Jews in Europe and Russia, and the Puritans and Quakers in England. Gordon Allport suggests that certain characteristics are necessary for a group to become a suitable scapegoat. The group must be (1) highly visible in physical appearance or observable customs and actions; (2) not strong enough to strike back; (3) situated within easy access of the dominant group and, ideally, concentrated in one area; (4) a past target of hostility for whom latent hostility still exists; and (5) the symbol of an unpopular concept.[23]

Some groups fit this typology better than others, but minority racial and ethnic groups have been a perennial choice. Irish, Italians, Catholics, Jews, Quakers, Mormons, Chinese, Japanese, Blacks, Puerto Ricans, Chicanos, and Koreans have all been treated, at one time or another, as the scapegoat in the United States. Especially in times of economic hardship, societies tend to blame some group for the general conditions, which often leads to aggressive action against the group as an expression of frustration. For example, a study by Carl Hovland and Robert Sears found that, between 1882 and 1930, a definite correlation existed between a decline in the price of cotton and an increase in the number of lynchings of Blacks.[24]

In several controlled experiments, social scientists have attempted to measure the validity of the scapegoat theory. Neal Miller and Richard Bugelski tested a group of young men aged 18 to 20 who were working in a government camp about their feelings toward various minority groups. The young men were reexamined about these feelings after experiencing frustration by being obliged to take a long, difficult test and being denied an opportunity to see a film at a local theater. This group showed some evidence of increased prejudicial feelings, whereas a control group, which did not experience any frustration, showed no change in prejudicial attitudes.[25]

Donald Weatherley conducted an experiment with a group of college students to measure the relationship between frustration and aggression against a specific disliked group.[26] After identifying students who were or were not highly anti-Semitic and subjecting them to a strongly frustrating experience, he asked the students to write stories about pictures shown to them. Some of the students were shown pictures of people who had been given Jewish names; other students were presented with pictures of unnamed people. When the pictures were unidentified, the stories of the anti-Semitic students did not differ from those of other students. When the pictures were identified, however, the anti-Semitic students wrote stories reflecting much more aggression against the Jews in the pictures than did the other students.

For more than 20 years, Leonard Berkowitz and his associates studied and experimented with aggressive behavior. They concluded that, confronted with equally frustrating situations, highly prejudiced individuals are more likely to seek scapegoats than are nonprejudiced individuals. Another intervening variable is that personal frustrations (marital failure, injury, or mental illness) make people more likely to seek scapegoats than do shared frustrations (dangers of flood or hurricane).[27]

Some experiments have shown that aggression does not increase if the frustration is understandable.[28] Other experiments have found that people become aggressive only if the aggression directly relieves their frustration.[29] Still other studies have shown that anger is a more likely result if the person responsible for the frustrating situation could have acted otherwise.[30] Clearly, the results are mixed depending on the variables within a given social situation.

Frustration–aggression theory, although helpful, is not completely satisfactory. It ignores the role of culture and the reality of actual social conflict and fails to show any causal relationship. Most of the responses measured in these studies were of people already biased. Why did one group rather than another become the object of the aggression? Moreover, frustration does not necessarily precede aggression, and aggression does not necessarily flow from frustration.

The Sociology of Prejudice

Sociologist Talcott Parsons provided one bridge between psychology and sociology by introducing social forces as a variable in frustration–aggression theory. He suggested that both the family and the occupational structure may produce anxieties and insecurities that create frustration.[31] According to this view, the growing-up process (gaining parental affection and approval, identifying with and imitating sexual role models, and competing with others in adulthood) sometimes involves severe emotional strain. The result is an adult personality with a large reservoir of repressed aggression that becomes *free-floating*—susceptible to redirection against convenient scapegoats. Similarly, the occupational system is a source of frustration: Its emphasis on competitiveness and individual achievement, its function of conferring status, its requirement that people inhibit their natural impulses at work, and its ties to the state of the economy are among the factors that generate emotional anxieties. Parsons pessimistically concluded that minorities fulfill a functional "need" as targets for displaced aggression and therefore will remain targets.[32]

Perhaps most influential in staking out the sociological position on prejudice was Herbert Blumer, who suggested that prejudice always involves the "sense of group position" in society. Agreeing with Kramer's delineation of three levels of prejudice, Blumer argued that prejudice can include beliefs, feelings, and a predisposition to action, thus motivating behavior that derives from the social hierarchy.[33] By emphasizing historically established group positions and relationships, Blumer shifted his focus away from the attitudes and personality compositions of individuals. As a social phenomenon, prejudice rises or falls according to issues that alter one group's position vis-à-vis that of another group.

Socialization

In the **socialization process,** individuals acquire the values, attitudes, beliefs, and perceptions of their culture or subculture, including religion, nationality, and social class. Generally, the child conforms to the parents' expectations in acquiring an understanding of the world and its people. Being impressionable and knowing of no alternative conceptions of the world, the child usually accepts these concepts without questioning. We thus learn the prejudices of our parents and others, which then become part of our values and beliefs. Even when based on false stereotypes, prejudices shape our perceptions of various peoples and influence our attitudes and actions toward particular groups. For example, if we develop negative attitudes about Jews because we are taught that they are shrewd, acquisitive, and clannish—all-too-familiar stereotypes—as adults we may refrain from business or social relationships with them. We may not even realize the reason for such avoidance, so subtle has been the prejudice instilled within us.

People may learn certain prejudices because of their pervasiveness. The cultural screen that we develop and through which we view the surrounding world is not always accurate, but it does permit transmission of shared values and attitudes, which are reinforced by others. Prejudice, like cultural values, is taught and learned through the socialization process. The prevailing prejudicial attitudes and actions may be deeply embedded in custom or law (e.g., the **Jim Crow laws** of the 1890s and the early twentieth century establishing segregated public facilities throughout the South, which subsequent generations accepted as proper and maintained in their own adult lives).

Although socialization explains how prejudicial attitudes may be transmitted from one generation to the next, it does not explain their origin or why they intensify or diminish over the years. These aspects of prejudice must be explained in another way.

Economic Competition

People tend to be more hostile toward others when they feel that their security is threatened; thus, many social scientists conclude that economic competition and conflict breed prejudice. Certainly, considerable evidence shows that negative stereotyping, prejudice, and discrimination increase markedly whenever competition for available jobs increases.

An excellent illustration relates to the Chinese sojourners in the nineteenth-century United States. Prior to the 1870s, the transcontinental railroad was being built, and the Chinese filled many of the jobs made available by this project in the sparsely populated West. Although they were expelled from the region's gold mines and schools and could obtain no redress of grievances in the courts, they managed to convey to some Whites the image of being a clean, hardworking, law-abiding people. The completion of the railroad, the flood of former Civil War soldiers into the job market, and the economic depression of 1873 worsened their situation. The Chinese became more frequent victims of open discrimination and hostility. Their positive stereotype among some Whites was widely displaced by a negative one: They were now "conniving," "crafty," "criminal," "the Yellow menace." Only after they retreated into Chinatowns and entered specialty occupations that minimized their competition with Whites did the intense hostility abate.

One pioneer in the scientific study of prejudice, John Dollard, demonstrated how prejudice against the Germans, which had been virtually nonexistent, arose in a small U.S. industrial town when times got bad:

> Local Whites largely drawn from the surrounding farms manifested considerable direct aggression toward the newcomers. Scornful and derogatory opinions were expressed about the Germans, and the native Whites had a satisfying sense of superiority toward them. . . . The chief element in the permission to be aggressive against the Germans was rivalry for jobs and status in the local woodenware plants. The native Whites felt definitely crowded for their jobs by the entering German groups and in case of bad times had a chance to blame the Germans who by their presence provided more competitors for the scarcer jobs. There seemed to be no traditional pattern of prejudice against Germans unless the skeletal suspicion of all out-groupers (always present) be invoked in this place.[34]

Both experimental studies and historical analyses have added credence to the economic-competition theory. Muzafer Sherif directed several experiments showing how intergroup competition at a boys' camp led to conflict and escalating hostility.[35] Donald Young pointed out that, throughout U.S. history, in times of high unemployment and thus intense job competition, nativist movements against minorities have flourished.[36] This pattern has held true regionally—against Asians on the West Coast, Italians in Louisiana, and

French Canadians in New England—and nationally, with the antiforeign movements always peaking during periods of depression. So it was with the Native American Party in the 1830s, the Know-Nothing Party in the 1850s, the American Protective Association in the 1890s, and the Ku Klux Klan after World War I. Since the passage of civil-rights laws on employment in the twentieth century, researchers have consistently detected the strongest anti-Black prejudice among working-class and middle-class Whites who feel threatened by Blacks entering their socioeconomic group in noticeable numbers.[37] It seems that any group applying the pressure of job competition most directly on another group becomes a target of its prejudice.

Once again, a theory that offers some excellent insights into prejudice—in particular, that adverse economic conditions correlate with increased hostility toward minorities—also has some serious shortcomings. Not all groups that have been objects of hostility (e.g., Quakers and Mormons) have been economic competitors. Moreover, why is hostility against some groups greater than against others? Why do the negative feelings in some communities run against groups whose numbers are so small that they cannot possibly pose an economic threat? Evidently, values besides economic ones cause people to be antagonistic to a group perceived as an actual or potential threat.

Social Norms

Some sociologists have suggested that a relationship exists between prejudice and a person's tendency to conform to societal expectations.[38] **Social norms**—the norms of one's culture—form the generally shared rules defining what is and is not proper behavior. By learning and automatically accepting the prevailing prejudices, an individual is simply conforming to those norms.

This theory holds that a direct relationship exists between degree of conformity and degree of prejudice. If so, people's prejudices should decrease or increase significantly when they move into areas where the prejudicial norm is lesser or greater. Evidence supports this view. Thomas Pettigrew found that Southerners in the 1950s became less prejudiced against Blacks when they interacted with them in the army, where the social norms were less prejudicial.[39] In another study, Jeanne Watson found that people moving into an anti-Semitic neighborhood in New York City became more anti-Semitic.[40]

John Dollard's study, *Caste and Class in a Southern Town*, provides an in-depth look at the emotional adjustment of Whites and Blacks to rigid social norms.[41] In his study of the processes, functions, and maintenance of accommodation, Dollard detailed the "carrot-and-stick" method social groups employed. Intimidation—sometimes even severe reprisals for going against social norms—ensured compliance. However, reprisals usually were unnecessary. The advantages Whites and Blacks gained in psychological, economic, or behavioral terms served to perpetuate the caste order. These gains in personal security and stability set in motion a vicious circle. They encouraged a way of life that reinforced the rationale of the social system in this community.

Two 1994 studies provided further evidence of the powerful influence of social norms. Joachim Krueger and Russell W. Clement found that consensus bias persisted despite the availability of statistical data and knowledge about such bias.[42] Michael R. Leippe and Donna Eisenstadt showed that induced compliance can change socially significant attitudes and that the change generalizes to broader beliefs.[43]

Although the social-norms theory explains prevailing attitudes, it does not explain either their origins or the reasons new prejudices develop when other groups move into an area. In addition, the theory does not explain why prejudicial attitudes against a particular group rise and fall cyclically over the years.

Although many social scientists have attempted to identify the causes of prejudice, no single factor provides an adequate explanation. Prejudice is a complex phenomenon, and it is most likely the product of more than one causal agent. Sociologists today tend either to emphasize multiple-cause explanations or to stress social forces encountered in specific and similar situations—forces such as economic conditions, stratification, and hostility toward an outgroup.

Stereotyping

One common reaction to strangers is to categorize them broadly. Prejudice at the cognitive level often arises from false perceptions that are enhanced by cultural or racial stereotypes. A **stereotype** is an oversimplified generalization by which we attribute certain traits or characteristics to a group without regard to individual differences. Sometimes stereotypes are positive—for example, that African Americans are good athletes and that Asians are good mathematicians. But even here, they can create pressures and problems—for example, for African Americans who are not athletic or for Asians who are weak in math. Stereotypes distort sociocultural truths but nevertheless are socially approved images held by one group about another.[44]

Stereotypes, which easily become ingrained within everyday thinking, serve to enhance a group's self-esteem and social identity—in accord with Blumer's concept of prejudice as a sense of group position. Even if an outgroup is economically successful, stereotyping it as clannish, mercenary, or unscrupulous enables other groups to affirm their own moral superiority.

Not only do stereotypes deny individuals the right to be judged and treated on the basis of their own personal merit, but also, by attributing a particular image to the entire group, they become a justification for discriminatory behavior. Negative stereotypes also serve as important reference points in people's evaluations of what they observe in everyday life. Following is an excellent illustration of how prejudice leads a person to attribute to other people's behavior motives and causes that are consistent with preexisting stereotypes:

> Prejudiced people see the world in ways that are consistent with their prejudice. If Mr. Bigot sees a well-dressed, white, Anglo-Saxon Protestant sitting on a park

bench sunning himself at three o'clock on a Wednesday afternoon, he thinks nothing of it. If he sees a well-dressed black man doing the same thing, he is liable to leap to the conclusion that the person is unemployed—and he becomes infuriated, because he assumes that his hard-earned taxes are paying that shiftless good-for-nothing enough in welfare subsidies to keep him in good clothes. If Mr. Bigot passes Mr. Anglo's house and notices that a trash can is overturned and some garbage is strewn about, he is apt to conclude that a stray dog has been searching for food. If he passes Mr. Garcia's house and notices the same thing, he is inclined to become annoyed, and to assert that "those people live like pigs." Not only does prejudice influence his conclusions, his erroneous conclusions justify and intensify his negative feelings.[45]

Once established, stereotypes are difficult to eradicate, even in succeeding generations. Evidence of the pervasiveness and persistence of stereotypes came from a study comparing responses of college students over three gen-

"Mutual: Both Are Glad There Are Bars Between 'Em!"
This visual stereotype of an apelike Irishman reinforced prevailing beliefs that the Irish were emotionally unstable and morally primitive. This cartoon appeared in *Judge* on November 7, 1891, and is typical of a worldwide tendency to depict minorities as apelike.

(*Source:* The Distorted Image, courtesy John and Selma Appel Collection)

erations. Providing a list of eighty-four adjectives, the researchers asked the students to select five that they thought described the most characteristic traits of ten racial and ethnic groups.[46] Although each group showed increasing reluctance to make such generalizations, a high level of uniformity nonetheless marked the responses.

Notably, students either tended to agree on the same adjectives others had chosen in earlier studies or to pick a similar new adjective. Positive stereotypes regarding work achievement continued for "Americans," Germans, Japanese, and Jews. Emotional stereotypes for the Irish and for Italians, a carefree image for "Negroes" (the accepted word then), a negative stereotype for Turks, a positive and conservative image for the English, and commitment to family and tradition for Chinese—all remained constant generalizations over the 35-year span of the study. Other studies have reported similar findings.[47]

Both majority-group and minority-group members may hold stereotypes about each other. Such generalized labeling often begins with some small basis in fact as applied to a few particular individuals that is then erroneously applied to everyone in that group. Social barriers between the two groups, mass-media portrayals reinforcing the stereotypes (see the accompanying Ethnic Experience box), and societal pressures to conform to the stereotype combine to give such thinking a false aura of validity, encouraging people to ignore contrary evidence.

Ethnophaulisms

An **ethnophaulism** is a derogatory word or expression used to describe a racial or ethnic group. This is the language of prejudice, the verbal picture of a negative stereotype that reflects the prejudice and bigotry of a society's past and present. Howard J. Ehrlich divides ethnophaulisms into three types: (1) disparaging nicknames (e.g., chink, dago, polack, jungle bunny, or honky); (2) explicit group devaluations (e.g., "jew him down" for trying to get something for a lower price, "luck of the Irish" suggesting undeserved good fortune, or "to be in Dutch" meaning to be in trouble); (3) irrelevant ethnic names used as a mild disparagement (e.g., "jewbird" for black cuckoos having prominent beaks, "welsh" on a bet signifying failure to honor a debt, or "Irish confetti" for bricks thrown in a fight).[48]

Both majority and minority groups coin and use ethnophaulisms to denigrate outgroups. Such usage helps justify discrimination, inequality, and social privilege for the majority, and it helps the minority cope with social injustices caused by others. Them-versus-us name-calling is divisive, but it also indicates the state of intergroup relations. Erdman Palmore, for example, concluded that all racial and ethnic groups use ethnophaulisms. He found a correlation between the number of them used and the degree of group prejudice, and he observed that they express and support negative stereotypes about the most visible racial or cultural differences.[49]

The Ethnic Experience
The Impact of the Media

As a reflector of society's values, the media have a tremendous impact on the shaping of our personal and group identities. Radio, television, films, newspapers, magazines, and comics can convey the rich textures of a pluralistic society or they can, directly or indirectly (by omission and distortion), alter our perception of other ethnic groups and reinforce our defensiveness and ambivalence about our own cultural backgrounds. As an Italian-American, I've realized this myself when comparing the ethnic invisibility of 50s television with modern shows that concentrate on Mafia hit men and multiple biographies of Mussolini. Having squirmed as I watched some of these portrayals, I can empathize with Arabs who resent being characterized as villainous sheikhs, Jews seen as mendacious moguls or even the current vogue for matching a Russian accent with a kind of oafish villainy. Although such stereotypes may or may not serve political ends, they share the cartoonlike isolation of a few traits that ignore the humanity and variety of a group's members.

What is the impact of ethnic stereotypes on TV and in film on how people feel about themselves and how they perceive other ethnic groups?

Although research in this area is limited, what is available suggests that TV and film's portrayal of ethnics does have a deleterious effect on perceptions of self and others. In my own clinical work, I have found that minority children and adults will often internalize negative stereotypes about their own group. Other studies have shown that ethnic stereotypes on television and in the movies can contribute to prejudice against a particular group—especially when the person is not acquainted with any members of that group. . . .

In studies of youngsters who commit hate acts—desecration of religious institutions, racial and anti-Semitic incidents—many youngsters apprehended reported they got the idea of performing vandalism from news coverage of similar acts (the copy cat syndrome). They saw media coverage as conferring recognition and prestige, temporarily raising their low self-esteem.

Add to TV fiction and news the rash of "truly tasteless" joke books, radio call-in shows that invite bigoted calls from listeners, late-night TV hosts and comedians who denigrate ethnic groups, and the impact on people's perceptions is considerable. While the media cannot be blamed for creating the bigotry, their insensitive reporting and encouragement of inflammatory comments establishes a societal norm that gives license to such attitudes and behavior.

Source: Joseph Giordano, "Identity Crisis: Stereotypes Stifle Self-Development," *Media and Values*, Winter 1987, p. 13. Reprinted by permission.

Ethnophaulisms seem to appear most often during times of major social and economic change, such as migration or immigration waves, rapid urbanization or technological change, recessions and depressions, or war. Linguistic experts have identified about 1,200 ethnic slur-names or epithets used historically in U.S. speech.[50] Most of them are obsolete today, although a few remain, and new ones appear almost yearly.

Sometimes members of a racial or ethnic minority group use an ethnophaulism directed against themselves in their conversations with one another. On occasion, they may use the term as a reprimand to one of their own kind for acting out the stereotype, but more often, they mean it as a humorous expression of friendship and endearment. However, when an outsider uses that same term, they resent it because of its prejudicial connotations.

Yet outsiders may use certain terms that are not derogatory even when others view them as such. In an analysis of heterosexist talk, British researchers found that in references to others' sexuality, such utterances do not necessarily have negativity built into them. Rather, they become prejudicial or troublesome among participants in those situations as their meaning becomes produced and negotiated. For example, such descriptive terms as "poof" or "dyke" could involve flexible, episodic practices that do not settle into stable, causal attitudes. In managing such talk, speakers may be (1) discounting heterosexism, (2) displaying a lack of understanding, (3) softening the blow, or (4) conceding positive features.[51] The context of words is important, as in "Dutch treat" and "luck of the Irish," which are no longer recognized as derogatory.

Ethnic Humor

Why do some people find ethnic jokes funny, whereas others find them distasteful? Studies show the response often reflects the listener's attitude toward the group being ridiculed. If you hold favorable or positive attitudes toward the group that is the butt of the joke, then you are less likely to find it funny than if you hold unfavorable or negative views. If you dislike a group about which a joke implies something negative, you will tend to appreciate the joke.[52]

Sometimes people tell or laugh at derogatory jokes about their own group. Jeffrey Goldstein suggests several reasons for this. One is to strengthen ingroup cohesiveness by reminding members of the perceptions and threats of outgroups. Another is to dissociate oneself from stereotypes of one's group through self-disparaging group humor. A third possibility is that we use ethnic humor to affirm ourselves, point out the absurdity of our predicaments, and objectify our faults and make them laughable. The key to ethnic humor, then, lies in both the joker's and the audience's attitudes.[53]

The Influence of Television

Virtually every U.S. household owns at least one television set, and families in the United States watch more than 7 hours of TV daily, on average. Does all this viewing make us think or act differently? Does it change our attitudes or shape our feelings and reactions about minority groups? Or is it only entertainment with no appreciable effect on perceptions and behavior? Abundant research evidence indicates television programming distorts reality, promotes stereotypical role models, and significantly shapes and reinforces our attitudes about men, women, and minority groups.

Perpetuation of Stereotypes

Twice in the late 1970s, the U.S. Commission on Civil Rights charged the television industry with perpetuating racial and sexual stereotypes in programming and news.[54] Besides criticizing the almost exclusively negative racial portrayals on police shows over the preceding 6 years, the report attacked the television industry for portraying

> a social structure in which males are very much in control of their lives, . . . older, more serious, more independent, and more likely to hold prestigious jobs. Women, on the other hand, were younger, often unemployed, more "family bound," and often found in comic roles. Those women who were employed were in stereotyped and sometimes subservient occupations.

In 1982, media expert George Gerbner continued the criticism, arguing that little had changed since the commission's reports.[55] A tiny percentage of Black characters, for example, were "unrealistically romanticized," but the overwhelming majority of them occupied subservient, supporting roles—such as the White hero's comic sidekick. Gerbner commented:

> When a black child looks at prime time, most of the people he sees doing interesting things are white. That imbalance tends to teach young blacks to accept minority status as naturally inevitable and even deserved.[56]

In the 1990s, the blatant stereotypes faded, but more subtle ones remained. Terrorists are still likely to be Arabs, single mothers to be African Americans on welfare, gang members to be Hispanic, and gardeners to be Asian. The once-popular television show *In Living Color* was denounced by some for perpetuating racial and gay stereotypes, although others disagreed. Still, African Americans, Asians, Hispanics, and women have made significant gains in television, both on and behind the camera.[57] On the other hand, numerous Italian American organizations have objected to HBO's phenomenally successful series *The Sopranos* for perpetuating the stereotype linkage of Italians with the Mafia.

Influencing of Attitudes

Television influences attitudes toward racial or ethnic groups by the status of the parts it assigns to their members, the kind of behavior they display within these parts, and even the type of products they promote. Television greatly influences children's attitudes in this area. Children watch television

Critically acclaimed and honored, *The Sopranos* nonetheless drew complaints from many Italian American individuals and organizations for helping perpetuate the stereotype linking Italians with organized crime. Yet, in Italy, the show drew no such criticism as Italians said, "Everyone knows it's just a show." What explains these different reactions?

(*Source:* Reuters/Hulton Archive)

during prime time more than any other time of day. Yet according to a 2002 Children Now's study, prime time remains overwhelmingly White, with people of color appearing largely in secondary and guest roles. Whites account for 73 percent of the prime time population, followed by African Americans (16 percent), Latinos (4 percent), Asian/Pacific Islanders (3 percent), and Native Americans (0.2 percent). However, prime time diversity dramatically increases as the evening progresses, with the 8 P.M. hour the least racially diverse and the 10 P.M. hour the most racially diverse. Thus, children and youths are more likely to see a much more homogeneous prime time world than are adults who watch television later in the evening.[58]

Due to the near invisibility of characters of color (and the often negatively stereotyped portrayals when they do appear), children of color who watch television extensively may have low self-esteem, feel alienated, and be reluctant to participate in activities outside their own community.[59] This impact on identity development can be especially strong for Latino, Asian, and Native American children, who almost never see people who look like them on television. Children in these and other underrepresented groups can receive a strong, clear message that the majority culture does not value or respect them.[60]

All in the Family, a popular comedy series in the 1970s and still in syndicated reruns, received an NAACP award for its contribution to race relations but divided critics over the question of whether it reduced or reinforced racial bigotry.[61] Offering an explanation for both views, Neil Vidmar and Milton Rokeach reported findings that selective perception and prior attitudes determining reactions to the situations on screen governed viewers' affective responses.[62] Liberal viewers saw the program as satire, with son-in-law Mike effectively rebutting Archie's ignorance and bigotry or minority members besting Archie by the end of the program. In contrast, prejudiced viewers— particularly adolescents—were significantly more likely to admire Archie over Mike and to perceive Archie as winning in the end. Although most respondents indicated they thought Mike made better sense than Archie, highly prejudiced adolescents were significantly more likely to perceive Archie as making better sense. Thus, the program was probably doing more to reinforce prejudice and discrimination than to combat it.

Ingroup and Outgroup Perceptions

Two months before a 1986 racial attack in the Howard Beach area of Queens in New York City made national headlines, a study of 1,200 students at a public high school in the area revealed their attitudes toward race and ethnicity in real life and on television.[63] The school had been chosen because it contained a multiethnic population, with large numbers of Black, Hispanic, and Italian American students and smaller groups of students of Irish and Asian descent. Reasons for watching television varied by ethnic group (Table 4.1).

TABLE 4.1   Reasons for Watching TV, by Ethnic Group (in Percentages)

	Ethnic Group						
Reasons for Watching	Asian	Black	Hispanic	Jewish	Italian	Irish	All
It brings my family together.	18	23	20	10	14	13	18
I learn a lot from it.	35	51	36	24	28	31	40
It shows how others solve problems I have.	41	38	36	31	34	27	37
I get to know different people.	35	42	33	24	26	27	34
It teaches things I don't learn in school.	26	32	26	16	17	11	27
It shows what life is really like.	29	28	27	14	19	13	25
I learn how to act.	9	12	11	2	7	2	10
It keeps me from being bored.	94	86	78	86	88	89	85

Source: S. Robert Lichter and Linda S. Lichter, *Television's Impact on Ethnic and Racial Images,* American Jewish Committee. 1986. Reprinted by permission.

Also, one-fourth of these students said that TV accurately depicts what life and people are really like and that TV influences their racial and ethnic attitudes. Their responses to twenty then-popular TV ethnic characters as positive or negative were both realistic and revealing of broad patterns of consistent responses. Generally, group members saw their portrayed group members more favorably and as more typical than did nonmembers.

The Influence of Advertising and Music

Social scientists are paying increasing attention to the impact of corporate advertising, rap music lyrics, and music videos on attitudes about men and women. Beyond the obviousness of marketing products and entertainment lie their powers of seduction, imagery, and conditioning of attitudes.

Advertising

The average American is exposed to more than 3,000 advertisements a day and watches 3 years' worth of television ads over the course of a lifetime. What effect do they have on our attitudes? In a content analysis of popular 1990s TV commercials designed for specific target audiences, researchers found the characters in them enjoyed more prominence and exercised more authority if they were White or male. Images of romantic and domestic fulfillment also differed by race and gender, with women and Whites disproportionately shown in family settings and in cross-sex interactions. In general, the researchers found that these commercials tended to portray White men as powerful, White women as sex objects, Black men as aggressive, and Black women as inconsequential. They suggest that these commercial images help perpetuate subtle prejudice against African Americans by exaggerating cultural differences and denying positive emotions.[64]

Exploitation of women in ads is worse today than ever before, writes Jean Kilbourne, best known for her documentary film work (*Killing Us Softly; Pack of Lies*) and her college lecture tours. Kilbourne's research points out that women—and girls, in particular—need to be mindful of the influential power of advertising. Women's bodies, frequently portrayed as headless torsos, have long been used to sell everything from toothbrushes to chain saws. In addition, endless glossy spreads in women's magazines feature beauty products, fashion, and diets to keep women focused on exterior "problems." She doesn't blame ads alone for demonizing fat women or causing binge drinking, teenage pregnancy, and violence against women. The cumulative effect is what appalls her. Taken together, she says, advertising fosters an inescapable, poisonous environment in which sexist stereotypes, cynicism and self-hatred, and the search for quick fixes flourish. Consumers may think they are unaffected, but advertisers successfully create a false consciousness and teach young women that they are appetizing only when "plucked, polished and painted."[65]

Music

One of the major criticisms of rap music is that it may affect attitudes and behavior regarding the use of violence, especially violence against women. Although some rap artists—such as Arrested Development and Queen Latifah—reflect a concern for humanity and offer inspiration and hope, others—such as Eminem, 2 Live Crew, Apache, N.W.A., and Scarface—routinely endorse violence, homophobia, and portray women as punching bags, strippers, or simply sperm receptacles. Such portrayals prompted the National Black Women's Political Caucus to seek legislation to control the access to rap music. In 1993, prominent Harlem minister Calvin O. Butts, III, encouraged people to bring him all offensive rap cassettes, CDs, records, and videos to throw in a pile in the street and crush with a steamroller.

Pop culture has enormous influence on how young men and women see themselves and each other in terms of sexuality and gender. Sut Jhally, best known for his documentary film *Dreamworlds* (which MTV tried to stop), says the powerful sexual imagery in hundreds of music videos, produced mostly by men, objectifies and dehumanizes women, frequently portraying them as existing solely for males' sexual satisfaction.

Social scientists and activists fight against this onslaught to eliminate the prejudices that television shows and commercials, advertisements, music lyrics, and videos promulgate.

Can Prejudice Be Reduced?

A great many organizations and movements dedicated to reducing prejudice have existed over the years. Although they have varied in their orientation and focal point of activity, they have usually adopted two basic approaches: to promote greater interaction between dominant and minority groups in all aspects of living, by either voluntary or compulsory means; and to dispense information that destroys stereotypes and exposes rationalizations (self-justifications). Neither approach has been successful in all instances, probably because the inequalities that encourage prejudicial attitudes still exist.

Interaction

Contact between people of different racial and ethnic backgrounds does not necessarily lead to friendlier attitudes. In fact, the situation may worsen, as has happened frequently when schools and neighborhoods have experienced an influx of people from a different group. In many instances, however, interaction does reduce prejudice.[66] It would also appear that many other variables determine the effect of interaction, including the frequency and duration of contacts; the relative status of the two parties and their backgrounds;

whether their meeting is voluntary or compulsory and competitive or cooperative; and whether they meet in a political, religious, occupational, residential, or recreational situation.[67]

A good example of the significance of the type of contact emerges from the experiments in **cooperative learning** of Elliot Aronson and Neal Osherow.[68] This research team observed that classroom competition for teacher recognition and approval often wreaked special hardship on minority children less fluent in English or less self-assured about participating in class. The researchers created interdependent learning groups of five or six children, each member charged with learning one portion of the day's lesson in a particular subject. The children learned the complete lesson from one another and then took a test on all the material. Because it creates interdependent groups, this technique is not the same as the cooperative learning approach so common in U.S. schools. In fact, Australian researchers compared use of the two approaches among children in grades 4 to 6 and found that the cooperative learning method produced significant improvements on measures of academic performance, liking of peers, and racial prejudice, in contrast to the effect of the cooperative approach that exacerbated preexisting intergroup tensions[69] (see the accompanying Ethnic Experience box).

Information

Many people have long cherished the hope that education would reduce prejudice. Some studies, such as that by Gertrude Selznick and Stephen Steinberg, have found a definite correlation between level of education and degree of tolerance,[70] but other studies have not.[71] Charles Stember's research led him to conclude that more highly educated persons were not more tolerant; they were simply more sophisticated in recognizing measures of bias and more subtle in expressing their prejudices.[72] In sum, it appears that formal education is far from a perfect means of reducing prejudice.

One reason for this failure is that people tend to use **selective perception;** that is, they absorb information that accords with their own beliefs and rationalize away information that does not. Another reason is the almost quantum leap from the classroom to real-life situations. Dealing with prejudice from a detached perspective is one thing; dealing with it in actuality is quite another because emotions, social pressures, and many other factors are involved.

Despite these criticisms, courses in race and ethnic relations certainly have value because they raise the students' level of consciousness about intergroup dynamics. However, a significant reduction or elimination of prejudice is more likely to occur by changing the structural conditions of inequality that promote and maintain prejudicial attitudes. As Herbert Blumer suggests, the sense of group position dissolves and racial prejudice declines when major shifts in the social order overtake the current definition of a group's characteristics.[73] As long as the dominant group does not react with fear and institute a

The Ethnic Experience
Reducing Prejudice through Cooperative Learning

The experience of a Mexican-American child in one of our groups serves as a useful illustration. We will call him Carlos. Carlos was not very articulate in English, his second language. Because he was often ridiculed when he had spoken up in the past, over the years he learned to keep quiet in class. He was one of those students . . . who had entered into an implicit contract of silence with his teacher, he opting for anonymity and she calling on him only rarely.

While Carlos hated school and was learning very little in the traditional classroom, at least he was left alone. Accordingly, he was quite uncomfortable with the jigsaw system, which required him to talk to his groupmates. He had a great deal of trouble communicating his paragraph, stammering and hesitating. The other children reacted out of old habits, resorting to insults and teasing. "Aw, you don't know it," Susan accused. "You're dumb, you're stupid. You don't know what you are doing."

One of the researchers, assigned to observe the group process, intervened with a bit of advice when she overheard such comments: "Okay, you can tease him if you want to. It might be fun for you, but it's not going to help you learn about Eleanor Roosevelt's young adulthood. And let me remind you, the exam will take place in less than an hour." Note how this statement brings home the fact that the reinforcement contingencies have shifted considerably. Now Susan does not gain much from putting Carlos down. And she stands to lose a great deal, not just from the teacher singling her out for criticism but because she needs to know Carlos's information.

Gradually, but inexorably, it began to dawn on the students that the only chance they had to learn about Carlos's segment was by paying attention to what he had to say. If they ignored Carlos or continued to ridicule him, his segment would be unavailable to them and the most they could hope for would be an 80 percent score on the exam—an unattractive prospect to most of the children. And with that realization, the kids began to develop into pretty good interviewers, learning to pay attention to Carlos, to draw him out, and to ask probing questions. Carlos, in turn, began to relax more and found it easier to explain out loud what was in his head. What the children came to learn about Carlos is even more important than the information about the lesson that they got from him. After a couple of days, they began to appreciate that Carlos was not nearly as dumb as they had thought he was. After a few weeks they noticed talents in him they had not seen before. They began to like Carlos, and he began to enjoy school more and to think of his Anglo classmates as helpful friends and interested colleagues rather than as tormentors.

Source: Elliot Aronson and Neal Osherow. "Cooperation, Prosocial Behavior, and Academic Performance: Experiments in the Desegregated Classroom," *Applied Social Psychology Annual* 1 (1980), 174–75. Reprinted by permission.

countermovement, the improvement of a minority's social position changes power relations and reduces negative stereotypes. Therefore, continued efforts at public enlightenment and extension of constitutional rights and equal op-

Cooperative learning, where each child tells the others about parts of the lesson, is now a common teaching technique in U.S. elementary schools. Experiments by social scientists show this approach is also an effective means of reducing the walls of prejudice and social distance and building self-esteem and motivation in minority youngsters, particularly in interdependent learning groups.

(*Source:* © Fritz Hoffman/The Image Works)

portunities to all Americans, regardless of race, religion, or national origin, appear to be the most promising means of attaining an unprejudiced society.

One measure of shifting group positions is the expanding inclusiveness of the mainstream U.S. ingroup; previously excluded minority groups, once victims of prejudice, are gaining the social acceptance of structural assimilation. In its over-200-year history, the United States has experienced a changing definition of *mainstream "American"*—from only those whose ancestry was English, to the British (English, Welsh, Scots, and Scots Irish), to peoples from Northern and Western Europe, and now to all Europeans. People of color, however, have yet to gain entry into this national cultural identity group, and that entry is the challenge before us.[74]

Diversity Training

A workplace environment that promotes positive intergroup interaction is more efficient, has higher morale, and retains experienced personnel. Conversely, a hostile work environment has lower productivity, disgruntled personnel, and a higher attrition rate. Moreover, if an organization develops a reputation for insensitivity to diversity, it will attract fewer qualified job applicants among women and people of color, and businesses will lose market share by attracting fewer clients from our increasingly diverse society for their goods and services.

With women and non-White males now constituting 75 percent of the people entering the U.S. labor force, and with nearly 40 percent of the nation's enlisted military personnel identifying themselves as a minority, it has become critical for all organizations to take steps to prevent prejudice from creating dysfunctions within their daily operations.[75]

As someone who has conducted numerous diversity training workshops for military leaders and corporate management (including health care), let me give you some insight into these programs. The best ones heighten awareness by providing informational insights into the diversity of cultural value orientations, as well as into the current and future demographics of employees and clients. Most valuable in broadening perceptions is the inclusion of interactive learning sessions such as role-playing demonstrations of wrong–right handlings of situations and the creation of small groups to discuss and offer solutions to hypothetical but realistic problems.

Although programs vary greatly in their length, structure, and content, the most effective ones are comprehensive, actively supported by management as part of the organization's general mission statement, and fully integrated into all aspects of the organization. The latter includes a diversity orientation session for new employees, occasional reinforcement sessions for continuing employees, and all levels of management working together to promote an inclusive, hospitable work climate. Such efforts can make a significant contribution to reducing prejudice in the workplace.

Retrospect

The psychology of prejudice focuses on individuals' subjective states of mind, emphasizing the levels of prejudice held and the factors of self-justification, personality, frustration, and scapegoating. The sociology of prejudice examines objective conditions of society as social forces behind prejudicial attitudes; socialization, economic competition, and social norms constitute major considerations.

Stereotyping often reflects prejudice as a sense of group position. Once established, stereotypes are difficult to eradicate and often are manifest in ethnophaulisms and ethnic humor. Television has a profound impact in shaping and reinforcing attitudes; unfortunately, it tends to perpetuate racial and sexual stereotypes instead of combating them.

Increased contact between groups and improved information do not necessarily reduce prejudice. The nature of the contact, particularly whether it is competitive or cooperative, is a key determinant. Information can develop heightened awareness as a means of improving relations, but external factors (economic conditions and social pressures) may override rational considerations.

The imagery in advertising, rap music lyrics, and music videos can have a cumulative effect in shaping values about men and women. These images and words help perpetuate subtle prejudice and a false consciousness.

Diversity in the workplace, whether corporate or military, has prompted many organizations to create a more positive, inclusive environment through diversity training workshops. The most effective ones are comprehensive, actively supported by management, and fully integrated into all aspects of the organization.

KEY TERMS

Action-orientation level of prejudice
Authoritarian personality
Cognitive level of prejudice
Cooperative learning
Displaced aggression
Emotional level of prejudice
Ethnophaulism
Jim Crow laws

Prejudice
Relative deprivation
Scapegoating
Selective perception
Self-justification
Social norms
Socialization process
Stereotype

REVIEW QUESTIONS

1. What is prejudice? What are some of its manifestations?

2. What are some of the possible causes of prejudice?

3. What role does television play in combating or reinforcing stereotypes?

4. In what ways can advertising be harmful to minorities?

5. What are the criticisms against some rap music and music videos?

6. How can we reduce prejudice?

SUGGESTED READINGS

Allen, Irving L. *Unkind Words: Ethnic Labeling from Redskin to WASP.* New York: Bergin & Garvey, 1990.
    Informative, highly readable insights into how ethnic animosities take many and devious forms in abusive slang.
Clark, Kenneth B. *Prejudice and Your Child.* Middletown, Conn.: Wesleyan University Press, 1988.
    A thorough examination of the effects of racial prejudice on children, both majority- and

minority-group members, with specific suggestions for overcoming prejudicial feelings in children.

Lester, Paul M. (ed.). *Images That Injure: Pictorial Stereotypes in the Media.* New York: Praeger, 1996.
A collection of essays that discuss media stereotypes, their impact on individuals and society, and the motivations of those who made the images.

Perlmutter, Philip. *Legacy of Hate: A Short History of Ethnic, Religious, and Racial Prejudice in America.* New York: M. E. Sharpe, 1999.
A comprehensive study of bigotry in the United States against various groups, from colonial beginnings to the present.

Sowell, Thomas. *Migrations and Cultures: A World View.* New York: HarperCollins, 1997.
A provocative book that draws from case histories of the Germans, Italians, Japanese, Chinese, Jews, and Asian Indians and argues that immigrants' habits and beliefs are more important to their fate than a country's economy, culture, or politics.

CHAPTER

8 Discrimination

Whereas prejudice is an attitudinal system, **discrimination** is actual behavior, the practice of differential and unequal treatment of other groups of people, usually along racial, religious, or ethnic lines. The Latin word *discriminatus*, from which the English word is derived, means "to divide or distinguish," and its subsequent negative connotation has remained relatively unchanged through the centuries.

Levels of Discrimination

Actions, like attitudes, have different levels of intensity. As a result, discrimination may be analyzed at five levels.[1] The first level is *verbal expression*, a statement of dislike or the use of a derogatory term. The next level is *avoidance*, in which the prejudiced person takes steps to avoid social interaction with a group. Actions of this type may include choice of residence, organizational membership, activities located in urban centers, and primary relationships in any social setting.

At the third level, *exclusion* from certain jobs, housing, education, or social organizations occurs. In the United States, the practice of **de jure segregation** was once widespread throughout the South. Not only were children specifically assigned to certain schools to maintain racial separation, but segregationist laws kept all public places (theaters, restaurants, rest rooms, transportation, etc.) racially separated as well. This exclusion can also take the form of **de facto segregation** as residential patterns become embedded in social customs and institutions. Thus, the standard practice of building and maintaining neighborhood schools in racially segregated communities creates and preserves segregated schools.

The fourth level of discrimination is *physical abuse*—violent attacks on members of the disliked group. Unfortunately, this behavior still occurs often in the United States. A new term, **ethnoviolence,** has entered our vocabulary. The Prejudice Institute defines ethnoviolence as encompassing a range of action—intimidation, harassment, group insults, vandalism, graffiti, swastika painting, arson, cross burning, physical assault, and murder—committed against people targeted solely because of their race, religion, ethnic background, or sexual orientation.[2] Thousands of incidents of ethnoviolence against members of various minority groups occur each year throughout the United States on college campuses and in both suburban and urban areas.

The most extreme level of discrimination is *extermination:* massacres, genocide, or pogroms conducted against a people. Such barbarous actions continue to occur sporadically, as in Bosnia and Rwanda in the 1990s and the 9/11 attacks in New York City and Washington, D.C., in 2001.

Relationships between Prejudice and Discrimination

Prejudice can lead to discrimination, and discrimination can lead to prejudice, although no certainty exists that one will follow the other. Our attitudes and our overt behavior are closely related, but they are not identical. We may harbor hostile feelings toward certain groups without ever making them known through word or deed. Conversely, our overt behavior may effectively conceal our real attitudes.

Prejudiced people are more likely than others to practice discrimination; thus, discrimination quite often represents the overt expression of prejudice. It is wrong, however, to assume that discrimination is always the simple acting out of prejudice. It may instead be the result of a policy decision protecting the interests of the majority group, as happens when legal immigration is curtailed for economic reasons. It may be due to social conformity, as when people submit to outside pressures despite their personal views.[3] Discriminators may explain their actions with reasons other than prejudice toward a particular group, and those reasons may be valid to the discriminators. Sometimes discriminatory behavior may precede prejudicial attitudes as, for example, when organizations insist that all job applicants take aptitude or IQ tests based on middle-class experiences and then form negative judgments of lower-income people who do not score well.

Robert Merton formulated a model showing the possible relationships between prejudice and discrimination (Figure 5.1). Merton demonstrated that, quite conceivably, a nonprejudiced person may discriminate and a prejudiced person may not. In his paradigm, Merton classified four types of people according to how they accept or reject the American Creed: "the right of equitable access to justice, freedom and opportunity, irrespective of race or religion, or ethnic origin."[4]

The Nonprejudiced Nondiscriminator. Nonprejudiced nondiscriminators are neither prejudiced nor practicers of discrimination. Of course, as Merton observes, these are virtues of omission, not commission. He criticizes members of this class who show no inclination to illuminate others and

Prejudiced	Discriminates	
	No	Yes
No	All-weather liberal	Fair-weather liberal
Yes	Timid bigot	Active bigot

FIGURE 5.1   Relationships between Prejudice and Discrimination

to fight actively against all forms of discrimination. They talk chiefly to others sharing their viewpoint, and so they deceive themselves into thinking that they represent the consensus of the community. Furthermore, because their "own spiritual house is in order," they feel no pangs of conscience pressing them to work collectively on the problem. On the other hand, some nonprejudiced nondiscriminators obviously are activists and do engage in dialogue with others who hold different viewpoints, thereby transforming belief into action.

The Nonprejudiced Discriminator.   Expedience is the byword for those in the category of the nonprejudiced discriminator, for their actions often conflict with their personal beliefs. They may, for example, be free of racial prejudice, but they will join clubs that exclude people who belong to outgroups, they will vote for regressive measures if they would benefit materially from these, and they will support efforts to keep African Americans out of their neighborhood for fear of its deterioration. These people frequently feel guilt and shame because they are acting against their beliefs.

The Prejudiced Nondiscriminator.   Merton's term *timid bigots* best describes prejudiced nondiscriminators. They believe in many stereotypes about other groups and definitely feel hostility toward these groups. However, they keep silent in the presence of those who are more tolerant; they conform because they must. If there were no law or pressure to avoid bias in certain actions, they would discriminate.

The Prejudiced Discriminator.   Prejudiced discriminators are active bigots. They demonstrate no conflict between attitudes and behavior. Not only do they openly express their beliefs, practice discrimination, and defy the law if necessary, but they consider such conduct virtuous.

The second and third categories—the nonprejudiced discriminator and the prejudiced nondiscriminator—are the most sociologically interesting classifications because they demonstrate that social-situational variables often determine whether discriminatory behavior occurs. The pressure of group norms may force individuals to act in a manner inconsistent with their beliefs.

Social and Institutional Discrimination

Discriminatory practices are encountered frequently in the areas of employment and residence, although such actions often are taken covertly and are denied by those who take them. Another dimension of discrimination, often unrealized, is **social discrimination**—the creation of a "social distance" between groups. Simply stated, in their intimate primary relationships, people tend to associate with others of similar ethnic background and socioeconomic level; dominant-group members thus usually exclude minority-group members from close relations with them.

Discrimination is more than the biased actions of individuals, though. In their influential book, *Black Power*, Stokely Carmichael and Charles Hamilton called attention to the fact that far greater harm occurs from **institutional discrimination**—unequal treatment of subordinate groups inherent in the ongoing operations of society's institutions.[5] Entrenched in customs, laws, and practices, these discriminatory patterns can exist in banking, criminal justice, employment, education, health care, housing, and many other areas in the private and public sectors. Critical to understanding this concept is the fact the practices are so widespread that individuals helping to perpetuate them may be completely unaware of their existence. Examples would be banks rejecting home mortgage applications of minorities at a higher rate, the sentencing inequities in our justice system, the concentration of minorities in low-paying jobs, the former "separate but equal" educational structure in the South, and segregated housing.

Hubert Blalock, offering conflict-perspective reasoning, suggested that, when the dominant group feels that its self-interests—such as primacy and the preservation of cherished values—are threatened, extreme discrimination usually results.[6] Blalock believed that the dominant group will not hesitate to act discriminatorily if it thinks that this approach will effectively undercut the minority group as a social competitor (see the accompanying International Scene box). Further, the dominant group will aggressively discriminate if it interprets minority variation from cultural norms as a form of social deviance that threatens society's sacred traditions (e.g., the large influx of Catholic immigrants in the nineteenth-century Protestant-dominated United States or the

The International Scene
Discrimination in Northern Ireland

Northern Ireland contains about 1 million Protestants with loyalties to the over-whelmingly Protestant United Kingdom and about 680,000 Catholics with a prefer-ence for unification with the Catholic-dominated Republic of Ireland. Despite some progress toward reconciliation since the 1998 peace agreement, it remains today a polarized society, its sporadic violence fed by centuries of deep-seated hostility.

Sociologically, Catholics are the minority group, with limited political power. They are more likely than Protestants to be poor, to suffer prolonged unemploy-ment, and to live in substandard housing in segregated communities. Catholics tend to be in low-status, low-skill jobs and Protestants in high-status, high-skill po-sitions. It is difficult, however, to determine whether these employment patterns result from overt job discrimination, from structural factors of community segre-gation, education, and class, or from both.

Although the degree of actual discrimination employed to maintain their dom-inance is unclear, Protestants rationalize about the situation through a set of negative beliefs about Catholics. Many Protestants stereotype Catholics as lazy welfare cheats who are dirty, superstitious, and ignorant. They also view them as oversexed (as "proved" by the typically larger size of Catholic families) and brainwashed by priests, whose primary allegiance, they say, is to a foreign entity—the Pope. Moreover, many Protestants suspect that Catholics are intent on undermining the Ulster government to force reunification with the Republic of Ireland. Most Protestants see no discrimi-nation on the basis of religion in jobs, housing, and other social areas. Catholics "get what they deserve" because of their values, attitudes, and disloyalty.

For their part, most Catholics in Northern Ireland strongly believe that they suffer from discrimination as a direct consequence of their religion. They view Protestants as narrow-minded bigots who stubbornly hold onto political power and have no desire to relinquish any part of it. A vicious circle of prejudice and dis-crimination, despite the peace accord, intensifies Protestant resistance to sharing power and Catholic reluctance to support the government.

As yet not fully implemented, the hard-fought pragmatism and promise of the 1998 peace accord could still fall victim to political opportunism, fickle public opinion, or the evil intent of the radicals on both sides, who have never agreed to forswear the use of bombs and murder to pursue their political ends.

In contrast, Protestants in the Republic of Ireland, who constitute only 3 per-cent of the population, live in harmony with their Catholic neighbors. They are fully integrated socioeconomically and do not, for the most part, experience prejudice.

Critical thinking question: What must be done to reduce the prejudice and discrimination that sows the seeds of violence in Northern Ireland?

---

appearance of "dishonest" Gypsies among "decent, hardworking" people). Discrimination, in this view, is "a technique designed to neutralize minority group efforts."[7]

The Affirmative-Action Controversy

At what point do efforts to secure justice and equal opportunities in life for one group infringe on the rights of other groups? Is justice a utilitarian concept—the greatest happiness for the greatest number? Or is it a moral concept—a sense of good that all people share? Is the proper role of government to foster a climate in which people have equal opportunity to participate in a competitive system of occupations and rewards, or should government ensure equal results in any competition? These issues have engaged moral and political philosophers for centuries, and they go to the core of the affirmative-action controversy.

The Concepts of Justice, Liberty, and Equality

Over 2,300 years ago, Plato wrote in the *Republic* that justice must be relative to the needs of the people who are served, not to the desires of those who

In 2003, as the U.S. Supreme Court justices heard arguments for and against the use of affirmative action in admissions decisions at the University of Michigan, demonstrators outside made their views known. The court's subsequent 5–4 ruling was a broad one, endorsing continuance of this practice, but under broad guidelines not intended for an indefinite period.

(*Source:* © AP/Wide World Photos)

serve them. For example, physicians must make patients' health their primary concern if they are to be just. In *A Theory of Justice*, John Rawls interprets justice as fairness, which maximizes equal liberty for all.[8] To provide the greatest benefit to the least advantaged, society must eliminate social and economic inequalities placing minority persons in offices and positions that are open to all under conditions of fair equality of opportunity. Both men see the ideal society as well ordered and strongly pluralistic: Each component performs a functionally differentiated role in working harmony; society must arrange its practices to make this so.

Anticipating the emergence of the equal-protection-under-the-law clause of the Fourteenth Amendment as a major force for social change, Joseph Tussman and Jacobus tenBroek examined the problems of the doctrine of equality 5 years before the 1954 Supreme Court school desegregation ruling. Americans, they argued, have always been more concerned with liberty than with equality, identifying liberty with the absence of government interference:

> What happens, then, when government becomes more ubiquitous? Whenever an area of activity is brought within the control or regulation of government, to that extent equality supplants liberty as the dominant ideal and constitutional demand.[9]

Tussman and tenBroek noted that those who insist on constitutional rights for all are not so much demanding the removal of government restraints as they are asking for positive government action to provide equal treatment for "minority groups, parties, or organizations whose rights are too easily sacrificed or ignored in periods of popular hysteria."[10] Responsibility for promoting individual rights has increasingly been placed on the federal government.

Affirmative Action Begins

We can trace the origin of government affirmative-action policy to July 1941, when President Franklin D. Roosevelt issued Executive Order 8802, obligating defense contractors "not to discriminate against any worker because of race, creed, color, or national origin." Subsequent executive orders by virtually all presidents continued or expanded the government's efforts to curb discrimination in employment. President Kennedy's Executive Order 10925 in 1961 was the first to use the term **affirmative action;** it stipulated that government contractors would "take affirmative action that applicants are employed, and that employees are treated during employment, without regard to their race, creed, color, or national origin."

The legal basis for affirmative action appears to rest on two points. Stanford M. Lyman argued in 1987 that passage of the Thirteenth Amendment, which abolished slavery, set the precedent for action against any vestiges of slavery manifest through racial discrimination.[11] Both supporters and opponents, however, point to Title VII, Section 703(j), of the 1964 Civil Rights Act as the keystone of their positions on affirmative action.

Title VII seems to address the need for fairness, openness, and color-blind equal opportunity. It specifically bans preference by race, ethnicity, gender, and religion in business and government. Opponents claim that this clear language outlawing preferences makes affirmative action unnecessary and illegal.[12] Supporters contend that President Lyndon Johnson's Executive Order 11246 is linked to Title VII by mandating employer affirmative-action plans to correct existing deficiencies through specific goals and deadlines. This was, supporters say, a logical step from concern about equal rights to concern about actual equal opportunity.[13]

Addressing an expanded list of protected categories (Asians, Blacks, Hispanics, Native Americans, women, the aged, people with disabilities, and homosexuals), an array of state and federal policy guidelines began to regulate many aspects of business, education, and government practices. Legislation in 1972 amended the 1964 Civil Rights Act, giving the courts the power to enforce affirmative-action standards. Preference programs became the rule, through reserved minority quotas in college and graduate school admissions and in job hirings and promotions, as well as through government set-aside work contracts for minority firms.[14]

Court Challenges and Rulings

The resentment of Whites over "reverse discrimination" crystallized in the 1978 *Regents of the University of California v. Bakke* case, when the U.S. Supreme Court ruled that quotas were not permitted but race could be a factor in university admissions. In a separate opinion, Justice Harry A. Blackmun stated:

> In order to get beyond racism, we must first take account of race. There is no other way. And in order to treat some persons equally, we must treat them differently. We cannot—we dare not—let the Equal Protection Clause perpetuate racial superiority.

For the next 11 years, the court upheld the principle of affirmative action in a series of rulings (see Affirmative Action box). Since 1989, however, a more conservative court has shown a growing reluctance to use "race-conscious remedies"—the practice of trying to overcome the effects of past discrimination by helping minorities. This has been true not only in affirmative-action cases involving jobs and contracts but in school desegregation and voting rights as well. The 1995 *Adarand Constructors v. Pena* decision scaled back the federal government's own affirmative-action program, mandating "strict scrutiny and evidence" of alleged past discrimination, not just a "general history of racial discrimination in the nation." In another 1995 decision, the Supreme Court declared that race could no longer be the "predominant fac-

Affirmative Action: Forty Years of Actions and Decisions

1964   The Civil Rights Act of 1964 established legal recourse against discrimination based on race, color, religion, sex, or national origin in public accommodations, transportation, public education, and federally assisted programs.

1972   Legislation gives the courts power to enforce affirmative-action standards.

1978   In *Regents of the University of California v. Bakke*, the Supreme Court, by a 5 to 4 vote, ruled that racial quotas are illegal but said that colleges and universities could consider race as one factor in admitting students.

1980   The Court ruled that a federal public works program that set aside 10 percent of its spending for minority contractors was constitutional.

1981   The Court ruled that the city of Hartford, Connecticut, could require that 15 percent of all workers on city-financed projects be women or minorities.

1987   For the first time, the Court upheld an affirmative-action plan for women, ruling that companies can give special preferences to hire and promote female employees to create a more balanced work force.

1989   The Court threw out a set-aside program in Richmond, Virginia, in which contractors on city building contracts were required to give at least 30 percent of the value of the project to firms at least one-half minority owned.

1990   The Court upheld federal policies favoring women and minorities in granting broadcasting licenses.

1995   The Court set a stricter standard on state programs or laws designed to help minorities. Only race-based preferences narrowly tailored to address identifiable past discrimination would be deemed constitutional.

1996   The Court declined to hear an appeal of a Fifth U.S. Circuit Court of Appeals ruling that "race itself cannot be taken into account" by the University of Texas in admitting students to its law school, which knocked down its affirmative-action admissions plan.

1996   The Court ordered the Virginia Military Institute to admit women or give up state funding. The decision also affected The Citadel, South Carolina's state-run military school.

1996   Californians voted to forbid any consideration of race, gender, or national origin in hiring or school admissions.

1997   The Court declined to hear a challenge to California's Proposition 209, the measure that banned race or gender from being a factor in state hiring or school admission.

1998   Washington State voters eliminated all preferential treatment based on race or gender in government hiring and school admissions.

2000   Florida ended the consideration of race in university admissions and state contracts, instead calling for more aid based on financial need.

2003   The Court upheld an affirmative-action program at the University of Michigan law school but struck down the university's system that awarded extra points to minorities in its points-based admissions policy.

tor" in drawing congressional districts—or by implication, any jurisdiction for any government body, from school boards to state legislatures.

In 1995, the California Board of Regents banned affirmative action for graduate and undergraduate admissions. The following year, California voters overwhelmingly passed the California Civil Rights Initiative, which prohibited the use of race, ethnicity, or gender "as a criterion for either discriminating against, or granting preferential treatment to, any individual or group," thereby dismantling state affirmative-action programs. Also in 1996, a sweeping ruling by the U.S. Circuit Court of Appeals in *Hopwood v. Texas* led the Texas attorney general to interpret the opinion as banning affirmative action in admissions, scholarships, and outreach programs.

Without affirmative action, California and Texas universities initially suffered minority enrollment drops in their undergraduate and graduate programs. However, both states then implemented percentage plans as a viable alternative to achieve a race/ethnic balance in higher education without the stigma of set-asides and lowered admission standards. California guaranteed university admission to the top 4 percent of high school graduates, and Texas guaranteed the top 10 percent. When Florida ended its affirmative-action program, it guaranteed college admission to the top 20 percent if students completed a minimum of 2 years of foreign language and other academic credits.

A major Supreme Court decision in 2002 preserved affirmative action in university admissions at the University of Michigan law school by a 5 to 4 vote, while at the same time striking down that university's undergraduate admissions program that used a point system based in part on race. In making a forceful endorsement of the role of racial diversity on campus in achieving a more equal society, the court's ruling was a broad one that applies to all admissions programs. Moreover, this ruling strengthened the solitary view of Justice Lewis Powell at the time of the *Bakke* decision that there was a "compelling state interest" in racial diversity. At the same time, the court suggested a time limit on such programs, with Justice Sandra Day O'Connor writing in the majority opinion, "We expect that 25 years from now the use of racial preferences will no longer be necessary to further the interest approved today."[15]

Adding significance to this ruling is the fact that it also sends a strong signal to the nation's employers that they should continue their own affirmative-action plans to hire more women and minorities. Perhaps demonstrating the commitment of business to affirmative action were the series of friend-of-the-court briefs filed by sixty-five corporations (including General Motors and Microsoft) in support of the university.[16]

This ruling, however, is not the final word on affirmative action, as numerous groups still oppose it. With several Supreme Court justices about to end their careers on the bench, new challenges to a differently constituted court may result in different rulings.

Has Affirmative Action Worked?

Evidence about the success of affirmative-action programs is as mixed as public debate on the subject. John Gpuhl and Susan Welch revealed in 1990 that the *Bakke* decision had little impact on the enrollment of African Americans and Hispanics in medical and law schools; their enrollment had already leveled off 2 or 3 years before this 1978 ruling.[17] However, in a 1995 study, Alfred Blumrosen found that 5 million minority workers and 6 million women had better jobs than they would have had without preferences and antidiscrimination laws.[18] In 1986, William Robinson and Stephen Spitz found increased minority and female hirings and "positive business results" in several large-scale studies on the effectiveness of affirmative action.[19] The Committee on the Status of Black Americans asserted in 1989 that the evidence on the program's success showed positive results.[20] Not all African Americans agree; many believe their circumstances in recent years have at best remained unchanged or have even worsened.[21]

No doubt some of the criticism against affirmative action is racist or sexist. However, some leaders of minority and women's groups believe it has had a destructive influence on their own communities. Thomas Sowell and Linda Chavez maintain that universities recruit talented minority students away from local colleges where they might do very well and into learning environments where the competition for grades is intense. Opponents also argue that affirmative action is "misplaced condescension" that has poisoned race relations—a view that seems to posit a golden age of race relations in the United States at some point prior to the advent of affirmative action. According to this line of reasoning, the achievements of minorities become tainted by the possibility that they resulted from special favorable treatment rather than being earned on merit.

Public Opinion

Negative public opinion about affirmative action gathered strength in the 1990s as the United States experienced a slow-growth economy, stagnant middle-class incomes, and corporate downsizing, all of which made the question of who gets fired—or hired—unusually volatile. James Q. Wilson and Seymour Martin Lipset cynically suggested that the long-term resentment of affirmative action by Whites influenced policy only when the remedy's effects finally touched the people who set the national agenda. The middle and upper classes, they argue, paid scant attention to mandated minority hirings among trade unionists or to busing orders in working-class neighborhoods. Now, however, women and minorities are competing for managerial positions that the elite once dominated and for admission to universities that the elites' sons and daughters also wish to attend.[22]

A *New York Times/CBS News* survey conducted in 1997 found that most Americans favored the goals of racial diversity in the schools and the workplace but rejected some of the main methods affirmative action used to secure them. But while opposed to preferences based on race and gender (Blacks less in opposition than Whites), most Americans seemed eager to support affirmative action based on economic class.[23] Under such a provision, for example, the White son of a poor coal miner in West Virginia could be eligible for special help, but the daughter of an affluent African American stockbroker would not.

Another poll, conducted by the Associated Press in 2003, just a few weeks before the Supreme Court ruling on the Michigan case, found that four in five Americans said it was important that colleges have racially diverse student bodies. However, only 51 percent thought affirmative-action programs were still needed to help Blacks, Hispanics, and other minorities, while 43 percent did not and 35 percent wanted them abolished. Among Blacks, 89 percent thought the programs were necessary. About six in ten young adults in the poll, from 18 to 34 years old, said affirmative action was still needed.[24] An obvious split along racial and generational lines exists on this subject.

Even as affirmative action withers in some states, it continues in others. Proposed federal legislation in the Congress would end it everywhere. Supporters of affirmative action argue "mend it, don't end it," whereas opponents urge that it be dismantled completely. The next few years undoubtedly will see a continuing battle and significant changes in affirmative action as we know it.

Racial Profiling

Although racial profiling has a long history, only in recent years have the government and public given it much attention. **Racial profiling** refers to action taken by law enforcement officials on the erroneous presumption that individuals of one race or ethnicity are more likely to engage in illegal activity than individuals of other races or ethnicities. Such thinking led authorities routinely to stop vehicles driven by Blacks and Latinos in the expectation of finding drugs in their possession.

Some argued that overall discrepancies in crime rates among racial groups justified such profiling in traffic enforcement activities to produce a greater number of arrests for nontraffic offenses (e.g., narcotics trafficking). Critics contended that an emphasis on minority-group drug use would naturally result in more minority arrests, but the evidence shows that about 85 percent of all illicit drug users are White.[25]

In the 1990s, racial profiling received a great deal of attention through media exposés, special reports, commissions, and legislative initiatives. In 2001, the Bush administration became the first to take action to ban it in federal law enforcement. However, the terrorist attacks later that year changed the government view of racial profiling from an undesirable police activity to one of necessity for national security. As a result, airline security, customs officials, and police place Arab and Muslim Americans under special scrutiny,

Although Whites are as likely to commit moving traffic violations as non–Whites, the tendency of police officers to stop a disproportionate number of minority drivers led to charges of biased actions through racial profiling. After 9–11, national security concerns extended racial profiling specifically to Arabs and Muslims, an action some see as necessary and others decry as biased.

(*Source:* © Tom Carter/PhotoEdit, Inc.)

and immigration officials prosecute them for minor violations often ignored for resident aliens of other ethnic backgrounds.

In 2003, the U.S. Department of Justice issued guidelines rejecting racial profiling. It argued that such activity is immoral and perpetuates negative racial stereotypes that are "harmful to our diverse democracy, and materially impair our efforts to maintain a fair and just society." However, in that same statement, it included a broad and largely undefined exception when "national security" concerns come into play.[26] At the present time, then, a dichotomy exists between racial profiling attitudes and actions.

Retrospect

Discriminatory behavior operates at five levels of intensity: verbal expression, avoidance, exclusion, physical abuse, and extermination. Discrimination is not necessarily an acting-out of prejudice. Social pressures may oblige non-prejudiced individuals to discriminate or may prevent prejudiced people from discriminating.

The debate over affirmative action involves these questions: Is it a democratic government's responsibility to provide a climate for equal opportunity or to ensure equal results? If the latter, at what point do efforts to secure equality for one group infringe on the rights of other groups? After several decades of implementation, affirmative-action programs face a mixture of support and dismantling through court decisions, public initiatives, and state action.

Racial profiling remains a serious concern, given its mixed interpretation since the 2001 terrorist attacks.

KEY TERMS

Affirmative action	Ethnoviolence
De facto segregation	Institutional discrimination
De jure segregation	Racial profiling
Discrimination	Social discrimination

REVIEW QUESTIONS

1. What is discrimination? What are some of its manifestations?

2. What is the relationship between prejudice and discrimination?

3. Why would institutional discrimination be difficult to eliminate?

4. What is the intent of affirmative action?

5. Discuss the pros and cons of affirmative action.

6. Is racial profiling an important tool in law enforcement?

SUGGESTED READINGS

Allen, Irving L. *Unkind Words: Ethnic Labeling from Redskin to WASP.* New York: Bergin & Garvey, 1990.
   Informative, highly readable insights into how ethnic animosities take many and devious forms in abusive slang.

Curry, George E., and West, Cornel (eds.). *The Affirmative Action Debate.* New York: Perseus Press, 1996.
   An excellent collection of essays that gives all sides equal voice in discussing this highly controversial topic.

Harris, David A. *Profiles in Injustice: Why Racial Profiling Cannot Work.* Nevada City, CA: New Press, 2003.
   A thoughtful and scrupulous analysis of racial profiling's history, its failure in crime prevention, and recent steps at improvement.

Irons, Peter H. *Jim Crow's Children: The Broken Promise of the Brown Decision.* New York: Viking Press, 2002.
Clearly exposes the gaping divide among our ideals, laws, and social realities as well as the interconnection of poverty, race, and education.

Lott, Bernice E., and Dianne Maluso (eds.). *The Social Psychology of Interpersonal Discrimination.* Guilford, Conn.: Guilford Press, 1995.
Provides an overview of current research focusing on behavior rather than attitudes and beliefs, exploring how and why people discriminate against others in everyday life.

Sowell, Thomas. *Migrations and Cultures: A World View.* New York: HarperCollins, 1997.
A provocative book that draws from case histories of the Germans, Italians, Japanese, Chinese, Jews, and Asian Indians that argues immigrants' habits and beliefs are more important to their fate than a country's economy, culture, or politics.

9

What Is White Privilege?

Reprinted from *Overcoming Our Racism: The Journey to Liberation*, (2003), by permission of John Wiley & Sons, Inc.

Now that you've read the analysis in the last chapter, it seems important to give you a concrete and formal definition of White privilege. White privilege is the unearned advantages and benefits that accrue to White folks by virtue of a system normed on the experiences, values, and perceptions of their group. White privilege automatically confers dominance to one group, while subordinating groups of color in a descending relational hierarchy; it owes its existence to White supremacy; it is premised on the mistaken notion of individual meritocracy and deservedness (hard work, family values, and the like) rather than favoritism; it is deeply embedded in the structural, systemic, and cultural workings of U.S. society; and it operates within an invisible veil of unspoken and protected secrecy.

THE DECONSTRUCTION OF WHITE PRIVILEGE

White privilege continues to be a taboo topic for White people in our society. It is an unacknowledged secret that is overtly and covertly denied and protected through the use of self-deception. It protects White folks from realizing that they benefit from racism; as long as it is hidden from consciousness, you can maintain the illusion that you are not responsible for the state of race relations because you do not knowingly engage in racist behaviors. The invisible nature of White privilege serves to keep you comfortable, confident, and relatively oblivious to how it has the opposite effects on persons of color and how it harms, intimidates, oppresses, alienates, and makes for discomfort. Making the invisible visible is the first step toward dismantling the unfair and harmful nature of White privilege. The deconstruction of White privilege requires an analysis of its five basic components.

Automatically Confers Dominance Versus "I Made It on My Own"

Because you live in a society normed and standardized on White Euro-American values, most of the structures, policies, and practices of your institutions are situated in such a manner as to pave the road for White folks while creating obstacles for other groups. The United States continues to favor White, Eurocentric ways of thinking, acting, and being that do not match the reality of racial/ethnic minorities in this country. In this respect, two sides of the coin are present: on the one side, White privilege automatically confers dominance, control, and power to White Americans; and on the other side, it automatically disempowers and oppresses people of color. On the one side, it automatically advantages one group; and on the other side, it automatically disadvantages the other. Peggy McIntosh, a White Wellesley professor, in her article "White Privilege: Unpacking the Invisible Knapsack" makes this last point as well: "As a white person, I realized I had been taught about racism as something which puts others at a disadvantage, but had been taught not to see one of its corollary aspects, white privilege, which puts me at an advantage."[1]

I could probably get you to acknowledge that persons of color, women, gays and lesbians, disabled, and other marginalized groups are often put in a disadvantaged position. Most of you would further admit that being a racial minority in this society subjects you to second-class citizenship. Yet it is intriguing that most White Americans would actively deny that they are advantaged automatically by this state of affairs. In the last chapter, for example, the Black salesman who says that White customers avoid him, view him as a well-dressed janitor, and always corroborate the information he dispenses with White salespeople is clearly disadvantaged (may make fewer sales). In addition, he must constantly cope with internal feelings of micro-invalidation that strike at the core of his self-esteem. White salespeople, however, fail to see that the African American presence in the showroom actually ensures that the White salespeople will make more sales (advantaged). The fact that White customers will seek them out and treat them as more knowledgeable and trustworthy validates them as superior sales representatives. The deception resides in the belief by White folks that the superior outcome (sales) reflects their individual efforts ("I made it on my own").

Many other examples can be given. The hostess and waiter who treated my friend Dave as the person in control made him feel confident, validated, and strong; they left me, however, feeling invalidated, belittled, and frustrated. Not too long ago, a well-known Black actor, Danny Glover, with upraised hand, watched cabs whiz by him in New York City, only to stop to pick up White pedestrians a short distance down the block. Store clerks who examine the identification of Black customers attempting to cash checks with greater frequency and care than they do for White customers are another of the countless examples of such everyday occurrences.

Because White folks tend to see racism as individual acts of meanness, they seldom consider that an invisible system of White privilege has automatically conferred racial dominance to them; it advantages and validates you but disadvantages and invalidates persons of color. The system protects unfair individual acts of racial dominance by denying their race-related meanings and offering alternative explanations of reality grounded on a White Euro-American perspective.

Exists on White Supremacy Versus "I'm Not Responsible for the Oppression of Others"

White privilege could not exist without White supremacy. In Chapter Five, we defined White supremacy as a doctrine of racial superiority that justifies discrimination, segregation, and domination of persons of color based on an ideology and belief system that considers all non-White groups racially inferior. The examples just cited are clear: the Black salesperson is less competent and capable than White salespersons; my friend Dave is seen as superior and the one in charge; both the Black actor and the Black customers are less trustworthy and prone to potential crime. But White supremacy is more all-encompassing and insidious than these individual examples. They are manifested not just in individual acts of bias and discrimination but also in the very institutional and cultural foundations of our society.

White supremacy and oppression go hand in hand. In his book *Pedagogy of the Oppressed*, Paulo Freire describes the ability of the dominant culture to control minorities through the ability to define their identities and roles. Minorities are defined as criminals, delinquents, untrustworthy, less intelligent, lacking moral character, primitive, uncivilized, prone to violence, aliens, illegal immigrants, and so forth. The roles they occupy are servants, housekeepers, janitors, or generally lower positions in our society.[2]

To maintain the conformance and silence of persons of color, White supremacy as a doctrine and belief is instilled through education and enforced by biased institutional policies or practices that punish those who dare raise their voices in objection to their second-class status. You are taught that Columbus discovered America, that the pioneers settled the West, that the internment of Japanese Americans was based not on racism but on national security, and that the Lewis and Clark expedition gave the United States a claim to the Oregon territory. You are taught to believe in the notion that differences are deviant, in the myth of the melting pot, in positive portrayals of White folks, and in negative portrayals of minority groups. A particularly noteworthy and powerful example of White supremacy was the *manifest destiny* argument in the 1840s: all land owned by Native Americans was decreed by God to belong to White people.

The irrational sense of entitlement is a dominant feature of White privilege. And even more insidious are the benefits that accrue to White folks from these historical events. Unless you are the indigenous peoples of this land, you benefit from the past injustices of those who took the land from the early inhabitants. Pretense and mystification about these facts only serve to perpetuate White supremacy. When my White brothers and sisters, for example, claim that they should not be blamed for the past actions of their ancestors (taking land from American Indians, enslaving Blacks from Africa, segregating Latinos, and taking businesses from Japanese Americans during their internment), they miss a vital point. They still benefit from the past injustices of their forebears!

So even if you are completely free of conscious racial prejudices and desire to forgo or disclaim White privilege, you still receive benefits automatically, and unintentionally. If you profit from White privilege, whether knowingly or unknowingly, then you serve an oppressor role.

Predicated on Favoritism Rather Than Meritocracy Versus "The Most Qualified Ought to Get the Job"

In referring to President George W. Bush, syndicated columnist Molly Ivins once commented, "George Bush was born on third base and believes he hit a triple." This statement represents the ultimate illusion of meritocracy, that those who occupy a favored position achieved their status through individual effort and merit alone. If you accept the concept of White privilege, then you must entertain the more realistic notion that many White folks did not succeed because of superior ability but due to favoritism. George Bush did not become president of the United States solely because of hard work or superior intellect but was born into a privileged family, given favored status by a White society (all his life attending the best White schools, living in the best White neighborhoods, obtaining the best White jobs, having to only deal with a White police force, and so forth), and had opportunities not available to persons of color. Using the baseball analogy, whereas President Bush started on third base, most persons of color cannot even make it to the batter's box!

In the United States, our society arose from the cherished concept of *rugged individualism*; it is part of the Protestant ethic that believes there is a strong relationship between ability, effort, and success. People who succeed in our society work harder, have more skills, or are more competent. People who fail to achieve much in our society are seen as lazy, less capable, or less intelligent. Democratic ideals such as "equal access to opportunities," "everyone can make it in society if they work hard enough," "liberty and justice for all," "God helps those who help themselves," and "fulfillment of personal destiny" are culturally conditioned into your thinking. Behind these phrases lies one major assumption: everyone operates on a level playing field. In the presence of White privilege, however, the playing field is tilted in such a way as to be an uphill trek for persons of color and a downhill one for Whites.

The idea that you are the "master of your own fate" unfairly blames minority citizens for their inability to achieve more in this society. It fails to take into consideration the systemic forces of racism, prejudice, and discrimination and the operation of White privilege. People of color who suffer in poverty and unemployment and who live in the ghettos or barrios are blamed as suffering from deficiencies in their lifestyles or as possessing personal inadequacies.

Yet the reasons may not be internal but external: denied jobs, refused apartments, stopped-and-searched, declared uneducable, and told by a society that they are incompetent, untrustworthy, less intelligent, and culturally deprived. There is a triple purpose to the existence of White privilege: to advantage White Americans, to disadvantage persons of color, and to attribute causes to individual deficiencies, thereby relieving White society of responsibility for perpetuating inequality. The ultimate conclusion drawn from an understanding of White privilege is that your achievement as a White person may not be due so much to meritocracy as to un-earned advantages and benefits. Likewise, the lower achievements of persons of color may not be due to personal inadequacies but to the unfair operation of White privilege.

Embedded Systemically in Society Versus "The Cream Always Rises to the Top"

I have already presented arguments challenging the belief that those with greater competence, superior skills, good work ethic, and high intellect automatically benefit from the rewards of society: "the cream always rises to the top." White privilege is not confined just to the individual perceptions or actions of Euro-Americans. Indeed, I have tried to make the case that institutional and cultural mani-festations of White privilege are more harmful because they are sys-temically embedded in our society and have large-scale effects that dwarf individual actions of prejudice or discrimination.

Discriminatory benefits that favor Whites are seen in all facets of our society: bank lending practices, access to health care, hous-ing, jobs, education, media portrayals, law enforcement, and court decisions that mete out justice. I am not talking about a few indi-viduals hurt by White privilege but about literally millions of mar-ginalized persons in our society. The existence of institutional racism shields the operation of White privilege through what I call standard operating procedures (SOPs), which represent the rules, habits, pro-cedures, and structures of organizations that oppress persons of color while favoring Whites. Two examples can be given to illustrate the pervasiveness of White privilege. Let us trace the institutional and societal SOPs pertaining to Felix Hernandez (Latino) and Randall Clay Jr. (White), two hypothetical figures but very representative of situations that constantly present themselves in the work site.

The Case of Felix Hernandez

Born and raised in the barrios of Los Angeles, Felix is the eldest of six children, whose mother and father migrated from Mexico to the United States several years before his birth. Both parents have no more than a fifth-grade education; the father works as a laborer and the mother as a housekeeper. Attempts to better their economic situation by trying to start a landscaping business met with failure, especially because banks would not lend Mr. Hernandez the necessary start-up funds. The father was considered not creditworthy, and the bank would not accept their home as collateral; it was in a neighborhood that seemed immune to the housing-appreciation boom in Los Angeles.

From the age of twelve, Felix worked at different odd jobs to help pay the mortgage and support the family. In addition to working part-time throughout middle and high school, he had financial responsibilities that extended his community college education to four years. Because he came from a poor community, the schools he attended were considered among the worst in the state; there was a high turnover rate of teachers and students, testing scores were low, physical facilities were in bad need of repair, school supplies and computers were nearly absent, and both delinquency and truancy were high.

In addition, Felix was exposed to a curriculum that seldom portrayed his group positively but was strong in reflecting the contributions, achievements, heritage, and cultures of White America. Oftentimes Felix found himself resentful and alienated from the material. Worst yet, he expended great psychological efforts to fight off viewing himself and his group as inferior.

At a young age, he was labeled a "yellow bird" by teachers and placed into special classes that were more custodial than educational. Another group of students were labeled "blue birds" and tracked into college prep course work. When Felix's mother observed that most of the students in the yellow-bird track were Brown or Black and nearly all those in the blue birds were White, she strenuously objected. The school psychologist attempted to appease her by administering several standardized IQ tests. The results, according to the psychologist, revealed that Felix was actually worse than expected. His scores were consistent with students in educable mentally retarded classes. From that point on, teachers expected little from Felix.

Despite his inferior education, Felix graduated from junior college, received a bachelor's degree in business from a four-year state college, and obtained an MBA at the age of thirty-five from a relatively unknown private school that many considered a "diploma mill." He was the first and only one in his family to obtain a college education and an advanced degree. He has been employed for the past five years as a project manager for a small computer software firm operated by Taiwanese-born partners.

The Case of Randall Clay Jr.

Born into an upper-middle-class family in Los Angeles, Randall Clay is the eldest of three children. His father was employed as a middle manager for a major technology company prior to starting his own software-computing firm. In her former life, Mrs. Clay was an elementary school teacher but is now a full-time homemaker. Mr. Clay credits his successful rise in business to hard work, good planning, and business acumen. After obtaining his bachelor's from the University of California-Los Angeles (UCLA), he saved money and purchased a fixer-upper in an affluent neighborhood of Los Angeles and saw his equity appreciate at an astounding pace. Years later, he used his home as collateral for a major loan from the bank to start his own business. Because of his high income, savings, and the location of his home, Mr. Clay was considered an excellent credit risk by the bank.

As a youngster, Randall attended the best public schools in Los Angeles; there was no formal tracking, the high school prided itself in producing college-bound graduates, teachers seldom left the district, student dropout rates were low, and the student body was relatively homogeneous (few students of color attended). The physical surroundings were more like a college campus, supplies and computer equipment were plentiful, and teaching was considered superior. Randall could relate well to the primarily Euro-American curriculum, never felt alienated, and worked hard throughout the high school years. Although he had considered a part-time job to increase discretionary funds for social activities, his father always stated, "School is your job; . . . just get a good education" and subsequently increased Randall's allowance.

Teachers seldom doubted Randall's intellectual abilities. Counselors gave him vocational and career advice, recommended his taking advanced placement (AP) classes, and even helped him select appropriate colleges. Though Randall received multiple offers from top-tier colleges, he chose to attend his father's alma mater, UCLA, majoring in business administration. He finished in four years and then attended the University of California-Berkeley, where he obtained an MBA at the age of twenty-five. Upon Randall's graduation, Mr. and Mrs. Clay expressed admiration for their son's accomplishments and praised Randall for his dedication and hard work. During Randall's job search, Mr. Clay had simply placed a call to colleagues at his former place of employment. Within a week after Randall's interview with the company, he was hired into a middle-management position at a high starting salary.

Afterword

Imagine that the lives of both of these men intersected several years later. In their aspirations to move up the career ladder, Felix and Randall applied for the director's position with a large nationally known Silicon Valley computer company. Though both were on the shortlist, the company offered the position to Randall because of his impressive academic credentials and the institutions he had attended, because of his greater experience in working for a "big national firm," because he seemed skilled in being able to supervise large groups of employees, because he "fit in better" with the corporate culture, because he had better letters of reference, and because he appeared, despite his youth, more accelerated than other candidates.

Although a few were impressed with Felix, the interviewers felt that he would have difficulty fitting into their corporate culture; despite his excellent grades, several questioned the quality of his education, his "small-time" experience in a local firm, and the apparent lack of leadership experience.

Did the "cream rise to the top"? That's an important question for you to ask. Certainly, if you were to inspect the résumés of both men, Randall Clay would appear to be clearly the superior candidate. He went to more competitive schools, earned better grades, took a harder curriculum (AP courses), finished his education at a faster pace, earned his MBA from a nationally renowned institution, had more work experience with a multinational corporation, supervised many more employees, and had greater work responsibilities.

In contrast, Felix Hernandez went to schools that had poor academic reputations, received mediocre grades, did not take AP courses in high school (none were offered), obtained his master's degree from a nationally unranked professional school, required an above-average amount of time to complete higher education, and his work experience was limited to a local start-up company. Indeed, as the project manager, Felix supervised only three employees on his team and did lack experience in supervising a large labor force.

What are hidden in the analysis of the résumés are the SOPs (institutional and societal policies, programs, practices, and structures) that have disadvantaged Felix and advantaged Randall. The SOPs may be applied equally to all groups but serve to maintain the status quo.

- Systemic societal forces that produce segregation, allowing only certain groups to purchase homes in affluent neighborhoods, resulting in differential worth of real estate

- Bank lending practices that consider creditworthiness on the basis of location, inevitably discriminating against minority communities

- Inequitable school financing in which property taxes of wealthy communities produce greater educational resources than poorer communities

- Segregated schools that dispense inferior education to one group, but advantaged education to another

- Biased curricula, textbooks, and materials that affirm the identity of one group while denigrating others

- Educational testing that is normed and standardized on a White-middle-class population, resulting in culturally biased test instruments used to track minority students into non-college-bound classes

- Teachers and counselors with expectations, attitudes, and racial perceptions that result in beliefs that students of color are less capable, often resulting in a self-fulfilling prophesy among minorities that it is true

- School tracking systems that may unfairly perpetuate inequities in education

- Hiring policies and practices that utilize the "old boy's network" to recruit and hire prospective employees

I therefore ask the question again: Did the "cream rise to the top"? It would seem from this analysis that another argument can be made. In light of the numerous hurdles placed in the path of Felix, his achievements can only be considered laudatory. And although Randall was obviously bright and hardworking, his trek to the top was paved with many advantages; foremost among them is a society structured in such a way as to benefit Whites.

The Unspoken and Protected Secret Versus "We Should Be a Color-Blind Nation"

The "invisible Whiteness of being" maintains its viability precisely because it is a protected and seldom spoken secret. In 1972, Ralph Ellison's book *Invisible Man* described the *invisible man syndrome*, where racial issues and color are diluted, ignored, or considered irrelevant.[3] When originally formulated, the concept of a color-blind society was seen as the answer to discrimination and prejudice: Martin Luther King, for example, advocated judging people not by the color of their skin but by their internal character.

Many White Americans, however, have distorted or conveniently used color blindness as a means of color denial or more accurately *power* denial. An understanding of White privilege ultimately unmasks a dirty secret kept hidden by White Americans: much of what they have attained is unearned, and even if they are not overtly racist, Whites cannot choose to relinquish benefits from it. In his own racial awakening, Robert Jensen, a White professor of journalism writes:

> I know I did not get where I am by merit alone. I benefited from, among other things, white privilege. That doesn't mean that I don't deserve my job, or that if I weren't white I would never have gotten the job. It means simply that all through my life, I have soaked up benefits for being white. I grew up in fertile farm country taken by force from non-white indigenous people.

I was educated in a well-funded, virtually all-white public school system in which I learned that white people like me made this country great. There I also was taught a variety of skills, including how to take standardized tests written by and for white people.

There certainly is individual variation in experience. Some white people have had it easier than me, probably because they came from wealthy families that gave them even more privilege. Some white people have had it tougher than me because they came from poorer families. White women face discrimination I will never know. But, in the end, white people all have drawn on white privilege somewhere in their lives.[4]

Getting White privilege out of the closet is difficult and resisted for several reasons.

- *The white-out phenomenon.* White privilege mimics the norms of fairness, justice, and equity by whiting out differences and perpetuating the belief in sameness. The denial of power imbalance, unearned privilege, and racist domination is couched in the rhetoric of equal treatment and equal opportunity. As mentioned earlier, the programs, policies, and practices of institutions may be monocultural. They are applied equally to all groups, so organizations and policymakers believe they are not discriminating and are being eminently fair. Educational policy regarding IQ testing, use of college admission test scores, and hiring and promotion criteria in employment decisions are applied equally across all groups. As in the case of Felix and Randall, however, they have damaging differential impact on persons of color. Unfortunately, the belief in equal treatment masks the fact that the universal standards are White.
- *Pretense of innocence.* As long as White Americans view racism, unfairness, and discrimination as residing in individual acts and believe that they did not overtly discriminate or consciously condone private acts of racism, they can alleviate guilt and respon-

sibility for its existence. "I didn't own slaves; don't blame me for the sins of my forefathers," and "I didn't take part in the internment of the Japanese Americans" are prototypical statements of this posture. The pretense of innocence is a conspiracy among Whites to deny the pain and suffering experienced by people of color, but more important, it's to absolve them of personal responsibility for perpetuating injustice and allow them to remain passive and inactive. Viewing racism as not deeply embedded in our culture and institutions but only in individual manifestations allows Whites to pretend that racism does not exist on a systemic level. They need not take collective action and risk possible censure from family, friends, and coworkers for revealing the ugly secret of White privilege.

• *Living a false White reality.* White Americans have power precisely because they are able to define reality. The authors of a report released in April 2001, *Off Balance: Youth, Race, and Crime in the News,* analyzed broadcast, magazine, and newspaper coverage of crime reporting from 1910 to 2000.[5] Blacks are overrepresented in the media as criminals and underrepresented as victims in proportion to the true crime statistics for their race. This imbalance in coverage creates a situation whereby persons of color are inaccurately perceived, whereas Whites are viewed as law-abiding. Indeed, the term *young Black male* has become synonymous with criminal.

Unfortunately, the reality that Whites live is a false one, clouding their ability to see themselves or their group in an accurate manner. The school shootings of children in Colorado, Oregon, Arkansas, Pennsylvania, Mississippi, and California have made Littleton and Santee household names. After the killing of two White children by a classmate, the mayor of Santee, California, stated, "We're a solid town, a good town, with good kids, a good church-going town, an All-American town." Interestingly, this reaction typifies the puzzlement of many White communities. "How could such a dreadful thing happen in our community?"

A recent FBI report indicates that there is no profile of a school shooter. Yet persons of color see a clear profile. These shootings of students by fellow classmates have occurred in primarily White suburbs and rural communities. White boy after White boy after White boy have been the shooters. There is plenty of violence in urban communities and schools, but it appears that White America can only see crime in minority communities. Tim Wise, a Nashville-based writer, reports the following facts: White children, not those in the urban ghetto, are most likely to use drugs. They are seven times more likely to use cocaine than Blacks, eight times more likely to have smoked crack, ten times more likely to have used LSD, seven times more likely to have used heroin, twice as likely to binge drink, and twice as likely to drive drunk. White youth, ages twelve to seventeen, are more likely to sell drugs and twice as likely to bring a weapon to school as Black males![6] Few Whites are aware of these statistics. It is obvious that White denial allows one to see White communities as healthy while minority communities are labeled easily as violent, dangerous, and infused with crime.

A LIST OF WHITE PRIVILEGE ADVANTAGES AND DISADVANTAGES

Having defined White privilege, its meaning, and its function in Euro-American society, a more specific list may help you understand precisely how it may be manifested in your everyday reality. The following is a list compiled from the writings of White women and men whose personal journey to understanding and combating racism resulted in an awakening to their own White privilege: Peggy McIntosh, Sara Winter, Robert Jensen, and Mark Maier.[7]

1. *Advantage:* When you attend school, you can be assured that your race will be portrayed positively; the curriculum will reflect your

heritage and contributions to your nation; you will be told that you made this nation what it is today. (*Disadvantage:* The contributions of racial/ethnic minorities are often ignored in the educational literature; they are portrayed negatively as problem people or in stereotypical fashion.)

2. *Advantage:* When you hail a cab, you don't have to worry about not being picked up because of your race, let alone even think about this matter. (*Disadvantage:* A recent study conducted by *Dateline* indicates that 25 percent of New York City taxi drivers will not pick up Black customers.)

3. *Advantage:* When you go for a job interview, you never worry or even think about how being White may be held against you. You are assured that employers will not presume you are less competent or capable because of your race. (*Disadvantage:* Studies support the fact that persons of color are often viewed as suspect in their qualifications, whereas Whites are not subjected to a similar evaluation because of their skin color.)

4. *Advantage:* When you read a magazine or newspaper or watch television, you are likely to see people of your race widely represented in different roles and at different levels. (*Disadvantage:* Minorities are consistently underrepresented in media; when portrayed, they usually are in lower-level positions.)

5. *Advantage:* When you apply for a loan, write a check, or use your credit card, you can count on your skin color not to work against you in determining reliability or creditworthiness. (*Disadvantage:* Persons of color are often suspected as poor credit risks, as not having financial resources, or of being less trustworthy in monetary transactions.)

6. *Advantage:* You will not, as a White person, feel obligated or be expected to "give something back to the White community" or to extend yourself outside work hours to bring others of your race into the opportunity structure. (*Disadvantage:* Persons of color are often singled out as being responsible for their group or as

representatives of their race. As a result, they are saddled with the additional expectation that they are obligated to "give back" to the community.)

7. *Advantage:* You can generally purchase a home in most neighborhoods and feel welcomed or at least be treated neutrally. (*Disadvantage:* Even with the financial means, many persons of color are made to feel unwelcome in many neighborhoods—they represent the wrong elements, will increase crime, or will lower the market value of homes in the neighborhood.)

8. *Advantage:* If a traffic cop stops you while driving, you can be pretty sure you were not targeted or profiled because of being White. (*Disadvantage:* Recent results of a New Jersey investigation of traffic stops suggest that racial profiling is all too prevalent. Among African Americans and Latinos, being stopped by police is called DWB, or "driving while Black or Brown.")

9. *Advantage:* You can arrange, most of the time, to be among people of your own race. (*Disadvantage:* White folks have the luxury of arranging to be among members of their own race, to disengage from other racial groups, and to avoid dialogue or confrontation. People of color have no such luxury. They operate in a society that is made for and run by White folks.)

10. *Advantage:* You can choose public accommodation without fearing that people of your race cannot get in or will be mistreated. (*Disadvantage:* Traveling throughout the country and seeking stays in local motels or even larger hotels, many people of color continue to be denied accommodations or made to feel unwelcome.)

11. *Advantage:* You can choose blemish cover or bandages in "flesh" color and have them more or less match your skin. (*Disadvantage:* This is a statement that brings home the point of how our society is structured and created primarily for Whites only.)

12. *Advantage:* You can remain oblivious of the language and customs of persons of color, who constitute the world's majority, without feeling in your culture any penalty for such oblivion. (*Dis-*

advantage: Persons of color cannot survive in this society by ignoring the language and customs of White folks. They are constantly vigilant and painstakingly aware of how their survival means understanding the minds and institutions of their oppressors.)

13. *Advantage*: You can criticize our government and talk about how much you fear its policies and behavior without being seen as a cultural outsider. (*Disadvantage*: Any critical statements by persons of color toward the United States are likely to be seen as coming from a foreigner. "If you don't like it here, go back to China, Mexico, or Africa.")

14. *Advantage*: When you enter a department store and browse through sales items, you can be assured that the security guards will not pay extra attention to your presence or follow you throughout the store. (*Disadvantage*: Persons of color are more likely than Whites to be perceived as criminals or "up to no good.")

15. *Advantage*: When you look at people on the organizational hierarchy, you are likely to see many others of your own race. People like you will be represented at higher levels. (*Disadvantage*: In an organizational hierarchy, people of color are more likely to occupy the lower rungs of the employment ladder.)

16. *Advantage*: You are seldom likely to be mistaken for a janitor. (*Disadvantage*: Persons of color are seldom perceived as leaders, as authoritative and knowledgeable.)

17. *Advantage*: You can purchase posters, postcards, picture books, greeting cards, dolls, toys, and magazines featuring people of your race. (*Disadvantage*: White Euro-American society continues not to reflect social and demographic reality.)

18. *Advantage*: When you hunt for an apartment, apply for a job, or seek admission to a club, you don't have to worry that your race will make you appear threatening. (*Disadvantage*: Again, persons of color are more likely to be perceived as untrustworthy.)

19. *Advantage*: You can criticize the United States government or its various institutions without fear that you will be perceived as

a foreign subversive or radical who is intent on overthrowing the government. (*Disadvantage:* Because persons of color are often perceived as aliens to begin with, voicing dissatisfaction with the country reinforces the belief that they are subversives.)

20. *Advantage:* The ultimate White privilege, however, is your ability to acknowledge your unearned privileged status but at the same time ignore its meaning. (*Disadvantage:* The ultimate White hypocrisy is to recognize that your privileged position was unfairly earned on the backs of minorities but to ignore its meaning. This, perhaps, is the most frustrating issue confronting people of color. Why, if you recognize White privilege, do you continue to do nothing?)

What You Can Do to Overcome Racism

Try the following exercises.

Exercise Number 1

Do you benefit from White privilege? Take the following inventory. Mark each of the following statements "true" or "false."

White Privilege Inventory	True	False
1. I can obtain legal or medical help without my race working against me.	_____	_____
2. I am seldom placed in a position where I am asked to speak for my race.	_____	_____
3. If I want, I can always arrange to be in the company of people of my race.	_____	_____
4. When I enter a department store to shop, I can be assured that security guards will not follow me or suspect me of shoplifting.	_____	_____

White Privilege Inventory	True	False

5. Store personnel will not be suspicious of my financial resources when I cash a check or use my credit card because of my race. _____ _____

6. When I am stopped by a traffic officer, I never worry that racial profiling was involved. _____ _____

7. I never worry whether my children will be given curricular material that show people of my race or if people of my race will be portrayed positively. _____ _____

8. The person in charge is generally a person of my race. _____ _____

9. Coworkers will never suspect that I obtained my job because of my race rather than my good qualifications. _____ _____

10. If I am loud in public or disturb the peace, my race is never put on trial. _____ _____

1. If you marked most of these to be true, you are the recipient of White privilege. What does that mean for you?

2. As we did in the last section of this chapter, for each statement identify the advantages that you experience because of your Whiteness. Now outline the disadvantages that people of color suffer because of White privilege.

Exercise Number 2

This chapter identified five components of White privilege: it (1) automatically confers dominance to one group, (2) owes its existence to White supremacy, (3) is premised on individual meritocracy rather than favoritism, (4) is embedded in the systemic workings of U.S. society, and (5) operates within an invisible veil.

In the cases of Felix Hernandez and Randall Clay Jr., we outlined how White privilege is embedded in the systemic workings of society, characteristic number four. As an exercise, can you do the same for the other four components? The other four components are listed in one column. Now how do they apply to both individuals? Use the following outline to discuss and record how White privilege is operating.

Components of White Privilege	Felix Hernandez	Randall Clay Jr.
1. Automatically confers dominance		
2. Manifested in White supremacy		
3. Based on favoritism instead of meritocracy		
4. Invisible		

Exercise Number 3

Think about these questions or discuss them with others.

1. If you accept the fact that White privilege exists, how does that make you feel? Are you guilty about it? Do you feel uncomfortable?

2. Realizing that White privilege exists, what does that mean for you?

3. If you believe that White privilege is unfair and a travesty to society, what do you plan to do about it? Try to list the actions you would take to dismantle White privilege. Does the task seem overwhelming? Are you having difficulty coming up with solutions?

4. What does giving up White privilege mean? Is it even possible for a White person to "disown" White privilege? What does this mean for you?

10 Old-Fashioned versus Modern Racism

Where Have All the Bigots Gone?

In the past, whites were comfortable with openly expressing prejudiced racial attitudes, because the culture in American society was such that overt hostility toward other races, discrimination, and segregation of other races from the white-dominated culture were the norm. Thus, not until the late 1920s was serious attention paid by psychologists to the problem of prejudice and stereotyping. Though it took American society over 30 more years to acknowledge its deep racial prejudice, researchers in the 1920s and 1930s were beginning to tackle questions such as: What is a stereotype and how does it form (Lippmann, 1922)? What is the content of racial stereotypes (Katz & Braly, 1933)? How strongly do prejudiced attitudes correspond to behavior in interracial interactions (LaPiere, 1934)? Implicit in these questions (and the answers the researchers were obtaining in their data) were the beginnings of a shift in the way prejudiced people were viewed. As Jones (1997) describes it, "There was a tendency to consider individuals who answered a question in a certain way not only as prejudiced, but as morally inferior human beings" (p. 42). As a result of this shift in perspective, prejudice and stereotyping were no longer viewed as a "normal" part of being human, but rather, were beginning to be seen as problems to be understood and reduced or eliminated whenever possible. That is, prejudice was no longer a "natural" thing, but it signified that the individual *chose* that negative view of certain others, through either a moral defect, mental laziness (as first discussed by Lippmann and later developed by social cognition researchers), or both.

Therefore, stereotypes were coming to be understood as attitudes (evaluations, rather than "pictures in our head") that some people endorse but others do not (Jones, 1997). Here was a turning point in understanding prejudice and stereotyping. If the basis of prejudice, stereotyping, and discrimination was a negative attitude (and not something inherent about being human), then if we can understand the nature of those attitudes, we can understand the nature of stereotyping and prejudice and then be in a much better position from which to address ways to reduce or eliminate stereotyping and prejudice. Why were some people prejudiced and others not prejudiced? Is it even possible to not have prejudice? These questions (and many more) occupied the thoughts of researchers in the early part of the 20th century, and likely will continue to be the focus of research for years to come, as the answers remain elusive despite tremendous advances in our knowledge over the decades.

The sections that follow examine how stereotyping and prejudice have changed form over the decades. The chapter also examines whether stereotyping and prejudice seem to be more or less prevalent today than they were in the past. The second half of the chapter focuses in some detail on the methods that social scientists have used to further the understanding of stereotyping and prejudice, examining the major avenues of measuring stereotypes, and highlighting the strengths and weaknesses of each approach. The chapter concludes with a discussion of the current state of the art in stereotype and prejudice measurement and fruitful directions for future research on measures of prejudice and stereotyping.

From Katz and Braly (1933) to Civil Rights, and Beyond

With Katz and Braly's (1933) landmark study, researchers obtained their first view of the content of racial stereotypes that whites held about blacks. Recall from our discussion of this classic study (in Chapter 1) that white college students were asked to indicate whether

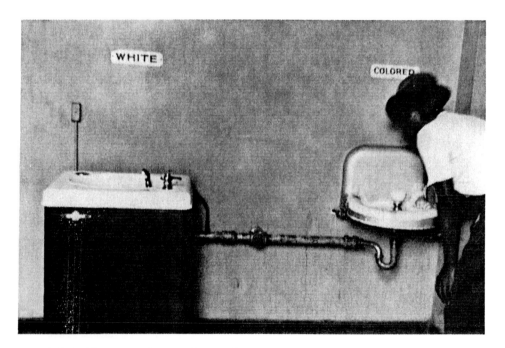

"Old-fashioned" racism is the type of openly-hostile prejudice that characterized much of the segregated southern United States prior to the landmark Supreme Court rulings of the 1950s and the civil rights movements of the 1950s and 1960s. Such prejudice led to state-sanctioned segregation of blacks and whites in all public places, based on the belief that blacks were inferior and whites deserved the privileged status in society, as evidenced here in a 1950 photo of segregated drinking fountains in North Carolina.

various traits (84 in all) described whites or blacks. Those early data suggested that whites held very negative views of blacks, and very positive views of whites. For instance, blacks were viewed by the white respondents as "superstitious," "lazy," and "ignorant," whereas they viewed whites as "industrious," "intelligent," and "ambitious." Few respondents were willing to attribute positive qualities to blacks or negative qualities to whites. However, over the years, data have been gathered using the adjective checklist procedure to attempt to gauge whether and how whites' stereotypes of blacks are changing. These data indicate that these attitudes have become less negative and increasingly positive (Dovidio & Gaertner, 1991; Dovidio, Brigham, Johnson, & Gaertner, 1996).

Certainly the changes in the social, legal, and political climate of the United States seem to correspond to the changes in whites' self-reported stereotypes of blacks. The changes in society, mentioned earlier, have been quite dramatic in the area of race relations. Segregation and discrimination were outlawed. Laws (Civil Rights Act of 1965) and social programs (e.g., Affirmative Action) were created to advance the economic status and job prospects for groups that had traditionally experienced discrimination. Movies (e.g., *Amistad*), television (e.g., *Roots*), and music were beginning to deal with stereotyping and prejudice, and other race relations issues. Blacks were being accepted into white American society on many levels. Most researchers agree that white Americans *have* indeed reduced their negative views of and prejudice toward blacks; however, compelling evidence suggests that the extent of this attitude and prejudice change is not as dramatic as was once believed (Fiske, 1998). The following sections examine this evidence, reviewing also criticisms of the Katz and Braly study and studies like it that rely on the adjective checklist methodology for assessing stereotypes.

Are Low-Prejudiced People *Really* Low-Prejudiced?

Some have questioned the adjective checklist procedure of Katz and Braly as a misleading measure of the stereotyping landscape. For example, Niemann, Jennings, Rozelle, Baxter, and Sullivan (1994) point to several problems with the Katz and Braly procedure, including (1) the subjects were predominantly white, upper-class men, which limits the generalizability of the data, and (2) the method requires the subject to rely on a rather controlled, cognitive process in which the individual is actively thinking about whether a particular trait "fits" into their schema for the group in question (Devine, 1989; Fiske & Neuberg, 1990). This is a limitation because much research suggests that stereotypes are activated automatically on encountering the stimulus (group label, or other indicator of the group) and can hold a wealth of affective and other cognitive information that drives the stereotype that cannot be represented on the adjective checklist (Fiske & Neuberg, 1990; Stangor & Lange, 1994; for an exception, see Lepore & Brown, 1997). Thus, as Neimann et al. (1994) suggest, "results using the checklist method may provide stereotypes that are more a function of the words presented on a list than of the schematic content of the respondents' stereotypes" (p. 380). Consider the following experiment. Ehrlich and Rinehart (1965) administered the Katz and Braly adjective checklist to half of their participants, and asked the other half to simply list all the words, traits, and characteristics they needed to adequately describe the group in question. The results showed that the words that participants used in the "open-ended" method were different from the words the participants checked in the Katz and Braly procedure. Subsequent research by Allen and colleagues (Allen, 1971; Potkay & Allen, 1988) has expanded the "open-ended" procedure to include values assigned to the words generated, and these values are analyzed to indicate the degree of favorability and un-favorability of the characterizations of the target. This technique, termed the *adjective generation technique,* is a good way to ascertain the content of stereotypes at a given point in time (Allen, 1996). The differences in words generated from time A to time B can indicate how stereotypes of the target group may be changing.

Other researchers suggest that the Katz and Braly procedure does not, as commonly believed, measure knowledge about stereotypes, but rather, personal beliefs about the truth of the stereotype. This position is exemplified by Devine and Elliot (1995), in their analysis of the decline in racial stereotypes. Devine and Elliot suggest that it is important to distinguish between personal beliefs about stereotypes, and knowledge about the stereotypes, and their analysis of the participant responses to the adjective checklist data accumulated over the years (e.g., Gilbert, 1951; Karlins, Coffman, & Walters, 1969) suggests that some participants construed the task as an assessment of their stereotype knowledge and others thought it was a measure of their personal beliefs about blacks and whites. Devine and Elliot compared these earlier data with more contemporary adjective checklist data on racial attitudes (i.e., Dovidio & Gaertner, 1986). Their analysis supports the notion that the adjective checklist, as it has been administered over the decades, is actually measuring personal beliefs (or willingness to publicly state those beliefs) about the truth of racial stereotypes. Thus, as we have seen earlier in this chapter, it is not surprising—given the change in American society on racial issues over the last 50 years—that the personal beliefs of whites (or willingness to publicly state such beliefs) about stereotypes of blacks indicate a strongly diminished belief in those stereotypes.

This analysis would suggest that some progress *has* been made in reducing the negative personal beliefs that whites have about blacks. But what about the negative stereotypes of blacks that used to be common in America? Have they diminished? According to Devine and Elliot (1995), the answer is, unfortunately, no. Their data suggest that when whites are asked about their knowledge (not personal beliefs) about the stereotypes of blacks, their responses indicate a high degree of negativity in the traits selected as stereotypic of blacks. These contemporary ratings are virtually identical to the negative adjective rating data collected since 1933. This suggests that although personal beliefs in negative stereotypes of blacks appears to have decreased, knowledge of the cultural stereotype of blacks has remained the same. In other words, whites rather unanimously know about the negative things (and few positive things) that are stereotypically associated with blacks through their early learning from parents, or other exposure to such information in society. What has seemed to change is their willingness to personally believe, and also overtly express, such negative racial attitudes.

In sum, the available evidence suggests that stereotypes themselves have not changed much over the last century, but the form in which they are expressed has changed. Before the social, legal, and political climate of the United States changed dramatically with the Civil Rights movement of the late 1950s and 1960s, stereotypes and prejudice were fairly easy to assess. Researchers could use simple self-report measures (e.g., Katz and Braly's adjective checklist procedure) to understand the content and extent of negative affect directed at other groups. However, the Civil Rights movement (and legislation) changed the social landscape with regard to stereotyping and prejudice. Stereotyping and prejudice "went underground." The negative affect and stereotypes were still there, but in a subdued, subtle form.

This "new form" of prejudice was not adequately conceptualized by models of stereotyping and prejudice that were applied before the 1960s. Researchers needed different theories that could better address these contemporary expressions of prejudice. The theories had to account for the ambivalence that seemed to characterize the attitudes of whites toward blacks in the post–Civil Rights environment. Most whites seemed to have an underlying association between blacks and undesirable characteristics and values; conversely, most whites overtly embraced egalitarianism, the values of equality for all, and nondiscrimination. Another way to think about this fundamental ambivalence that characterizes current expressions of racism and prejudice is the "trouble with equality." The hard-won fight for the civil rights of blacks in society was an easy rallying point for most justice-minded Americans, because the overt discrimination, prejudice, and segregation of one group of people in a democratic society violated all standards of morality, ethics, and justice. Thus, that fight was for the *freedom* of blacks. However, the post–Civil Rights era can be thought of as the search for the *equality* of blacks. Three major theories of contemporary forms of prejudice and racism attempt to explain the origins of the ambivalence that whites experience in their attitudes toward blacks. This chapter examines the basic tenets of each, as well as the empirical support for each theory. A discussion of ways to *measure* stereotyping and prejudice follows. The endorsement of negative stereotypes and expressions of prejudice have changed over the decades, so researchers have had to modify the methods and instruments they use to assess prejudice.

Modern Racism

According to McConahay (1983, 1986), the theory of *modern racism* asserts that some whites have an ambivalence toward blacks because of the conflict between their antiblack feelings and their beliefs that racism and discrimination is wrong. For modern racists, the issue is not whether blacks *should* be equal, but *how* that equality should be implemented in policy, law, and employment. As with the symbolic racism perspective (discussed later), the theory of modern racism suggests that modern racists have a problem with giving "special treatment" (e.g., hiring preferences, as in Affirmative Action) to blacks, because they believe it violates the work ethic that says that one only advances in life based on their own achievements and hard work, not on "unfair" shortcuts. Modern racists believe that (1) discrimination is a thing of the past; (2) blacks are too pushy, trying to get into places where they are not welcome; (3) the demands of blacks are unfair; and (4) their gains (due to social programs that provide economic, housing, and other opportunities to blacks) are undeserved and unfair (McConahay, 1986).

Modern racists do not consider themselves to be racists for two reasons. First, they regard racism as associated with the pre–Civil Rights, "old-fashioned" racism in which open hatred and feelings of superiority are shown by the racist (McConahay, 1986). Second, their subtle negative feelings toward blacks are disguised (to prevent the dissonance associated with acknowledging the hypocricy of prejudice and egalitarian values) as negative attitudes toward *anyone* who violates what they believe are traditional American values (McConahay & Hough, 1976). The theory of modern racism has good empirical support (e.g., McConahay, Hardee, & Batts, 1981), and the self-report scale (called the "Modern Racism Scale") that McConahay (1986) has devised to measure this subtle prejudice has been shown to have fair reliability and validity (McConahay, 1986). For over a decade, the Modern Racism Scale (MRS) was one of the most widely used measures of contemporary prejudice toward blacks. However, recall from our discussion in Chapter 3 that a number of criticisms of the MRS led researchers to search for better ways to measure racial attitudes (Biernat & Crandall, 1999). The strongest criticism is that modern racism is not conceptually distinct from old-fashioned racism (Fazio, Jackson, Dunton, & Williams, 1995). Later in this chaper, these criticisms are discussed in more depth. Next, we turn to the theory of "symbolic racism."

Symbolic Racism

Kinder and Sears (1981; Sears, 1988) have proposed a different approach to understanding the origins of the prejudice of contemporary white Americans toward blacks. They suggest that old-fashioned overt racism has been replaced with what they term *symbolic racism.* This is defined as a "blend of anti-black affect and traditional American moral values embodied in the Protestant Ethic" (Kinder & Sears, 1981, p. 416). According to this view, whites who would be classified as symbolic racists tend to resist changing the racial status quo (i.e., white dominance) in all areas of life, economically, socially, and politically. The use of the term *symbolic* is used to describe this resistance that originates not out of self-interest, but out of the general belief that blacks violate traditional American values (such as self-reliance, individualism, hard work, obedience).

The symbolic racist can also deny holding racist attitudes (and they may in fact believe that they are not prejudiced), because, in their view, a racist is one who exhibits "old-fashioned" racist beliefs of the inherent superiority of one race over another, and negative affect toward a group based on such beliefs. The negative affect and negative attitudes that symbolic racists may hold toward another group are converted into derision for groups that do not seem to value traditional American values. According to this position, then, symbolic racists would have no problem with other groups if those other groups were self-reliant, hard-working, and individualistic. However, because their view of how closely the other group is adhering to those values is tainted by their prejudice, it is unlikely that that group would ever be perceived as adhering to those ideals. In this way, symbolic racists are able to keep their negative affect and stereotypes of the outgroup, and even express these sentiments overtly, while still claiming that the source of such negative evaluations is the "objective difference" between whites and the outgroup in their support of traditional American values.

Critics of the symbolic racism concept argue that (1) it is an ill-defined concept (Bobo, 1988; Eagly & Chaiken, 1993), and (2) other explanations, such as realistic group conflict (Bobo, 1983) and social dominance theory (Sidanius, Devereux, & Pratto, 1992) can just as easily explain whites' opposition to social programs that reduce the inequity between blacks and whites. Perhaps the most damaging attack on symbolic racism comes from numerous studies that suggest that symbolic racism does not appear to be a distinct concept from more traditional (old-fashioned) forms of racism (Lea, Bokhorst, & Colenso, 1995; Raden, 1994; Sniderman & Tetlock, 1986; Weigel & Howes, 1985). However, the debate is not settled on the symbolic racism concept. Indeed, Eagly and Chaiken (1993) and Wood (1994) have noted that one of the redeeming qualities of the theory is that it rightly highlights the importance of the link between values and racial attitudes. Although it seems unlikely that symbolic racism represents a whole new ideology of racism (Schuman, Steeh, Bobo, & Krysan, 1997), it would be fruitful for researchers to further explore what particular set of values seem to co-occur with a more negative view of other racial groups. Research by Katz and Hass (1988) indicates that value conflict in whites leads to ambivalent attitudes toward blacks, and exploring what implications such ambivalence may have for the strength with which prejudicial feelings and beliefs are held would be interesting (Thompson, Zanna, & Griffin, 1995).

Aversive Racism

According to Gaertner and Dovidio (1986), the racist history of American culture combined with the cognitive tendency to categorize information (Fiske & Taylor, 1991) results in subtle, yet commonplace racist beliefs and feelings in white Americans. *Aversive racism* is a term Gaertner and Dovidio use to describe white Americans who possess these racist beliefs and feelings as well as strong egalitarian values. Thus, aversive racism reflects an ambivalence in whites between their learned negative attitudes (from early childhood to adulthood) toward blacks, and their commitment to egalitarian values and beliefs. Because egalitarian ideals and beliefs are central to the aversive racist's self, they may deny conscious awareness of their negative attitudes and prejudice toward blacks. Indeed, they will take great pains to *not* do or say anything that appears to be prejudiced, because they truly believe that they are not prejudiced. However, their underlying biases may be expressed as pro-white behaviors, such as ingroup favoritism, rather than the old-fashioned prejudicial expressions of outgroup derogation. When they are in a situation in which it is unclear whether there are social prohibitions against expressing negative racial beliefs, the aversive racist's negative feelings about blacks may be expressed in subtle, easily rationalizable ways. However, when the social norms are clearly anti-prejudice, then the aversive racist will not behave in a racist fashion, and they may even appear very strongly egalitarian (Katz, 1981; McConahay et al., 1981). In contrast to "old-fashioned" racism, in which the racist openly displays hatred for, and beliefs of superiority to, blacks, aversive racists experience more subtle feelings of "discomfort, uneasiness, disgust, and sometimes fear" in the presence of blacks (Gaertner and Dovidio, 1986, pp. 62–63).

In a recent paper, Dovidio and Gaertner (2000) analyzed data from 1988 to 1989 on hiring decisions of white participants regarding black and white job applicants, and compared those data with similar data gathered in 1998 to 1999. The aversive racism theory suggests that self-reported expressions of prejudice should decline over time, but that subtle, underlying prejudice should remain constant. Consistent with the theory, results of the analysis found that self-reported prejudice levels of the 1998 to 1999 participants were indeed lower than those of their counterparts a decade earlier. When presented with a clearly superior black applicant, participants did not show any underlying prejudice against the applicant or preference for the white applicant, and tended to hire the well-qualified minority. However, when the qualifications of the black applicant were rather ambiguous, their subtle, underlying hostility toward black applicants emerged, and the white participants tended to prefer to hire the white candidate.

Summary of Contemporary Theories of Prejudice

Although symbolic and modern racism differ from aversive racism in that they are found primarily in political conservatives, whereas aversive racism is associated with liberals (Dovidio & Gaertner, 1996), these theories are all very similar. For example, Ward (1985) found support for the common argument made by modern, aversive, and symbolic racism theories that negative racial attitudes are acquired early in childhood (primarily through parental attitudes), and that this forms the basis for a rather stable bedrock of anti-black affect beneath later egalitarian beliefs learned in school, from peers, and society. The theories of modern, symbolic, and aversive racism also suggest that because whites' negative affect toward blacks manifests itself subtly in terms of opposition to social programs and voting behavior that are aimed at bringing more blacks into society, they actually may have little awareness of their negative feelings toward blacks (Dovidio et al., 1996).

Another important feature is the common thread of racial ambivalence that runs throughout these contemporary theories of prejudice. By virtue of growing up in America, whites learn, through American society, culture, parents, and peers, what stereotypes are associated with various groups, and feelings of negative affect get attached to these groups in the white's memory. However, society also teaches values of equality, freedom, nondiscrimination, and values that embody the "protestant work ethic" (hard work, independence, and self-sufficiency), which whites also tended to embrace. The clash between these values with regard to perceptions of how various racial outgroups violate cherished values that embody the Protestant work ethic leads the white to feel ambivalence (conflicted) toward blacks. The stronger their ambivalence, the more inconsistent their behavior will be toward blacks. The determining factor in whether negative attitudes toward blacks may be displayed tends to hinge on the context. Relatively minor aspects of the situation can influence the whites' racial attitude and behavior to be either positive or negative toward blacks (Crocker, Major, & Steele, 1998; Fiske, 1998).

The similar motivational and behavioral manifestations of prejudice in modern, aversive, and symbolic racists suggests support for the underlying theme of racial ambivalence that characterizes many whites' racial attitudes in contemporary American society. However, as we have seen, much disagreement occurs over whether some of these theories (e.g., modern and symbolic racism) are really identifying distinct forms of racism, or whether they are simply "old wine in new bottles" (relabeling old-fashioned racism). Clearly, the *expression* of racial prejudice and stereotyping has changed over the decades. But, has the *form* of prejudice changed? That is, are the contemporary theories of prejudice describing a type of prejudice conceptually distinct from "old-fashioned" prejudice? The end of the chapter takes up this question. First, let us consider the ways that researchers attempt to assess prejudice and stereotyping.

Measures of Stereotyping and Prejudice

One of the biggest challenges for researchers studying prejudice and stereotyping involves the question of how best to accurately measure prejudiced attitudes. This is a formidable obstacle for researchers. Consider the questions that must be addressed to devise a sound measure of prejudice: What is the *nature* of the motivation that underlies the expression of prejudice and stereotypes about others (Allport, 1954)? Is the prejudice more likely to be expressed under certain affective or cognitive conditions (Mackie & Hamilton, 1993)? Are some personality types more likely to be prejudiced (e.g., Adorno et al., 1950)? Once the nature of the prejudice and its relation to personality and situational influences (e.g., cognitive load) have been identified, the researcher can then attempt to create a self-report measure to measure the participant's level of that particular type of prejudice. The next sections examine the various ways researchers have attempted to measure prejudice and stereotyping, addressing the criticisms and supportive evidence for each approach. Last, the chapter examines the current state of the science of measuring prejudice and discusses the future trends in measuring prejudice.

Self-Report Questionnaires

There is an old saying among social scientists, "If you want to know how someone feels about something, ask them." This practical approach to ascertaining the attitude of an individual has guided psychologists, sociologists, opinion pollsters, and other researchers for over 60 years. Sometimes, as in opinion polls or interviews, the respondent is asked about their attitudes on a variety of topics, and the questioner records the reply on their questionnaire or computer database. However, this is not the most popular method of obtaining attitude data, because of its labor-intensive nature. Interview methods such as this require an interviewer, and attitudes of individuals can only be ascertained one person at a time (i.e., one interviewer and one respondent). A much more efficient way to find out how people feel about something is to have them complete a questionnaire themselves (hence the term *self-report*). In this method, a researcher can administer hundreds of questionnaires simultaneously to hundreds of participants. The self-report quickly became, and remains, the most popular method of attitude assessment in psychology today. The big advantage of self-report questionnaires is their efficiency: one can obtain lots of attitude data from lots of people very quickly. For example, the researcher could mail out hundreds (or thousands) of questionnaires to potential respondents, or they might bring an equal number of questionnaires to various classes on a college campus, and obtain the data from student volunteers. Sometimes, the researcher does not even need to be present: the potential subject could stop by the psychology department to pick up a questionnaire packet (complete with informed consent, the questionnaire(s), and a debriefing sheet), and return it to the department later.

However, self-report measures have some serious drawbacks. First, the responses to the questions are usually restricted to the response alternatives provided on the questionnaire (unless it is a free-response, open-answer format in which the individual can write anything they want in response to the question). Thus, the researcher gets a general, if somewhat imprecise, measure of the respondent's attitudes. Second, and perhaps more importantly, people do not always provide their true attitudes on self-report measures. This may be due to a couple of reasons. People may not have conscious awareness of their true, underlying attitudes toward an issue, because of the sensitive nature of the issue. A good example of this is racial attitudes. In the past, stereotyping others and holding prejudiced attitudes were the norm, and there were no legal or societal prohibitions against overtly displaying such negative attitudes. Over time, this has changed dramatically, and it is no longer tolerated in mainstream society. However, old habits die hard, and research on modern racism, aversive racism, and symbolic racism suggests that, for many people, their negative feelings toward other groups may not have been eliminated, but are just hidden more carefully.

Even some people who believe they are low in prejudice still harbor underlying negative racial attitudes. Consider the following quote by Pettigrew (1987, as cited by Devine, Monteith, Zuwerink, & Elliot, 1991, p. 817): "Many Southerners have confessed to me, for instance, that even though in their minds they no longer feel prejudice toward blacks, they still feel squeamish when they shake hands with a black. These feelings are left over from what they learned in their families as children." Thus, the anxiety and cognitive dissonance that are aroused with awareness of the underlying attitude may motivate such individuals to shut off those feelings from their awareness, to deny their existence, to maintain a desired image of themselves as persons with no prejudice. Other individuals may be aware of their negative feelings toward other groups, but they do not express these attitudes because of the negative social (and sometimes legal) consequences for such behavior. Thus, interpersonally and on questionnaires, they express little or no prejudice, whereas they may indeed harbor negative attitudes toward certain groups. This tendency to present oneself in a positive light is termed *social desirability*, and it presents a big obstacle for the attitude researcher. In these situations, the person who is providing their attitudes is concerned with presenting responses that are socially acceptable, and hiding any attitudes that are socially unacceptable. Because the researcher only wants to get the honest, accurate responses from the individual, he or she must take extra measures to enhance the likelihood that the respondent will provide his or her true attitudes, even if they are unpopular.

The researcher can decrease the influence of social desirability in the subject's responses in several ways. For most experiments investigating attitudes, the researcher can tell the subjects that their responses will be completely anonymous. If it cannot be anonymous, the next best thing is to make the responses confidential (i.e., only the principal investigator—or other responsible professionals—will have access to the data, and for research purposes only). This helps alleviate any anxiety that the subject may have about their responses being identifiable with them. Another instruction researchers will give to subjects when asking for their attitudes on various issues is that it is important that the subject provide his or her *honest* responses, not how they think they *should* respond (i.e., the socially desirable response). Honesty in responding to the questionnaire or the researcher's questions is emphasized as paramount, in the hope of appealing to the participant's desire to be a "good subject" by correctly following directions and helping the researcher.

Finally, virtually all respondents to attitude measures are tempted to try to "figure out" the purpose of the attitude questionnaire (what it is measuring; for example, whether the person is prejudiced against homosexuals). Aspects of the questionnaire and the testing situation that encourage the subject to make his or her own hypotheses about what answers are expected (or what is being measured) are called *demand characteristics,* and these represent an unwanted bias in the research. If the subject is responding to his or her own ideas of what the questionnaire is measuring, or what the researcher wants the subject to say, then they are not providing their truthful opinions on the items. In these instances, the researcher may use "filler items" in the questionnaire, to make the purpose of the questionnaire less obvious to the respondent (to "throw them off the scent"). Filler items are those items that have no relation to the hypotheses under investigation and are included in the questionnaire as a way to distract the respondent from the hypotheses of the researcher. For example, one may only be interested in responses to seven items dealing with attitudes toward homosexuality, and there may be 43 other items that examine other issues (such as attitudes toward recycling). This often has the intended effect of making it difficult for the respondent to formulate hypotheses of what is under investigation in the questionnaire, and without the bias of that potential demand characteristic, participants should therefore be more likely to provide their honest responses to the items. The problem with these techniques is that they are not a guarantee that there will be no social desirability or other biases in the participant's responses. In fact, research suggests that these techniques that are designed to enhance the validity of self-report measures are only partially effective (Schuman & Kalton, 1985). Thus, researchers have developed other methods of getting attitude information.

The Bogus Pipeline

This technique, devised by Jones and Sigall (1971), was inspired in part by a paper by Karlins, Coffman, and Walters (1969). Karlins et al. reported that whites in the United States reported more favorable attitudes toward blacks over the course of many decades, and showed little prejudice and little stereotyping of blacks, according to their responses on the questionnaires in the study. Jones and Sigall believed that such a sudden shift in how whites viewed blacks was unlikely, especially given the turbulent interracial climate of the 1960s. Jones and Sigall suspected that attitudes had not changed dramatically, but people's willingness to express overt negative racial attitudes was likely diminishing. Thus, they reasoned that some of the respondents in the Karlins et al. study were more likely providing the socially appropriate attitudes about other races, and keeping their prejudices to themselves. Sigall and Page (1971) designed a study to examine this, using an apparatus that subjects are led to believe can assess one's true attitudes. In other words, the subject is told that the experimenter will have a direct reading—a "pipeline"—to their attitudes on the issues under examination. The apparatus looks much like a polygraph machine, with dials, lights, buzzers, and electromyographic (EMG) electrodes that are attached to the person's arms.

The procedure for the bogus pipeline study (as it was carried out by Sigall and Page) is as follows: One half of the participants are either assigned to a rating condition in which they indicate their attitudes on the issue in question (e.g., racial attitudes) aloud when the experimenter asks the question. The other half are assigned to an EMG condition, in which they are asked to provide their ratings by turning a wheel, attached to a computer, that moves a dial to the left or right, corresponding to more negative or more positive attitudes (or disagreement vs. agreement) to the question being asked of the participant. Participants in the rating condition were asked to turn the wheel device to move the pointer to the number (from a range of −3 to +3) that corresponds to their attitude on the item. For half of the rating condition participants, the experimenter read a list of 22 traits (e.g., *superstitious, ambitious*) and asked the participant to indicate on the wheel device how representative each trait was of "Americans." The other half of the participants were asked to indicate how representative each trait was of "blacks." Typically, these ratings indicated that participants (in the Sigall & Page study, all participants were white, and all were men) rated both Americans and blacks positively.

In the EMG condition, participants were told of the EMG machine, and that the intent of the study was to further validate the measures it provides. Participants in this condition were first given a five-item inventory asking their attitudes on relatively neutral topics such as music, sports, movies, etc. The experimenter then took the questionnaire and led the participant into the room with the EMG machine at the wall opposite the door. The experimenter casually places the completed questionnaire on a table by the door as they enter, and he leaves the door slightly ajar. The subject is seated at the machine with his back to the wall. As the experimenter is explaining the EMG machine and procedure to the subject, another researcher silently gets the questionnaire and copies the answers and returns the questionnaire to the table.

After the experimenter has explained the procedure, the participant has electrodes attached to his forearm. The experimenter explains that the machine can assess the participant's "implicit muscle movements," and it will tell the experimenter the strength with which the participant is about to turn the wheel (i.e., how strong, and in what direction the participant's attitude is on the item in question). To convince the participant of the accuracy of the machine, the experimenter asked the participant to hold the wheel and concentrate on his answers to the 5-item inventory he completed earlier. The experimenter read the question, turned a switch on the machine, and the machine buzzed for a few moments and then was silent as the needle (controlled by the researcher's associate in the other room, who had copied the participant's answers) moved to a number. On the fourth item, the experimenter asked the subject to try to "trick" the machine by moving the wheel in the opposite direction of his attitude, and to think about the opposite attitude as well. The machine was not "fooled" and gave the attitude number that the subject had indicated earlier on the questionnaire. After the fifth item, the experimenter retrieved the subject's questionnaire from the table and compared it with the machine's readings, and showed the subject that the machine was extremely accurate. The participant is then read the 22 traits and asked to provide his honest attitudes about each of them. As with the rating condition, half of the participants in the EMG condition are asked about the typicality of the traits for "Americans," and the other half are asked how well these traits describe "blacks."

When the results from the rating and EMG conditions were compared, some very striking differences emerged. Generally speaking, EMG participants were more confident than their rating condition peers that "Americans" had more positive traits, and less negative traits. For example, ratings participants thought that the trait "honest" was not very typical (−.27) of Americans, but EMG participants thought it was more typical (+.60). Ratings subjects thought that Americans were not lazy (−.40), and EMG participants were even more adamant that this was the case (−.80).

However, the results were different for perceptions of blacks. Generally, although ratings participants evaluated blacks rather favorably, EMG participants rated blacks as having more undesirable and fewer desirable traits. For example, ratings participants thought that the trait "unreliable" was not indicative of blacks (−.67), while EMG participants believed that it was characteristic of blacks (+.27). On the trait of "honesty," ratings participants believed that it was characteristic of blacks (+.60) whereas EMG participants believed that it was not very typical of blacks (−.33).

These results supported Jones and Sigall's suspicions that the dramatic decline in prejudiced attitudes that was reported by Karlins et al. (1969) did not reflect a revolution in the attitudes of whites toward blacks. Many whites were not as low-prejudiced as their egalitarian responses on self-report measures of prejudice would suggest. Thus, although negative attitudes of whites toward blacks had not declined dramatically, what had changed was the willingness of whites to overtly express these negative racial attitudes. As Sigall and Page describe the results, the EMG participants provided more negative attitudes toward blacks (compared with those in the ratings condition) because they believed that the machine could accurately assess their attitudes, and if they attempted to portray themselves as those in the ratings condition (i.e., as nonprejudiced), the machine would show to the researcher that the subject had lied. Thus, rather than risk being seen as a liar, the subject indicates (via his negative responses about blacks) that he is prejudiced!

Does the Bogus Pipeline technique work, and is it a viable means to accurately assess prejudice? Although Schlenker, Bonoma, Hutchinson, and Burns (1976) were unable to completely replicate Sigall and Page's findings, and others found no differences between self-reported attitudes and attitudes provided using the bogus pipeline (Broverman, Bloom, Gunn, & Torok, 1974; Cherry, Byrne, & Mitchell, 1976), the bulk of the research suggests that it does indeed reduce attitude distortion (due to social desirability and other self-presentational goals) (Page & Moss, 1975; Riess, Kalle, & Tedeschi, 1981; Quigley-Fernandez & Tedeschi, 1978). A recent comprehensive meta-analysis of 31 bogus-pipeline studies also showed that the technique does indeed work to reduce socially desirable responding and leads to more truthful responses from the participants (Roese & Jamieson, 1993). Interestingly, other research, in which the subject is led to believe that their self-reported attitudes will be later validated for accuracy, shows similar reductions in attitude distortion (e.g., Evans, Hansen, & Mittelmark, 1977; Hill, Henderson, Bray, & Evans, 1981).

Although the data indicate that the bogus pipeline (and variations thereof) is a particularly accurate (i.e., little attitude distortion) measure of attitudes, it is almost never used in modern prejudice research. The reason is simple: it is very labor-intensive to conduct research with bogus-pipeline–type measures. The experiment involves elaborate deception, and extensive training of the experimenters, and the experimenter needs to devise an accurate replica of the "EMG" machine (the bogus pipeline) and convince today's more psychologically savvy subjects that the machine is valid, and that the experimenter is being upfront with the subject.

Measuring Stereotyping

Though it was once a useful gauge of stereotypes, the Katz and Braly adjective checklist is rarely used in contemporary research because of the aforementioned problems associated with the measure. Other researchers have used a "diagnostic ratio" measure of stereotyping (McCauley & Stitt, 1978). This procedure asks the participant to provide estimates of the percentage of the target group who possess a given characteristic (e.g., honesty), and also what percentage of "people in general" possess the given characteristic. To the degree that participants' responses for the target group differ from those they indicated for the general population, positive or negative attributes (depending on the perceived differences on the trait[s] in question) are thus attributed to the target group. Perhaps because of its perceived complexity, the diagnostic ratio measure of stereotyping has not been a very popular method to assess stereotyping (Allen, 1996). Researchers have come back to the free-response technique, exemplified by the Adjective Generation Technique (AGT) procedure (Potkay & Allen, 1988), as a robust and accurate measure of the stereotypes individuals hold about outgroups at a given time (e.g., Devine, 1989; Esses, Haddock, & Zanna, 1994). Free-response measures also have a distinct advantage over earlier measures of stereotyping in that they can more accurately predict subsequent prejudice-related behavior toward the outgroup (Stangor, Sullivan, & Ford, 1992). The down side to free-response measures of stereotyping is that (1) they are not always better predictors of prejudice and discrimination, and (2) the task of coding the free-response data generated by the participants is often time-consuming and requires lengthy reliability analyses that some researchers might consider too labor-intensive (Stangor & Lange, 1994). Nevertheless, if the goal is to understand the content of sterotypes toward a certain target at a particular time, free response measures are an excellent method to achieve that end.

A primary approach to research in stereotyping and prejudice is to ascertain the conditions that facilitate and inhibit the use of stereotypes in making judgments about others. In other words, when are we more or less likely to use a stereotype when thinking about, or forming an impression of, another person? One useful approach to assess the proclivity to use stereotypes in social judgments is to examine the degree to which participants in a study use the category membership of the target as a heuristic in helping them arrive at conclusions about that target. Though a variety of measures exist, a popular version has been Bodenhausen's (1990) Student Court Questionnaire (SCQ). Participants are asked to read a short description about a disciplinary hearing that will be held against a student on campus involving either academic dishonesty or possession of drugs. The paragraph presents a brief outline of the offense and the evidence that implicates the defendant. However, the information is ambiguous as to the guilt or innocence of the defendant (i.e., there is equal evidence that suggests he is innocent and that he likely committed the offense). Participants are then asked, on eight Likert-type items, about the likelihood that the defendant is guilty, severity of punishment if he is guilty, etc. There are two versions of the SCQ. One names the defendant in the paragraph with an "ethnically nondescript" name, such as "Dan Jensen." The other version is identical to the first except for the name of the defendant, which is an "African American–sounding" name, such as "Darnell Jackson." Within all experimental conditions, half of the participants get the nondescript version, and the other half get the African American version. To the degree that responses on the two versions of the questionnaire differ significantly in terms of judgments of greater guilt, more severe punishment deserved, etc. for the black defendant, the researcher can then conclude that the independent variable for that condition either increased, or had no effect on, the tendency to use a stereotype in social judgments. The SCQ is popular because it is nonreactive, easy to administer and score, very brief, and has little or no demand characteristics associated with it. Using this measure (and variants thereof), researchers have found that when people are happy (Bodenhausen, Kramer, & Süsser, 1994), they are more likely to use a stereotype in their judgments about a target. Research also indicates that people are more likely to stereotype others when they are angry, but not when they feel sad (Bodenhausen, Sheppard, & Kramer, 1994). Research also indicates that when people are cognitively busy they are more likely to use stereotypes when thinking about a target (Bodenhausen & Lichtenstein, 1987; Fiske & Neuberg, 1990).

Measuring Prejudice

In addition to discovering the conditions under which stereotyping is likely to occur, researchers have been equally interested in understanding the relation between negative intergroup affect (prejudice) and subsequent attitudes and behavior toward outgroups. To this end, a considerable amount of effort has been directed toward devising self-report measures of prejudice. Recall that a good self-report measure must be fairly nonreactive, reliable, relatively short, valid, and be easy to score and interpret if it will be useful to the research community. Questionnaires on sensitive issues such as prejudice have an additional burden of overcoming inevitable biases in responding because of social desirability, reactivity, and unawareness of one's underlying attitudes (as in the case of aversive racists, and to a lesser extent, modern and symbolic racists). As a result of these difficult measurement obstacles, some theorists have suggested that contemporary forms of prejudice cannot be measured by self-report questionnaires (Gaertner & Dovidio, 1986).

Nevertheless, many researchers have devised self-report measures of prejudice, with varying degrees of success. Although far too many exist to discuss in this chapter (for a comprehensive review of published prejudice measures, see Biernat & Crandall, 1999), we will focus on the most popular measure of prejudice, the Modern Racism Scale (MRS; McConahay, Hardee, & Batts, 1981; McConahay, 1986). McConahay (1986) designed the MRS to measure the subtle form of anti-black prejudice that characterizes prejudice today, according to Modern Racism Theory. The scale comprises seven statements to which the respondent indicates his or her agreement or disagreement on a 5-point Likert scale. Agreement with the items indicates the presence of modern racist beliefs, such as the belief that discrimination is no longer a problem in the United States, that blacks get unfair special treatment in government policy, and that they should not "push themselves where they are not wanted." The inability to empathize with the plight of blacks is also an indicator of modern racism (as in the reverse-scored item "It is easy to understand the anger of black people in America"). To avoid reactivity, social desirability, and demand characteristics, most researchers also include many more filler items (that tap similar social attitudes) randomly interspersed between the seven MRS items, to conceal the true purpose of the measure. The reader will note that the basis for the items is quite similar to the underlying beliefs that underlie the symbolic and aversive racism theories. For that reason, many researchers have used the MRS as a measure of general subtle prejudice that characterizes some whites' attitudes toward blacks in contemporary American society.

Of course, one of the first questions researchers ask about any measure is, "is it valid and reliable?" McConahay (1986) reported that the test–retest reliability was between .72 to .93, and that it showed fair convergent validity (Biernat & Crandall, 1999). The problem with the MRS is that it does not show very good discriminant validity. Specifically, it does not fail to correlate with measures of a different construct, old-fashioned racism (McConahay [1986] reported correlations between old-fashioned and modern racism between .33 and .66). Other researchers have found similar high correlations (.65, Weigel & Howes, 1985; .86, Swim, Aikin, Hall, & Hunter, 1995) between measures of old-fashioned racism and scores on the MRS (Weigel & Howes, 1985). Another problem with the MRS is that, contrary to McConahay's (1986) assertions, it does appear to be reactive. Jackson and Fazio (1995) found that when high-prejudice individuals (as indicated by earlier MRS scores) completed the MRS again with a black experimenter, they shifted their responses on the MRS to appear less prejudiced. Those who were given the MRS by a white experimenter showed no significant attitude shift. The researchers suggest that the shift in the black experimenter condition indicates the reactivity of the scale, and that subjects respond in socially desirable ways in certain situations.

Priming and Reaction Times—The True Measure?

For the reasons above, the MRS has become less popular as a means to measure prejudice. Researchers have recently investigated the merits of reaction-time methods for measuring prejudice. Reaction-time measures are desirable in assessing racial attitudes, because they bypass the controlled cognitions that may mask underlying negative racial affect (Dovidio & Gaertner, 1996). Research by Gaertner (Dovidio & Gaertner, 1993; Gaertner & McLaughlin, 1983) found that white participants were more likely to associate positive characteristics with the racial category word *white* than with the word *black*. However, there were no differences in association between negative characteristics and the group labels. In other words, this research supports the research discussed earlier in this chapter, which concluded that though many whites are still prejudiced against blacks, the prejudice seems to take the more mild form of favoritism toward the ingroup, rather than outgroup derogation.

Consider a recent compelling series of studies reported by Fazio, Jackson, Dunton, and Williams (1995). Fazio et al. wanted to examine the relationship between participant MRS scores and reaction times to (positive and negative) words that follow photos of faces of different races. Based on earlier research by Fazio and his colleagues (Fazio, Sanbonmatsu, Powell, & Kardes, 1986), Fazio et al. reasoned that people tend to associate negative or positive words and traits with different racial groups, and these words are automatically activated in memory on seeing a member of that group. According to the spreading-activation theory of memory, this activation should facilitate the recognition of the related words (Collins & Loftus, 1975). On presentation of a black face, the degree to which whites show faster recognition times for certain words, and not others, would indicate the types of words that are most strongly associated with blacks (the same applies with photos of individuals of other ethnicities and races).

Because activation of category-related concepts in memory is an automatic process, it cannot be corrupted by social desirability, reactivity, or other biases that taint self-report measures (Dovidio & Fazio, 1992; Fazio, 1990). Thus, if white participants show faster recognition for negative words (and not for positive words) after the black photo prime, and faster recognition times for positive words after photos of individuals of their own race, we would conclude that the individual is prejudiced against blacks and favors their own race (ingroup bias). Fazio et al. asked participants whose MRS scores were in the top and bottom 10% of the pretesting sample (i.e., the most high- and low-prejudiced individuals) to participate in a study of word meanings and recognition of faces. They randomly presented 48 photos of white, black, Asian, and Hispanic students' faces (which were obtained from volunteers before the study) to the participant for 315 milliseconds. The faces served as the prime for the subsequent presentation of trait words. Participants then saw a randomly presented trait word and were asked to press a key labeled either "good" or "bad," depending on their categorization of that trait. As shown in Figure 5.1, the results indicated that when white participants viewed a black prime, they showed greater facilitation for the recognition of negative trait words, but when they saw a white prime, they showed greater facilitation for positive trait words. This pattern did not differ between those who scored high or low on the MRS. Black participants showed the opposite result. The authors found the same results when using participants with a range of MRS scores (rather than the top & bottom 10%; Experiment 2).

Using this reaction-time measure of prejudice, Fazio et al. have demonstrated a strong case for the idea that the MRS is a highly reactive and blatant measure of prejudice. When high and low MRS scorers took the reaction-time measure of prejudice, the results indicated that *both low- and high-prejudice* whites showed stronger negative attitudes linked to the black category, and stronger positive attitudes linked to the white category (this finding was also supported by similar findings reported by Wittenbrink, Judd, & Park, 1997). Finally, the data obtained in Fazio et al.'s second experiment revealed that participants' scores on the MRS were not correlated with the reaction-time measure of prejudice. This indicates that that two measures are not assessing the same

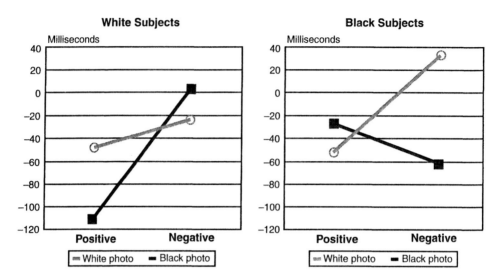

FIGURE 5.1 **In group favoritism and priming.** In a series of compelling experiments, Fazio and his colleagues showed that when we think of our own group (primed by a photograph of a person from our ingroup), we are quicker to recognize positive trait words, and slower to recognize negative trait words. However, when participants were primed with a photograph from a member of their outgroup, they were faster at recognizing negative trait words and slower to recognize positive trait words. The effect holds for both black and white participants. This research suggests that activation of one's ingroup category facilitates cognitive access to positive information, and activation of outgroup categories facilitates cognitive access to negative information. Note: the higher the mean recognition time as plotted on the *y* axis (the less negative, in terms of milliseconds), the greater the facilitation of the prime for recognition of the trait words. (Copyright © 1995 by the American Psychological Association. Reprinted with permission.)

construct. Even stranger than the lack of correspondence is the fact that the MRS and the reaction-time measure were weakly ($r = 0.28$, $p < 0.06$) *negatively correlated.* That is, those with the lowest (least prejudiced) scores on the MRS showed the highest amount of negativity (fastest facilitation for most negative traits after the black prime) on the reaction-time measure.

Rather than being a nonreactive measure of prejudice toward blacks, the MRS should be thought of as a measure of one's *willingness* to express negative racial attitudes (Biernat & Crandall, 1999; Jackson & Fazio, 1995). What can we conclude from the fact that both high- and low-prejudiced persons (as indicated by MRS scores) showed facilitation for negative trait words after the black prime? Does that mean that all whites are prejudiced toward blacks? No. Recall that the MRS measures one's willingness to express negative feelings toward blacks, whereas the reaction-time measure used in Fazio et al.'s research seems to measure something else. Despite Fazio et al.'s assertions that reaction-time measures are indeed a true indicator of prejudice, the reaction-time methodology appears to be assessing the strength of the association between the category and associated traits. Faster facilitation to various words gives the researcher an indication of the strength of the associations, and the most-facilitated words after the category prime give an indication of the content of the stereotype that the individual has for that prime category.

The fact that these two measures are tapping different constructs would account for the lack of correlation between them in Fazio et al.'s Study 2, but it would not account for the weak negative correlation (the negative correlation is an odd finding, and one that Fazio et al. do not attempt to interpret). This explanation would also account for the finding that both high- and low-prejudiced whites showed more facilitation to negative words after the black prime than with the white prime. Specifically, the results indicate simply that whites are more likely to associate negative traits with blacks. As Devine (1989) has demonstrated, however, there is an important difference between knowledge of the stereotype and personally believing or endorsing the stereotype. She found that high- and low-prejudiced whites had the stereotype automatically activated on presentation of the category, but that low-prejudiced individuals quickly suppressed the expression of such stereotypes, whereas high-prejudiced individuals showed no attempt to suppress expression of their stereotypes. Thus, knowing the stereotype does not mean that one personally believes or endorses the prejudice.

If reaction-time measures give us a glimpse into the content of the individual's stereotype of a group, and the strength of the association of the traits and the category, are they therefore an inappropriate method for measuring prejudice? Maybe not. Lepore and Brown (1997) found that although high- and low-prejudiced individuals did not differ in the content of the traits associated with blacks, they did differ in the strength of the associations between the category blacks and positive and negative traits (see also Wittenbrink et al., 1997). They speculate that this difference between high- and low-prejudiced individuals is caused by the facilitating and inhibiting effects of the category on related positive and negative words. Lepore and Brown suggest that high-prejudiced whites tend to have stronger associations between the category label and negative characteristics, and that though their associations between the category black and positive traits are activated, these are inhibited. For low-prejudiced persons, the same positive and negative traits are also activated on thinking of the category, but the associations for positive traits are facilitated in recognition whereas the associations for negative traits are inhibited. Thus, Lepore and Brown propose that high- and low-prejudiced persons have the same positive and negative traits associated with a category, but that the strength of these specific associations differs between the two groups because of different patterns of facilitation and inhibition.

If this sounds similar to the model proposed by Devine (1989), it is, with one important difference. Both models (and the results of the Fazio et al. [1995] studies) suggest that high- and low-prejudiced persons know the stereotypic information associated with a given racial outgroup (in these experiments, the outgroup was blacks, but the model can apply to other outgroups). Devine says that low-prejudiced persons consciously inhibit the activated stereotype. Lepore and Brown (1997) say that the inhibition of the stereotype also occurs, but that it is automatic (nonconscious). Which approach best accounts for the differences between high- and low-prejudiced persons? At this point, the evidence is mixed, and there is a need for much more future research on the subject before we can arrive at a definitive conclusion.

As measures of the content and strength of stereotypic information associated with outgroups, reaction time measures are perhaps the best method researchers have today. However, as measures of prejudice, much more research is needed on reaction time measures to demonstrate the conditions under which high- and low-prejudiced persons can be distinguished in terms of their negative feelings toward the outgroup, and not only in terms of the strength of the associated traits with the outgroup category. Currently, researchers must infer the presence of prejudice (negative feelings toward the group) from knowing that a given person has stronger associations between negative traits and the category. However, to be more confident about an individual's prejudice, paper-and-pencil measures, and even reaction-time measures, should be correlated with the individual's verbal and nonverbal behaviors in intergroup contexts. As Devine et al. (1996) cogently argue, researchers currently know very little about the dynamics of the interracial interaction. By understanding the verbal and nonverbal behavior of the majority and minority member in such a context, we can begin to understand the reciprocal nature of negative expectancy confirmation, misattribution, and misunderstandings that perpetuate prejudices. Such a context also provides for a more externally valid measure of outgroup prejudice.

Summary: Is There Such a Thing as Modern Prejudice?

Over the last century, prejudice has evolved in the way people express it. Before the mid-1960s, expressions of prejudice were openly expressed in the United States. America was overtly hostile toward equal rights for women, anything dealing with homosexuality, and, most notably, blacks. Indeed, this prejudice was so entrenched in society that it was condoned by our government in its policy of "separate but equal" segregation of schools, restaurants, and other public places into "white" and "colored" facilities. However, with the great social changes in the 1960s, such open prejudice was no longer tolerated in society. Researchers noticed that with these changes, the old methods of measuring prejudice were no longer adequate to ascertain a person's level of prejudice. We discussed how researchers came up with new ways to measure prejudice, which revealed that some people who *said* they were not prejudiced on self-report measures of prejudice, were indeed quite prejudiced, as indicated by the new measures. Earlier in this chapter, we left unanswered the question of whether current expressions of prejudice represent a different type of prejudice from the prejudice expressed in the past. That is, are theories of "modern prejudice" describing a qualitatively different type of prejudice from old-fashioned prejudice, or are they describing new ways to measure the more subtle contemporary versions of old-fashioned prejudice?

This is a difficult question, and one that researchers are still attempting to answer. One step in this direction comes from a paper by Kleinpenning and Hagendoorn (1993). They suggest that when one looks at the components of attitudes toward ethnic groups (such as stance on segregation, rights for outgroups, threat from outgroup members, and adjustment of outgroups), people can be reliably distinguished along a continuum of attitudes toward ethnic groups. That is, the nonracist represents the absence of negative attitudes toward other ethnic groups, followed (in increasing order of negativity toward ethnic outgroups) by aversive racists, symbolic racists, and biological (old-fashioned) racists. Given the consistent findings of strong correlations between the various measures of "modern prejudice" and "old-fashioned" prejudice, Kleinpenning and Hagendoorn's model accounts for the correlations by suggesting that these measures *should* be correlated to some degree because they are all assessing various degrees of prejudice toward ethnic outgroups. Kleinpenning and Hagendoorn suggest that today's prejudice is not independent of, but rather is a first step toward, old-fashioned prejudice. Whether old-fashioned, overt, and openly hostile, or covert, subtle, and virtually undetectable, research shows that each type of prejudice still results in negative behavior, affect, and cognitions about the stereotyped target, and that of course can have negative influences on the individuals who are targets of such prejudice. In the next chapter, we turn to an in-depth examination of how prejudice, both overt and subtle, affects those who are targets of prejudice.

GLOSSARY

aversive racism   Anti-black prejudice in individuals who believe they are very egalitarian, but who also have negative feelings and attitudes toward blacks. This prejudice is more likely to be expressed as ingroup favoritism, rather than outgroup derogation.

bogus pipeline   Technique for assessing attitudes that reduces social desirability, but is very labor-intensive. The participant is connected to a device similar to a lie detector, and the participant is led to believe that the device will give the experimenter an accurate reading of the participant's true attitudes.

demand characteristics   Aspects of the experimental situation that lead the participant to form their own hypotheses about what the experiment is about (and what behavior the experimenter would like them to show).

modern racism   A subtle form of prejudice that is only expressed when the individual believes it is safe, acceptable, or easily rationalizable.

social desirability   Presenting oneself and one's attitudes as very positive, to give the most socially acceptable attitude/behavior, even if it deviates from one's true attitudes.

symbolic racism   Anti-black prejudice originating out of the belief that blacks violate traditional American values.

DISCUSSION QUESTIONS

1. Do you believe that stereotyping and prejudice (any type, racial, ethnic, gender, age, etc.) has declined or increased over the last century? What do you think accounts for the increase/decrease?

2. What are the legitimizing myths that modern racists hold about blacks? In what ways do they rationalize their prejudice toward blacks?

3. What, in your opinion, is the best way to measure prejudice and endorsement of stereotypes?

4. What are the strengths and weaknesses of Fazio's reaction-time measure of prejudice?

5. In your opinion, will prejudice and stereotyping always be a part of our society, and not decrease, but merely change focus or form? Why?

INTERNET RESOURCES

departments.colgate.edu/psychology/web/dovidio.htm home page of Dr. John Dovidio, a leading researcher on prejudice, discrimination, and stereotyping

www.udel.edu/psych/fingerle/sgaertner.htm home page of Dr. Sam Gaertner, another leading prejudice researcher

jones.socialpsychology.org Internet site for Dr. James Jones, a prominent prejudice researcher and author of the excellent book, *Prejudice and Racism* (1997)

www.psych.indiana.edu/cogsci/fazio.html home page of Dr. Russell Fazio, prominent social cognition researcher

CHAPTER

11 Experiencing Prejudice

In the search for understanding the processes that lead to the formation, maintenance, and reduction of stereotypes and prejudice, researchers have taken a certain view of the process that is implicit in one underlying common fact about all the writings, experiments, and theorizing that characterized the research: prejudice originated and was maintained within the majority perceiver of the minority target. It is a fairly intuitive notion to think that if a perceiver holds prejudice toward a target, and if we want to understand the processes that lead to the formation, maintenance, and reduction of that prejudice, we need to understand more about that perceiver. Indeed, this is how much of the research literature has approached prejudice and stereotyping.

We know much about how various personality characteristics are more likely to foster prejudice (Adorno et al., 1950), and how various affective states (Bodenhausen, 1993), expectancies (Devine, Evett, & Vasquez-Suson, 1996), cognitive capacity (Mackie & Worth, 1991), and motivational (Isen & Simmonds, 1978) deficits can lead to increased reliance on stereotypes in social judgments. However, as Devine et al. (1996) note, this literature only gives us an incomplete picture of the context in which stereotyping occurs. Stereotyping and prejudice are not processes that involve a perceiver regarding an inactive target of stereotyping. Rather, stereotyping and prejudice occur in a dynamic social context involving the perceiver and target reacting to each other. It is a two-way street, involving feedback from the target that often confirms the expectations of the perceiver, and the perceiver's behavior then often confirms the expectations of the target. This is discussed in detail later, but suffice it to say that it is important, if we want to more thoroughly understand stereotyping and prejudice, that we consider the perspective of the target in this social interaction. This chapter explores what it means to be the target of prejudice and stereotyping. What effect does it have on one's motivations, expectancies, self-esteem, and approach to interactions with members of the stereotyping majority? The chapter also explores how the target's expectations influence the perceiver in the social context, and how each individual's expectations bias the way they view the social interaction, such that they emerge from the situation with their stereotypes of the other newly confirmed, and their prejudices strengthened.

Social Stigma

Suppose I asked you, "Have you always been 'normal'?" Your reply may likely be, "What do you mean by 'normal'?" By 'normal' I mean 'mainstream' in your attitudes, dress, appearance, and personality. Normal in that these aspects of yourself are not extreme in any respect, such that you 'fit in' with the majority of society at any given point in your life. When I put it that way, it is likely that you might have a difficult time answering my initial question in the affirmative. At some point in our lives, it is likely that we have *all* been unusual in some respect. Perhaps you had a leg brace as a child, or wore glasses, or wore a funny-looking hat during winter (because it was the only one you had), or you had a bad case of acne. Perhaps you were quite short, or your pituitary glad was active early, and you were significantly taller than your peers, or maybe you were brighter or less bright compared with your peers. The examples are endless.

The point, for our purposes in this chapter, is to think back to those times, to remember as vividly as you can, how people regarded your "uniqueness." How were you treated, and how did it make you feel? How did others' treatment influence your self-esteem and your attitudes toward those others? It is likely that the treatment from others was not especially positive, and this probably made you feel negatively toward those others, and negatively about yourself. No one likes to be the subject of such negative evaluations from others. That is precisely why so many people try to "fit in" with the majority, so they will not be singled out for ridicule or treated negatively by others. Such treatment is fairly overt among children, who—not learning socially sophisticated methods of expressing disapproval—have no compunction about telling everyone and the individual in question about the target's deficiencies (sometimes entailing laughter, cruel jokes, or physical hostility). Among adults, those negative evaluations may take the form of subtle negative comments, rude behavior, or other subtle expressions of prejudice. For many people, these unusual aspects about them are temporary (for example, wearing braces on your teeth, or having acne), and they are no longer subject to ridicule as time goes on. But for others, being the object of negative evaluations from society is something they deal with each day of their lives.

Noted sociologist Erving Goffman (1963) referred to the unusual characteristics that engender negative evaluations as being indicators of *stigma.* The stigmatized person is one who is "reduced in our minds from a whole and usual person to a tainted, discounted one" (Goffman, 1963, p. 3). Stigmas are characteristics that "mark" the individual as "deviant, flawed, limited, spoiled or generally undesirable" (Jones, Farina, Hastorf, Markus, Miller, Scott, & French, 1984, p. 8). The reader will note that stigma encompasses all of the more familiar situations in which prejudice is shown (e.g., racial, religious, gender, age, sexual orientation), but it also covers any physical, behavioral, or psychological marker that elicits negative evaluation from society. Goffman denoted three types of stigmas: "abominations of the body" (physical deformities, being overweight, etc.; Crandall, 1994), "blemishes of individual character" (e.g., drunkenness), and "tribal stigmas of race, nation, and religion" (e.g., prejudice against another race; p. 4).

Although researchers know much about how nonstigmatized persons view stigmatized individuals (e.g., Heatherton, Kleck, Hebl, & Hull, 2000; Jones, 1997a), comparatively little research has been conducted on the experiences of the stigmatized person, and how stigmatized and nonstigmatized individuals regard each other in social interactions. This chapter explores in some detail the extant research that has addressed the problem of understanding how the stigmatized are influenced by prejudice, stereotyping, and discrimination. Ways to understand how prejudice is maintained and, indeed, reinforced as a result of intergroup interactions is addressed. Finally, the chapter concludes with a look at unanswered questions and empirical challenges prejudice researchers should address in the future.

Group Identification

Previous research indicates that individuals faced with external threats (such as prejudice) show stronger ingroup identification (Janis, 1968). Research has confirmed this general effect with Jewish persons (Dion & Earn, 1975; Radke, Trager, & Davis, 1949; Rollins, 1973), blacks (Cross & Strauss, 1998), and women (Swim & Hyers, 1997, as cited in LaFrance & Woodzicka, 1998). However, subsequent research has indicated that whether the individual has already strongly personally identified with their stigmatized group will have a major impact on the degree to which that individual disassociates from the group. Doosje and Ellemers (1997) found that people differ in the degree to which they identify with their stigmatized group. "High identifiers" are much more likely to associate themselves with their group, even when (and especially when) it has a negative image. High identifiers derive much of their self-esteem from their identification as a group member. They are much more likely to seek collective strategies to group threat. They tend to make it clear that they are fully committed, loyal group members, who are (to coin a phrase) in it for the long run. "Low identifiers," however, are much more likely to disassociate themselves from the group, especially when the group has a negative image. They feel no special affinity toward, or self-esteem from, their group. Doosje and Ellemers conclude that low identifiers "seem quite prepared to let the group fall apart" when the group is threatened or has a negative image (p. 271). Low identifiers are thus much more individualistic and opportunistic in that they will only identify themselves with the group when it would positively affect their social identity.

Stereotype Threat

For most groups, there exist a few (perhaps more) widely known stereotypes. From early on, children learn these stereotypes (Jones, 1997a) and are aware of how their own group and other groups are sometimes negatively viewed by others (Rosenberg, 1979). In addition to the negative implications that stereotypes of one's group have for one's self-concept and self-image, such stereotypes represent another problem with which one must contend. Specifically, individuals in stereotyped groups often find themselves ever-vigilant to not behave in ways that confirm stereotypes about one's group. Doing so would appear to lend evidence to support the legitimacy of the stereotype in eyes of others, and even in the individual's view of himself or herself. Steele and Aronson (1995) refer to this situation as *stereotype threat*. On the face of it, it would seem that if you were aware of the stereotype, and you decided to behave in ways that disconfirm the stereotype, you would behave in that counterstereotypical fashion, and that would be it. No problem, and no hassle. However, research indicates that, for many stereotypes, the negative implications of confirming the stereotype are important enough that they can impair one's ability to behave in a counter-stereotypic way (Baumeister, 1984; Steele & Aronson, 1995; Steele, 1997; Aronson, Quinn, & Spencer, 1998). In other words, the anxiety that one feels in thinking about possibly confirming the stereotype can be so debilitating that it actually impairs one's performance on the stereotype-relevant dimension, thereby having the paradoxical effect of confirming the stereotype.

In the research on this relatively new area of inquiry, most of the attention has focused on stereotypes that revolve around intellectual ability and performance. For blacks, a common stereotype suggests that they perform poorly compared with others on measures of intellectual ability (Steele, 1992). As Cose (1993) describes:

> In some places things are much as they were when I was a schoolboy and heard one teacher say that Blacks had "lazy tongues," and another announce that he didn't care whether anyone learned anything since he was getting paid anyway, and yet another explain, when challenged over handing out brain-deadening assignments, that kids like us were incapable of handling difficult material. Scholastic attainment may not generally be discouraged in so brutal a manner, but legions of Black kids still have it instilled in them that they are not particularly intelligent; and at least partly as a result of such indoctrination, many give up on academic achievement at a very young age (p. 162).

In fact, statistics on results of standardized aptitude and intelligence tests over the decades suggest that blacks consistently average about 15 points less on such measures compared with whites (Loehlin, Lindzeg, & Spuhler, 1975). Most researchers on the reasons for this gap agree that it is due to socioeconomic disadvantages that blacks experience that affect their academic environment, cultural biases embedded into standardized intelligence tests, as well as discrimination and prejudice that they face from others (Schiele, 1991). However, this does not explain the finding that even when blacks and whites have the same preparation, blacks still achieve less (i.e., poorer subsequent GPA, time to graduation, etc.; Steele & Aronson, 1995). Steele and Aronson (1995; see Fig. 6.1 on p. 134) suggest that the debilitating effects of stereotype threat may account for the gap in subsequent achievement between similar-scoring blacks and whites. Their research supported this idea. They found that when black participants believed that a difficult verbal test was a measure of their intellectual ability (compared with those who were not told this), they underperformed compared with whites in the ability-diagnostic condition (intellectual ability) but performed as well as whites in the nondiagnostic condition. They also found that just making the stereotype salient impaired the performance of blacks on the task, even in nondiagnostic conditions (see Fig. 6.2 on p. 135).

Research with women reveals similar results, implicating the stereotype threat effects. For women, a commonly held stereotype has been that they are less capable in science and mathematics (Aronson et al., 1998). Quinn and Spencer (1996, as cited by Aronson et al., 1998) manipulated the diagnosticity of a math examination (i.e., by either telling participants that the math examination was diagnostic or not diagnostic of their math ability) for male and female participants with matched math backgrounds and skills (as measured by their SAT scores and calculus grades). Results indicated that when women believed that the examination was diagnostic, they performed poorly compared with their male counterparts. When women believed it was not diagnostic, they performed as well as the other male participants. Simply completing a math test in a group in which she is the sole woman (with two other men) seems to make salient the stereotype of women's poor math performance, and women in these situations do indeed perform poorly compared with women doing a math test in a group of two other women (Inzlicht & Ben-Zeev, 2000). In addition to race and gender, researchers have also examined the stereotype threat that is attached to being poor. When low-socioeconomic-status individuals believe that they

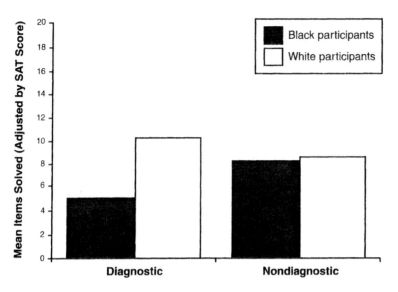

FIGURE 6.1 Stereotype threat and performance on a difficult verbal test. When Steele and Aronson presented black and white students with a test of verbal ability, the way the test was introduced to the black student had an impact on his/her performance. Steele and Aronson told half of the participants that the test was diagnostic of intellectual ability (stereotype threat condition) and the other half were told that it was a problem-solving task unrelated to intellectual ability. Statistically controlling for participants' SAT verbal scores, Figure 6.1 shows that blacks and whites performed equally in the nondiagnostic condition. However, when blacks believed there was a danger that their performance on the test potentially could confirm a stereotype about blacks (the diagnostic condition), the anxiety associated with that belief impaired their performance relative to whites in the same condition. (Copyright © 1995 by the American Psychological Association. Reprinted with permission.)

might confirm a common stereotype of them (specifically, that they perform poorly on measures of intellectual ability relative to those who are not poor), their performance suffers on perceived diagnostic measures relative to those who are not poor. When the examination is seen as nondiagnostic, they do just as well as their more affluent peers (Croizet & Claire, 1998).

In an interesting twist on the stereotype threat research, Cheryan and Bodenhausen (2000) examined the influence of salient *positive* stereotypes on one's task performance. That is, if the stereotype about your group is that you do especially well on a task, could that stereotype potentially enhance or impair one's performance? Cheryan and Bodenhausen focused on the stereotype that Asians have a special aptitude for mathematical problems. Asian American women were exposed to an "identity salience" manipulation, in which they were to complete a survey about either their ethnic group (e.g., "Overall, my race is considered good by others"), their gender, or their individual identity. They then completed a test of math skills. The results showed that when participants' ethnic identity was made salient, their math performance was significantly worse compared with when their personal identity or gender identity was made salient. These results suggest that the

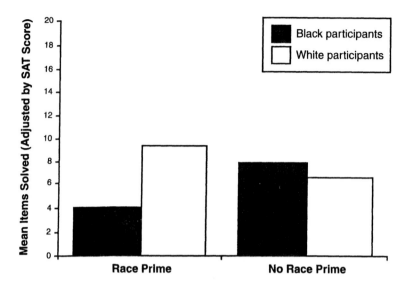

FIGURE 6.2   The slightest prime unleashes stereotype threat. Steele and Aronson also found that it does not take much priming at all to activate feelings of stereotype threat. In one variation of the study described in Figure 6.1, Steele and Aronson did not tell participants anything about the diagnostic nature of the verbal test. However, they primed half of the participants to think about their race merely by having the participants indicate their race in a demographic questionnaire. That simple difference was enough to cause black participants to feel stereotype threat when doing the verbal test, and, as can be seen in Figure 6.2, their performance suffered compared to that of whites who also had their race primed. (Copyright © 1995 by the American Psychological Association. Reprinted with permission.)

pressure to confirm a positive stereotype can be just as debilitating to one's performance as is the pressure to disconfirm a negative stereotype about one's ingroup.

Accumulated evidence indicates support for the notion that stereotypes about one's group can impair one's performance on salient, ego, and identity-relevant tasks (Stone, Lynch, Sjomeling, & Darley, 1999). Paradoxically, although stereotype-threatened individuals are motivated to do well on the tasks, they tend to be inefficient in their work, in large part because their attention is split between their alternating assessment of the correct answers to the task and their worry that their performance may confirm a stereotype for their group (Steele & Aronson, 1995). Still, why do stereotype-threatened individuals who score similarly to non–stereotype-threatened persons (e.g., European Americans) on intelligence and aptitude tests achieve less than their European American counterparts? Steele (1992, 1997) suggests that the answer may lie in a process called *disidentification.* In disidentification, individuals disengage their identity from the achievement domain in question, such that their self-esteem and sense of self-competence is preserved and shielded from the negative effects of associating identity with performance on a stereotype-relevant dimension (Aronson et al., 1998). In practical terms, then, a woman may disidentify with achievement in science and mathematics, and blacks may disidentify from academics (Major, Spencer, Schmader, Wolfe, &

A stereotype about women is that they are not as adept as men are at mathematical and scientific reasoning. In the 1980s, in what was to bring a tremendous amount of negative publicity, toy maker Mattel released a talking Barbie doll that had a repertoire of a few sentences, one of which was "Math is hard!" Following a storm of controversy after the doll hit the store shelves, Mattel quickly removed that particular Barbie doll.

Crocker, 1998; Osborne, 1995). Again, the disidentification process allows the stigmatized to retain their self-esteem.

This is an interesting point that bears some elaboration. Intuitively, it would seem clear that people who are stigmatized should have lower overall self-esteem compared with nonstigmatized persons. Much research suggests that this is not the case, however. In fact, research suggests that blacks, for example, show self-esteem that is as high as or higher than that of European Americans (Crocker & Major, 1989; Porter & Washington, 1979). Interestingly, although the stigmatized are more likely than the nonstigmatized to show disidentification, they are less likely to see the stereotype-threat dimension (e.g., academics) as unimportant (Crocker & Major, 1989; Major & Schmader, 1998). Thus, although disidentified stigmatized individuals agree that the stereotype-threat dimension is important, it is not important *for them* and for their self-identity.

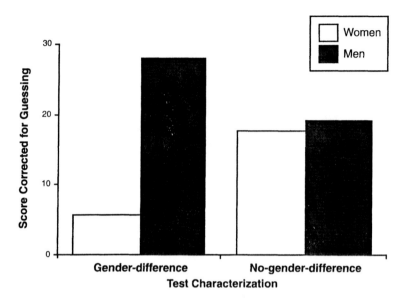

FIGURE 6.3 **The experience of stereotype threat for women.** Steele and his colleagues also examined stereotype threat among women. As with the experiment procedure described for Figure 6.1, Steele et al. invited males and females who were good at math, and who considered math ability to be an important part of their identity, to take a difficult math test. For half of the participants, the test was described as generally showing gender differences in performance on the test. As can be seen in Figure 6.3, when women believed the test did not show gender differences in performance, they performed just as well as men. However, when women were led to believe that males and females perform differently (activating the stereotype about women not being as adept at math as were men), their performance on the test was much worse than men in the same condition. (Copyright © 1995 by the American Psychological Association. Reprinted with permission.)

What might trigger disidentification? Major and Schmader (1998) suggest that, by either *devaluing* the importance of the stereotype-threat domain or *discounting* the validity and self-diagnosticity of outcomes on the stereotype-threat dimension, the stigmatized can psychologically disengage from the stereotype-threat dimension and protect their self-esteem. Indeed, some disenchanted blacks may devalue academic achievement by derogating other blacks who pursue achievement in academics by saying they are "acting white" (Fordham, 1988; Fordham & Ogbu, 1986). In other words, the belief is that achievement in academics is something that whites can accomplish, and blacks who aspire to academic achievement are "selling out" and disidentifying themselves from their black identity.

Indeed, some academics have suggested that blacks who achieved academic success did so by adopting behaviors and attitudes that distanced themselves from their culture of origin, and that this results in increased depression, anxiety, and identity confusion (Fordham, 1988; Fordham & Obgu, 1986). In a careful examination of these predictions, Arroyo and Zigler (1995) found that academically achieving blacks were indeed more likely to experience feelings of depression and anxiety compared with their peers who were not academically successful. However, achievement in academics does not necessarily lead to racial identity confusion. Arroyo and Zigler found that both high- and low-achieving blacks were more likely to negatively evaluate and psychologically distance themselves from their racial group when they believed that their group was negatively evaluated by others. Thus, paradoxically, achieving academic success can have important psychological consequences for blacks.

Some evidence suggests that these processes may arise in the individual's early teen years. Osborne (1995) found that the correlation between blacks' self-esteem and academic outcomes remained strong until about eighth grade. Then, Osborne writes, ". . . something happened to weaken their identification. . . . It is probable that the African American students . . . may begin to see the academic environment as discriminatory and lacking in rewards, and begin disidentifying" (p. 453). Steele (1997) suggests that the "something" that happened is stereotype threat. In one experiment (cited in Steele, 1997), he varied the strength of the threat that female subjects were under by telling some subjects that differences between men and women in mathematics ability was due either to genetic differences (in other words, an innate limitation of being female) or to social/learned causes (i.e., discrimination, social roles). Participants' identification with mathematics and math-related careers was measured either before or after taking a difficult math test. Results indicated that women under stronger stereotype threat (i.e., the genetic limitation females have in mathematics) tended to disidentify more with math careers than women under weak stereotype threat (see Fig. 6.3 on p. 137).

Stereotype threat has implications for how one perceives one's ingroup, and, importantly, one's relation to the ingroup. Lee and Ottati (1995) investigated how one's social identity may be affected by stereotype threats that are either consistent or inconsistent with self-perceived stereotypes about one's ingroup. According to Tajfel and Turner's Social Identity Theory (SIT; 1986), we derive our identity and self-esteem through two avenues. One is through our own accomplishments, and the other is through our group membership. SIT suggests that when one belongs to a devalued or threatened group, continued identification with the group threatens one's self-esteem. Threatened individuals may therefore disidentify with their ingroup to protect their self-esteem.

Lee and Ottati examined how Chinese participants would respond to negative stereotypic threats that are inconsistent or consistent with one's ingroup perceptions. They found that negative stereotypes that are inconsistent with the ingroup stereotype lead ingroup members to increase their perceptions of ingroup homogeneity, or solidarity/unity. That is, participants' identification with their ingroup increased. However, when participants were exposed to a negative stereotype-consistent threat (that is, partially consistent with stereotypes about Chinese), the participant had a more difficult time denying the validity of the stereotype expression. Participants protected their social identity by emphasizing that not all members of their group are characterized by the negative stereotype. In doing so, participants were emphasizing more ingroup heterogeneity, which may reflect a weakening identification with their ingroup as a whole (Spears, Doosje, & Ellemers, 1997).

Although this psychological disidentification may be a temporary response to a particular situation (Markus & Kunda, 1986), continued exposure to stereotype threat may lead stigmatized individuals to chronically disengage psychologically from the stereotype-threat dimension (Major & Schmader, 1998). What are the consequences for the stigmatized individual who has disidentified from the stereotype-threat domain? Disidentification can be both adaptive and maladaptive. Because of prejudice, discrimination, and disadvantage the stigmatized person may encounter in the stereotype-threat domain, disidentification can be viewed as a healthy, effective coping response that allows the individual to protect their self-concept and self-identity (Crocker, Major, & Steele, 1998; Major & Schmader, 1998). However, Steele (1997) and Major and Schmader (1998) note that the paradox of disidentification is that although it saves the self-esteem, it imperils the individual's chances for success and achievement in domains that society may regard as important.

There are ways to reduce stereotype threat. Steele (1997) suggests that it is not enough to merely prevent disidentification of stigmatized students. It is important to simultaneously enhance the individual's identification with the stereotype-threatened domain. Techniques such as Aronson's "jigsaw classroom" (see Chapter 9) can be an effective way to help students enjoy school and can lead to higher self-esteem and higher examination scores (Aronson & Bridgeman, 1979; Wolfe & Spencer, 1996). Steele (1997) suggested some additional useful strategies: optimistic student–teacher relationships, challenge instead of remediation, stress that intelligence is expandable, affirming domain belongingness, valuing multiple perspectives, having visible successful role models, and building self-efficacy.

Recent evidence suggests that such an approach may work (Steele, Spencer, Hummel, Carter, Harber, Schoem, & Nisbett, 1998, as cited in Aronson et al., 1998). Steele et al. (1998) implemented a program for the reduction of stereotype threat and enhanced domain identification for black college freshman at the University of Michigan. The researchers used three ways to reduce stereotype threat: (1) students were "honorifically recruited" for the program by emphasizing that they were bright enough to be admitted to the University of Michigan (this taps into domain belongingness); (2) students participated in weekly seminars to get to know each other and share common problems; and (3) participants attended subject master workshops that exposed them to advanced material outside the material discussed in class. Results after 4 years of the program indicated that participants had grade point averages about $4/10$ higher than nonprogram peers, and they were more likely to finish college. Interviews with participants indicated that the program did in fact reduce stereotype threat, increased domain identification, and led to better grades (Aronson et al., 1998).

Self-Esteem

It seems intuitive that those who are stigmatized quickly become aware of the negative way that many in society view them. This should have a negative effect on the self-esteem of the stigmatized. However, the data are mixed on this issue. Some research concludes that stigmatized persons suffer no damage to their self-esteem, and in some cases, their self-esteem is higher than that of nonstigmatized counterparts (Porter & Washington, 1979; Rosenberg, 1979; Simmons, Brown, Bush, & Blyth, 1978). In fact, studies have failed to show decreased self-esteem for such stigmatized groups as blacks, the physically challenged, developmentally disabled, or mentally disabled (for a review, see Crocker & Major, 1989). Conversely, other studies have indicated that some stigmatized individuals (e.g., overweight persons; Crocker, Cornwell, & Major, 1993) do suffer lower self-esteem.

What seems to account for why some stigmatized individuals are able to protect their self-esteem and others seem to feel miserable about themselves has much to do with the perceived controllability (and hence, the justifiability) of the stigma (Crocker et al., 1998). Those individuals who believe that their stigmatizing condition is controllable (and thus indicates some personal flaw on their part) may be more likely to feel that negative evaluations of themselves are justified and will be more likely to feel lower self-esteem. However, believing that one's stigma is uncontrollable will lead the stigmatized individual to resist the "blame" for the stigma, to attribute negative evaluations to prejudice, and to maintain self-esteem (Crocker & Major, 1994).

A comprehensive meta-analysis of 261 comparisons of self-esteem differences between whites and blacks showed that, in general, blacks tend to have higher self-esteem than whites (Gray-Little & Hafdahl, 2000). Although this finding has been reached in earlier studies, the authors note that past researchers would disregard the findings as flawed, because of the assumption that members of a stereotyped group *had* to have lower self-esteem as a result of how the larger society held negative views of blacks, but not of whites. Gray-Little and Hafdahl further suggest that the reason for the higher self-esteem of blacks lies in the fact that they do not (as was assumed) base their self-worth on the way others view them. If they did, it might be the case that they would feel more negatively about themselves. However, Gray-Little and Hafdahl found that the reference groups for blacks are other blacks, and not society. They are a distinctive minority group, and by embracing that disctinctiveness and their positive ethnic/racial identity, they maintain as high, and often higher, self-esteem relative to their Caucasian counterparts.

Another explanation for the inconsistent findings concerning the influence of prejudice on the self-esteem of the target of prejudice centers on a problem with the way researchers have conceptualized and measured self-esteem. In a recent analysis, Crocker and Quinn (2000) argued that researchers assumed that self-esteem was a stable aspect of personality, and that when the target of prejudice would experience prejudice, stereotypes, or discrimination, they would internalize the shame or psychological pain, and this then would damage the individual's self-esteem. However, the literature on self-esteem do not support these assumptions. Crocker and Quinn make the compelling case that it is more accurate to conceptualize self-esteem as a kind of "working self-esteem," which is multiply determined and constructed by the situational, motivational, and interpersonal factors in a given situation, and by one's salient beliefs and values at that time. Such a conceptualization would account well for the inconsistency in the self-esteem studies, and it is important to continue research on this intriguing perspective to examine whether it holds up to empirical and theoretical scrutiny, and to ascertain its parameters with regard to the data.

Denial of Discrimination

Other research has shown another way by which stigmatized individuals maintain their self-esteem. Researchers have found that, often, stigmatized persons are able to deny that they have been personally discriminated against, or that (because of their stigma) they have suffered prejudice, discrimination, or other mistreatment (Crosby, 1984). This denial of personal discrimination has been found in blacks (Abeles, 1976) and women (Crosby, 1984), in addition to other minority groups. What is especially interesting about these data is that the stigmatized person acknowledges that their group suffers discrimination and prejudice in society, but they have not personally had such negative experiences. Such a disconnect (or cognitive distortion) allows the stigmatized person to avoid the uncomfortable reality that the world may not be a just or fair place (Lerner, 1980), and that their life may be negatively (and seemingly unavoidably) affected by their stigma (Crosby, 1984). Given the negative implications of believing the latter two statements about the world, it is easy to understand why stigmatized persons would deny personal discrimination. Such a perspective appears to hold no negative psychological, emotional, or adjustment consequences, and it may indeed be an adaptive way to deal with the unfair treatment one often receives as a result of being a member of a stigmatized group.

In a compelling line of recent experiments, Taylor and his colleagues (Ruggiero & Taylor, 1995; Ruggiero & Taylor, 1997; Taylor, Wright, & Porter, 1994; Taylor, Wright, Moghaddam, & Lalonde, 1990) have explored the factors that underlie the denial of personal discrimination (what they term the "personal/group discrimination discrepancy"). Ruggiero and Taylor (1995) suggest that the explanation of denial for this discrepancy may be premature. Their research indicated that situational ambiguity is an important determining factor in whether group members perceive personal discrimination. Women in two experiments received negative feedback and were led to believe that their evaluator was or was not prejudiced against women. When it was certain that they had been discriminated against because of their membership in a stigmatized group, participants attributed their failure to discrimination. However, when the reasons for their failure were ambiguous, women minimized the possibility of discrimination and tended to attribute their failure to themselves. Subsequent research with women, blacks, and Asians supported these findings.

Ruggiero and Taylor (1995) speculate that minimizing the possibility of discrimination is a two-edged sword. It results in a hit to one's self-esteem (i.e., I received negative feedback because of my own failings, not because of discrimination), but it also leads to an increased feeling of personal control over one's life. In other words, if my perspective was that I was always discriminated against, and I explained all my negative outcomes in terms of discrimination, I would likely feel little control over my life and feel quite powerless to influence outcomes in my life. However, if I believed that discrimination happened only occasionally, I would feel that had much more control over events in my life (that positive and negative outcomes were due to my abilities, or lack thereof, which are things I can control).

Self-Fulfilling Prophecy

Attributing negative feedback from a nonstigmatized individual to prejudice often, but not always, works as a technique for the stigmatized to protect their self-esteem. Sometimes, the ubiquity of the stereotype about one's stigmatized group can indeed influence one's self-concept. For example, Stephan and Rosenfield (1982) analyzed several studies and literature reviews of the attitudes of blacks and whites toward their own groups and toward the other group, and found that whites' views of their own group was largely positive (with the exception of the characteristic "materialistic"), and their view of blacks was very negative (with the exception of "musical," "peace-loving," and "proud"). Blacks tended to view whites in very negative terms as well (with the exception of attributing the positive characteristics "intelligent" and "industrious" to whites). Finally, although blacks viewed their own group in positive terms, they also believed some negative stereotypes about their group (they attributed the characteristics "lazy" and "superstitious" to blacks).

What might explain the process whereby a stigmatized group comes to accept and believe some negative stereotypes about itself? One possible mechanism whereby this may occur is through a *self-fulfilling prophecy*. The self-fulfilling prophecy refers to the phenomenon whereby a perceiver's expectations about a target eventually lead that target to behave in ways that confirm those expectations (Rosenthal & Jacobson, 1968). Thus, some researchers have hypothesized that one reason for the finding that some stigmatized groups view themselves as having a small number of stereotypic, negative characteristics is that the group members have internalized the negative views of the group that the majority members (and, to a large extent, society) directly and indirectly communicate to them (Word, Zanna, & Cooper, 1974). Allport (1954) believed that this may occur in minority groups because if the minority group acknowledged that one's group had as much worth as other groups in society, it would bring about tremendous psychological discomfort in that it causes the stigmatized individual to question the structure of social reality (Crosby, 1984).

The process works as follows. The majority member's stereotype influences how they interact with the member of the minority group. These behaviors elicit behaviors that fit the majority member's initial expectancies (Hamilton & Trolier, 1986). This may be difficult to ignore if you are a member of the stigmatized group. If you are finding that your fellow stigmatized colleagues are demonstrating the stereotyped characteristics (in response to the expectancies of the nonstigmatized group, see Snyder & Swann, 1978), and you recall yourself acting the same way, it is not surprising then, that you accept as valid that your group (including you) tends to demonstrate that characteristic. In other words, faced with the evidence from within and outside the stigmatized group that points to that conclusion, the stigmatized individual may be likely to internalize that stereotype for their group.

However, note that self-fulfilling prophecies do not occur when the target is aware of the perceiver's expectations (Hilton & Darley, 1985). Although the self-fulfilling prophecy is a robust phenomenon (Rosenthal & Rubin, 1978), recent research indicates that its effect in maintaining stereotypes and eliciting stereotypic behavior in stigmatized individuals is limited. Jussim and Fleming (1996) reviewed the literature on self-fulfilling prophecy effects in intergroup interactions and found that most of the naturalistic studies show that the effect of the stereotyped expectations on the stigmatized tends to be quite small (correlation of .2, and a .2 regression coefficient). Thus, although the idea that self-fulfilling prophecies may elicit more stereotype-consistent behaviors in the stigmatized (and may even lead them to believe their group possesses some negative stereotyped characteristics), and although it is an interesting explanation for the data reported by Stephan and Rosenfield (1982), few data support it as a factor in the stereotype-relevant behavior of the stigmatized.

In sum, Major and her colleagues (Crocker & Major, 1989; Major & Schmader, 1998) suggest four ways the stigmatized can maintain their self-esteem: (1) They may attribute the negative evaluations and reactions of others to prejudice; (2) they may devalue outcomes in which their group compares poorly with other groups (recall the discussion on Stereotype Threat, above); (3) they may compare their stigmatized ingroup with other stigmatized groups, rather than with nonstigmatized groups; and (4) they may psychologically disengage their self-esteem from feedback in domains in which their group is at a disadvantage. Self-esteem in stigmatized individuals seems to be fairly resilient against the negative influence of prejudice and stereotyping from others.

Intergroup Interactions

Research has yielded little information on how the expectations and affective states of majority and minority groups in actual intergroup interactions influence their perceptions of the behavior of their interaction partner. Past research has attempted to understand the perceptions of an *imagined* intergroup interaction partner (e.g., Devine, Evett, & Vasquez-Suson, 1996; Islam & Hewstone, 1993; Stephan & Stephan, 1985). In one such experiment, Langer, Fiske, Taylor, and Chanowitz (1976) found that people experience discomfort and a desire to avoid interactions with physically different (pregnant women and physically challenged) persons, because of their conflict over whether to stare at the individual. They found that the tendency to stare at an outgroup member is primarily attributable to curiosity about a group with whom the subjects infrequently come into contact. Interestingly, people did not derogate the physically different persons, so staring (and avoidance behavior) was not due to feelings of disgust or dislike. Staring and avoidance were reduced when people had more time to get accustomed to the physically different person (via simple habituation).

However, prior research has tended to only address majority and minority groups separately. Research on the majority groups (e.g., whites, young, heterosexuals) has explored how stereotypes and prejudices arise in these individuals (to reduce or even eliminate such negative intergroup attitudes). Investigations with minority groups (e.g., blacks, homosexuals, the elderly) have examined how minority group members feel about their stigma, and how the stigma influences their self-perceptions and behavior toward others (Devine et al., 1996). However, to assess how affect, perceptions, and expectations influence how one perceives the outgroup member in an intergroup context, it is important to understand the dynamics of the intergroup interaction.

Dynamic Nature of Interactions

Devine et al. (1996) make the compelling argument that researchers today must turn their attention toward understanding the dynamic *live* interactions between majority and minority group members, and how their thoughts, feelings, and behavior both *change the interaction* and *are changed* by their perception of the interaction on a moment-by-moment basis. As I have mentioned throughout this text, much research suggests that the typical intergroup interaction is characterized by some (or a significant degree of) anxiety (see Fiske, 1998; Stephan & Stephan, 1985). The potential causes for the anxiety are different for each member in the intergroup interaction. For high-prejudiced majority members, their anxiety may be due to their discomfort (sometimes driven by strong negative feelings, such as disgust or anger) with the minority group, and their preference to avoid the minority group altogether (Devine, Monteith, Zuwerink, & Elliot, 1991; Monteith, 1993). The behaviors of the minority group individual in response to the high-prejudiced majority member are likely to be seen by the latter as supportive evidence for their stereotypes. For low-prejudiced individuals, however, it is important to distinguish between those who have had many intergroup experiences ("intergroup skilled") from those who have had little intergroup interactions ("intergroup unskilled"). Both groups are highly motivated to indicate to the minority group individual that they are not prejudiced. For the intergroup-skilled majority member, they have a good idea of how best to present their low-prejudiced self to the other individual, and they feel little or no anxiety in the interaction. This is conveyed to the minority member through a relaxed behavior and demeanor. The model contends that in this situation, the minority member is thus less likely to misinterpret the behavior of the low-prejudiced majority member as indications of underlying prejudice. Rather, the minority group member is likely to respond in similar fashion.

In the case of the low-prejudiced, intergroup-unskilled majority member, Devine and her colleagues (1996) suggest that the intergroup context holds the potential for much misunderstanding, because of the different motivations, expectations, and perceptions the majority and minority individuals bring to the interaction. The intergroup unskilled individual is in a very difficult spot. Because they have had little intergroup contact, they do not know what behaviors are appropriate, what might (unintentionally) communicate prejudice where it does not exist, and what to expect from the minority member. This uncertainty leads to anxiety. This anxiety is evidenced in more avoidant nonverbal behaviors, such as decreased eye contact, nervous laughter, and increased interpersonal distance (Word et al., 1974). These behaviors often result in conveying precisely the *opposite* impression to the minority group member: that the majority member is nervous because they are uncomfortable around minorities (because of feelings of prejudice toward the minority). According to Devine and her colleagues, at this point in the interaction, the minority member may respond with withdrawal, dismissal (being indifferent to the majority group member), or hostility. Next, if the majority individual does not perceive that the minority member's reaction is in response to perceived prejudice, they may perceive the minority's behavior as an indicator of prejudice toward the majority. Thus, intergroup interactions can often be fraught with misunderstandings, misperceptions, and reaffirmed prejudices. As is the case in social interactions in general, the perceived motives and expectations can often affect one's behavior toward the other person, and this often results in confirmed expectations and behavior confirmation (Snyder & Swann, 1978).

An experiment by Weitz (1972) shows that it is easy to see why minority group members might be suspicious about the true attitudes and motives of the majority group interaction partner. She asked 80 whites men to participate in an interaction with another individual. Racial attitudes were measured earlier (all participants selected for the study were low in self-reported prejudice toward blacks) and then the experimenter asked the partner to read some information about the partner with whom the man would interact. Among this information, the participant read that the interaction partner was either black or white. Measures of anxiety in the participant's voice (participants recorded a brief taped message) and behavior (participants were asked to choose how long and how closely they would like to work on the task with the partner, whether they would like to wait with the partner, and how far apart they should sit during the task) were taken to assess whether there was any discrepancy between attitudes and behavior. Results indicated that very favorable racial attitudes were strongly correlated with avoidant, unfriendly behavior. Thus, although they claimed to be low in prejudice, their nonverbal behavior indicated otherwise. This certainly represents a confusing situation for the minority at the receiving end of this behavior. Weitz suggests that because vocal and behavioral cues are more illustrative (more trustworthy), the minority would more than likely pay attention to these cues and respond in like fashion (i.e., negatively toward the white). Unfortunately, this would likely contribute to the white's unease and confirm their negative feelings about the minority group, and prejudice and misunderstanding would thus be perpetuated by both interactants.

What if one's stigmatized status was not obvious (e.g., being on welfare); would that individual's interaction with the nonstigmatized differ in important ways from interactions between visibly stigmatized persons and the nonstigmatized? It is an interesting question. One might imagine that, because of the immediacy and obvious nature of some stigmas (e.g., race, gender, physical characteristics), stigmatized persons in these groups would tend to be more defensive, more alert to signs that they are being treated unfairly by others. This could most assuredly influence how that person approaches interactions with a nonstigmatized person. In an experiment to examine this question, Frable, Blackstone, and Scherbaum (1990) found that, indeed, whether one's stigma is visible or "invisible" makes a big difference in that person's interaction with a nonstigmatized person. Forty-four pairs of women were unobtrusively videotaped although they waited for the experimenter to begin the study. Their interpersonal behavior, attitudes toward their interaction partner, and memory for the interaction and environment were measured. Some participants had invisible stigmas (they had been raped, they were bisexual, or they were victims of incest), and others' stigmas were visible (being more than 60 pounds overweight, they were black, or they had severe facial acne). Stigmatized persons were always paired with a nonstigmatized person. Results indicated that invisible and overtly stigmatized persons reacted differently to the interaction. Individuals with invisible stigmas were more likely to take their partner's perspective, to remember what occurred in the interaction, and to remember details about what the partner said. Those with visible stigmas were much less likely to remember the interaction details, but remembered details about the partner's appearance and the room. Frable et al. (1990) suggest that invisible deviants need to pay close attention to all information that might be relevant to exposing their condition. In that respect, paying attention to what was said is very important. Those with visible stigmas have a "spoiled identity" (Goffman, 1963), and are engaged in "damage control" in that they are more vigilant about nonverbal behavior in an effort to ascertain the true attitude of the nonstigmatized person toward their stigmatized group.

Interestingly, an analysis of the participants' perceptions of the interaction and their attitudes toward their partner showed that nonstigmatized participants showed a lot of effort, encouraging their partners to participate, and tended to talk, smile, and initiate conversation. Although the stigmatized participated, the nonstigmatized did not remember their contributions, and in fact reported that they disliked their stigmatized partner. Because the nonstigmatized person tended to devalue the contribution (or distort the extent of their own contribution and effort in the interaction), their negative preconceptions and stereotypes of the stigmatized group were more likely to be confirmed. These findings again illustrate the difficulty of overcoming stereotypes and the potential for misunderstanding in intergroup interactions.

To put it simply: if you enter a social interaction expecting it to go poorly, it is likely to turn out poorly. A study by Ickes (1984) supports this conclusion. Ickes examined the unstructured interactions of intergroup dyads composed of blacks and whites. Results revealed that although white dyad members displayed more smiling, gazing, and talking relative to their black partner, they also perceived the interaction as more stressful and uncomfortable. Ickes concluded that these results are likely attributable to differences between blacks and whites in terms of intergroup contact experiences. By virtue of their minority status, blacks are much more likely to have contact with whites (and thus should feel more comfortable in interactions with whites) than whites are to have contact with blacks. Thus, the lack of intergroup experience can lead to anxiety about the intergroup interaction. The more anxiety one feels, the more one is likely to perceive the reaction of an interaction partner to oneself as more negative (Pozo, Carver, Wellens, & Scheier, 1991).

Devine's model of the dynamic nature of intergroup interactions is an important contribution to the extant prejudice and stereotyping literature. It clearly articulates how expectations, motivations, and prejudices can influence and be influenced by the perceptions of the other individual's behavior. The model is also unique in attempting to explain how moment-to-moment changes in social interactions influence both interactants. The model is also unique in taking into account the perspective, expectations, motivations, and behavior of the minority individual in the intergroup context in an analysis of how these factors influence and are influenced by the majority individual. Understanding this dynamic process is an important next step to understanding the complexity of intergroup interactions. However, testing a dynamic model such as this in an experimental setting poses daunting challenges for the researcher. First, in a typical social psychological experiment, there usually are clearly defined causal variables, and the researcher is interested in examining the effects on participants when this variable is manipulated. In other words, there is a unidirectional linear cause and effect implicit in the experiment. Although this makes life easy for the experimenter, such experiments represent an incomplete picture of how natural social interactions affect (and are affected by) the interactant's behavior. As we have seen, the behavior of the majority (or minority) member in the intergroup context does not occur in a vacuum. Rather, behavior, expectations, and perceptions change and are changed by the other's behavior. Second, this dynamic model suggests that there is no single clear cause and effect in a continuous interaction, but that there are many many mini cause–effect sequences all encompassed in a dynamic feedback loop (for further discussion, see Nelson, 1993). For these reasons, we know very little about how the dynamics of the intergroup interaction influence the interactants. This discussion of the dynamic nature of intergroup interactions is revisited in greater detail in Chapter 10. Below, we explore how expectations, metastereotypes, and intergroup anxiety affect intergroup interactions.

Expectations

Another factor that fuels the negative expectancies for the intergroup interaction is the notion that the majority and minority have different perspectives from which they approach an understanding of the world. As Gates (1995, as cited by Jones, 1997b) suggests, "people arrive at an understanding of themselves and the world through narratives—narratives purveyed by schoolteachers, newscasters, "authorities," and all the other authors of our common sense. Counternarratives are, in turn, the means by which groups contest the dominant reality and the fretwork of assumptions that supports it . . . much of Black history is simply counternarrative" (p. 57). Thus, the narratives and counternarratives define reality for various individuals. Jones (1997b) suggests that oftentimes the reason why the minority approaches contact with the majority with negative expectations is that the majority "are strongly biased toward their own experiences, values, beliefs, and the products of their culture," whereas the minority "who have so often been victimized by those very beliefs and cultural outcroppings, mistrust them and ultimately dislike them" (p. 257).

Intergroup Anxiety

Most of the past research on reactions to the outgroup has typically involved imagining (or reading) an intergroup scenario, and how you might think and feel in such a situation. Ideally, we would like data that speak to how people react in an actual intergroup interaction (to compare the data for how we *think* we would react to how we *actually* react). Unfortunately, few studies exist that compare anticipated with actual behaviors in the intergroup context. However, the direction of the research in stereotyping seems to be changing to answer Devine et al.'s (1996) call to explore the uncharted waters of expectations and impressions of other individuals in live intergroup interactions.

In one such experiment, Hyers and Swim (1998) examined the reactions of minority and majority members in an actual intergroup interaction. Black or white women participated in triads in which they were either the sole representative of their ethnic group (i.e., one black and two whites) or they were a nonsolo member. The subject was being covertly videotaped although they worked on a group task. Each group consisted of one subject and two confederates. They were told that they were to decide 10 best occupations that would be useful for starting a new society on a desert island. They were to provide their suggestions to the group with justification for their responses. After the group task was completed, the participants were ostensibly interviewed separately (however, only the subject was interviewed; the confederates—unbeknownst to the subject—were not interviewed). The subject was told that the purpose of the study was to examine how the group interacted, and she was told that she was videotaped. After the subject agreed to authorize the use of the videotape for the study, they viewed their reactions on the videotape and wrote down their thoughts and feelings about different points of the group task. Hyers and Swim expected that, because white women likely did not have as much intergroup experience, they would feel more negative affect than black subjects. However, this hypothesis was not supported. Also, whether the subject was the sole representative of her ethnic group did not influence her reactions to the intergroup encounter. Results did indicate that white women showed decreased task attention. The authors suggested that blacks showed little affective, cognitive, or behavioral negative experiences in the intergroup interaction, attributable, in large part, to their greater intergroup experience.

Metastereotypes

Sigelman and Tuch (1997) introduced the term *metastereotype* to refer to one's perceptions of another group's stereotypes of one's group. For example, what do whites believe that blacks believe about whites? Similarly, what stereotypes about blacks do blacks believe whites endorse? If minorities share a common experience in their stigmatization at the hands of the majority, it seems logical that the majority might have a common view of how the minority group views them. To examine metastereotypes, Vorauer, Main, and O'Connell (1998) examined white Canadians' perceptions of how Aboriginal Canadians viewed them. Results indicated that white Canadians have a common negative stereotype about how they are viewed by Aboriginal Canadians, and that the belief in these metastereotypes was associated with more negative affect and expectancies regarding potential intergroup interactions. Additionally, when the white Canadians endorsed these metastereotypes, they experienced decreased self-esteem and worsened self-concept clarity.

While there is a substantial literature on the stereotypes that majority members have about minorities, we know relatively little about the perceptions of minorities of the majority members, and little to nothing about their metastereotypes. To address this issue, Sigelman and Tuch (1997) examined data gathered from the National Opinion Research Center (Davis & Smith, 1990) on blacks' perceptions of whites' views of blacks. The attitudes of blacks and whites toward each other also were examined. Finally, the degree of stereotype endorsement for each group was examined. The authors uncovered some surprising data. Two thirds of the black participants in the survey indicated that they believed that whites endorsed *every* stereotype about blacks. This is not as alarming when one considers that the researchers also found that most whites in the survey did in fact view blacks in very stereotyped terms! It appears, therefore, that the metastereotypes of the black participants were largely accurate. However, not all blacks were as strong in their belief that whites endorsed stereotypes about blacks. The data from the survey showed that black women, younger blacks, and higher-income blacks were less likely than their older, male, and lower-income counterparts to view whites as holding positive stereotypes (positive views) about blacks. Paradoxically, according to Sigelman and Tuch, it seems that those who have more contact with whites are least likely to believe that whites hold positive views of blacks.

Intergroup interactions are also doomed when the interactants are prejudiced against each other's groups. Pettigrew (1979) suggested that the prejudice of the individual taints their perception of both positive and negative behavior on the part of the disliked outgroup member. When the outgroup member does something that is perceived as negative, the prejudiced perceiver is more likely to attribute the action to internal, genetically determined factors, compared with the same act committed by an ingroup member. When the prejudiced perceiver views a positive action from the outgroup member, they will most likely attribute it to luck, exceptional effort, the "exceptional case" (in other words, *subcategorization;* Weber & Crocker, 1983).

Attributional Ambiguity

One of the most fundamental components of our social lives concerns the attempt to understand the behavior of other people. As Heider (1958) phrased it, we are all "amateur scientists," trying to arrive at reasonable explanations (theories) for the data (behavior) that confront us. In trying to understand others' behavior toward us, we are trying to decide whether the individual's actions were caused by some internal force or stable characteristic about the individual (e.g., an enduring personality trait), or a situational force (e.g., a role the individual is playing, or that the person was forced to behave in some fashion). This is the basic problem of attribution. To which of these two major causes do we attribute the other's behavior? For most people, there are always various individuals and situations that make it difficult to arrive at a clear answer to the attribution question. However, there is a difference between the stigmatized and nonstigmatized, in terms of their daily experiences in understanding the causes of other's behavior toward them. Most of the time, for most nonstigmatized individuals, this task is fairly straightforward: other people behave toward them based on the personality or performance of the nonstigmatized individual. Stigmatized individuals, however, face a different set of circumstances.

In attempting to understand the reasons for others' behavior toward them, the stigmatized are confronted with another possible causal explanation for the other's behavior: their reaction (often based on stereotypes and prejudices) to the individual's stigma. Thus, because the stigmatized are well familiar with the stereotypes and prejudices that exist about their group (Jones, 1997a), they are continually faced with deciding whether to attribute others' behavior toward them as a reaction to their stigma (and thus, to stereotypes and prejudice), or to their reaction to the aspects of the stigmatized individual that are not associated with the stigma (i.e., the stigmatized person's personality). This constant attributional calculus has been termed *attributional ambiguity* (Crocker & Major, 1989; Major & Crocker, 1993). Major and Crocker (1993) suggest that the chronic uncertainty that the stigmatized experience regarding the causes of others' behavior toward them has important consequences for the self-esteem, mood, motivation, and interpersonal behavior of the stigmatized. For example, it is one thing to believe that the store manager told you that the job they listed in the want ads has been filled, but quite another to believe that the manager told you that because of the color of your skin (or your gender, age, or the fact that you are in a wheelchair, etc.).

For many stigmatized, self-esteem can be protected by regarding the negative behavior of others toward them as a reflection of underlying prejudice, and not as a consequence of their personal traits (Goffman, 1963; Jones et al., 1984). Some readers who are members of nonstigmatized groups might respond, "That sounds like an awfully cynical way to go about life." Before you rush to such an assessment, consider the following. If you had a noticeable stigma, one that is associated with a number of negative stereotypes, you likely would come to learn, as you grew up, that this stigma was universally noticed by others. Given this, you are faced with the very difficult task of understanding what the motives are for the behavior of the nonstigmatized outgroups toward you. Given the pervasiveness of prejudice and stereotypes in American society, it is likely that most people are aware of, and some percentage of them believe, stereotypes about your group. The assessment you need to make is a probability assessment (Fiske & Taylor, 1991; Kahneman, Slovic, & Tversky, 1982). Specifically, what is the likelihood that the nonstigmatized individual with whom I am interacting is behaving according to some stereotypes he/she has about my group?

In answering this question, trying to understand the (potential) stereotyper and the context in which the behavior occurred is helpful. Attempting to find out whether the stereotyper had the ability and motivation (and background learning history) that would enable him/her to behave in nonstereotyped ways is useful. What the stigmatized person is attempting to understand here is the *intent* of the stereotyper (Fiske, 1989). The reasons for the behavior of the nonstigmatized person may be clear with an assessment of the context in which the negative intergroup behavior occurred. If it is "*nondominant,*" then other persons surrounding the stereotyper are thinking and acting in nondiscriminatory terms, and in this instance, the behavior of the stereotyping majority member is especially likely to be regarded as caused by prejudice of the individual (because of a basic perceptual contrast effect). However, if the context is such that everyone else is emitting similar stereotyping behaviors as the individual in question, the question of intent becomes cloudier, and the context holds a fair amount of attributional ambiguity for the stigmatized individual.

One way to avoid the frustration of trying to ascertain the true motive behind the other's behavior is to just assume that no behavior that others exhibit toward you is related to your stigma. This is an "innocent until proven guilty" approach. Although apparently logical and reasonable, this perspective has some self-relevant pitfalls that make it unattractive. You know that such a perspective is a fair way to view others, but American society is—more often than not—unfair in the way your stigmatized group is viewed (Fiske, 1998; Swim & Stangor, 1998). Given that conclusion, your conclusion is likely to be that most (not all) nonstigmatized outgroup members will react to you based in some part on their stereotypes and prejudices about your stigmatized group (the "guilty until proven innocent" approach).

In a fascinating experiment, Kleck and Strenta (1980) investigated the effects of having negatively valued characteristics on one's perceptions of an interaction partner. Women participants were told that they would be interacting with another participant (who was a confederate) in a brief discussion of tactics people use to make friends. Participants were randomly assigned to one of three characteristics conditions: allergy, epilepsy, or facial scar. Participants were told that the experimenter wanted to assess whether the partner's behavior would be affected by the participant's physical condition. Participants were asked to complete a biographical questionnaire and indicate their condition on the second page (unbeknownst to the participant, the partner/confederate was not shown the second page). Those in the scar condition had a fake scar applied to their face, which was quite noticeable. Participants confirmed the presence of the scar with a mirror, and were asked not to touch it or discuss it unless the partner mentioned it. Before the participant interacted with the partner, the experimenter informed her that he needed to moisturize the scar so that the adhesive would not crack. While doing so, he removed the scar, without the participant's knowledge! The experimenter then brought the participant's biographical information to the partner in the other laboratory room, and then the two were brought together and seated in a room. After a 6-minute discussion, they went back to their separate laboratory rooms, and the participant evaluated the partner's behavior, and provided her attitude toward the partner.

Results indicated that participants who were in the negative stigma conditions (scar and epilepsy) believed that their conditions had a strong impact on the behavior of the partner. Those in the allergy condition did not have this belief about their partner. Specifically, scar and epilepsy participants were more likely to perceive that their partner was tense and patronizing. Additionally, they believed that their partner liked them less and found them less attractive. These data highlight the strong influence of expectancies in clouding our perceptions of others' reactions to us. Even though there was no stigma presented to the confederate, and the confederate's behavior toward the participant was virtually the same for all participants, those who believed that their partner was regarding them as negatively stigmatized perceived their partner's behaviors as reflecting tension and derision toward the participant. Our expectancies about someone can cause us to regard that person's normal, innocuous behavior as symptomatic of the attributed motive, characteristic, or personality of the other individual (Fiske & Taylor, 1991; Rosenhan, 1973).

With this assessment, it would be difficult to take the "innocent until proven guilty" perspective, because you are making your self-esteem and self-identity vulnerable to the negative effects of others' behavior (that is likely based on unfair evaluations of you because of stereotypes about you). In short, you may perceive that you are treated fairly, when in fact, the probability is that you are not being treated fairly. In that instance, you may feel foolish, gullible, and hurt. To protect the self, the stigmatized individual may take a "guilty until proven innocent" approach to interacting with nonstigmatized individuals (Jones et al., 1984; Major & Crocker, 1993; Swim, Cohen, & Hyers, 1998).

Research also indicates that positive feedback from nonstigmatized individuals to the stigmatized can present an attributionally ambiguous situation. To what does the stigmatized person attribute the positive evaluation he or she has received? Is it due to a patronizing and artificial positive evaluation of the person that is related to their stigma, or is it due to purely the performance or personal characteristics of the stigmatized individual? In other words, the stigmatized individual may ask themselves, "Did this person give me this positive feedback because I am black (or a woman, or Hispanic, Asian, etc.) and they do not want to appear prejudiced, or is it because they really like me (or what I did) for who I am as a person?" This is a difficult question to answer in most instances.

Consider the following illustration of the problem. Several studies have demonstrated that nonstigmatized individuals give more positive ratings to stigmatized (compared with nonstigmatized) individuals in impression formation experiments (e.g., Carver, Glass, Snyder, & Katz, 1977). This led some researchers to explain the findings in terms of a "sympathy" effect. However, further analysis indicates that there could be three possible explanations for these findings. They may reflect true positive biases of the majority members, or they may reflect unconscious distortions of true negative feelings, or, finally, they may represent conscious distortions of true negative feelings, due to social desirability effects (Carver, Glass, & Katz, 1978).

In a clever experiment, Carver, Glass, and Katz (1978) investigated how white women evaluated black and physically handicapped target individuals. Participants were asked to read a transcript of an interview with the target individual (either a white man, or a black man, or a physically handicapped man) who was described as of lower socioeconomic status, who had no plans for the future, and who had few friends. Basic demographics of the target individual, and their group identifier (if any, e.g., "handicapped" or "black") were provided at the top of the interview transcript. Participants in the control condition read the transcript, and then provided their ratings of the target individual. The other half of the participants were given a "bogus pipeline" procedure (recall our discussion of this method in Chapter 5). Participants were hooked up to what appeared to be a very real physiological measuring device to their arms, chest, and fingertips. It was explained that this would allow researchers a direct assessment of the participant's reaction to the interview transcript, and hence, the researcher would know what the participant's true attitudes were toward the target. As a measure of "reliability," however, participants were asked to complete the rating sheet (as the control condition participants had), so that the investigator could compare the two types of attitude information.

Results indicated that participants in the control and bogus pipeline conditions were identical in their ratings of the handicapped individual. They also agreed in their ratings of the white man. As predicted, ratings of the handicapped person were significantly higher than ratings of the white. Control condition participants who read about a black interviewee rated him as positively as the ratings that the handicapped individual garnered. However, participants who were in the bogus pipeline condition rated the black target significantly lower than those in all other conditions. Carver et al. (1978) explained these data as suggesting that perceptions of stigmatized individuals are not homogeneous. It appeared that the favorable ratings of the handicapped reflected a true underlying positive attitude toward the handicapped. However, the favorable ratings of the black target seemed to reflect an attempt to cover underlying negative feelings toward blacks. The authors explain the difference in reaction to the two targets as possibly attributable to different perceptions of the degree to which each target has hurdles in life they must overcome. They speculate that perhaps participants gave handicapped persons more "credit" for having to overcome physical, mental, and social difficulties. They may have conversely regarded the black individual as not facing as many difficult challenges in life as the handicapped. Another possible explanation may be that observers viewed the negative life circumstances of the black person as caused by lack of motivation, whereas the situation for the handicapped individual could have been attributed to circumstances beyond his control (Carver et al., 1978).

If we could experimentally manipulate the situation, such that sometimes the nonstigmatized person's reaction (positive or negative) to the stigmatized person is based only on an evaluation of the stigmatized person's character (and not the stigma), and other times, it was less clear, we might be able to more clearly understand the consequences for the self-esteem of the stigmatized. Well, just such an experiment has been published (you knew I was going to say that, didn't you?). Crocker, Voelkl, Testa, and Major (1991, Experiment 2) asked black students to participate in an experiment ostensibly on friendship. When each participant arrived at the laboratory, they were told that another participant had arrived earlier and was seated in an adjacent room (there really was no other participant). The experiment room in which the black participant was seated had a one-way mirror (obscured by closed blinds) in the wall to the adjacent room (where the other participant was supposedly seated). The black participants were told that the experimenters were interested in same-race and cross-race friendship formation, and in this instance, the participant would be paired with a white participant. Participants were asked to complete a self-description questionnaire (that did not indicate their race) and a measure of self-esteem. Participants were told that their responses would be shared with the other participant, and they would use it to determine whether the two of them could become friends.

Participants were next told that either the blinds would be raised so their partner could see them (but they could not see their partner) and use this information in their judgment of whether they wanted to be further acquainted with the participant, or they were informed that the blinds would not be raised, so that the other person would not be biased by appearance of the participant. The experimenter brought the black participant's self-description to the next room, ostensibly to let the "other participant" evaluate it. The experimenter then brought back either a positive or negative evaluation and gave it to the participant. Participants read it, and then completed a few questionnaires, including another measure of their self-esteem and a measure of current mood.

The results were quite interesting. When black participants received positive feedback, their self-esteem *increased* when they believed they could not be seen, but for those who were in the "blinds up" (seen) condition, positive feedback from the white partner brought about a *decrease* in self-esteem. In the not-seen condition, the positive feedback can only be attributed to information about the participant that was on his/her self-description. Thus, the conclusion the black participant may make is, "the white person likes me because I have a good personality, and may have similar interests." Of course, we all like to be liked by others, and this type of feedback about our personality makes us feel good about ourselves. However, in the "seen" condition, the black participant is faced with attributional ambiguity. It is unclear why they received positive feedback from the white partner. In this instance, black participants attributed the positive feedback to a patronizing, false-positive feedback that was probably given so the white participant would not appear prejudiced. Such an attribution (that it is likely that their stigma determined another's evaluation of them) led black participants to feel worse about themselves.

Negative feedback from the white partner had different effects on the self-esteem of black participants. When participants believed they were seen, their self-esteem remained *unchanged*. When they believed they were not seen, their self-esteem *decreased*. These data indicate that when a stigmatized individual believes that others have evaluated them negatively solely on the basis of a self-description (and not on race, as in the unseen condition), the only possible attribution for such an evaluation is that there is something unlikeable about the individual, which naturally makes the stigmatized individual feel negatively (and results in a decreased self-esteem). Conversely, when a stigmatized person receives negative feedback from a nonstigmatized person who can see him/her, he/she is presented with an attributionally ambiguous situation. Here, participants resolved this ambiguity in a way that protected their self-esteem, and in terms of the most likely probable cause of the negative evaluation: they attributed the negative evaluation to the prejudice of the nonstigmatized participant. Unfortunately, although such an attribution may protect the self-esteem of the stigmatized individual, it also may result in feelings of helplessness and depression (Major & Crocker, 1993). A related study by Britt and Crandall (2000) examined whether black and white participants accepted positive and negative feedback from an evaluator after they were informed not only about the race of their evaluator, but also about the *motive* of the evaluator: whether the evaluator was pro- or anti-black/white. Results indicated that black and white participants discounted (were not affected by) positive feedback when they were seen by a pro-black (or pro-white, respectively) evaluator. Similarly, participants tended to discount negative feedback from anti-black (or anti-white) evaluator.

The attributional ambiguity of positive and negative feedback also may have consequences for the motivation of the stigmatized individual. Because it is unclear why the stigmatized individual received the feedback, he/she thus has little information about his/her true ability/characteristics on that dimension, and this uncertainty may lead the stigmatized person to more likely engage in *self-handicapping* behaviors (e.g., drinking and staying out late the night before an important morning examination) that are designed to provide a ready excuse (anticipated poor performance) on that dimension (Arkin & Baumgardner, 1985; Berglas & Jones, 1978; Major & Crocker, 1993). This uncertainty also may result in decreased motivation to engage in behaviors on the relevant domain (e.g., aca-demics . . . see the earlier discussion of Stereotype Threat).

The Paradoxical Effects of Affirmative Action

Members of stereotyped groups, such as racial and ethnic minorities, women, and the elderly, are sometimes the beneficiaries of programs and regulations that are designed to help them economically, occupationally, or educationally. For example, affirmative action programs are designed to overcome the effects of past discrimination and current stereotypes and help these underrepresented minorities get good employment in the workplace. However, critics of affirmative action regard such programs as mere "reverse discrimination," charging that they represent an unfair attempt to place preference on minority status above job qualifications in hiring decisions (Blanchard & Crosby, 1989; Kravitz, Klineberg, Avery, Nguyen, Lund, & Fu, 2000). Research indicates that when both the beneficiaries and critics of affirmative action programs perceive the program as unjustified, they will each react negatively to the program (Taylor & Dube, 1986). Although affirmative action programs have succeeded in helping more minorities into the workplace, many observers have suggested that, overall, the success of the program has been limited (Murrell & Jones, 1996). Aside from any potential limitations in the program's ability to fulfill its purpose, another concern has been voiced by critics. Specifically, some argue that affirmative action may have psychological costs for those who benefit from the program. Steele (1990) suggests that it implies that the recipients of affirmative action are, a priori, inferior and in need of help from society (i.e., the majority).

Some evidence supports this argument. Schneider, Major, Luhtanen, and Crocker (1996) reasoned that because minorities are more likely to be stereotyped as having lesser abilities, they will be more susceptible to potential negative psychological effects of offers of help from members of the majority. The idea here is that it is likely that, because of the attributional ambiguity of the situation (is this majority member offering me help because they are a nice person, or because they think I am incompetent because of my minority status?), the minority member may be more likely to attribute helping behavior to veiled prejudice and stereotypes (Major, Feinstein, & Crocker, 1994). Such an attribution would clearly have implications for the minority member. Schneider et al. further hypothesized that if the minority believes that others see them as incompetent, it may negatively affect their self-esteem and views of their own work competence. Heilman, Block, and Lucas (1992) reported data to support this idea. They found that just mentioning that a woman was an Affirmative Action hiree led perceivers to view her as less competent and less qualified than a non–Affirmative Action female hiree or a male hiree.

In the Schneider et al. (1996) study, white and black participants were assigned to either a help or no-help condition. Black students who received help from a white student reported lower self-esteem compared with blacks in the no-help condition. Blacks who received help also reported more depressed affect than those who did not receive help; however, they did not evaluate the helping majority member negatively. In a related investigation, Nacoste (1985) found that when women perceived that they were given membership in a group primarily based on their category membership, they felt that the admission procedure was less fair, and they displayed fewer positive emotions compared with those women admitted based on their qualifications. These results are consistent with other research that suggests that being the recipient of help can negatively influence one's self-esteem and feelings of competence (Blaine, Crocker, & Major, 1995; Fisher, Nadler, & Whitcher-Alagna, 1982; Schroeder, Penner, Dovidio, & Piliavin, 1995).

The prognosis is not as bleak as it may appear for minorities who are the beneficiaries of affirmative action. Pratkanis and Turner (1996) acknowledge that although much research suggests that the stigma attached to individuals who benefit from affirmative action is real, and is quite negative, further analysis indicates that the pernicious consequences for the recipient's self-esteem and competence evaluations can be short-circuited. Pratkanis and Turner suggest that when help was given to a minority individual (i.e., an Affirmative Action hiring decision) who appears not to conform to societal values and suggests that the recipient lacks competence or qualification, nonminorities feel defensive and hostile, whereas the minority recipient tends to experience decreased self-esteem. However, if the same help is framed such that it is aimed at removing past discriminatory barriers, the minority and nonminority perceivers do not experience negative reactions to such help. When help is presented in this way, it is less threatening, and is seen as social support and an indicator of societal concern for overcoming the negative effects of stereotypes and past discrimination.

Perceived Controllability of the Stigma

Some stigmas are seen as controllable (e.g., homelessness, substance abuse, being overweight), and others (e.g., race, gender) are not perceived as controllable or reversible. This has tremendous implications for the affect, self-esteem, and motivation of the stigmatized individual, as well as their reactions to the nonstigmatized. If one receives negative feedback, and believes that it is attributable to the nonstigmatized person's reaction to the individual's observable, but noncontrollable stigma, the stigmatized person will tend to attribute the negative reaction to prejudice, and they will not suffer any loss of self-esteem (Crocker et al., 1991). However, individuals with perceived controllable stigmas face a different set of circumstances. First, the nonstigmatized are likely to have less sympathy for, and feel more derision toward the stigmatized person, because the stigma is believed to be due to lack of effort, ability, or will (Crocker et al., 1998; Weiner, Perry, & Magnusson, 1988). Second, when those with perceived controllable stigmas receive this negative feedback from the nonstigmatized, they are more likely to feel decreased self-esteem, and more negative affect. However, they do not blame the nonstigmatized person for the negative evaluation. It is as if the stigmatized person says, "Yes, I know I have this negative, controllable condition. I feel bad about it. I don't blame you for noticing it, and telling me I should change it." Third, prejudice toward those who have a controllable stigma is seen as more justifiable than prejudice toward those who have an uncontrollable stigma (Rodin, Price, Sanchez, & McElligot, 1989).

To examine this unique reaction of those with (perceived) controllable stigmas, Crocker, Cornwell, and Major (1993) investigated the attributions of overweight and "normal" weight women when they received positive and negative feedback from nonoverweight males. Women were led to believe that another male participant in an adjoining room was also participating in the study (in actuality, there was no other participant). The study was ostensibly about how dating relationships form, and what things people look for when they have a limited amount of information. Women were weighed, and their height was measured. On a self-description sheet, the women were to indicate these measurements, as well as a number of other demographic and personality characteristics, as well as other self-descriptions. Men would ostensibly do the same. The experimenter took her self-description to the man, and they exchanged the sheets. Women read that the man was fit, unattached, and was a premed major. Overweight women were shown either a positive or negative evaluation from the man that either did or did not indicate a strong desire to date her.

The self-esteem of the female subjects before and after the feedback was measured, as well as their mood, and attributions for the male's feedback. Results indicated that when overweight women were rejected, they attributed it to their weight, and they did not blame the man for the negative feedback (one problem that Crocker et al. note is that measuring the subject's weight and height may have made this a salient reason for any feedback she may later receive, and this may be a possible confound). In addition, they felt significantly more (compared with their "normal weight" counterparts) negative affect, depression, and hostility, and lower self-esteem, as a result of attributing the negative feedback to their weight.

Thus, the literature suggests that the perception by others and oneself of the controllability of one's stigma can have tremendous implications for how one is actually regarded by the nonstigmatized (e.g., with sympathy or anger), and how one feels in response to such feedback. Those with uncontrollable stigmas may be energized, in the face of negative feedback, to fight prejudice, and overcome obstacles in society to achieve their goals. They do not blame themselves for their "stigma" (they rarely regard their situation as a stigma). Rather, they protect their self-esteem in response to negative feedback from the nonstigmatized through an attribution of prejudice. However, the data indicate that those with controllable stigmas not only feel worse about themselves and their abilities, they hold no malice toward the negative evaluator, and blame themselves for their condition (Crocker & Major, 1994). They are also more likely to try to change their stigmatizing condition, and regard themselves as a failure when they fail to do so (Crocker et al., 1998).

Summary

Being a member of a stigmatized group has important and lasting effects on one's self-concept, self-esteem, intergroup interactions, motivation and achievement, expectations, attributions, and affect. This chapter has illustrated how the nonstigmatized treat those with stigmas, and has attempted to highlight many (but not all) of the ways that the stigmatized react to their group status and its influence on their self-identity. Whereas self-reported prejudice toward the stigmatized has declined dramatically (Gaertner & Dovidio, 1986), much evidence suggests that what has declined is not necessarily prejudiced attitudes, but the willingness to publicly state those (now socially inappropriate) negative attitudes (McConahay, 1986). The research we reviewed in this chapter shows that prejudice is alive and well in America, and this has important implications for the future of intergroup relations. If we are to better understand prejudice, and ways we can reduce prejudice, we need to understand more fully the perspective of those who experience prejudice and discrimination in large and small ways every day of their lives. We know much about how majority members think, feel, and behave toward minority members, but little empirical attention has been devoted to undersanding prejudice from the minority's perspective (for a notable exception, see Swim & Stangor, 1998). Much more attention is needed in this neglected area of prejudice research. Finally, a more three-dimensional view of prejudice will likely be obtained when researchers begin to take Devine et al.'s (1996) challenge to tackle the methodologically and theoretically complex problem of prejudice in actual, dynamic intergroup interactions. When we consider how motives, behavior, expectancies, feelings, and attitudes all interact in response to the context and the perceptions of the partner on a moment-by-moment basis, we will have a much richer understanding of how prejudice and stereotypes are maintained and reinforced. Hopefully, we will also be closer to understanding how to reduce prejudice.

GLOSSARY

attributional ambiguity   Situation in which it is difficult for the perceiver to ascertain whether the target's behavior was due to the influence of the situation or to the individual's personality or attitudes.

disidentification   The process by which people disengage their identity from their performance on a stereotype-relevant dimension, in order to protect their self-esteem.

metastereotypes   A person's beliefs regarding the stereotype that outgroup members hold about his or her own group.

self-fulfilling prophecy   Process by which a perceiver's expectations about a target lead that target to behave in ways that confirm those expectations.

self-handicapping   A self-presentation strategy whereby the individual seeks to provide ready excuses for anticipated failure on a self-relevant dimension.

stereotype threat   Situation in which negative expectations about ability (due to stereotypes about the group's ability on that dimension) lead the stigmatized person to experience anxiety at the thought of performing poorly and confirming the stereotype. This anxiety often has the unfortunate effect of inhibiting performance, and confirming the stereotype.

stigma   The possession of a characteristic or attribute that conveys a negative social identity.

DISCUSSION QUESTIONS

1. In your opinion, why do people tend to single out people who are different from themselves, and treat them negatively, and form prejudices and stereotypes about them? Have you ever been the target of ridicule? If so, how did it make you feel?

2. Are there any ingroups of yours with which you feel especially strongly identified? Why?

3. What are some stereotypes about any of your ingroups? Do you think you make deliberate efforts to avoid confirming those stereotypes?

4. In what ways might increased intergroup contact reduce feelings of anxiety among individuals in an intergroup interaction?

5. In dealing with the attributional ambiguity related to their stereotyped group, how do you think members of that group interpret the behavior of others toward themselves: with a predominantly "guilty till proven innocent," or "innocent until proven guilty" approach? Why?

INTERNET RESOURCES

www.isr.umich.edu/rcgd/stigma/   web page of Dr. Jennifer Crocker, social cognition researcher, who examines stigma, attributional ambiguity, and other prejudice-related phenomena

www.u.arizona.edu/~jeffs/index.html   home page of Dr. Jeff Stone, social psychologist examining stereotype threat as well as cognitive dissonance and other social-cognitive phenomena

www.stanford.edu/~jbonham/steele/   home page of Dr. Claude Steele, eminent social psychologist and pioneer of stereotype threat research and self-affirmation theory

12 Dominant–Minority Relations

So far, we have looked at people's behavioral patterns in relating to strangers, the role of culture and social structure in shaping perceptions and interactions, and the complexity of prejudice and discrimination. In this chapter, we examine response patterns that dominant and minority groups follow in their dealings with each other.

The following pages suggest that these patterns occur in varying degrees for most groups, regardless of race, ethnicity, or time period. They are not mutually exclusive categories, and groups do not necessarily follow all these patterns at one time. To some degree, though, each minority or dominant group in any society shares these pattern commonalities. Before we examine the patterns, we must consider two notes of caution. First, all groups are not alike, for each has its own unique beliefs, habits, and history. And second, variations *within* a group prevent any group from being a homogeneous entity.

Minority-Group Responses

Although personality characteristics play a large role in determining how individuals respond to unfavorable situations, behavioral patterns for the group in general are similar to those of other groups in comparable circumstances. External factors play an important role, but social interpretation is also a critical determinant, as explained in the next section on ethnic- and racial-group identity. Also, the minority group's perception of its power resource—its power to change established relationships with the dominant group in a significant way—to a large extent determines the response it makes.[1] The responses include avoidance, deviance, defiance, acceptance, and negative self-image.

Ethnic- and Racial-Group Identity

Any group unable to participate fully in the societal mainstream typically develops its own group identity. This is a normal pattern in ingroup–outgroup relationships. In the field of race and ethnic relations, group identity can serve as a basis for positive encounters, a source of comfort and strength, or entry into the mainstream. It can also be a foundation for prejudice and discrimination, negative self-image, a detriment to social acceptance, or a source of conflict.

Ethnic-group identity exists when individuals choose to emphasize cultural or national ties as the basis for their primary social interactions and sense of self. Leaving the taken-for-granted world of their homeland, immigrants—as strangers in a strange land—become more self-conscious of their group identity. Even as the acculturation process and ethnogenesis unfold, these group members retain some of the "cultural baggage" they brought with them and see themselves—as does the mainstream society—as possessing distinctiveness because of their ethnicity.

Many factors determine the duration of an ethnic-group identity. A cohesive ethnic community, continually revitalized by the steady influx of newcomers, will maintain a strong resilience. Ethnic minority media can play a significant role in strengthening that sense of identity. Indeed, minority media can even affect the assimilation process, either by promoting it (as did the New York *Daily Forward* newspaper among Jewish immigrants in the late nineteenth and early twentieth centuries) or by delaying that process by stressing the retention of language, customs, and values.

Socialization into one's own ethnic group also engenders this identity. Often, part of the growing-up process for minorities involves the existence of a dual identity: one in the larger society and another within one's own group. This multiple reality affects one's roles and behavior, and sense of self, depending on the social setting and other participants.

Ethnic-group identity can be especially protracted on the basis of religion. Some good examples are persistent subcultures such as the Amish, Hutterites, and Hasidic Jews mentioned in Chapter 2. Although a group identity usually remains among the adherents of any faith, its existence along other ethnic lines depends on racial and assimilation considerations. For example, Catholic immigrants in the nineteenth century and other Catholic and Jewish immigrants in the early twentieth century once stood apart not only for their religion but for their other subcultural traits as well. Although traces of anti-Catholicism and anti-Semitism remain today in the United States, most members of these religious groups hold a mainstream-group identity alongside their religious-group identity, which was not the case a few generations ago. More recent arrivals—such as Buddhists, Hindus, Muslims, and Sikhs—are not only religiously distinct from the previously three main U.S. religions but are culturally distinct in other ways along with their usual racial differences. Currently, their ethnic-group identities embody all these aspects (religion, race, culture), and only time will tell what evolution in group identity will occur among them.

For most but not all European groups, everyday ethnicity eventually yields to assimilation over the generations, and ethnic-group identity declines. That change is possible because gradually the group identifies more and more with mainstream society and its subcultural "marks" (clothing, language, customs, behavior, residential clustering) disappear, making the group less noticeable to the rest of society as they become absorbed into the dominant White culture.

Because of the social definition of race, this metamorphosis is difficult for non-Europeans in a color-conscious society. Physical identification through skin color, facial features, and/or hair texture thus maintains differences between the mainstream racial group and others. With their race an inescapable feature affecting their social acceptance and interaction patterns, non-Europeans typically develop a *racial-group identity*. This ingroup bonding satisfies the human need for a sense of belonging while simultaneously serving as a basis for racial and cultural pride. Such an arrangement can foster a healthier, more positive self-identity than would otherwise develop among racial minorities relegated to secondary social status.

People of color—whether black, brown, yellow, or red—typically affirm their identity and heritage in a variety of ways. These include combating their stereotypes, teaching the younger generation about their racial history and achievements, adopting slogans (e.g., "Black is beautiful" and "La Raza" [the race]), and using a dual identity (e.g., African American, Mexican American, Korean American, Native American) as a positive designator of their dual reality. The more militant racial group members often use ethnophaulisms against their own whom they criticize for "thinking or acting White" and call them, depending on the racial group, an "oreo," "coconut," "banana," or "apple"—that is, one color on the outside, but White on the inside.

Ethnic- or racial-group identity, then, can have positive and negative consequences. Examining it in both a social and historical context will lead to a more complete understanding of this social phenomenon.

Avoidance

One way of dealing with discriminatory practices is through **avoidance,** if this avenue is available. Throughout history, minority groups—from the ancient Hebrews to the Pilgrims to today's new arrivals—have attempted to solve their problems by leaving them behind. One motive for migrating, then, is to avoid discrimination. If leaving is not possible, minorities may turn inward to their own group for all or most of their social and economic activities. This approach insulates the minority group from antagonistic actions by the dominant group, but it also promotes charges of "clannishness" and "nonassimilation." Lacking adequate economic, legal, or political power, however, the minority group may find avoidance the only choice open to it.

By clustering together in small subcommunities, minority peoples not only create a miniature version of their familiar world but also establish a safe place in which they can live, relax, and interact with others like themselves, who understand their needs and interests. For some minority groups, seeking shelter from prejudice is probably a secondary motivation, following a primary desire to live among their own kind.

Asian immigrants, for example, have followed this pattern. When the Chinese first came to this country, they worked in many occupations in which workers were needed, frequently clustering together in neighborhoods close to their jobs. In the United States, prejudicial attitudes had always existed against the Chinese, but in the post–Civil War period, they became even more the targets of bitter hatred and discrimination for economic and other reasons. Evicted from their jobs as a result of race-baiting union strikes and limited in their choice of residence by restrictive housing covenants, many had no choice but to live in insular Chinatowns within the larger cities. They entered businesses that did not compete with those of Whites (curio shops, laundries, restaurants, etc.) and followed their old-country tradition of settling disputes among themselves rather than appealing to government authorities for adjudication.

Deviance

When a group continually experiences rejection and discrimination, some of its members can't identify with the dominant society or accept its norms. People at the bottom of the socioeconomic ladder, particularly members of victimized racial and ethnic groups, may respond to the pressures of everyday life in ways they consider reasonable but that others view as **deviance.** This situation occurs in particular when laws serve to impose the moral standards of the dominant group on the behavior of other groups.

Many minority groups in the United States—Irish, Germans, Chinese, Italians, African Americans, Native Americans, and Hispanics—have at one time or another been arrested and punished in disproportionate numbers for so-called crimes of personal disorganization. Among the offenses to the dominant group's morality have been public drunkenness, drug abuse, gambling, and sexual "misconduct." It is unclear whether this disproportion reflects the frequency of misconduct or a pattern of selective arrests. Moreover, some types of conduct are deviant only from the perspective of the majority group, such as cockfighting or female genital mutilation, whereas other types, such as wife beating, may also be deviant within the minority community.

Part of the problem with law enforcement is its subjective nature and the discretionary handling of violations. Many people have criticized the U.S. criminal justice system for its failure to accord fair and equal treatment to the poor and to minority-group members as compared with people from the middle and upper classes.[2] Criticisms have included (1) the tendency of police to arrest suspects from minority groups at substantially higher rates than those from the majority group in situations where discretionary judgment is possible; (2) the overrepresentation of certain dominant social, ethnic, and racial groups on juries; (3) the difficulty the poor encounter in affording bail; (4) the poor quality of free legal defense; and (5) the disparities in sentencing for members of dominant and minority groups. Because social background constitutes one of the factors that the police and courts consider, individuals who belong to a racial or ethnic group with a negative stereotype find themselves at a severe disadvantage.

When a particular racial or ethnic group commits a noticeable number of deviant offenses, such as delinquency, crime, drunkenness, or some public-nuisance problem, the public often extends a negative image to all members of that group even if it applies to only a few. Some common associations, for example, are Italians and gangsters, Irish and heavy drinking and fighting, Chinese and opium, African Americans and street crimes such as mugging and purse snatching, Puerto Ricans and knife fighting. Even though a very small percentage of a group actually engages in such behavior, the entire group may become negatively stereotyped. A number of factors—including values, behavior patterns, and structural conditions in both the native and adopted lands—help explain the various kinds of so-called deviance among different minority groups. The appropriate means of stopping the deviance is itself subject to debate between proponents of corrective versus preventive measures.

Deviant behavior among minority groups occurs not because of race or ethnicity, as prejudiced people think, but usually because of poverty and lack of opportunity. Clifford Shaw and Henry McKay, in a classic study of juvenile delinquency in Chicago, suggested that structural conditions, not membership in a particular minority group, determine crime and delinquency rates.[3] They found that the highest rates of juvenile delinquency occurred in areas with poor housing, few job opportunities, and widespread prostitution, gambling, and drug use. The delinquency rate was consistently high over a 30-year period, even though five different ethnic groups moved in and out of those areas during that period. Nationality was unimportant; the unchanged conditions brought unchanged results. Other studies have demonstrated a correlation between higher rates of juvenile or adult crime and income level and place of residence.[4]

Because many minority groups are heavily represented among low-income populations, studies emphasizing social-class variables provide insight into the minority experience. For example, Albert Cohen found that a lack of opportunities encourages delinquency among lower-class males.[5] Social aspirations may be similar in all levels of society, but opportunities are not. Belonging to a gang may give a youth a sense of power and help overcome feelings of inadequacy; hoodlumism becomes a conduit for expressing resentment against a society whose approved norms seem impossible to follow.[6] Notwithstanding the economic and environmental difficulties they face, the large majority of racial-group and ethnic-group members do not join gangs or engage in criminally deviant behavior. But because some minority groups are represented disproportionately in such activities, the public image of the group as a whole suffers.

Some social factors, particularly parental attitudes about education and social ascent, appear to be related to delinquency rates. For example, parental emphasis on academic achievement may partially explain the low rate of juvenile delinquency among second-generation Jews compared with the high

258

rate of juvenile delinquency among second-generation Italians, whose parents often view formal education as a frill.[7]

Defiance

If a minority group is sufficiently cohesive and conscious of its growing economic or political power, its members may act openly to challenge and eliminate discriminatory practices—**defiance.** In defying discrimination, the minority group takes a strong stance regarding its position in the society. Prior to this time, certain individuals of that group may have pioneered the movement (e.g., by challenging laws in court).

Sometimes the defiance is violent and seems spontaneous, although it usually grows out of longstanding conditions. One example is the Irish draft riot in New York in 1863 during the Civil War. When its volunteer armies proved insufficient, the Union used a military draft to secure needed troops. In those days, well-to-do males of draft age could legally avoid conscription by buying the military services of a substitute. Meanwhile, because the Irish were mostly poor and concentrated in urban areas, many of them had no recourse

Ethnic festivals, such as the Cinco de Mayo Festival in Los Angeles where Hispanics line up to buy food at booths, provide an opportunity to celebrate one's cultural heritage and reafirm ethnic identity. At the same time such events enable nongroup members to enrich their intercultural experiences by enjoying the foods, music, and crafts that are part of America's diversity.

(*Source:* © David Young-Wolff/PhotoEdit)

when drafted. Their defiance at what they considered an unfair practice blossomed into a riot in which Blacks became the scapegoats, with lives lost and property destroyed or damaged. Similarly, the 1991 Washington, D.C., Hispanic riot after a Black female police officer shot a Salvadoran immigrant and the 1992 Los Angeles riot following the acquittal of police officers videotaped beating Rodney King may both have been spontaneous reactions, but only within the larger context of smoldering, deep-seated, longstanding resentments.

A militant action, such as the takeover of a symbolic site, is a moderately aggressive act of defiance. The late 1960s witnessed many building takeovers by African Americans and other disaffected, angry, alienated students on college campuses. In many instances, the purpose of the action was to call public attention to what the group considered society's indifference toward or discrimination against their people. Similar actions occurred in this period to protest the war in Vietnam. A small group of Native Americans took this approach in the 1970s to protest their living conditions; at different times, they seized Alcatraz Island in California, the Bureau of Indian Affairs in Washington, D.C., and the village of Wounded Knee in South Dakota. Media attention helped validate and spread the idea of using militant actions to promote a group's agenda.

Any peaceful action that challenges the status quo, though less aggressive, is defiant nonetheless; parades, marches, picket lines, mass meetings, boycotts, and demonstrations are examples. Another form of peaceful protest consists of civil disobedience: deliberately breaking discriminatory laws and then challenging their constitutionality, or breaking a discriminatory tradition. The civil-rights actions of the 1960s—sit-ins, lie-ins, and freedom rides— challenged decades-old Jim Crow laws that restricted access by Blacks to public establishments in the South. Shop-ins at stores that catered to an exclusively White clientele represented deliberate efforts to break traditional store practices.

Acceptance

Many minority people, to the frequent consternation of their leaders and sympathizers, accept the situation in which they find themselves. Some do so stoically, justifying their decision by subtle rationalizations. Others are resentful but accept the situation for reasons of personal security or economic necessity. Still others accept it through false consciousness, a consequence of the dominant group's control over sources of information. Although **acceptance** maintains the superior position in society of the dominant group and the subordinate position of the minority group, it does diminish the open tensions and conflicts between the two groups.

In some instances, conforming to prevailing patterns of interaction between dominant and minority groups occurs subconsciously, as the end result of social conditioning. Just as socialization can inculcate prejudice, so too it can cause minority-group members to disregard or be unaware of alternative status possibilities. How much acceptance of lower status takes this form

Thousands of people demonstrated in 1997 at the New York City Hall to protest the police assault and sodomy of unarmed Haitian immigrant Abner Louima. Four police officers from the 70th Precinct were convicted of criminal charges in 1999 and imprisoned, but in 2002, a federal appeals court overturned the convictions of three of the officers. Protest demonstrations are a common form of defiance by groups to challenge openly their grievances.

(*Source:* Stacy Walsh Rosenstock/Newsmakers/Getty Images)

and how much is characterized by resentful submission have not been completely settled. However, Brewton Berry and Henry Tischler state, "It is not uncommon for one to conform externally while rejecting the system mentally and emotionally."[8]

African Americans, Mexican Americans, and Native Americans have experienced a subordinate position in the United States for multiple generations. Until the 1960s, a combination of structural discrimination, racial stratification, powerlessness, and a sense of the futility of trying to change things caused many to acquiesce in the situation imposed on them. Similarly, Japanese Americans had little choice when, following the bombing of Pearl Harbor and the subsequent rise in anti-Japanese sentiment, the U.S. government in 1942 dispossessed and imprisoned 110,000 of them in "temporary relocation centers."

Acceptance as a minority response is less common in the United States than it once was. More aware of the alternative ways of living presented in the media, today's minorities are more hopeful about sharing in them. No longer do they passively accept the status quo, which denies them the comfortable life and leisure pursuits others enjoy. Simultaneously, through court decisions, legislation, new social services, and other efforts, society has created a more favorable climate for improving the status of minority groups. Televised news features and behavioral-science courses may have heightened the public's social awareness as well.

Consequences of Minority-Group Status

Minority groups that experience sustained inequality face four possible outcomes: negative self-image, a vicious circle of continued discrimination, marginality, and status as middleman minorities.

Negative Self-Image

The apathy that militant leaders find among their own people may result from a **negative self-image,** a common consequence of prejudice and discrimination. Continual treatment as an inferior encourages a loss of self-confidence. If everything about a person's position and experiences—jobs with low pay, substandard housing, the hostility of others, and the need for assistance from government agencies—works to destroy pride and hope, the person may become apathetic. To remain optimistic and determined in the face of constant negative experiences from all directions is extremely difficult.

Kurt Lewin once observed that minority-group members had a fairly general tendency to develop a negative self-image.[9] The pervasiveness of dominant-group values and attitudes, which include negative stereotypes of the minority group, may cause the minority-group member to absorb them. A person's self-image includes race, religion, and nationality; thus, individuals may feel embarrassed and inferior if they see that one or more of the attributes they possess are despised within the society. In effect, minority-group members begin to perceive themselves as negatively as the dominant group originally did.

Negative self-image, or self-hatred, manifests itself in many ways. People may try to "pass" as members of the dominant group and deny membership in a disparaged group. They may adopt the dominant group's prejudices and accept their devalued status. They may engage in ego defense by blaming others within the group for the low esteem in which society holds them:

> Some Jews refer to other Jews as "kikes"—blaming them exclusively for the anti-Semitism from which all alike suffer. Class distinctions within groups are often a result of trying to free oneself from responsibility for the handicap from which the group as a whole suffers. "Lace curtain" Irish look down on "shanty" Irish. Wealthy Spanish and Portuguese Jews have long regarded themselves as the top of the pyramid of Hebraic peoples. But Jews of German origin, having a rich culture,

view themselves as the aristocrats, often looking down on Austrian, Hungarian, and Balkan Jews, and regarding Polish and Russian Jews at the very bottom.[10]

Negative self-image, then, can cause people to accept their fate passively. It also can encourage personal shame for possessing undesired qualities or antipathy toward other members of the group for possessing them. Minority-group members may attempt to overcome their negative self-image by changing their name or religion, having cosmetic surgery, or moving to a locale where the stereotype is less prevalent.

But Lewin's view that negative self-image is a fairly general tendency among minority-group members may be too broad. For example, members of tightly cohesive religious groups may draw emotional support from their faith and from one another. The insulation of living in an ethnic community, strong ingroup loyalty, or a determination to maintain a cultural heritage may prevent minority-group members from developing a negative self-image.

Recent experiments have shown that people who are stigmatized can protect their self-esteem by attributing the negative feedback they receive to prejudice. In a study analyzing minority children's attitudes toward their own group, Frances E. Aboud suggested group visibility as a possible link to positive self-image. In another analysis, Margaret Beale Spencer argued that, since parents are the first source of a child's "sense of self," their instilling racial pride contributes to resilience and may lead to coping strategies against prejudice that have positive consequences.[11]

The Vicious Circle

Sometimes the relationship between prejudice and discrimination is circular. Gunnar Myrdal refers to this pattern as **cumulative causation**—a **vicious circle** in which prejudice and discrimination perpetuate each other.[12] The dynamics of the relations between dominant and minority groups set in motion a cyclical sequence of reciprocal stimuli and responses. For example, a discriminatory action in filling jobs leads to a minority reaction, poverty, which in turn reinforces the dominant-group attitude that the minority group is inferior, leading to more discrimination and so on.

Myrdal points out that the pattern of expectation and reaction may produce desirable or undesirable results. The expectations held about the newcomers determine the pattern that develops.[13] If the dominant group makes the newcomers welcome, they in turn are likely to react in a positive manner, which reinforces their friendly reception. If the new group is ignored or made to feel unwelcome, the members may react negatively, which again reaffirms original attitudes and actions. As Allport says, "If we foresee evil in our fellow man, we tend to provoke it; if good, we elicit."[14] In other words, negative expectations engender negative reactions, broadening the social distance between the groups and causing the vicious circle to continue.

When Jews were denied access to many U.S. vacation resorts during the nineteenth century, their reactions served to reinforce their negative stereotype in the minds of some, reinforcing their discriminatory behavior. Some Jews demanded equal access, which the resort operators took as proof that Jews were "pushy." When Jews responded to this discriminatory policy by establishing and patronizing their own resorts in the Catskill Mountains of New York, the majority group labeled them "clannish." Similarly, the Irish encountered severe job discrimination in the mid-nineteenth century; the resulting poverty forced many of them to live in urban slums, where they often had trouble with the law. Given this evidence of their "inferiority" and "undesirability," majority-group employers curtailed their job opportunities further. In the same way, discrimination by Whites against Blacks, based partly on the low standard of living endured by many of the latter, exacerbates the problems of poverty, fueling even more the antipathy of some Whites toward Blacks.

Marginality

Minority-group members sometimes find themselves caught in a conflict between their own identity and values and the necessity to behave in a certain way to gain acceptance by the dominant group. This situation—**marginality**—usually arises when a member of a minority group is passing through a transitional period. In attempting to enter the mainstream of society, the marginal person internalizes the dominant group's cultural patterns without having gained full acceptance. Such individuals occupy an ill-defined position, no longer at ease within their own group but not yet fully a part of the *reference group,* the one by whose standards they evaluate themselves and their behavior.[15]

Over the years, sociologists have differed in their interpretation of the effects of marginality. Robert E. Park, who gave this social phenomenon its name, believed that it caused the individual a great deal of strain and difficulty. A marginal person, he observed, is one "whom fate has condemned to live in two societies and in two not merely different but antagonistic cultures."[16]

According to Park, this situation can cause the marginal person, whether an adult or a child, to suffer anxiety over a conflict of values and loyalties. Adults leave the security of their cultural group and thereby risk being labeled renegades by their own people. They seek sustained social contacts with members of the dominant group, which may view them as outsiders. No longer comfortable with the old ways but nonetheless influenced by them and identified with them, marginal adults often experience feelings of frustration, hypersensitivity, and self-consciousness.

Children of immigrants likewise find themselves caught between two worlds. At home, their parents attempt to raise them in their social heritage, according to the established ways of the old country. Meanwhile, through school and other outside experiences, the children are exposed to the U.S. culture and want to be like other children in the society. Moreover, they quickly learn that the dominant group views their parents' ways as inferior and that they too are socially rejected because of their background. Consequently, many young people in transition develop emotional problems and are embarrassed to bring classmates home.

According to this view, marginality is an example of cultural conflict caused primarily by the clash of values within the individual. Many sociologists now believe, however, that the reaction to marginal status depends largely on whether the individual receives reassurances of self-worth from the surrounding community. Thus, successfully defining the situation and adjusting to it are contingent on the individual's sense of security within the community.[17] Supportive ethnic subcommunities and institutions and a sense of solidarity among members of the ethnic group contribute to that sense of well-being. These observations have led some sociologists to emphasize that the transitional phase involves stable individuals in a marginal culture rather than marginal persons in a dominant culture.[18] Individuals in a marginal culture share their cultural duality with many others in primary-group relationships, in institutional activities, and in interacting with members of the dominant society without encountering any dichotomy between their desires and actuality.

Whether this phase of the assimilation process represents an emotionally stressful experience or a comfortably protected one, minority-group members nonetheless pass through a transitional period during which they are not fully a part of either world. An immigrant group may move into the mainstream of U.S. society within the lifetimes of the first-generation members, it may choose not to do so, or it may not be permitted to. Usually, marginality is a one- or two-generation phenomenon. After that, members of the minority group either have assimilated or have formed a distinctive subculture. Whichever route they take, they are no longer caught between two cultural worlds.

Middleman Minorities

Building on theories of marginality, Hubert Blalock suggested the model of **middleman minorities**.[19] This model, based on a dominant–subordinate stratification system, places middleman minorities in an intermediate rather than a low-status position.[20] Feudal and colonial societies, with their ruling elite and large peasant masses, often rely on middleman minorities to forge mediating commerce links between the two. Consequently, such minorities commonly are trading peoples whose history of persecution (Jews, Greeks, and Armenians) or sojourner orientation (Chinese, Japanese, and Koreans) have obliged them to perform risky or marginal tasks that permitted easy liquidation of their assets when necessary.[21]

Middleman groups often serve as buffers and hence experience hostility and conflict from above and below. Jews in Nazi Germany and Asians in Uganda in the early 1970s, for instance, became scapegoats for the economic turmoil in those societies. Their susceptibility to such antagonism and their nonassimilation into the host society promote high ingroup solidarity.

About 12 percent of all Korean Americans are self-employed, more than any other minority group. This store owner's family lives above his deli and also works in the store—common patterns among many immigrants of no separation of work and residence and of the necessity of combined family work efforts.

(*Source:* Corky Lee)

Systematic discrimination can prolong the duration of a group's middleman-minority status, as in the case of European Jews throughout the medieval period. Sometimes the entrepreneurial skills developed in trade and commerce provide middleman minorities with adaptive capabilities and competitive advantages, enabling them to achieve upward mobility and to assimilate more easily; this occurred for Jewish immigrants to the United States and may similarly occur for Korean Americans. In other cases, a group may emerge as a middleman minority because of changing residential patterns. One example is Jewish store owners in city neighborhoods where they once served their own people; when their original neighbors moved away and they found themselves unable to follow them, these urban merchants served new urban minority groups who were situated lower on the socioeconomic ladder.

Dominant-Group Responses

Members of a dominant group may react to minority peoples with hostility, indifference, welcoming tolerance, or condescension. The more favorable responses usually occur when the minority is numerically small, not perceived as a threat, or both. As the minority group's population increases, threatening the natives' monopoly on jobs and other claims to privileged cultural resources, the dominant group's attitude is likely to become suspicious or fearful. If the fear becomes great enough, the dominant group may take action against the minority group.

Dominant groups often use religion in varying aggressive ways against minority groups. Besides religious persecution (a push factor in many migrations throughout world history), they often use missionaries to convert minorities. Dominant groups do not necessarily conduct these sometimes forced conversions with the intent of assimilating a minority group. For example, teaching Christianity to slaves enabled Southern Whites to create a false consciousness among the Africans in accepting their fate but working hard to please their masters. In the case of Native Americans, the federal government gave reservation land to several Protestant religions in an effort to convert the "heathens" and remake them in the White man's image, while maintaining their isolated, segregated confinement.

Legislative Controls

If the influx of racial and ethnic groups appears to the dominant group to be too great for a country to absorb, or if prejudicial fears prevail, the nation may enact measures to regulate and restrict their entry. Australia, Canada, and the United States—the three greatest receiving countries in international migration—once had discriminatory immigration laws that either excluded or curtailed the number of immigrants from countries other than those of northern and western Europe. Through similar patterns of policy change, Canada (in 1962), the United States (in 1965), and Australia (in 1973) began to permit entry from all parts of the world.

To maintain a paternalistic social system, the dominant group frequently restricts the subordinate group's educational and voting opportunities. This denial assures the dominant group of maintaining its system of control, whether over internal minorities, such as Blacks in the Old South and various ethnic minorities in the former Soviet Union, or over colonized peoples, such as those ruled by the Belgians, British, Dutch, French, Japanese, and Portuguese. Most colonial powers have committed themselves to stability, trade, and tapping the natural resources of a country rather than to developing its infrastructure and preparing it for self-governance. As a result, the usual experience of native populations under colonial rule has been largely ceremonial leadership from figureheads, who lack real power in important matters, installed and approved by the colonial authority; limited educational opportunities; and restricted political participation. Other means of denying political power have included disenfranchising voters through high property qualifications (British West Indies), high income qualifications (Trinidad), and poll taxes (United States), although none of these practices exists today in these areas. The most conspicuous recent example of rigid social control was in South Africa, where a legislated apartheid society denied Blacks not only equal education and the ballot but also almost every other privilege.

Segregation

Through a policy of containment—avoiding social interaction with members of a minority group as much as possible and keeping them "in their place"—the dominant group can effectively create both spatial and social segregation.

Spatial segregation is the physical separation of a minority people from the rest of society. This most commonly occurs in residential patterns, but it also takes place in education, in the use of public facilities, and in occupations. The majority group may institutionalize this form of segregation by law (de jure segregation) or establish it informally through pervasive practice (de facto segregation).

Spatial segregation of minorities has a long history. Since the days of the preindustrial city, with its heterogeneous populations, the dominant group has relegated racial and ethnic minorities to special sections of the city, often the least desirable areas.[22] In Europe, this medieval ecological pattern resulted in minority groups being situated on the city outskirts nearest the encircling wall. Because this pattern remains in much of Europe today, Europeans, unlike people in the United States, consider it a sign of high prestige to live near the center of the city.[23]

The dominant group may use covert or overt means to achieve spatial segregation of a minority group. Examples of covert actions include restrictive covenants, "gentlemen's agreements," and collusion between the community and real estate agents to steer "undesirable" minorities into certain neighborhoods.[24] Overt actions include restrictive zoning, segregation laws, and intimidation. Both covert and overt methods of segregation have been found unlawful by U.S. courts since the mid-1970s.

An important dimension of spatial segregation is that the dominant group can achieve it through avoidance or residential mobility. Usually referred to as the invasion-succession ecological pattern, this common process has involved different religions and nationalities as well as different races. The most widely recognized example in the United States is previously all-White neighborhoods becoming Black, but any study of old urban neighborhoods would reveal the same pattern as successive waves of immigrants came here over the years. Residents of a neighborhood may resist the influx of a minority group but eventually abandon the area when their efforts are not successful. This pattern results in neighborhoods with a concentration of a new racial or ethnic group—a new segregated area.

Social segregation involves confining participation in social, service, political, and other types of activities to members of the ingroup. The dominant group excludes the outgroup from any involvement in meaningful primary-group activities and in secondary-group activities. Organizations use screening procedures to keep out unwanted types, and informal groups act to preserve their composition.

Segregation, whether spatial or social, may be voluntary or involuntary. Minority-group members may choose to live by themselves rather than among the dominant group; this is an avoidance response, discussed previously. On the other hand, minority-group members may have no choice about where they live because of economic or residential discrimination.

Whether by choice or against their will, minority groups form ethnic subcommunities, whose existence in turn promotes and maintains the social distance between them and the rest of society. Not only do minority-group members physically congregate in one area and thus find themselves spatially segregated, but they do not engage in much social interaction with others outside their own group.

Under the right conditions, frequent interaction reduces prejudice, but when interaction is severely limited, the acculturation process slows considerably. Meanwhile, values regarding what is normal or different are reinforced, paving the way for stereotyping, social comparisons, and prestige ranking.

Expulsion

When other methods of dealing with a minority group fail—and sometimes not even as a last resort—an intolerant dominant group may persecute the minority group or eject it from the territory where it resides—**expulsion.** Henry VIII banished the Gypsies from England in the sixteenth century, Spanish rulers drove out the Moors in the early seventeenth century, and the British expelled the French Acadians from Nova Scotia in the mid-eighteenth century. More recent examples include Idi Amin, who decreed in 1972 that all Asians must leave Uganda, Muammar Ghadafi, who expelled Libya's ethnic Italian community in 1970, and Serbs, who forced ethnic Albanians out of Kosovo in 1999.

The United States also has its examples of mass expulsion. In colonial times, the Puritans forced Roger Williams and his followers out of Massachusetts for their nonconformity; the group then settled in what became Rhode Island. The forcible removal of the Cherokee from fertile Georgia land and the subsequent "Trail of Tears," during which 4,000 perished along the 1,000-mile forced march to Oklahoma Territory, is another illustration.

Mass expulsion is an effort to drive out a group that is seen as a social problem rather than attempting to resolve the problem cooperatively. This policy often arises after other methods, such as assimilation or extermination, have failed. Whether a dominant group chooses to remove a minority group by extermination or by expulsion depends in part on how sensitive the country is to world opinion, which in turn may be related to the country's economic dependence on other nations.

Xenophobia

If the dominant group's suspicions and fears of the minority group become serious enough, they may produce volatile, irrational feelings and actions. This overreaction is known as **xenophobia**—the undue fear of or contempt for strangers or foreigners. This almost hysterical response—reflected in print, speeches, sermons, legislation, and violent actions—begins with ethnocentric views. Ethnocentrism encourages the creation of negative stereotypes, which in turn invites prejudice and discrimination and can escalate through some catalyst into a highly emotional reaction (see the accompanying International Scene box).

Many examples of xenophobia exist in U.S. history. In 1798, the Federalists, fearful of "wild Irishmen" and "French radicals" and anxious to eliminate what they saw as a foreign threat to the country's stability, passed the Alien and Sedition Acts. When a bomb exploded at an anarchist gathering at Chicago's Haymarket Square in 1886, many Americans thereafter linked foreigners with radicals. The Bolshevik Revolution in 1917 led to the Palmer raids, in which foreign-born U.S. residents were illegally rounded up and incarcerated for their alleged Communist Party affiliation; some were even deported. In 1942, 110,000 Japanese Americans, many of them second- and third-generation U.S. citizens, were interned in concentration camps as a result of irrational suspicions that they would prove less loyal during the ongoing World War II than German Americans and Italian Americans. The U.S. English movement's current efforts to pass English-only laws reflect a xenophobic fear that foreigners won't learn English.

Annihilation

The Nazi extermination of more than 6 million Jews brought the term *genocide* into the English language, but the practice of **annihilation**—killing all the men, women, and children of a particular group—goes back to ancient times. In warfare among the ancient Assyrians, Babylonians, Egyptians, Hebrews, and others, the usual practice was for the victor to slay all the enemy, partly to prevent their children from seeking revenge. For example, preserved in Deuteronomy are these words of Moses:

> . . . when Sehon offered battle at Jasa, coming out to meet us with all his forces. . . . We made an end of him and of his sons and of all his people, took all his cities there and then, putting all that dwelt there, men, women, and children, to the sword, and spared nothing except the beasts we drove off for our use, and such plunder as captured cities yield.

> . . . Og, that was king of Basan, came out to meet us with all his forces, and offered battle at Edrai. . . . So the Lord our God gave us a fresh victory over Og, king of Basan, and all his people, and we exterminated them, there and then laying waste all his cities. . . . We made an end of them as we had made an end of Sehon, that reigned in Hesebon, destroying all the inhabitants of their cities, men, women, and children, plundering their cattle and all the plunder their cities yielded.[25]

The International Scene
Xenophobia in Germany

Under communist rule, East Germany imported thousands of workers from other Marxist countries, particularly Angola, Cuba, Mozambique, and Vietnam. With the fall of the Berlin Wall in 1989 and of communism itself soon thereafter, about two-thirds of the 90,000 sojourners returned to their homelands. Despite this, after unification with West Germany, a wave of xenophobia swept eastern Germany in the early 1990s, fueled by a steady influx of immigrants from the Soviet Union.

Facing high unemployment levels and an uncertain future, alienated German youths committed a series of violent attacks on foreigners. The wave of violence in 1992 and 1993—during which more than 1,800 attacks on foreigners and 17 deaths occurred—brought Germans to the frightening realization that this rampant xenophobia reflected much more than the random vandalism of a minority of alienated youths. Hundreds of thousands of people held mass marches and candlelight vigils in most major German cities to show their opposition to the violence. In a survey taken at the end of 1992, 69 percent of Germans surveyed said they rejected the "Foreigners Out!" slogan, up from 43 percent earlier in the year. Finally, the political system responded by tightening police protection of foreigners and enacting asylum legislation that curtailed the number of refugees who could be admitted into Germany. Still, xenophobic responses continued. The total number of such incidents was higher in 1995 than in 1992. Although these incidents have dropped since then, they still number in the thousands each year.

Politics also reflects the xenophobic mood of some Germans. In local elections in 1992, the anti-immigrant German People's Union (Deutsche Volks Union, or DVU) and the Republikaner Party (REPS), led by former SS officer Franz Schonhuber, won seats for the first time in two state parliaments. In response, the government banned a 130-member neo-Nazi group, the Nationalist Front, as well as radio or television airing of extremist right-wing music. Such measures did not reduce the growing anti-foreigner mood. In April 1998, 13 percent of the electorate—and 27 percent of the voters under age 30—in the small eastern German state of Saxony-Anhalt voted for the DVU. This share of the vote was the highest achieved by the extreme right in a state election since the Federal Republic's founding in 1949. The extremists did not fare well, however, in the 1998 national elections, which resulted in the election of center-left Social Democrat Gerhard Schröder as chancellor. Since then, the DVU split into two factions and the government acted to ban NPD, the most extreme right-wing party. In the 2002 election both the DVU and REPS also fared poorly

Critical thinking questions: How does the United States compare to Germany in anti-foreigner sentiment, violence, and politics? Why doesn't the United States, like Germany, ban extremist political parties or music?

In modern times, various countries have used extermination as a means of solving a so-called race problem. Arnold Toynbee once said that the "English method of settlement" followed this pattern.[26] The British, through extermination and close confinement of survivors, annihilated the entire aboriginal population of Tasmania between 1803 and 1876.[27] The Dutch considered South African San (Bushmen) to be less than human and attempted to obliterate them.[28] When native peoples of Brazil resisted Portuguese settlement of their lands, the Whites solved the problem by systematically killing them. One favored means of doing so was to place the clothing of recent smallpox victims in their villages and allow the contagion to destroy the native population.[29] In the 1890s and again in 1915, the Turkish government systematically massacred hundreds of thousands of Armenians, events still solemnly remembered each year by Armenian Americans. One of the largest genocides in U.S. history occurred at Wounded Knee in 1890, when the U.S. Seventh Cavalry killed about 200 Native American men, women, and children. In the past 50 years, campaigns of genocide have occurred around the globe in such countries as Sudan, Burundi, Rwanda, Nigeria, Indonesia, Iraq, Bangladesh, Bosnia, and Kosovo.

Lynchings are not a form of annihilation because the intent is not to exterminate an entire group but to set an example through selective, drastic punishment. Nonetheless, the victims usually are minority-group members. Although lynchings have occurred in the United States throughout its history, only since 1882 have reasonably reliable statistics on their frequency been kept (Figure 6.1). Sources such as the *Chicago Tribune* and the Tuskegee Institute, which have kept data on this subject, reveal that at least 5,000 lynchings have occurred since 1882. They have taken place in every state except the New England states, with the Deep South (including Texas) claiming the most victims.

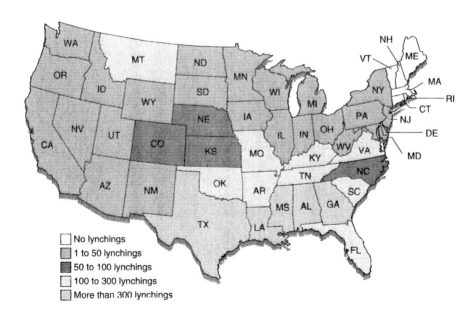

No lynchings
1 to 50 lynchings
50 to 100 lynchings
100 to 300 lynchings
More than 300 lynchings

FIGURE 6.1   Lynchings in the United States Since 1882

In fact, 90 percent of all lynchings during this period have occurred in the southern states; Blacks have accounted for 80 percent of the victims. The statistics do not, however, cover lynchings during the nation's first 100 years, including those in the western frontier, when many Native Americans and Hispanics also met this fate.[30]

Annihilation sometimes occurs unintentionally, as when Whites inadvertently spread Old World sicknesses to Native Americans in the United States and Canada, to Inuit (Eskimos), and to Polynesians. Having no prior exposure to such ailments as measles, mumps, chicken pox, and smallpox, the native populations had little physiological resistance to them, and thus succumbed to these contagious diseases in unusually high numbers. Other forms of annihilation, usually intentional, occur during times of mob violence, overzealous police actions, and the calculated actions of small private groups.[31]

Hate Groups and Hate Crimes

Like most nations, the United States has had its share of hate groups and hate crimes. Most prominent among hate groups of the past were the Know-Nothings of the mid-nineteenth century and the Ku Klux Klan in the late nineteenth and early twentieth centuries. In fact, bias crimes against Europeans, Native Americans, Asians, and numerous religious groups occurred frequently in the nineteenth and twentieth centuries. Deplorably, this ugly pattern remains a brutal force in U.S. society.

Although experts usually associate an increase in hate groups with difficult economic times, the number of U.S. hate groups in the prosperous 1990s grew by an alarming 20 percent. The Intelligence Project of the Southern Poverty Law Center reported that the number of organized, active hate groups in the United States in 2002 was 708, fueled by racist religious groups, White power rock 'n' roll music, and Internet propaganda (Figure 6.2).[32]

Neo-Nazi organizations comprised 220 of these 708 hate groups, with Klan groups accounting for another 133, followed by 27 of the Christian Identity following, which identifies Whites as the Bible's chosen people and Jews as satanic. Neo-Confederate groups, which oppose most non-White immigration and all interracial marriages, total 91. An additional 18 groups were defined as skinheads, 91 were neo-Confederates, and 82 were Black separatists, including the Nation of Islam. Although the Nation of Islam was not involved in political violence in 2002, its tenets are based on racial hatred according to the Intelligence Project. The remaining 137 hate groups followed a hodgepodge of hate-based doctrines.

California and Texas contained the largest number of hate groups (48 each), followed by Florida (44), South Carolina (42), Alabama (34), Georgia and North Carolina (31 each), Mississippi (27), Ohio (26), and New York (25). Every state except Vermont had at least one such group in 2002.

Reported hate crime offenses—only some of which are committed by members of organized hate groups—numbered 7,462 in 2002 and claimed 9,222

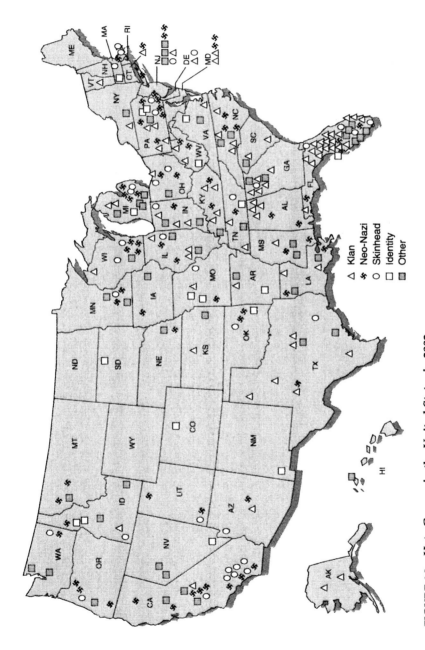

FIGURE 6.2 Hate Groups in the United States in 2002

Source: Adapted from the Southern Poverty Law Center, Intelligence Project, 2003.

victims. Racial bias motivated 49 percent of the incidents, religious bias another 19 percent, sexual-orientation bias 18 percent, and ethnicity/national origin bias 15 percent (Table 6.1). Crimes against persons accounted for 64 percent of hate crime offenses, while damage/destruction/vandalism of property constituted 36 percent. Ten persons were murdered in hate-motivated incidents.[33]

To combat hate crimes—commonly defined as any criminal offense against a person or property that is motivated in whole or part by the offender's bias against a race, religion, ethnic/national origin, group, or sexual orientation—many states have passed laws mandating severe punishments for persons convicted of such crimes. Federal law (18 U.S.C. 245) also permits federal prosecution of a hate crime as a civil-rights violation if the assailant intended to prevent the victim from exercising a "federally protected right" such as voting or attending school. Despite these sanctions, however, the numbers of hate groups and hate crimes continue to rise.

TABLE 6.1 Bias Motivation of Hate Crime Incidents in 2002

	Percentage of Category	Percentage of Total
Race		48.8
Anti-Black	68.3	
Anti-White	19.7	
Anti-Asian/Pacific Islander	6.0	
Anti-multiracial group	4.3	
Anti–Native American	1.7	
Religion		19.1
Anti-Jewish	65.3	
Anti-Islamic	10.9	
Anti-Protestant	3.9	
Anti-Catholic	3.7	
Anti-multireligious group	2.2	
Other	14.0	
Ethnicity/National Origin		18.1
Anti-Hispanic	43.6	
Other	56.4	
Sexual Orientation		14.7
Anti-male homosexual	66.3	
Anti-female homosexual	13.8	
Anti-homosexual	17.8	
Anti-heterosexual	0.8	
Anti-bisexual	1.2	

Source: FBI Uniform Crime Reports, accessed online at http://www.fbi.gov/ucr/hatecrime2002.pdf [December 6, 2003].

Exploitation

Countless writings have documented instances of the **exploitation** of minority groups in various countries. Sometimes the perpetrators of this abuse are members of the same group—the operators of Asian sweatshops in U.S. cities, for instance, and the *padroni* of old Italian immigrant communities, both of whom often benefited at the expense of their own people. Most often, however, members of dominant groups exploit minority groups.

Middle-range conflict theories are often helpful in understanding specific forms of exploitation, such as the internal-colonialism theory discussed in Chapter 3. Another analytical explanation comes to us from Edna Bonacich, who suggests a split-labor-market theory as a means of understanding the ethnic antagonism arising from economic exploitation.

Bonacich theorizes that ethnic antagonism results from a combination of economic exploitation by employers and economic competition between two or more groups of laborers that produces a wage differential for labor.[34] She contends that much ethnic antagonism is based not on ethnicity and race but on the conflict between higher-paid and lower-paid labor—the **split-labor-market theory:**

> Ethnic antagonism is specifically produced by the competition that arises from a price differential. An oversupply of equal-priced labor does not produce such antagonism, though it too threatens people with the loss of their job. However, hiring practices will not necessarily fall along ethnic lines. . . . All workingmen are on the same footing, competing for scarce jobs. When one ethnic group is decidedly cheaper than another (i.e., when the labor market is split), the higher paid worker faces more than the loss of his job; he faces the possibility that the wage standard in all jobs will be undermined by cheaper labor.[35]

If the higher-paid labor group is strong enough, it may be able to block the cheaper competition through an exclusionary movement or a caste system. To some degree, the United States's restriction of Chinese and Japanese immigrant labor and Australia's restriction of Asian and Polynesian immigrants represent victories for organized labor against lower-paid competition. In a caste system, higher-paid labor controls certain high-paying jobs exclusively and limits the minority group to other lower-paying jobs (often lacking health benefits and pension plans). This creates an aristocracy of labor and submerges the labor-market split by stratifying the differentially priced workers. This phenomenon can be seen in the job differentials between Blacks and Whites—and between men and women in certain trade unions.

Among the factors that lower the price of one group's labor are exploitation by management, unfamiliarity with wage standards, limiting language skills and customs, and lack of economic resources. All of these factors force them into low-paying jobs, into making contractual commitments be-

Sweatshops today remain a form of economic exploitation just as they did three generations ago. One difference is the children in the shops alongside their working mothers. Many Asian and Hispanic newcomers, many of them undocumented aliens, work under appalling conditions for long hours and low pay.

(*Source:* © Lina Pallotta/Impact Visuals)

fore emigrating, or into seeking political support from a labor organization or government:

> Governments vary in the degree to which they protect their emigrants. Japan kept close watch over the fate of her nationals who migrated to Hawaii and the Pacific coast. . . . In contrast Mexican migrant workers to the United States have received little protection from their government, and African states were unable to intervene on behalf of slaves brought to America.[36]

When a labor market splits along ethnic lines, racial and ethnic stereotyping becomes a key factor in the labor conflict, and prejudice, ethnic antagonism, and racism become overt. The conflict is not due to religious differences and does not depend on which group was first to move into the area because examples of ethnic antagonism can be found in which these variables were controlled. Bonacich argues that the one characteristic shared by all societies where ethnic antagonism is acute is an indigenous working class that earns higher wages than do immigrant workers. Not everyone agrees with this theory, however. In the case of the anti-Chinese movement led by labor unions, racism was the motivating factor, and White workers offered to work for lower wages if this meant that the Chinese would be removed from their jobs.[37]

In applying the split-labor-market theory to the history of the Chinese in America between 1848 and 1882, Mike Hilton suggested several modifications. If the economy expands and labor shortages occur, ethnic antagonisms are disarmed. Most important, an ethnic bourgeoisie necessarily evolves because of the existence of an ethnic labor force:

> Native capitalists are seldom equipped to locate and reproduce that ethnic labor force by themselves. Unfamiliarity with the language and customs of Chinese workers made it necessary that white capital rely on an intermediary class of Chinese businessmen for two purposes. First, locating and hiring an adequate number of Chinese workers required that capital act through an intermediate class of Chinese compradors. Second, once obtained, the Chinese labor force had to be provisioned according to their accustomed tastes. This requirement fostered the development of a class of Chinese merchants.[38]

Hilton argued that the ethnic bourgeoisie is both exploitative, in that it benefits from the ethnic worker, and benevolent, in that it solidifies the ethnic community and provides for its social needs. The ethnic bourgeoisie can greatly influence a split-labor market because its stronger economic and political base and often higher educational level enable it to act on behalf of the ethnic group. Although it does not always do so, the ethnic bourgeoisie can articulate the injustices of a caste system and challenge restrictive institutions.

A bourgeoisie arises from within the ranks of any ethnic group at some stage in its members' adjustment to life in the United States. Most notable are the *padroni* among the Italian and Greek immigrants and the *padrinos* among Puerto Rican and Mexican laborers.

Retrospect

Ethnic- and racial-group identity is a normal pattern in ingroup–outgroup relationships. It can have positive and negative results depending on the social context in which it exists. A group identity based on immigrant status is normally of shorter duration than one based on religion or race. Minorities typically experience a dual identity, one in the larger society and another within their own group.

Minority-group responses to prejudice and discrimination include avoidance, deviance, defiance, and acceptance depending in large measure on the group's perception of its power to change the status quo. After prolonged treatment as an inferior, a person may develop a negative self-image. Continued inequality intensifies through a vicious circle or cumulative causation.

Marginality is a social phenomenon that occurs during the transitional period of assimilation; it may be either a stressful or a sheltered experience depending on the support system of the ethnic community. Some groups become middleman minorities because of their historical background or sojourner orientation; they may remain indefinitely in that intermediate place in the social hierarchy, a potential scapegoat for those above and below them, or they may achieve upward mobility and assimilation.

Dominant-group actions toward the minority group may take various forms, including favorable, indifferent, or hostile responses. When the reaction is negative, the group in power may place restraints on the minority group (e.g., legislative controls and segregation). If the reaction becomes more emotional or even xenophobic, expulsion or annihilation may occur. Sensitivity to world opinion and economic dependence on other nations may restrain such actions. Another dominant response is exploitation as illustrated by the internal-colonialism theory, discussed in Chapter 3, or by the split-labor-market theory, in which differential wage levels can spark ethnic antagonism. An ethnic bourgeoisie may arise that is both exploitative and benevolent.

KEY TERMS

Acceptance	Marginality
Annihilation	Middleman minorities
Avoidance	Negative self-image
Cumulative causation	Social segregation
Defiance	Spatial segregation
Deviance	Split-labor-market theory
Exploitation	Vicious circle
Expulsion	Xenophobia

REVIEW QUESTIONS

1. What are some common minority-group responses to prejudice and discrimination?

2. What are some common majority-group responses to minorities?

3. What is marginality? Why may it be a stressful experience in some cases but not in others?

4. What are middleman minorities? How do they affect acceptance?

5. Discuss three conflict viewpoints about the exploitation of minorities.

SUGGESTED READINGS

Blalock, Hubert M., Jr. *Toward a Theory of Minority Group Relations*. New York: Wiley, 1967.
    An influential work that describes conceptual frameworks for understanding dominant–minority relations, including self-serving discrimination and middleman minorities.

Bonacich, Edna, and John Modell. *The Economic Basis of Ethnic Solidarity.* Berkeley: University of California Press, 1981.
> Building on middleman-minority theory, an examination of how Japanese cohesiveness has led to socioeconomic advancement.

Gourevitch, Philip. *We Wish to Inform You That Tomorrow We Will Be Killed with Our Families.* New York: Farrar Straus Giroux, 1998.
> A journalist's dramatic narrative of the 1994 Hutu massacre of 800,000 Tutsi within 100 days in Rwanda—its history, aftermath, and the temptation for revenge in the refugee camps.

Knobel, Dale T. *"America for the Americans": The Nativist Movement in the United States.* Boston: Twayne, 1996.
> A detailed account of the xenophobic spirit in the United States and the nativist fear that the newcomers threaten U.S. culture.

Mahler, Sarah J. *American Dreaming: Immigrant Life on the Margins.* Princeton, N.J.: Princeton University Press, 1995.
> The struggles of immigrants who fled troubled homelands in search of a better life, only to be marginalized by the U.S. society they had hoped would embrace them.

Massey, Douglas S., and Nancy A. Denton. *American Apartheid: Segregation and the Making of the Underclass,* reprint ed. Cambridge, Mass.: Harvard University Press, 1993.
> A richly documented account of how segregation and dissociation from other cultures and ways of life lie at the root of many problems facing African Americans today.

The Native Americans

ifferent in race, material culture, beliefs, and behavior, the Europeans and the Native Americans initially were strangers to each other. The Europeans who first traded with and then conquered the natives showed little interest in or understanding of them. Brutalized and exploited, the Native Americans experienced all the dominant-group response patterns: legislative action, segregation, expulsion, xenophobia, and—for some tribes and groups—annihilation. In turn, they reacted with varying patterns of avoidance, defiance, and acceptance, steadfastly remaining numerous and persistent subcultures with a marginal existence.

SOCIOHISTORICAL PERSPECTIVE

Most ethnohistorians place the number of Native Americans who lived in what later became the United States before European colonization at between 6 and 10 million. Divided into several hundred tribes with discrete languages and lifestyles, these original inhabitants had cultures rich in art, music, dance, life-cycle rituals, belief systems, social organization, coping strategies, and instruction of their young. Although the tribes varied in their values, customs, beliefs, and practices, their cultures rested primarily on living in harmony with the land.

Early European explorers and settlers, reflecting ethnocentric views, condemned the aspects of Native American culture that they did not understand and related to other aspects only in terms of their own culture. Some considered the indigenous people to be savages, even though Native American societies had a high degree of social organization. Others idealized them as uncorrupted children of nature who spent most of their time engaging in pleasurable activities. In Europe, intellectual debate raged over how the presence of people so isolated from other human beings could be explained. Were they descended from the inhabitants of Atlantis, Carthage, ancient Greece, East Asia? Were they the Lost Tribes of Israel?[1] Were they no better than beasts, or were they intelligent, capable beings?

In colonial and frontier days, the **stereotype** of the Native Americans often was negative, especially when they obstructed Europeans from occupying the Native Americans' land. As a result of *self-justification*—the denigration of others to justify maltreating them—some whites viewed Native Americans as cruel, treacherous, lying, dirty heathens. Although that very negative stereotype no longer prevails, even today Native Americans are portrayed in films, TV shows, and comic strips as colorfully dressed but unemotional, humorless, and uncommunicative individuals (*Dances with Wolves* being a notable exception). Supposedly, all they desired during the frontier period were scalps, firearms, and "firewater." Contemporary Native Americans often are stereotyped as backward, unmotivated, or continually drunk, or they are regarded as romantic anachronisms.

Outsiders frequently overgeneralize about Native Americans, thinking of the many tribes as one people even though the tribes have always differed from one another in language, social structure, values, and practices. Of the approximately 300 different Native American languages spoken in 1492 within the modern borders of the United States, only about half still exist. At present there are 275 Native American reservations, and the Bureau of Indian Affairs recognizes 556 different tribal entities in the United States.[2] Figure 7.1 shows the principal Native American tribes living in the United States today.

Native Americans share several distinguishing physical characteristics. Most have thick, black, straight hair but very little facial or body hair. They tend to be dark-eyed with rather prominent cheekbones. Beyond these similarities, they vary greatly in physical stature and features. The ethnophaulism *redskin* is not at all accurate; their skin coloring ranges from yellowish to coppery brown.

The Native Americans' experiences in the American colonies were unique in one respect: The whites, not the Native Americans, were the newcomers, and the whites were the minority for many years. The relationship between Native Americans and whites often was characterized by distrust, uneasy truces, or violent hostilities. Even in colonial Massachusetts and New Netherland, where peaceful coexistence initially prevailed, the situation deteriorated.

As the two peoples interacted more fully, each group grew more antagonistic toward the other. The Native Americans could not understand the European settlers' use of beatings, hangings, and imprisonment as means of social control. The settlers could not understand the Native Americans' resistance to Christianity and to the whites' more "civilized" way of life. These were but peripheral considerations, however; the major issue was whose way of life would prevail and whether the land would be further developed or allowed to remain in its natural state, abounding with fish and wildlife.

FIGURE 7.1 Principal Native American Tribes in the Continental United States (Where They Live Today)

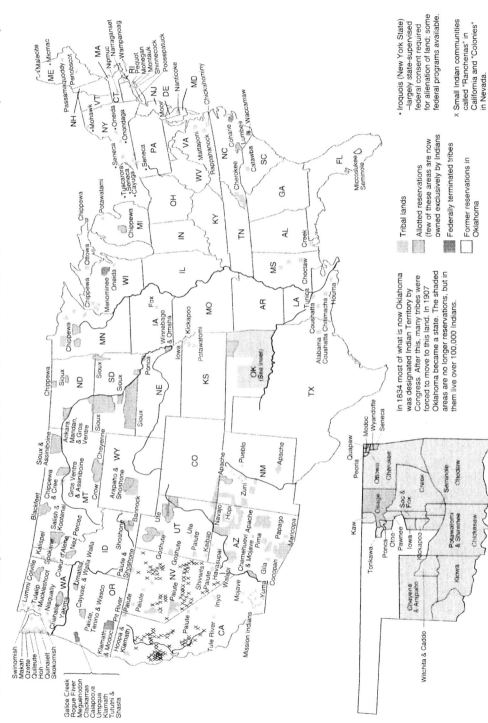

Source: Based on data from U.S. Department of the Interior, Bureau of Indian Affairs, "Indian Land Areas, General" (map), (Washington, DC: U.S. Government Printing Office, 2001).

The conflict increased as the settlers encroached on more and more Native American lands. Eventually, fighting broke out. Many killings occurred in Virginia in 1622 and in Connecticut in 1637. Metacom, the leader of the Wampanoag, who was known as King Philip, united the Nipmuc and Narraganset tribes behind him in 1675 and attacked 52 of the 90 New England settlements, completely destroying 12 of them. The colonies seemed in danger of total defeat, but in 1676 Philip was slain, and subsequently the Native American bands were wiped out one by one. Fighting between Native Americans and settlers continued sporadically and locally throughout the westward movement of whites until the 1880s.

In the mid-19th century, the U.S. government adopted a policy of forced relocation in dealing with Native American tribes and encouraging westward expansion. The government used military force to displace the many tribes and resettle them on wilderness reservations, where they remained unless new settlement plans or the discovery of oil and valuable minerals caused further displacement. This program of compulsory segregation and dependence, compounded by attempts to impose "Americanization," reduced the Native Americans' status to that of a subordinate colonized people—wards of the government—living at a subsistence level. Reflecting changing attitudes and interests in the late 19th and early 20th centuries, Congress enacted various pieces of legislation ostensibly designed to help the Native Americans. These laws, to be discussed shortly, actually worked to the Native Americans' further disadvantage, worsening their already low and dependent status.

One short-lived Pan-Indian association of the 20th century, the Society of American Indians, which existed from 1910 until 1920, failed to unify the tribes into an effective pressure group or to generate much outside support. In 1944 a group of World War II veterans formed the National Congress of American Indians (NCAI). In the early 1960s another organization, the National Indian Youth Council (NIYC) came into existence. New moves toward unity began in the 1960s, and new legislation and greater government sympathy helped the Native Americans' cause.

The most significant factor in the Native Americans' success, however, was the civil-rights movement, which heightened the nation's social consciousness and inspired the Native Americans to renew their campaign for self-determination. Although they had never been silent, they now became more vocal and organized, and they found outsiders more receptive. They became more militant, too, as demonstrated by the occupation of Alcatraz Island in 1969; the takeover of the Bureau of Indian Affairs in Washington, DC, in 1972; the long confrontation in 1973 at Wounded Knee (site of an 1890 massacre); and the march on Washington in 1978. A new generation of "Red Power" advocates took up the fight for Native American rights. Some attempted to achieve their goals through a national, or Pan-Indian, movement, whereas others preferred to emphasize individual tribal culture and practices.

Throughout the 500-year history of Native American–white relations, the Native Americans have rejected the notion that the whites' religions and lifestyles are superior to theirs. To understand the nature of the relations between these two groups, we must comprehend the roles of **ethnocentrism,** stereotyping, cultural differences, and power differentials in intergroup relations.

Early Encounters

In the first encounters between Native American and Europeans, two human races with vast differences in culture, knowledge, and lifestyle were seeing each other's physical distinctions for the first time. Each group was a source of wonder to the other. Columbus's first impressions of the Arawak tribe in the Caribbean reflected ethnocentrism:

> I knew they were a people who would better be freed and converted to our Holy Faith by love than by force. . . . they are all generally of good height, of pleasing appearance and well built. . . . They must be good servants and intelligent . . . and I believe that they would easily become Christians, as it appeared to me that they had no sect.[3]

This wood engraving of 17th-century Dutch colonists along the Hudson River trading for hides and furs with Native Americans illustrates the cooperation and reciprocal gains of early contact. Soon, however, the Native Americans became less self-sufficient and more dependent on products of European manufacture, which, together with continual land encroachment, led to tensions and ultimately violent conflicts. (*Source:* The Granger Collection)

Although he admired the Native Americans, Columbus essentially saw them as potential servants, and he assumed that they had no religious convictions because he found no trappings of religion or written codes such as he was accustomed to seeing in Europe.

As Europeans became more curious about Native Americans, an idealistic concept of the Native American as the Noble Savage took hold. Michel de Montaigne, a 16th-century French philosopher, had numerous talks with "a simple, crude fellow" who had lived in Brazil for 10 or 12 years; from the descriptions of this traveler—who, Montaigne concluded, "has not the stuff to build up false inventions and give them plausability; and wedded to no theory"—Montaigne drew the following portrait of these indigenous people:

> [They have] no sort of traffic, no knowledge of letters, no science of numbers, no name for a magistrate or for political superiority, no custom of servitude, no riches or poverty, no contracts, no successions, no partitions, no occupations but leisure ones, no care for any but common kinship, no clothes, no agriculture, no metal, no use of wine or wheat. The very words that signify lying, treachery, dissimilation, avarice, envy, belittling, pardon—unheard of.[4]

Although some Europeans romanticized Native Americans and a positive mystique about the Native Americans swept Elizabethan England and other parts of Europe, others viewed them as bloodthirsty barbarians and cruelly exploited them. The early phases of Spanish military activity, particularly in Mexico, Peru, and the North American Southwest, involved enslavement, plunder, rape, and slaughter of Native Americans. The Spanish put the peaceful Arawak tribe of the Caribbean islands into forced labor, using members of the tribe in land clearing, building, mining, and plantation work. Because they had no weapons to match those of their conquerors, the subjugated peoples often responded by committing mass suicide and mass infanticide. Within a few decades of the European discovery of the New World, the Native American population began to decline rapidly as a result of disease, warfare, and self-destruction.

The **dichotomy** of views of the Native American either as a Noble Savage or as a bloodthirsty barbarian was epitomized in the great debate between Bartolomé de las Casas, a bishop serving in the New World, and Juan Ginés de Sepulveda, a Renaissance scholar. The latter considered the Native Americans no better than "beasts" who should be enslaved. Las Casas presented a picture of the Native Americans as naifs, both artistically and mechanically inclined, with intellectual capabilities for learning and a willingness to coexist with the Spanish intruders.[5] In 1550 King Charles V appointed the Council of the Indies, a panel of distinguished theologians and counselors, which met at Valladolid. The council heard the arguments of the two antagonists, agreed in large measure with Las Casas, and thereupon fundamentally altered Spanish policy toward the Native Americans.

As part of his long struggle to protect the Native Americans, Las Casas had returned to Spain in 1517 to plead their case directly to the king. In doing so, he revealed the extent of their decimation: "At my first arrival in Hispaniola [1497], it contained a million inhabitants and now there remain scarce the hundredth part of them." He believed the Native Americans could survive only if another labor force replaced them. By convincing the Spanish authorities that Africans were sturdier and better adapted to agricultural operations, he opened the doors for the subsequent massive slave trade of blacks to the Spanish possessions in the New World. It is cruelly ironic that the humane efforts of Las Casas on the Native Americans' behalf encouraged the brutalization and exploitation of black people and racial discrimination against them that has lasted for more than 400 years.

The Native American populations in the United States and Latin America differ in their social, economic, and political status. Nevertheless, Native Americans are indigenous to the land, regardless of present-day national boundaries (such as the Mohawk in New York State and Canada). Several factors, including habitability of terrain, migration patterns, degree of industrialization, and especially different governmental and social attitudes in the various countries have accounted for the differences. In the United States, the 19th-century policy of removal, relocation, and Native American dependence on the federal government prevented most tribes from becoming full participants in U.S. society.

In Latin America, however, Spain adopted a more benevolent policy toward the Native Americans in 1550, following the recommendations of the Council of the Indies; and greater interaction, intermarriage, absorption, and gradual acculturation occurred among the Native Americans and the Spanish. Except for those living in the central Andes and other remote areas, the indigenous peoples became fuller participants in their society than did their counterparts in the United States and lived in relative cultural and racial harmony with the white, black, *mulatto* (of mixed black and white ancestry), and *mestizo* (of mixed Native American and white ancestry) populations. Along with the other nonwhite groups, they were part of the large low-ranking social class, in sharp contrast to the small high-ranking class. Despite the climate of comparative racial harmony, however, they have had very little opportunity for upward mobility; and most Latin American nonWhites live in economic stagnation. In contrast, most North American tribes have experienced both economic stagnation and a lack of racial harmony.

Native American populations in Latin America and North America were decimated by various sicknesses that resulted from earlier contact with white explorers or traders. When the early settlers in New England found deserted Native American villages, they rejoiced; they considered this to be mute testimony of the judgment of Divine Providence on these "heathens" as well as on their own undertaking. The Lord had smitten the pagan to make way for the righteous! This accidental annihilation often resulted from a serious contagion such as smallpox, tuberculosis, or cholera. Native Americans were also fatally susceptible to such diseases as measles, mumps, and chicken pox because they had not developed immunities to these Old World illnesses.

Cultural Strains

In many areas, when the white settlers were few in number and depended on Native American assistance, the Native Americans were hospitable and the whites were receptive to them. The Native Americans along the East Coast helped the colonists to get settled by teaching them what to plant and how to cultivate their crops, as well as imparting to them the knowledge and skills they needed to survive in the wilderness. As the settlements became stabilized, relations between the two races became more strained, as the following excerpt from Douglas Edward Leach's study of 17th-century New England reveals:

> Ever since the coming of the white men there had been economic intercourse between Indians and English traders. At first it had seemed that the flourishing trade in furs, tools, cloth, and foodstuffs was as beneficial to the Indians as to the colonists, but as time went on and the English extended their activities the Indians grew more and more dissatisfied with the situation. It became apparent that they were gradually sinking into a position of complete economic subservience. Indian villages which had once enjoyed almost total self-sufficiency were now increasingly dependent upon products of English manufacture. . . .
>
> In the meantime, some of the Indians were exchanging their forest ways for the security and comfort of English habitations by engaging themselves as servants or laborers to the settlers, whose ambitious expansionism was fostering a continual shortage of labor. This meant that members of the two races were now being brought into frequent contact with each other on the streets of colonial villages, producing still more interracial friction. Furthermore, the migration of individual Indians to the English plantations was disturbing to the other Indians who chose to cling to their old independence, and who saw with dismay the weakening of tribal and family bonds. . . .
>
> At the same time, the English colonists were being hardened in the conviction that the Indians were a graceless and savage people, dirty and slothful in their personal habits, treacherous in their relations with the superior race. To put it bluntly, they were fit only to be pushed aside and subordinated, so that the land could be occupied and made productive by those for whom it had been destined by God. If the Indians could be made to fit into a humble niche in the edifice of colonial religion, economy, and government, very well, but if not, sooner or later they would have to be driven away or crushed.[6]

Throughout the westward movement, if contact led to cooperation between the two cultures, the resulting interaction and cultural diffusion usually worked to the disadvantage of the Native Americans. They lost their self-sufficiency and became economically dependent on whites. The whites, in turn, insisted on full compliance with their demands as the price of continued peaceful relations. Even if the Native Americans complied with the whites' demands, however, many whites continued to regard them as inferior people destined for a subservient role in white society.

Differing Values

Benjamin Franklin offered a classic example of different values in his account of a treaty signed between the whites and the Iroquois in 1744:

> After the principal Business was settled, the Commissioners from Virginia acquainted the Indians by a Speech, that there was at Williamsburg a College, with a Fund for

Educating Indian youth; and that, if the Six Nations would send down half a dozen of their young Lads to that College, the Government would take care that they should be well provided for, and instructed in all the Learning of the White People. . . . [The Indians'] Speaker began . . . "We are convinc'd . . . that you mean to do us Good by your Proposal; and we thank you heartily. But you, who are wise, must know that different Nations have different Conceptions of things; and you will therefore not take it amiss, if our Ideas of this kind of Education happen not to be the same with yours. We have had some Experience of it; Several of our young People were formerly brought up at the Colleges of the Northern Provinces; they were instructed in all your Sciences; but, when they came back to us, they were bad Runners, ignorant of every means of living in the Woods, unable to bear either Cold or Hunger, knew neither how to build a Cabin, take a Deer, or kill an Enemy, knew our Language imperfectly, were therefore neither fit for Hunters, Warriors, nor Counsellors; they were totally good for nothing. We are however not the less oblig'd by your kind Offer, tho' we decline accepting it; and, to show our grateful Sense of it, if the Gentlemen of Virginia will send us a Dozen of their Sons, we will take great Care of their Education, instruct them in all we know, and make *Men* of them."[7]

Almost 100 years later, George Catlin offered insight into another manifestation of differing value orientations. Catlin, a 19th-century artist famous for his paintings of Native Americans and his sensitivity to their ways, described how each of the two cultures viewed the other:

The civilized world look upon a group of Indians, in their classic dress, with their few and simple oddities, all of which have their moral or meaning, and laugh at them excessively, because they are not like ourselves—we ask, "why do the silly creatures wear such great bunches of quills on their heads?—Such loads and streaks of paint upon their bodies—and bear's grease? abominable"! and a thousand other equally silly questions, without ever stopping to think that Nature taught them to do so— and that they all have some definite importance or meaning which an Indian could explain to us at once, if he were asked and felt disposed to do so—that each quill in his head stood, in the eyes of his whole tribe, as the symbols of any enemy who had fallen by his hand—that every streak of red paint covered a wound which he had got in honourable combat—and that the bear's grease with which he carefully anoints his body every morning, from head to foot, cleanses and purifies the body, and protects his skin from the bite of mosquitoes, and at the same time preserves him from colds and coughs which are usually taken through the pores of the skin.

At the same time, an Indian looks at the civilized world, no doubt, with equal, if not much greater, astonishment, at our apparently, as well as really, ridiculous customs and fashions; but he laughs not, nor ridicules, nor questions—for his natural good sense and good manners forbid him,—until he is reclining about the fireside of his wigwam companions, when he vents forth his just criticisms upon the learned world, who are a rich and just theme for Indian criticism and Indian gossip.

An Indian will not ask a white man the reason why he does not oil his skin with bear's grease, or why he does not paint his body—or why he wears a hat on his head, or why he has buttons on the back of his coat, where they can never be used—why he wears whiskers, and a shirt collar up to his eyes—or why he sleeps with his head towards the fire instead of his feet—why he walks with his toes out instead of turning them in—or why it is that hundreds of white folks will flock and crowd round a table to see an Indian eat—but he will go home to his wigwam fireside, and "make the welkin ring" with jokes and fun upon the ignorance and folly of the knowing world.[8]

These two selections sharply illustrate how culture shapes an individual's view of reality. When people use their own group as a frame of reference in judging another group, the resulting ethnocentric judgments declare the outgroup to be strange and inferior.

One Native American nation, the Iroquois, had a pronounced influence on some of the provisions of the U.S. Constitution. Iroquois is a name given to five Native American tribes located in New York State and the Ohio River Valley—the Cayuga, Mohawk, Oneida, Onondaga, and Seneca—who united in a league in 1570. They added a sixth tribe—the Tuscarora—in 1722 and took other groups, including the Delaware, under their protection. The League was still expanding and maturing when it was curtailed by white settlers; by 1851 it had virtually disappeared.

In its time, the League's democratic processes were so effective that romanticists called the Iroquois the "Greeks in America," and many aspects of their system served as models for the colonists. Called the Great Law of Peace, the Iroquois constitution gave each of the five tribes an equal voice, guaranteed freedom of political and religious expression, and had amendment and impeachment processes.[9]

VALUES AND SOCIAL STRUCTURE

Although the cultures of the many tribes differed (and still differ today) from one another, some marked similarities have existed among them. For one thing, the Native Americans have lived in close and intimate relationship with nature, respecting and not abusing the land. They have traditionally maximized the use of any animal prey—using its skin for clothing and shelter, its bones for various tools and implements, its sinews for thread, its meat for food, its bladder for a container, and so on.

Native American approaches toward possessing the land itself ranged from individual to joint to tribal ownership, depending on the tribe. Most frequently, the land belonged to the tribe; as tribal members, individuals or families could live on and possibly farm certain portions. Land no longer cultivated by one Native American could be cultivated by another. However, the nominal owner could not dispose of the property without considering the land-use rights of the current user. More emphasis was thus placed on the rights of the user than on the rights and power of the nominal owner.[10] In terms of shared access, this practice resembles a law in present-day Sweden that roughly translates as "every person's right." In that country, a landowner cannot deny others access to the land, since all are entitled to enjoy its beauty. Thus campers and hikers do not encounter no-trespassing signs; because all respect the land, littering and other forms of abuse are quite rare.

With regard to personal interaction, Native Americans established primary relationships either through a clan system (descent from a common ancestor) or through a friendship system, much like the systems of other tribal societies:

> Kin relationships were the basic building blocks of Indian society. These blocks were formed into social and political structures ranging from nuclear families to vast empires. The Indians, in their initial attempts to establish a basis of cooperation with the immigrant whites, attempted to incorporate the newcomers into the familiar kinship system. When proffered marriage alliances were turned down by the whites, the Indians sought to establish relationships based on the reciprocal responsibilities of brother to brother, nephew to uncle, and, finally, children to father. The white man refused the proferred relationships, misinterpreted Indian speech as weakness, and increasingly imposed his will on the disheartened remnants of once proud Indian nations.[11]

Native American children grow up under the encouragement and discipline of the extended family, not just the nuclear family. A generalized love of all children in the tribe, rather than just their own progeny, is common among Native Americans.[12] This factor may help explain the permissive and indulgent child-rearing practices many early Europeans reported.[13] Whether the Native American tribe was a hunting, fishing, or farming society, the children were raised in a cooperative, noncompetitive, affectionate atmosphere. Considered from the outset as an individual, the child developed a sense of responsibility and interdependence at an early age. Unrestrained displays of affection or temper and the use of corporal punishment have rarely been part of traditional Native American child-care practices. Instead, the means of social control are shame and ridicule, and the Native American matures into an individual keenly aware of any form of conduct that would lead other members of the tribe to react negatively. Sometimes the price of emphasizing these forms of social control is heavy, for a great deal of psychological harm can be caused by shame and ridicule.

Closely related to sensitivity to shame and ridicule is the Native American concept of personal honor, including the honor of one's word. Once pledged, whether to a white person or to another Native American, that word was considered inviolate. Exceptions did exist; Albert Britt reports that chiefs "lied only as a war measure, personal or tribal—later, in an attempt to please the white."[14] Some tribes had no word for *thief,* although an enemy's goods were always fair game. Sometimes, as among the Sioux, Crow, and Blackfeet, young men of one tribe would steal from another tribe as a form of sport or a joke; but normally they would not steal from one another.[15]

The Native American woman's role differed from the man's. Women's functions were to work and to raise children. However, the notion that women held a subservient position and labored long and hard while the men idled away their time is inaccurate. Actually, a cooperative but not egalitarian arrangement existed between the sexes, with the men doing the heavy work and the women doing tasks that would not conflict with their child-rearing responsibilities. In hunting and fishing societies, the men would be away from the village for extended periods searching for food. In farming societies, the men cleared and cultivated the land,

and the women tended the crops, collected edible foods, and gathered firewood while the men sought a fresh meat supply. Each member of the tribe, according to sexually defined roles, had kinship and tribal responsibilities to fulfill.

STEREOTYPING OF NATIVE AMERICANS

One popular misconception was that the Native American was a bloodthirsty savage. Some tribes, such as the Apache and Ute, were warlike, but most sought to avoid conflict if they could. Rivalries did exist among various tribes, however; and the French, English, and (later) U.S. settlers often exploited these rivalries for their own advantage. Native Americans believed strongly in retributive justice: A wrong had to be repaid, even if it took years, but not to a greater degree. Scalping, often depicted in films as a standard Native American practice, was not common. Even tribes that did scalp frequently did so because of their belief in retributive justice. Some historians argue that the Native American first learned about scalping from white settlers:

> Whatever its exact origins, there is no doubt that scalp-taking quickly spread over all of North America, except in the Eskimo areas; nor is there any doubt that its spread was due to the barbarity of White men rather than to the barbarity of Red men. White settlers early offered to pay bounties on dead Indians, and scalps were actual proof of the dead. Governor Kieft of New Netherland is usually credited with originating the idea of paying for Indian scalps, as they were more convenient to handle than whole heads, and they offered the same proof that an Indian had been killed. By liberal payment for scalps, the Dutch virtually cleared southern New York and New Jersey of Indians before the English supplanted them. By 1703 the colony of Massachusetts was paying the equivalent of about $60 for every Indian scalp. In the mid-eighteenth century, Pennsylvania fixed the bounty for a male Indian scalp at $134; a female's was worth only $50. Some White entrepreneurs simply hatcheted any old Indians that still survived in their towns.[16]

Another side of the Native American stereotype is the portrayal of them as silent or aloof. This image probably grew out of normal behavior in ambiguous situations, such as those faced by Native Americans transported to Europe for exhibition, transported to Washington, DC, for treaty negotiations, or interacting with strangers. Because they had developed from childhood a strong inclination to avoid acting in any way that might bring about shame or ridicule, Native Americans often remained silent for fear of speaking or acting improperly. This practice is still common in courtship, in the greeting offered to children returning from boarding school, and in the face of harsh, angry words from a white. In each instance, the practice among most tribes is to allow some time, perhaps days or months, to elapse before the uncertainty is sufficiently reduced to permit conversation. Native American silence is a precautionary device to preserve respect and dignity on both sides.[17] It does not represent aloofness, and it is temporary, continuing only until the situation lends itself to speaking.

In a larger context, William Lang has identified the fundamental difference in values that separates European Americans from Native Americans. European Amer-

Throughout the American Southwest, Native Americans selling handcrafted jewelry is a common sight at numerous roadside stands or a sidewalk bazaars, such as this scene in Santa Fe. With limited occupational choices available, utilizing artistic skills of one's heritage preserves the past and helps meet present-day economic needs.
(*Source:* © Karen Preuss/The Image Works)

icans have a tendency to separate and categorize elements of experience in the belief that this process leads to ultimate knowledge. Statistical truth thus becomes the key to knowledge and to understanding human behavior. This approach has led to spectacular advances in science and technology but also to an "attitude of arrogant superiority" that dismisses other approaches as unsophisticated and inadequate (see the accompanying Ethnic Experience box). In contrast, says Lang, Native Americans have a holistic, or symbiotic, view of existence, seeing it as a great circle, or sacred hoop, representing unity and equality, linking all aspects of culture—art, religion, ritual, social organization, language, law, and lifestyle. Life is thus a complex matrix of entities, emotions, revelations, and cooperative enterprises; and the hallmark of the Native American approach is to experience rather than to interpret human existence. Because everything is interconnected, Native Americans believe a unified approach to life is more satisfying than a fragmentary one.[18]

CHANGES IN GOVERNMENT POLICY

Official European and U.S. government policy toward the Native Americans has changed frequently over the years (see Figure 7.2). In 1763, King George III of

The International Scene
A New Treaty Ends Exploitation

*T*hroughout the 20th century, fishing, lumber, and mining companies have removed millions of dollars' worth of natural resources from the rugged Nass Valley in northwestern British Columbia. The Nisga'a Indians who live in this spectacular mountain valley laid claim to the fish, timber, and minerals taken from their territory all along, but never received any compensation whatsoever. With no control over their own land and few other economic options, the Nisga'a lived in poverty in substandard housing and typically had a 60 percent unemployment rate.

The Nisga'a had sought a treaty since 1887 to protect their rights and land claims. After two decades of negotiations, the Canadian government and the tribe reached agreement in August 1998. The 5,500-member tribe will receive $126 million in cash over a 15-year period, title to 745 square miles in the Nass Valley, and return of about 250 Nisga'a artifacts from museums in Hull, Quebec, and Victoria, British Columbia. In return, the tribe will relinquish claim to the other nine-tenths of their original land claim as well as their tax-exempt status, although they will retain the right to self-government,

with their own justice system (judges, police, and jails).

Some dissenters in the tribe think too much was given up, and the opposition British Columbian Liberal Party objects to creating "a whole new order of government" and "entrenching inequality based on race." For its part, the right-wing Reform Party opposes the treaty as "an unwelcome step toward creation of mini-states for each of British Columbia's native communities." Nevertheless, the Nisga'a approved the treaty in 1998 and slightly more than a year later both the British Columbia and Canadian legislatures did the same. In May 2000, the treaty—the first between a North American tribe and a national government since the 19th century—went into effect. The government transferred the land to the Nisga'a Nation, and created Bear Glacier Provincial Park and a water reservation. Two months later the B.C. Supreme Court upheld the legislation and treaty as "constitutionally valid."

Critical thinking question: Why doesn't the United States negotiate treaties with its Native American tribes?

Source: Adapted from David Crary, "Indian Treaty Splits British Columbia," Associated Press, August 4, 1998.

England issued a proclamation declaring that thenceforth the Native American tribes would be treated as independent nations and denying the colonies any jurisdiction over them. Thereafter, if the colonists wanted to obtain additional Native American lands or negotiate trade pacts, they had to do so through the English government and not directly with the Native Americans.

FIGURE 7.2 Government Actions Toward Native Americans

1763 English Royal Proclamation: Tribes accorded independent nation status; all lands west of the Appalachian mountains are Native American country; the royal government must approve all land purchases.

1778 Continental Congress: Reaffirms the old British policy as U.S. policy.

1787 Northwest Territory Ordinance: Opens the Midwest for settlement; declares the U.S. government responsible for Native American property, rights, and liberty.

1824 Bureau of Indian Affairs is created under the jurisdiction of the Secretary of War.

1830 Indian Removal Bill: Mandates all Indians must move west of the Mississippi River.

1830–1843 Except for Iroquois and Seminole, more than 100,000 eastern Native Americans are forcibly relocated westward. About 12,000 die on the "Trail of Tears."

1850–1880 Most reservations are established, as forced segregation becomes the new Native American reality.

1871 Appropriations bill rider: Declares tribes no longer are independent nations; legislation, not negotiation, is to determine any new arrangements.

1887 Dawes Act: Reservations surveyed, divided in tracts, and allotted to individual tribal members; surplus land sold.

1898 Curtis Act: Terminates tribal governments that refuse allotment; the President is to appoint tribal chiefs henceforth.

1906 Burke Act: Eliminates Native Americans' right to lease their land, with the intent to force Native Americans to work the land themselves.

1924 Indian Citizenship Act: Grants U.S. citizenship to Native Americans.

1934 Indian Reorganization Act: Ends allotment; encourages tribal self-government; restores freedom of religion; extends financial credit; promotes the revival of Native American culture and crafts.

1952 Relocation Program: Moves Native Americans at government expense to urban areas for better job opportunities.

1953 Termination Act: Authorizes elimination of reservation systems, with an immediate end to federal services and tax immunity.

1973 Menominee Restoration Act: Revokes termination and restores the Menominee's reservation and tribal status.

1974 Indian Finance Act: Facilitates financing of Native American enterprises and development projects through grants and loans.

1975 Indian Self-Determination and Education Assistance Act: Expands tribal control over reservation programs; provides funding for new public schools on or near reservations.

1976 Indian Health Care Improvement Act: Provides funds to build or renovate hospitals, add more personnel, and give scholarships to Native Americans to enter Indian Health Service.

1978 Education Amendments Act: Gives substantial control over education programs to local Native American community.

1978 Tribally Controlled Community College Assistance Act: Provides grants to tribal community colleges.

1978 Indian Child Welfare Act: Restricts placement of Native American children by non–Native American social agencies in non–Native American homes.

1978 American Indian Religious Freedom Act: Protects religious rights of Native Americans, including their use of peyote.

1993 Religious Freedom Restoration Act: Restores standards of review for American Indian Religious Freedom Act that were overturned by a Supreme Court ruling in 1990.

1993 Omnibus Indian Advancement Act: Establishes foundation for gifts to BIA schools; increases economic development opportunities for tribes; improves tribal governance.

Historians cite enforcement of this policy as an indirect cause of the American Revolution. In addition to the delay involved in drawing up petitions, crossing the ocean back and forth, and waiting for bureaucratic processing, the colonists fumed over the fact that heathens were being accorded higher official status than they enjoyed. Yet when the colonies declared their independence from England, they adopted the same policy, in 1778; and the tribes retained quasi-national status. Congress reaffirmed this policy when it passed the Northwest Territory Ordinance in 1787, declaring the federal government—and not the states—responsible for Native American property, rights, and liberty.

Indian Removal Act

In 1830, by a close vote, Congress passed the Indian Removal Act recommended by President Andrew Jackson. This act called for **expulsion** of all Native Americans from the southeastern states and their relocation to the territory west of the Mississippi River. The legislation was prompted in part by the state of Georgia, which for several years had been annexing the fertile land of the Cherokee for its expanding cotton industry. The Cherokee had rejected Georgia's assertion of legal authority to settle disputes over all lands within its borders, and petitioned the U.S. Supreme Court for protection, citing their "foreign nation" status and treaties with the federal government.

Combining two cases, *Cherokee Nation v. Georgia* and *Worcester v. Georgia*, Chief Justice John Marshall delivered the majority opinion on February 28, 1832, establishing the foundation that has shaped U.S. Native American policy ever since. The Cherokee were not a foreign nation, the court ruled, and therefore could not sue Georgia. They were instead a "domestic dependent nation," a "distinct community, occupying its own territory." Because of this definition, the court said, the laws of Georgia had no jurisdiction, and the court thus ruled in favor of the Cherokee keeping the land.

President Jackson reportedly responded, "John Marshall has rendered his decision, now let him enforce it." Indeed, two of the three branches of government favored removal of the Cherokee, and Jackson interpreted his overwhelming re-election in November as a mandate from the electorate to pursue that policy. Jackson thus moved to enforce the Indian Removal Act, launching one of the ugliest episodes in the nation's history.

Expulsion. After signing the Treaty of Dancing Rabbit Creek (1830) under compulsion, the Choctaw of Mississippi were the first to face removal. The government forcibly relocated 20,000, of whom 5,000 died from famine and disease along the march to Indian Territory in Oklahoma. In 1836, the army moved against the Creek in Alabama, forcing 17,000 westward; 2,000 died from exposure, famine, and disease en route, and another 3,500 died within three months of arrival. About 1,000 Chickasaw in Mississippi died during their forced march.[19] The Seminole in Florida successfully resisted expulsion by adapting guerrilla-warfare tactics in the Everglades, killing almost 2,000 soldiers and costing the U.S. Army more than $20 million before it gave up the fight.[20]

The Cherokee.   In about 1790, the Cherokee, after some 14 years of warfare with the whites, decided to adopt U.S. customs and culture. In other words, they actively sought assimilation in an effort to live harmoniously with a different civilization. Over the next 40 years, their success in achieving this goal was remarkable. They converted their economy to one based on agriculture and commerce, strengthened their self-governing political system, and prospered. They cultivated farmlands in the fertile soil of the tristate region of Georgia, Tennessee, and North Carolina, and reaped bountiful harvests. The Cherokee patterned themselves after the whites, setting up churches, schools, sawmills, grist mills, and blacksmith shops. They acquired spinning wheels, looms, plows, and all the other implements of white society.

Most extraordinary of all was the achievement of a Cherokee named Sequoyah. In 1821, after a 12-year struggle, he succeeded in inventing a phonetic syllabary notation system for the Cherokee language. This immense accomplishment was unprecedented in world history. An untrained man had been able to write a language by himself, and to do so in a way that could be learned easily. Remarkably, within three years almost all the Cherokee could read and write their own language. By 1828, the tribe had its own newspaper and had adopted a written constitution, a code of laws, a bicameral legislature, and an appellate judiciary.

By U.S. standards, the Cherokee were the most "civilized" tribe in the country. Driven by a desire for self-improvement, they had educated themselves, converted to Christianity, and learned the whites' ways of agriculture, business, and government. They had successfully acculturated. Only one problem remained: The whites wanted their rich land for cotton growing, and consequently the Cherokee now faced eviction, too.

With U.S. public opinion against the Cherokee, the voices of John Marshall, Daniel Webster, Henry Clay, Sam Houston, Davy Crockett, and others could not help the Cherokee cause. Georgia confiscated Cherokee lands and redistributed them to whites through land lotteries, with the state militia stationed in the region to preserve the peace should the Native Americans resist:

> The premeditated brutality of the militia's daily conducts suggested their
> commanders' hope of provoking a Cherokee reaction which might provide
> an excuse for their immediate physical expulsion. The carefully disciplined
> Cherokee instead patiently submitted even when the provocations extended to the
> burning of their homes, the confiscation of their property, the mistreatment of
> their women, the closing of their schools, and the sale of liquor in their churches.[21]

The Cherokee retreated into the forests and continued their desperate legal maneuvering to avoid expulsion. Although federal troops removed the Choctaw and Chickasaw in Mississippi and the Creek in Alabama, they did not move against the Cherokee, who had won worldwide sympathy and whose efforts to obtain recognition of their rights in the courts continued to be successful. Instead, the federal government intensified its efforts to promote disunity among the Cherokee through bribery, jailings, persecution, and denial of the services and support guaranteed under treaties. Most of the Cherokee remained loyal to their president, John Ross, and rejected the proposed treaty of removal and its $5 million compensation payment.

Government officials finally succeeded in getting the treaty signed on December 29, 1835, by convening an ad hoc council of President Ross's Cherokee opponents. Fewer than 500 of the 17,000 Cherokee appeared, but they signed the treaty, and the Senate ratified the pact on May 18, 1836. Ross and the Cherokee people fought this fraudulent treaty; and in January 1838, Ross presented the Senate with a petition signed by 15,665 Cherokee repudiating the document. The Senate rejected the petition by a vote of 37 to 10. A new wave of public protest against the government's conduct toward the Cherokee swelled in the North, including an impassioned open letter to President Van Buren by Ralph Waldo Emerson, but these results did not alter the outcome. On April 10, 1838, Van Buren ordered General Winfield Scott to remove the Cherokee immediately, using whatever military force was necessary. The U.S. government, through its military forces, acted against an entire people who had willingly adapted to the changing world around them. Soldiers forced them at gunpoint from their homes, first to stockades and then westward, far from all that had been theirs:

> Families at dinner were startled by the sudden gleam of bayonets in the doorway and rose up to be driven with blows and oaths along the weary miles to the stockade. Men were seized in their fields or going along the road, women were taken from their wheels and children from their play. In many cases, on turning for one last look as they crossed the ridge, they saw their homes in flames, fired by the lawless rabble that followed on the heels of the soldiers to loot and pillage. So keen were these outlaws on the scent that in some instances they were driving off the cattle and other stock of the Indians almost before the soldiers had fairly started their owners in the other direction. Systematic hunts were made by the same men for Indian graves, to rob them of the silver pendants and other valuables deposited with the dead. A Georgia volunteer, afterward a colonel in the Confederate service, said: "I fought through the Civil War and have seen men shot to pieces and slaughtered by thousands, but the Cherokee removal was the cruelest work I ever knew."[22]

The Cherokee suffered extensively during this mass expulsion. Beginning in October 1838, army troops marched the Cherokee westward along what the Cherokee later called the Trail of Tears: 10 to 20 Native Americans died each day from exposure and other miseries. By March 1839, fewer than 9,000 of the 13,000 who had set out survived to reach the Indian Territory, which is now Oklahoma. At the midpoint of this sad episode—December 3, 1838—President Van Buren's message to Congress announced,

> It affords me sincere pleasure to apprise the Congress of the entire removal of the Cherokee Nation of Indians to their new homes west of the Mississippi. The measures authorized by Congress at its last session have had the happiest effects. . . . They have emigrated without any apparent reluctance.[23]

Reservations and Dependence

A shift in U.S. government policy in the mid-nineteenth century changed Native American lifestyles to such an extent that its aftereffects remain visible today on any reservation. Instead of using annihilation and expulsion to deal with the Native Americans, the government embarked on a policy of segregation and isolation. Between 1850 and 1880, it established most of the nation's Indian reservations, which now number more than 300.

In 1871, Congress tacked onto an appropriations bill a rider that ended federal recognition of the Native American tribes as independent, **sovereign** nations—or "domestic dependent nations," for that matter—and made them wards of the government instead. Bureaucrats became responsible for the welfare of the Native American peoples, issuing them food rations and supervising every aspect of their lives. The results were devastating. Proud and independent people who had been taught self-reliance at an early age now depended on non–Native American government agents. Many of the tribes had been nomadic and found it difficult to adjust to reservation life. Such problems as inadequate administration by the government agents and irregular delivery of food, supplies, and equipment made matters worse.

The government was still not through restructuring the Native Americans' lifestyles, either, for U.S. leaders at the time believed that what they were doing was "for the best." Americanization became the goal. This meant destroying tribal organizations, suppressing "pagan" religions and ceremonies, allowing only English to be the language of instruction in the schools, requiring "white" hair and clothing styles, and teaching only the dominant (white) group's culture and history:

> Most of the attention of the Americanizers was concentrated on the Indian children, who were snatched from their families and shipped off to boarding schools far from their homes. The children usually were kept at boarding school for eight years, during which time they were not permitted to see their parents, relatives or friends. Anything Indian—dress, language, religious practices, even outlook on life (and how that was defined was up to the judgment of each administration of the government's directives)—was uncompromisingly prohibited. Ostensibly educated, articulate in the English language, wearing store-bought clothes, and with their hair short and their emotionalism toned down, the boarding-school graduates were sent out either to make their way in a white world that did not want them, or to return to a reservation to which they were now foreign.[24]

One value promulgated was the rugged individualism of white society, rather than the cooperative, noncompetitive approach of the Native American. This was the purpose of the General Allotment Act of 1887. Its sponsor, Senator Dawes, genuinely believed that the law would engender in the Native American that spirit of self-interest that he considered the major force in white civilization.

In reality, this legislation deprived the Native Americans of even more land. Its goal was to break the backbone of Native American culture by ending communal ownership of reservation lands and instead giving each Native American a share. Many of the Native Americans had no technical knowledge of farming and neither the cash nor the credit to obtain farm implements. Some Native American peoples believed it was sacrilegious to plow the earth. Loopholes in the Dawes Act enabled unscrupulous whites to plunder the Native Americans' lands, either through low-cost, long-term leases or by convincing Native American owners to write wills leaving their property to white "friends." This practice was widespread, and a mysterious increase in the number of Native American deaths followed; some of these deaths were later proved to have been murders.[25]

In 1898, faced with tribes that refused to accept the allotment policy, the government passed the Curtis Act. This law terminated the tribal governments of all tribes that resisted allotment, and it made their tribal chiefs presidential appointments thereafter. By 1914, the 138 million acres of Native American holdings had been reduced to 56 million acres of eroded, poor-quality land.[26]

Indian Reorganization Act

After 1933, Franklin Roosevelt's administration shifted from a policy of forced assimilation to one of pluralism. Secretary of the Interior Harold L. Ickes and Bureau of Indian Affairs (BIA) Commissioner John Collier, in particular, deeply sympathized with the Native American cause. One outcome was the Indian Reorganization Act of 1934, which ended the land-allotment program, encouraged tribal self-government, extended financial credit to the tribes, gave preference in BIA employment to Native Americans, and permitted consolidation of Native American lands split up through inheritance. Furthermore, the Native Americans were encouraged to revive their ancient arts and crafts, their languages, their religions and ceremonies, and their customs and traditions. In keeping with an administrative philosophy of treating the Native Americans with dignity, the act was permissive, not mandatory; each tribe could vote to accept or reject the new law. Most chose to accept it.

In the 1950s, new top administrative personnel in President Eisenhower's Interior Department and the BIA espoused a different philosophy and tried to shift the BIA back to assimilationist policy. Some critics of the 1934 legislation considered it regressive. Now these people, believing that the only way to end the chronic poverty, disease, overpopulation, and hopelessness among the Native Americans was to end the isolation of reservation life, tried some new approaches.

The Relocation Program

Beginning in 1952 while President Truman was still in office, the Bureau of Indian Affairs attempted to lessen the problem of overpopulation on the reservations. The BIA provided financial and other assistance to individuals or families who wanted to obtain jobs and living accommodations in urban areas. For many Native Americans, the word relocation had terrible connotations. That euphemism had been used for the internment camps in which 110,000 Japanese Americans had been placed during World War II. Furthermore, Dillon S. Myer, the government administrator who had been in charge of those camps, was now in charge of the Native American relocation program.

Most Native Americans who enrolled in this program (out of about 40,000 total) went to work in low-status unskilled or semiskilled jobs and found housing in the poorer sections of the cities. Some adjusted and became acculturated; others felt uprooted and were driven to alcoholism or other problems. More than one fourth of the total number returned to the reservations. The program tapered off after 1960, due mostly to other efforts to improve Native American life.

The Termination Act

A series of bills passed in 1953–1954 sought to end federal responsibility for welfare and administration of Native Americans by ending all federal services and federal liaison with tribal organizations and by dispensing receipts from the sale of reservation land among all tribal entities. Medical care, schools, road maintenance, and other federal services guaranteed under treaty obligations were immediately halted, instead of being gradually withdrawn to allow a period of transitional adjustments. Tribes such as the Menominee of Wisconsin were forced to sell lakefront property to maintain essential services. The termination acts affected 109 tribes and bands, a total of 13,263 Native Americans, and over 1.3 million acres of trust land.[27]

Two of the more prosperous tribes, the Klamath of southern Oregon and the Menominee of Wisconsin (both of whom owned considerable tracts of valuable timberland), as well as some Paiute and Ute in Utah, and several other tribes were among the first to be affected by this legislation. For the Klamath, a tribe of 668 families totaling some 2,000 individuals, termination threatened to obliterate their tribal identity. In the spring of 1968, when 77 percent of the tribe's members voted to withdraw from the tribe and receive a cash payment for their share of the land-holdings, many government and business officials feared that liquidating tribal assets when the lumber market was already depressed would threaten the Pacific Northwest economy. Instead of selling the lumber, Congress voted to purchase the land, which it used to create the Winema National Forest. A federal trusteeship for adults declared incompetent to handle their own affairs and for minors kept the government involved in the affairs of 48.9 percent of the tribe members.[28]

In the case of the Menominee, the new policy brought economic disaster:

> Almost overnight, many millions of dollars of tribal assets disappeared in the rush to transform the Menominee reservation into a self-supporting county. The need to finance the usual hospital, police, and other services of a county and pay taxes imperiled the tribe's sawmill and forest holdings, alienated tribal lands, threatened many Indians with the loss of their homes and life savings, and saddled Wisconsin with a huge welfare problem which it could not underwrite and which had to be met by desperate appeals for help from the same federal government that had thought it had washed its hands of the Menominees.[29]

The standard of living dropped sharply as the tribe lost its ability to furnish water, electricity, and health care. Shortly after termination, a tuberculosis epidemic swept through the Menominee. Washington's reckless policy shift cost the Menominee their hospital, their sawmill, and some of their best land, which they had to sell because they could not afford the taxes on it. President Nixon officially repudiated the termination policy in 1970, and Congress reversed the termination

TABLE 7.1 Formerly Terminated Native American Tribes Now Restored

Tribe or Band	State	Population	Acres
Alabama–Coushatta	Texas	450	3,200
California Rancherias (37–38 rancherias)	California	1,107	4,315
Catawba	South Carolina	631	3,388
Coyote Valley Ranch	California	NA	NA
Klamath	Oregon	2,133	862,662
Lower Lake Rancheria	California	NA	NA
Menominee	Wisconsin	3,270	233,881
Ottawa	Oklahoma	630	NA
Peoria	Oklahoma	640	NA
Ponca	Nebraska	442	834
Southern Paiute	Utah	232	42,839
Western Oregon (61 tribes and bands)	Oregon	2,081	3,158
Wyandotte	Oklahoma	1,157	94

Note: NA = not available.
Source: Bureau of Indian Affairs.

of the Menominee in December 1973. The Restoration Act re-created their reservation, but the Menominee never got back their old hospital or their sawmill.

The following year, the Menominee took over the abandoned 64-room Alexian Brothers monastery to serve as their new hospital. It had been built on Menominee land at a time when any church group could take as much Native American reservation land as it needed to build religious structures. Local whites, who had bought tribal land cheaply when the tribe had to sell, objected, although the Alexian Brothers did not. When bloodshed seemed imminent, the governor of Wisconsin called out the National Guard to maintain order. A peaceful accommodation was reached, and the Menominee won permanent possession of the building. Between 1977 and 1990, most of the other tribes that had been terminated also had their federal recognition restored (see Table 7.1) but, in many cases, not their land.

PRESENT-DAY NATIVE AMERICAN LIFE

Of all the minorities in the United States, according to government statistics on income, employment, and housing, Native Americans are "the poorest of the poor." It is cruelly ironic that most of the Native Americans' problems are due not only to their subordinate position as a result of conquest but also to their insistence on their right to be different, to continue living as Native Americans. In a society that has long demanded assimilation, this insistence has not been popular.

Population

By 2000, the Native American population was 2.5 million, up from 2.1 million in 1990.[30] Some of this increase reflects a rise in the number of people claiming Native American ancestry who had not heretofore done so; but in addition, the Native American birth rate is almost twice the national average.

As Figure 7.3 indicates, the age distribution of the Native American population (including Alaska Natives) is weighted toward the younger years to a much greater extent than that of the total U.S. population. The greater ratio of the population in childbearing age groups suggests continued faster rates of population increase among Native Americans. They are far from being the "vanishing Americans" some observers have claimed. Yet half live on reservations that provide inadequate economic support for those already living there.

Employment

Chronic unemployment is a serious problem, exceeding 50 percent on most reservations and on reaching as high as 95 percent at the Rosebud reservation in South Dakota. Up to 75 percent of those who do work are on federal payrolls, providing

FIGURE 7.3 **Native American Population, 2000 (in percentages)**

Native American Population			Age	Total U.S. Population		
Males		Females		Males		Females
	0.8	1.3	75+		2.2	3.7
	0.6	0.8	70-74		1.4	1.7
	0.9	1.1	65-69	Median age 31.7	1.6	1.8	Median age 34.1
	1.3	1.4	60-64		1.8	2.0
	1.8	1.9	55-59		2.3	2.4
	2.5	2.7	50-54		3.1	3.1
	3.4	3.3	45-49		3.5	3.6
	3.7	3.9	40-44		4.0	3.9
	4.0	4.1	35-39		4.0	4.0
	3.8	3.7	30-34		3.7	3.5
	3.8	3.7	25-29		3.5	3.3
	4.1	3.9	20-24		3.4	3.2
	4.8	4.6	15-19		3.7	3.4
	5.0	4.8	10-14		3.7	3.4
	4.9	4.8	5-9		3.7	3.4
	4.4	4.2	0-4		3.5	3.2

Percentage   Percentage

Source: U.S. Bureau of the Census.

education, health care, and social services to their fellow tribespeople. Others eke out an existence from fishing, from raising small herds of sheep or cattle, or from small-plot gardening (if they have enough water).[31]

Tribal Enterprise.   Some tribes have succeeded through their own efforts. The Mississippi Choctaw are one of the 10 largest employers in that state, with enterprises that include five auto-parts factories and one greeting-card operation; overall, they employ over 8,000 workers.[32] Similar successful operations can be found among the Salt River Pima Maricopa of Arizona, New Mexico's Jicarilla Apache, and the Devils Lake Sioux of North Dakota. The Oklahoma Cherokee now receive half of their funds from commercial ventures, including Cherokee Nation Industries, which constructs military components. Most successful have been the Maine Passamaquoddy, whose diversified investments from a land-claims settlement netted a $60 million profit from the sale of a cement plant in 1988. Owning the patent rights to an antipollution technology known as a recovery scrubber, which turns harmful sulfur dioxide and dust into limestone and fertilizer, the tribe has a financially secure future.[33]

The Pequot tribe in Mashantucket, Connecticut, owns Foxwoods, a spectacular example of a successful gambling casino bringing great wealth to tribal members. However, it is one of a few exceptions, for most tribal gambling casinos are small-time bingo or poker gambling halls, whose revenues do little to combat the poor economic conditions that plague so many reservations.

(*Source:* © Michael Dwyer/Stock Boston)

The "New Buffalo."   Because federal law permits them to offer any form of gambling not prohibited in other parts of the state, some tribes have improved their financial situation with casinos. Nicknamed the "new buffalo" because of their role in providing for the tribes' well-being, most of these casinos are little more than glorified bingo halls, in some instances permitting poker games as well. About half of the 275 reservations now have casinos of some sort. The most successful gambling operations are run by the Mashantucket Pequot in Connecticut, the Florida Seminole just outside Miami, and the Cabazon near Palm Springs, California.

Life Expectancy

Demographic statistics (see Table 7.2) testify to the harshness and deprivation of reservation life and the despair accompanying it.[34] The average life span in some tribes is 45 years.[34] Nationally, the Native American life span is about 10 years less than the national average. Leading causes of death among Native American adults include motor vehicle accidents, chronic liver disease and cirrhosis, diabetes, homicide, and suicide—all higher than the national average.[35]

Deaths by suicide among Native American males aged 15 to 24 are more than twice as frequent (41.8 per 100,000) as among the general population's youth (18.5 per 100,000).[36] Recent studies reveal that teens who take their lives typically belong to tribes that have loose social integration and are undergoing rapid socioeconomic change. Young persons with a high risk of suicide include substance abusers, and

TABLE 7.2   Age-Adjusted Death Rates in the United States per 100,000 Population, 1998

Cause of Death	Native Americans	All Races	Ratio
Cardiovascular disease	97.1	126.6	0.7
Malignant neoplasms (cancer)	83.4	123.6	0.7
Motor-vehicle accidents	31.8	15.6	2.1
Diabetes mellitus	29.6	13.6	2.0
Cerebrovascular disease	19.6	25.1	0.8
Chronic liver disease and cirrhosis	22.0	7.2	2.8
Pneumonia, influenza	14.1	13.2	1.1
Suicide	13.4	10.4	1.2
Homicide	9.9	7.3	1.2
HIV (AIDS)	2.2	4.6	0.4

Source: National Center for Health Statistics, *Health, United States 2000* (Hyattsville, MD; NCHS, 2000), Table 30, pp. 163–164.

individuals who have had or have caused a pregnancy, who believe their family doesn't care, or who have family members or friends who have committed suicide. Another possible related factor is the fact that, in a comparison survey in rural Minnesota, 11 percent of Native American teens reported that at least one of their parents was dead, compared with 5 percent of white teens in the same region.[37]

Suicide isn't the only violence in the world of Native Americans. In 1999, the U.S. Justice Department, in its first-ever comprehensive analysis of Native Americans and crime, reported that they are more than twice as likely as others to become victims of violent crime. Although their murder is no higher than for whites and only a fifth as high as among blacks, they are three times as likely as whites and twice as likely as blacks to be victims of rape or aggravated assault. Alcohol abuse, tensions with non-Indians, poor law enforcement services, and other factors may all play a part in generating such high rates of violent crime.[38]

Alcohol Abuse

The most serious social problem facing Native Americans today is alcohol abuse, which is also a major factor in their high mortality rate. Death from alcohol-related causes is five times the national average. Native American people 25 to 34 years old have a rate of terminal liver cirrhosis nearly three times the national rate;[39] and 75 to 80 percent of Native American suicides involve the use of alcohol. Crimes related to consumption of alcohol and other drugs occur up to 20 times more often among Native Americans than among whites in the same geographic areas.[40]

Despite popular misconceptions about Native Americans' susceptibility to alcohol problems, no research to date has found Native Americans to be different from other people regarding the physiology of alcohol metabolism. As Philip A. May reports, scientific evidence shows that Native Americans metabolize alcohol as rapidly as, or more rapidly than, matched controls of non–Native Americans; alcohol metabolism and alcohol genetics are traits of individuals, and there is more variation within any ethnic group than there is between ethnic groups.[41] Moreover, some recent evidence suggests that tribal people may actually drink less than the total U.S. population. Surveyed tribes reported a 40 percent drinking rate compared to the national rate of 70 percent.[42]

Problem drinking sets in early among Native American youth. A 1992 report based on a nationwide survey found a correlation between both high emotional stress and pessimism about the future among adolescents and heavy drinking. The rate of such drinking triples between the 7th and 12th grades, to 27.3 percent. Although white youths' alcohol consumption begins to diminish after age 22, no comparable decline occurs among Native American youths.[43]

Michael Nofz suggests that cultural marginality is a key factor in understanding problem drinking among Native Americans.[44] On the one hand, Native Americans seek to maintain their tribal identity and traditional cultural heritage, even though they are not always certain what their heritage means in the context of modern life; on the other hand, they desire respect, success in the world of work and careers, and the standard of living enjoyed by the dominant society. Inner conflict occurs because the two sets of standards of Native Americans attempt to reconcile are not always consistent. What mainstream society deems appropriate may be undesirable according to tribal values, and vice versa.[45]

Education

Some significant changes have occurred since 1969, when a Special Senate Subcommittee on Indian Education issued a scathing report on the BIA school system, particularly its boarding schools:

> We are shocked at what we discovered. . . .
>
> We have developed page after page of statistics. These cold figures mark a stain on our national conscience, a stain which has spread slowly for hundreds of years. They tell a story, to be sure. But they cannot tell the whole story. They cannot, for example, tell of the despair, the frustration, the hopelessness, the poignancy, of children who want to learn but are not taught; of adults who try to read but have no one to teach them; of families which want to stay together but are forced apart; or of 9-year-old children who want neighborhood schools but are sent thousands of miles away to remote and alien boarding schools.
>
> We have seen what these conditions do to Indian children and Indian families. The sights are not pleasant.
>
> We have concluded that our national policies for educating American Indians are a failure of major proportions. They have not offered Indian children—either in years past or today—an educational opportunity anywhere near equal to that offered the great bulk of American children. Past generations of lawmakers and administrators have failed the American Indian. Our own generation thus faces a challenge—we can continue the unacceptable policies and programs of the past or we can recognize our failures, renew our commitments, and reinvest our efforts with new energy.[46]

In 1976, the American Indian Policy Review Commission criticized the BIA for failing to resolve any of these problems.[47] Singled out for especially sharp condemnation were the 19 boarding schools described as "dumping grounds for students with serious social and emotional problems," which "do not rehabilitate" but "do more harm than good."[48]

Moreover, the BIA violated official policy by not sending students to the school closest to their homes.[49] For example, Alaskan Native American children were sent to Fort Sill, Oklahoma. Others, classified as "problems," such as a girl in Washington State who objected to a history test that called her ancestors "dirty savages," were sent to distant boarding schools, as well. Not financial considerations, but the conscious intention of forcing a separation between children and their parents and between "children and the idea of the reservation" determined the location of schools.[50] (See the accompanying Ethnic Experience box.)

Others have frequently commented on the teaching of U.S. culture and history in reservation schools and on insensitivity and nonreceptivity to Native American culture and history. A typical example is a composition topic given to Chippewa children at a reservation school in the Northwest: "Why We Are All Happy the Pilgrims Landed."

The Educational Amendments Act of 1978 gave substantial control over school policy and programs to the Native American communities. Local school

The Ethnic Experience
Boarding School Experiences

"We lived for a few years on Devil's Lake Reservation in North Dakota. . . . I spoke no English until I was four years old. Everything we spoke in the house was Sioux. The religion that my mother and my father both professed was that of their respective tribes. My father had taken on the Sioux religion and my mother was Mohawk. . . .

"I can tell you more about the actual life of a reservation-born Indian, drawing from my mother's experience, than on my own. When my mother was eight years old, economic pressures and also family pressures from the point of view of social justice forced all of the five children of her family to be sent to the Haskell Indian Institute for their education. There was so little future for them if they remained on the reservation, so little possibility of an education. . . .

"My mother was still on crutches. She had had a very serious operation and she was six years between crutches and wheelchair and

had to have the operation repeated. Yet she was never excused from any one of the regimental disciplines that were rampant at Haskell. For example, the first statement off the bus was, 'You will be up at five o'clock in the morning. From this moment on there is to be no Indian spoken and the punishments are very severe for anyone who violates this law. You must speak English.'

"My mother had learned first Indian and then some French. She knew not a word of English and yet no one was allowed to ask any companion [for] even the slightest translation. My mother saw severe punishments inflicted on my aunts and uncles, but she herself, because she was so sick, was never punished. However, she was very careful not to violate the rules. Despite the fact she was still in a wheelchair, she had to be out at reveille in the morning. They were up at five o'clock. By five-fifteen they had reveille: You had to be dressed, your face washed, and you had to be

Source: Sioux–Mohawk woman whose mother went to boarding school in the 1940s.

boards and school authorities now ensure that the curriculum addresses the unique aspects of Native American culture and heritage. Further, bilingual Native American language programs in 17 states help preserve ancestral languages and teach English to children who were raised in households where only their tribal language was spoken.

Today 12 percent of Native Americans are aged 10 to 19, compared to 9 percent of other U.S. racial/ethnic groups. Unfortunately, compared to those same minority groups, fewer Native American teens will graduate from high school (65.6 percent versus 80.9 percent), and fewer still will complete college (9.4 percent versus 22.2 percent).[51] On average, if 100 Native American students enter the ninth grade, only 66 will graduate from high school. Of these graduates, fewer than half will enter college, and only about 9 will earn a degree (see Table 7.3 on page 264).

standing in military formation. Then the roll call was called. It was all with the viewpoint of checking who had escaped during the night, because escape was rampant. There was actually some kind of barbed wire around the enclosure at that time.

"My mother, however, did say she had never found a better school. Afterward she went to different schools and she had to admit the education she received at Haskell was superior. She went all the way to business college, and she got six good years of violin training, which prepared her well enough so that she was accepted by the Juilliard School of Music. So she always had admiration for the education that was afforded the Indians. However, the absolute cutoff and isolation from the tribal customs and from the language brought about a lot of culture shock. And the big thing at Haskell was to try to fool the white folks. The Indians always felt that they were on the other side of the line and that nothing would ever overcome that barrier. . . .

"The Indians were forced to take on a Christian religion. Either you adhered to a Christian religion or you were assigned to heavy duty on Sunday mornings, and nobody wanted that. So my mother simply joined the Methodist Church not out of any conviction whatsoever, but because she had had a delicate operation on the hip; and when she saw that the Catholics were bundled off in a pickup truck whereas those who went to the Methodist church had a comfortable, plush school bus, that was the cause for her choice of religion. She never, however, really joined the church, was never baptized. She simply conformed because, she said that was the way to keep the white people off her back.

"Now they say that the whole setup has changed a lot and there is none of that rigid discipline."

Approximately 80 percent of Native American students attend public schools. The rest—about 40,000 students—attend 180 BIA-operated schools in 23 states, two thirds of which are boarding schools and one third of which are on reservations.[52] Isolated reservation students often rise quite early to catch a school bus and spend hours traveling long distances, when weather permits such travel. Similarly, many secondary students are bused many miles to continue their education.

Another 1978 legislative act, the Tribally Controlled Community College Assistance Act, provides federal grant money to tribally controlled colleges in 11 western and midwestern states. About 10,000 Native Americans—a full-time equivalent of about 4,500 students—are enrolled.[53] In 1994 President Clinton signed a law giving the 29 tribally controlled colleges the status of land-grant institutions, which makes them eligible for more program grant money.[54]

TABLE 7.3   Socioeconomic Characteristics of Native Americans, 1990

	No. Persons	% HS Grad or Higher	% Coll Grad or Higher	% Families Below Poverty	% Persons Below Poverty
Cherokee	369,035	68.2	11.1	19.4	22.0
Navajo	225,298	51.0	4.5	47.3	48.8
Sioux	107,321	69.7	8.9	39.4	44.4
Chippewa (Ojibwe)	105,988	69.7	8.2	31.2	34.3
Choctaw	86,231	70.3	13.3	19.9	23.0
Pueblo	55,330	71.5	7.3	31.2	33.2
Apache	53,330	63.8	6.9	31.8	37.5
Iroquois	52,557	71.9	11.3	17.3	20.1
Lumbee	50,888	51.6	9.4	20.2	22.1
All Native Americans	1,937,391	65.6	9.4	27.2	31.2

Source: U.S. Bureau of the Census, *1990 Census of Population: Characteristics of American Indians by Tribe and Language,* 1990 CP-3-7.

Housing

One of the most visible signs of Native Americans' economic deprivation is re-servation housing, called "open-air slums" by some critics. Mostly located down back roads and therefore rarely seen by reservation visitors, the various tribes live in small, overcrowded western-style houses, in mobile homes, or in hogans—traditional one-room, eight-sided log houses with sod roofs. Many Native American homes lack indoor plumbing, and residents must haul water from a mile or more away. The Indian Health Service says that in some parts of "Indian country" 35 percent of homes don't have safe water and sewage systems.[55] Because many Native Americans live in crowded dwellings without running water, infectious dis-eases spread more rapidly. A 1990 study of New Mexico Native Americans found their **mortality rate** from such infectious diseases as tuberculosis, influenza, pneu-monia, kidney infection, meningitis, and parasitic diseases to be greater than that of other population groups.[56]

NATURAL RESOURCES

Encroachment on Native American land to obtain natural resources or fertile land continues. The need for water and energy has led government and industry to look covetously at reservation land once considered worthless. In July 1978, 2,000 Native Americans participated in a 2,700-mile march to Washington, DC. There they successfully demonstrated against several proposed bills that would have allowed strip mining and siphoning of groundwater from tribal land, although both have since occurred on some reservations.

Exploitation and Emerging Control

Under 53 million acres held by 22 western tribes, lie some of the nation's richest reserves of natural gas, oil, coal, and uranium, worth billions of dollars. In fact, one-third of the nation's low-sulfur coal and at least half its uranium deposits are on tribal land. Some tribes, such as the oil-rich Osage in Oklahoma, benefit from sale of these resources. Only 14 percent of Native Americans, however, live on reservations that receive natural-resource revenues equal to $500 or more annually per reservation resident.[57]

Even when a tribe thinks its timber, mining, or fishing royalties have secured it a measure of financial stability, such may not be the case. A 1982 federal audit, for example, found that decades of sloppy bookkeeping by the Bureau of Indian Affairs had left the Red Lake band of Minnesota Chippewa more than $800,000 short in their trust fund. In 1989 the BIA simply deducted $1.2 million from the tribe's trust fund account to adjust for accounting mistakes, forcing the tribe to sue for recovery of its money. Federal auditors in September 1991 warned that fiscal mismanagement of the $2 billion in BIA trust funds may cost the taxpayers untold millions to cover hundreds of tribal claims.[58]

Because the BIA was unable to account for billions of dollars in Indian trust fund accounts, a 1996 class-action suit on behalf of all tribes brought results. In December 1999, a federal judge held officials in the Department of Interior (who oversee the BIA) in contempt of court for failing to provide relevant materials. A court-appointed special investigator determined government officials had shredded 162 cartons of ledgers listing transactions and disbursements plus record of uncashed checks—some 100 years old—that never reached their intended Indian recipients. Finally, Treasury Department officials admitted it received many millions of dollars from the Interior Department with no instructions, so they just put it in a general fund where it was used, among other things, to bail out New York City during its 1975 fiscal crisis, to save Chrysler Corporation from going under, and even to reduce the national debt. The BIA had also leased large tracts of Indian land to gas and oil companies and failed to collect any money.

Calling the situation "fiscal and governmental irresponsibility in its purest form," the court fined the government $625,000 and officially assumed oversight on efforts to reform the trust program and required quarterly updates. An appeals court panel upheld the ruling, and the administration opted not to appeal. In the second half of the lawsuit, begun in mid-2001, the court will determine how much the Native American plaintiffs will receive, with some estimates ranging from $20 to $40 billion.[59]

Blackfeet. The Sweet Grass Hills are 1,000-foot-high volcanic pyramids standing on the plains of Montana. The hills receive twice the rainfall the plains do, and some observers say the grass grows sweeter in the meadows of these hills than anywhere else. Native Americans from across the continent travel here to collect it for their ceremonies, braiding and drying it, then burning it to "smudge," or purify, people and objects with its sweet, sacred smoke.

As both a burial ground and a place where the Blackfeet of Montana have practiced their religion, the hills are sacred to this tribe, once the fiercest of the northern Plains peoples. In 1995, the land faced the threat of strip mining for gold under the Mining Act of 1872. About 150 miles east-southeast of the Sweet Grass Hills are the Little Rocky Mountains, where previous gold mining has scarred the land, silted in the creeks, and leached cyanide (used by miners to bond and remove finely disseminated gold) into the water. Because the hills are a critical source of water for surrounding ranches and farms, an unusual coalition of environmentalists, farmers, ranchers, and the Blackfeet are fighting to stop two mining companies from changing the Sweet Grass Hills forever. In 1997, the Forest Sevice placed a ban on oil and gas drilling in a nearby region for 10–15 years while determining if it is eligible for designation as a "traditional cultural property." That would not ban development but would add major safeguards, and possibly help preserve the Sweet Grass Hills as well.[60]

Navajo. More than 180,000 Navajo live on the nation's largest Native American reservation, larger than the state of West Virginia; its 16 million acres surround the four-corner junction of Arizona, New Mexico, Colorado, and Utah. Beneath this harsh, barren land, 2.5 billion tons of coal and 55 million pounds of uranium deposits lie untouched in the ground.[61] Ironically, high-voltage wires run across vast tracts of the Navajo Nation, carrying electricity to California but not to two thirds of the Navajo living under them.[62]

The 12,000 Navajo who lived on Big Mountain in northern Arizona fell victim to another form of exploitation. An attorney, working secretly as a hired agent of Peabody Coal Company—the world's largest privately owned coal company—helped persuade Congress to pass the Navajo–Hopi Land Settlement Act in 1978, dividing 1.8 million acres between the two tribes. Any member of either tribe on the wrong side of the line was forced to move. At the time, 100 Hopi were living on territory assigned to the Navajo, and 10,000 Navajo on lands now officially Hopi. Coincidentally, the Hopi side contains most of the region's known coal reserves, which Peabody wanted for strip mining. The attorney then concocted a "Hopi tribal council" of pro-mining leaders from 3 of the 12 Hopi villages, which signed leases to his company covering 100 square miles of coal reserves. Peabody was already strip-mining coal at nearby Black Mesa, an operation that had destroyed over 4,000 burial and other sacred sites and caused wells to run dry across both Navajo and Hopi reservations.[63]

By 1993, all but 200 Navajo families had moved, motivated partly by a $5,000 stipend they received in return for abandoning their small adobe shelters and moving to government-built housing, and partly by a federal law requiring an immediate 90 percent reduction in livestock grazing on lands now assigned to the Hopi and giving Hopi tribal police the right to impound Navajo livestock. Ill-equipped to succeed in an urban economy, many of the relocated Navajo soon lost their homes after the $5,000 was gone. These Navajo suffered far higher rates of unemployment, alcoholism, and suicide than other Navajo.[64]

On most reservations, Native Americans live away from areas where tourists are permitted. Living in isolation from society and often in substandard housing lacking electricity and indoor plumbing, the children typically live in a protective, warm tribal environment, but one nevertheless overwhelmed by poverty and limited life opportunities.
(*Source:* © Jim Noelker/The Image Works)

As the 1993–1994 winter approached and the 200 remaining families attempted to cling to their ancestral homes, BIA agents began confiscating their firewood, along with their axes and saws, and denied the Navajo access to the area water supply. They demolished all new construction projects, began daily raids to confiscate all the free-range Navajo livestock (mostly sheep) they could find, and increased the fee for recovering impounded livestock 10-fold. Still the families held out, unwilling to renounce their claim to sacred sites in the area or to accept the prohibition against burying their dead on the land—a stipulation that strikes at the very core of Navajo custom.

Finally, in 1997, unsuccessful in addressing their grievances in U.S. courts, the Navajo filed a complaint with the United Nations, accusing the U.S. government of violating the Universal Declaration of Human Rights through forced relocation, religious persecution, and environmental degradation of native lands. In the summer of 1998, for the first time in history, the UN Commission on Human Rights conducted a formal investigation of alleged human-rights violations inside the United States. An organized, international protest march in 2000 did nothing to stop the remaining two dozen families from receiving eviction notices.[65]

Lake Superior Chippewa (Ojibwe).   Each spring in northern Wisconsin, walleyed pike gather in the shallows of Lake Minocqua to spawn, and members of the

Chippewa come to exercise their special treaty rights to harvest these large fish by spearfishing. Resentful local non–Native American fishermen (who are forbidden by state law to capture walleyed pike during spawning season) stage vocally abusive and sometimes violent protests at the site, fearful that the Native Americans' traditional spearfishing will deplete the supply of walleyed pike and drive away sport fishermen. Although the Chippewa have voluntarily limited the size of their annual catch, the protesters' animosity continues. Recent bumper stickers read "Save a walleye. Spear a pregnant squaw." Antifishing protesters carried spears topped with fake Native American heads and hurled rocks and insults. A bulletin board at a bowling alley in the northern Wisconsin town of Eagle Rock in 1990 warned against shooting Native Americans:

> That will only get more sympathy for them, but if you put holes in their boats, they can't spear and holes in their tires they can't get to the lakes. Stop being wimps. Yelling or simply watching will not intimidate anyone. . . . Force confrontation and overreactions, escalate. . . . Nothing will change until you escalate.[66]

Claiming "the exercise of treaty rights is not in tune with contemporary society," northern Wisconsin protesters have aligned with the Citizens Equal Rights Alliance (CERA), a national anti–Native American organization. Stop Treaty Abuse (STA), which claims 3,000 members, has publicly dedicated itself to pursuing a course of disruption until all citizens can equally use resources on Native American lands. Understandably, large development corporations support these organizations. In 1997, Wisconsin's governor sought to reduce Chippewa hunting and fishing rights in exchange for renewal of their casino licenses.[67]

Council of Energy Resource Tribes. Twenty-five Native American tribes formed the Council of Energy Resource Tribes (CERT) in 1975. Modeling the council after the OPEC oil cartel, Native American leaders believed this new organization could prevent further exploitation and secure far greater revenues in return for tribal mineral resources. Aided by a $2 million federal grant, CERT hired technical experts to negotiate with private corporations. An early spectacular success was a contract with Atlantic Richfield (ARCO) for $78 million in tribal royalties over a 20-year period, after the company had opened negotiations with a $300,000 offer.

Since 1975, CERT has doubled the number of tribes it represents and has expanded its services to include advisement on monitoring nuclear-waste management on tribal lands. CERT also seeks to increase the employment of Native American youth by increasing their engineering and technical skills and by developing proposals to industrialize reservations with royalties from resource development. Critics, including other Native Americans, worry about environmental destruction and disruption of traditional values and culture caused by extensive mining operations.

"Dances with Garbage and Nuclear Waste"

With landfills filling up or shutting down because pollutants are leaching into groundwater, disposal companies are looking for cheap new sites for the 320 billion tons of solid-waste materials and 3 billion tons of toxic-waste materials produced annually in the United States.[68] Native American lands are not subject to the same set of environmental regulations as the rest of the country. Poor, but possessing large tracts of isolated land, Native Americans in recent years have seen their reservations recommended as toxic-waste dumping grounds. Although more than 100 tribes have been approached, most of them have rejected the disposal companies' cash offers and employment promises.[69]

In contrast, the Rosebud Sioux tribal council in South Dakota voted to allow O&G Industries of Connecticut to build a 6,000-acre mega-regional trash site on the reservation. Previously rejected by the Sioux community at the neighboring Pine Ridge reservation, the huge dump will hold millions of tons of garbage, incinerator ash, coal ash, sewage-sludge ash, and shredded tires. Despite company promises of financial riches for the tribe's 18,000 members, they receive only $1 per ton of trash even though similar dumps charge up to $80 a ton.[70]

The Mescalero Apache—a 3,400-member tribe living in southern New Mexico—made a controversial $2 billion deal with the nation's nuclear utilities to house radioactive waste (spent uranium fuel rods) in a remote corner of their scenic 720-square-mile reservation. Called everything from hapless victims of

Strip mining is aesthetically unattractive and one of the most irreversible abuses of land, as this stark scene at Black Mesa in northern Arizona shows. This process removes the upper level of soil cover that contains mineral deposits, pollutes groundwater with heavy metals, and permanently alters the condition of the ecosystem. For the Navajo, or Dineh, it is also a desecration of more than 4,000 burial and sacred sites.
(*Source:* © Dan Budnik/Woodfin Camp & Associates)

environmental racism to unscrupulous opportunists selling out their heritage by despoiling Mother Earth for profit, tribal leaders reject all such criticism. With an average 18 percent unemployment rate despite a profitable sawmill, ski resort, and convention center, the Mescalero see their acceptance of a nuclear waste dump as providing them with between $15 and $25 million a year.[71]

Another tribe had little choice about its contact with waste. The St. Regis Mohawk reservation on the St. Lawrence River near Massena, New York, was inundated with chemical garbage for decades. Located downstream, downwind, and downgradient in an industrial corridor extending 100 miles west to Lake Ontario, the reservation suffers from both aquatic poisoning and airborne toxins and has experienced a high number of birth defects, thyroid disease, and diabetes.[72] Its water and land food chains are permeated with PCBs discharged by General Motors, Reynolds Metal, and other corporate polluters. The Environmental Protection Agency in 1983 fined GM $507,000 for illegal use and disposal of PCBs—the largest fine ever levied for violating of the Toxic Substance Control Act—and it dredged 30 tons of contaminated soil from the St. Lawrence and hauled toxic sludge from lagoons on company property. Yet problems with the two resulting waste sites, their 35-foot high mounds covered by impermeable sheaths, still remain. An impasse presently exists between GM, which wants to seal the dumps permanently, and the Mohawk, who want the toxic sludge dug out and removed forever. Meanwhile, the Mohawk lifestyle has changed: no one fishes or lives off the land now.[73]

Water Rights

Nevada's Pyramid Lake, a spectacular 30-mile expanse of water, belongs to the Paiute, whose water rights the federal government was and is supposed to protect. Instead, in 1906, the government developed an irrigation project to divert 9.8 billion gallons of water each year before it reached the lake. By the 1940s, the water level had dropped 80 feet, killing the trout on which the Paiute depended. In 1944, the U.S. Supreme Court decided the water-rights case, awarding the tribe $8 million in damages. However, in settling the case on their behalf, the Justice Department did nothing about the fish crisis, the water level in the lake, or imposing restrictions on future irrigation. Finally, the Justice Department, formally confessing its "breach of faith with the Indians," petitioned the Supreme Court in 1983 to reopen the case to allow the Paiute to refill their lake.[74] A 1996 agreement settled the lawsuit, as three localities and the Department of the Interior agreed to fund a $24 million program to improve river flows, water levels, and wildlife conditions over a five-year period.

Water-rights cases are complex. The McCarran Amendment of 1952 waived the sovereign immunity of the United States on behalf of Native American water rights in general stream adjudications, granting state courts the power to decide these issues. Also, although the U.S. Supreme Court has been reluctant to deny to Native Americans prerogatives to water rights, it has occasionally denied Native

American claims in cases that had previously been adjudicated. Such was the situation with Pyramid Lake: The Court rejected the Paiute claim because of an earlier decision in 1940.[75]

Water disputes are sharpest in the Southwest, where the water table is the lowest. Urban sprawl and agribusiness have prompted whites to sink deep wells around reservations in Arizona, siphoning off the water reserves of several tribes. In New Mexico, for example, farmers simply "appropriated a viable water system the Pueblo Tribe had built two hundred years before Cortes set sail," leaving that tribe without an adequate water supply.[76]

Water rights are the western tribes' most valuable rights, providing a basis for achieving economic independence. Loss of water dooms them to an even worse existence. On the bright side, 10 water-rights cases were settled in the 1980s at a total cost to the government of $600 million. In 1990 Congress approved payment of $25 million to the Mojave Apache of the Fort McDowell reservation near Phoenix. In 1992 a $56.5 million settlement with the Northern Cheyenne in Montana was delayed for budgetary reasons. In 2001, the U.S. Supreme Court supported claims by five tribal reservations to water rights for the Colorado River, reflecting the continuing struggle for water in the Southwest.[77]

Suburban sprawl is not only impacting on water usage. As it encroaches on the nation's green spaces, a growing number of sacred Native American sites are under threat from housing developments and industrial plants. From North Dakota and Minnesota to Arkansas, from Florida to Nevada, Native American groups are fighting battles with state and federal governments to protect places, including burial sites, to prevent construction from destroying the cultural integrity of these locations.[78]

RED POWER

As Alvin M. Josephy, Jr., noted, Native Americans have never been silent about their needs and wishes.[79] Beginning with Seneca Chief Red Jacket's visit to Washington, DC, in 1792, Native Americans have repeatedly told the federal authorities what their people wanted and what was acceptable to them. Because they were seen as savages, the Native Americans found that government representatives usually ignored their views. When the forced-removal programs and the bloodshed came to an end in the late 19th century, the government began trying to change the reservation Native Americans' way of life, to eliminate their poverty, and to encourage further integration.

In the 20th century, Native American militancy was quite rare until the 1960s. In the mid-1960s, Native Americans changed their approach, partly because the social climate was different. Many social forces were at work—the civil-rights movement, the Vietnam protest, the idealism of the Great Society, and a growing social awareness within mainstream society itself. Perhaps taking their cue from other movements, a new generation of Native American leaders asserted themselves.

Pan-Indianism

Pan-Indianism—a recent social movement that attempts to establish a Native American ethnic identity instead of just a tribal identity—has its roots in the past. The growing Iroquois Confederation of the 17th century, the mobility and social interaction among the Plains Tribe in the 19th century, and the spread of the Ghost Dance religion in the 19th century are earlier examples of Pan-Indianism. As Native American youths found comfort in one another's presence, first in boarding schools and later in urban areas, they discovered a commonality in their identity as Native Americans.

Several organizations dedicated to preserving Native American identity and gaining greater political clout have evolved from this emerging group consciousness. The Society of American Indians (SAI) and the National Congress of American Indians (NCAI) were the first 20th-century attempts to organize. More recently, the National Indian Youth Council (NIYC) and the American Indian Movement (AIM) have attracted many young people who object to discrimination and white domination. The NIYC staged fish-ins to protest treaty violations of Native American rights in Washington State. In the ensuing legal battle, the Supreme Court ruled in favor of the Native Americans.

The Pan-Indian movement has not been completely accepted, however, even among young people. Many Native Americans prefer to preserve their tribal identities and to work for the cultural enrichment and social betterment of their own tribe rather than to engage in a national movement. As part of this tribal emphasis, these individuals also learn and teach their people silversmithing, pottery and blanket making, and other crafts that are part of their heritage. In an effort to increase tribal pride and economic welfare, they also establish cultural centers to exhibit and sell their artistic works and wares.

Alcatraz

On November 20, 1969, a group of 78 Native Americans under the name Indians of All Tribes occupied Alcatraz Island, a former federal prison. This move, the first militant Native American action in the 20th century, was both symbolic and an effort to establish a cultural center. The sarcasm in this excerpt from their proclamation attacks the paternalism, neglect, and deprivation fostered on Native American tribes past and present:

> We will give to the inhabitants of this island a portion of that land for their own, to hold in perpetuity—for as long as the sun shall rise and the rivers go down to the sea. We will further guide the inhabitants in the proper way of living. We will offer them our religion, our education, our life-ways, in order to help them achieve our level of civilization and thus raise them and all their white brothers up from their savage and unhappy state. We offer this treaty in good faith and wish to be fair and honorable in our dealings with all white men. We feel that this so-called Alcatraz Island is more than suitable for an Indian Reservation, as determined by the white

man's own standards. By this we mean that this place resembles most Indian reservations in that

1. It is isolated from modern facilities, and without adequate means of transportation.
2. It has no fresh running water.
3. It has inadequate sanitation facilities.
4. There are no oil or mineral rights.
5. There is no industry and so unemployment is very great.
6. There are no health care facilities.
7. The soil is rocky and nonproductive; and the land does not support game.
8. There are no education facilities.
9. The population has always exceeded the land base.
10. The population has always been held as prisoners and kept dependent upon others.

Further, it would be fitting and symbolic that ships from all over the world, entering the Golden Gate, would first see Indian land, and thus be reminded of the true history of this nation. This tiny island would be a symbol of the great lands once ruled by free and noble Indians.[80]

This militant action did not succeed. The group's cohesiveness collapsed when the 12-year-old daughter of its leader, Michael Oakes, a Mohawk, fell down an elevator shaft on the island and died. Oakes, the unifying and motivating force, left Alcatraz with his daughter's body. Federal authorities then stepped in and removed the Native Americans. Oakes himself was later shot to death in California, supposedly mistaken for a trespasser. Today Alcatraz Island is a tourist attraction as a former prison, and its conversion to a gambling casino has been discussed.

Wounded Knee

On February 27, 1973, about 200 members of the American Indian Movement seized control of the village of Wounded Knee, South Dakota, taking 11 hostages. The location was symbolic because Wounded Knee had been the site of the last Native American resistance in 1890, when 150 Miniconjou Sioux from the Cheyenne River Reservation, including men, women, and children, were massacred by the U.S. Cavalry. Many were killed from behind, and the wounded were left to die in a blizzard the following night.[81]

A 71-day siege following the 1973 seizure was a staged media event aimed at directing national attention to the plight of the Native Americans. Some Native American leaders criticized the action as rash, but most Native Americans appeared to sympathize with it. The holdout ended May 8, 1973, with two Native Americans killed, injuries on both sides, including a U.S. marshal paralyzed, and $240,000 in damage to property.[82]

The militants had demanded, among other things, that the government deal with the Sioux on the basis of an 1868 treaty that guaranteed them dominion over the vast northern Plains between the Missouri River and the Rocky Mountains, land that the U.S. government confiscated in 1876. That Native American land claim has been described by Sioux representatives as the "largest, most historically and socially significant and, in terms of time taken in the courts, the oldest Native American land claim on record."

Native Americans were not unified in their resistance to cultural domination. James Fenelon and Rod Brod point out that "near civil war conditions" existed on the Pine Ridge Sioux reservation in the 1970s because "Culturicidal policies targeted and to a large measure destroyed internalized confederations on the community and tribal-band level." Differing forms of resistance evolved into a triad of primary actors including Tribal Council enforcement arms, sociopolitical activists such as AIM's organizing efforts, and the "traditionals" including spiritual leaders and those retaining cultural knowledge and practice. The fourth group on Pine Ridge is the rest of the "general (Indian) population" who could be associated with any or all of the preceding actor-agents.[83]

THE COURTS

With more than 700 Native American lawyers practicing by 1990, legal efforts to force the government to honor tribes' treaty rights have been more numerous and successful. In 1980, the U.S. Supreme Court reaffirmed a lower court's award of $105 million to compensate 60,000 Sioux living on eight reservations in South Dakota, Montana, and Nebraska for the government's illegal seizure of the Black Hills. Native American activist Russell Means urged Sioux chiefs to reject the U.S. offer and demand the land instead, claiming that the Black Hills land was "our graveyard, our church, the center of our universe and the birthplace of our people . . . everything we hold sacred and dear, and this is the reason it is not for sale."[84]

The Oglala Sioux then filed suit for return of the western half of South Dakota and for $1 billion in damages for "hunger, malnutrition, disease, and death" caused by loss of the land. It also demanded restoration of tribal hunting rights on the land, a ban on removal of natural resources, and a ban on federal interference with Sioux use of the land for "subsistence and religious purposes."[85] In June 1981, the U.S. Court of Appeals rejected the suit, saying it had no jurisdiction in the matter because Congress had created the Indian Claims Commission—since disbanded—as the sole remedy for Black Hills claims.[86]

The cash settlement offer for the Black Hills rested in part on a 1950 precedent, when the U.S. Court of Claims awarded $31.2 million to the Colorado Ute for lands illegally taken from them. This amounted to about $10,000 for each tribal adult and child. A precedent also existed for return of land. The Taos Pueblo of New Mexico had regarded the lands at and near Blue Lake as sacred since the 14th century. Demanding the land back from the Forest Service instead of a proffered cash settlement, the Taos ultimately regained 48,000 acres in 1970 through congressional action at President Nixon's urging.

In 1977, the Passamaquoddy and Penobscot laid claim to about 5 million acres, or nearly one third of Maine. The Carter administration threw its support behind the Native Americans and in 1978 reached an out-of-court settlement: a lump-sum payment of $25 million cash, plus an additional $1.7 million a year for 15 years, and the sale to the two tribes of 300,000 acres at $5 an acre. The basis for the claim was that the Native American land had been bargained away in violation of the Nonintercourse Act of 1790, which reserved to Congress the power to negotiate with Native American tribes. The tribes then wisely developed an investment portfolio that included purchasing manufacturing plants for audio cassettes and video cassettes and the largest cement factory in New England. Unemployment among the two tribes has dropped from 50 to 8 percent since the investments began.[87]

Elsewhere, after losing 76 of 80 court battles with various Native American tribes, the state of Washington broke new ground, dealing with the tribes as if they were governments. Reaching agreement on salmon management, they are now also cooperating on health policy, child-welfare agreements, and water rights. Wyoming, Colorado, and New Mexico have also negotiated directly with tribes to avoid costly and possibly losing court battles.[88] In New York, the Mohawk, Oneida, Cayuga, Onondaga, Seneca, and Tuscarora nations of the Iroquois Confederacy all have filed sizable land claims, given impetus by a 1985 Supreme Court ruling that New York's treaty with the Oneida violated the Nonintercourse Act, setting a precedent for its treaties with the other Iroquois tribes. Years of negotiation ended (at least temporarily) in 1996, when state officials abruptly broke off negotiations over sales tax issues. In 1998, the Oneida Nation filed an amended complaint in the land claim. The U.S. Justice Department filed a similar complaint in support of the Oneidas. As this book goes to press, the case is pending.[89]

BUREAU OF INDIAN AFFAIRS

The Bureau of Indian Affairs was created in 1824. It has many critics among federal officials, sociologists, anthropologists, and Native Americans (see box on next page). Some observers view it as a bureaucracy staffed by able, dedicated people (90 percent of them Native Americans) whose ability to act is frustrated by an inefficient organization; others see it as an inept agency that "loses" trust funds, administers ineffective programs that are supposed to reduce unemployment and poverty, and maintains a paternalistic trustee relationship with the tribes. Since 1993, Ada Deer, a Menominee, has been BIA commissioner, but non–Native Americans continue to hold many of the other high positions.

Native American hostility toward the BIA goes beyond complaints about unsympathetic, incompetent, or patronizing personnel; it is directed against the bureau's very structure. Although different government agencies touch all Americans in some ways, few non–Native Americans realize how thoroughly the BIA dominates the lives of Native Americans residing on reservations. The agency is in charge of everything, from tribal courts and schools to social services and law enforcement.

The Ethnic Experience
A Formal Apology to the Indian People

"*T*he works of this agency have at various times profoundly harmed the communities it was meant to serve. From the very beginning, the Office of Indian Affairs was an instrument by which the United States enforced its ambition against the Indian nations and Indian people who stood in its path. . . .

"As the nation looked to the West for more land, this agency participated in the ethnic cleansing that befell the western tribes. . . In these more enlightened times, it must be acknowledged that the deliberate spread of disease, the decimation of the mighty bison herds, the use of the poison alcohol to destroy mind and body, and the cowardly killing of women and children made for tragedy on a scale so ghastly that it cannot be dismissed as merely the inevitable consequence of the clash of competing ways of life. This agency and the good people in it failed in the mission to prevent the devastation. . . .

"Nor did the consequences of war have to include the futile and destructive efforts to annihilate Indian cultures. After the devastation of tribal economies and the deliberate creation of tribal dependence on the services provided by this agency, this agency set out to destroy all things Indian.

"This agency forbade the speaking of Indian languages, prohibited the conduct of traditional religious activities, outlawed traditional government, and made Indian people ashamed of who they were. Worst of all, the Bureau of Indian Affairs committed these acts against the children entrusted to its boarding schools, brutalizing them emotionally, psychologically, physically, and spiritually. Even in this era of self-determination, when the Bureau of Indian Affairs is at long last serving as an advocate for Indian people in an atmosphere of mutual respect, the legacy of these misdeeds haunts us. The trauma of shame, fear and anger has passed from one generation to the next, and manifests itself in the rampant alcoholism, drug abuse, and domestic violence that plague Indian country. Many of our people live lives of unrelenting tragedy as Indian families suffer the ruin of lives by alcoholism, suicides made of shame and despair, and violent death at the hands of one another. So many of the maladies suffered today in Indian country result from the failures of this agency. Poverty, ignorance, and disease have been the product of this agency's work.

"And so today I stand before you as the leader of an institution that in the past has

Source: Excerpts from a speech by Assistant Secretary of the Interior for Indian Affairs Kevin Gover at a ceremony on September 8, 2000, commemorating the BIA's 175th anniversary, at the BIA in Washington, DC.

It must approve virtually every tribal decision regarding the use of tribal resources—even the disposition of cash settlements that the Navajo and other tribes have won in lawsuits against the BIA itself.

Mere suspicion by a BIA official that certain individuals cannot properly handle their money or their personal affairs is sufficient to impose a requirement that

committed acts so terrible that they infect, diminish, and destroy the lives of Indian people decades later, generations later. These things occurred despite the efforts of many good people with good hearts who sought to prevent them. These wrongs must be acknowledged if the healing is to begin.

"Let us begin by expressing our profound sorrow for what this agency has done in the past. Just like you, when we think of these misdeeds and their tragic consequences, our hearts break and our grief is as pure and complete as yours. We desperately wish that we could change this history, but of course we cannot. On behalf of the Bureau of Indian Affairs, I extend this formal apology to Indian people for the historical conduct of this agency. . . .

"Never again will this agency stand silent when hate and violence are committed against Indians. Never again will we allow policy to proceed from the assumption that Indians possess less human genius than the other races. Never again will we be complicit in the theft of Indian property. Never again will we appoint false leaders who serve purposes other than those of the tribes. Never again will we allow unflattering and stereotypical images of Indian people to deface the halls of government or lead the American people to shallow and ignorant beliefs about Indians. Never again will we attack your religions, your languages, your rituals, or any of your tribal ways. Never again will we seize your children, nor teach them to be ashamed of who they are. Never again.

"We cannot yet ask your forgiveness, not while the burdens of this agency's history weigh so heavily on tribal communities. What we do ask is that, together, we allow the healing to begin: As you return to your homes, and as you talk with your people, please tell them that the time of dying is at its end. Tell your children that the time of shame and fear is over. Tell your young men and women to replace their anger with hope and love for their people. Together, we must wipe the tears of seven generations. Together, we must allow our broken hearts to mend. Together, we will face a challenging world with confidence and trust. Together, let us resolve that when our future leaders gather to discuss the history of this institution, it will be time to celebrate the rebirth of joy, freedom, and progress for the Indian Nations. The Bureau of Indian Affairs was born in 1824 in a time of war on Indian people. May it live in the year 2000 and beyond as an instrument of their prosperity."

formal BIA approval be obtained for any transactions those persons make. Only by comprehending the total pervasiveness of this bureaucracy can we begin to fathom the dependence, despair, and frustration the system engenders.

Yet the BIA continues with its sorry record of waste, corruption, and fiscal mismanagement. A 1999 study by the National Academy of Public Administration (NAPA) detailed acute shortcomings in the agency's ability to manage finance, information technology, records, and procurement operations. Its overall ranking by the Federal Performance Project in 2000 was a "D." In 2001, the executive director of the Harvard Project on American Indian Economic Development said, "We can't find a single case of sustained economic success where the BIA is in control."[90] In fact, when tribes took over the managing and management of tribal forests, they surpassed the BIA in harvest productivity and selling price.[91]

URBAN NATIVE AMERICANS

As many as 70 percent of all Native Americans live in urban areas or do not live on reservations (see Figure 7.4).[92] Los Angeles claims the largest concentration (more than 87,000), but that constitutes only 0.6 percent of the city's total population. San Francisco's Native American population is almost 44,000, or 0.7 percent of the total. Other cities with sizable numbers—usually exceeding 16,000—are Boston, Chicago,

FIGURE 7.4 **Where Native Americans Live, 2000**

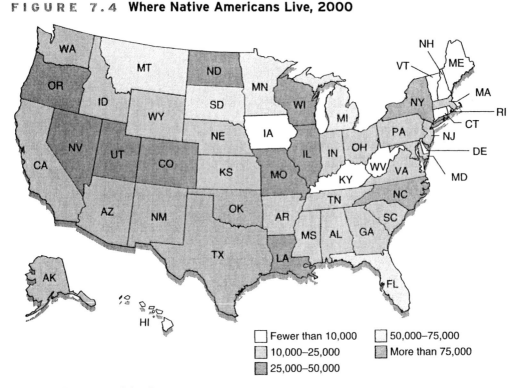

Legend:
- Fewer than 10,000
- 10,000–25,000
- 25,000–50,000
- 50,000–75,000
- More than 75,000

Source: U.S. Bureau of the Census.

Cleveland, Dallas, Detroit, Denver, Houston, St. Louis, Miami, Minneapolis-St. Paul, New York City, Omaha, Philadelphia, Phoenix, San Diego, and Seattle.[93]

Although urban Native Americans are more widely dispersed in residence than are blacks and Chicanos, approximately three fourths of them live in poverty in the poorer sections of the cities. For example, 40 percent of the 14,000 Native Americans living in New York City in 1986 were unemployed, and eight out of nine Native American families there lived below the poverty level.[94] Often lacking job skills and adequate education, these Native Americans generally experience the same poverty they left behind, but without the familiar environment and tribal support system. Researchers have found that urban migration does not immediately improve Native American well-being. Findings consistent with those of other studies show that, although urban Native Americans are more likely to be employed than those who remain behind on the reservations, they do not achieve any improved income earnings, on average, until after five years of residence in the city.[95]

Even though urban Native Americans are not gathered in ethnic enclaves, their other behavior patterns are similar to those of European immigrants. Situated in a social arena where they constitute a minority, new arrivals experience the culture shock of urban living away from the solidarity of the tribe. This shock sometimes leads to personal disorientation, and Native Americans seldom get relief or assistance from the dominant society.

Members of urban Native American populations generally drink more and have a higher rate of problem drinking than do most members of reservation populations. Such heavy drinking is most common among the lower social strata of urban Native Americans and relates highly to such occupational considerations as prestige and satisfaction.[96] In 1994, a 10-year study of urban Native Americans and Alaska Natives living in Washington State revealed that they fared far worse in virtually every health dimension than did urban whites. Infant mortality, tuberculosis, and injury- and alcohol-related death rates were higher for them than for urban whites, African Americans, and rural Native Americans and Alaska Natives.[97]

Native Americans who succeed in adapting to urban living, usually over a two- to five-year period, settle into semiskilled or skilled jobs. Once they have gained some economic security, they frequently move out of the city to racially mixed suburban areas. Although this shows some degree of acculturation and convergent social adaptation, the trend appears to be limited. Many middle-class urban-adapted Native Americans form their own ethnic institutions, including churches, powwow clubs, social centers, and athletic leagues.[98] Most Native Americans attempt to preserve their ethnic identity and do not interact socially with non–Native Americans to any noticeable degree.[99]

CULTURAL IMPACT

Perhaps no other ethnic group has had as great an impact on U.S. culture as the Native Americans, primarily because this group was already here when the first

Europeans arrived; and the whites, who had to adapt to a new land, found it advantageous to learn from the **indigenous** people. Cities, towns, counties, states, rivers, lakes, mountains, and other geographic entities by the thousands bear Native American names today. More than 500 words in our language are Native American, including *wigwam, succotash, tobacco, papoose, chipmunk, squash, skunk, toboggan, opossum, tomahawk, moose, mackinaw, hickory, pecan, raccoon, cougar, woodchuck,* and *hominy.*[100]

The Native Americans' knowledge of wild herbs and the more than 80 plants they domesticated brought whites a wide variety of new tastes. Native Americans introduced the Europeans to corn, white and sweet potatoes, kidney beans, tomatoes, peanuts, peppers, pumpkins, avocados, pineapples, maple sugar, chicle, and cacao, as well as tobacco and long-fiber cotton. The Native Americans' knowledge of medicinal plants is also part of their legacy:

> At least fifty-nine drugs, including coca (for cocaine and novocaine), curare (a muscle relaxant), cinchona bark (the source of quinine), cascara sagrada (a laxative), datura (a pain-reliever), and ephedra (a nasal remedy), were bequeathed to modern medicine by the Indians.[101]

Native Americans also made various articles that many people still use today—canoes, kayaks, snowshoes, toboggans, moccasins, hammocks, pipes, parkas, ponchos, dog sleds, and rubber syringes, among other items. Native American influence on jewelry, clothing, art, architecture, literature, and scouting is substantial. Traditional Native American reverence for the land parallels beliefs that conservationists support. The Iroquois influence on the Constitution for House—Senate conferences has already been mentioned. In addition, appreciation and adaptations of Native American child-rearing practices, group-directed activities, cooperatives, and ministrations to a patient's mental state are common today.[102]

NATIVE AMERICAN ASSIMILATION

That hundreds of thousands of Native Americans are not assimilated into mainstream society has certainly not been through lack of effort by the dominant group. After following a policy of frontier genocide, expulsion, and forced segregation on reservations, the federal government adopted other methods to "kill the Indian, but save the man," according to a popular saying between 1860 and 1930.[103]

On reservation land set aside for churches, missionaries attempted to "civilize" the "heathens." Taken from their homes at a young age, Native American children attended boarding schools, had their long hair cut short, and their clothing replaced with clothing of the whites. There they suffered harsh physical punishment if they spoke their native language or practiced their cultural traditions. On the reservations meanwhile, the Dawes Act of 1887 disrupted their traditional approach to communal landholding in an attempt to force them to conform to the social and economic structure of the dominant society.[104] Another dimension to this cultural onslaught occurred in the 1890s with the outlawing of indigenous religions. In the 1950s the termination and relocation programs represented another federal effort to get Native Americans to assimilate.

All these efforts had a major impact on Native Americans and their way of life, much of it negative. Earlier sections of this chapter, for example, offered statistics about rates of suicide, alcoholism, violence, disease, poverty, educational attainment, and unemployment. Today, many live in two worlds—their own ethnic community and the mainstream community—forcing them to maintain a bicultural ethnic identity.

Native Americans are not a homogeneous group, and they differ greatly in their level of acceptance and commitment to specific tribal values, beliefs, and practices through a variance of customs, language, and family structure. Moreover, their socioeconomic status and geographic setting (urban, rural, or reservation) affect other individual differences.[105] Michael Garret and Eugene Pichette suggest that a five-level continuum of five levels of acculturation would best describe Native Americans:

- **Traditional:** May or may not speak English, but generally speak and think in their native language; hold only traditional values and beliefs and practice only traditional tribal customs and methods of worship.
- **Marginal:** May speak both the native language and English; may not, however, fully accept the cultural heritage and practices of their tribal group; not fully identify with mainstream cultural values and behaviors.
- **Bicultural:** Generally accepted by dominant society and tribal society/nation; simultaneously able to know, accept, and practice both mainstream values/behaviors and the traditional values and beliefs of their cultural heritage.
- **Assimilated:** Accepted by dominant society; embrace only mainstream cultural values, behaviors, and expectations.
- **Traditional:** Assimilated Native Americans who have made conscious choice to return to the "old ways." They are generally accepted by dominant society but seek to embrace previously lost traditional cultural values, beliefs, and practices of their tribal herbal heritage. Therefore, they may speak both English and their native tribal language.[106]

Caught between two cultures, many Native Americans experience pressure to compromise their basic cultural values and behaviors to meet societal expectations and standards. Thus acculturation influences serve as a mediating factor in maintaining one's cultural values in the process of identity development.[107] More Native American students report feelings of rejection, depression, and anxiety than do other students. By the fifth or sixth grade, many have become sullen, resistant, and indolent, which, experts say, is caused by their failure to reconcile cultural differences, leading to a high percentage of school dropouts.[108] The challenge remains to find ways for Native Americans to establish a healthy and meaningful cultural identity through bicultural competence.

SOCIOLOGICAL ANALYSIS

Both Hollywood and the BIA rely on stereotypes in their characterization and treatment of Native Americans, even though extensive differences between tribes have always existed. In this chapter, we have looked at their similarities and differences, noting changes in attitude and public policy toward them over the years. Our three theoretical frameworks not only provide a coherent approach to understanding the experiences of Native Americans but also provide insights into their problems.

The Functionalist View

Whites may never have fully understood the traditional Native American social system, but anthropologists have found that these tribal societies functioned with a high degree of social organization. Kin relationships, from the nuclear family to a vast clan system, formed the basis of interaction. Clearly defined interdependent work roles for young and old, male and female, in cooperative tasks of living fostered a rather stable society. Living off the land and espousing a pantheistic belief system, they were conservationists, maintaining a harmonious relationship with their natural environment. They were self-sufficient people with institutionalized practices of gift giving and property control—such as the willful destruction of personal property in a competitive display of wealth among some Pacific Coast tribes—which helped sustain a fairly equitable society without great extremes of poverty or riches.

Even early contacts with white explorers, trappers, and settlers tended to be harmonious, with both sides benefiting from what each had to offer the other. Dysfunctions occurred as Native Americans slipped into economic subservience, their way of life further threatened by encroachment on their land by steadily increasing numbers of white settlers. Whites saw the Native Americans as a hindrance to their making the land productive, so they forcibly removed them. Forced segregation on nonproductive reservations completely destroyed Native American society as a self-sufficient entity while reinforcing other aspects of the culture. The systemic disorganization of the society—entrenched for over 100 years—restricted life opportunities. Continued poor education, low income, bad housing, poor health, alcoholism, and other pathologies are costly to society and the people who endure them.

Functionalists stress that the most effective method of resolving these problems is to reorganize our social institutions to put the Native American social system back into balance. However, the plight of the Native Americans is functional to the few reservation Native Americans employed by government agencies to provide services and to BIA employees whose jobs rest on continued paternalistic control, as well as to whites living near reservations who dominate these regions' economy. These individuals, Native American and white alike, would find adjustments in the system dysfunctional to themselves and therefore oppose such changes.

The Conflict View

Lieberson's power theory provides an obvious model for studying Native American–white relations. As discussed in Chapter 4, the white newcomers, superior in technology compared to the indigenous population, engaged in early conflict. The native population suffered numeric decline from warfare, disease, and disruption of sustenance activities, and its social institutions were undermined. Westward expansion, the nation's "Manifest Destiny," occurred by pushing aside the people who already possessed the land, without regard for their rights or wishes. Formal government agreements and treaties became meaningless to those in power if further land confiscation or exploitation for natural resources offered profits.

What about today? Who benefits from Native American deprivation now? The battle over the precious commodity of water in the Southwest offers one answer. Water might enable these tribes to gain some income, but it has been stolen out from under them by mining companies, farmers, and land developers. Prolonged court battles enable powerful business interests to maintain their dams, wells, and aqueducts at the expense of the Native Americans. You have read of abuses of other natural resources as well.

Why doesn't Congress do something? Legislators respond to public pressure. Those not living near Native Americans are not motivated or sufficiently concerned to insist that corrective action be taken. Those living near Native Americans have a vested interest in maintaining the status quo, and they are the constituency with the power to influence their district's or state's national legislative representatives.

Yet Native Americans have achieved some positive results. They did so through an emerging group consciousness, whether tribal or Pan-Indian (involving all Native Americans). Protest marches and demonstrations, militant acts of defiance—the Alcatraz, Wounded Knee, and BIA occupations—and class-action lawsuits have all brought public attention and some efforts to remedy their situation. Conflict theory suggests that organized social movements by the exploited can bring about social change. Native Americans are increasingly discovering that redress of their grievances will not occur without concerted public pressure.

The Interactionist View

Consider again the words of Columbus, Franklin, and Catlin earlier in this chapter. Ethnocentric views of Native American culture prompted a definition of the native population as inferiors, savages, and even nonhumans! Once you create such social distance between groups by dehumanizing them, it is easy to justify any action taken against them. Compounding the negative labeling process was racial differentiation. European Americans viewed even the acculturated Native Americans working as servants or laborers in colonial villages, or the entire Cherokee people, as members of an inferior race fit to be subordinated and relegated to a noninterfering, humble role in society.

For their part, the Native Americans at first found white customs, fashions, and behavior outlandish and astonishing. Later they perceived the whites as threats to their existence, and as liars and treacherous people. The ensuing hostilities reaffirmed each group's negative view of the other, and the conflict ended with total subjugation of the Native Americans.

Government policy today mistakenly interprets the needs of all tribes in broad terms, and treats all tribes alike: the biggest and smallest, the agrarian and fishing, the ones with economic land bases and the ones without. Many dominant-group people in the United States view Native Americans as perpetuating their own problems by remaining on reservations, depending on government support, and refusing to blend in with white society. Growing up on reservations, Native Americans find security in tribal life, viewing the outside world as alien and without promise. Now the strangers in their own land, they believe they have the right to preserve their culture and to receive government assistance because of past abuses, including broken treaties. With so many different interpretations of the current situation, the problems of the reservation appear difficult to resolve.

High levels of prejudice against Native Americans still exists in the West, especially on the edges of the reservations where there is a climate that tolerates violence, say the experts. A 1999 study released by the Justice Department revealed that Native Americans are the victims of violent crime at a rate of more than twice the national average for blacks. Unlike blacks and whites, they are most likely to be the victims of violent crimes committed by members of a race other than their own. Clearly, the negative labeling and dehumanizing processes that led to past acts of violence against Native Americans remains a problem today.[109]

RETROSPECT

The white strangers who appeared among the Native Americans eventually outnumbered them, overpowered them, and changed their way of life. Once a proud and independent people, the Native Americans were reduced to a state of poverty, despair, and dependence. The land they had known so well and roamed so freely was no longer theirs. Forced to live within an alien society that dominated all aspects of their lives, they became strangers in their native land. Misunderstood and categorized as savages, they observed the taken-for-granted world of the Whites more keenly than most Whites did theirs.

Physical and cultural differences quickly became the basis for outgroup hostility as the groups competed for land and resources. Like other groups, the Native

Americans faced the familiar patterns of stereotyping, prejudice, discrimination, and conflict because of their alleged inferiority and actual lack of power. Isolation on the reservations not only prevented assimilation (which most Native Americans did not desire anyway) but also created for them a world of dependence and deprivation. Subsequent efforts at forced assimilation—boarding schools, relocation, and termination of the reservation—failed because of Native American resiliency and the Bureau of Indian Affairs' lack of thoroughness in personal preparation, assistance, and follow-through.

The Native Americans are still misunderstood and exploited. One, two, or three hundred years ago, people who lived far from the Native Americans idealized them, and those who lived nearest often abused and exploited them. It is no different today. Many people are oblivious to their problems and consider them quaint relics of the past; others find them either undesirable or in the way. Some want their land and will use almost any means to secure it. Native Americans still encounter discrimination in stores, bars, and housing, particularly in cities and near the reservations. They are frequently beaten or killed, and their property rights infringed on.

Since the 1960s, some Native Americans have become more assertive. Many young, better-educated Native Americans are forgetting tribal differences and finding a common bond—pan-Indianism—uniting in the struggle to protect what they have and to restore what they have lost. Others prefer a more individualistic approach within the tribe. Some gains have been made, and more non–Native Americans are becoming aware of the situations, but at present the Native Americans still are one of the poorest minorities in the United States.

KEY TERMS

Dichotomy	Indigenous	Sovereign
Ethnocentrism	Mortality rate	Stereotype
Expulsion	Pan-Indianism	

REVIEW QUESTIONS

1. Why do some social scientists call the Native Americans the first victims of racism? Why is racism an integral part of their experiences?

2. Cite some examples of ethnocentrism and stereotyping regarding Native Americans.

3. Why is the power differential so crucial in understanding the Native Americans' past and present problems?

4 Why have most government efforts to "help" the Native Americans failed?

5 In what ways has little changed in the exploitation of the Native Americans?

SUGGESTED READINGS

Brown, Dee. *Bury My Heart at Wounded Knee,* reprint ed. New York: Holt, 2001.
A Native American viewpoint of past Native American–white interrelations, offering a valuable corrective to traditional historical coverage.

Deloria, Vine, Jr. *Red Earth, White Lies: Native Americans and the Myth of Scientific Fact.* Fulcrum Publishing, 1997.
Challenges assumption that numerous scientific "facts," such as the Bering Strait theory of the peopling of America, are more truthful than traditional Native American versions

Fixico, Donald L. *The Urban Indian Experience in America.* Tuscon: University of Arizona Press, 2000.
An ethnohistorical narrative that deals with such issues as relocation, stereotypes, alcoholism, the Indian middle class, and urban-Indian identity crisis.

Fixico, Donald L. *The Invasion of Indian Country in the Twentieth Century: American Capitalism and Tribal Natural Resources.* Niwot: University Press of Colorado, 1998.
A bicultural perspective on the cultural conflict over land and natural resources, with case studies of the Muskogee Creek, Osage, Pueblo, Klamath, Chippewa, and Sioux.

Jaimes, M. Annette (ed.). *The State of Native America.* Boston: South End Press, 1992.
An anthology of writings, mostly of Native Americans, that explore the situations faced by present-day tribes.

Josephy, Alvin M., Jr. *The Indian Heritage of America,* rev. ed. Boston: Houghton Mifflin, 1991.
Encompasses the whole historical and cultural range of Indian life in North, Central, and South America, with many insights into cultural attributes and legacies.

Lazarus, Edward. *Black Hills, White Justice.* New York: HarperCollins, 1991.
A thorough chronicle of the ongoing legal battle of the Sioux nation for its land, from colonial times to the present.

Nielson, Nancy J. *Reformers and Activists.* New York: Facts on File, 1997.
Profiles of Native Americans who have worked to improve living conditions for their people and reformers who have fought injustice.

Prucha, Francis P. *American Indian Treaties: The History of a Political Anomaly.* Berkeley: University of California Press, 1995.
Analyzes ratified and unratified treaties, the treaty system during various periods and its collapse and 20th-century issues related to treaties.

Weatherford, J. McIver. *Native Roots: How the Indians Enriched America.* New York: Fawcett Columbine, 1992.

A rich detailed account of the cultural legacy of Native Americans found in many aspects of present-day U.S. society.

INTERNET LINKS

Go to *http://www.ablongman.com/parrillo* for numerous links relevant to this chapter under "Internet Readings and Exercises."

Black Americans

Most Africans who arrived in America from 1619 until the end of the slave trade, in 1808, immigrated unwillingly; but 20th-century voluntary emigration to the United States from Africa has been substantial (see Figure 10.1). Between 1899 and 1922, 115,000 African blacks and over 25,000 West Indian blacks arrived. The restrictive immigration law of 1924 reduced the number of new immigrants from these groups; Africans, for example, were limited to only 122 newcomers annually.[1] In recent years, Africa has been averaging about 43,000 immigrants a year, and over 96,000 West Indians are now moving to the United States each year.

Differences in culture have prevented any unifying racial bond from forming between black immigrants and native-born blacks. The newcomers are strangers in a new land; many native-born blacks—like Native Americans—are strangers in their own land; and both groups are strangers to each other. The new arrivals come from areas where their race is the majority, or where a tripartite color system prevails, or where color is not a primary factor in group life; and they enter a society where color is an important determinant of social and cultural identity. They find that white Americans identify Africans with a partially assimilated and socially restricted native black population that itself does not accept or relate well to them.

The role of blacks in U.S. society, together with the recurring racial problems of prejudice and discrimination, has often been discussed, particularly in the past three decades. This chapter attempts to place black–white relations in perspective by showing their similarities with and differences from the patterns of dominant–minority interaction of other racial and ethnic groups. Other major themes are the long-lasting impact of cultural conditioning and the changes wrought by the civil-rights movement.

SOCIOHISTORICAL PERSPECTIVE

During the age of exploration, black crew members served under Columbus and under such 16th-century Spanish explorers as Balboa, Cortéz, Pizarro, and de Soto. The first-known group of African immigrants consisted of 20 voluntary immigrants who landed in Jamestown in August 1619, a year before the Pilgrims landed at Plymouth Rock. They came as indentured servants (as did many whites), worked off their debt, and became masters of their own destiny. They were the fortunate few, for the labor demands of the southern colonies soon resulted in the enslavement of millions of other Africans and their forced migration to the United States. Slavery quickly replaced indentured servitude in the South. Blacks were forcibly taken from their African homelands and sold into lifelong slavery in a land they did not choose and in which they had no opportunity to advance themselves because they were not free.

FIGURE 10.1 **Africa**

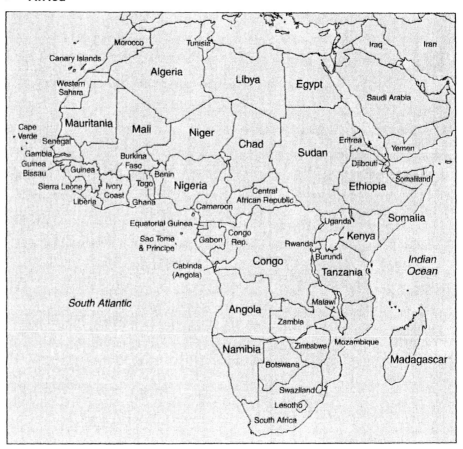

The Years of Slavery

To ease their transition to a new land, other ethnic groups re-created in miniature the society they left behind; but the Africans who came to the United States were not allowed to do so. Other groups could use education to give themselves and their children a better future, but state laws in the South made educating black slaves a criminal offense. Other groups may have encountered some degree of hostility and discrimination, but through hard work and perseverance many were able to overcome nativist fears and prejudices. For blacks, however, 200 years of master–slave relations did much more than prevent their assimilation; they shaped values and attitudes about the two races that are still visible today.

As the industrial North and the slaveholding, agrarian South evolved into different societies, they developed different norms. To be sure, the institution of slavery created an inferior status for blacks and led to much prejudice and discrimination. Yet there were free blacks in the South, too (nearly half a million by 1860)—people who had been emancipated by their owners or who had purchased their freedom or who were descendants of free mothers. They lived in such urban areas as New Orleans, Mobile, and Charleston; in the tidewater regions of Virginia and Maryland; and in the piedmont region of western North Carolina and Virginia. Those who lived in southern cities worked in a wide variety of skilled and unskilled occupations; some were architects, teachers, store and hotel managers, clerks, and milliners. In the North, although there was some variance, blacks faced considerable discrimination in education, housing, employment, and voting rights. Because in the North no operative caste system delineated norms and interaction patterns, many whites reacted more strongly to blacks in their midst. As a result, northern blacks had considerable difficulty achieving economic security.

Racism and Its Legacy

Although some ancient civilizations considered themselves superior to others, they tended to do so on the basis of culture or special religious status, not race. Most historians agree that racism did not emerge as an ideological phenomenon until the 16th and 17th centuries.[2] This was the period of European exploration and imperialism, during which Europeans were brought into contact with many physically different, less technologically advanced peoples. The physical characteristics, values, and ways of life of these people differed from their own, so the Europeans naively concluded that there must be some relationship between how the people looked and how they behaved. This was another instance in which prejudices and stereotyping resulted from ethnocentric rationalization.

Myths about the racial inferiority of blacks emerged as a rationalization of slavery. Although slavery was by no means uncommon under earlier systems, ancient civilizations did not link skin color and social status. Statues and paintings from ancient Egypt, for example, depict slaves and rulers alike as both white and black.[3] Speculation about how racism arose includes such factors as (1) the rise of seagoing power among European nations and increased contact with red, brown, black, and yellow peoples; (2) the influence of Christianity, linking slavery and skin color with the Curse of Ham (Noah's second son, cursed by his father in Genesis 9:20–29); and (3) European technological and military superiority over native peoples throughout the world. In the 19th century, with racism firmly implanted in U.S. culture, a mangled and scientifically unsound form of evolutionary theory was developed to support racist thinking, for some argued that the white race was more highly evolved than the others.

W. E. B. DuBois interpreted the rise of racism as follows:

> Labor was degraded, humanity was despised, the theory of "race" arose. There came a new doctrine of universal labor: mankind were of two sorts—the superior and the inferior; the inferior toiled for the superior; and the superior were the real men, the inferior half men or less. . . . Luxury and plenty for the few and poverty for the many was looked upon as inevitable in the course of nature. In addition to this, it went without saying that the white people of Europe had a right to live upon the labor and property of the colored peoples of the world.
>
> In order to establish the righteousness of this point of view, science and religion, government and industry, were wheeling into line. The word "Negro" was used for the first time in the world's history to tie color to race and blackness to slavery and degradation. The white race was pictured as "pure" and superior: the black race as dirty, stupid, and inevitably inferior; the yellow race as sharing, in deception and cowardice, much of this color inferiority; while mixture of the races was considered the prime cause of degradation and failure in civilization. Everything great, everything fine, everything really successful in human culture, was white.
>
> In order to prove this, even black people in India and Africa were labeled as "white" if they showed any trace of progress; and, on the other hand, any progress by colored people was attributed to some intermixture, ancient or modern, of white blood or some influence of white civilization.[1]

Although a rather small percentage of white southerners actually owned slaves, these were the wealthiest, most influential people in southern society; and other southern whites strongly supported the system. The total separation of U.S. slaves from the rest of society, unlike the partial separation of slaves in Latin American countries (where they had greater family stability and gradational conditions of freedom), produced important social consequences. As the dominant element of the southern economy, plantation slavery affected the region's cultural lifestyle and its societal institutions. Illiteracy, nonexistent social and economic organizations, itinerant preachers, strictly white local law enforcement and protection, lack of medical and learning facilities, isolation, and dependency were the social realities of blacks.

As a result of the racial ideology, stereotyping, and social isolation that survived the end of slavery, blacks in the United States—despite their adaptability, willingness, and competence—were more thoroughly excluded from participation in the free community than were the former slaves of Latin America. Once established, the master–slave social system and the theory of racial inferiority that supported it conditioned values, attitudes, and the development of capacities that lasted far beyond the Civil War. Treated as if they were biologically inferior, blacks became socially inferior, first as a result of slavery and then as a result of discrimination in jobs, housing, and education.

Overcoming 200 years of social conditioning is not easy. A generation after the close of the Civil War, many blacks were making economic progress in the South, but whites retained deep-seated belief in their own racial superiority. Previous discussions of the vicious circle and the long-lasting effects of stereotypes help explain the persistence of institutionalized racism long after the end of slavery.[5]

In 1876, when Reconstruction ended and the status of blacks became a southern question rather than a national issue, blacks were assigned a formalized inferior status. Segregation, disfranchisement, **black codes** (state laws designed to keep blacks in subservient positions), job discrimination, and occupational eviction occurred. Not until the 1960s did many deliberate segregationist practices end in the South.

Although many laws now protect people against discrimination, racist beliefs continue to exist. They can be seen in the reasons people give for moving out of racially changing neighborhoods or in their attitudes toward cities, crime, and welfare. Fear of crime, violence, and other problems of the inner city may be justified, but some individuals incorrectly attribute such troubles to race. Deviance, it must be remembered, occurs among all groups who are poor, powerless, and victims of discrimination.[6]

The problem with racism is twofold: its legacy and its subtlety. *Legacy* here refers not only to its institutionalization within society but also to its transmission from one generation to the next. Slavery and segregation may end, but some people continue to believe blacks are inferior. This is part of the subtlety of racism, because people usually draw such conclusions from their observable world. They are not aware that this "objective" reality has been socially constructed over generations. The alleged inferiority is a myth, except as a social product. People see primarily the effects of prolonged racist attitudes and actions. Even a person's own attitudes, actions, and reactions may unwittingly contribute to the propagation of racism.[7]

INSTITUTIONALIZED RACISM

Institutionalized racism, which occurs when laws attempt to legitimize differential racial treatment, took a new form after slavery in the United States was abolished. At first, though, racial equality seemed to have some chance of developing. During the Reconstruction period and almost to the end of the 19th century, southern blacks generally had greater access to stores, restaurants, public transportation, bars, and theaters than in the first half of the 20th century. A typical pattern was for whites to live on one street in large homes, while behind them on the parallel street were the lesser dwellings of blacks, many of whom worked as domestics. Although a clear status distinction existed, in most places no severe social distance divided the two races. Blacks lived in close proximity to whites and frequently interacted with them in secondary relationships through their occupational roles as domestic or service workers. In education, marriage, political participation, and major economic enterprises, however, blacks did not share any commonality with whites (see the accompanying Ethnic Experience box).

The Ethnic Experience
How Northerners Differ from Southerners

"*I* had heard so much talk about New York. People would say things were so good in New York until I felt that if I would get to New York, I would find money on the streets and wouldn't have no more worries. All my problems would be solved. When I got to New York, things were much different than that. Jobs were very hard to find, and the people were very different than in West Virginia.

"Finally I did get a job through the State Employment Office, working as a cook in the Brooklyn Navy Yard in a private canteen. I stayed there a year and then the war closed up—was over. Then I got another job in a seafood house on 34th Street and 3rd Avenue and I stayed there a year. Then a friend of mine and I went into our own business selling raw fish. Opened a store in Brooklyn selling raw fish. And, of course, it didn't pan out that way. The problem with that business was that we didn't have enough capital to carry us over the rough spots. And then my wife started having babies, and so I had to give up that job and seek another, which I did, and finally I got a job right away at another seafood house.

"In the South we had whites live here, Colored live there and everybody would speak to you whether they knowed you or not. But when I got to the North, I'd be out on the street, maybe walking around, before I got the jobs, looking around, trying to find my way around, and I would be saying, 'Good morning,' and 'Good evening,' whichever way the situation was, and people would look at me as if I was some dope or something. People would say, 'What's wrong with him?' People are not as friendly up here.

"And I also found out when we bought a house here, that the whites started right away moving out. They started selling their houses, putting up signs for sale. That didn't bother me any. Only thing was that I was just saying to myself that I thought New York was so great. Why should this be happening? And in the South, where I was living, it didn't happen that way. Blacks and whites lived side-by-side there, and we didn't have no problems with that. That kind of upset me that in New York, after hearing so much about it, this did go on."

Source: Black migrant from West Virginia who came North in 1944 at age 26.

Immigration and Jim Crow

The change in black–white relations during the late 19th and early 20th centuries is an example of **cultural drift,** a gradual and pervasive change in a people's values. Economic problems, scandals, and frustrations endured by southern whites appear to be some of the factors that reshaped their attitudes. In a region where they had long been considered inferior, many blacks were achieving socioeconomic respectability and becoming economic competitors. Resentment at black upward mobility, amplified by a historical undercurrent of racist attitudes, was further increased by economic troubles (declining cotton prices and unemployment). Because blacks were racially distinct, they became a convenient scapegoat for the frustrations and hostility of southern whites.

Less liberal attitudes in the North were another factor that led to an increased incidence of racist acts of discrimination in housing, labor, associations, unions, schools, and churches throughout the United States.[8] What caused this change in the North? The change in racial attitudes occurred just when great numbers of southern and eastern European immigrants were settling in northern urban areas. The arrival of so many dark-eyed, dark-haired, dark-complexioned newcomers set in motion a nativist reaction culminating in restrictive immigration laws. Northerners became more sensitive to the influx of foreigners and "anarchists" as well as to southern blacks coming north to seek work. The racial overtones of racism in the North's ethnocentric reaction to the "new" immigrants prompted greater empathy for the South's reaction to blacks from northern nativists. As a result, the North ceased to pressure the South regarding its treatment of blacks and allowed the Jim Crow laws to emerge without a challenge.

In the 1870s and 1880s, Californians succeeded in making the Chinese question a national issue and cleverly related it to that of blacks whenever necessary. Political deals were made; and later, southern representatives voted overwhelmingly in favor of the Chinese Exclusion Act of 1882 and the 1921 immigration bill restricting southern and eastern Europeans, most of whom were settling in the North.

In 1896, the U.S. Supreme Court ruling on *Plessy v. Ferguson* upheld the principle of "separate but equal" railroad accommodations for blacks and whites. Only a few southern states had had mandatory segregation laws covering train passengers before the turn of the century. Between 1901 and 1910 though, most southern states passed multiple, activity-specific **Jim Crow laws** as part of a rolling snowball effect of such legislation. Segregation became the norm in all areas of life—bars, barbershops, drinking fountains, toilet facilities, ticket windows, waiting rooms, hotels, restaurants, parks, playgrounds, theaters, and auditoriums. Through literacy tests, poll taxes, and other measures, the southern states also succeeded in disfranchising black voters.

Effects of Jim Crow

The segregation laws, mostly of 20th-century vintage, reflected racist attitudes that remained strong throughout the South decades after slavery had ended. When the 1954 Supreme Court ruling overturned school segregation laws, 17 states had mandatory segregation: Alabama, Arkansas, Delaware, Florida, Georgia, Kentucky, Louisiana, Maryland, Mississippi, Missouri, North Carolina, Oklahoma, South Carolina, Tennessee, Texas, Virginia, and West Virginia. Four other states—Arizona, Kansas, New Mexico, and Wyoming—permitted segregation as a local option.

The South.   It is impossible to exaggerate the impact on society of legalizing such discriminatory norms. These laws existed for two or three generations. During that

For the first six decades of the 20th century, Jim Crow laws maintained a racially segregated society in the South. All aspects of public interaction, including the entrance and seating accommodations of this movie theater, determined use and accessibility by race. Such pervasive norms socialized many people into accepting a world of institutionalized discrimination as "normal."
(*Source:* Bern Keating/Black Star)

time, both white and black children grew up in a society in which the two races were distinguished from each other and treated differently simply because of that racial difference. Because the white world of reality was one in which differential treatment was the norm, the inferior status of blacks was taken for granted. For most whites growing up in such an environment and in turn transmitting values and attitudes to their children, this reflected objective reality.

Structural discrimination in the South was pervasive. Despite legal challenges by the National Association for the Advancement of Colored People (NAACP) and by other groups and individuals, most blacks and whites appeared to accept the situation. To whites, the inferior status of blacks in southern society appeared to justify continued differential treatment. It was, as Gunnar Myrdal concluded in his study of U.S. race relations, a perfect example of the vicious circle, in which "discrimination breeds discrimination."[9] Because blacks' education and job opportunities were restricted, the end result of segregation was reinforcement of the attitude supporting segregation. The consequences of deprivation and limited opportunity only aggravated the situation. Blacks were a group of easily recognizable people who did not hold lucrative jobs or become educated; who lived in squalor amidst poverty, disease, crime, and violence; and who were not "good enough" to use the same facilities as whites. This gave whites more ammunition to bolster their aversion to blacks and increased their prejudicial attitudes and discriminatory actions. Myrdal calls this intensification a **cumulative causation,** in which an almost perpetual sequence of reciprocal stimuli and responses produces complex interactive results.[10]

The North. But what about the North, where few segregationist laws existed? Although there had been some migration to the North earlier, prior to 1914 almost all blacks resided in the South; then, however, large numbers of blacks began to migrate to the northern urban areas. Clearly the Jim Crow laws and poor economic conditions were the major push factors for moving north, and promises of better wages, education, and political freedom were the primary pull factors (see the accompanying Ethnic Experience box).

> By 1915, the North needed labor. The war was under way in Europe and Northern industry was reaping the benefits from it. The large supply of foreign immigrant labor was rapidly dwindling. In the fourteen years after 1900, over twelve million immigrants found their way to the United States. More than one million immigrants reached the United States in 1914 alone. The next year this figure was cut to about one third, in 1916 to about one fourth, and, by 1918, only 110,618 new arrivals landed on the shores of the United States, while 94,585 left. Other sources of labor were needed and Southern Negroes appeared as an available and willing substitute. . . .
>
> The larger pay and increased economic opportunities in the North were heady inducements to migrants. But it was not only for economic reasons that the desire to come North existed in so many. . . . The desire of adults to see their children able to obtain an education caused many to move North. . . . According to a *New York Times* editorial (January 21, 1918), higher wages would have been far less attractive if the colored man had not felt, and felt for a long time and bitterly, that in the North and West he would not, as in his southern home, be reminded of his black skin every time he met a policeman, entered a street car, railway station or train, and in a hundred other less conspicuous ways in the course of a day.[11]

So Jim Crow segregation in the South was an important cause of migration to the North. By 1925, more than 1.5 million blacks lived in the North. As their counterparts on the West Coast had done in response to Asian immigrants, labor unions in the North organized against the blacks. Seeing them either as an undesirable social element or as economic competition, many workers quickly became antagonistic toward them. It was one more instance of people being progressives at a distance but reactionaries at close range. Although African Americans did find greater freedom in the North, the dominant group's animosity toward them led to majority patterns of avoidance and discrimination.

Race riots, basically an urban phenomenon reflecting the growing hostility in the North, swept through a number of cities during World War I. In 1917, in East

The Ethnic Experience
Adjusting to Northern Urban Life

"*I* came to the North not because of a lack, not being able to cope with economic situations in the South, because I was doing all right economically. I came, more or less, for a change of environment and for a higher income for the work I was doing.

"I was educated in the South and by the time I left I was not sharecropping any longer. I was teaching and so my standard of living was different from back when I was a child growing up. I had heard many rumors about the North when I was a child. I had heard there was no segregation in the North. You were at liberty to ride buses, use all facilities, no discrimination in jobs. And I found all of this was, more or less, a fairy tale in a lot of respects. As an adult, I had a more accurate picture of what the North was all about since I had relatives living in Detroit, Washington, and New Jersey.

"I worked at different jobs—office worker, in a nursery school, a dietician—before going to grad school and becoming a public school teacher as I was in the South.

"The biggest adjustment to me going from a rural to an urban setting was getting accustomed to rushing, rushing, rushing city life. To me the people were always running instead of walking. There was always the hustle-bustle to catch the buses and catch subways and this kind of thing. And this was the hardest thing for me to get accustomed to, and the rate at which people worked. The people in the North move much, much faster than people in the South.

"I lived in an apartment with my sister four months, got married and moved to another apartment with my husband. We lived there a year and then moved to the suburbs where we bought our house. Now things here have deteriorated to the extent we have higher unemployment in the North than we do in the South. The overcrowding situation and your housing situation is badly in need of improvement, too."

Source: Black migrant from South Carolina who came north in 1954 at age 22.

St. Louis, Illinois, 39 blacks and 8 whites were killed and hundreds seriously injured in one of the worst of these riots. In 1919 the crisis became even more acute, with returning war veterans seeking jobs and more blacks moving north:

> That year there were race riots large and small in twenty-six American cities including thirty-eight killed in a Chicago riot of August, from twenty-five to fifty killed in Phillips County, Arkansas; and six killed in Washington. For a day, the city of Washington, in July, 1919, was actually in the hands of a black mob fighting against the aggression of the whites with hand grenades.[12]

The riots intensified the hostile racial feelings even more. The South had **de jure segregation,** but Jim Crow—as a cause of black migration and a model for northern attitudes and actions—played an important role in the development of *de facto* **segregation** in the North. With race the determinant for various life opportunities in both the North and the South, succeeding generations of blacks encountered the same obstacles to upward mobility. So the effects of Jim Crow on black assimilation into the mainstream of U.S. society went beyond the South and lasted longer than just the first half of the 20th century.

The Ku Klux Klan

Originally organized in the South during Reconstruction, primarily to intimidate blacks so that they would not exercise their new political rights—at a time when any man who had fought on the Confederate side during the Civil War was barred by law from voting or holding office—the Ku Klux Klan (KKK) reorganized in the 20th century with a broader range of target groups. In 1915, William J. Simmons resurrected the movement, formalized its rituals and organization, and dedicated it to white supremacy, Protestant Christianity, and "Americanism."

Protest or reactionary groups generally do not become popular unless they address or exploit a shared awareness of the problems or concerns important to a distinct segment of society. The Klan was no exception, both in the 1870s and again in the 1920s, when a combination of factors—the agricultural depression, Prohibition, immigration, and isolationism—caused it to expand rapidly. By 1923, the Klan claimed 3 million enrolled members and operated in virtually every state in the union, with public ceremonies and parades.

At first the Klan concentrated on maintaining white supremacy by intimidating white employers as well as black workers and potential voters. Although this remained an important theme, as the Klan spread northward, its racist orientation broadened into a more general nationalism and nativism. Fears and condemnation of Jews and foreigners, especially Catholics, led the Klan into a campaign of promoting an Anglo-Saxon version of Americanism with evangelical zeal. The hooded Klansmen used mass raids, tarring and featherings, floggings, and other strong-arm tactics to enforce their notions of moral propriety or to stabilize the old order. In reality, their actions only fomented additional strife and cruelty.

After a series of internal struggles, exposés of corruption, and mounting anti-Klan opposition, the Klan empire came apart. Although it retained some influence in rural regions of New York, Pennsylvania, Indiana, and the South, its heyday ended in the mid-1920s. It remains active, however, particularly during times of racial troubles. Ironically, in the 1970s the Klan sought to recruit Catholics—one of its major targets in the past—from the South Boston area who opposed school busing.

The Ku Klux Klan thus evolved into a multixenophobic organization in which southern and eastern European Catholics and Jews, as well as blacks, were seen as a threat to the nation's character. The Klan's enormous popularity in the early 1920s reflected the times, because these minority peoples were felt to present an economic threat to more established residents. As prosperity increased and immigration decreased, thereby reducing the tensions, support for the Klan ebbed. Its success, like the success of the Native American Party and the Know-Nothing

Party of the 19th century, indicates that many people were receptive to its philosophy and goals.

The Ku Klux Klan is not just a relic from the past. Wherever racial strife occurs, its members come to sermonize, recruit, and stir up trouble. They have harassed and intimidated blacks in southern California and Vietnamese along the Texas Gulf Coast. When unemployment rises, they seek out the vulnerable white victims, offering a convenient black scapegoat for their troubles. In the backwoods of several states, they run paramilitary camps, practicing riflery and battle tactics for what they see as an inevitable racial war. Klan members indoctrinate their children at these camps, too, passing on a legacy of hate. Meanwhile, on equal-access local cable channels, they telecast programs promoting their bigotry.

THE WINDS OF CHANGE

In the past, blacks made many concerted efforts to improve their lot. The Colored National Farmers' Alliance claimed 1,250,000 members in 1891, but it faded from the scene by 1910. In the 20th century, several black leaders arose to rally their people: Booker T. Washington, W. E. B. DuBois, Marcus Garvey, and A. Philip Randolph. In the 1920s, 1930s, and 1940s, the NAACP and other groups filed court cases that achieved limited success but laid the basis for the 1954 school-desegregation ruling, which produced a massive restructuring of black–white relations.

Desegregation: The First Phase

Having experienced life outside their cultural milieu, many blacks who fought in World War II returned home with new perspectives and aspirations. The GI Bill of Rights, the Veterans Authority, and the Federal Housing Authority offered increased opportunity for education, jobs, and housing. Expectations increased, and the growing popularity of television sets brought into more and more homes insights into lifestyles that previously could only be vaguely imagined.

Several court cases challenging school-segregation laws of Delaware, Kansas, South Carolina, and Virginia reached the U.S. Supreme Court in 1954. After consolidating the several suits, the justices ruled unanimously that the "separate but equal" doctrine was unconstitutional. Social-science data, through *amicus curiae* briefs, played an important role in the decision.[13] The following year, the Court established a means of implementing its decree by giving the federal district courts jurisdiction over any problems relating to enforcement of the ruling. The Court insisted that the states move toward compliance with "all deliberate speed," but this guideline was vague enough to allow the states to circumvent the ruling at first.

Although the NAACP quickly began a multipronged challenge to school districts in the 17 states where statutorily mandated school segregation existed, its efforts met with mixed success. Many whites, perceiving their values, beliefs, and

Under presidential orders to enforce court-mandated school integration, federal troops escort black students as they arrive in a U.S. Army station wagon at Central High School in Little Rock, Arkansas, during the first week of integration in September 1957. This action followed the state governor's use of National Guard troops to deny entry to black students. President Eisenhower then put the Guard under U.S. Army control. (*Source:* AP Photo)

practices to be threatened by outsiders, resisted desegregation. State legislatures passed bills to stave off integration, whites used economic and social pressures to intimidate any blacks who attempted to integrate local schools, and the school districts themselves procrastinated in dealing with the problem. For three years, the battle of wills resulted in a stalemate, continuing the status quo despite the Supreme Court ruling.

On another front, an event occurred in Montgomery, Alabama, in 1955 that foreshadowed other minority actions in the 1960s. Rosa Parks, a tired black seamstress on her way home from work, found the seats in the black section of the bus all occupied and so sat down in an open seat in the section reserved for whites; when she refused the bus driver's demand that she relinquish the seat, she was arrested. Through the organizing efforts of Martin Luther King, Jr. in the black community, a successful bus boycott occurred. Four months later, the NAACP argued the case in the Federal District Court, which ruled against segregated seating on municipal buses. The U.S. Supreme Court upheld the decision.

The confrontation in the fall of 1957 at Little Rock Central High School in Arkansas was a watershed event in desegregation. Here the state's defiance of the Supreme Court could not be ignored, because the governor called out the National

Guard to forcibly block a concerted effort to integrate the high school in accordance with a federal court order. President Eisenhower, who had personally opposed the 1954 ruling, acted decisively by federalizing the National Guard and sending regular army troops to Little Rock to ensure compliance.

With all legal avenues of appeal exhausted and the federal government insisting that all citizens, including black children, be accorded equal rights, southern resistance ebbed. Desegregation in the public schools, although sometimes slight in effect because of neighborhood-based districting plans, became the norm throughout the southern states. That is not to say that everything was harmonious. Some whites established private academies to avoid sending their children to integrated schools, and some southern leaders publicly committed themselves to upholding southern tradition at all costs. Still, Jim Crow had been dealt a severe blow, and opponents readied themselves for the next assault.

Desegregation: The Second Phase

In the 1960s the civil-rights movement gained momentum, attracted many more followers, and moved against the remaining Jim Crow legislation. Sit-in demonstrations began in Greensboro, North Carolina, on February 1, 1960, when four freshmen from the all-black Agricultural and Technical College sat at the all-white lunch counter at the local Woolworth's store and refused to leave. During the spring of 1960, similar sit-ins occurred throughout the South. From the sit-ins evolved a fourth social organization—the Student Nonviolent Coordinating Committee (SNCC)—to compete with the NAACP, the Congress on Racial Equality (CORE), and the Southern Christian Leadership Conference (SCLC), which Dr. King had formed after the bus boycott.

The success of the sit-ins convinced many people that direct action was a quicker and more effective means of achieving total desegregation than protracted court battles. James Farmer of CORE organized Freedom Rides from Washington, DC, to selected southern locations in 1961 to challenge the segregated facilities in bus terminals. These were followed by freedom marches, voter-registration drives, and continued litigation challenging the constitutionality of Jim Crow legislation.

All of these movements were symptomatic of the times. John Kennedy's election as president in 1960 and his speaking of "a new generation of leadership" had inaugurated a period of high hopes and ideals. It was a time of political commitment and societal change, of VISTA and the Peace Corps, of promise and reachable goals. As the civil-rights movement grew, "We Shall Overcome" became the rallying theme song, and Bob Dylan's "Blowin' in the Wind" captured the spirit of the times.

Civil-rights activity met with fierce resistance. Dr. King urged nonviolence, but younger black activists grew impatient with such an approach:

> Nonviolence was for him [King] a philosophical issue rather than the tactical or strategic question it posed for many younger activists in SNCC and CORE. The aim was "to awaken a sense of moral shame in the opponent." Such a philosophy

presumed that the opponent had moral shame to awaken, and that moral shame, if awakened, would suffice. During the 1960s many civil rights activists came to doubt the first and deny the second. The reasons for this did not lie primarily in white Southern terrorism as manifested in the killing of NAACP leader Medgar Evers, of three civil rights workers in Neshoba, Mississippi, of four little girls in a dynamited church in Birmingham, and many others. To a large extent, white Southern violence was anticipated and expected. What was not expected was the absence of strong protective action by the federal government.

Activists in SNCC and CORE met with greater and more violent Southern resistance as direct action continued during the sixties. Freedom Riders were beaten by mobs in Montgomery; demonstrators were hosed, clubbed, and cattle-prodded in Birmingham and Selma. Throughout the South, civil rights workers, Black and White, were victimized by local officials as well as by nightriders and angry crowds. It was not surprising, then, that student activists in the South became increasingly disillusioned with nonviolent tactics of resistance.[14]

Two events in 1963—the March on Washington and the integration of the University of Alabama—gave two civil-rights activists, King and Kennedy, the opportunity to express the mood of the times. On August 28, 1963, tens of thousands of marchers of all races from all over the country and from many walks of life gathered before the Lincoln Memorial. Dr. King addressed them (in part) as follows:

> There are those who are asking the devotees of civil rights, "When will you be satisfied?" We can never be satisfied as long as the Negro is the victim of the unspeakable horrors of police brutality. We can never be satisfied as long as our bodies, heavy with the fatigue of travel, cannot gain lodging in the motels of the highways and the hotels of the cities. We cannot be satisfied as long as the Negro's basic mobility is from a smaller ghetto to a larger one. We can never be satisfied as long as a Negro in Mississippi cannot vote and a Negro in New York believes he has nothing for which to vote. No, no, we are not satisfied, and we will not be satisfied until justice rolls down like waters and righteousness like a mighty stream. . . .
>
> I say to you today, my friends, that in spite of the difficulties and frustrations of the moment I still have a dream. It is a dream deeply rooted in the American dream.
>
> I have a dream that one day this nation will rise up and live out the true meaning of its creed: "We hold these truths to be self-evident; that all men are created equal." . . . I have a dream that my four little children will one day live in a nation where they will not be judged by the color of their skin but by the content of their character.

On April 4, 1968, an assassin's bullet prevented Martin Luther King from seeing his dream move closer to reality. President Kennedy had been assassinated 4½ years earlier, on November 22, 1963, before Congress could pass the civil-rights legislation he had proposed after sending troops to enforce the integration of the University of Alabama that same year. In explaining his actions, Kennedy had told the public in a television address:

> This nation was founded by men of many nations and backgrounds. It was founded on the principle that all men are created equal, and that the rights of every man are diminished when the rights of one man are threatened. . . .

Over 200,000 people jammed the area in front of the Lincoln Memorial, and on either side of the Reflecting Pool all the way to the Washington Monument. The 1963 March on Washington ended with Martin Luther King's "I Have a Dream" speech, which effectively gave a vision about the goals sought by the civil rights movement.
(*Source:* Hulton/Archive by Getty Images)

It ought to be possible, therefore, for American students of any color to attend any public institution they select without having to be backed up by troops. It ought to be possible for American consumers of any color to receive equal service in places of public accommodation, such as hotels and restaurants, and theaters and retail stores without being forced to resort to demonstrations in the street.

And it ought to be possible for American citizens of any color to register and to vote in a free election without interference or fear of reprisal.

It ought to be possible, in short, for every American to enjoy the privileges of being American without regard to his race or his color.

In short, every American ought to have the right to be treated as he would wish to be treated, as one would wish his children to be treated. But this is not the case. . . .

One hundred years of delay have passed since President Lincoln freed the slaves, yet their heirs, their grandsons, are not fully free. They are not yet freed from the bonds of injustice; they are not yet freed from social and economic oppression.

And this nation, for all its hopes and all its boasts, will not be fully free until all its citizens are free.

The Civil Rights Act of 1964 was the most far-reaching legislation against racial discrimination ever passed. It mandated that equal standards be enforced for voter eligibility in federal elections. It prohibited racial discrimination and refusal of service on racial grounds in all places of public accommodation, including eating and lodging establishments and places of entertainment, recreation, and service. It gave the attorney general broad powers to intervene in private suits regarding violation of civil rights. It banned racial discrimination by employers and unions and by any recipient of federal funds, and it directed federal agencies to monitor businesses and organizations for compliance and to withhold funds from any recalcitrant state or local agency.

Congress passed additional legislation in 1965 to simplify judicial enforcement of the voting laws and to extend them to state and local elections. In 1968, further civil-rights legislation barred discrimination in housing and gave Native Americans greater rights in their dealings with courts and government agencies at all levels. Congress also set stiff federal penalties for persons convicted of attempting or conspiring to intimidate or injure anyone who was exercising any of the civil rights provided by congressional action.

In 1966, Stokely Carmichael, the head of SNCC, advanced the slogan "Black Power"—a declaration that civil-rights goals could be achieved only through concerted black efforts. It symbolized the attainment of what Kurt Lewin called a "sense of peoplehood" and what Franklin Giddings identified as a "consciousness of kind." The word *black* rather than *Negro* became the accepted way of referring to this racial group in the 1970s. Unfortunately, Carmichael was also a major force in the purge of whites from the SNCC leadership—an isolationist act that alienated many white sympathizers to SNCC's cause.

Four decades later, we can readily see the gains in black power in the political arena. The number of black elected officials increased dramatically, from about 170 in 1964 to almost 8,900 in 1999, about two thirds of these in the southern states.[15] Blacks also improved their rate of participation in other areas; including voter registration. Perhaps "stateways" will change "folkways," as legislation opens doors to blacks, thereby providing long-term opportunities for the social conditioning of people's attitudes toward racial harmony.

URBAN UNREST

As the civil-rights movement gained momentum, it spread northward as well. Protests against discrimination in employment and housing and against *de facto* segregation in northern schools began in the early 1960s, in New York City and Philadelphia, and quickly spread:

> None of the problems of the blacks in the North—slum schools, unemployment or residential segregation—were new, but an intensified awareness of them had grown. Part of this new awareness reflected the economic cramp that developed during the latter part of the fifties, particularly in the burgeoning ghettoes of northern and western cities. Ideological cramp was being felt outside the South, too. The promise of a new equality for all blacks, the struggle of southern blacks to realize this promise, and the complacency of white America as the white South turned the new equality into token equality spread disillusionment into black neighborhoods all over the nation. Ironically, the plaintive and oft-repeated plea of white southerners that the problem of race relations was not just a Southern problem finally began to be heard—but only because it was now sounded by black voices.[16]

In the North, ideological support for the black cause waned as the percentages of blacks in northern cities increased. Changes—in particular, open housing and busing—were demanded nearer home. By 1964 Charles Silberman observed,

> And so the North is finally beginning to face the reality of race. In the process, it is discovering animosities and prejudices that had been hidden in the recesses of the soul. For a brief period following the demonstrations in Birmingham in the spring of 1963—a very brief period—it appeared that the American conscience had been touched; a wave of sympathy for the Negro and of revulsion over white brutality seemed to course through the nation. But then the counteraction set in, revealing

a degree of anti-Negro prejudice and hatred that surprised even the most sophisticated observers.[17]

As blacks experienced some gains and some frustrations, a pattern of increased alienation, cynicism, hostility, and violence ensued. When a social movement achieves some goals, its expectations are increased and so are its frustrations, which leads to greater militancy.[18] Militant leaders such as Malcolm X, Eldridge Cleaver, Huey Newton, and Bobby Seale emerged to speak of the grievances of northern blacks. New organizations, such as the Black Panthers, and older ones, such as the Black Muslims, attracted many followers as they set out to meet the needs of northern blacks in the ghettos.

The 1960s Riots

In the summer of 1964, blacks rioted in the tenement sections of Harlem, Rochester, and Philadelphia, attacking both police and property. The following summer, the violence and destruction were more massive; outbursts occurred first in the Watts section of Los Angeles and then in Chicago; Springfield, Massachusetts; and Philadelphia. Ghetto violence continued. In the summer of 1966, 18 different riots occurred and in the summer of 1967, 31 cities experienced riots, of which those in Newark (26 killed) and Detroit (42 killed) were the worst.

The increase in the number and intensity of riots in 1967 prompted an in-depth study of 75 of the disorders, including those in Newark and Detroit, by the National Advisory Commission on Civil Disorders. It concluded that, although specific grievances varied somewhat from city to city, there were consistent patterns in who the rioters were, how the riots originated, and what the rioters wanted. The most intense causal factors were police practices, unemployment and underemployment, and inadequate housing. In its 1968 report, the so-called Kerner Commission warned that the United States was "moving toward two societies, one black, one white—separate and unequal."[19]

The assassination of Martin Luther King, Jr., in April 1968 prompted violence to erupt anew in 125 cities. The Justice Department reported 46 people killed in one week of unrest. Several years of civil-rights legislation now set changes in motion. Government action at all levels sought to correct the conditions that encouraged the violence, and U.S. cities experienced no further major disturbances for several years.

Several factors contributed to the cooling of black urban violence. First, a new social movement protesting the war in Vietnam, to which many black youths were sent, became a focus of public concern. Second, many black leaders were assassinated (King, Evers, and Malcolm X) or imprisoned (Carmichael, Newton, and Seale), or went into exile (Cleaver). Third, many blacks redirected their energies toward community self-help programs, some leaders were co-opted into leadership roles within the system, and other blacks began to strive for the black power goal Carmichael had enunciated. Perhaps, also, the realization that the destruction of their neighborhoods had left a trail of economic devastation without producing any tangible benefits helped stop the rioting.

The 1980s Miami Riots

In Miami in May 1980, black economic frustrations and resentment against the growing Cuban community—sparked by an all-white jury's acquittal of four white police officers accused of bludgeoning a black man to death—set off three days of the worst outbreak of racial violence in 13 years. When it ended, 18 were dead, more than 400 were injured, and property damages exceeded $200 million.[20] In January 1989, violence erupted in Miami again, in the Overtown section, after a policeman shot and killed a black motorcycle rider.

The 1992 Los Angeles Riot

Five days of rioting erupted in Los Angeles in 1992, after a jury acquitted four white city police officers of criminal wrongdoing in the videotaped beating of black motorist Rodney King. In the aftermath of the prolonged riot, officials reported 58 deaths, 4,000 injuries, 11,900 arrests, and damage ranging as high as $1 billion.[21] The events seemed like a flashback to the 1960s and some observers predicted a new wave of rioting across the United States in response to a decade of retreat by the federal government from its earlier role as a champion of the disadvantaged; but U.S. society had changed. Most of the nation's 30 million African Americans did not take to the streets. Those who did were part of a relatively small urban underclass clearly distinct from the 40 percent of all African American families now middle class or upwardly mobile working class. Moreover, whereas the 1965 Watts riot was black versus white, the 1992 riot was multiracial warfare: blacks preying on other blacks, Latinos on whites, blacks and Latinos on Koreans and other Asian Americans.[22] The Rodney King verdict was the spark that detonated a powder keg built of the pathologies resulting from poverty—squalid living conditions, frustration, alienation, anger, and family disintegration.

In Chapter 8, I discussed some aspects of the black–Korean conflict. Part of that animosity stems from the growing presence and economic success of Korean merchants in black neighborhoods where poverty and unemployment are widespread. As previously mentioned, 1 in 10 Korean Americans is self-employed, compared to 1 in 67 African Americans. African Americans are more likely to be in public-sector employment.[23] Limited education is not a barrier to self-employment for Korean Americans because of their informal networks of assistance and advice. Poorly educated African Americans, however, lack similar support networks and are less likely to become entrepreneurs in the central city.[24] As these blacks witness the economic gains of strangers in their midst while they themselves are mired in deprivation, their resentment sometimes reaches the flashpoint of violence when triggered by an incident.

How can the United States prevent such violence? The primary answer lies in taking steps to meet black expectations and to eliminate the economic despair that fuels riots. We must focus on overcoming depressed urban economies, chronic unemployment, a poorly skilled and poorly educated labor force, substandard housing, and unsafe streets.

Reducing the social distance among urban residents through community interaction offers another promising approach. When "we" replaces "us versus

Riots not only occur because of race relations problems. Los Angeles, still infamous for its 1992 multiracial riot that left 58 people dead and 4,000 injured, with $1 billion in property damage, experienced another riot in June 2000. Here a car burns during a riot that followed a victory celebration by L.A. Lakers fans after the team's win in the NBA finals.
(*Source:* © Jason Kirk/Online USA/NEWSMAKERS/Getty Images)

them," violence becomes less likely. Still another approach is to increase the number of African American entrepreneurs in the central city. African American proprietors would act as positive role models and could provide initial employment opportunities to urban African American youth. Local mom-and-pop stores could become bonding anchors in the neighborhood, reinforcing community life around work and thereby helping generate and sustain informal associations.[25]

Postviolence Exodus

For several complex reasons, a significant white middle-class migration from cities to suburbs began in the 1950s, and urban violence has clearly been a major factor in this movement. The 1960s riots gave added impetus to white flight, with many stores and businesses following close behind. Because many major cities—especially in the Northeast and Midwest—also experienced population declines, this resulted in a larger concentration of people of color in these cities.

Riots also induced many middle-class minorities to leave the embattled neighborhoods in south-central Los Angeles and elsewhere.[26] Violence, burning, and looting thus destroy the neighborhood economy, stability, and potential as its middle class flees.

THE BELL-CURVE DEBATE

In 1994, *The Bell Curve*, by Richard Herrnstein and Charles Murray, set off a firestorm of controversy.[27] Rejecting conventional theories about the role of environment and culture in creating dependence and crime, the authors argued that intelligence is the best single explanation of wealth, poverty, and social status. They asserted that the United States was becoming increasingly stratified by intellectual ability—with a "cognitive elite" of brilliant, highly educated business leaders, politicians, and professionals; a large cognitive middle class of about 125 million with IQs measuring between 91 and 110; and a growing underclass of dullards with IQs of 90 or below.

The authors also contended that social pathologies such as poverty, welfare dependence, illegitimacy, and crime were all strongly related to low IQ. Most explosive was their argument that blacks as a group were intellectually inferior to whites as a group because the mean, or average, IQ score for blacks was 15 points lower than that for whites. Herrnstein and Murray then attacked affirmative action in college admissions and in the workplace, characterizing it as a futile policy designed to help the cognitively disadvantaged; not-so-smart people, they implied, can never become middle class.

Another volatile theme of the book was the proposition that the cognitive elite pass on their genetic advantages to their children while members of the low-IQ underclass pass on genetic disadvantages. Herrnstein and Murray, noting the higher birth rate among the underclass, argued that government subsidies to welfare mothers were responsible for a gradual decline in the national IQ. Therefore, they argued, such programs as Aid to Families with Dependent Children should be terminated.

Critics attacked the book for its selective use of data to fit its political arguments, such as ignoring the difference between actual intelligence and IQ as measured by tests. Others found factual contradictions, such as the claim that the national IQ had declined when actually group scores have been rising slowly but steadily since the 1930s.[28] Still others attacked the book's scholarship, methodology, and analytical techniques.[29]

Early IQ Tests

Although Herrnstein and Murray offered some new wrinkles, their argument is an old, discredited one. The intelligence test, first developed by Alfred Binet in 1905, became a popular means of comparing the intelligence of different racial and ethnic groups, although that was not Binet's intention. This supposedly objective, scientific instrument was intended to measure an individual's innate intelligence, uninfluenced by any beneficial or detrimental effects of environment. As misappropriated and applied to groups of people, however, the test invited researchers to compare groups' intellectual ability. Early studies showed that northern and western Europeans—and often the Chinese and Japanese—scored consistently and decidedly higher than southern and eastern Europeans, blacks, Mexicans, and Native Americans.[30] Conveniently ignoring the results for Asians, nativists and segregationists seized on these studies as arguments for immigration restrictions against "inferiors," for the forced assimilation of Native Americans, and for Jim Crow laws in the South.

Gradually, as nativist antipathy against the "new" immigrants abated, the argument shifted primarily to intelligence differences between blacks and whites. The disparity in the test results, which most authorities believe actually reflects a cultural bias within the tests, became a basis for claiming white intellectual superiority.

In 1958, Audrey Shuey's book *The Testing of Negro Intelligence* appeared and caused a furor. Shuey surveyed some 240 studies of 60 different intelligence tests that had been given over a 44-year span to hundreds of thousands of servicemen from World Wars I and II and thousands of schoolchildren of all ages through college, from all regions of the country. She concluded that the "remarkable consistenc[ies] in test results . . . all point to the presence of some native differences" between blacks and whites "as determined by intelligence tests."[31]

For any scientist, the interpretation of findings is as crucial as the findings themselves and the methods employed to obtain them. Shuey was accurate in observing the consistent lower scoring of blacks on intelligence tests. However, many scientists disagreed with her conclusion that this was due to intellectual inferiority of the race. The conclusion of innate or genetic differences was a quantum leap from her findings, which did not prove any such thing.

In the late 1960s, the IQ controversy centered on claims made by two California professors: Arthur R. Jensen, an educational psychologist at the University of California (Berkeley), and William B. Shockley, a Nobel Prize–winning physicist at Stanford University. Jensen argued that the 10- to 20-point IQ differential between blacks and whites involved only certain mental functions. He pointed out that blacks and whites tested equally well in such brain functions as rote learning and memory but that blacks did more poorly in problem-solving, in seeing relationships, and in abstract reasoning. Because this material does not depend on specific cultural information, he maintained, the blacks' lower scores must be due to their genetic heritage.[32] Shockley declared in the mid-1960s that the conceptual intelligence of blacks, as measured by many different IQ tests, was significantly lower than that of whites, and that some of this variance was genetically caused and therefore not correctable.

IQ Test Performance by Other Groups

Refuting this position, Thomas Sowell argued that, on average, white ethnic groups, such as the Poles, Jews, and Italians, scored in the 80s on IQ tests administered during the 1920s but as a group had gained 20 to 25 points by the 1970s after experiencing upward mobility.[33] Groups of European ancestry who have not experienced upward mobility, as well as Mexican Americans and Puerto Ricans, continued to score in the 80s on IQ tests. Most significantly, at various times and places, other low-IQ groups have also done poorly on the abstract portions of mental tests. Studies of immigrant groups in 1917, of white children in isolated mountain communities, of working-class children in England, and of early Chinese immigrants all show marked deficiencies on the abstract sections. Concerning the Chinese Americans, recent studies show them to be strongest on the abstract portions of the mental tests, suggesting that upward mobility helps to improve powers of abstract reasoning. Other patterns—children's IQ scores declining as they become adults and females consistently scoring higher than males—also are frequent among low-IQ groups, not just blacks. Again, these results change once the group achieves a higher socioeconomic status.

Another problem with IQ tests is that they purport to measure only some forms of intelligence—analytical, conceptual, and verbal (see Figure 10.2). We are only beginning to understand how and why the brain functions as it does. Until we know more, any assumption of intellectual superiority or inferiority based

---

FIGURE 10.2   Black Intelligence Test of Cultural Homogeneity

The purpose of this tongue-in-cheek "test" was to demonstrate both the subcultural language or understandings of a group and the unfairness of culture-loaded IQ tests on low-income people. Many of you will probably do badly on these questions, regardless of your ability, if the questions are alien to your cultural background, and that is the point of demonstrating cultural bias in tests.

1. Alley Apple is a (a) brick, (b) piece of fruit, (c) dog, (d) horse.
2. CPT means a standard of (a) time, (b) tune, (c) tale, (d) twist.
3. Deuce-and-a-quarter is a (a) money, (b) a car, (c) a house, (d) dice.
4. The eagle flies means (a) the blahs, (b) a movie, (c) payday, (d) deficit.
5. Gospel Bird is a (a) pheasant, (b) chicken, (c) goose, (d) duck.
6. "I know you, shame" means (a) You don't hear very well. (b) You are a racist. (c) You don't mean what you're saying. (d) You are guilty.
7. Main Squeeze means (a) to prepare for battle, (b) a favorite toy, (c) a best girlfriend, (d) to hold up someone.
8. Nose Opened means (a) flirting, (b) teed off, (c) deeply in love, (d) very angry.
9. Playing the dozens means (a) playing the numbers, (b) playing baseball, (c) insulting a person's parents, (d) playing with women.
10. Shucking means (a) talking, (b) thinking, (c) train of thought, (d) wasting time.
11. Stone fox means (a) bitchy, (b) pretty, (c) sly, (d) uncanny.
12. T.C.B. means (a) that's cool baby, (b) taking care of business, (c) they couldn't breathe, (d) took careful behavior.

Answers: 1-a, 2-a, 3-b, 4-c, 5-b, 6-d, 7-c, 8-c, 9-c, 10-d, 11-b, 12-b.

Source: Robert L. Williams, Ph.D.

on IQ scores is conjectural. Moreover, the only demonstrated value IQ scores have is in predicting how well students will do in a traditional school setting. They do not predict performance in nontraditional approaches to education or in any job situation. Does a professor with a 135 IQ teach better than one with 120? Not necessarily, and that is another reason IQ scores should not be a factor in questions of social interaction.

LANGUAGE AS PREJUDICE

Words are symbols connoting meanings about various phenomena in the world around us. That the very words used to describe the two races—*white* and *black*—usually convey positive and negative meanings, respectively, is unfortunate. For example, *white* often symbolizes cleanliness, purity, or heroes (clothes, armor, hats, and horses), and *black* often stands for dirt, evil, or villains. A snow-covered landscape is beautiful, but a sky laden with black smoke is not. Black clouds are seen as threatening, but white clouds are not.

The power of words is such that the pervasiveness of positive and negative meanings for these two words can easily influence minds and attitudes. Ossie Davis had such concerns in mind when he said,

> A superficial examination of Roget's *Thesaurus of the English Language* reveals the following facts: the word "whiteness" has 134 synonyms, 44 of which are favorable and pleasing to contemplate. For example: "purity," "cleanness," "immaculateness," "bright," "shiny," "ivory," "fair," "blonde," "stainless," "clean," "clear," "chaste," "unblemished," "unsullied," "innocent," "honorable," "upright," "just," "straightforward," "genuine," "trustworthy," and only 10 synonyms of which I feel to have been negative and then only in the mildest sense, such as "gloss-over," "whitewash," "gray," "wan," "pale," "ashen," etc.
>
> The word "blackness" has 120 synonyms, 60 of which are distinctly unfavorable, and none of them even mildly positive. Among the offending 60 were such words as "blot," "blotch," "smut," "smudge," "sullied," "begrime," "soot," "becloud," "obscure," "dingy," "murky," "low-toned," "threatening," "frowning," "foreboding," "forbidding," "deadly," "unclean," "dirty," "unwashed," "foul," etc. In addition, and this is what really hurts, 20 of these words—and I exclude the villainous 60 above—are related directly to race, such as "Negro," "Negress," "nigger," "darkey," "blackamoor," etc.
>
> If you consider the fact that thinking itself is subvocal speech (in other words, one must use words in order to think at all), you will appreciate the enormous trap of racial prejudgment that works on any child who is born into the English language.[34]

When *black* has so many negative connotations—blackening the reputation, being black-hearted, blacklisting or blackballing someone, being a blackguard, using black magic, running a black market, and so on—it is easy to see how language by itself can precondition a white person's mind against black people and can lead a black person's mind into possible self-hatred.

FIGURE 10.3   Age-Sex Composition of the Black Population, 2000 (in percentages)

	Black Population		Age	Total U.S. Population	
	Males	Females		Males	Females
	1.2	2.3	75+	2.2	3.7
	0.8	1.3	70-74	1.4	1.7
Median age 26.6	1.1	1.5	65-69	1.6	1.8
	1.4	1.7	60-64	1.8	2.0
	1.7	2.1	55-59	2.3	2.4
	2.4	2.8	50-54	3.1	3.1
	3.0	3.5	45-49	3.5	3.6
	3.7	4.1	40-44	4.0	3.9
	3.8	4.3	35-39	4.0	4.0
	3.6	4.0	30-34	3.7	3.5
	3.5	3.9	25-29	3.5	3.3
	3.7	3.9	20-24	3.4	3.2
	4.3	4.2	15-19	3.7	3.4
	4.6	4.4	10-14	3.7	3.4
	4.7	4.6	5-9	3.7	3.4
	4.1	4.0	0-4	3.5	3.2

Median age 29.5   Median age 31.7   Median age 34.1

Source: U.S. Bureau of the Census.

SOCIAL INDICATORS OF BLACK PROGRESS

As Figure 10.3 shows, a larger percentage of blacks than whites are young. This demographic fact suggests both a more rapid future population growth for blacks and the importance of the socioeconomic environment in which young people grow up. The more enriched their childhood socialization, the greater their adult life opportunities. The more deprived their environment, the more limited their adult life opportunities.

Where are we today? How far has the United States gone toward true equality for blacks and whites? Sociologists use quantifiable measurements of social indicators to identify specifically a group's achievements in comparison with others', as well as its mobility within the stratification system. Three of the most common variables—education, income, and occupation—offer an objective portrait of what gains have been made and of how much the gap between the two races has narrowed.

Education

Since 1960, as a greater proportion of the population stays in school longer, the percentage gap between blacks and whites completing four years of high school

TABLE 10.1   **Educational Attainment by Race (in percentages)**

	1960	1970	1980	1990	2000
Completed 4 years of high school or more					
Black males	18.2	30.1	50.8	65.2	78.7
White males	41.6	54.0	69.6	79.1	84.8
Black females	21.8	32.5	51.5	66.5	78.3
White females	44.7	55.0	68.1	79.0	85.0
Completed 4 years of college or more					
Black males	2.8	4.2	8.4	11.2	16.3
White males	10.3	14.4	21.3	25.3	28.5
Black females	3.3	4.8	8.3	10.8	16.7
White females	6.0	8.4	13.3	19.0	23.9

Source: U.S. Bureau of the Census, *Statistical Abstract of the United States 2001.* (Washington DC: U.S. Government Printing Office, 2001), Table 216, p. 139.

or beyond has steadily lessened for both males and females (see Table 10.1). At the college level, more blacks than ever before are completing four years of college or more, but proportionately the gap between black attainment compared to white attainment has steadily widened. Improvement in high school completion also manifests itself in the changed dropout rates. From a dropout rate twice that of white students in 1970, the black student dropout rate by 1995 had fallen to about the same level as that of white students and surpassed them in 1999 in 16–17 years range (see Table 10.2). These statistics offer a hopeful sign for the next generation's socioeconomic progress.

Another barometer is comparative test scores. The College Entrance Examination Board, which administers the Scholastic Aptitude Test (SAT), reports that between 1987 and 2001 the mean SAT scores of black students rose by 5 points on the verbal section and by 15 points on the math section, whereas the mean scores of whites rose by 5 points on the verbal section and by 17 points on the math section. However, a significant difference in scores remains: 529 to 433 in verbal scores and 530 to 426 in math scores for whites and blacks, respectively.[35]

Income

Historically, black family income has always been significantly lower than white family income. Civil-rights legislation and the War on Poverty began to create a slow, steady improvement until the 1980s, when economic problems and a reduc-

TABLE 10.2 **High School Dropouts, by Race and Age (in percentages)**

Race and Age	1970	1980	1990	1999
White*	10.8	11.3	10.1	9.3
16–17 years	7.3	9.2	6.4	5.3
18–21 years	14.3	14.7	13.1	13.1
22–24 years	16.3	14.0	14.0	12.5
Black*	22.2	16.0	10.9	10.8
16–17 years	12.8	6.9	6.9	4.9
18–21 years	30.5	23.0	18.0	16.8
22–24 years	37.8	24.0	13.5	14.8

*Includes persons 14–15 years, not shown separately.
Source: U.S. Bureau of the Census. *Statistical Abstract of the United States 2001*,
(Washington, DC: U.S. Government Printing Office, 2001), Table 258, p. 163.

tion in federal support for remedial programs eroded some of the gains. As Table 10.3 indicates, the 2000 median family income was $45,904 for whites and $30,439 for blacks. Put differently, the average black family earned 66 cents for every $1 the average white family earned, its best ratio ever. Although the median black family income is steadily rising, the actual income gap between the two groups has only begun to recede as well.[36]

An important social indicator is the poverty rate among blacks. After its significant drop from 48.1 percent in 1959 to 29.5 percent in 1970, it held fairly constant

TABLE 10.3 **Median Family Income, 1950-2000, Selected Years**

Year	White Income	Black Income	Black Income as a Percentage of White Income	Actual Income Gap
1950	$ 3,445	$ 1,869	54.3	$ 1,576
1960	5,835	3,230	55.4	2,602
1970	10,236	6,279	61.3	3,957
1980	21,904	12,674	57.9	9,230
1990	36,915	21,423	58.0	15,492
2000	45,904	30,439	66.3	15,465

Source: U.S. Bureau of the Census, *Money Income in the United States 2000*. (Washington, DC: U.S. Government Printing Office, 2001), P60-213, September 2001.

until dropping again in the prosperous 1990s. Today less than 1 in 4 blacks live in poverty compared to less than 1 in 12 whites. Through good times and bad, the black poverty rate has consistently remained three times that of the white rate (see Figure 10.4).

One significant factor has been the **feminization of poverty**—the high percentage of impoverished families headed by women.[37] Many women lack education and job skills, and their earning potential is limited further by the unavailability or unaffordability of child-care centers, making families headed by women especially vulnerable to living in poverty. Among black female-headed families, 39 percent lived in poverty in 2000.[38] Approximately 56 percent of all black children under 18 lived in a single-parent home in 1998, a matter of grave concern to African American leaders and government officials alike.[39]

For black Americans, progress and regression have occurred simultaneously. A larger segment than ever before has secured better-paying positions and greater economic stability. At the same time, we have witnessed the growth of a multi-generational poor underclass that is mired in urban ghettos and habitually unemployed or underemployed.

A sizable African American middle class has evolved. About 31 percent of U.S. black families have incomes of $50,000 or more, and most of these affluent individuals live in a suburban home.[40] At the same time, we have witnessed the collapse of inner-city neighborhoods. Entry-level urban manufacturing jobs are mostly gone, as are black, middle-class role models in those areas. Instead a welfare and underground economy exists, where the only successful people with money are drug pushers, pimps, and prostitutes. It is a world where the men often lack jobs and the

FIGURE 10.4 **Black and White Families Below the Poverty Level in Selected Years, 1959-2000 (in percentages)**

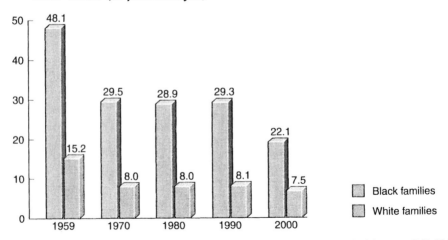

Source: U.S. Bureau of the Census. *Poverty in the United States 2000* (Washington, DC: U.S. Government Printing Office, 2001).

women often lack husbands. A large proportion of the African Americans living in poverty make up this hard-core poor, trapped in a seemingly unending cycle of broken homes, joblessness, welfare, drugs, crime, and violence—a reality that culture-of-poverty advocates cite in support of their position.

Blauner's internal-colonialism theory can be applied productively to this trapped segment of the black population. The segregated black ghetto appears to be a more permanent phenomenon than those of European immigrants, with few individuals able to escape it. Until some large-scale improvement occurs—and none seems imminent—our urban ghettos will remain sinks of despair, decay, and fear.

Occupation

Because the nature of a person's work provides an important basis for societal esteem, the occupational distribution of an entire group serves as a comparative measure of its status in the larger society. Table 10.4 offers a statistical breakdown of this measure. Although African American representation in managerial, professional, technical, and white-collar occupations has grown slowly but steadily, significant differences remain.

Black men were more likely to be employed as operators, fabricators, or laborers than in any other occupational group (31 percent). In contrast, white men were more likely to be employed in managerial and professional occupations (32 percent). Black men were also twice as likely as white men to work in service occupations (17 versus 8 percent). These occupations include police, firefighters, food-service workers, health aides, public-transportation workers, social-welfare aides, and cleaning and building service workers.

TABLE 10.4   **Occupational Distribution by Sex and Race, 16 Years and Over, 2000 (in percentages)**

	Male		Female	
Classification	**Black**	**White**	**Black**	**White**
Managerial, professional	20.4	32.5	27.7	37.3
Technical, sales, administrative support	17.4	19.0	35.4	38.8
Service occupations	15.7	7.3	24.7	14.0
Precision production, crafts, repair	15.4	20.7	2.2	2.2
Operators, fabricators, laborers	28.9	17.1	9.7	6.4
Farming, fishing, forestry	2.1	3.5	0.1	1.2

Source: Adapted from U.S. Bureau of the Census, *Statistical Abstract of the United States 2001* (Washington, DC: U.S. Government Printing Office, 2001), Table 595, p. 384.

Both black and white women were more likely to be employed in technical, sales, and administrative support occupations than elsewhere (38 percent and 41 percent respectively). Black women were more likely to work in service occupations (27 percent versus 15 percent); meanwhile, meanwhile, 35 percent of white women were employed in managerial and professional occupations compared to 24 percent of black women.

Housing

To a large extent, the quality of one's housing reflects one's occupation and income. By 2000 housing units occupied by black owners accounted for over 47 percent of all black housing.[41] However, racial discrimination has continued to affect urban neighborhoods and population distribution. The 1968 Fair Housing Act made it "unlawful . . . to refuse to sell or rent . . . a dwelling to any person because of race, color, religion, or national origin," but three decades later *de facto* segregation persists in U.S. metropolitan areas.

Redlining. One continuing problem is **redlining**—the refusal by some banks to make loans on property in lower-income minority neighborhoods, which are indicated on city maps with red pencil lines. Such a practice accelerates the deterioration of older housing because owners have difficulty obtaining funds to improve buildings and potential buyers cannot secure mortgages. To overcome this problem, the Community Reinvestment Act (CRA) of 1977 stipulated that banks have an "affirmative obligation" to lend in lower-income neighborhoods. When it has been seriously applied, the CRA has proved effective in helping turn neighborhoods around, and thousands of lower-income people have become home owners.[42]

Formal redlining has led banks to close branch offices in poor neighborhoods, thereby removing a crucial financial anchor from many communities. In 12 major U.S. cities analyzed in a 1995 study, three times as many banks per 100,000 residents existed in white areas as in minority areas; but in 1970, the areas had been fairly equal in their number of banks per 100,000 residents.[43]

Residential Segregation. Most African Americans now live outside central cities (see Figure 10.5), continuing an outmigration to the suburbs that began over 30 years ago. Does this mean there is less black–white residential segregation? Analysts, using two measurement tools called a *dissimilarity index* and a *hypersegregation index*, reported that 2000 census data show that, although blacks remain the most segregated group, they are less segregated than they were in 1990. Hispanics, however, are more segregated than they were a decade ago. This pattern held true from coast to coast, in city and suburb, and in every region of the country.

Nationally, less than 4 in 10 non-Hispanic whites live in nearly all-white neighborhoods compared to more than half in 1990. Only in the Midwest do the majority of blacks live in nearly all-black neighborhoods. The lowest levels of black–white segregation are in the high-growth Sunbelt, which attracts both whites and minorities, thereby generating a growing share of Americans living in areas

FIGURE 10.5 **Population Living Inside and Outside Central Cities, Blacks and Non-Hispanic Whites, in 1960 and 2000 (in percentages)**

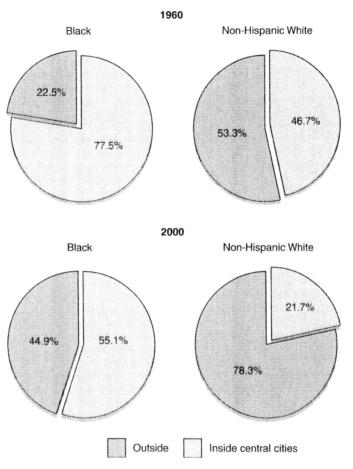

1960

Black   Non-Hispanic White

22.5%   46.7%
77.5%   53.3%

2000

Black   Non-Hispanic White

44.9%   55.1%   21.7%
                               78.3%

☐ Outside   ☐ Inside central cities

Source: U.S. Bureau of the Census.

where the two races mix freely. Meanwhile, Hispanics are increasingly living in ethnic enclaves where none existed a decade ago, and Asian segregation also increases in numerous metropolitan areas.[44]

Racial segregation remains stubbornly rooted in the nation's older cities, where blacks and whites have always lived apart. Such urban residential segregation limits job opportunities for youth and prevents minorities from moving closer to suburban jobs.[45] Suburbia is also becoming more integrated, although its outer rings are still mostly white. Despite the notion advanced by some that middle-class blacks are almost as segregated from whites as are poor blacks, researchers, controlling for numerous socioeconomic characteristics, found that they are not.

These suburban blacks have far more white neighbors than do low-income, inner-city blacks, although their white neighbors are often less affluent than they are. It would appear that race still powerfully shapes their residential options, even if they are less segregated than poor blacks.[46]

RACE OR CLASS?

Despite economic gains made by many African Americans, nearly one in four remains mired in poverty. The causes of this split, or **bipolarization,** within the black community has stirred heated debate. Is it the result of continuing racial discrimination or of socioeconomic conditions?

In *The Declining Significance of Race* (1978), sociologist William J. Wilson touched off the debate by arguing that the life chances of blacks—their economic opportunities—are now determined far more by their social class than by their race.[47] Educated blacks can compete equally with whites, enjoying unprecedented opportunities for better-paying jobs. At the same time, Wilson said, increasingly stringent job qualifications in this high-technology age may permanently trap the black underclass in economic subordination. Although race is not insignificant, Wilson stressed that social class, not racial discrimination, denies upward mobility to the black poor. Affirmative action helps middle-class blacks, not the poor. Until we recognize the dependent nature of welfare and the need to provide skills and education to the urban poor, we cannot effectively attack the problem of inequality.

Economist Thomas Sowell echoed this view, pointing out in *Ethnic America* (1981) the parallels between blacks and other ethnic groups in social class and upward mobility as key factors in their acceptance and socioeconomic mainstreaming.[48] Similarly, Carl Gershman, a white civil-rights activist and former research director of the A. Philip Randolph Institute, called the current problem class-caused, suggesting that black leaders remained preoccupied with racial bias as the sole cause of ghetto poverty and ignored the reality of a bipolarization of U.S. blacks.[49]

Other black social scientists, however, disagreed with Wilson, Sowell, and Gershman. Sociologist Charles V. Willie in *Caste and Class Controversy* (1979) maintained that economics is but one facet of the larger society and should therefore not be considered in isolation. White racism permeates all social institutions, controlling entry to all desirable positions in education, employment, earnings, housing, and social status. By surrendering their cultural identity, blacks may gain middle-class status, said Willie, but they become psychologically chained in a white world that permits only token entry while retaining actual power, control, and wealth.[50]

Psychologist Kenneth B. Clark called Wilson's position "wishful and premature optimism."[51] Death, retirement, and entry into judicial, political, or corporate careers removed the most effective civil-rights leaders from their organizing and activist roles, subverting their efforts to remedy continuing and worsening racial problems. Blacks in corporate, government, or university life do not occupy genuine decision-making positions so much as they do created positions of racial tokenism, with limited influence and a disinclination to jeopardize their "personal gains and affable acceptance of their white colleagues." Institutionalized racism remains, said Clark, as seen in the failure of whites to resolve the problem of the urban ghettos and in the use of such racial code words as *busing, quotas, reverse discrimination, meritocracy,* and *maintaining standards,* which imply that efforts to correct racial injustice weaken the fiber of society. Two decades later, this debate continues.

The Black Middle Class

In a comprehensive study of the black middle class, Bart Landry tracked its three phases and its 10-fold expansion from about 3 percent of the black population in 1910. For almost 100 years after emancipation, the black middle class was mostly a mulatto elite that owned businesses in service industries (barbers, caterers, tailors), often serving a white clientele.[52] By 1960, the black middle class had grown to about 13 percent, entering the professions (accountants, doctors, lawyers, undertakers), but serving mostly a black clientele and living within the black community.[53] After the civil-rights movement, a new black middle class emerged, employed in the predominantly white corporate world, universities, and government agencies, and with

One false stereotype defines African Americans as living in poverty. Almost 1 in 4 do fall into that category; but with 7 in 10 belonging to the working or middle class, the clothing, home furnishings, and lifestyle revealed in this photo are far more typical of most African Americans.
(*Source:* © Myrleen Ferguson/Photo Edit)

little ties to the black community. This group—with its greater economic power, suburban homes, and desire to integrate into the mainstream—prompted Wilson and others to suggest that economic, not racial, factors were now the primary constraints on African Americans.

Among those economic constraints is the reality that the average earnings of the black middle class remain lower than those of the white middle class. Also, black entrepreneurs often have limited cash resources, making their businesses riskier ventures and thus more susceptible to economic recessions and failure. Racism also remains a factor, whether in the form of a glass ceiling limiting blacks to middle-range managerial positions or in verbal epithets from strangers, harassment from police, poor restaurant service, or difficulty hailing a cab.[54]

The Black Poor

In 1987, Wilson argued further that, unlike in the past, today's inner-city neighborhoods face social isolation.[55] The flight of middle- and working-class black families from inner-city neighborhoods removes essential role models and undermines supportive social institutions. Furthermore, outsiders avoid these communities, which are plagued by massive unemployment, crime, and substandard schools. Consequently, area residents—women and children on welfare, school dropouts, teenage mothers, and aggressive street criminals—are cut off from mainstream society.[56] Gary Orfield effectively noted the magnitude of this isolation:

> To a considerable extent the residents of city ghettos are now living in separate and deteriorating societies, with separate economies, diverging family structures and basic institutions, and even growing linguistic separation within the core ghettos.[57]

Current social indicators about this segment of the black population do not provide any cause for optimism that significant improvement will occur in the near future. Unless some bold, innovative action addresses the multiple problems of limited education and job skills, high unemployment, and the growing number of single-parent, welfare-dependent families, the situation shows every sign of perpetuating the black underclass.

The Racial Divide

In 1835, French visitor Alexis de Tocqueville observed in *Democracy in America* that blacks and whites were "two foreign communities." In 1944, Swedish scholar Gunnar Myrdal argued in *An American Dilemma* that blacks could not escape the caste condition into which they were born. In 1992, Andrew Hacker used statistics much like those cited earlier in this chapter to present a pessimistic picture of a socio-economically segregated nation.[58]

Although African Americans have made significant gains since the 1960s, few sociologists would argue that racism is a thing of the past. Wilson said racism had become less prevalent, but he acknowledged that it still existed. Conservative Dinesh D'Souza, however, in a controversial 1995 book, *The End of Racism,* held that racism originated and continues as a "rational discrimination" that is now limited to the inner cities, where the "streets are irrigated with alcohol, urine and blood."[59] Asserting that repeal of the Civil Rights Act of 1964 and of affirmative action would somehow end racism, he endorsed the need for "colorblindedness" in attitudes and laws while at the same time proposing separatist solutions. (Blacks should get together and "reform their community.")

In stark contrast, Stephen Steinberg's 1995 book *Turning Back* attacked the so-called arrival of a color-blind society as a "spurious justification for maintaining the racial status quo."[60] His contention—in essence, the liberal position—is that programs such as affirmative action are necessary to "confront the legacy of slavery and resume the unfinished racial agenda," since part of that legacy is the continued existence of racist institutions and practices. Jill Quadagno noted that racism was a major factor both in developing policies to help those in need and in undermining the war on poverty.[61]

As these arguments rage along ideological lines among intellectuals, minority leaders, and politicians, the general public seems divided more along racial lines. Many whites believe either that a level playing field now exists—thanks to changed attitudes, majority-group enlightenment, and antidiscrimination laws— or that an uneven playing field tilted in favor of minorities exists. Many African Americans believe systemic racism against black people permeates all social institutions and everyday life.

The vastly differing racial perceptions between whites and blacks were starkly illustrated by their reaction to the 1995 jury verdict in the O. J. Simpson trial. Public-opinion polls indicated that 83 to 87 percent of African Americans believed justice was served, so deeply ingrained is their distrust of the entire criminal-justice system. Among white Americans, however, the opposite viewpoint prevailed: From 78 to 86 percent believed justice was denied, that a murderer escaped conviction because defense attorneys played the "race card" effectively. Clearly, we have a long road yet to travel before we achieve interracial understanding and cooperation.

AFRICAN IMMIGRANTS

Although many nonblacks simply use Negroid racial features as the basis of group classification, much cultural diversity exists among blacks in the United States. Generalizing about them is just as inaccurate as generalizing about whites. Regional and social-class differences create distinctions among U.S. blacks, and cultural differences make West Indian black immigrants unlike native-born blacks. Recent black immigrants from Africa are culturally distinct not only from the two former groups but also from one another when they have different countries of origin. (See Table 10.5.) In addition, although many native-born U.S. blacks call themselves African Americans, a wide cultural gulf separates them from the more recent

TABLE 10.5   Number of Africans Living in the United States, 2000

Nigerian	137,002
Cape Verdean	79,366
Ethiopian	73,661
Ghanian	41,563
South African	37,357
Liberian	28,983
Kenyan	14,875
Sudanese	12,167
Sierra Leonean	6,165
Ugandan	4,727

Source: U.S. Bureau of the Census.

African immigrants.[62] This fact is demonstrated at the student level when, for example, both black and African student organizations form at the same college.

Value Orientations

Professor Muruku Waiguchu, an immigrant from Kenya, contrasted some of the value orientations of black American and African college students in the United States.[63] He found that African students tended to show some degree of contempt and arrogance toward black American students, commonly using such ethnophaulisms as *Negro* or *nigger* to refer to them. Africans are frequently more achievement-oriented and competitive than black American students, in part because they have help from white supporters and no "history of denials and exclusion" from white America. African college students are also less racially conscious in the U.S. sense and therefore are more likely to participate in interracial primary relationships (parties, dating, marriage) than are black American college students. Waiguchu concludes that the two black groups do not share a greater trust and understanding because both have been victimized by white social conditioning:

> Unlike any other people, much of our history, and therefore our cultural continuity, has been written by our detractors and oppressors. The inevitable consequence has been that we look at one another through the eyes given and provided to us through the education process and other forms of communication owned and operated by white people. . . . We do not articulate our interests collectively because we oftentimes do not understand one another and waste valuable time labelling one another with the stereotypes we have collected from the white man.[64]

Whether whites are the ultimate cause of African American–African misunderstanding is debatable. It is true, though, that different cultural orientations and ethnocentrism play important roles. Just as dominant and minority white groups have often mistrusted each other, so different black groups may display outgroup negativism despite racial similarity.

Immigration Patterns

As Table 10.6 shows, African immigration has significantly increased in the past few decades. Chain migration, Americanization of foreign students enrolled in U.S. colleges, economic opportunities, and homeland events are the major push–pull factors at work.

Immigration from Africa remained low until the 1950s, when about 14,000 immigrants arrived. This number doubled to about 29,000 in the 1960s, more than doubled to 81,000 in the 1970s, and did so again to 177,000 in the 1980s. Over 300,000 Africans arrived in the 1990s. Ethiopia, Ghana, and Nigeria are currently the primary countries from which black Africans immigrate to the United States.[65] Overall, Nigerians constitute the largest immigrant group from continental Africa, followed by Ethiopians and Ghanians.[66]

Cultural Adjustment

African immigrants face two handicaps in trying to adjust culturally to life in the United States. First, in their homelands, they were members of the racial (although

TABLE 10.6 **African Immigration to the United States, by Country of Origin, 1971-1998**

Country	1971–1980	1981–1990	1991–2000
Cape Verde	5,531	7,876	9,182
Ethiopia	3,881	27,214	49,848
Ghana	5,195	14,876	35,638
Kenya	4,505	7,853	14,010
Liberia	2,400	8,058	16,004
Nigeria	8,767	35,365	67,306
Sierra Leone	1,265	5,194	11,274
Sudan	N/A	1,953	12,619
Republic of South Africa	11,459	15,738	22,647
Tanzania	2,989	4,181	4,247
Uganda	3,370	3,881	4,014

Source: Adapted from U.S. Immigration and Naturalization Service, *Statistical Yearbook 2000,* (Washington, DC: U.S. Government Printing Office, 2002), Table 3.

not always the ethnic) majority, but here they are not; and in various social and work settings, many encounter racism for the first time. Second, because of their cultural distinctions, Africans do not identify with American blacks, and American blacks do not identify with them. Successful American blacks interested in helping the less fortunate of their race usually concentrate on U.S.-born poor, not on newcomers from Africa. As a matter of preference and necessity, the African immigrants seek out one another for mutual support and refuge.

A high percentage of African immigrants are well educated and possess occupational skills that enable them to secure economic security quickly. Having achieved a middle-class socioeconomic status, or at worst working-class stability, these first-generation Americans usually prefer to retain their African identity rather than to blend in with the black American community.

Cape Verdean Americans

About 400 miles off the coast of West Africa, near the equator, lie 10 islands known as the Cape Verde archipelago. Until 1975, these islands were a Portuguese colony. The opportune location of the Cape Verdes relative to trade winds and ocean currents made them strategically important for maritime traffic. From the early 18th to the mid-19th century, whalers from the United States often sought shelter or fresh provisions there and sometimes took on Cape Verdeans as crew members.

Whereas some remained as crew members or became harpooners, captains, and even shipowners, most worked to pay their passage to the United States to escape the poverty and intermittent famines they faced on the islands. Once the textile mills began appearing in the United States in the mid-19th century, the number of Cape Verdean immigrants to New England increased from a steady trickle to hundreds, sometimes thousands, annually.

Cape Verdeans, like many other people of color, vary widely in their physical appearance, even within the same family. Although U.S. residents classified them as "black," they saw themselves as "Portuguese" and "white," believing that their sociocultural identity set them apart from Africans and American blacks. However, rejection by the more numerous white Portuguese in New England and simplistic racial stereotyping by other U.S. natives resulted in the Cape Verdeans setting themselves apart as a separate social category—as nonblack Portuguese Cape Verdeans.[67]

The pursuit of a nonblack identity, despite a physical appearance suggesting to most U.S. outsiders that they are indeed black, has encouraged the continuance of such "ethnic markers" as language (Crioulo), music, and cuisine. Musical sounds come from the guitar, mandolin, and drums. Cape Verdean festivities attract friends and family who have moved away from the community clusters. Through communications and transportation technology, a strong interactional network remains. Any family crisis (childbirth, illness, death) demands social visits. Endogamy remains the norm, with marriage to a U.S. black treated as grounds for social ostracism.[68]

Almost 8,000 Cape Verdean immigrants arrived in the United States in the 1980s, and an average of 900 have continued to arrive annually since 1990. Over

51,000 Americans claim Cape Verdean ancestry, making them the second largest group of recent arrivals from sub-Saharan Africa, behind the Nigerians. Massachusetts is home to over 29,000 Cape Verdean Americans, and another 10,000 live in Rhode Island. Small numbers can be found in all states except Alabama, Delaware, Idaho, Iowa, North and South Dakota, Montana, West Virginia, and Wyoming.[69]

Some Cape Verdeans work in the cranberry bogs of Massachusetts and Rhode Island, but most work in factory and service occupations. Many second- and third-generation Cape Verdean Americans are graduating from college and entering white-collar occupations.[70]

Nigerian Americans

Nigeria is Africa's most populous country and ranks tenth in the world in population, at approximately 127 million people in 2001. With 44 percent of this population under the age of 15, Nigeria's annual growth rate should continue to rise rapidly in the near future.[71]

Population pressures, economic difficulties, and political unrest are the push factors that caused immigration to the United States to increase significantly. The number of Nigerian immigrants quadrupled from about 8,800 in the 1970s to 35,400 in the 1980s. Some 53,000 immigrants arrived in the period from 1991 to 1998, already making the 1990s the decade of greatest Nigerian immigration.[72]

More African Americans claim ancestry from Nigeria than from any other country of origin. The primary states of residence of Nigerian Americans are Texas, California, New York, Maryland, Georgia, Illinois, and New Jersey.

About 28 percent of these immigrants enter white-collar occupations, and another 9 percent enter blue-collar and service occupations. The remainder are homemakers, children, and unemployed or retired persons.[73]

WEST INDIAN AMERICANS

English- and French-speaking Caribbean people have also emigrated to the United States in substantial numbers. Although they come from the same region, their languages and cultures set them apart from each other and from the Hispanic peoples as well. Most of them are dark-skinned; encountering racial discrimination in housing, jobs, and other social interactions is a common (though new) experience for them.

Guadeloupe, Martinique, and French Guiana send very few immigrants. English-speaking immigrants from the Bahamas, Barbados, Bermuda, the British Virgin Islands, Dominica, and other small islands arrive at a rate of a few hundred or less each year. Trinidad and Tobago average about 5,000 immigrants yearly. Currently, the two major donors are Haiti and Jamaica, whose immigrants we will now briefly examine.

The Haitians

Most members of the first wave of about 4,400 Haitian immigrants, who came to the United States in the 1950s, were well-educated members of Haiti's upper class who were fleeing the harsh regime of President François Duvalier. In the 1960s, almost 35,000 Haitians, mostly of the middle class, arrived in the United States. The third wave, primarily illiterate peasants and unskilled urban workers with little or no education, including "boat people," has been emigrating since the mid-1970s. Over 56,000 legal immigrants entered the United States in the 1970s, and more than 138,000 came in the 1980s.[74]

Over 157,000 legal Haitian immigrants entered the United States in 1991–1999. In the 1990s, thousands of others, the "boat people," have fled their homeland and entered the United States as **undocumented aliens.** Federal policy, consistent through Republican and Democratic administrations has been to deny refugee status to almost all of them, to discourage their entry, and to deport them. A 1992 Supreme Court ruling supported this government policy of forced repatriation, and the 1997 Nicaraguan Adjustment and Central American Relief Act failed to include Haitians among the undocumented aliens it made eligible for permanent status.

Emigration from Haiti will probably continue for a long time. In their homeland, hunger is widespread, and less than one fourth of the population has access to clean drinking water. Rates of infant mortality, tuberculosis, and HIV are among the highest in the world. Only one third of the land is arable, but population pressure puts 43 percent under cultivation. The struggle of the people to eke out a living through subsistence agriculture has led to overcultivation, soil erosion, and deforestation. Haiti's forests and woodlands have been reduced to 4 percent of the total land area.[75]

Haiti has the highest birth rate and death rate and the highest rate of natural increase in the Western hemisphere. With a population of 6.9 million in a land area only slightly larger than Maryland, its population density measures 642 inhabitants per square mile. Some 55 percent of all Haitians over age 15 are illiterate.[76]

Many of today's Haitian arrivals speak only Haitian Creole. French is the language of the educated elite in Haitian government, commerce, and education. Fluency in one language does not mean comprehension of the other. Nevertheless, because of the prestige attached to things French and the assumption by many U.S. residents that all Haitians speak French, Haitians often pretend to be able to speak it, to enhance their status.[77]

Most Haitians are Roman Catholics, with an increasing segment attracted to evangelical Protestantism. A significant minority practice *voudou,* a religion with African roots that combines belief in the existence of a *bon Dieu,* or good God, and *lwas,* spirits who offer protection, advice, and assistance in resolving spiritual and material problems.[78]

Alex Stepick and Carol Dutton Stepick found that Haitian immigrants in south Florida live in tightly clustered neighborhoods, with 86 percent reporting little or no interaction with Anglos.[79] Their social isolation results in part from their belief that both whites and African Americans discriminate against them and in part from their inability to speak English. Only 20 percent of the immigrants in the Stepicks' extensive study claimed to speak English at least reasonably well.

In Florida, where more than 266,000 Haitians live, and in New York, where another 182,000 reside, their unemployment rate is four times the national average.[80] Living in crowded, substandard housing, they find work in low-paying jobs in service industries. About one third of all migrant farm laborers on the East Coast are Haitians.

The Jamaicans

Another fairly recent group, the Jamaicans, constitute the largest non-Hispanic immigrant population from the Caribbean. Of the 622,000 Jamaican Americans living in the United States in 2000, 79 percent were foreign born. Although California claimed over 18,000 Jamaican Americans by 2000, giving it by far the largest concentration west of the Appalachian Mountains, most Jamaicans settle on the East Coast in urban environments. According to the 2000 census, the leading states in Jamaican American population were New York (257,600), Florida (162,600), New Jersey (26,900), and Connecticut (27,200).[81]

Annual Jamaican immigration now averages over 13,000, and the continual large influx augments the Jamaicans' ethnic communities and cultural vitality. The presence of Jamaicans is perhaps most visible to other Americans through West Indian food stores and reggae music. Speech is another indicator, because Jamaicans speak English but in a *patois* characterized by rapid speech patterning and a clipped accent, which sometimes causes difficulty for a first-time listener.

Jamaica itself is a pluralistic society, with three layered segments: a small white population at the top, a black segment comprising about four fifths of the population at the bottom, and a brown population in between.[82] Within this "hierarchically arrayed mosaic of total communities," each provides its members with the entire range of life experience.[83] Most of the immigrants who come to the United States are blacks, reflecting their status as their nation's racial group in greatest economic need. On the island, this group practices a folk culture containing numerous elements reminiscent of African societies and Caribbean slavery.[84]

Economic opportunity is the primary motivation for immigration. Tourism in Jamaica and the limited economy cannot support the growing population base. Adapting quite easily to U.S. society, first-generation Jamaican Americans find their initial encounters with racism to be bitter and difficult experiences. Some become disillusioned and return home, but most remain to pursue their goals. Second-generation Jamaican Americans appear to be integrating into society as black Americans. It remains to be seen whether the present Jamaican communities will become more structured, encouraging cultural pluralism through the continued arrival of newcomers, or whether the short-term integration process will continue.[85]

BLACK AMERICAN ASSIMILATION

Any discussion on the subject of black American assimilation must first consider the diversity of the black population in the United States. Native-born blacks face racial issues in their social acceptance, but they grow up and live within the

American culture. However, they are by no means a single entity. Socioeconomic differences affect whether they live within the mainstream or margins of society. Moreover, those raised in the Northeast are likely to differ in lifestyles and interaction patterns from those raised in the South.

Race is obviously an important factor in the U.S. experiences of West Indians and Africans also, but compounding theirs are adjustment and acculturation processes all immigrants undergo. Today's first-generation black Americans thus illustrate many of the everyday ethnic realities and patterns of other immigrant groups: chain migration, residential and occupational patterning, parallel social institutions, ingroup solidarity, and endogamy. Yet, as Mary C. Waters details in *Black Identities: West Indian Immigrant Dreams and American Realities* (1999), ethnic heterogeneity among immigrant blacks eventually yields to racial hegemony. In what still remains a color-coded society, the dominant group views them as undifferentiated "blacks" and therefore relegates all to a separate, minority status.[86]

Black American culture remains a resilient component of U.S. society, despite the high level of cultural assimilation among most native-born blacks. Although gaps remain, secondary structural assimilation (education, income, occupation, housing) is greater than ever before, as detailed earlier. It would be a mistake, however, to assume that economic good times in the 1990s were solely responsible for renewed hope in the black communities. Even as the strong economy made bigger dreams possible, a strong resurgence of black self-confidence and self-determination made their realization more probable. In a 1999 *Newsweek* poll, for example, nearly three fourths of blacks surveyed expressed confidence that their family incomes would increase over the next 10 years, and most credited black churches and black self-help for the upturn in black conditions. Of course, not all have benefited. More black men are in prison than ever before, more young black men commit suicide, and black academic achievement still trails that of whites.[87]

Although blacks and whites interact more frequently than in the past, most of these interactions occur within secondary groups and are therefore superficial and segmented. Primary structural assimilation (friendships, primary-group memberships) remains limited, as easily witnessed on most college campuses in cafeterias or other informal settings, as well as in fraternities and sororities. We are far from an idealized racial order with black–white friendships, such as portrayed in the *Lethal Weapon* film series.[88] And as friendships are segregated, even among adolescents, it is not surprising that marital assimilation (intermarriage) remains lowest among black Americans in comparison to other racial groups.[89] Parrillo's social-distance findings about African Americans, discussed in Chapter 1, show both our progress and the continuing social distance between the races.

Historically, the unique experience of slavery hindered black assimilation, but even after emancipation, the fierce refusal of many white Americans to accept black Americans as fellow citizens undermined it further. Many changes have occurred since the civil-rights movement of the 1960s, but more are needed before skin color ceases to be a factor in social acceptance and assimilation.

SOCIOLOGICAL ANALYSIS

Blacks have been victims of slavery, restrictive laws, or racial discrimination for most of the years they have lived in the United States (see the accompanying International Scene box). Despite many improvements since the 1960s, problems remain. Some argue that the unique experiences of black people in the United States require separate analysis, that their situation cannot be compared to that of other ethnic

The International Scene
The Perception of Race in Brazil

*L*ike the United States, Brazil was colonized by Europeans (primarily the Portuguese) who subjugated the native population and imported Africans as slave laborers. In fact, Brazil today is second only to the United States in the number of its citizens of African descent outside Africa itself. Despite these similarities, race relations in Brazil have followed a very different path from that in the United States.

The United States maintains a fairly rigid biracial system, classifying people as white or nonwhite. This simplistic "us" and "them" categorization has long promoted racial prejudice, segregation, and hostility. Moreover, it is becoming increasingly unrealistic. In 1999, the Census Bureau identified over 1.3 million interracial married couples, up from 310,000 in 1970. According to the Population Reference Bureau, the United States is presently experiencing a boom in mixed-race babies. Biracial children numbered well over 2 million in 2000, compared to a total of 460,000 reported in 1970. With such increases, how well do U.S. racial categories serve the nation's emerging multiracial society?

In Brazil, a multiracial classification system exists. In its broadest categories, the society has three population types: *pretos* (blacks), *brancos* (whites), and *pardos* (mulattos). In 1995, the racial mixture was 54 percent white, 5 percent black, 41 percent mulatto, and 1 percent Asian.

Mulattos in the United States are classified with blacks, but they constitute a separate group in Brazil. Moreover, Brazilian mulattos may be further categorized into about 40 subclassifications of color variations. To identify each of these separate racial categories, Brazilians use dozens of precise terms reflecting minute distinctions in skin shading, hair, and facial features.

Since the first days of Portuguese settlement, miscegenation has been common, although usually within similar color gradients rather than between couples at opposite ends of the color line. Brazil's more fluid color continuum deters formation of a racist ideology or segregated institutions, although whites remain traditionally in a higher social class than most of the people of color.

Critical thinking question: Should the United States adopt a multiracial classification system? Why or why not?

groups. Others maintain that, despite certain significant dissimilarities, sufficient parallels exist to invite comparative analysis in patterns of dominant–minority relations. Use of the three major perspectives incorporates both views.

The Functionalist View

Inequality exists in all societies because people value certain occupational roles and social positions over others. A value consensus develops about their functional importance in meeting the needs, goals, and priorities of society. Status, esteem, and differential rewards depend on the functionalist orientation of the society and the availability of qualified personnel. As one example, slavery offered the South a practical and effective means of developing an agricultural economy based on cotton; slaves provided a cheap labor force to work long hours, and the job required only physical endurance—no unusually high level of training, skills, talent, or intelligence. The system worked, leaving slave owners free for "genteel" artistic, intellectual, and leisure pursuits while reaffirming in their minds the "inferiority" of their toiling "darkies."

This value consensus survived the social disorganization of the postbellum South. A generation later, Jim Crow laws once again formalized a system of inequality through all social institutions. A new tradition became entrenched, restricting opportunities and participation based on old values but feeding on itself for justification of the existing order. In the North, blacks filled a labor need but remained unassimilated. This lack of societal cohesion and the continued presence of blacks generated prejudice, avoidance, and reciprocal antagonism. In both the North and the South in the 20th century, these system dysfunctions—the waste of human resources and lost productivity—produced social problems of poor education, low income, unemployment, crime and delinquency, poor housing, high disease and mortality rates, and other pathologies.

System corrections, in the form of federal judicial and legislative action, helped restore some balance to society, reorganizing social institutions and eliminating barriers to full social, political, and economic opportunities. Other dysfunctions—the Vietnam War, rampant inflation during the 1970s, structural blue-color unemployment, and sporadic economic downturns—curtailed some gains by blacks. Further adjustments are necessary to overcome the remaining problems, most especially those in the inner city.

The Conflict View

Slavery is an obvious example of past economic exploitation of blacks, but more recent practices may be less obvious. Job discrimination, labor-union discrimination—particularly in the building trades—and prejudices in educational institutions leading to low achievement and high dropout rates have forced many blacks into low-paying, low-status, economically vulnerable jobs. For many years, confining blacks to marginal positions preserved better-paying job opportunities for whites.

Maintaining a low-cost surplus labor pool that was not in competition for jobs sought by whites benefited employers and the dominant society, providing domestic and sanitation workers and seasonal employees, as well as job opportunities for whites in social work, law enforcement, and welfare agencies.

Both de jure segregation and de facto segregation illustrate how successfully those with power protected their self-interests by maintaining the status quo. Control by whites of social institutions limited blacks confined to certain occupations and residential locations, away from participation in the political process and out of the societal mainstream. Although a black and mulatto elite did arise and some positive white actions occurred, such as President Roosevelt's 1941 executive order banning racial discrimination in defense industries, blacks mostly remained severely oppressed.

Blauner's internal-colonialism model is appropriate here: The outside control of black segregated communities is by employers, teachers, social workers, police, and politicians who represent the establishment, making the administrative, economic, and political decisions that govern the ghetto. Unlike European groups, Blauner maintained, blacks did not gain control and ownership of their own buildings and commercial enterprises within a generation, remaining instead a subjugated and dependent colonized population.[90]

The civil-rights movement of the 1960s, a culmination of earlier efforts and court decisions, fits the Marxian analysis of social change. Blacks developed a group cohesiveness, overcoming a false consciousness that equality was unattainable, and formed an effective social movement. Sweeping changes through civil-rights legislation, punctuated by urban violence during the years from 1964 to 1968, brought improved life opportunities to blacks and other minorities.

The Interactionist View

Just as our attraction to strangers is based on perceived similarities, our antipathy to strangers can be based on learned prejudices. In the United States, skin color often triggers negative responses about busing, crime, housing, jobs, and poverty. Where did such attitudes originate? Earlier we examined multigenerational stereotyping and social isolation of blacks as the legacy of racism. If beliefs about a people, culturally transmitted and reinforced by external conditions, center on their differences or alleged inferiority, then avoidance, exploitation, and subjugation can become common responses.

The opposition to integration efforts usually comes from fear of these "unlike" strangers. Although expressed reasons may include preserving neighborhoods or neighborhood schools, the real reason often is concern that blacks will "contaminate" the area or school. Beliefs that the crime rate, school discipline, property values, and neighborhood stability will be adversely affected by their presence often prompts whites to resist proposed integration. Similarly, unfounded beliefs that blacks are less reliable, less honest, and less intelligent than whites frequently influence hiring and acceptance decisions. The unfairness and inaccuracy of such sweeping generalizations is less significant than the fact that people act on them. Too many white people have spun a gossamer web of false reality and believe it.

Black racism works in much the same way. Black racists see all whites as the enemy and all blacks as right, and they respond with suspicion to any friendly action by whites or any white criticism of a black person. Because both sides define situations in a particular way, the interpretation they assign usually reinforces their original biases. Upward mobility—in education, occupation, and income—does much to alter people's interpretations. Eliminating residential segregation and encouraging more primary interactions will further that process.

RETROSPECT

Through 200 years of slavery and 100 additional years of separate-and-unequal subjugation, blacks found society unresponsive to their needs and wants. Negatively categorized by skin color, they saw clearly that two worlds existed in this country: the white and the nonwhite. Many blacks remain trapped in poverty and isolated in urban ghettos; many who have achieved upward mobility find that they are still not accepted in white society, at least in meaningful primary relationships.

Numerous similarities exist between the black experience in the United States and the experiences of other minority peoples. Like Asians and Native Americans, blacks frequently have been judged on the basis of their skin color and not their individual capabilities. They have experienced (as have many immigrant groups) countless instances of stereotyping, scapegoating, prejudice, discrimination, social and spatial segregation, deprivation, and violence. When they have become too visible in a given area or have moved into economic competition with whites, the dominant group has perceived them as a threat and reacted accordingly. All this is a familiar pattern in dominant–minority relations.

More than 200 years of slavery exacted a heavy toll on the black people of the United States, and the exploitation and discrimination did not end with the abolition of slavery. As a result of generations of social conditioning, many whites preserved a master–slave mentality long after the Civil War. Two generations later, when blacks had made some progress, Jim Crow laws eliminated those gains and reestablished unequal treatment and life opportunities, thereby increasing prejudice.

A change in values and attitudes became evident with the historic Supreme Court decision of 1954 on school desegregation. Although school integration was slow, it did come about, and both blacks and whites were encouraged to seek even more changes. The resurgent civil-rights movement peaked in the mid-1960s, when a broad range of laws were passed to guarantee black people a more equitable life experience.

Almost half a century has elapsed since the 1954 court decision. A great many changes have taken place in the land, and observable improvements have occurred in all aspects of life for many African Americans. Still, problems remain. A disproportionate number of nonwhite poor continue to be concentrated in the cities, frequently trapped in a cycle of perpetual poverty. Despite all the legislation and court decisions, most blacks still engage only in primary relationships with other blacks. Social distance between blacks and whites in informal and private gatherings remains great. *De facto* segregation remains a problem, too, with the majority of whites living in suburbs farther away from the city and the majority of blacks living in more adjacent ones.

Greater interaction occurs between the two races in places of public accommodation, and this may eventually reshape white and black attitudes. That, together with improved educational opportunities, may lead to greater structural assimilation for African Americans. One element crucial to any such progress is the condition of the economy. Its ability to absorb African Americans into positions in the labor force that permit upward socioeconomic mobility will, in large measure, determine their future status in U.S. society.

KEY TERMS

Bipolarization	*De facto* segregation	Jim Crow laws
Black codes	*De jure* segregation	Redlining
Cultural drift	Feminization of poverty	Undocumented aliens
Cumulative causation	Institutionalized racism	

REVIEW QUESTIONS

1. In what ways is the black experience in the United States unique?

2. What similarities exist among the experiences of blacks, Native Americans, and Asians in the United States?

3. What similarities are there between the responses of blacks and of European immigrants to prejudice and discrimination?

4. What factors have delayed African Americans in gaining economic and political power as European and Asian immigrant groups did?

5. What is the present status of African Americans in the United States, according to the leading social indicators?

6. How are the cultural orientations of African and West Indian immigrants dissimilar to those of U.S.-born blacks?

7. What insights into the black experience do the three major sociological perspectives provide?

SUGGESTED READINGS

Bell, Derrick. *Faces at the Bottom of the Well: The Permanence of Race*. New York: Basic Books, 1992.
A pessimistic look at racism, arguing that our progress against it is illusory because it is an integral component of U.S. society.

Billingsley, Andrew. *Climbing Jacob's Ladder: The Enduring Legacy of African American Families*. New York: Simon & Schuster, 1992.
Research into the structures and strengths of the black family in varying socioeconomic hierarchies, with a focus on the urban poor.

Blackwell, James E. *The Black Community: Diversity and Unity*, 3rd ed. New York: HarperCollins, 1991.
An examination of the institutional structure, status, and aspects of daily life among African Americans.

Dent, David J. *In Search of Black America: Discovering the African American Dream*. New York: Simon & Schuster, 2000.
A rich and layered look at middle-class black Americans, showing them to be a complex group of people with a myriad of opinions, viewpoints, and beliefs.

Hacker, Andrew. *Two Nations: Black and White, Separate, Hostile, Unequal*. New York: Scribner's, 1992.
A data-extensive comparison of social indicators and power that assesses the relative status of blacks and whites.

Pinkney, Alphonso. *Black Americans*, 4th ed. Englewood Cliffs, NJ: Prentice Hall, 1994.
An excellent portrait of the history and contemporary situation of African Americans, with emphasis on power, social class, and Gordon's assimilation variables.

Tatum, Beverly D. *Why Are All the Black Kids Sitting Together in the Cafeteria? And Other Conversations About Race*, rev. ed. New York: Basic Books, 1999.
A helpful book for whites and blacks in understanding racial issues and behavior, and why identity still matters to young people in a society struggling to become more color-blind.

West, Cornel. *Race Matters*. Boston: Beacon Press, 1993.
An optimistic look at race relations that analyzes issues affecting black Americans and suggests remedies necessary to end racism.

Wilson, William J. *When Work Disappears: The World of the New Urban Poor*. New York: Knopf, 1996.
Sociologist Wilson continues his in-depth examination of the social and economic transformation of the inner city and its impact on the "ghetto underclass."

INTERNET LINKS

Go to *http://www.ablongman.com/parrillo* for numerous links relevant to this chapter under "Internet Readings and Exercises."

East and Southeast
Asian Americans

With high immigration doubling their numbers from 6.7 million in 1970 to 10.2 million in 2000, Asians and Pacific Islanders are transforming the face of America.[1] In California, 1 in 9 residents is now Asian; in San Francisco County, 31 percent are Asian.[2] Throughout the United States, the Asian American population is noticeably increasing, sometimes generating resentful, even hostile, reactions from other local residents (Figure 8.2). In this chapter we look at immigrant ethnic groups from East and Southeast Asia (see Figure 8.1). In Chapter 9, we'll turn our attention to groups from West Asia and the Middle East.

SOCIOHISTORICAL PERSPECTIVE

The Chinese first came to the United States during the California gold rush in the 1850s. Japanese, Koreans, and Filipinos began to arrive on the West Coast between 40 and 60 years later to seek their fortune. Some came to stay, but many came as **sojourners,** intending to return home after earning enough money. This view of the United States as a temporary overseas job opportunity—together with the racism they faced and, in the case of the Chinese, a tradition of separate associations wherever they went—led the early Asian immigrants to form subsocieties. Throughout the first third of the 20th century, this social organization enabled Asians to overcome the structural discrimination that sharply limited their work and life opportunities.

The Chinese encountered racial hostility almost as soon as they arrived in California, despite the overwhelming need for manual

FIGURE 8.1 **Southeast Asia**

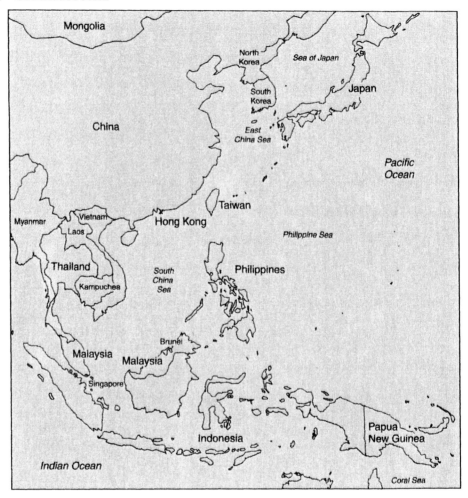

labor in the mid-19th century. They were often expelled from the mining camps, forbidden to enter schools, denied the right to testify in court, barred from obtaining citizenship, and occasionally murdered. After the Civil War, anti-Chinese tensions increased, culminating in the Chinese Exclusion Act of 1882. Japanese, Koreans, and Filipinos who came to the West Coast later encountered racism and discrimination similar to what the Chinese had faced. Many of them went to work as farm laborers in rural areas or as unskilled workers in urban areas.

A major social problem affecting most Asian immigrants through the 1940s was the shortage in this country of Asian women. Not only was this imbalance in the sex ratio significant in their personal, social, and community life, but it also provided the basis for racist complaints about prostitution and miscegenation. For the Chinese, the sojourner orientation, the custom that wives should remain in

FIGURE 8.2 Asian and Pacific Islander Population, 2000 (in percentages)

	Asian or Pacific Islander Population		Age		Total U.S. Population	
	Males	Females			Males	Females
	1.2	1.7	75+		2.2	3.7
	0.9	1.2	70-74		1.4	1.7
Median age 28.7	1.2	1.5	65-69	Median age 31.7	1.6	1.8
	1.6	1.8	60-64		1.8	2.0
	2.0	2.2	55-59		2.3	2.4
	2.8	3.3	50-54		3.1	3.1
	3.4	3.9	45-49		3.5	3.6
	3.9	4.4	40-44		4.0	3.9
	4.3	4.6	35-39		4.0	4.0
	4.5	4.8	30-34		3.7	3.5
	4.7	4.9	25-29		3.5	3.3
	4.0	4.0	20-24		3.4	3.2
	3.7	3.6	15-19		3.7	3.4
	3.4	3.2	10-14		3.7	3.4
	3.4	3.2	5-9		3.7	3.4
	3.3	3.3	0-4		3.5	3.2

Median age 30.8 (Asian or Pacific Islander Females). Median age 34.1 (Total U.S. Females).

Percentage (6 5 4 3 2 1 0 1 2 3 4 5 6)   Percentage (6 5 4 3 2 1 0 1 2 3 4 5 6)

Source: U.S. Bureau of the Census.

the household of the husband's parents, and subsequent immigration restrictions, all help explain this disproportionate sex ratio. By the turn of the century, the shortage of Chinese women in the United States had led to the rise of brothels in Chinatowns, and public condemnation. The Filipinos also were mostly male and similarly affected by the shortage of same-ethnicity women. Whether the Asians patronized prostitutes or sought the company of white women who were not prostitutes, racist whites expressed moral indignation, and negative racial stereotypes resulted. Legislators in 14 states passed laws against **miscegenation** (interracial intermarriage or breeding) to prevent Asians from marrying Whites.

By 1920, the Japanese sex ratio was largely balanced. Following World War II, a greater number of Asian women migrated to the United States, and the sex ratio for other Asian immigrant groups improved as well. Refugees and war brides from the Japanese, Korean, and Vietnamese wars account for part of the change, as do the brides of servicemen stationed overseas during the intervening years. The Immigration Act of 1965, which included provisions giving preference to relatives of U.S. residents, finally ensured both sexes equal opportunity to enter the United States.

After World War II, immigrants from these countries and from other parts of East and Southeast Asia entered a much more industrialized society. Many also came from lands affected by Western contact. Some were political refugees, better educated and more skilled than earlier Asian immigrants. Many preferred living in

These Asian youths line up for a medical examination in 1910 at the Angel Island
Immigration Station. Situated in San Francisco Bay, this western counterpart to
Ellis Island was the primary processing center for Asian immigrants. Experiencing
the same societal hostility that confronted many Italian immigrants at Ellis Island,
many Asians were detained at Angel Island by U.S. officials or denied admission
to the country.
(*Source:* The Granger Collection, New York)

California, and others moved to the East Coast or elsewhere. Entering various occupations, these postwar immigrants were spared the violent hostility of previous times, although many encountered resentment and discrimination nonetheless.

CULTURAL ATTRIBUTES

The great social distance between themselves and Asians often causes white and black Americans to view Asians as a homogeneous group. They are not. Not only do they differ in their nationality, language, religion, and culture, but they are also diverse within each of their own cultures. Consequently, no single model can reflect the wide disparities in occupational choices or acculturation and acceptance experiences.

Although we need to look beyond racial stereotypes to understand the different Asian immigrant groups more fully, we can identify certain cultural hallmarks that Asians tend to share. The degree to which individuals internalize these norms and values depends significantly on social class, length of residence in the United States, and acculturation.

Generally, traditional Asian values emphasize appropriate behavior, strict control of aggressive or assertive impulses, and a self-conscious concern for conduct in the presence of others. Sibling rivalry is discouraged, and older children are socialized to set an example for younger siblings in politeness, gentleness, and unselfish sacrifices for another's pleasure. Unlike U.S. children, who are encouraged to develop an inner sense of guilt as a social-control mechanism, Asian children experience the external sanctions of shame, or losing face—of bringing disgrace or dishonor to the family name.

Within the family, open displays of emotion or affection are rare, except with infants and small children. Uniting the family is the important value of filial piety. Elders in the family (even those only slightly older) command respect and obedience; younger family members never talk back to them. Traditional sex-role definitions require the men to provide for and protect the women and the women to submit to the decisions of the men. Fathers and eldest sons are thus the most powerful family members.

As in most immigrant groups, the extended family is predominant among Asian Americans. A cohesive structure exists, encouraged in part by the sense of duty and responsibility arising out of filial piety but also by values stressing ancestor worship and the importance of the family name. Loneliness and isolation for the unmarried or aged seldom occur because the extended family embraces and absorbs them. No typical Asian American family model exists, however; and the blending of U.S. and Asian cultures affects the family structure, especially in promoting a more egalitarian role for women.

THE CHINESE

U.S. residents on both coasts of North America knew something about the Chinese long before they first came to the United States. The United States had established trade relations with China as early as 1785, and many Protestant missionaries went there after 1807. Newspaper reports and magazine articles, inspired by the Anglo-Chinese War (1839–1842)—the so-called Opium War—and subsequent rebellions and incidents, featured lurid descriptions of filth, disease, cruel tortures, and executions. Americans gradually developed an unfavorable image of the Chinese based on these ethnocentric distortions and exaggerations. In 1842, seven years before the gold rush, the *Encyclopaedia Britannica* offered this unflattering portrait of the Chinese people:

> A Chinaman is cold, cunning and distrustful; always ready to take advantage of those he has to deal with; extremely covetous and deceitful; quarrelsome, vindictive, but timid and dastardly. A Chinaman in office is a strange compound of insolence and meanness. All ranks and conditions have a total disregard for truth.[3]

Structural Conditions

Most Chinese who came to the United States in the 19th century were farmers, artisans, craftsmen, political exiles, and refugees. The discovery of gold in California proved to be an opportunity not only for easterners and Europeans but for the Chinese from Kwangtung province, who could reach the gold rush country easily and who sought to recoup their losses from flood, famine, and the Taiping Rebellion (1850–1864). A combination of push–pull factors thus brought the Chinese to the United States. Chinese males set out alone, in many cases leaving wives and children in the village and the kinship circle of the extended family. The first wave of migrants came as sojourners, intending to earn some money and then return home.

Visible because of their race, appearance, and behavior, the Chinese aroused both curiosity and suspicion. The sounds and characters of their language seemed most peculiar to the non-Chinese, as did their religion. Their "strange" clothes and hair worn in *queues* (a braid of hair in the back of the head) also seemed out of place in the crude pioneer surroundings. With little or no command of English, they kept mostly to themselves and viewed California as a temporary workplace. As a result, the Chinese remained an enigma to most Americans.

By 1860, California's population included a large and varied ethnic segment. About 38 percent were foreign born, and many others were Spanish-speaking natives or children of European immigrants.[4] The Chinese constituted about 9 percent of the state's population in 1860, but because they were mostly adult males, they accounted for close to 25 percent of the labor force.[5] As the general population increased, however, the percentages of the total and working populations that they represented decreased.

Hired as laborers who worked in gangs, the Chinese built much of the western portion of the transcontinental railroad for the Central Pacific. As many as 9,000 Chinese a year toiled through the High Sierra country, digging tunnels and laying tracks, and the task was completed sooner than expected. Leland Stanford, then president of the Central Pacific Railroad, described the Chinese as "quiet, peaceable, industrious, economical." Although Chinese laborers received the same wages as non-Chinese, they fed and housed themselves, unlike the white workers, and thus cost the railroad company two thirds as much as whites to maintain.[6] The Chinese did not, however, pose an economic threat to the non-Chinese workers:

> Hiring Chinese resulted not in displacement of non-Chinese but in their upgrading. To the unskilled white railroad laborer of 1865, the coming of the Chinese meant his own advancement into that elite one-fifth of the labor force composed of strawbosses, foremen, teamsters, skilled craftsmen. And one final reason was perhaps more cogent than all the others. No man with any choice would have chosen to be a common laborer on the Central Pacific during the crossing of the High Sierra.[7]

At the same time that the railroad was being built, West Coast manufacturing was increasing. Demands on eastern U.S. industries during the Civil War and the high cost of transporting eastern goods encouraged this growth.[8] A shortage of available women and children prompted the textile industry to hire many Chinese.[9] The end of the Civil War, however, brought veterans seeking jobs and eastern manufacturing concerns seeking West Coast markets, helped by efficient, low-cost shipment of goods over the transcontinental railroad. Fired when their work was completed, Chinese railroad laborers sought other jobs; but economic conditions worsened across the nation, culminating in the Panic of 1873. Labor supply exceeded demand, and laborers, union organizers, and demagogues mounted racist denunciations of Chinese "competition."

Among the most popular ethnophaulisms directed against the Chinese during this period of labor agitation were accusations of their being "dirty" and "disease-ridden." These epithets had originated decades earlier. In the 1840s, Americans first became aware of the relationship between germs and dirt and disease. Negative stereotypes about the supposed Chinese preference for eating vermin and the crowded, unsanitary Chinatowns caused whites to associate the Chinese with leprosy, cholera, and bubonic plague. By the 1870s, the labor issue had become predominant; but as the labor unions closed ranks against the Chinese, they labeled them a menace to both the economy and the health of U.S. society. The *real* issue by 1877, however, was race, disguised as labor conflict.

Societal Reaction

Racist attacks against the Chinese continued throughout the remainder of the 19th century. Some antagonists compared them with blacks in terms of "racial inferiority"; and others attacked the "vices" of the "Oriental" race. In the 1850s, one antislavery southerner attempted to draw parallels among several groups that were supposedly inferior:

> No inferior race of men can exist in these United States without becoming
> subordinate to the will of the Anglo-Americans. . . . It is so with the Negroes
> in the South; it is so with the Irish in the North; it is so with the Indians in New
> England; and it will be so with the Chinese in California. . . . I should not wonder,
> at all, if the copper of the Pacific yet becomes as great a subject of discord and
> dissension as the ebony of the Atlantic.[10]

Cries for restrictions on Chinese immigration increased as racial antagonism rather than economic competition came to the forefront. In particular the myth of an Asian proclivity for despotic government was propagated by hostile Western media. "Oriental despotism" soon became as much a catch-phrase as "heathen Chinese." In 1865, the *New York Times* expressed alarm at the supposed effect of increased Asian immigration on U.S. civilization, religion, morals, and political institutions:

> Now we are utterly opposed to the permission of any extensive emigration of
> Chinamen or other Asiatics to any part of the United States. There are other points
> of national well-being to be considered beside the sudden development of material
> wealth. The security of its free institutions is more important than the enlargement
> of its population. The maintenance of an elevated national character is of higher
> value than mere growth in physical power.

. . . We have four millions of degraded negroes in the South . . . and if there were to be a flood-tide of Chinese population—a population befouled with all the social vices, with no knowledge or appreciation of free institutions or constitutional liberty, with heathenish souls and heathenish propensities, whose character, and habits, and modes of thought are firmly fixed by the consolidating influence of ages upon ages—we should be prepared to bid farewell to republicanism and democracy.[11]

In 1867, California Democrats used an anti-Chinese platform to such advantage that they swept the state elections, including the gubernatorial chair. Democrats elsewhere saw a bonanza in this issue because many Republicans were identified with the railroads and with companies that recruited and employed the Chinese, and because the Democrats—identified with the defeated Confederacy and slavocracy—could not use Negro-baiting effectively outside the South after 1865. Republicans secured the Burlingame Treaty of 1868 between China and the United States, providing for unrestricted travel between both countries "for the purpose of curiosity, or trade, or as permanent residents." Still, public hostility in the United States against the Chinese continued to grow.

To some, the Chinese posed a serious immigrant threat to the idealized concept of the melting pot. Individuals who held this belief argued that German and Irish Catholics, at least, were physically similar to the Protestant northern and western Europeans. An 1868 *New York Times* editorial offered this display of racial bigotry:

> Although they are patient and reliable laborers, they have characteristics deeply imbedded which make them undesirable as part of our permanent population. Their religion is wholly unlike ours, and they poison and stab. The circumstance would need be very favorable which would allow of their introduction into our families as servants, and as to mixing with them on terms of equality, that would be out of the question. No improvement of race could possibly result from such a mixture.[12]

As the prejudices of the 1850s distilled into the almost hysterical sinophobia of the 1870s and 1880s, the negative stereotype of the "yellow peril" emerged. In 1879, Senator James G. Blaine of Maine, a Democratic party leader and presidential hopeful, even attacked Chinese family values because of the sojourner orientation:

> The Asiatic cannot go on with our population and make a homogeneous element. This idea . . . comparing European immigration with an immigration that had no regard to family, that does not recognize the relation of husband and wife, that does not observe the tie of parent and child, that does not have in the slightest degree the enabling and civilizing influence of the hearthstone and the fireside.[13]

His erroneous comments ignored not only the intense cohesiveness of Chinese family structure but also the common practice of European males' coming to the United States ahead of their families.

Legislative Action

Over 225,000 Chinese came to the United States between 1850 and 1882. As Chinese sojourners came to the United States and returned to China in steady numbers, steamship companies found passenger trips a highly profitable operation and so encouraged Chinese immigration. In 1881, about 12,000 Chinese disembarked; and in 1882, the number jumped to almost 40,000.[14]

Another cycle of economic woes and labor agitation against the Chinese led to increasing pressures for restrictions. President Arthur vetoed the first restriction bill, which would have barred all Chinese immigration for 20 years. A few months later, however, he signed a revised bill that barred Chinese laborers for a 10-year period but permitting Chinese businessmen, clergy, students, and travelers to enter. The Chinese Exclusion Act of 1882 marked a significant change in national policy toward immigrants. For the first time in the nation's history, the federal government enacted a human embargo on a particular race of laborers. Sufficient exceptions remained to allow 8,000 legal Chinese immigrants in 1883,

THE ARGUMENT OF NATIONALITY.

Excited Mob—"We don't want any cheap-labor foreigners intruding upon us native-born citizens."

Violence against the Chinese was all too common in the United States in the late 19th century. This nasty satirical cartoon uses stereotypical images to denote race and ethnicity, as well as the hypocrisy of the mob lynching.
(The Library of Congress)

but legislative action in 1884 tightened the restrictions further, and in 1885 the number of Chinese immigrants dropped to 22.[15]

Violence directed against Chinese immigrants, which had sporadically flared up prior to the legislation, continued. In 1871, 21 Chinese had been massacred in Los Angeles, and anti-Chinese riots had occurred in Denver in 1880. Such hostile actions became much more widespread after 1882. For example, at Rock Springs, Wyoming, in September 1885 a mob attacked and murdered 28 Chinese, wounded many others, and drove hundreds from their homes. A concerted plan against the Chinese was put into effect by labor unions and politicians in various localities across the western United States. In Tacoma, Seattle, Oregon City, and many smaller towns, angry mobs expelled hundreds of Chinese residents, with considerable loss and destruction of property.

Congress extended the Chinese Exclusion Act for 10 years in 1892 and extended it indefinitely in 1902. Other Anglo-Saxon–dominated countries on the Pacific Rim also restricted Chinese immigration. Australia passed legislation in 1901, but Canada did not take such action until 1923. U.S. commentators frequently criticized Canada, especially the province of British Columbia, because Chinese entered the United States from there. Reverse migration also occurred after 1858, when the United States served as a point of entry into Canada for many Chinese.

Organized labor's creation and instigation of the anti-Chinese issue is illustrated in an 1893 American Federation of Labor (AFL) convention resolution, which held that the Chinese brought to the United States "nothing but filth, vice, and disease." It also maintained they had corrupted "a part of our people on the Pacific Coast to such a degree that could it be published in detail the American people would in their just and righteous anger sweep them from the face of the earth."[16] These wild, racist charges had little basis in fact except that filth and disease did exist in some Chinatown districts—as indeed they did in Irish, Italian, and other ethnic urban slums.

Avoidance and Segregation

How did the Chinese immigrants react to all the abuse, vilification, and discriminatory legislation? Some reluctantly returned to China. Some sought redress in the courts, winning all cases involving state immigration restrictions but few based on assault or property damage complaints. The latter were difficult to maintain in California, at least, because from 1854 to 1870 the California courts did not allow Chinese to testify against whites.

Expelled from various trades and occupations as well as from many residential areas, Chinese immigrants had little choice but to congregate in Chinatowns and rely on their own benevolent and protective associations for assistance. A large number congregated in San Francisco, but others moved to the larger eastern and midwestern cities and formed ethnic enclaves there. These Chinatowns were in low-rent ghetto areas, usually situated close to major means of transportation, which at least gave the Chinese ready access to friends and relatives. For example, in New York City and San Francisco, they are near the docks; and in Boston, Pittsburgh, and St. Louis, near the railroad stations.

In seeking redress of grievances through the courts, the Chinese petitioned for equal rights. They won the right to have their children attend public schools, and then they fought to desegregate the schools. Housing codes kept them in the ghetto, where they found themselves segregated both socially and spatially. Securing jobs through the associations or from Chinese merchants, most entered occupations that either did not compete with whites (such as in art and curio shops or Chinese restaurants) or that involved serving only their own people. They settled disputes among themselves, partly because this was their custom and partly because they distrusted the white people's court. The traditional associations and the family clan offered them the familiarity and protection they needed. Chinese temples, newspapers, schools, and Old World festivals all represented efforts to preserve their cultural and traditional practices.

Examining the early growth of Chinatowns across the United States and analyzing the modern status of New York's Chinatown, D. Y. Yuan identified a four-stage process of development.[17] The first stage was marked by involuntary choice in response to societal prejudice and discrimination. Defensive insulation came next, as protection against racial hostility. Then, as a group consciousness emerged, voluntary segregation became the third stage, with Chinatown residents sharing culture and problems of adjustment. The final stage was gradual assimilation, a process markedly slowed by voluntary segregation and social isolation.

Albert Palmer drew on his firsthand experience as a white growing up near San Francisco's Chinatown in the late 19th century to develop his social analysis of the stereotyped dominant view of these "foreign settlements":

> Those who know only the picturesque Chinatown of today can hardly realize what the Chinatown of the eighties and nineties was like. It was dirty, overcrowded, rat-infested, and often diseased. It was poorly built with narrow alleys and underground cellars and secret passages, more like a warren of burrowing animals than a human city. It seemed uncanny because inhabited by a strange yellow race who wore "pigtails," talked an outlandish lingo in high falsetto voices, were reputed to eat sharks' fins and even rats, and to make medicine out of toads and spiders, and who sprinkled garments for ironing by sucking their mouths full of water and then squirting it out over the clothes. And Chinatown was accounted vicious because it was the haunt of gambling, opium smoking, lotteries, tong wars and prostitution, where helpless little slave-girls were bought and sold. . . .
>
> Now, fear is a great disturber, and it largely created the old Chinatown. It did this partly, in fact, by herding Chinese into narrow, squalid quarters and surrounding them by hatred and suspicion; and partly in imagination, by creating the weird and distorted picture of their outlandish character. . . . Chinatown was never quite so bad as the prejudice and fear imagined it.[18]

In analyzing organizational life in San Francisco's Chinatown between 1850 and 1910, Stanford M. Lyman found that the traditional associations quickly came in conflict with one another.[19] As the clans (lineage bonds), *hui kuan* (ethnic or regional bonds), and secret societies (outlaw or protest bonds) fought to secure the allegiance of immigrants and to dominate the community, the Chinese faced strife from both inside and outside their community:

> The organizational developments and internecine fights that took place in Chinatown from 1850 to 1910 indicate that forming an overseas Chinese community was not an easy task. Principles of clan solidarity, barriers of language and dialect, allegiance to rebellious secret societies, and their own competitive interest in making enough money to permit retirement in China divided the loyalties of the Chinese immigrants. Yet during the same period the depredations of anti-Chinese mobs, the difficulties and indignities imposed by restrictive immigration legislation, the occupational discrimination created by state and local laws prohibiting or limiting the employment of Chinese, and the active opposition of the American labor movement to the Chinese workingman all seemed to call for a community united in the face of its enemies. What emerged out of this condition of pressures from without the ghetto and divisions within was a pattern alternating between order and violence. By 1910 this pattern had assumed a complex but recognizable sociological form: that of the community whose members are bound to one another not only because of external hostility but also because of deadly internal factionalism.[20]

One constant of Chinese immigrant life was discrimination and hostility in the white world:

> During most of this period, the lives of average Chinese in the United States were difficult and irregular. No matter how well educated they were, in their living quarters they were confined to a crowded Chinatown. . . . College training in engineering or other technical subjects did not guarantee decent positions to Chinese. If one should go out, dressed casually for a walk, or go to a club, or even to a church, he was liable to be picked up by the immigration officers on suspicion of illegal residence. For many years officials made a practice of picking up persons in the street or in public places on the suspicion that they were aliens illegally in this country. Such arrests were reported to be very common, especially in the late 1920s. . . . It was up to the Chinese to prove he was not an illegal alien or even an illegal citizen. But proof is sometimes difficult and takes time. Eventually he would solve his difficulty, but only after suffering much trouble and anxiety.[21]

Not all Chinese migrated to the crowded Chinatowns of the cities. A few hundred, many of whom became merchants, settled in the Mississippi Delta. Chinese grocers catered mostly to blacks, extending them credit and providing other essential services (such as assisting illiterate rural blacks with government forms and making telephone calls). Some Chinese married black women; others brought their families over from China.

In this transition from sojourner to immigrant, Chinese men with families tried to evade their "black" status and avoid discrimination against their children, who were attending white public schools. In the 1920s, however, as a result of segregationist actions, Chinese children were expelled from the white schools, and the action was upheld by the courts "to preserve the purity and integrity of the white race, and prevent amalgamation." Separate schools for the Chinese were established, as the Mississippi Chinese developed parallel institutions when they were excluded from the white prototypes. By 1950 their status had improved, and white churches and schools were opened to them. Recently, second-generation Mississippi Chinese have been migrating to other parts of the United States.

On U.S. campuses today, another form of segregation occurs—between mainland Chinese and Taiwanese students, who lead very different lives and rarely interact. Class and political differences promote separate churches, student organizations, and prejudices in the two groups.[22]

Social Factors

In the 19th century, single Chinese women rarely ventured alone to the United States in search of economic opportunity; and Chinese tradition demanded that the wife remain with her husband's parents, even if he worked far from home. About half the Chinese sojourners were married.[23] The imbalance in the male–female ratio in the United States was very significant: 1,858:1 in 1860; 1,284:1 in 1870; 2,106:1 in 1880; 2,678:1 in 1890; and 1,887:1 in 1900. By 1920, the gender ratio, although still very much out of balance, had lessened to 695:1.[24] The ratio continued to decline steadily thereafter. By 1990, Chinese immigration had reached parity in sex distribution: 49 percent male and 51 percent female from mainland China, and 47 percent male and 53 percent female from Taiwan.[25]

In earlier years, however, the overabundance of Chinese males and the scarcity of Chinese females led to organized prostitution in Chinatowns. Numerous brothels dotted the Chinatowns, some of them run or protected by the secret societies and staffed with young women kidnapped from their villages, sold by impoverished parents, or lured abroad by the deceit of a proxy marriage.[26]

> With the vast Pacific Ocean separating him from domestic joys and companionship, the Chinese sojourner relied on the tong-controlled brothels for sex, attending the gambling and opium dens for recreation and respite from the day's toil, and paid homage and allegiance to his clansmen, *Landsmänner,* and fraternal brothers to secure mutual aid, protection, and a job.[27]

Intermarriage was extremely difficult for the Chinese; indeed, 14 states had passed laws expressly forbidding miscegenation. Furthermore, in 1884, a federal court ruled that only wives of those males exempt from the Chinese Exclusion Act of 1882—namely, merchants and businessmen—could emigrate to the United States. For nearly all the Chinese laborers in the United States, establishing a family was impossible. By 1890, 40 years after the Chinese had first arrived, only 2.7 percent of the total Chinese population was U.S.-born. The figure climbed to 30 percent by 1920. Legislation in 1943 allowed Chinese women to enter the country, enabling the U.S.-born Chinese population to pass the halfway point in 1950. By 1960, U.S.-born Chinese accounted for approximately two thirds of the total.[28]

Recent Patterns

Congress ended the ban on immigration from China in 1943 and in its place instituted a quota system, despite lingering anti-Chinese feeling. Speaking against the repeal, however, Congressman White of Idaho in 1943 condemned the Chinese as a race unable to accept U.S. standards, citing the actions of a few to create a false stereotype of an entire group:

> The Chinese are inveterate opium-smokers most of the day. They brought that hideous opium habit to this country. . . . There is no melting pot in America that can change their habits or change their mentality. . . . If there are any people who have refused to accept our standard and our education, it is the Chinese.[29]

In any case, the 1943 legislation permitted only 105 Chinese immigrants to enter the United States each year, and that quota included anyone in the world of Chinese descent, not just citizens of China. Special and separate legislative acts covering refugees, displaced persons, and brides allowed more Chinese to enter. Not until passage of the Immigration Act of 1965, however, could the Chinese enter under regular immigration regulations.

Since 1965, the Chinese American population has increased rapidly, growing more than fivefold since 1970 to about 2.4 million in 2000 (see Table 8.1). Although immigration dropped in the 1990s, over 40,000 still arrive annually. As a result, the Chinatowns in San Francisco, Los Angeles, and New York have almost doubled in population in the past decade, spilling over their traditional boundaries and into adjacent neighborhoods. The arrival of so many "FOB" (fresh off the boat) immigrants and refugees has raised commercial rents, squeezing out old-line shops.

TABLE 8.1   **East and Southeast Asian American Populations**

Nationality	1970	1980	1990	2000
Chinese	435,000	806,000	1,645,000	2,433,000
Filipino	343,000	775,000	1,407,000	1,850,000
Vietnamese*	NA	262,000	615,000	1,123,000
Korean	70,000	355,000	799,000	1,077,000
Japanese	591,000	701,000	848,000	797,000
Cambodian*	NA	16,000	147,000	172,000
Laotian*	NA	48,000	149,000	169,000
Hmong*	NA	5,000	90,000	169,000
Thai*	NA	45,000	91,000	113,000

Note: NA = not available.
*Virtually all have entered the United States since 1970.
Source: U.S. Bureau of the Census.

With the Chinatowns unable to absorb all the newcomers, Chinese are flourishing in outlying areas as well—in the Corona, Flushing, and Jackson Heights sections of Queens in New York City, and in the Richmond and Sunset neighborhoods of western San Francisco. Upward mobility and outward migration have converted Monterey Park, east of Los Angeles, from an almost entirely white residential suburb into "Little Taipei," where the majority are now Chinese Americans.[30]

The San Francisco, Los Angeles, and New York Chinatowns, paradoxically, are both tourist attractions and slum communities. They are filled with overcrowded, dilapidated buildings and troubled by the problems of youth gangs and high tuberculosis rates, but nonetheless they retain historical, picturesque, and commercial importance. Less evident to tourists are the Chinese garment shops, or sweatshops, notorious for their long hours and meager compensation.[31] Also hidden above and behind the street-level storefront façades is a population density that is 10 to 12 times the city average and a tuberculosis risk rate that is 13 times the general population's. Compounding the problem are crime syndicates in China, known as *triads*, that smuggle perhaps as many as 80,000 Chinese into the United States each year (only about 10 percent are caught).[32] Estimates place the number of illegal aliens in big-city Chinatowns as one in five residents.[33]

Within the Chinatowns, streets mark off the sections containing residents of different regional origins and dialects, much as in an early-20th-century Little Italy. In New York City, for example, which is the largest Chinese enclave in the western hemisphere, Burmese Chinese concentrate on Henry Street, Taiwanese on Centre Street, Fukienese on Division Street, and Vietnamese Chinese on East Broadway.[34]

A Chinatown concern in recent years has been the increasing rebelliousness, criminality, and radicalism of many Chinese American youths. The formation of delinquent gangs, particularly in New York City and San Francisco, has resulted in a growing number of gang wars and killings. The rise of youthful militancy and delinquency appears to reflect the marginal status of those in the younger generation, who experience frustration and adjustment problems in the United States. Many recent arrivals from Hong Kong are unfamiliar with the language and culture; they are either unemployed or in the lowliest jobs, and they live in overcrowded, slumlike quarters with no recreational facilities. For some youths, gang behavior helps fill status and identity needs.[35]

Socioeconomic Characteristics

In 1994, over 55 percent of the elderly Chinese immigrants who came to the United States between 1980 and 1987 depended on public assistance. Many did not want to live with their adult children, now established in the United States, and did not object to acknowledging their financial dependence on the government.[36] Nevertheless, far more elderly Chinese and Japanese live in extended-family households than do non-Hispanic whites.[37]

Chinese Americans present a bipolar occupational distribution: 30 percent occupy professional and technical positions as against 15 percent of the white labor force; but the Chinese are also heavily overrepresented among low-skilled

In a scene photographed around 1912, U.S. flags fly in New York City's Chinatown. This blend of the distinctive features of an ethnic community and the U.S. influence illustrates the ongoing processes of acculturation and ethnogenesis—the absorption of some cultural elements of the host society while elements from one's own cultural heritage are retained or adapted.
(National Archives)

service workers, with 24 percent as compared to 7 percent of the white labor force. Such employment characteristics reflect in part educational and immigration patterns. Also notable is a higher median family income for Chinese Americans than for other U.S. ethnic groups. However, more than 62 percent of Chinese families have more than one wage earner, compared to the 57 percent of the total population of families, which may account for the difference.[38]

THE JAPANESE

When Commodore Matthew Perry sailed into Tokyo Bay in 1853, his arrival marked the beginning of a new era for Japan. For more than 200 years, the Japanese had lived in government-enforced isolation. The emperors had prohibited travel and foreign visitors, although castaways were treated hospitably and allowed to leave unharmed. No one was permitted to build large boats, and any attempt to emigrate was punishable by death.

The situation began to change in 1860, when the Japanese government sent its first official emissaries to Washington. U.S observers thought the Japanese lacked emotional expression:

> [A San Francisco reporter wrote:] "This stoicism, however, is a distinguishing feature with the Japanese. It is part of their creed never to appear astonished at anything, and it must be a rare sight indeed which betrays in them any expression of wonder."
>
> In the 85 years which passed between the arrival of Japan's first embassy and the end of World War II, this "distinguishing feature" of the Japanese became the cardinal element of the anti-Japanese stereotype. Characterized by journalists, politicians, novelists, and film-makers as a dangerous enemy, the Japanese were also pictured as mysterious and inscrutable.[39]

Beginning in 1868, the Japanese began emigrating, first as laborers and eventually as permanent settlers. Their numbers on the U.S. mainland were small at first. U.S. Census records show only 55 in 1870 and 2,039 in 1890. After that, they came in much greater numbers, reaching 24,000 in 1900, 72,000 in 1910, and 111,000 in 1920.

Economic Competition

Because many families in Japan still followed the practice of **primogeniture** (in which the eldest son inherits the entire estate), many second and third sons came to the United States to seek their fortunes. They settled in the western states, where anti-Chinese sentiment was still strong, most of them becoming farmers or farm laborers. Their growing numbers, their concentration in small areas, and their racial visibility led to conflict with organized labor, vegetable growers, and shippers in California.

Early Japanese immigrants entered various manufacturing and service occupations. Hostility from union members, who resented Asians' willingness to work for lower wages and under poor conditions, produced the inevitable clashes. Members of the shoemakers' union attacked Japanese cobblers in 1890, and members of the union for cooks and waiters attacked Japanese restaurateurs in 1892. Finding that employment was difficult to obtain, most Japanese gravitated to the outlying areas and entered agricultural work, first as laborers and eventually as tenant farmers or small landholders; other Japanese became contract gardeners on the estates of whites.

Their industriousness and knowledge of cultivation placed the Japanese in serious competition with white and Hispanic farmers, and they encountered further acts of discrimination. In 1913, the California legislature passed the first alien landholding law, prohibiting any person who was ineligible for citizenship from owning land in the state, and permitting such persons to lease land for no more than three years in succession. Under the United States Naturalization Act of 1790, then still in effect, citizenship was available to "any alien, being a free *white* person" (italics mine). In 1868, the government had modified this law to extend citizenship to persons of African descent (the recently freed slaves), but the Japanese continued to be excluded.

Because their children born in this country were automatically U.S. citizens, the Japanese held land in their children's names, either directly or through land-holding companies whose stock they owned collectively. After World War I, new agitation arose against the Japanese. In 1920, the California legislature passed a law prohibiting aliens from being guardians of a minor's property or from leasing any land at all. The U.S. Supreme Court upheld the constitutionality of this law in 1923; and New Mexico, Arizona, Louisiana, Montana, Idaho, and Oregon passed similar statutes. Because their opportunities were still best in agriculture, many Japanese continued to work as tenant or truck farmers. Morton Grodzins suggests that their immense success (the Japanese raised 42 percent of California's truck crops by 1941) helps to explain why white vegetable growers and shippers pressed for their evacuation during World War II.[40]

National Policy

Most non-Californians had no strong feelings about Japanese immigrants, but they were aware of Japan's growing military power after the Japanese defeated Russia in 1905 after two years of warfare. The catalyst that triggered a change in national policy toward the Japanese was a local incident. In 1906, the San Francisco Board of Education passed a resolution transferring 93 Japanese children scattered throughout the city's 23 schools into a segregated "Oriental" school in Chinatown. This action made national headlines and had international ramifications. Under pressure from the Japanese government, President Theodore Roosevelt instructed the attorney general to initiate lawsuits challenging the constitutionality of this action.

As a compromise, the school board rescinded its resolution, the government dropped its legal action, and Roosevelt issued an executive order (which remained in effect until 1948) barring the entry of Japanese from a bordering country or U.S. territory. Thus Japanese who stayed even briefly in Hawaii, Canada, or Mexico could no longer enter the mainland United States. In addition, President Roosevelt secured the so-called Gentlemen's Agreement of 1908, whereby Japan agreed to restrict, but not eliminate altogether, the issuance of passports. The big loophole in the Gentlemen's Agreement was permission for wives to enter. Many Japanese married by proxy and then sent for their "picture brides." Several thousand Japanese entered the United States every year until World War I, and almost 6,000 a year came after the war.

As men brought their wives here and children were born, fearful nativists made exaggerated claims that the Japanese birth rate could lead to the Japanese "overrunning" the country. Questions about Japanese immigration began to shift from economic competition to the "assimilability" of the Japanese because of their race, lifestyle, and alleged birth rate. The anti-Japanese stereotype, long a part of dominant-group attitudes, played a key role:

> The anti-Japanese stereotype was so widespread that it affected the judgements of sociologists about the possibilities of Japanese assimilation. Thus, in 1913 Robert E. Park was sufficiently depressed by anti-Japanese legislation and popular prejudice to predict: "The Japanese . . . is condemned to remain among us an abstraction, a symbol, and a symbol not merely of his own race, but of the Orient and of that vague, ill-defined menace we sometimes refer to as the 'yellow-peril.'" Although Park later reversed his doleful prediction, his observations on Japanese emphasized their uncommunicative features, stolid faces, and apparently blank character.[41]

The Immigration Law of 1924—which severely restricted the number of southern, central, and eastern Europeans who could enter the United States—specifically barred the Japanese, because it denied entry to all aliens ineligible for citizenship. The bill passed by large majorities (323 to 71 in the House and 62 to 6 in the Senate), indicating widespread support for limiting immigration to the supposedly "assimilable" peoples. The Japanese government vehemently denounced this legislation, taking it as a national affront, a violation of the terms of the Gentlemen's Agreement, and an insult to a world power only recently courted by the United States. Nevertheless, the legislation remained in effect until 1952. (See the accompanying International Scene box about a latent function of Japanese national policy on immigrants.)

Expulsion and Imprisonment

By 1940 about 127,000 ethnic Japanese lived in the United States, 94,000 of them in California. About 63 percent were U.S.-born, and only 15 percent were of voting age. Japan's attack on Pearl Harbor in 1941 and the subsequent war led to what was subsequently referred to as "our worst wartime mistake."[42] More than 110,000 Japanese, many of them second- and third-generation Americans with as little as one eighth Japanese ancestry, were removed from their homes and placed in "relocation centers" in Arkansas, Arizona, eastern California, Colorado, Idaho, Utah, and Wyoming.[43]

> The evacuees loaded their possessions onto trucks. . . . Neighbors and teachers were on hand to see their friends off. Members of other minority groups wept. One old Mexican woman wept, saying, "Me next. Me next."
> . . . People were starting off to 7 o'clock jobs, watering their gardens, sweeping their pavements. Passers-by invariably stopped to stare in amazement, perhaps in horror, that this could happen in the United States. People soon became accustomed to the idea, however, and many profited from the evacuation. Japanese mortgages were foreclosed and their properties attached. They were forced to sell property such as cars and refrigerators at bargain prices.[44]

The International Scene
The Difference Between Race and Culture

After decades of Japanese refusal to let in unskilled foreigners, tens of thousands of Bangladeshis, Pakistanis, Thais, and other Asians entered Japan in the 1980s on tourist visas and stayed illegally. Worried that it might be flooded by foreigners, as France and Germany had been, Japan enacted tougher immigration curbs on unskilled workers in 1989 and began expelling the estimated 100,000 illegal immigrant Asians. Still needing a labor pool and not wanting to open its doors to outsiders, Japan next changed its immigration laws in 1990 to encourage immigration of foreigners whose parents or grandparents already lived in Japan, expecting a homogeneous blending.

About 150,000 unskilled ethnic Japanese fleeing the troubled economy of Brazil quickly entered Japan to take dirty, difficult, and dangerous jobs at construction sites, factories, and foundries or low-status jobs in restaurants and shops unwanted by native-born Japanese. But what objectively appeared to be a mutually beneficial arrangement created numerous adjustment problems for both sides, neither of which was prepared for the resulting culture shock.

The Japanese expected the Brazilians to be Japanese, but culturally they were not. They spoke Portuguese—and little or no Japanese—when they arrived and for a long time afterward. They dressed differently, talked more noisily, and laughed and embraced one another in public, all unlike the native-born Japanese. Their ethnicity became more visible with the advent of numerous Portuguese-language radio programs and newspapers, restaurants, stores, and social clubs. Brazilian street festivals in Tokyo flavored with samba and salsa attracted large crowds.

The immigrants complain that they are looked down on and treated with suspicion. They say they suffer discrimination in stores and restaurants, where they are either made to feel unwelcome or treated as probable shoplifters. Another problem they face is the lack of health benefits and worker's compensation if they are injured at work. The government, meanwhile, has opened a dozen centers to assist the foreign-born laborers.

Today about 270,000 Brazilians live in Japan, about 3,500 of them in a public-housing complex in Toyota City. Numerous slights by Japanese against Brazilians, and the natives' generalization that all Brazilians are criminals, served as preludes to confrontations, and in May 1999 to a brawl between Japanese and immigrant youth gangs. The Toyota City government then formed a committee to work on improving relations between the two nationalities, but the committee did not include any Brazilians.

Critical thinking question: What similarities to the above situation do you find between native-born African Americans and immigrants from Africa?

The mass expulsion of the Japanese from the West Coast was unnecessary for national security, although that reason was cited as the primary justification. The traditional anti-Asian sentiment on the West Coast, fear of the "perfidious" character of the Japanese, and opposition to Japanese producing a sizable share of the area's agricultural products may all have been factors. There was no mass evacuation of the 150,000 ethnic Japanese in Hawaii, which was much more strategic and vulnerable to attack because of its location. The differences in the Japanese experience in Hawaii and on the mainland can perhaps best be understood by looking at the differences in structural discrimination. In Hawaii, the Japanese were more fully involved in economic and political endeavors, partly because they lived in an environment of greater racial harmony. On the West Coast, the Japanese were more isolated from mainstream U.S. society, and certain labor and agricultural groups saw them as an economic threat. Also, anti-Asian attitudes and actions had prevailed in that area for almost 100 years.

Besides the trauma that resulted from being uprooted and interned, the Japanese had to adjust culturally to their new surroundings. Instead of their preferred deep hot baths, they had only showers and common washrooms. Central dining halls prevented families from eating together intimately as a family unit. Outside and sometimes distant toilet facilities, not partitioned in the early months,

A Japanese-American assistant teacher leads a kindergarten class in singing an English folk song at the Tule Lake "internment relocation center" in May 1943. This photo speaks volumes about attempts at normalcy within a wartime concentration camp for civilians, most of them U.S. citizens, and about official Americanization efforts. (*Source:* AP Photo)

were a hardship for the old and for the parents of small children. Almost 6,000 babies were born while these centers were in existence, and proper hospital facilities were not always available. Only partial partitions divided rooms occupied by different families in the same barracks, permitting minimal privacy. Ted Nakashima, a second-generation Japanese American, offered a frightening portrait of what the early months of life in the Tule Lake, California, camp were like:

> The resettlement center is actually a penitentiary—armed guards in towers with spotlights and deadly tommy guns, fifteen feet of barbed wire fences, everyone confined to quarters at nine, lights out at ten o'clock. The guards are ordered to shoot anyone who approaches within twenty feet of the fences. No one is allowed to take the two-block-long hike to the latrines after nine, under any circumstances. The apartments, as the army calls them, are two-block-long stables, with windows on one side. Floors are . . . two-by-fours laid directly on the mud, which is everywhere. The stalls are about eighteen by twenty-one feet; some contain families of six or seven persons. Partitions are seven feet high, leaving a four-foot opening above. . . .
>
> The food and sanitation problems are the worst. We have had absolutely no fresh meat, vegetables or butter since we came here. Mealtime queues extend for blocks; standing in a rainswept line, feet in the mud, waiting for the scant portions of canned wieners and boiled potatoes, hash for breakfast or canned wieners and beans for dinner. Coffee or tea dosed with saltpeter and stale bread are the adults' staples. Dirty, unwiped dishes, greasy silver, a starchy diet, no butter, no milk, bawling kids, mud, wet mud that stinks when it dries, no vegetables—a sad thing for the people who raised them in such abundance. . . .
>
> Today one of the surface sewage-disposal pipes broke and sewage flowed down the streets. Kids played in the water. Shower baths without hot water. Stinking mud and slops everywhere.
>
> Can this be the same America we left a few weeks ago? . . . What really hurts most is the constant reference to us evacuees as "Japs." "Japs" are the guys we are fighting. We're on this side and we want to help.
>
> Why won't America let us?[45]

Although the harsh physical conditions and sanitation problems improved, the Japanese Americans remained prisoners because of their background. They tried to make life inside the barbed wire fences a little brighter by fixing up their quarters and planting small gardens. However, these "residents" of the "relocation centers" still lived, for the most part, in concentration camps. About 35,000 young Japanese Americans left these centers by the end of 1943, going voluntarily to the East and Midwest for further schooling or a job. For those obliged to remain in the camps, life was monotonous and unproductive. The evacuation brought financial ruin to many Japanese American families; they lost property, savings, income, and jobs for which they were never adequately compensated.

By weakening Japanese subcommunities and institutions, the evacuation program encouraged acculturation. The traditional authority of the first-generation Japanese Americans (*Issei*) lessened; family structure and husband–wife roles underwent changes and became more equal because of camp life; and second-generation Japanese (*Nisei*) who resettled found new opportunities. Of the Japanese who relocated to the Midwest and to the East Coast, a large number later returned to the West. Many became more a part of U.S. society in the postwar period because they had been forced to do so.

In 1944, the Supreme Court upheld the Japanese evacuation by a 6-to-3 vote (*Korematsu v. United States of America*), although the dissenting justices gave strong minority opinions. Justice Francis Murphy called approving the evacuation "the legalization of racism." Justice Robert H. Jackson, who later prosecuted the Nazi war criminals at Nuremberg, wrote,

> But once a judicial opinion rationalizes such an order to show that it conforms to the Constitution, or rather rationalizes the Constitution to show that the Constitution sanctions such an order, the Court for all time has validated the principle of racial discrimination in criminal procedure, and of transplanting American citizens. The principle then lies about like a loaded weapon ready for the hand of any authority that can bring forward a plausible claim of an urgent need. Every repetition imbeds that principle more deeply in our law and thinking and expands it to new purposes.[46]

Soon after, another case, *Endo v. United States,* brought an end to this forcible detention—as of January 2, 1945—when the U.S. Supreme Court unanimously ruled that all loyal Japanese Americans be set free unconditionally. In 1976, President Ford signed an executive order officially closing the camps, but such mass, ethnicity-based evacuations could conceivably recur because of the judicial precedent set by the Court in upholding the action.

Justice Jackson's 1944 dissenting opinion seemed prophetic 35 years later, when the seizure of U.S. hostages at the U.S. Embassy in Iran prompted calls by some politicians for Iranian students then attending U.S. colleges to be rounded up and detained in the very same concentration camps.

While they were internees and during the years following their mass incarceration, Japanese Americans sought redress through the Japanese American Citizens League (JACL). This organization fought to restore and reopen frozen bank deposits to their owners, obtain compensation for owners of confiscated land, and regain lost retirement benefits owed to civil-service workers. The Evacuation Claims Act of 1948 brought token repayment of about 10 percent of actual Japanese American losses.[47] In 1988, new legislation brought a formal apology to the former internees for violating their "basic civil liberties" because of "racial prejudice." The bill also awarded a tax-free payment of $20,000 to each of the 60,000 surviving detainees.[48]

Recent Patterns

Because homeland influences are important in understanding immigrant orientations, changes in Japan since World War II are worth mentioning. U.S. occupation of the country and foreign-aid-based reconstruction led to significant and rapid social change in Japan. Westernization and industrialization affected Japanese values and lifestyles; it also altered U.S. attitudes. The 25,000 Japanese war brides who accompanied returning GIs to the United States at first encountered suspicion and hostility, but such attitudes eventually disappeared. Some were not accepted by the Japanese American ethnic community, but Japanese wives of whites were usually looked on as unthreateningly exotic by the dominant group.[49]

Traditionally, Japanese parents have encouraged their children to get a good education; and since the 1940s, Japanese-American males and females have performed well above the national norms of those completing high school and college. The culture's emphasis on conformity, aspiration, competitiveness, discipline, and self-control helps to explain the high educational attainments of Japanese Americans.[50] Encouraged by their *Nisei* (second-generation) elders and the upwardly mobile *Sansei* (third generation), the *Yonsei* (fourth generation) and *Gosei* (fifth generation) have increasingly entered professional fields, especially engineering, pharmacy, electronics, and other technical fields. Most Japanese Americans are U.S.-born, and their higher education levels translate into their having incomes above those of any other ethnic group, including all white Americans.[51]

The social organization and social controls within Japanese culture have been strong enough to withstand most problems of marginality, as evidenced by low rates of divorce, crime, delinquency, mental illness, and suicide. As Harry H. L. Kitano, a Japanese American sociologist who was interned during World War II, observed,

> The ability of the Japanese family and community to provide ample growth opportunities, to present legitimate alternatives, to provide conditions of relative tolerance and treatments, to provide effective socialization and control, as well as the relative congruence between Japanese culture and middle-class American culture, has aided the group in adapting to acculturative changes with a minimum marginal population. Relatively few Japanese seek social friendships in the social cliques and organizations outside their own ethnic group. And those who do seek outside contacts appear to have many of the necessary requisites for such activity—high education, good training, and adequate income.[52]

With half their number now native-born Americans, Japanese Americans have become arguably the best-assimilated of all Asian Americans.[53] Both of Hawaii's U.S. senators, Daniel Akaka and Daniel Inouye, are of Japanese ancestry. On the mainland, structural assimilation, for example, is evident among the *Sansei* and *Yonsei,* whose outgroup dating and exogamy have significantly increased, surpassing 50 percent or more, according to some studies.[54] This trend prompted Masako M. Osako to suggest that Japanese Americans may become "the first nonwhites to merge biologically into the dominant American society."[55]

Japanese immigration to the United States in the 1980s amounted to 47,000 and over 60,000 in the 1990s—far less than the totals of most other East Asian countries.[56] Consequently, the Japanese-American population represents a steadily declining proportion of the Asian American community (8 percent in 2000). Two out of every three Japanese Americans live either in California (36 percent) or Hawaii (29 percent). About half of all new arrivals are skilled and professional workers who find many similarities between U.S. society and their homeland. Most are adherents of Buddhism, a religion whose U.S. membership is growing because of the continuing entry of Japanese and other Asian believers in this faith.

One special group in the United States is that of the *Kai-sha*—businesspeople and employees of large corporations on two- or three-year assignments with their companies' U.S. branch offices. Their presence is more noticeable in the New York metropolitan region than ever before. Many suburban towns near New York City, particularly those along the Metro train line north into Westchester County and northeast along the New Haven line have experienced a large influx of Japanese *Kai-sha* and their families. Long-time residents of such suburban communities as Scarsdale, Hartsdale, Larchmont, and Mamaroneck, unaccustomed to Asian neighbors, have seen their neighborhoods extensively integrated in a short time.[57]

THE FILIPINOS

The Filipinos came to the United States with a unique status. In 1898, the Philippines became a U.S. possession, so for the next several decades the inhabitants were considered U.S. nationals, although not U.S. citizens. Consequently, they were not designated as aliens, and there was no quota restriction on their entry until 1935. The geographic locale of their homeland and their Spanish heritage complicated their status, however, because the federal government argued that they were not whites. The U.S. Supreme Court upheld this official position in a 1934 ruling on a case challenging the 1790 naturalization law limiting citizenship to foreign-born whites:

> "White persons" within the meaning of the statute are members of the Caucasian race, as Caucasian is defined in the understanding of the mass of men. The term excludes the Chinese, the Japanese, the Hindus, the American Indians and the Filipinos.[58]

Early Immigrants

Like so many other immigrant groups, the early Filipino immigrants did not think of themselves in nationalist terms. Instead they placed themselves in one of several native language subgroupings: the Tagalogs, Visayans, or Ilocanos. Their social hangouts—the clubhouse, bar, or poolroom—often reflected that separation. U.S. society lumped them together, however, and soon societal hostility forged a common ethnic identity among them.

After the Gentlemen's Agreement of 1908 curtailed Japanese emigration, the Hawaiian Sugar Planters' Association recruited laborers from the Philippines to work the plantations. Fifteen years later, the modest number of Filipinos in the continental United States (5,603 in 1920), began to increase. Why? California growers, faced with the loss of Mexican labor because of quota restrictions in the pending Immigration Act of 1924, turned to the Filipinos as an alternative labor source. By 1930 the number of Filipinos in the continental United States had increased to over 45,000, with more than two thirds living in California.

Many Filipinos worked in agriculture at first, particularly in California and Washington. However, the lure of the city attracted many young Filipino males to urban areas, where they sought jobs. Discrimination, along with lack of education and job skills, resulted in their getting only low-paying domestic and personal-service work in hotels, restaurants, other businesses, and residences. They were employed as bellboys, waiters, cooks, busboys, janitors, drivers, house boys, elevator operators, and hospital attendants. By 1940 their employment in these areas peaked, with 9 out of 10 Filipinos so employed.[59] Feeling that they were being exploited by their employers, they often joined unions (or formed their own unions when denied membership in existing unions) and went on strike, intensifying management resentment. Ironically, the union hierarchy also disliked them and later joined in efforts to bar them from the United States.

As the Depression of the 1930s worsened and jobs became scarcer, dominant-group critics increased their objections to the presence of the Filipinos. Race riots erupted in Exeter, California, on October 24, 1929, and in Watsonville, California, on January 19, 1930, when one Filipino was killed. In both instances, several hundred white men beat Filipinos, shattered windows in cars and buildings, and wrecked property. Other clashes occurred in San Jose and San Francisco, followed on January 28, 1930, by the bombing of the Filipino Federation of America Center in Stockton, called "the Manila of California" because of its large Filipino population.

The Scarcity of Filipino Women

Of every 100 Filipinos coming to California between 1920 and 1929, 93 were male; almost 80 percent were single and between 16 and 30 years of age. Because there were few Filipina women available, these males sought the company of women of other races. This situation enraged many white men, as the following racist statement illustrates:

> The Filipinos have . . . demanded the right to run dance halls under the alias of clubs, with white girls as entertainers. And the excuse they have openly and brazenly given for their demand is that the Filipinos "prefer" white women to those of their own race and that besides there are not enough Filipino women in the country to satisfy their lust. . . . If that statement is not enough to make the blood of any white man, of any other decent man boil, then there is no such thing as justified indignation at any advocacy of immorality.[60]

This bigoted, demagogic statement reflects the sort of sexually oriented charges often directed against minority racial groups. Filipino men's association with white women through intermarriage, dance hall encounters, and affairs led to increased tensions in Filipino–white relations. The Filipinos' reputation as great lovers emerged as a stereotype, and probably was enhanced when a San Francisco judge commented:

> Some of these boys, with perfect candor, have told me bluntly and boastfully that they practice the art of love with more perfection than white boys, and occasionally

one of the girls has supplied me with information to the same effect. In fact, some of the disclosures in this regard are perfectly startling in nature.[61]

Filipino responses followed quickly. Sylvester Saturday, editor of the Filipino Poets League in Washington, DC, stated,

We Filipinos are tickled at being called "great lovers." Surely, we are proud of this heritage. We love our women so much that we work ourselves to death to gain and keep their affections.[62]

A Filipino from Chicago chided,

And as for the Filipinos being "great lovers," there is nothing surprising about that. We Filipinos, however poor, are taught from the cradle up to respect and love our women. That's why our divorce rate is nil compared with the state of which Judge Lazarus is a proud son. If to love and respect our womenfolks is savagery, then make the most of it, Judge. We plead guilty.[63]

White U.S. residents were not amused. Several western states passed laws prohibiting marriages between Filipinos and whites. The Tyding–McDuffie Act of 1935 granted deferred independence to the Philippines and imposed an immediate rigid quota of 50 immigrants a year. Repatriation efforts from 1935 to 1937 succeeded in returning only 2,190 U.S. residents to the Philippines.[64]

Because of the lack of Filipino women and legal restrictions on intermarriage, many Filipino males remained single. These early immigrants became lonely old men with no family ties, living in poverty after years of hard work, although a small number did intermarry with Mexicans, Native Americans, mulattos, Asians, and whites.[65]

Unlike the Chinese, who had a tradition of being sojourners and who formed benevolent and protective associations, the Filipinos did not establish the support institutions usually found in immigrant communities. Their lack of families and the seasonal, transitory nature of their employment were primary reasons for this. As a result of housing discrimination, they lived in hotels and rooming houses in less desirable sections of town. The pool hall and taxi-dance hall became their recreational outlets.[66]

Postwar Immigrants

With the Philippines a strategically important ally during World War II, the social climate in the mainland United States became more liberal toward Filipinos. In January 1942, legislation was passed enabling Filipino residents to become naturalized U.S. citizens. They could buy land in California, and many did—often from Japanese Americans who were being removed from certain areas, such as Los Angeles. Many Filipinos bought farms in the San Fernando Valley, the San Joaquin Valley, and the Torrance–Gardena area.[67]

Since the Immigration Act of 1965, Filipino immigration has been quite high. An unstable political situation at home toward the end of the Marcos regime (which was peacefully overthrown in 1986) and continuing economic limitations in the Philippines have served as the major push factors. Like the Japanese, new Filipino arrivals tend to have better educational and occupational skills than most of their ethnic cohorts born in the United States. Over two thirds are professional and technical workers in medicine, law, engineering, and education. Because of licensing and hiring problems, however, many are unable to secure jobs commensurate with their education, skills, and experience.[68]

Filipinos are fragmented socially, linguistically, and politically. Unlike the Koreans, few are entrepreneurs; and seldom do Filipinos form cooperative credit associations to raise business capital. Filipino youth, unlike other East Asian American youth but like the Indochinese, often reject traditional family discipline and are becoming assimilated. About half of all Filipino Americans speak only English.[69]

The largest concentration of Filipinos living outside the Philippines is in Hawaii, where they comprise 60 percent of all hotel maids and porters. On the mainland, Filipinos tend to settle on either the West Coast or the East Coast. Mostly Roman Catholics, with a strong loyalty to family and church, today's Filipino Americans otherwise present diverse socioeconomic characteristics of education, occupation, income, and residence. Time of immigration and age appear to be the key variables. The old-timers—retired laborers—usually are single males with meager incomes. Second and third generations born in the United States typically share such problems as lack of social acceptance, low income, low educational achievement, and negative self-image. In contrast, new arrivals often are college graduates seeking white-collar jobs in the economic mainstream.[70]

Filipino Americans more than doubled in number between 1970 and 1980, going from 343,000 to 775,000, and doubled again—to nearly 1.9 million—by 2000. Today they are the second-largest Asian and Pacific Islander ethnic group in the United States, comprising 18 percent of the total U.S. Asian population. The continuing arrival of new immigrants, now averaging 35,000 annually, points to further substantial population increases.[71]

THE KOREANS

By the middle of the 19th century, English, French, and Russian whaling ships sailed Korean waters, and many Catholic missionaries had come to Korea. The United States, however, became the first Western nation to sign a treaty with Korea, when it formalized a relationship of friendship and trade in 1882. Other nations quickly followed suit, and all attempted to displace China as the pre-eminent foreign power in Korea.

Despite various treaties and declarations by the different nations purporting to guarantee Korea's independence, Japanese hegemony, both political and economic, continued. Japan's victory over Russia in 1905 solidified Japanese domination of Korea, and Japan exercised colonial control until the end of World War II. Even then, Korea did not gain national independence, however, for an Allied military agreement in 1945 mandated that Soviet troops accept the Japanese surrender in the region north of the 38th parallel and U.S. troops do the same in the region south of it. This temporary line, created out of military expediency, became a permanent demarcation that still defines the split between North and South Korea.

Early Immigrants

The Hawaii Sugar Planters' Association, needing laborers to replace the Chinese, who were excluded by the 1882 legislation, recruited 7,226 Koreans, 637 of them women, between 1903 and 1905. This was the first large group of Koreans to migrate to the United States. The Koreans, mostly peasants, sought economic relief from the famines plaguing their country at the turn of the century. In Hawaii, they worked long hours for meager wages under harsh conditions. Of the original group, about 1,000 returned to Korea, 2,000 males and 12 women went on to the mainland United States, and the rest remained in Hawaii.[72] The males were almost all between the ages of 20 and 40.[73] (See the accompanying Ethnic Experience box.)

Between 1907 and 1924, several thousand more Korean immigrants—mostly "picture brides," political activists fighting Japanese oppression, and students—migrated to the United States. As a result of the age disparity between the picture brides and the older males, many second-generation Korean Americans spent a good portion of their formative years with non–English-speaking widowed mothers who had had limited formal schooling.[74]

Recent Immigrants

Not until the end of the Korean War and passage of the Refugee Relief Act in 1953 did Koreans emigrate in substantial numbers. As refugees or war brides, Koreans came to the United States in growing numbers, beginning in 1958. The continued presence of U.S. troops in South Korea and the cultural influence on South Korea that resulted were constant inducements to the Koreans to intermarry or contemplate living in the United States. The liberalized immigration law of 1965 opened the doors to Asian immigrants and allowed relatives to join family members already in the United States. This chain-migration pattern resulted in an impressive fivefold population increase in 10 years, from 70,000 in 1970 to 355,000 in 1980 and in a doubling of that number to 799,000 in 1990. By 2000, the Korean American population increased by a third to 1.1 million.

The Role of the Church

Almost 70 percent of the Korean American population identifies itself as Christian, a significantly higher proportion than the 30 percent Christian population living in Korea. Mostly Presbyterian and Methodist, Korean American congregations

The Ethnic Experience

The First Korean Women in the United States

The following comments, through the courtesy of Harold and Sonia Sunoo, are a composite of taped interviews with three Korean women who were among the first 12 women to come to the U.S. mainland:

"We left Korea because we were too poor. We had nothing to eat. . . . There was absolutely no way we could survive.

"At first we were unaware that we had been 'sold' as laborers. . . . We thought Hawaii was America in those days. . . . We cut sugar canes, the thing you put in coffee. . . .

"I'll never forget the foreman. No, he wasn't Korean—he was French. The reason I'll never forget him is that he was the most ignorant of all ignoramuses, but he knew all the cuss words in the world. . . . [I] could tell by the sound of his words. He said we worked like 'lazy.' He wanted us to work faster. . . . He would gallop around on horseback and crack and snap his whip. . . . He was so mean and so ignorant!

". . . If all of us worked hard and pooled together our total earnings, it came to about fifty dollars a month, barely enough to feed and clothe the five of us. We cooked on the porch, using coal oil and when we cooked in the fields, I gathered the wood. We had to carry water in vessels from water faucets scattered here and there in the camp area. . . .

"My mother and sister-in-law took in laundry. They scrubbed, ironed, and mended shirts for a nickel apiece. It was pitiful! Their knuckles became swollen and raw from using the harsh yellow laundry soap . . . but it was still better than in Korea. There was no way to earn money there."

On the mainland, the Koreans encountered even worse problems than in Hawaii because of the more highly charged racial tension and the severe weather conditions, as the following account indicates:

"We had five children at that time—our youngest was three and a half. I was paid fifteen cents an hour for weeding. Our baby was too young to go to school, so I had to take him along with me to the fields—it was so early when we started that he'd be fast asleep when we left so I couldn't feed him breakfast. Returning home, he'd be asleep again because he was so tired. Poor child, he was practically starved. He too suffered so much. . . . [In February] the ground . . . was frozen crisp and it was so cold that the baby's tender ears got frozen and blood oozed from him. . . . For all this suffering, I was paid fifteen cents an hour."

Source: Three Korean immigrants who came to Hawaii between 1903 and 1905 at ages ranging from 19 to 25.

now exceed 2,000, compared to fewer than 75 in 1970. Ethnic churches, including Korean ones, make important contributions to immigrant communities, serving more than religious purposes. The church becomes a social organization, providing religious and ethnic fellowship, a personal community, and a family atmosphere within an alien and urban environment.[75]

One study of the role of Korean churches in the ethnic community of Chicago, where more than 50,000 Koreans live, found patterns reminiscent of those of earlier European immigrants.[76] Church affiliation was 57 percent, compared to 12 percent in Korea. This heightened interest in church membership and frequent attendance at worship services is common among new immigrant groups seeking a communal bond in their ethnic identity. Not surprisingly, the study found that religious involvement was the primary motive, but over 95 percent listed "loneliness and seeing friends and relatives" as secondary reasons for involvement in church activities. Because the greater the participation, the greater the identification with homeland and culture, Korean American churches, like similar institutions in other ethnic communities, serve as a focal point for enhancing ethnic identity.

Occupational Adaptation

In Los Angeles County, where over 200,000 Korean Americans live, 40 percent of the males operate their own businesses.[77] Nationwide, the 12 percent self-employment rate of Korean Americans is the highest of all ethnic or racial groups, including whites. Whereas better than 1 in 10 Korean Americans is a business owner, the figure for blacks is 1 in 67 and for nonminorities 1 in 15.[78] So deeply entrenched is self-employment in the Korean immigrant ethos, a survey revealed, that 61 percent of South Koreans planning to emigrate to the United States expected to go into business for themselves, even though most had never been self-employed in their homeland.[79]

In many cities and **exurbs,** small Korean family-operated businesses are especially conspicuous. In Los Angeles, Korean Americans now dominate the retail wig and liquor businesses. In Washington (DC), Philadelphia, New York City, and Chicago, Korean Americans are especially visible as grocery-store owners and fruit-stand operators. Many other Korean Americans work as employees in these small stores and firms, which penetrate the black and Hispanic markets.[80] Because the Koreans occupy an intermediate position in trade and commerce between producer and consumer, they play the role of a middleman minority.[81] As we will see later, their visibility in other racial or ethnic neighborhoods has sometimes made them targets of community hostility.

Widespread use of rotating-credit associations has greatly aided the Koreans in establishing their own businesses. Like the *hui* among the Mandarin Chinese, the *tanomoshi* among the Japanese, and the *susu* of Caribbean Islanders, the **kye** of the Koreans provides startup funds for their ethnic entrepreneurs. In the arrangement's simplest form, each member contributes a fixed amount monthly to a fund and has rotating access to the pot. The first borrowers pay extra loan interest. Dating back to Korean farming villages of the 16th century, the *kye* helps newcomers get started in business while simultaneously functioning as a social club to bind immigrants together.

Overall, Koreans are more highly educated than most other nonwhite groups. Their income, however, in proportion to their number of college graduates, lags behind that of native-born Americans, although their earnings are similar to those of other Asian American groups.[82] Koreans have fared rather poorly in social acceptance, as indicated by social-distance measures, an important indicator of structural assimilation. In his 1956 and 1966 studies, Emory S. Bogardus found Koreans at or near the bottom in preference rankings, below all other East Asian peoples. In his 2001 study, Vincent N. Parrillo found that Koreans had improved in preference rankings although they remained in the bottom tier (see Chapter 1).[83]

THE VIETNAMESE

In April 1975, as the Vietnam War ended, 127,000 Vietnamese and 4,000 Cambodian refugees entered the United States. As they waited in relocation centers at military bases for sponsors to materialize, public-opinion polls showed that most U.S. citizens, especially members of the working class, believed the refugees would take jobs away from people already living in the United States. Labor and state officials raised serious objections to "flooding" the labor market and welfare rolls with so many aliens at a time when the economy was mired in a recession. Yet all the refugees were resettled within seven months across all 50 states.

Like the Cuban exiles of the 1960s and later, many of these Vietnamese were middle class, migrating for political rather than economic reasons. Many were well educated, with marketable skills, and nearly half spoke English.[84] They were relatively cosmopolitan people, mostly from the Saigon region, and many had previously lived elsewhere, particularly in North Vietnam.

In 1979, tens of thousands of Vietnamese "boat people"—many of them actually ethnic Chinese residents of Vietnam—sought refuge in other countries, setting sail in flimsy, overcrowded boats. Many drowned or were killed by pirates, but several hundred thousand reached refugee camps in Thailand and other countries (see the accompanying Ethnic Experience box). President Carter authorized admitting 14,000 refugees per month for 15 months, bringing over 200,000 additional Indochinese refugees into the United States.

Immigration from Vietnam remains significant. About 281,000 Vietnamese immigrated to the United States in the 1980s, and over 250,000 arrived in the 1990s. From a virtual nonpresence in the United States in 1970, the Vietnamese numbered 1.1 million in 2000, making them the third largest East Asian group, and constitute 11 percent of the total Asian American population. Most of these more recent arrivals speak little English and have few occupational skills, making their adjustment and attainment of economic self-sufficiency more difficult.

Cultural Differentiation

Unlike most people in the United States, who believe in free will and self-determination, many Vietnamese believe in predestination, with very limited individual control over events.[85] Two of the more important factors that the Vietnamese believe determine a person's destiny are *phuc duc* and astrology. These are core elements within the family infrastructure of filial piety and ancestor worship, and they provide important insights into the Vietnamese ability to adapt to a new society with minimal emotional anxiety.

The concept of *phuc duc* refers to the amount of good fortune that comes from meritorious or self-sacrificing actions. This accumulation of rewards, secured primarily by women for their family, also affects the lives of succeeding generations into the fifth generation. *Phuc duc* is quantifiable, in that improper conduct diminishes the amount one has, whereas the nature of one's actions and one's degree of personal sacrifice determines the amount one acquires:

> To a great extent *phuc duc* acts as the social conscience of the nation, a collective superego. The children are conscientiously instructed in the ways of living that result in *phuc duc*. It is, in great part, related to the Confucian concept of Li [propriety and etiquette], although it is actually Buddhist-Confucian in origin and unique to Vietnam. It has its place in future reincarnations but primarily it relates to the family and to future generations of the family. Thus the responsibility that it represents is impressively exacting: the future destiny of one's loved ones and those yet unborn depends upon one's conduct.[86]

So strong is the Vietnamese belief in horoscopes that parents accept no responsibility for a child's personality, believing that the configuration of the celestial bodies at the moment of conception fixes the character of that individual. At the time of birth, a Vietnamese astrologer specifically predicts the personality and events to come for the newborn infant. This often becomes a self-fulfilling prophecy because the predictions influence actual behavior (the parents' child-rearing practices as well as the child's own actions, including mate selection as an adult). The Vietnamese way of life thus includes belief in a deterministic life force over which the individual has minimal control. This concept has greatly influenced the accommodation of the Vietnamese to the United States:

> For many this is the second or third time that they have been refugees. It is not something that one ever gets used to, but there is a philosophic acceptance of fate. And this the Vietnamese can accept. It is assigned to bad *phuc duc*, to the heavens, to the land on which one's ancestors are buried, or whatever. The cause, however, is externalized and inasmuch as this is universally concurred in by one's peers, these adverse events are integrated into one's psychic apparatus with a minimum of emotional dislocation.[87]

Han T. Doan points out that the Vietnamese believe human nature is basically good but corruptible.[88] Diligence is thus necessary in all activity: One must continually exercise caution, self-control, meditation, honor, modesty, and moderation. Vietnamese are strongly tradition bound, revering their ancestors, homeland, and family traditions. They tend to live in harmony with nature rather than to dominate it. Instead of favoring individualism, Vietnamese culture is oriented toward achievement of group goals, primarily within the extended family:

> The doctrine of the "Golden Mean" of Confucius and that of the "Middle Path" of Buddha have been ingrained in the Vietnamese thinking and have dominated

The Ethnic Experience
A Desperate Bid for Freedom

"*O*ur boat was kind of lucky, 'cause 70 percent of boats get captured by Vietnamese Coast Guard. That day there was no moon. It was totally dark. . . . Luckily we make it. . . . After one day and one night we get out of the control of the Vietnamese. Now we know we're free! . . . Our boat was 30 feet long and about 7 feet wide and, totally, we had about 103 people. It was so crowded, almost like a fish can, you know? Can you imagine?

". . . There was only enough water for one cup for each person in one day. So we rarely drank the water for, if we don't have water, we're going to die in the sea. The first day everyone got seasick. Nobody got used to it, the kind of high waves and ocean. So everyone got seasick and vomited. . . . But by the second day and the third day, we felt much better.

"We kept going straight into the international sea zone and we met a lot of ships. We tried to get signal for help, we tried to burn our clothes to get their attention. We wrote the big S.O.S. letter in our clothes and tried to hang it above the boat. No matter how we tried, they just passed us by. I think they might feel pity for us, have the good compassion, but I think they're afraid their government going to blame them because the law is, if you pick up any refugee in the ocean, your country got to have responsibility for those people. So finally we so disappointed because we got no help from anybody and our boat is now the only boat and we have only 3 h.p. motor.

"We have too many people and the wave is extremely high, about 5 feet. It is so dangerous. You can see the boat only maybe like 1 feet distant from the sea level. But we got no choice. We decide to keep going straight to Malaysia. The fifth day, the sixth day, we saw

Source: Vietnamese refugee who came to the United States in 1980 at age 17.

Vietnamese thoughts. These doctrines account for the harmony maintained in social relationships among Vietnamese and between Vietnamese and other peoples. In their relations with others, Vietnamese, in order to maintain the "just middle," try to avoid injuring others and hurting their susceptibility; they compromise. They are also delicate and tactful, gentle, polite, and flexible: what belongs to others is pretty and what belongs to them is ugly. Also, it is desirable for Vietnamese to show respect to their superiors and kindness to their inferiors. The desire to please others can be found in old folk sayings that "since one does not have to buy nice words, one should choose those pleasant to others' ears." To make others happy, one sometimes has to bend low and to live up to their expectation.[89]

According to Confucian thinking, a hierarchical system is the natural order of things. It is necessary, therefore, that individuals know their position in the system and behave as befits that position.[90] Thus cultural values of courage, stoicism, and

nothing. The only thing we saw is water, sun, and at night the stars. It's just like upside-down moon. And the sea. If you look down into the ocean, you get scared, because the water—color—is so dark. It's like dark blue. If you look down into the water, you had the feeling like it invite you, say 'Go down with me.' Especially at night, the water—it's black, like evil waiting for you. Say, 'Oh, 103 people. I was waiting for you. Come down with us.' We kept going, but we don't know where we're going to be, if we have enough food and water to make it. . . . We don't even know if we're going the right way . . . we just estimate by looking at the sun and the stars.

". . . The sixth day we saw the bird and a couple of floating things, so we are hoping we are almost come to the shore. We had some hope and we kept traveling one more day, the seventh day. That day is the day—our wa-ter—we have only one more day left. And the gasoline is almost gone. And we saw some fire, very little fire, very far away. And we went to that fire. One hour, two hours. And finally we saw that fire offshore drilling platform of Esso Company. Everybody's screaming and so happy because we know at least we have something we can turn to. . . . We know we cannot go any further. Most of the women and children in my boat are exhausted, and some of the children unconscious. Some of the children had been so thirsty, they just drank the water from the sea. And the water from the sea is terrible. The more you drank, the more you got thirsty. And the children, starving, got a bad reaction from the seawater. We all got skin disease and exhausted. . . . They took us in their boat to the refugee camp in Malaysia."

adaptation through conformity, have helped make the refugees' adjustment somewhat easier. Peter I. Rose adds that other cultural values also have been effective: a strong sense of family; great respect for education; high motivation to achieve, especially for a better life for their children; and an emphasis on discipline, responsibility, and hard work.[91]

Acculturation

Refugees' adaptation to U.S. life appears to vary. One study found that a higher educational level and degree of Americanization prior to immigration eased the acculturation process.[92] Contradictorily, another study found that higher education meant poorer adjustment because of underemployment.[93] Both studies

At an Austin, Texas school, Vietnamese Americans learn of their children's progress at a parent-teacher conference. The high educational achievement among so many different Asian American groups results from a strong value orientation of education as a means to a successful life.
(*Source:* © Bob Daemmrich/The Image Works)

agreed, however, that Vietnamese who possessed relatively traditional views faced the greatest culture shock and difficulty in adaptating.

Adaptation problems continued into the third and fourth year after arrival. Physical complaints often were due to psychological stresses and were psychosomatic. Women were more likely than men to suffer from depression, anxiety, and tension. A greater frequency of feelings of inadequacy, anger, tension, and sensitivity occurred among these Vietnamese refugees than in the general population. Principal causes of mental stress were loneliness, lack of community life, breakup of the family, uncertainty about the future, homesickness, grief over losses in fleeing the homeland, and frustration in coping with life in the United States. As was found in earlier studies of Cuban and Hungarian refugees, assuming hostile and aggressive attitudes toward the host society or fellow refugees often proved an effective adaptive style. This emotional arousal helped Vietnamese to overcome the passivity of their traditional cultural values and to find better ways to survive and surmount their problems.[94]

Contributing to Vietnamese immigrants' adjustment problem was the federal government's policy of scattering the refugees throughout the United States. Intended as an integration program to accelerate acculturation, it denied the Vietnamese a social and emotional support network of ethnic communities comparable to those developed and used by other immigrant groups. Initially, no mutual-assistance organizations were formed, and early studies showed varying degrees of success in the refugees' adaptation to life in the United States.

Gradually, Vietnamese Americans began to relocate near one another, particularly in California, Texas, Virginia, and New York. Here their concentrations, aided by subsequent "normal" immigration, have led to the development of ethnic neighborhoods and social networks characteristic of first-generation Americans. In Orange County, California, for example, a "Little Saigon" has blossomed where the language, signs, shops, offices, and music all convey a distinctly Vietnamese atmosphere. Similarly, Anaheim now has its own Little Saigon.

As with most immigrant groups, age determines the immigrants' degree of acculturation. The elderly come to be with their families but show little interest in giving up their cultural values or assimilating. Youths find their traditional family values inconsistent with those of the dominant group in U.S. society. Traditionally, Vietnamese parents play a major role in determining their adolescents' social interactions. Vietnamese culture emphasizes achieving one's identity and sense of worth through close relationships with family adults and as a member of an extended family. U.S. adolescents are more autonomous and concerned about peer approval. These ways attract Vietnamese youths, encouraging them to reject parental guidance and enter into situations without parental consent. Intergenerational conflict is thus exacerbated by the gap between the cultural values of the adults and those learned by their children.[95]

Vietnamese—like other Southeast Asians—have lower labor-force participation and median family incomes, higher poverty and unemployment rates, and disproportionate representation in low-skill, low-paying jobs than most East Asian American groups. These economic disadvantages particularly manifest themselves among the refugee population and seem likely to continue, although second- and third-generation Southeast Asians should fare better thanks to their higher education levels and English proficiency.[96]

OTHER SOUTHEAST ASIANS

Cambodians and Laotians, like the Vietnamese, came from the area of Southeast Asia formerly colonized and administered as French Indochina. For centuries prior to the arrival of the French, however, these three groups were linguistically, culturally, and ethnically distinct from one another, and differences exist within each nationality group as well. Of the approximately 1 million Indochinese Americans identified by the 2000 census, about 24 percent were from Laos, 15 percent were from Cambodia (Kampuchea), and 61 percent were from Vietnam.

Thailand, formerly Siam, is another Southeast Asian nation that has sent significant numbers of immigrants to the United States. Although over 131,000 Thai now live in the United States, relatively little has been written about this group,

In a wonderful example of ethnogenesis, these immigrants from Thailand gather together on a suburban backyard patio for a typical American weekend barbecue, using a satay (skewered meat) recipe from their homeland. Their hairstyle and clothing reflect the mixture of cultural influences from their native and adopted lands. (*Source:* © Bob Daemmrich/The Image Works)

except in groupings with other Southeast Asians (see the accompanying Ethnic Experience box).

The Laotians

About 169,000 Laotians now call the United States home. These refugees include several subgroups, including the Tai Dam, over 3,000 of whom live prosperously in Iowa. Most refugees from Laos, however, are the lowland Lao, although more has been written about the Hmong (pronounced *mung* and meaning "free people").

A traditional mountain people living north of the Plain of Jars in Laos, the Hmong had been little exposed to the modern world—Western or Eastern—practicing slash-and-burn farming on hilltops, attributing disease to evil spirits, and relying on the stories of their parents and grandparents for their education. Their belief in spirits includes the idea that a frightening or shameful experience leads to illness caused by the individual spirit fleeing the body. To lock the soul inside so it cannot leave, the Hmong wear copper or silver bracelets, anklets, and necklaces as special protective jewelry.[97]

The Ethnic Experience
The Struggle to Adapt

"*I* came to the U.S. for the adventure. I had heard much about this country and seen many American films. My parents are Chinese and migrated to Thailand about twenty years before I was born. My father is a very successful businessman, having his own lumber business and a few hotels. So I really came here only to satisfy my own curiosity, but I stayed here for my undergraduate and graduate course work and I haven't returned yet.

"It's almost as if I sensed this before I left. I was going to America because I wanted to see that country, but before my parents took me to the airport, I cried. At the airport a lot of people came to say farewell to me and I just waved to them. I had the feeling I would never come back here. Especially when I got into the airplane, I felt that I was losing the things that I really love, and I wanted to get off. It's a very lonely and scary feeling. . . .

"Things seemed strange to me at first. Oriental people all have dark hair. Here I saw many people with different features, with blond hair, brown hair, and so on. At that time they looked funny to me. I had seen some American soldiers in Thailand, but they were a small minority. Now everyone around me was so very different. Another thing was being driven [so fast] on the highways. . . . We have few good highways in Thailand and this was a new experience.

"I can't describe to you how lonely and depressed I was in this country. I at first wished I had never come. The family I stayed with in New Hampshire was friendly and tried to teach me about America, but the language and cultural barriers were overwhelming in those first six or eight months. I was withdrawn because I was afraid of the people and didn't know how to do. Most people were impatient with me and so avoided me. I was sad and didn't like this country, but I felt obliged to my parents to stay for the year even though I was very homesick.

"At the end of the school year I went back home. I discovered I had changed. I was more independent and stubborn, and I enjoyed doing some things that Thai people thought were silly, like getting a suntan. Also, I really wanted to be somebody and make my parents proud, and I thought the best way was to get an education in the U.S. So I came back here and earned my bachelor's degree. This summer I'll finish my master's degree and then I'll go back home to my parents and give them my diplomas. They really belong to my parents because they gave me material and emotional support. I'll come back here . . . and maybe someday be a college professor."

Source: Thai immigrant who came to the United States in 1971 at age 19.

Recruited as U.S. allies during the secret war in Laos in the early 1970s, thousands of Hmong men and boys went to work for the CIA, rescuing downed U.S. pilots, sabotaging communist war supplies, and gathering intelligence on North Vietnamese troop movements. About 15,000 Hmong were killed in combat with the Viet Cong. When communist Pathet Lao forces took control of Laos, the new government systematically attempted to wipe out the Hmong, forcing them to flee.

Many Americans felt a special concern and commitment to the Hmong, and tens of thousands were admitted into the United States as refugees. Coming from a society that had no written language until 40 years ago and no cash economy, the Hmong have faced enormous difficulties in making the quantum leap to living in U.S. society.

Hmong society is patrilineal: the traditional role of the wife is devotion to her husband. An extremely strong extended family and clan system binds the individuals together. This is why, after initially being scattered across the country by the U.S. government, many Hmong have resettled near kin and clan members. Today, 89 percent of the Hmong population in the United States reside in three states: California, Minnesota, and Wisconsin.[98] Although problems of language, economic naiveté, and lack of job skills initially plagued the Hmong, placing a large percentage on welfare, some recent studies suggest that a gradual, successful acculturation has begun.[99]

As the children become "Americanized" adolescents, cultural dissonance typically affects the Hmong family. Parents lack personal experience and role models for dealing with the adolescent experience in the United States, because adolescence as such did not exist in Laos. There, succeeding generations married young and assumed parental responsibilities early. Dating without an adult chaperone, and any overt public display of affection, such as kissing or holding hands in public, violates Hmong tradition. Attracted to the U.S. way of life, Hmong teenagers often challenge their parents' authority on these matters.[100]

Although the Hmong have suffered from poverty since their arrival in the United States, their experience of severe destitution earlier in refugee camps in Thailand appears to have helped them cope. Moreover, they do not expect to stay poor, because they encourage many family members to work, and they show a strong commitment to educating their children.[101]

ETHNOVIOLENCE

A report of the National Asian Pacific American Legal Consortium identified 486 violent incidents against Asian Pacific Americans in 1999, a 57 percent increase in anti-Asian incidents over the previous year.[102] Viewed in isolation, each violent outbreak may seem to be a local incident, but it also may be a symptom of a more pervasive xenophobic fear escalating into a pattern of violence. In the 1980s Vietnamese fishermen were beaten and their boats torched in Texas and California. Tire slashings, windshield smashings, and attempted porch firebombings against Cambodians occurred in Revere, Massachusetts. In Seattle, shots were fired into homes of Southeast Asian refugees. In Detroit an unemployed auto-industry foreman beat Vincent Chin, a 27-year-old Chinese American, to death with a baseball bat enraged because Chin, celebrating his wedding engagement, had had the temerity to stand up to a white man's unprovoked racial slurs. Subsequently, the killer and his accomplice (his 23-year-old son) received lenient sentences and were acquitted of federal civil-rights charges. Soon after, a baseball-bat slaying of an Asian Indian occurred in Jersey City, New Jersey, and other baseball-bat beatings of a Laotian in Philadelphia and of another Asian Indian in Jersey City followed. In May 1993, a Baton Rouge jury acquitted a white man of manslaughter after the man admittedly shot and killed a 16-year-old Japanese exchange student who knocked on his door and whom he allegedly mistook for a housebreaker; this case received extensive coverage in Japan, and the verdict angered many.

In December 1986, a popular black disk jockey in Philadelphia reportedly said on the air that Koreans "suck our blood" and that blacks should "use kerosene" to stop them. That incident led to a public apology by the radio station, but dozens of firebombings of Korean stores in Harlem, Philadelphia, Washington, DC, and in other urban locales ensued.

By the time the May 1992 Los Angeles riots erupted, damaging or destroying about 2,300 Korean-owned stores and causing losses estimated in excess of $400,000, a nationwide pattern of black–Korean conflict was well established.[103] Like Jewish and Italian immigrants before them, thousands of Koreans owned inner-city retail stores, serving as a middleman minority to blacks and Hispanics in virtually every major U.S. city. Working long hours and relying on low-paid family labor to eke out a profit, they succeeded in neighborhoods where many area residents lived a marginal existence.[104]

Black resentment stems partly from the Koreans' ease in borrowing through the *kye* and their mercantile success in black neighborhoods. Blacks accurately complain that Koreans take money out of the community but rarely hire non-Koreans. They also interpret Koreans' limited English and brusque cultural interactions with customers as rudeness. Social distance, economic frustration, envy, alienation, and a sense of being exploited all help explain the racial tensions that erupt into **ethnoviolence.** An increase in the number of inner-city black entrepreneurs and concerted outreach by Korean merchants to the communities they serve would do much to lessen the problem.[105]

Other incidents of harassment, intimidation, graffiti, vandalism, and assault continue to serve as painful reminders of the continuing presence of widespread racism, bigotry, and discrimination. These violent episodes may match the familiar pattern of actions taken against earlier immigrant groups, but that offers no comfort for the victims or for a U.S.-born generation that considers itself more sophisticated and tolerant than past generations.

THE MODEL-MINORITY STEREOTYPE

Since 1966, when William Petersen first praised Asian Americans as a "model minority," the term has become entrenched in the public mind.[106] Images of Chinese engineers, Japanese financiers, Filipino nurses, Korean entrepreneurs, and Vietnamese restaurateurs abound, helping to reinforce this positive stereotype. Asian American educational and economic successes apparently demonstrate that people of color can realize the American Dream through hard work and self-reliance (see Figure 8.3). These achievements are seeming testimony to the possibility of color-free, problem-free, government-intervention–free integration

FIGURE 8.3 Social Indicators of Asian-American Progress (in percentages)

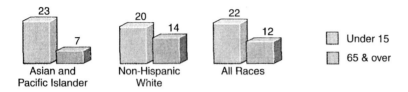

Age

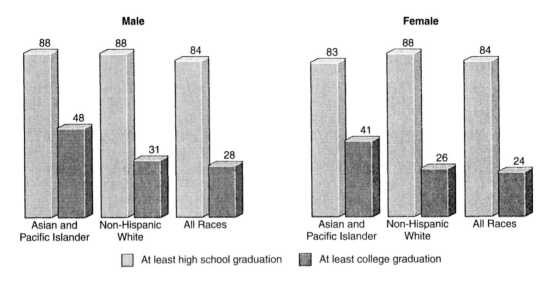

Education (of persons age 25 and over)

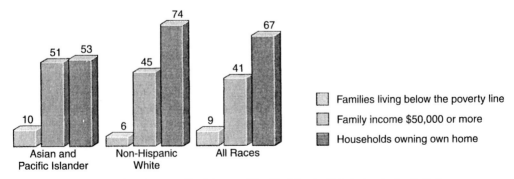

Economic Status

Source: U.S. Bureau of the Census, *The Asian and Pacific Islander Population in the United States,* March 2000.

into U.S. society. Like all stereotypes, however, that of the model minority is misleading and ignores the diversity of the Asian American population:

> Beneath a thick crust of scientists, professionals, and entrepreneurs are thicker
> layers of struggling families—peddlers and waiters and office cleaners and sweater
> stitchers who eke out a bare living by dint of double jobs and the presence of
> multiple wage earners.[107]

Other examples also contradict the stereotype. Many Southeast Asian refugees still require welfare aid. Not all Asian American students are strong academically. The criminal activities of major Asian American drug rings, smaller-scale Asian American extortion gangs, and Asian American youth gangs are seen as an often brutal menace. Some Asian Americans live in crowded dwellings and suffer from tuberculosis or depression, and some live without hope.

The idea of a model minority also creates a harmful and unrealistic example for the dominant group to use as a cudgel to blame others for their difficulties in achieving success. Commentators often unfairly criticize other minority groups for failing to attain comparable levels of achievement, ignoring that much of the success of Asian American youths is attributable to their being (in many cases) children of professionals, as well as to their coming from cultures that have prized educational achievement for many generations. Moreover, through thousands of interviews with Asian Americans, researchers agree that fear is a compelling motive for their intense academic effort; they seek protection against discrimination through academic success.[108]

EAST AND SOUTHEAST ASIAN ASSIMILATION

As with all groups, rates of acculturation and assimilation vary widely both among and within them, depending on various socioeconomic factors and length of residence. We can, however, make a few general observations. Because minority groups have less economic, political, and social power than the societal mainstream, such indicators as income, education, political participation, residential patterns, and intermarriage provide insights into the comparative status of Asian Americans.

As a group Asian Americans have the highest median family income ($55,521 in 2000 compared to $45,904 for whites). They have the lowest poverty rate of all minority groups, one that is only slightly higher than that of whites (12.5 percent versus 10.5 percent in 1999). Over 37 percent have at least a college degree, compared to 25 percent of non-Hispanic whites, 14 percent of blacks, and 8 percent of all Hispanics.[109] These positive indicators suggest substantial progress in the area of civic assimilation.

Citizenship is the first step toward political participation and influence. A greater proportion of Asian immigrants become U.S. citizens than any other immigrant group, a pattern partly influenced by the greater distance between their homelands and the U.S. Although their numbers will not give them the same political muscle as the larger black and Hispanic groups, their influence is growing, as evidenced by the election of Chinese American Gary Locke of Washington as the first Asian governor outside Hawaii.

Residential segregation is an important dimension of social relations between minority- and majority-group members. Although Asian Americans are predominantly concentrated in just a few states and are a mostly urban population, they tend to live in less segregated areas than other minority groups.[110] Moreover, the 2000 census revealed that they are dispersing more and more throughout the United States.

Racial intermarriages do not necessarily indicate complete acceptance between members of two groups, as racial boundaries may still exist despite their meaninglessness to those who do intermarry.[111] Nevertheless, comparative intermarriage statistics can give us some indication of a group's social acceptance, as least with respect to other groups. By 2000, about half of all U.S.-born Asian Americans had a non-Asian spouse, reflecting a growing trend. As more Asian Americans outmarry, future generations of Asian Americans may increasingly blend with other U.S. racial and social groups, mirroring the experience of European ethnic groups in the last century.[112]

Finally, Kyeyoung Park discussed an acculturation pattern found among Korean American families that we could easily apply to most other Asian groups as well.[113] Often the balance of power between generations shifts as older parents become dependent on their children, who must translate for them. Often his more successful younger brothers, who frequently immigrate before him, usurp the position of the esteemed oldest son. Women's labor-force participation in the United States is an important factor in changing relations between husbands and wives and in the capital-accumulation process.

SOCIOLOGICAL ANALYSIS

Some of this chapter's discussion of Asian immigrants has covered events that occurred in previous generations; other parts have focused on the contemporary scene. If we apply the sociological perspective to these individual group chronologies, we find that the time span involved is irrelevant to understanding the continuing patterns of intergroup relations.

The Functionalist View

The Chinese who came to the United States in the 19th century fulfilled important social needs—working on railroads, farms, and ranches and in stores and factories. Their work contributed significantly to the building of a transcontinental transportation system, the manufacture of needed goods, and the provision of valuable services. Although racial antagonism had existed earlier, nationwide economic hard times in the 1870s made the situation much worse. Economic dysfunctions set off intensified labor antagonism, culminating in a system adjustment of immigration restrictions. Despite occasional internal strife, the withdrawal of the Chi-

nese into their Chinatowns helped to promote ethnic solidarity and to offer a social network for their interaction in a hostile white society. Later, these Chinatowns
functioned as absorption centers for tens of thousands of new arrivals, once the
immigration restrictions were lifted.

Japanese, Korean, and Filipino farm laborers, both in Hawaii and on the mainland, helped agriculture expand and prosper. An urbanizing West Coast offered
many domestic and personal-service jobs—jobs filled mostly by Filipinos who
liked city life and its educational opportunities. Major societal dysfunctions—the
trauma of a desperate war begun with a surprise attack and of a severe, long-lasting
depression—triggered negative actions against the Japanese and Filipinos, respectively. Eventually, a restoration of system balance enabled these minority
groups to overcome past discrimination and become more fully assimilated. Problems remaining with Filipino immigrants stem from their unemployment or underemployment and their rapid increase in population, compounded by the
recent recession and the changing occupational structure of society.

Cultural traditions and family cohesiveness have been positive functions easing the adjustment of most East and Southeast Asian immigrants into U.S. society.
Family dysfunctions have also occurred, however, particularly with Americanized
Asian adolescents. These difficulties range from disputes over dating to problems
with self-identity and esteem, leading some Asian youths—unsupervised because
of their parents' working long hours—into gangs.

Korean, Vietnamese, and other Asian refugees allowed U.S. natives to act on
one of their commonly held values—humanitarianism—by opening their doors
to people from war-ravaged lands. Just as the U.S. host society has provided freedom and opportunity for these Asian peoples, so too has the society gained from
their labors and contributions to U.S. culture.

The Conflict View

When employers—railroads, farmers, urban businesses, and Hawaiian plantation
owners—needed inexpensive alien labor, they recruited it and reaped the profits.
When times turned bad, those with power used intergroup ethnic antagonisms to
divide the working class and thereby protect their interests. So it was that the series of electoral victories by the anti-Chinese Workingmen's Party in California
caused the Republican and Democratic political parties to commandeer the anti-
Chinese cause in order to defuse this new political movement. Similarly, white California growers advocated Japanese removal in 1942 to eliminate their competition
in the marketplace. Labor organizations campaigned against the Chinese in the
1870s and against the Filipinos and other groups in the 1930s to prevent their taking increasingly scarce jobs.

Originally applied to the historical example of labor antagonism against the
Chinese, the split-labor-market theory explains the experiences of several other
Asian groups equally well. Coming from low-income countries, Asian workers accepted wages that, although reasonable by their standards, undermined the wage
scale of the native workers. For instance, when the Chinese entered the shoemak-
ing trade extensively in the 1870s, weekly wages in the trade dropped from $25 to

$9. Complaints about unfair competition by Japanese farm laborers included their "willingness" to work for less than whites, or to accept payment in crops or land instead of wages. More recently, white shrimpers burned Vietnamese-owned boats in Galveston Bay, Texas; blacks in Harlem and Brooklyn urged boycotts of Korean stores; Hispanics in Denver housing projects attacked Indochinese refugees; and black–Filipino animosity on the East Coast occasionally manifested itself among medical-service workers competing for certain hospital jobs.

Economic exploitation or competition generates other forms of ethnic antagonism. The Chinatown sweatshops exploit immigrant labor and undermine the position of unionized garment workers, who are further affected adversely by imports from places like Taiwan and Hong Kong. Auto workers and steel workers experience layoffs and job insecurity because of Japanese products. As black, white, and Hispanic workers treat Asian Americans as the enemy, the real culprits are those who benefit most—the sweatshop employers, the corporations that avoid capital-modernization expenditures to maximize profits, and the U.S.-based multinational corporations that establish factories in low-income countries, marketing their products in the United States and elsewhere for higher profits.

The Interactionist View

Westerners have used the word *inscrutable* almost exclusively to describe Asians, especially the Chinese and Japanese. The concept that Asians defy understanding rests on their markedly non-Western physical appearance, language, belief systems, customs, stoicism, and observable behavior. Consistent with the connection between perceived similarity factor and acceptance of strangers, the extreme social distance between native-born U.S. citizens and Asian immigrants becomes understandable. As the groups farthest from the dominant group's interaction patterns, Asians offer easy targets for negative stereotyping, prejudice, scapegoating, and discrimination. Cultural differences become intertwined with physical differences in the minds of many Americans, allowing racism to predominate in value judgments and avoidance–dominance responses.

Asian immigrants in the late 19th and early 20th centuries gave the West Coast an immigrant experience similar to the European migration in the eastern United States. Hispanic Americans and Native Americans were already indigenous to the West, so Asians created the new subcommunities, worked for low wages, and received the scorn and resentment of earlier arrivals. The Asian newcomers were replicating patterns already exhibited by European immigrants in the eastern United States, but people in the West interpreted these as threats to their own economic security and mainstream culture. This social interpretation of reality set in motion the interaction problems that followed. Attitudes translated into actions, setting off reactions and reinforcing attitudes on both sides; thus, the vicious circle intensified and perpetuated the ingroup's perception of the outgroup.

Recent Asian immigrants offer a bipolar model. Those who come from preliterate societies wedded to a tradition of subsistence living face a bewildering leap into an urban society. Schutz's observation, discussed in Chapter 1, that every taken-for-granted situation for the native presents a crisis for the stranger, is overwhelmingly true for many Southeast Asians. Their adjustment and integration into U.S. society may be long and difficult. Other Asians bring education and skills that enable them to enter the economic mainstream more easily. Nonetheless, their racial and cultural differences presently limit their social integration or structural assimilation.

RETROSPECT

A combination of racial and non-Western cultural differences caused a great many Asian immigrants from 1850 to 1940 to remain outside the U.S. mainstream all their lives. Lack of acceptance and social interaction in the dominant society and frequent hostile actions directed against them reinforced the Asians' awareness of the differences in the people and culture around them. Each succeeding wave of Asian immigrants, from whatever country, encountered some degree of hostility because of their racial and cultural visibility. To some Americans, the Asians posed a serious challenge to the cherished notion of a melting pot because of their race, their non-Christian faith (though some were Christians), their language and alphabet, and their customs and practices. That many chose to settle on the West Coast near their port of entry, much as European immigrants had in the East, only underscored their presence and led whites to exaggerate their actual numbers. Many also believed that these immigrants posed an economic threat to U.S. workers, which further encouraged racist reactions.

Many white Americans came to accept negative stereotypes, first about the Chinese and later about the Japanese and Filipinos. Normal ethnocentric judgments about a culturally distinct people, coupled with racial visibility that offered a distinct link to the stereotype, caused generalized societal antagonism toward the Asians. The vast differences in culture and physical appearance, augmented by racist fears and fantasies of threats to economic security or to white womanhood from "lascivious Orientals," led to sporadic outbreaks of violence and a continuing current of hostility.

Until 1940, Japanese Americans were concentrated mostly in rural areas on the West Coast. On the mainland, racist antagonisms and fears culminated in 1942 with the militarily supervised removal of Japanese Americans from their homes and jobs. Although a few Japanese Americans were rounded up in Hawaii, no mass evacuation occurred there because Hawaii presented a less racist environment and offered fuller political and economic participation.

Filipinos, too, encountered overt racial discrimination prior to 1940. Following changes in U.S. immigration law in 1965, over 1.2 million Filipinos have migrated to the United States. Although many are underemployed, they and new arrivals among the Chinese and Japanese encounter less hostility today than did their predecessors.

Koreans, Vietnamese, Cambodians, Laotians, and Thais are more recent East and Southeast Asian immigrants. Some are war refugees, and all come from non-Western cultures and are racially distinct from white and black Americans. They enter a country that is far less racially hostile toward Asians than it historically has been. Many are either dependents of U.S. servicemen or individuals with marketable job skills. Most come from a region of the world where patience, stoicism, quiet industriousness, and the cohesiveness of an extended family are long-standing traditions. These values aid the newcomers' transition to a new life.

Asia is currently the major source outside the western hemisphere of immigrants to the United States. Approximately 40 percent of all immigrants now come from Asia. Obviously, that part of the world is profoundly altering the ethnic composition of the U.S. population. In the years ahead, the United States will become even more a land of racial and cultural diversity.

KEY TERMS

Ethnoviolence	*Kye*	Primogeniture
Exurbs	Miscegenation	Sojourners

REVIEW QUESTIONS

1. Discuss the interrelationship between labor conflict and racism with regard to the Chinese, Japanese, and Filipinos.

2. How did the Chinese immigrants of the late 19th century respond to hostility and discrimination?

3. What explains the different treatment of Japanese Americans in Hawaii and on the mainland during World War II?

4. How do the concepts of "ethnic church" and "middleman minority" apply to Korean Americans?

5. What are some cultural characteristics of Vietnamese Americans?

6. Discuss the legislation and court rulings historically directed against Asian Americans.

7. How do today's Asian immigrants differ from their predecessors? How and why does society respond to them differently?

8. How do the three major sociological perspectives approach the Asian experience in the United States?

SUGGESTED READINGS

Bloom, Barbara Lee. *Immigrants in America: The Chinese-Americans.* Farmington Hills, MI: Lucent Books, 2001.

Despite discrimination and legal exclusion in their early years of labor in the United States, the book recounts how Chinese Americans found success and acceptance.

Bulosan, Carlos. *America Is in the Heart.* Seattle: University of Washington Press, 2000.
A moving autobiography of a Filipino living in California in the 1920s.

Carino, Benjamin V. *The New Filipino Immigrants to the United States.* Honolulu: East-West Center, 1990.
A demographic and socioeconomic profile of recent Filipino newcomers, including their settlement patterns and community life.

Fong, Timothy P. *The First Suburban Chinatown.* Philadelphia: Temple University Press, 1994.
A detailed portrait of the evolution of Monterey Park, east of Los Angeles, into a mostly Chinese American community from a mostly white residential suburb.

Freeman, James M. *Changing Identities: Vietnamese Americans, 1975–1995.* Boston: Allyn and Bacon, 1995.
An ethnographic profile of Vietnamese refugees over a 20-year period, assessing their family transition, education, occupations and changing images.

Kim, Kwang Chung (ed.). *Koreans in the Hood: Conflicts with African Americans.* Baltimore: Johns Hopkins University Press, 1999.
A series of essays offering informative insights into recent conflicts between these two racial groups in Chicago, Los Angeles, and New York City.

Kitano, Harry H. L., and Roger Daniels. *Asian Americans: Emerging Minorities,* 2nd ed. Englewood Cliffs, NJ: Prentice Hall, 1995.
A thorough sociohistorical profile of each of the different Asian peoples who have migrated to the United States.

Min, Pyong Gap. *Caught in the Middle: Korean Communities in New York and Los Angeles.* Berkeley: University of California Press, 1996.
Profiles of Korean life, the middleman role, the social and structural factors underlying Korean–Black hostility, and the effect these conflicts have had on Korean ethnic solidarity.

Ng, Franklin (ed.). *Asian American Family Life and Community.* New York: Garland Publishing, 1998.
Essays examining the role of the family, generational changes, and the significance of kinship, networks, newspapers, and credit associations in various Asian American groups.

Springstubb, Tricia. *Immigrants in America: The Vietnamese-Americans.* Farmington Hills, MI: Lucent Books, 2001.
Portrays how the traditional values of these refugees from war and repression serve them well in retaining their old culture and in playing an increasingly large role in their new culture.

INTERNET LINKS

Go to *http://www.ablongman.com/parrillo* for numerous links relevant to this chapter under "Internet Readings and Exercises."

16

est Asian and Middle Eastern immigrants come from a part of the world situated between the area of Western thought and history on one side and the area of Eastern thought and philosophy on the other (see Figure 9.1). From Turkey through the Middle East to Bangladesh, the Muslim religion predominates, but the cultures are as diverse as elsewhere in the world.

Although some of these peoples immigrated to the United States before 1965 and had encounters similar to those of earlier racial and ethnic groups, most have come since the 1965 Immigration Act. Their acceptance as strangers and their adjustment to U.S. life has differed from the experience of pre-1920 immigrants because structural conditions in both the sending and the host countries have changed. As a result of the occupational-preference ranking adopted by the 1965 legislation, many newcomers are professional, managerial, or technical workers. Some are underemployed, but others have found employment in their occupational roles. Either way, most tend to be isolated from informal social contact with other people outside their nationality group. As with many East and Southeast Asians, the social distance between most first-generation West Asian or Middle Eastern Americans and native-born U.S. citizens is considerable.

SOCIOHISTORICAL PERSPECTIVE

Aside from special legislation of temporary duration allowing political or war refugees to enter the United States, immigration regulations before 1965 effectively limited the number of immigrants from the non-Western world. Because few had migrated to the United

FIGURE 9.1 The Middle East and Central Asia

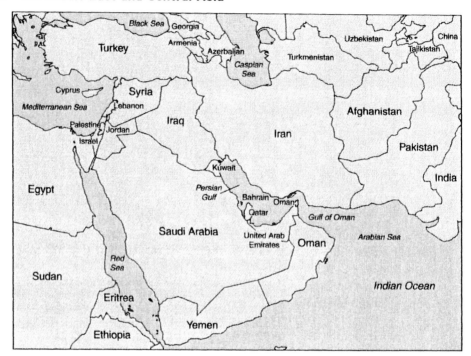

States prior to 1890, the year on which the 1924 immigration legislation based its quotas, very few non-Western immigrants were able to gain approval to migrate to the United States. Eliminating this restrictive national-origins quota system thus opened the door to many different peoples who had previously been denied entry.

Since the 1965 change in the immigration laws, a third major wave of immigration has occurred, again creating dramatic changes in the composition of the nation's population. For example, immigration from India between 1991 and 1999 easily exceeded that from Germany, Ireland, and Italy combined, previously three of the top suppliers of immigrants.[1] The 2000 census count identified over 400,000 foreign-born Arab Americans, a number that exceeds the combined foreign-born population from Greece and Spain.[2]

The Push-Pull Factors

For many non-Western immigrants, overpopulation and poverty so seriously limit the quality of life in their homelands that they seek a better life elsewhere. Sometimes restrictive government actions or limited socioeconomic opportunities push people to look elsewhere. The United States, with its cultural diversity, economic opportunities, and higher living standards, is influential throughout the world and a magnet to those dissatisfied with their situation. For others, the United States offers educational, professional, or career opportunities. Rapid air travel and instant communications, which reduce the psychological distance from a person's native country, are further inducements.

Structural Conditions

The non-Western immigrants discussed in this chapter follow the same patterns as have other ethnic groups who emigrated to the United States. They usually settle in urban areas near their compatriots, with whom they develop close primary social contacts.

Because many are trained professionals or skilled technicians, however, their job situation differs markedly from that of the mostly unskilled poor in the 1880–1920 immigrant groups. They usually do not settle in decaying sections of cities, because with their income they can find better places to live. The economic profile of these non-Western Americans ranges from the older and more affluent to the newer and struggling. Some are suburbanites, some live in working-class urban neighborhoods, and others cope with poverty. Wherever they congregate to live and work, various support facilities have arisen: churches or temples, grocery stores and restaurants specializing in native foods, social clubs or organizations, and perhaps their own schools and newspapers. They soon send for other members of their family or write home telling of their good fortune, prompting others to come to the United States. The chain-migration pattern of earlier immigrants recurs.

Many of the new immigrants do not fit the acculturation patterns that worked for other immigrant groups. For instance, prosperity in oil-rich Middle Eastern countries and the Western world's generalization of Arabs as a single group not only have strengthened that group's ethnic solidarity in the United States but also have encouraged some to plan to return to their native country eventually. A Saudi Arabian, for example, might return from the United States after acquiring an advanced education or experience that will permit a better life back home. Saudi Arabia collects no taxes whatsoever and offers free education and medical care, and its standard of living is improving rapidly. Although the number of immigrants from Saudi Arabia may be extremely low, a greater number of newcomers from other Arab countries are seeking permanent residence in the United States, as Table 9.1 indicates.

Because many members of this group of non-Western immigrants have marketable skills, they can obtain professional and salaried jobs without first having to adopt a subservient role in the economy. They need not yield to pressures to assimilate fully to gain middle-class respectability. Their income is high enough to enable them to enjoy the lifestyle they want, and as a result they are free to continue their own cultural behavior patterns. Some Americanization undoubtedly occurs, but these first-generation immigrants do not have to make substantial cultural sacrifices in order to "make it" in U.S. society.

Another sizable segment of non-Westerners in the United States consists of nonimmigrant (sojourner) students, workers, and businesspeople. Although they usually remain for only two to five years, their growing numbers make their

TABLE 9.1   **Arabic Immigrants Admitted to the United States**

Country	1971–1980	1981–1990	1991–2000
Algeria	1,123	1,511	6,326
Egypt	25,495	34,259	46,714
Iran	46,152	165,267	112,597
Iraq	23,404	22,211	40,749
Jordan	29,578	36,032	38,749
Lebanon	33,846	45,770	43,469
Morocco	4,431	7,158	20,442
Saudi Arabia	700	4,180	7,716
Syria	13,339	22,230	26,109
Yemen	5,170	5,634	16,319

Source: Adapted from U.S. Immigration and Naturalization Service Annual Report. *Statistical Yearbook 2000* (Washington, DC: U.S. Government Printing Office, 2002), Table 3.

presence a matter of significant concern in the field of race and ethnic relations. In 1998, for example, nearly 302,000 Asian students arrived in the United States to study, and about 995,000 Asians came to this country as temporary business visitors.[3]

In many respects these temporary visitors—visible to others in work, residential, shopping, and entertainment settings—resemble U.S. citizens who work for multinational corporations overseas. Even if assigned to another country for a considerable number of years, they seldom lose their sense of ethnic or national identity. They live within the culture and enjoy the available opportunities without contemplating abandoning their own cultural ties and becoming assimilated in the host country. Many aliens working in the United States have no interest in U.S. citizenship or assimilation, whether they work for one of their own country's multinational corporations or for some U.S. employer. Today's sojourners may be more sophisticated than their predecessors, but their resistance to assimilation is just as strong. At the same time, however, other non-Western immigrants are highly motivated to become part of U.S. society, as demonstrated by the fact that, among immigrants admitted since 1982, those from Cambodia, China, India, Korea, Laos, the Philippines, Taiwan, and Vietnam were proportionately higher than most other countries in becoming U.S. citizens.[4]

Societal Reaction

About 5,000 Asian Indians and 325,000 Middle Easterners migrated to the United States between 1880 and 1920. These early arrivals encountered far more prejudice and discrimination in the United States than their compatriots do today. Americans are now more tolerant of the differences in appearance and customs of non-Western immigrants. Terrorist attacks on September 11, 2001, in New York City and Washington, DC, however, increased suspicions about Arab Muslims, although their social acceptance remains fairly strong (see Table 1.1). People do categorize others and make judgments based on visible impressions, and this often leads to stereotyping. Distinguishing racial features and distinctive apparel, such as a dashiki, turban, or sari, set the newcomers apart. Although little overt discrimination occurs, limited social interaction takes place in most cases.

In recent surveys of social distance among various minority groups, racially distinct non-Western immigrants scored at the bottom, most notably Arab and Muslim Americans since September 11, 2001.[5] Many newcomers find themselves accepted in their professional, managerial, and technical occupational roles by members of the dominant society, but excluded from outside social activities. Once the workday or work week ends, they seldom receive social invitations from dominant-group members; thus they interact mostly with family and compatriots. Economic mainstreaming may have occurred for many non-Western immigrants, but they have yet to achieve social integration.

THE ASIAN INDIANS

Emigration from India to the United States happened in two distinct phases. In the early 20th century, several thousand poorly educated Indian agricultural laborers migrated to the West Coast and settled in rural regions in Washington (lumbering) and California (agriculture). Almost all the early immigrants were Sikh males who came from the Punjab region of northern India. Distinctive in their traditionally worn beards and turbans, they soon experienced hostile racism and violent attacks. In the 1970s and 1980s, a second group of immigrants—many of them provisioned with substantial monetary capital and "cultural capital" in terms of college education or professional training—arrived. Since the 1980s, less educated relatives of earlier immigrants have come, typically entering such family-owned businesses as groceries, motels, and newspaper stores, or driving taxis or limos.[6]

Early Immigrants

Between 1820 and 1900, fewer than 800 immigrants came to the United States from India. In the next two decades, a small wave of almost 7,000 agricultural laborers from northern India journeyed to the West Coast of the United States, and still others entered Canada. Almost entirely male, this group—like so many other immigrant groups—intended to accumulate some savings and then return home. Between 1908 and 1920, a total of 1,656 did leave, and another 249 were deported as undesirable aliens.[7]

This Sikh businessman is among the tens of thousands of non-Western professionals who have migrated to the United States in recent years. Their marketable skills—of great value to the U.S. economy—enable them to earn good incomes and to enjoy a comfortable, middle-class lifestyle, often in a suburban setting, thereby enriching their neighborhood by increasing its cultural heterogeneity.
(*Source:* © Peter Menzel/Stock, Boston)

Societal Reaction

Even though the Japanese, Chinese, and Filipinos far outnumbered the Asian Indians, the latter, too, experienced discrimination and dominant-group aggression because of their visibility and identification as Asians. Near a lumber camp in Bellingham, Washington, on September 5, 1907, several hundred whites raided the living quarters of Indian workers, forcing about 700 of them to flee across the Canadian border. Two months later, in Everett, Washington, several hundred whites drove the Indian workers out of town. Racial prejudice manifested itself also in Port Angeles, Washington, where real estate brokers published in the local newspaper the terms of their covenant not to sell to "Hindoos or Negroes." They justified their action on the ground that wherever these groups settle, they "have depreciated [the] value of adjacent property and injured the reputation of the neighborhood, and are generally considered as undesirable."[8]

The San Francisco–based Asiatic Exclusion League quickly included Asian Indians among its targets and warned the public that these people were a "menace." League officials declared that the East Indians were untrustworthy, immodest, unsanitary, insolent, and lustful.[9] National hostility toward Asian Indians during the period from 1908 to 1910 led immigration officials to reject 1,130 would-be immigrants from India at their ports of entry. Pro-immigration pressure from the Western Pacific Railroad in 1910 enabled 1,462 of them to enter between 1911 and 1920, but another 1,762 were denied entry, mostly on grounds that they would become public charges.[10] The popular magazine *Collier's*, influenced by the Asiatic Exclusion League's exaggerated claim that 10,000 Asian Indians already lived in California, printed an article warning its readers about the "Hindu invasion."[11] *Hindu* was a popular ethnic epithet for Indians in those days, undoubtedly used because so much of the Indian subcontinent (including 80 percent of India's population today) was Hindu. However, these immigrant victims were mostly Sikhs, a religious minority people composing just 2 percent of present-day India's population.

> In this atmosphere of marked hostility toward Asians, the few thousand East Indians gradually established themselves primarily in California and relied chiefly on agriculture as a means of livelihood. Typically the Indians sought work in groups with a leader serving as their agent in negotiating with employers. Owing in part to the desire of many farmers to break the Japanese monopoly on the labor supply in those areas, they had little difficulty finding employment in the Sacramento and San Joaquin valleys. Also, Indians moved into the Imperial Valley, another rapidly growing agricultural area.[12]

In 1923 the U.S. Supreme Court reversed previous lower-court decisions and ruled that Asian Indians were nonwhites and thus ineligible for citizenship under the terms of the 1790 Naturalization Act. The government then revoked naturalization certificates that had previously been granted to 60 or 70 Asian Indians. The decision also prevented Asian Indians in California from owning or leasing land in their own names because state legislation prohibited alien landholding. The Asian Indians thus became itinerant farm laborers. Few of them had any family life because of the migrant nature of their work and the lack of women they could marry.

Minority Response

Juan Gonzales, Jr., points out that the social and economic restrictions imposed by discriminatory immigration and **miscegenation** laws created and magnified the social isolation of the early immigrants. Unable to travel, send for wives or future brides, or marry women outside their own group, East Indian immigrants could neither participate fully in U.S. society nor produce a second generation of U.S. citizens to aid their movement into the mainstream of American life.[13]

About 3,000 Asian Indians returned home between 1920 and 1940. A few hundred more were deported. The population dwindled from 5,441 in 1920 to 3,138 in 1930 and to 2,405 in 1940.[14] A few of those who remained married Mexican American women. Most, however, lived in communal groups apart from the rest of society. Some Sikhs congregated in Stockton, California—the site of a large Filipino community—and built a temple there for worship.

In July 1946 the Luce–Celler Bill removed Asian Indians from the "barred zone" established in 1917 to prevent most Asians and Pacific Islanders from immigrating to the United States. Thenceforth, 100 Asian Indians could enter annually. In addition, males already living here could bring over their wives and children or make marital arrangements with women living in the old country. Finally, Asian Indians were permitted to become naturalized citizens, an opportunity taken by 1,772 of them between 1948 and 1965.[15]

By the mid-1950s, Gary R. Hess reports, the Asian Indian community in Sutter County in north-central California numbered about 900 and had grown stronger and more unified.[16] This came about because the men preferred to marry Asian Indian women and because the caste system in India had a negligible influence in the United States, except perhaps in terms of status. Because they rarely intermarried and they retained important aspects of their culture, the rural Asian Indians, Hess concluded, remained only slightly acculturated even though they had adopted certain material comforts, dress, and other features of life in the United States.

Physical appearance was an important factor setting these immigrants apart. In the early 20th century, the full beards prescribed by the Sikh religion were not fashionable. Moreover, all the men wore turbans and were sometimes belittled as "ragheads." The Indian women who arrived before the Depression—like those who have arrived since the more liberal Immigration Act of 1965—were quite distinct in wearing the *sari,* a lightweight outer garment with one end wrapped about the waist and the other draped over the shoulder or covering the head. Most cultural differences—appearance, food taboos, and social interaction—were an integral part either of the Hindu caste system or of the Sikh religion in India. Therefore, Asian Indians not only seemed strange to non-Indian U.S. natives but had difficulty assimilating because they were reluctant to abandon their customs and practices.

Recent Immigrants

Statistics reveal a dramatic change in the number of immigrants from India. Only 15,513 entered the United States over the 65-year period from 1901 to 1965. In the next 5 years, that total was easily surpassed: 24,587 immigrated between 1966 and 1970. Then the immigrant totals sky-rocketed: about 164,000 newcomers from India arrived in the 1970s; 251,000 in the 1980s; and 324,000 between 1991 and 1999.[17] The Asian Indian presence is now substantial, with a nearly 1.7 million in 2000—more than twice the number in 1990. Now the third largest Asian American population, 35 percent of all Asian Indians live in the Northeast, 24 percent in the South, 23 percent in the West, and 18 percent in the Midwest.[18]

Of the post-1965 immigrants from India, the largest number have been Hindu-speaking, followed by Gujarati, Punjabi, and Bengali speakers. Ethnic Asian Indians also emigrate from East Africa and Latin America, particularly from the Caribbean islands and British Guyana, where earlier generations had immigrated as indentured plantation laborers.[19]

The Immigration Act of 1965 alone does not explain the increase in Asian Indian migration. Conditions in India are another important factor. India is the world's second most populous country after mainland China, with 16 percent of the world's population occupying 2.5 percent of the world's land mass. The population density is nearly 11 times greater in India than in the United States.

The problem of overpopulation is quite serious. India's population has grown from 439 million in 1960, to over one billion in 2001. The rapid rise is not due to any increase in the birth rate but to a decline in the mortality rate. Even so, 1 million of the 18 million babies born in India each year die before they reach their first birthday, and about 500,000 more from every cohort die before they complete childhood. Hundreds of thousands of people die annually from infectious or parasitic diseases contracted from contaminated water and other unsanitary conditions in a country where the life expectancy at birth is only 60 years for males and 61 for females.[20] Nevertheless, the population is increasing by about 1.5 million people each month.

With over three fifths of the population engaged in agriculture, a literacy rate of 66 percent among males and 38 percent among females, and problems of severe poverty, hunger, and inadequate resources, India offers many of its citizens little economic security. However, many recent immigrants to the United States have been professional workers such as physicians, dentists, teachers, and skilled workers—the very people India needs most to retain if the quality of life there is to improve. Most developing nations face this **brain-drain** problem.

With their education and occupational skills, many of these newcomers achieve economic security, but also experience cultural strains. For example, they are uneasy with the sexual mores in the United States. Parents have considerable difficulty convincing their children that the Indian custom of not dating before an arranged marriage has merit. Although some second-generation Indian young people still yield to their parents' traditional prerogative to arrange marriages, this is one area where **ethnogenesis** is apparent. Most young people tolerate their parents' introduction to eligible mates but insist that the final choice is entirely their own.[21]

About 68 percent of all newly admitted Asian Indians pursue professional or managerial occupations.[22] The others typically operate convenience stores, gas stations, or family-managed hotels and motels. In fact, as Indian ownership of such establishments now approaches 20 percent across the land, they have found a family-labor economic niche as ubiquitous as the Korean greengrocery.[23] (See the accompanying International Scene box for a description of their jobs in South Africa.)

Racial ambiguity marks the Asian Indian acceptance pattern. The skin colors of Asian Indians range from light brown to almost black, although most of the U.S. immigrants are of a light hue. Americans perceive them as racially different but have difficulty categorizing them. Defined as "white" sometimes, "Asian" at other times, and "brown" or "black" at still other times, Asian Indians tend to classify themselves as "white" and identify with the majority group (see the accompanying Ethnic Experience box).[24]

ARAB AMERICANS

Arab is a broad term covering people of diverse nationalities, religions, and socioeconomic backgrounds. Although Arab Americans may share a sense of peoplehood, they come from 22 nations of North Africa and the Middle East. Not

The International Scene
Asian Indians in South Africa

*O*f the 43.4 million people living in South Africa, over 1 million are Asian Indians. They are mostly descendants of laborers recruited since the 1860s to work on the sugar estates or of traders who migrated before enactment of restrictive immigration laws in the early 20th century.

Their heritage of struggling against white oppression began a century ago with the arrival of a young lawyer named Mohandas Gandhi. His efforts to improve the circumstances of his compatriots living in South Africa led to the development of his strategy of *satyagraha*, or nonviolent mass defiance of discriminatory laws, later used in India's independence struggle. In 1894, Gandhi became the first secretary of the Natal Indian Congress (NIC); and before returning to India in 1914, he won concessions from Afrikaner leaders on taxes, marriage law, and rights of movement. In many respects, the NIC served as a model for the African National Congress (ANC), whose leader Nelson Mandela became president of South Africa when majority rule was finally achieved.

The infamous Group Areas Act in 1950 forced 75,000 Indians and 8,500 "Coloured" (mixed-race people) to vacate what had become valuable inner suburban land for more distant settlements with rudimentary services. When the ANC was banned in 1960 and its leaders arrested or exiled, Indian leaders and the NIC played a key role in keeping the ANC

together. By the 1980s their political alliance was indicated by the presence of 8 Indians on the 50-member ANC executive council.

As a middleman minority, the Indians fared better than the indigenous Africans, moving into middle-echelon jobs in accounting, sales, banking, and factory management, as well as becoming owners of many business and service enterprises. Their success has generated some African resentment and hostility. Violent attacks in 1992 against Indian businesses in black areas forced their owners to sell out and move back to major cities.

In postapartheid South Africa, the economic success of Indians continue to cause tension. Polls in 1994 showed that the majority of Indian voters, a group that had previously supported the ANC, now leaned toward the National Party. This conservative shift has been attributed to an Indian fear of losing economic power to the growing black business class.

Finding themselves both courted and pressured by various black and white political factions, South Africa's Indians guardedly approach an uncertain future in a turbulent land.

Critical thinking question: How similar or dissimilar is the Asian Indian experience in the United States compared to that in South Africa today?

surprisingly, many cultural differences separate them from one another, and their ethnic identities remain rooted in their nationalities and specific homelands.

Over 1 million Arab Americans live in the United States. About half descended from immigrants who arrived between 1880 and 1940, and the rest immigrants or

The Ethnic Experience
Values, Identity, and Acceptance

"You ask me if I came here to settle down. Yes, I came here to settle down. I changed myself a lot. I cut my hair. I took my sari off and I wore skirts and dresses. I dressed all-American. So it hurt to go outside and have people ask, 'Are you Indian?' We don't ask a white person, 'Are you French, British, Polish?' We are all Americans.

"I made a choice when I came to this country. My choice was to become an American citizen, and I have become one. I think we are wrong going into all these labels of cultural heritage. Our main goal is to keep America strong—America No. 1. And we can do that by communicating with each other; and in order to communicate and understand each other, we need to have one channel of culture and language.

"And it is difficult for us to forget about India because it is part of our culture. I spent 29 years there. I consider India as my mother—my womb. It gave me birth and my values. America is my father: It gave me my dream. They are both equally important. Maybe my children won't have to fight bigotry if we stop putting these labels on government forms, job applications, and on television. We must stop that. We should want to help people be part of us. We are Americans of Asian heritage. As long as they don't classify us, it will be easier for our children to be all Americans.

"My children are completely Americanized. I believe when in Rome, do as the Romans. I never forced on them the Indian language. In fact, they don't speak one word of the Indian language. They are very strong with Indian values, but I don't think they are Indian values alone. Those are universal values. Every American, Indian, Chinese, Japanese, Black, Puerto Rican—no matter what nationality you are, what racial group, all parents want that their children are well behaved, go to school, have good careers, don't hang out in the street and get into drugs or other trouble. I don't think the values are, you know, set for any one ethnic group. I don't find any American mother different from any Indian mother.

"The news media plays a very big role in spreading diversity. I'll give you an example. Every news media on television labels a person Black, White, Indian, and so on. Why? We are all Americans!

"What happened with my older daughter, who graduated college, was people kept asking her all the time, 'Are you Indian?' 'Are you Indian?' 'Are you Indian?' And then, at the age of 22, she turned around and said, "Hey, gee, if they're always asking me if I'm Indian, why don't I think about India, find something out about India. And if you're going to see after 50 years, different pockets of different ethnic groups, we too have to blame our own television media and our news media. If we keep giving people labels then, I don't know what is going to happen in America in the future."

Source: Asian Indian woman who came to the United States in 1970 at age 29.

descendants of immigrants who arrived after World War II. Over 250,000 Arab Americans live in southeastern Michigan, giving that area one of the largest concentrations of Arabs outside the Middle East.

Dearborn, Michigan, a suburb of Detroit, became a favorite destination of many working-class Arab immigrants after the 1967 Arab–Israeli war. Several thousand Muslim Palestinians, Yemenis, and southern Lebanese arrived there, making it today the largest Muslim community in the United States. Because of the concentration of so many first-generation Arab Americans, Dearborn today resembles more completely a "Little Arabia" than any other Arab American community. Nearby Detroit suburbs, such as Livonia, house large numbers of middle-class Arab Americans.

Despite the concentration of Arab Americans in cities of the Midwest (Cleveland, Chicago, and Toledo, in addition to the Detroit metropolitan area), an even greater proportion live in the Northeast. About 40 percent of all Arab Americans live in the Northeast, compared to about 28 percent in the Midwest, 20 percent in the South, and 12 percent in the West. Arab Americans in the Northeast are more likely to be U.S.-born, whereas those in the West are more likely to be immigrants. Different Arab subgroups are fairly evenly dispersed, although Saudi Arabians are concentrated in the West, Assyrians in the Midwest, and Syrians in the Northeast.[25]

Social Organization

Many of today's Arab Americans are sophisticated, cosmopolitan people whose lifestyle matches that of other middle- or working-class U.S. citizens. Like many other past and present immigrant groups, Arab Americans have established institutions to help preserve their cultural heritage, strengthen their ethnic identity, and unite the community. More than four dozen Arabic newspapers and some 50 Arabic radio programs broadcast in such cities as Chicago, Detroit, New York, and San Francisco, aid in this effort. Religious and community organizations provide important emotional, social, and financial services to help sustain the Arab community. Among professional organizations, two of the better known are the National Association of Arab Americans and the Association of Arab American University Graduates.

As with most immigrant groups, kinship links play an important role in stabilizing community life.[26] Exchanges of letters, gifts, and family visits help maintain bonds between the immigrants and their relatives back home. Another important element is belief in an integrated economic family unit. Family members pool their income and resources in a common fund for all to share, even if the family is dispersed. Each month many Arab Americans send vast amounts of money overseas to their relatives, helping them buy land, build homes, or purchase modern agricultural equipment such as tractors, plows, and irrigation pumps. Ironically, greater acculturation appears to be associated positively with satisfaction with life in the United States, but negatively with family satisfaction.[27] Perhaps marginality and the clash of values contribute to this outcome.

Enjoying a slice of pizza, these children of Arab immigrants, like most immigrant children, will likely acculturate more rapidly than their parents. Through the impact of the media, schools, and everyday life, and with their ability to learn a new language more easily than adults can, they will identify more closely with the land where they grow up than with the land of their parents' youth.
(*Source:* © Steven Rubin/The Image Works)

Residential Patterning

Arab Americans are repeating the pattern of many earlier European immigrants by settling almost exclusively in urban areas. Whereas only about 75 percent of the U.S. population lives in urban areas, 91 percent of all Arab Americans are urban. Arab immigrants are even more likely to reside in urban areas (97 percent) than are U.S.-born Arab Americans (87 percent).[28] Some first-generation Arab Americans live in recognizable ethnic neighborhoods in close proximity to one another, but others adopt slightly more dispersed residential patterns.

In an extensive field study of almost 6,000 Arab immigrants living in the Paterson, New Jersey, metropolitan area, my investigators and I found them to be a religiously diverse group: 34 percent Moslem, 30 percent Orthodox Christian, 25 percent Melkite Catholic, and 10 percent Protestant.[29] Lebanese refugees, mostly of the middle class, tended to live in nearby suburbs; and Circassians, Jordanians, Palestinians, and Syrians lived on the northern and southern peripheries of the city, spilling over into adjacent exurbs. This pattern of Arab immigrants settling on the edges of cities instead of in historically inner areas or transition zones has been found in other U.S. cities, too.[30]

In the Paterson area, we found that a few families would live fairly close to one another, but that the next grouping would be situated several blocks away. Nevertheless, a shared sense of community and frequent interactional patterns existed. Ethnic solidarity was maintained through a cosmopolitan network of communication and life-cycle rituals, homeland concerns, political activism, or limited social situations (work, school, and nearby families). Instead of maintaining a territorial ethnic community as other immigrant groups have, Arab immigrants maintain an interactional community.

In the Paterson study, racial composition of the neighborhood did not appear to be a factor in choice of residence or desire to relocate. No interracial tensions or conflicts were reported; Arab Americans shared a common assumption that those who lived where they did—white or black—were respectable people. Coming from a part of the world steeped in religious rather than racial prejudices, Arab Americans appear to be unconcerned about racial differences in the more secular society of the United States.

Fighting Stereotypes and Group Blame

Any discussion of Arab American problems with stereotyping or violence must distinguish conditions before and after September 11, 2001, the day of major terrorist attacks on the United States. Although Islamic radicals committed these atrocities, some Americans saw little distinction between those radicals and anyone identified as Arab, Muslim, or both.

Before those attacks films and television shows rarely portrayed Arabs as ordinary people. More often, they were oil-rich billionaires or cold-blooded terrorists. They ranged from broadly stereotypical TV wrestling villains as Abdullah the Butcher to cartoon villains such as Ali Boo-Boo, the desert rat in a Heckle and Jeckle animated feature. In the 1987 film *Wanted Dead or Alive,* starring Gene Simmons of the rock group Kiss, an Arab terrorist conspired with Arab Americans to poison the people of Los Angeles. The 1992 Disney film *Aladdin* gave the villainous Jaffar a distinctly Arabic accent, whereas Aladdin and Jasmine sound like typical U.S. teenagers. In *Martial Law* (1999), Middle Eastern terrorists detonate bombs in New York City and the federal government forces all Arab and Muslim Americans into detention camps.

Such widespread media portrayals have a cumulative, conditioning effect, and it is not a positive one. Adding to their difficulty in overcoming these stereotypical perceptions, Arab Americans have had to dissociate themselves from real-life terrorism. Bombings of the World Trade Center in 1993 and of U.S. embassies in Africa in 1998 caused the Arab American community some anxiety about the potential stigmatizing of all Arabs for the violent acts of just a few radicals.

The mass destruction and killing of nearly 4,000 people in attacks on the World Trade Center and Pentagon shocked everyone, including Arab Americans, many of whom had migrated here to get away from violence in their homelands. Although most Americans did not assign group blame, anti-Arab invective and sporadic acts of violence did occur. Such actions were remindful of the backlash that many Irish Americans felt in the 1870s over the terrorist activities of the Molly Maguires, or that many immigrants experienced when a bomb exploded in the midst of police officers at an immigrant labor rally at Haymarket Square in Chicago in 1886. Perhaps though, it is a tribute to the increased tolerance of U.S. society of 2001 that there were no calls for an action similar to that taken against Japanese Americans in 1942 after the bombing of Pearl Harbor.

However, it became more difficult to be an Arab American. Wanting to fly anywhere made one an immediate subject of intense scrutiny. Verbal abuse, vandalism, and physical attacks occurred.[31] Because some hijackers had lived in communities a year or more, many first-generation Arab Americans found their loyalties questioned. Ingroup–outgroup boundaries solidified more between Arab and other Americans, as reported in the 2001 social-distance survey discussed in Chapter 1.

Presented with so much negative stereotyping and suspicions, one might falsely conclude that predominantly Arab nations are our enemy. In fact, the United States maintains friendly relations with 19 or 21 such countries, and most were allies during Operation Desert Storm in 1991. The million-plus Arab Americans living in the United States are normal human beings pursuing the American Dream, but the media seldom report that. Failure to grasp the humanity of the Arab people increases the social distance between non-Arabs and Arabs.

THE SYRIAN/LEBANESE

A number of factors have contributed to a confusion of ethnic identities and a lack of accurate official U.S. statistics regarding immigrants from Syria and Lebanon. In the late 19th and early 20th centuries, the entire Arabian peninsula and the lands directly north of it were part of the Ottoman Empire; and its inhabitants were Turkish citizens until the end of World War I. Although much cultural diversity existed in this geographic region, all the inhabitants spoke Arabic and, except for the Sinai Egyptians, used the term *Syrian* to identify themselves. Still, the immigrants had Turkish passports; U.S. officials therefore identified them as Turkish until 1899, when a separate category for Syrians was begun. Although approximately 85 percent of the immigrants came from the area now known as Lebanon, only in the 1930s did the term *Lebanese* gain acceptance. Some Lebanese resisted the change in designation, preferring to continue calling themselves Syrians, whereas some people from what is now Syria began calling themselves Lebanese.

Ethnic Identity

In the past, Arab Americans tended to identify themselves by family name, religious sect, and village of origin. Rarely did they cross religious or village lines to set up common organizations. Instead, social clubs and fraternal organizations had a clannish focus, often leading to factionalism within the community. Neither political authority nor specific regional residence determined group affinity; rather, religion defined the goals and boundaries of the "Syrian" community:

> Theological differences of Jews, Christians and Moslems have become translated into social and structural realities with each community becoming socially separate from the others. What the people believe is not so important as the fact that people who believe similarly are considered to belong to some social order qualitatively different from that of the rest. Since religion deals with things of primary importance, a different religious persuasion turns others into members of a somewhat distinct society or "nation."
>   . . . Since the religions of the Middle East were all structurally and socially separate from one another, the Jewish community and the immigrant Moslem and Christian community continued this pattern of separation in the United States.[32]

Migration and Settlement

Although religious differences kept the three groups separate, the push–pull factors that led them to emigrate to the United States affected them similarly. Essentially, a combination of harsh living conditions—hunger, poverty, and disease—and Turkish oppression, particularly of Christians, led many Syrians to leave. The pull of the United States was the result of reports by missionaries and steamship agents of economic opportunities and religious and political freedom. Emigration to the United States began in the 1870s, reaching an estimated 100,000 between 1890 and 1914 as the harshness of Turkish rule increased. The peak years were 1913 and 1914, when more than 9,000 migrated to avoid conscription into the Turkish army, then being prepared for combat in World War I.

A seven-block area along Washington and Rector streets in lower Manhattan became a thriving Syrian community during the late 19th century. Other Syrians settled in downtown Brooklyn and elsewhere throughout the entire country. Most Syrian immigrants came either from cities or from densely populated villages; they usually chose to reside in U.S. cities of 100,000 or more and had little difficulty adjusting to urban life.

Between 1890 and 1895, the New York community established three Arab Christian churches: Melkite, Maronite, and Eastern Orthodox. Before then, Syrians had simply joined U.S. churches. Maronites and Melkites usually became Roman Catholics; members of the Eastern Orthodox Church generally became Episcopalians.[33]

Culture Conflicts

Newly arrived Syrians often replaced departing Irish American residents in old city neighborhoods. This is an example of the sociological concept of **invasion–succession,** in which one group experiencing vertical mobility gradually moves out of its old neighborhood. It is then replaced by another group living at the previous residents' original socioeconomic level. Sometimes hostility develops between the old and new groups. In the case of the Syrians, religious tension resulted in a clash with the Irish, as this 1920 account about the Dublin District of Paterson, New Jersey, reveals:

> When the Syrians came to live there, the rentals became higher. This caused hard feelings between the Irish and the Syrians, which developed into a feud between the two nationalities. The fight started in the saloon on Grand and Mill Streets, first with bitter arguments and harsh words, and then threatening fist fights. From the saloon, the fight came out to the streets. It was like two armies in opposition facing each other. . . . The police force was called in to put an end to this fight. All they could do was to throw water on them to disperse them. These fights continued for three days in the evening. Finally, a committee of Syrians went to talk to Dean McNulty of St. John's, explaining to him that they were Christians coming from the Holy Land, not Mohammedans or Turks, as the Irish used to call them. They were good Catholics and they wanted to live in peace with everybody. Then the good Dean, at Sunday masses, urged the Irish to stop fighting with the Syrians, who were like them, Catholics. He succeeded in stopping this fighting better than the police.[34]

Another problem the Syrian immigrants encountered before World War I was racial classification. In 1909, the U.S. District Court in St. Louis ruled them ineligible for naturalization on the basis of the 1790 legislation, declaring them to be nonwhite. Many Syrian Christians were blond and blue-eyed, but the racial barrier was determined by their country of origin. The Circuit Court of Appeals reversed this decision. Shortly thereafter, the matter was again raised, this time in the U.S. District Court in New York, which ruled that they could be naturalized.

Early Patterns

Syrian males usually came alone and then sent for their wives and children. Although poor, most were literate and insisted that their children complete primary school. Married Syrian women were more emancipated and less dependent on their husbands than were their counterparts in other ethnic groups at that time. Both mother and children—after they completed grade school—worked together for the family's economic welfare. The family structure proved to be an important factor in the Syrians' economic success.

Generally Syrians preferred to work as traders and shopkeepers because trading was a time-honored occupation in their native land. Many Syrians became peddlers and traveled throughout the United States, bringing essential and exotic goods to far-flung communities. In the late 19th and early 20th centuries, such peddlers filled an economic need and were welcome visitors to remote homes and communities. About one in three Syrian men became peddlers; others tried various commercial ventures, started restaurants, or, in a few cases, worked in factories.

The choice of peddling by so many Syrians expedited their acculturation. It took them into U.S. homes, quickly teaching them the hosts' language and customs. It prevented their cultural isolation by way of ghetto settlement patterns, instead dispersing them throughout the country. By 1914, most Syrian peddlers had switched to being shopkeepers, with the majority operating dry-goods or grocery stores.

Upward Mobility

Syrian Americans achieved economic security quickly, often in the first generation. This is especially significant because fewer than one fourth of those who came were professional or skilled workers. Aiding them in their adjustment, acceptance, and upward mobility were (1) wide dispersal, negating any significant opposition to their presence; (2) business expertise and self-employment, which allowed them greater rewards; and (3) cultural values of thrift, industriousness, and investment that were comparable to the middle-class values of the host society:

> Even while they were still in the lower income brackets and in working class occupations, the "Syrians" displayed the social characteristics of the middle classes in American urban centers. Studies of these Arab immigrants in Chicago, Pittsburgh and the South reveal a common pattern: low crime rates, better than average health, higher I.Q.'s, and more regular school attendance among the children, few intermarriages and divorces.[35]

Coming from a country in which nearly every man owned the house he lived in, determined to be independent, and highly motivated to succeed, the Syrians accumulated money rapidly and invested it either in property or in business ventures. By 1911, Syrians worked in almost every branch of commerce, including banking and import–export houses, and the government reported that their median income was only slightly lower than the $665 annual income of the adult native-born male.

> Unlike other immigrant groups who had to wait two or three generations to exert their independence from ghetto life and to satisfy their desire for mobility, it was the Syrian immigrants (first generation) who amassed the wealth that their sons used as a lever for bringing themselves into wider contacts with society.[36]

Rapid economic success and lack of either unfavorable stereotypes or discrimination barriers once they were known as Syrians rather than Turks, allowed Syrian/Lebanese immigrants to assimilate into U.S. society quite easily, so they did not need to duplicate the host society's institutions. True, they had social organizations and their own newspapers; but their mobility, wide dispersal, differing religions, and emphasis on the extended family rather than on ethnic organizations resulted in their being assimilated rather easily (see the accompanying Ethnic Experience box).

By the mid-1950s, Syrian Americans had completely abandoned their "nomadic" occupations. They had entered the mainstream of U.S. economic and social life and were represented in virtually every industry and profession.[37] Because they were prosperous, their children were able to enter the sciences, the professions, politics, and the arts; and many have distinguished themselves in these fields.

Over 56,000 Lebanese and 31,000 Syrians have left their homeland for the United States since 1988. Either joining friends and relatives who are already assimilated and dispersed or coming as middle-class refugees, they usually blend in easily with the rest of U.S. society in their work and residence. Syrian and Lebanese Americans maintain a strong social network of communication and interaction

This early-20th-century Syrian Christian peddler near Williston, North Dakota, was one of thousands of his countrymen who chose this occupation. Serving an important economic need, the Syrian peddlers acculturated quickly and encountered very little discrimination.
(Smithsonian Institution)

in social events. Their extended families have tended to do things together, including vacationing and relocating to different geographic areas.[38] In recent years, large-scale intermarriage has occurred, which Milton Gordon asserts is the last stage of the assimilation process.[39]

THE PALESTINIANS

About 100,000 Palestinian Americans now live in the United States, with Palestinian communities clustered in California, Illinois, Michigan, New Jersey, New York, and Texas.[40] Most Palestinian Americans are Muslims, although a significant proportion are Christian, mostly members of the Antiochian Orthodox Church. Many Palestinians work as sojourners in other Arab countries and then come to the United States directly from these countries.

Homeland Influence

Until recently, most Palestinian Americans tried to keep a low profile. Faced with stereotypes that labeled them as terrorists, they became disheartened by the actions of Palestinian extremists in their homeland. Yet they also felt bitterness over violent acts against their people, such as when Irgun, the Zionist underground army led by Menachem Begin, prior to the creation of Israel by international fiat later that year, massacred 254 Arab men, women, and children at Deir Yassin in 1948

The Ethnic Experience
First Encounters with U.S. Ethnicity and Language

"*I* am of Circassian origin, having been born in Syria. My father worked in government with the interior ministry. When the government changed from a moderate socialist to a radical socialist government following the Arab–Israeli War in 1968, my father was arrested as a pro-Western sympathizer. He escaped from jail, and we all fled to Jordan, where we received asylum. We migrated to West Germany, but very few Circassians live there, and so we came to the U.S. where other Circassians who had fled from Russia now lived.

"Before we came here, the idea I had about America was that the people were the same, that everybody was an American except the blacks because they were different in color. I thought everybody would be an American, but when we came here—especially as soon as I went to high school—I found everyone identified with their parents' origin. In other words, they would call themselves Italian-American, Dutch-American, and so on. It was a little confusing to me because I expected them to say they were Americans. Instead they said their nationality first and then said American.

"Most Circassians live in northern New Jersey or in California, and so we settled in New Jersey where my father already knew some people. I did have a lot of trouble with the language here. I spoke two languages—Circassian and Arabic—but starting as a sophomore in high school, I had trouble relating to the people. You know how high school kids are. They're immature. Sometimes in class I might say something with a super-heavy accent, and perhaps even say it completely wrong, and they would laugh at me. I didn't have many friends in high school because I worked after school, and besides, we didn't interact very much with the Americans because the Circassian community had its own activities and clubs. Our language and culture were different and the Americans weren't so friendly. Besides, once you know you have an accent, that does stop you from even trying to make friends. It's a barrier. You're still trying to learn a language and it's hard. With my brothers I spoke Arabic, with my parents who were so nationalistic we had to speak Circassian, and in school I had to learn English, and it was all very confusing."

Source: Syrian immigrant who came to the United States in 1968 at age 15.

and stuffed their bodies in a well. In 1998, Palestinian Americans created and passed from city to city a gigantic quilt composed of 418 patches to commemorate the fiftieth anniversary of that many Palestinian communities eliminated when the Jewish state came into existence.

When the Palestinian *intifada* uprisings against Israel began in 1988, Palestinian Americans took a strong interest in the cause, watching network news telecasts and listening to shortwave-radio reports. Inspired by the demonstrations and by the Arab League's recognition of an independent Palestinian state, sec-

This Afgan grocery store owner displays both his American patriotism and a poster with an X across Osama bin Laden. The store, located in "Little Kabul" in Fremont, California, where about 10,000 Afgans call home, was one of many publicly rejecting terrorism and demanding bin Laden's removal from their country.
(*Source:* © Norbert Schwerin/The Image Works)

ond- and third-generation Palestinian Americans have gained a new sense of ethnic identity and belonging. Changes in Israeli leadership and government policy culminated in the agreement signed by Palestinian leader Yasir Arafat and Israeli Prime Minister Yitzhak Rabin in 1995 that transferred control over much of the West Bank of occupied Jordanian territory to its Palestinian residents. Despite Rabin's assassination in 1996 and the subsequent impasse in Israeli–Palestinian talks, Palestinian self-rule continues to evolve, and that homeland influence has renewed the pride of Palestinian Americans in their ethnic identity. Continued Israeli–Palestinian conflict, especially the suicide bombers, and links to terrorist motivation against U.S. targets contribute to strained relations between Palestinian Americans and other U.S. citizens.

The American Federation of Ramallah

Many recent Palestinian arrivals from the Middle East lack advanced education or occupational skills for various white-collar positions, so they find employment in various working-class trades. One source of assistance is the American Federation of Ramallah, named after a town of 40,000 inhabitants ten miles north of Jerusalem. It is a nationwide ethnic organization, with local and regional social clubs designed to help people of Palestinian heritage adjust to life in the United

States. The organization provides financial assistance, guaranteed bank loans, and expertise to enable the newcomers to start mom-and-pop grocery, liquor, and variety stores. The newcomers gradually repay the loans, adding a small percentage to help others who follow them.

The federation also conducts many social activities, such as parties and picnics, through its local branches. These events help maintain ethnic bonding and provide opportunities for young people to meet potential marriage partners. A youth department offers summer-camp programs and cultural-heritage classes.

Community Life

For middle-class Palestinian Americans, the community's mosques and churches serve many purposes. They meet religious needs, of course; but they also function as ethnic centers for social occasions, temporary hostels for new arrivals not yet situated, cultural learning centers for youth, meeting places for Arab organizations, and reception centers for visiting dignitaries.

Working-class Palestinian American males, many of whom live in urban neighborhoods, often congregate in coffeehouses in their free hours, much as earlier Greek immigrants did. These neighborhood social centers provide places to relax, exchange news about the community or homeland, and perhaps learn of work opportunities.

Endogamy remains the norm among Palestinian Americans. Each summer, marriage-age Palestinian American singles throng East Jerusalem, the West Bank, and the Gaza Strip in search of a spouse. Some engagements last one to two years, but it is not uncommon for a couple—with their families' assistance—to meet, become engaged, and marry within a few weeks. Most such couples are college educated and happy with the nuptial arrangement because they share the same culture, religion, and expectations as they start new families in the United States.[41]

THE IRANIANS

Iran, formerly called Persia, is not an Arab country. The great majority of its people speak their own language, Farsi, not Arabic; and their culture has unique qualities that set it apart from the culture of neighboring Arab states. Immigration patterns and societal reaction to Iranian immigrants have fluctuated greatly in the past 30 years, depending on the political climate. Immigration to the United States from Iran is a relatively new phenomenon. During the reign of the westernizing Shah Mohammed Reza Pahlevi, about 50,000 Iranian students studied in the United States annually. They maintained a sense of community among themselves, forming associations and interacting with one another. Fear of political repression under the shah kept many from returning to their homeland until after his fall from power, in 1979.

Other Iranians living in the United States in the late 1970s were skilled professionals working as sojourners, who had no intention of remaining, or political refugees hoping to return home someday. At that time, only the Iranian college students maintained an ethnic community or network. Other Iranians kept to themselves, partly for fear that members of the shah's secret police force (SAVAK) would report something about them, bringing harm to relatives still in Iran. Minority emigrants from Iran—Armenians, Baha'is, and Jews—showed great cohesiveness, intending to become U.S. citizens, but they constituted a very small percentage of all Iranian immigrants.

In a study of his fellow Iranian immigrants, Maboud Ansari found that the Iranian migration in the late 1970s consisted mostly of male middle-class professionals. Although physically separated from their families, typical Iranian immigrants still viewed their extended family at home as their only source of primary relations, which they maintained through regular telephone calls. These men did not form a territorially compact community or develop close ties with their compatriots.[42] Most remained physically and socially distant from other Iranians in the United States and did not come together except at Now-Ruz, the Iranian New Year, celebrated on the first day of spring:

> The Now-Ruz party (which takes place in many major American cities) is the only major national event for Iranians in America. As the only publicly visible ceremony, it creates an atmosphere of national identity and a sense of belonging. However, it seems that somehow the ceremony has lost the meaning originally attached to it. For example, one of the most important aspects of Now-Ruz is to review or to extend friendships. The Iranians who attend the festivities in America are apt to come together as strangers and leave without exchanging any addresses or gaining any new friendships. Most of the festivities are characterized by a lack of intimacy and excessive self-consciousness in maintaining of social distance.[43]

In the 20 years since this study, Iranians have become more organized and socially interactive with one another, no longer fearful of Iranian secret police (SAVAK) or repercussions against family members still in Iran. Both older and more recent arrivals openly participate in a variety of ethnic activities, and few yearn to return to Iran.

In the 1970s though, Ansari found that Iranians fell into four self-designated categories. Only about 20 percent called themselves *mandegar* (settlers), or Persian Yankees. Many of these were older, former exchange students who opted to stay permanently. The majority were in the second category, the *belataklif*, or ambivalent Iranians. Torn by a nostalgic love and guilt feeling for what had been left behind, yet growing attached to what lay ahead in the United States, the *belataklif* remained undecided about staying or returning. Yet the longer one remained, the less likely one was to return, thus becoming a *mandegar*. The other two categories were the *siyasi*, political exiles who viewed their host society only as a necessary refuge; and the *cosmopolitans*, who were committed to their profession and not to their nationality—citizens of the world at home anywhere.[44] Today, the first and fourth categories primarily describe Iranian Americans.

Anti-Iranian feelings ran high in the United States throughout 1980 when the hostage crisis at the U.S. Embassy in Iran remained unresolved. Verbal abuse, boycotts, arson against Iranian American businesses, and physical attacks against Iranian students on several college campuses occurred. Iranian Americans who harbored no anti-U.S. feelings themselves became the scapegoats of U.S. frustration, suffering indignities and discrimination. Even into the 1990s, residual hostility was still much in evidence following the earlier "Irangate" controversy in Washington, DC, with revelations about weapons-for-hostages secret arrangements in 1980.

Iranian immigration in the 1980s totaled 116,000, up significantly from 45,000 in the 1970s; then dropped to 62,000 in the 1990s.[45] About 46 percent of Iranian immigrants choose California as their state of intended residence.[46] With more than 225,000 Americans now claiming Iranian ancestry, the presence of Iranian Americans is more readily noticed by outsiders. Although found in most major cities, distinct Iranian neighborhoods exist in Queens, New York, and Beverly Hills, California. As in the Washington, DC–Arlington, Virginia, area, classes in Farsi, the primary Iranian language, take place in these enclaves. Also located in these four areas are Islamic centers and mosques, further evidence of the emerging Iranian community.

Born to mostly middle-class professional parents, today's second-generation Iranian Americans grow up in a child-centered family with equalitarian norms, quite unlike the *patriarchal* and authoritarian character of families in Iran.[47] Nonetheless, many parents are concerned about preserving their Iranian heritage and make efforts to preserve the positive aspects of the culture, despite the inevitable Americanization process.

Living as a despised and persecuted religious minority in Iran, many Baha'is have emigrated to the United States, establishing centers in several major U.S. cities. The population of Baha'is in the United States is greater than anywhere else in the world, including the religion's cradle, Iran.[48]

THE IRAQIS

We must distinguish between the immigrants from Iraq who arrived before and those who came after World War II because political, social, and economic changes in the Middle East have made these groups of immigrants very different. Studying one Iraqi subcultural group of Chaldeans living in the Detroit metropolitan area, Mary Sengstock observed significant pre- and postwar changes caused by the evolution of Iraq into a modern nation-state and the heightened Arab consciousness caused by Arab–Israeli tensions.[49]

The early immigrants formed a community of village-oriented entrepreneurs whose religious traditions served as their primary identification. They maintained a *gemeinschaft* subsociety within the U.S. society. Family orientations were strong, and many Iraqis were self-employed, operating grocery stores and other small businesses. They were, for the most part, a self-enclosed ethnic community.

Not only do recent Iraqi immigrants to Detroit have different value orientations from their predecessors', reflecting their increased education and their more urbanized backgrounds, but these newer orientations have had an effect on the self-perceptions and behavior of the earlier immigrants. Although the Chaldeans are Christian, they feel the pull of Arab nationalist loyalties, and this national consciousness is infectious.[50] Most now think of themselves as Arabs or Iraqis, not as Chaldeans or Telkeffes, another Iraqi subcultural group. Recent immigrants are less likely to be self-employed and more likely to be involved in bureaucratic endeavors that bring them into contact with people of different backgrounds. Recent Iraqi immigrants thus rely more on formal organizations and interact more with outsiders. They are likely to join non-Chaldean organizations and to develop social relationships, including close friendship ties and marriage, with people from other backgrounds. With new immigrants arriving all the time (the Detroit community now exceeds 8,000), these patterns may well continue and be the norm.

From 1981 to 1999, over 57,000 Iraqi immigrants came to this country.[51] With thousands of newcomers arriving annually and following a chain-migration pattern of settlement, this ethnic group has experienced a slow, steady ethnic revitalization.

Interestingly, the Gulf War against Saddam Hussein's troops did not generate subgroup-specific hostility against Iraqi Americans living in the United States. Several factors probably contributed to this lack of societal animosity. Given their relatively small numbers and tendency to live within the larger Arab American community, Iraqi Americans are not particularly visually distinct. Furthermore, they were mostly supportive of the brief military action against their homeland's dictator.

THE TURKS

The U.S. Immigration and Naturalization Service reports that a total of more than 445,000 Turkish immigrants have come to the United States since 1820. Ordinarily, that number would place Turkey in the top 20 suppliers of emigrants. However, various subjugated peoples of different languages and cultures left the Ottoman Empire with only Turkish passports prior to World War I. Over 300,000 people, three fourths of the total "Turkish" immigrants, entered the United States during this period (see the Appendix). Although immigration officials identified them as Turkish by their passports, they really were Armenians, Syrians, Lebanese, or other nationalities. Over 70,000 ethnic Turks have immigrated since 1971, making this 30-year period the time of their largest immigration.

Factors Against Immigration

Several factors explain the earlier low level of emigration from Turkey in comparison with other poor, undeveloped nations during the great migration period. Perhaps foremost, Muslim Turks had waged a relentless campaign against the Christians within their empire and would hardly be inclined to settle in an almost exclusively Christian country. Second, the Turks had traditionally migrated in large groups. Consequently, there was little beyond the country's borders to attract families or individuals. In 1923, Turkey barred any emigrant from ever returning, even as a visitor. This law remained in force until 1950. With laws against emigration, few Turks chose to seek a better life elsewhere. Since 1965, however, an increasing number of Turkish immigrants have migrated to the United States because Turkey has been a military ally of the United States for several generations.

Societal Attitudes

Although relatively few Turks emigrated to the United States before World War I, feelings toward the Turks in the United States were mostly negative, primarily because of the Ottoman Empire's political and religious repression:

> Such sentiment towards Turkey as existed in America was largely anti-Turkish. We had of course inherited the ordinary western European prejudice against the Turks as champions of Islam. In addition, many groups in America had espoused the cause of one or another of those Ottoman subject peoples who in the nineteenth century were fighting to gain their independence from the Empire. Immigrants from that Empire had helped foster pro-Greek or pro-Macedonian or pro-Bulgarian sentiments in this country. What had principally aroused American interest in Turkey, however, and what had especially directed that interest towards the non-Turks were certainly the long-standing presence and activities of American missionaries in the Ottoman world. It was chiefly the Armenians' aspirations and woes to which those missionaries gave currency.[52]

The Ottoman Empire's efforts to suppress Armenian and Syrian/Lebanese Christians were often brutal. Annihilation of enemies occurred frequently, and Turkish massacres of thousands of Armenians in the 1890s and again in 1915 stirred the wrath of many Americans. To this day, many Americans of Armenian descent mark the anniversary of these Turkish pogroms. American hostility toward the Turks was common during those times, which helps explain the initial hostility Syrian/Lebanese immigrants encountered in the United States when they were misidentified as Turks. In his survey of **social distance** in 1926, Emory S. Bogardus found that Turks ranked 27th out of 30, above only Chinese, Koreans, and Asian Indians. In 1946, 1956, and 1966, Turks shifted a position or two, finishing 26th in 1966, above Koreans, Mexicans, blacks, and Asian Indians.[53] In the same surveys, Armenians ranked from 5 to 11 positions higher than Turks.

Immigrant Patterns

When the Balkan War of 1912 began, many young unmarried Turkish males came to the United States to avoid military service. When war-ravaged Europe achieved peace again in 1919, more than 30,000 of them returned to Turkey. The few thousand who remained settled primarily in New York, Massachusetts, Michigan, Illinois, and Indiana.

Most Turkish immigrants who came before World War II were illiterate and secured jobs as unskilled laborers. They settled mostly in New York City and Detroit, and they kept to themselves. Some gradually became acculturated, while others remained socially segregated within U.S. society.

More-recent Turkish immigrants are better educated than their predecessors. Many are professionals or experienced businesspeople who settle in a relatively dispersed pattern. Others are working-class tradesmen and laborers who usually cluster together in urban areas in sufficient numbers to induce the establishment of bilingual programs in neighborhood schools. Annual immigration to the United States numbers in the thousands, helping maintain ethnic vitality. It appears that structural assimilation will be at least a two-generation process.

THE PAKISTANIS

In recent decades, immigrants from Pakistan have become a significant presence in the United States. In the 1980s Pakistani immigration reached over 61,000, and the total for the 1990s exceeded 100,000.[54] Three in five are white-collar workers

Marchers in a Pakistani Day parade in New York City celebrate their heritage and interact with friendly onlookers. Many past and present racial and ethnic groups have used annual parades as rallying events for group solidarity. This popular activity instills ethnic pride in the younger generation, helping negate any marginality they may experience growing up as members of a minority group.
(*Source:* © Michael Dwyer/Stock Boston)

or professionals, and the rest are craftsmen, service workers, or laborers.[55] Another common occupation of Pakistani immigrants in many cities is taxicab driver. In New York City, for example, immigrants from Pakistan, Bangladesh, and India made up less than 0.5 percent of the population in 1994 but composed 30 percent of its taxicab drivers.[56]

Pakistani Americans have a widely dispersed settlement pattern, although 25 percent settle in the New York City metropolitan region. The Chicago, Washington (DC), Houston, and Los Angeles metropolitan areas are other locuses of residential clustering.[57] The Pakistanis' acculturation and assimilation patterns are similar to those of other groups considered in this chapter.

OTHER ASIAN AND MIDDLE EASTERN ASSIMILATION

Structural assimilation among immigrant groups is rarely a first-generation occurrence. Because most people claiming ethnicity from this part of the world are newcomers, sufficient time has not yet elapsed to give us a perspective on their assimilation. However, studies are emerging to give us some insights into their acculturation as immigrants. First, though, let us consider the assimilation of those who are not foreign born. This would include the descendants of Asian Indians, Lebanese, Syrians, and Turks who arrived in the early or mid-20th century. For the most part, their multigenerational life in the United States means only vestiges of ethnicity remain, and they are as much a part of the American mainstream as the descendants of European immigrants.

Those recent arrivals of middle-class backgrounds whose education and occupational skills enabled them to settle in upscale urban neighborhoods or suburban communities are part of the economic mainstream, but they often have not yet overcome social barriers to full acceptance. Like similarly situated Asian Americans discussed in the previous chapter, everyday ethnicity is still a real part of their lives, even though they may be living and working in a larger society. They are living in two worlds—private and public—old and new.

Uma Segal examined generational conflicts in Asian Indian families.[58] She found that these conflicts revolved around adolescents' power struggles for independence and freedom and around poor communication between parents and teens. Not surprisingly, the clash of cultures over sexual relationships and arranged marriages highlighted problematic areas. As young people identify with the country in which they live, and parents try to instill in their children the values they cherish from their homeland, such conflicts are a normal part of the immigrant experience.

Researchers studying Arab American adults found that acculturation and satisfaction with life in the United States and with family life were stronger with longer U.S. residence, younger age at immigration, not having recently visited their country of origin, and being Christian. Discrimination experiences influenced reduced satisfaction with life in the United States but not with acculturation in general.[59] Such findings would seem to reinforce assimilationist theory that length of residence and cultural affinity are key determinants of adjustment and acceptance.

SOCIOLOGICAL ANALYSIS

The non-Western immigrants discussed in this chapter have mostly arrived since 1965. Because only a few have lived in the United States longer than one generation, their experiences lack sufficient historical perspective to permit full analysis. Furthermore (as noted at the beginning of the chapter) because most are educated with marketable occupational skills, they do not entirely fit the theoretical framework of past immigrants. How well do the three theoretical perspectives explain their situation? As we will see, each provides a focus that promotes further understanding.

The Functionalist View

How has the social system been able to adapt relatively smoothly in absorbing the newcomers, many of whom are racially and religiously different? Functionalists would point to the immigration laws ensuring either sufficient earning power in occupational preference (higher admission priorities for skilled workers) or a support system in relative preference (higher admission priorities for close relatives). These better educated, better skilled, better connected individuals quickly adjust, contribute to the economy, and seem to integrate into society with a minimum of problems. Most currently rank low on the social-distance scale, but they become functionally integrated fairly easily. Their economic power allows them to live in middle-class neighborhoods, accessible through fair-housing laws. Some may even integrate areas, their comparable values and lifestyle making their native-born neighbors more receptive to them as a racially or culturally distinct people.

Less skilled non-Westerners have helped fill a population void in urban and ex-urban neighborhoods. Although they may encounter some minor problems, these newcomers bring stability to neighborhoods, preventing their decline and helping maintain a racial balance. Urban density gives the immigrants close proximity to one another, enabling ethnic solidarity to develop and be sustained. Living near their work, these newcomers find jobs other U.S. residents are unwilling to take. They also fulfill societal needs. As they struggle to succeed in the United States, they find better opportunities than they had known in their home countries, while society benefits from their work, purchasing power, and cultural contributions.

The Conflict View

Early non-Western immigrants provide grist for the analytical mill of conflict theorists. Industrialists often used Syrian/Lebanese men as strikebreakers in the Northeast, particularly during the intense labor unrest in the early 20th century.

Just as the Syrian/Lebanese offered factory owners a cheaper labor alternative, Asian Indians on the West Coast enabled farmers, lumber companies, and railroads to benefit from their low-cost labor. Other workers resented their presence, fearing that the newcomers' growing numbers would jeopardize their own positions. Once again, the split-labor-market theory seems applicable. Economic competition between two wage-level groups generated ethnic antagonism and violence.

More recent arrivals suggest a different analysis. In this case, tensions arise in the United States among African Americans and Hispanics at the bottom of the socioeconomic ladder who see foreign-born non-Westerners leapfrogging over them. Resentment builds against the new arrivals whose hiring appears to deny upward mobility to native-born minority groups. Foreigners benefit at the expense of U.S. natives, they think. In addition, the movement of non-Western immigrants into white, middle-class apartment complexes and suburban neighborhoods changes the prior racial or cultural homogeneity, which sometimes stirs hostilities among the old-timers against the newcomers.

Although conflict may be less intense regarding these groups than toward previous waves of immigrants, an undercurrent of tension and resentment may exist, as evidenced by occasional eruptions of public protest over the building of a Sikh temple in a suburban community or over the effort to provide bilingual education to a group of Turkish American children in an urban school (two actual incidents).

The Interactionist View

Because visual clues are a major means of categorizing strangers, people with different clothing or physical characteristics get classified as dissimilar types. Is it surprising to learn that the racially different (Africans and Asians) and the religiously different (Buddhists and Muslims) score lower on the social-distance scale? If this perception of others as being very different is coupled with a sense of overwhelming numbers of newcomers, fears of a "Hindoo invasion" or something similar can easily lead to acts of exclusion, expulsion, and violence. Consider the case of the Irish in Paterson who attacked the Syrians moving into their neighborhood, supposing them to be Turks or "Mohammedans." Only when a respected religious leader from their own community redefined the situation for the Irish did the fighting stop. In recent years, Palestinian Americans have struggled against U.S. natives who presume they are all terrorists because of a few extremists. Misinterpretations about an ethnic group often cause problems for the group's members, and the peoples in this chapter are no exception.

Because many recent immigrants can join the economic mainstream, their coworkers or neighbors assume that they have integrated socially as well. Interaction may occur in work-related relationships, but socially the middle-class newcomers tend to become "unknown ethnics," at least in primary relationships. Socially isolated except on rare occasions, the non-Westerners by necessity interact with compatriots, remaining a generalized entity in the minds of members of the dominant group. This social segregation appears to result more from an attraction toward similarly perceived others than from overt avoidance. Whatever the reason, non-Westerners are mostly social outcasts in the leisure activities of other U.S. residents. Variety may be the spice of life, but we do not apply that principle to racial and ethnic personal relationships.

RETROSPECT

Relatively few members of the racial and ethnic groups discussed in this chapter came to the United States before 1940. The experiences of those who did were generally similar to the experiences of other non-Western peoples in the United States and depended on the then-prevailing policies and regional attitudes.

For the most part, the immigrant experience of people from central and southwestern Asia is current. Although they are still identifiable because of physical and cultural differences, they usually have little difficulty with the U.S. mainstream because of their occupational status, their urban locale, and the relaxation of U.S. norms about newcomers. Nevertheless, as strangers they are keenly aware of the society in which they find themselves, and U.S. natives generally tend to avoid interacting with them in meaningful primary relationships. These non-Westerners are somewhat unusual in that many are able to secure a respectable social status via education, occupation, income, and residence; but because of their cultural differences, they have minimal social participation with native-born U.S. residents. This often is a two-way arrangement.

As larger numbers of immigrants from central and southwestern Asian countries come to the United States, they are making their presence felt more and more. One aspect of this impact is in religion. Waves of immigrant peoples have changed the United States from an almost exclusively Protestant country to one of three major faiths. Now this Judeo-Christian population composition, if present trends continue, may be modified further as the numbers of Muslims, Hindus, Buddhists, and adherents of other Eastern religions swell.

As the United States becomes culturally diverse in the areas of religion, physical appearance, and value orientation, more U.S. residents are becoming conscious of the differences in the people around them. Some argue that Americans today are more tolerant because of a resurgence of ethnicity and a more liberal government attitude toward cultural pluralism. Others contend that the past nativistic reaction to Asians in the West and to southern and eastern Europeans in the East is being replicated today against the non-Western immigrants. Riots and violent confrontations may have disappeared, but more subtle and sophisticated acts of discrimination occur, including calls for increased immigration restrictions against non-Western immigrants.

How accurate this analysis is remains to be determined. Recent central and southwestern Asian immigrants are better educated and better trained, often speak English before they arrive, and thus enter U.S. society at a higher socioeconomic level than earlier immigrants did. Their ethnic community is more interactional than territorial for the most part, although some groups are more clustered and visible than others. They seem to adjust fairly easily to life in the United States, although ingroup socializing is quite common, as was the case with past immigrant groups. Perhaps we are still a generation away from being able to measure the full impact of their role within U.S. society.

KEY TERMS

Brain drain	Invasion–succession	Structural assimilation
Ethnogenesis	Miscegenation	
Gemeinschaft	Social distance	

REVIEW QUESTIONS

1. Why do differences in economic power between non-Western immigrants and earlier immigrants make assimilation less necessary now than before?

2. What parallels exist between Asian Indian and east and southeast Asian immigrant experiences, both past and present?

3. How have structural conditions in the home countries reshaped ethnic identity and attitudes among Arab immigrants to the United States?

4. Discuss problems of stereotyping and prejudice encountered by non-Westerners because of outgroup perceptions and the media.

5. What insights do the three sociological perspectives offer about non-Western immigrants?

SUGGESTED READINGS

Angelo, Michael. *The Sikh Diaspora: Tradition and Change in an Immigrant Community.* New York: Garland Publishing, 1997.

Explores the dynamics of acculturation and the maintenance of cultural traditions in a compact, middle-class Sikh immigrant community in upstate New York.

Ansari, Maboud. *The Making of the Iranian Community in America.* New York: Pardis Press, 1993.

A fine and authoritative sociological study of Iranian emigrés and immigrants, their values and acculturation patterns.

Lessinger, Johanna. *From the Ganges to the Hudson: Indian Immigrants in New York City.* Boston: Allyn and Bacon, 1995.

An ethnographic study of the ethnic infrastructure, family and gender relations, and social activism in one urban community.

McCarus, Ernest (ed.). *The Development of Arab-American Identity*. Ann Arbor: University of Michigan Press, 1994.

A fine collection of essays on the Arab American immigrant experience: adaptation; facing stereotypes, prejudice, and violence; and maintaining values and identities in a new society.

Naff, Alixa. *The Arab Americans*. New York: Chelsea House, 1998.

A clear, well-written introduction to Arab Americans, examining their culture and acculturation experiences in the United States.

Sheth, Pravin. *Indians in America: One Stream, Two Waves, Three Generations*. Jaipur, India: Rawat Publishing, 2001.

An ambitious portrayal of a multigenerational saga within a multilingual ethnic group, covering its historical, cultural, and economic elements.

INTERNET LINKS

Go to *http://www.ablongman.com/parrillo* for numerous links relevant to this chapter under "Internet Readings and Exercises."

Hispanic Americans

erhaps no ethnic group attracts more public attention these days than do the Hispanic people. Their large numbers, their residential clustering, and the bilingual programs and signs associated with them make them a recognizable ethnic group. Hispanics, or Latinos, who live in poverty or are involved in gangs, drugs, or other criminal activity gain notoriety and generate negative stereotypes; but other Hispanic Americans live in the societal mainstream as working-class or middle-class citizens. Although their cultural backgrounds, social class, and length of residence in the United States differ in many ways, Hispanic Americans share a common language and heritage. Because of this commonality, outsiders often lump them all together despite their many differences.

SOCIOHISTORICAL PERSPECTIVE

Spanish influence in what is now the United States is centuries old. Long before the English settled in their colonies in the New World, Spanish explorers, missionaries, and adventurers roamed through much of the western hemisphere, including Florida and the Southwest. In 1518, the Spanish established St. Augustine, Florida; and in the same year (1609) that the first permanent English settlement (Jamestown) was established, the Spanish founded Santa Fe in what is now New Mexico. Spanish cultural influence was extensive throughout the New World in language, religion, customs, values, and town planning (e.g., locating church and institutional buildings next to a central plaza).

The nation's largest Hispanic groups—Mexicans and Puerto Ricans—became involved with the United States through two 19th-century wars 50 years apart. Through the fortunes of war, the places where they lived became part of the United States, functioning under a different set of laws of a country in which they were now a minority.

For the Mexicans, the Treaty of Guadalupe Hidalgo that ended the Mexican-American War in 1848 brought Texas, New Mexico, Arizona, and California into the United States and U.S. citizenship to about 75,000 Mexican nationals still living there one year after the treaty. Viewed as a conquered and inferior people, they soon lost title to the land where they and their ancestors had lived because they could not prove ownership in the Anglo court system. By 1892, official policy toward Mexican Americans was so biased against them that the federal government allowed anyone except them to get grazing privileges on public lands in the Southwest. Nor did the violence against them end. In fact, the interethnic violence between Anglos and Mexican Americans thereafter was so extensive that some experts believe there were more killings of Mexican Americans than lynchings of black Americans between 1850 and 1930.[1] Experienced in farming, ranching, and mining—concentrated along the fertile river valleys—the Mexican Americans proved a valuable labor pool and were incorporated within the white economy as lower-strata laborers.

Ruled by Spain for over 400 years, Puerto Ricans became U.S. nationals when the Treaty of Paris in 1898 ended the Spanish-American War and made their land U.S. territory. Until 1948, when Puerto Rico became a commonwealth with full autonomy and its people could elect their own governor, the island was a colony with appointed governors and its legislative actions subject to annulment by the U.S. Congress, which reserved the right to legislate for the island if it wished. As just one example of the island's colonial status, U.S. officials decreed that all education was to be in English. That edict remained in effect until 1991, when Puerto Ricans voted to restore Spanish as the island's official language.

Structural Conditions

The Hispanic American experience varies greatly, depending on the particular ethnic group, area of the country, and period involved (see Figure 11.1). In the Southwest, agricultural needs and the presence of Mexican Americans are crucial factors in dominant–minority relations. In the East, industrial employment, urban problems, and the presence of Cubans or Puerto Ricans provide the focal points of attitudes and actions.

In the past, low-skilled immigrant groups—including Puerto Ricans and Mexicans—typically obtained jobs such as unskilled factory work that had low status, low pay, and little mobility, but at least provided sufficient income to achieve some degree of economic security. Unlike past groups from less industrialized nations, however, today's Hispanic immigrants enter a postindustrial society where fewer unskilled jobs are available. As a result, many lack the necessary skills to adjust easily to working in the United States. Furthermore, the suburbanization of industry means that older cities (where poor immigrants traditionally lived and

FIGURE 11.1   Central America, Caribbean, South America

worked out of economic necessity) no longer have enough manufacturing jobs for the newcomers. And whereas the unions of the past helped European immigrants to obtain job security, better wages, and improved working conditions, today's unions are smaller and weaker, and in many service occupations nonexistent.

Overpopulation throughout Latin America is a significant factor in the continued migration of large numbers of Hispanics to the United States (see Table

TABLE 11.1 Legal Hispanic Immigration to the United States, 1961-1999

	1961–1970	1971–1980	1981–1990	1991–1999
Mexico	453,937	640,294	1,655,843	2,077,673
Caribbean	470,213	741,126	872,051	892,912
Central America	101,330	134,640	468,088	464,207
South America	257,954	295,741	461,847	484,264
Total	1,283,434	1,811,801	3,457,829	3,919,056

Source: U.S. Immigration and Naturalization Service, *Statistical Yearbook 1999,* (Washington, DC: U.S. Government Printing Office, 2001), Table 2, p. 22.

11.1). High birth rates, improved sanitation, reduction of child mortality, and negative cultural and religious attitudes toward birth control have led to population booms in countries whose resources and habitable land cannot support so many people. The total population of Latin America and the Caribbean grew from over 285 million in 1970 to over 525 million by 2000. Current projections indicate that the population will reach about 697 million by 2025.[2]

Suffering from poor living conditions, inadequate schools, limited job opportunities, and economic hardship, many Latinos seek a better life in the United States—indeed, significantly more people than legal channels can accommodate. As a result, some enter illegally along the 2,000-mile border between the United States and Mexico or into port cities by boat. Throughout the 1980s and 1990s, U.S. government agents have apprehended an average of 1.3 million **undocumented** (illegal) **aliens** annually. In 1998, the figure was 1.7 million, most of them from Mexico, with other large clusters from El Salvador, Honduras, Guatemala, and the Dominican Republic.[3] Of the estimated 5 million undocumented aliens residing in the United States, officials believe that about 54 percent are Mexicans. About 16 percent of the Mexican and about 36 percent of the Central American illegals entered with temporary visas and then remained after their visas expired.[4] Undocumented aliens strain local and state social services and generate dominant-group hostility, but they also make substantial economic contributions as consumers and as low-skilled workers.

Cultural Differentiation

The cultures of the peoples from the various Caribbean and Central and South American countries differ. Value orientations within a particular country also vary, depending on such factors as degree of urbanization, amount of outside contact, and social class. With these qualifications in mind, we will examine some cultural traditions that most Latinos share to a greater or lesser degree and that differ from traditional U.S. values. Before doing so, we should recognize that in areas of considerable acculturation, such as New Mexico, some of these cultural traits are muted, and Latinos have adopted many Anglo (the Latino term for mainstream white U.S.) behavior patterns.

The Cosmic Race. One cultural concept associated with Hispanics—especially Mexicans—is that of *La Raza Cosmica,* the cosmic race. The Mexican intellectual José Vasconcelos coined the term in 1925 to refer to the amalgamation of the white, black, and Indian races that he believed was occurring in Latin America.[5] In his old age he dismissed the idea as a juvenile fantasy, but the concept evolved into a group categorization similar to what Kurt Lewin calls the recognition of an "interdependence of fate." In essence, *La Raza Cosmica* suggests that all the Spanish-speaking peoples in the western hemisphere share a cultural bond and that God has planned for them a great destiny that has yet to be realized.

From this mythic construct, activists sought to unify compatriots around a common political goal based on the nationalism of an imagined community. Although those cultural resources remained dormant for much of the late 20th century, *La Raza* lived on as the name of an influential newspaper and of a strong political organization representing Chicano interests. Given the growing Mexican American presence, the cultural resources found in the concept of *La Raza* may soon animate activism toward greater social and economic justice for its people.[6]

Machismo. Overstated in the Anglo stereotype, **machismo** is a basic value governing various qualities of masculinity. To Hispanic males, such attributes as inner strength in the face of adversity, personal daring, bravado, leadership, and sexual prowess are measures of one's manhood.[7] The role of the man is to be a good provider for his family, to protect its honor at all times, and to be strong, reliable, and independent. He should avoid indebtedness, accepting charity, and any kind of relationship, formal or informal, that would weaken his autonomy. The culture and family system are male dominated. The woman's role is within the family, and women are to be guarded against any onslaught on their honor. Machismo may also find expression in such forms as perceived sexual allure, fathering children, and aggressive behavior. **Marianismo** is the companion value, describing various qualities of femininity, particularly acceptance of male dominance, emphasis on family responsibilities, and the nurturing role of women.

The concept of machismo is not strictly Latin American. Such traditional sex-role orientations are common throughout most undeveloped countries, whether African, Eastern, Middle Eastern, Western, or Pacific Island. For Latinos, machismo diminishes with increasing levels of education, assimilation, and multigenerational residence in the United States.

The result of these values can be not only a double standard of sexual morality but also difficulty adjusting to U.S. culture. Women have more independence in the United States than in most Hispanic countries. Instead of men being the sole providers, women can also find employment, sometimes earning more money than the men of the family. The participation of Hispanic women in the labor force seems to be related to educational level. More highly educated Cuban, Central American, and South American women participate in the labor force at rates similar to those of white women in the United States, whereas Mexican and Puerto

Rican women have especially low rates. Overall, the participation of Hispanic women in the labor force is comparable to the national average for all women.[8]

Dignidad.   The cultural value of **dignidad** is the basis of social interaction; it assumes that the dignity of all humans entitles them to a measure of respect. It is primarily "a quality attributed to all, regardless of status, race, color or creed."[9] Regardless of status, each person acknowledges others' *dignidad* in a taken-for-granted reciprocal behavior pattern. Therefore Hispanics—particularly Puerto Ricans—expect to be treated in terms of *dignidad*. Because it is an implicit measure of respect, one cannot demand it from others. Instead, one concludes that others are rude and cold if they do not acknowledge one's *dignidad*. More broadly, the concept includes a strong positive self-image.

Racial Attitudes

In most Latin American countries, skin color is less important than social class as an indicator of social status. There seems to be a correlation between darker skin color and lower social standing, but the racial line between whites and blacks that is sharply drawn in the United States is less distinct in Latin America. A great deal of color integration occurs in social interaction, intermarriage, and shared orientations to cultural values. There is also a much wider range of recognized color gradations, which helps to blunt any color prejudice. Still, in some places, such as Puerto Rico, color prejudice has increased, perhaps as a result of social and economic changes from industrialization.[10]

Color often serves as an unexpected basis of discrimination for Latinos coming to the United States. Being stereotyped, judged, and treated on the basis of one's skin color is essentially unknown to these brown-skinned peoples. Therefore, encountering prejudice and discrimination based on their skin color is a traumatic experience for them. Before long, they realize the extent of this ugly aspect of U.S. society. Some adapt to it, while others forsake it and return home; but practically all resent it.

Other Cultural Attributes

Hispanics generally have a more casual attitude toward time than do others in the United States and a negative attitude toward rushing. Another cultural difference— one that could easily lead to misunderstanding—is their attitude about making eye contact with others. To them, not looking directly into the eyes of an authority figure such as a teacher or police officer is an act of respect; but native U.S. residents may interpret it as shyness, avoidance, or guilt. Like some Europeans, Hispanics regard physical proximity in conversation as a sign of friendliness, but Anglos are accustomed to a greater distance between conversationalists. One can envision an Anglo being made uncomfortable by the seemingly unusual nearness of a Hispanic person and backing away, the latter reestablishing the physical closeness, the Anglo again backing away, and the Hispanic concluding that the Anglo is a cold or aloof individual. Each has viewed the situation from a different cultural perspective, leading to very different interpretations of the incident.[11]

Current Patterns

Hispanics are the largest ethnic group in the United States and are steadily increasing in number all the time. At 35.3 million residents in 2000 (a 58 percent increase over their 22.4 million in 1990, compared to an increase of 13.2 percent for the total U.S. population), they now constitute about 13 percent of the total U.S. population.[12] Moreover, they are now the nation's largest minority group, surpassing American blacks sooner than the Census Bureau projected. Reasons include a higher birth rate than Africans Americans, a high immigration rate from Spanish-speaking countries, and a low average age of these immigrants (over 40 percent are under 21).[13] See Figure 11.2.

In 2000, half of all Hispanics lived in just two states: California and Texas, where they are about one third of each state's total population. About 77 percent lived in

FIGURE 11.2 **Hispanic Population as a Percentage of Total Population by State, 2000**

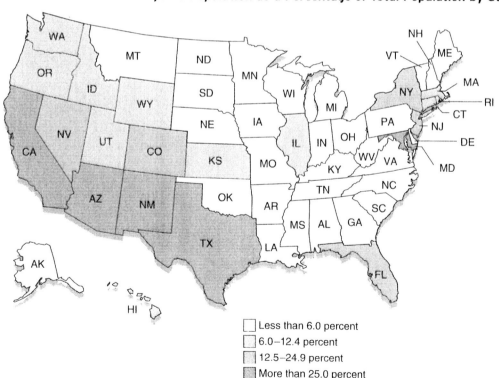

Less than 6.0 percent
6.0–12.4 percent
12.5–24.9 percent
More than 25.0 percent

Source: U.S. Bureau of the Census.

seven states with Hispanic populations of 1 million or more (California, Texas, New York, Florida, Illinois, Arizona, and New Jersey). The Hispanic percentages of some of the nation's 10 largest cities are New York (27 percent), Los Angeles (47 percent), Chicago (26 percent), Houston (37 percent), Philadelphia (8 percent), Phoenix (34 percent), San Diego (25 percent), Dallas (36 percent), San Antonio (59 percent), and Detroit (5 percent).[14]

What do these growing numbers and extensive population clusters suggest for future dominant–minority relations? There is no simple answer, because of the variance in the education, socioeconomic background, and occupational skills of the Hispanic newcomers. Despite nativist fears, however, English language mastery is a common goal of Hispanic parents for their children.[15] Concerns about ethnic tribalism or about the need to enshrine English as the "official" language of the United States seem unfounded, as we will discuss in the last chapter.

Cultural vitality, long an attribute among Mexican Americans in the Southwest, so near their homeland, will likely remain within other Latino communities, too. The dynamics of cultural pluralism are fueled by the large Hispanic presence, current migration patterns, psychological ties to the homeland, rapid transportation and communications, government policy, and societal tolerance. Acculturation and mainstreaming will no doubt occur for most Hispanics, as it has for members of other groups, but the dynamics of cultural pluralism suggest that the Hispanic influence will be long-lasting in U.S. society. Hispanics will not simply blend in with the rest of society. Rather, like the French who influenced the Louisiana region, Hispanic Americans will probably fundamentally affect U.S. culture itself (see the accompanying International Scene box).

SOCIAL INDICATORS OF HISPANIC PROGRESS

As Figure 11.3 shows, a much larger percentage of Hispanics than non-Hispanics are young, with proportionately more children and fewer elderly. Higher fertility, particularly among the foreign born, and the high percentage of young adult immigrants in their reproductive years create this differential. However, Hispanic groups vary in their migration and fertility patterns. For example, 15 percent of Cuban Americans are children under 15, compared to 33 percent among Mexican Americans. In contrast, children under 15 constitute 19 percent of non-Hispanic white people, and 26 percent of African Americans.[16]

Diversity among various Hispanic cultural groups also manifests itself in such social indicators as education, income, and occupation (see Figure 11.4). These indicators support mixed findings on the status of Hispanic Americans and provide some cause for concern.

Education

Perhaps the most important indicator of societal mainstreaming is education, for it provides the means for greater job opportunities. Unfortunately, as Table 11.2

The International Scene
Cultural Diffusion in Argentina

*B*ecause almost all Argentinians are descendants of relatively recent immigrants from Europe, their culture has a stronger European orientation than that of neighboring Latin American countries. The people of Buenos Aires, the *porteños*, often call their city the Paris of South America; and with its culture and glamour, it probably earns that name. Buenos Aires is often described as Latin America's most European city. The population consists largely of the descendants of immigrants from Spain and Italy who came to Argentina in the late 19th or early 20th century. There are also significant minorities of Germans, British, Jews from central and eastern Europe, and Middle Eastern peoples, who are known collectively as *turcos*.

Since the 1930s, most immigrants to the city have come from the northern portion of Argentina, where the population is predominantly *mestizo* (mixed Indian and European). Today, the *mestizos* make up between one-fourth and one-third of the population in the metropolitan area; they tend to live in the poorest sections of the city, in the *villas miserias* and the distant suburbs. The area's black and mulatto population is of negligible size.

There are no ethnic neighborhoods, strictly speaking, but many of the smaller minorities typically settle close to one another in tightly knit communities. Villa Crespo, for example, is known as a Jewish neighborhood; the Avenida de Mayo is a center for Spaniards; and Flores is the home of many *turcos*. The assimilation of these groups has been less than complete, but the Argentinian identity has been flexible enough to allow ethnocentric mutual-aid societies and social clubs to emerge. Even the dominant Spanish language has been affected by other European cultures and has undergone changes: in the slums and waterfront districts, an Italianized dialect has emerged; and Italian cuisine is popular in the city.

Another hybrid of the Old and New Worlds is the tango, which emerged from the poor immigrant quarters of Buenos Aires toward the end of the 19th century and quickly became famous around the world as Argentina's national dance. Influenced by the Spanish tango and, possibly, by the Argentinian *milonga*, it was originally a high-spirited local dance but soon became an elegant ballroom form danced to melancholy tunes.

The combination of Old and New World cultures is also seen in the Argentinian diet. Southern European influences appear especially in the city where breakfast is often a light serving of rolls and coffee; and supper is taken, in the Spanish tradition, after nine o'clock at night. The Italian influence is seen in the popularity of pasta dishes. But the New World asserts itself in the Argentinian passion for beef, which is overwhelmingly preferred to other meats and fish. *Maté*, a native tealike beverage brewed from *yerba maté* leaves, is popular in the countryside.

Critical thinking question: What examples of Hispanic cultural diffusion in the United States can you name?

Source: "Argentina: The People and Cultural Life" (online) accessed at *www.eb.com:180/cgi-bin/ g?keywords=immigrants+in+Argentina,* October 5, 1998.

FIGURE 11.3 **Age-Sex Composition of the Hispanic Population, 2000 (by percentage)**

| | Hispanic Population | | Age | | Total U.S. Population | |
	Males	Females			Males	Females
	0.7	1.1	75+		2.2	3.7
	0.6	0.7	70-74		1.4	1.7
Median age 25.0	1.0	0.9	65-69	Median age 26.1	1.6	1.8
	1.0	1.1	60-64		1.8	2.0
	1.3	1.4	55-59		2.3	2.4
	1.9	2.0	50-54		3.1	3.1
	2.5	2.5	45-49		3.5	3.6
	3.3	3.2	40-44		4.0	3.9
	4.2	3.8	35-39		4.0	4.0
	4.7	4.1	30-34		3.7	3.5
	5.2	4.4	25-29		3.5	3.3
	5.3	4.3	20-24		3.4	3.2
	4.8	4.2	15-19		3.7	3.4
	4.6	4.4	10-14		3.7	3.4
	5.2	5.0	5-9		3.7	3.4
	5.4	5.1	0-4		3.5	3.2

Median age 31.7 Median age 34.1

Percentage

Source: U.S. Bureau of the Census.

(p. 434) shows, in 2000, from 25 to 50 percent of all Hispanics ages 25 and older had not completed high school. As a result, not only are their employment options limited, but their children face a greater risk of dropping out of school, becoming teen parents, and experiencing difficulties in the job market.[17] All Hispanic groups lag significantly behind the non-Hispanic population in producing high school graduates, with Mexicans having the fewest. About 43 percent of all Latinos ages 25 or older never finished high school in 2000, compared to 11 percent of non-Hispanic whites. The comparison for holding a college degree is 11 to 28 percent.[18]

Reasons cited for the education gap between Hispanics and non-Hispanics include the limited formal education of parents, less preschool experience for Hispanic children compared to whites and blacks, and cultural/linguistic differences encountered in school. Also important is the increased proportion of immigrants in the U.S. Hispanic population. Few educational differences exist between males and females, and—except for Mexicans—between different Hispanic subgroups. Cuban Americans have the highest percentage of college graduates, and Mexican Americans have the lowest.

We can find two promising notes within other educational data. U.S.-born Hispanics in all ethnic groups are likelier than the foreign born to have higher

FIGURE 11.4   **Differences Among Hispanic Subgroups in Age, Education, and Economic Status, in 2000 (in percentages)**

Age

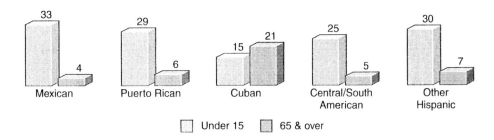

Under 15   65 & over

Education (of persons age 25 and over)

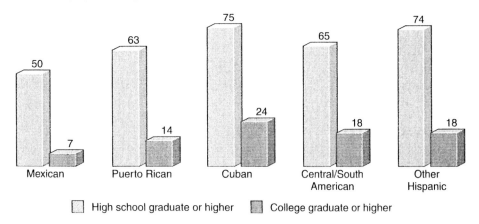

High school graduate or higher   College graduate or higher

Economic Status

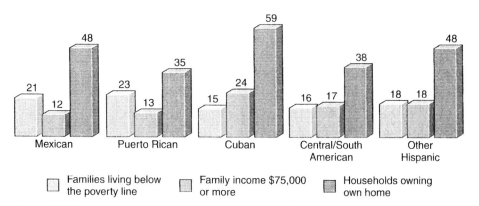

Families living below the poverty line   Family income $75,000 or more   Households owning own home

Source: U.S. Bureau of the Census, *Current Population Reports*, Series P20–535.

TABLE 11.2   **Educational Attainment, Ages 25 and Over, in 2000 (in percentages)**

Males	Non-Hispanic	Mexican	Puerto Rican	Cuban	Central/South American	Other Hispanic
8th grade or less	4.8	32.3	18.4	16.0	20.8	13.5
9th to 12th grade	7.9	17.5	18.6	8.7	13.8	12.6
H.S. graduate	32.3	27.0	29.7	32.3	30.2	32.0
Some college or AA degree	25.3	16.5	19.6	18.7	17.6	24.4
Bachelor's degree or more	19.0	4.9	9.5	15.6	11.8	10.0
Advanced degree	10.7	1.8	4.2	8.8	5.8	7.5
Females						
8th grade or less	4.7	32.2	16.9	20.0	23.5	16.4
9th to 12th grade	8.5	16.0	17.7	9.2	13.0	14.0
H.S. graduate	35.0	25.7	29.3	33.6	28.8	32.5
Some college or AA degree	26.9	18.9	23.8	15.5	17.4	25.2
Bachelor's degree or more	17.3	5.3	7.8	12.3	11.8	8.0
Advanced degree	7.7	1.8	4.5	9.5	5.4	4.0

Source: U.S. Bureau of the Census, "Hispanic Population in the United States," *Current Population Reports,* March 2000, Series P20–535.

percentages of high school and college graduates. In 1998, 44 percent of foreign-born Hispanic adults were high school graduates compared with 70 percent of U.S.-born Hispanic adults.[19] Further, sociologist Rubén Rumbaut—in the largest long-range survey of immigrant offspring in the nation—found that second-generation Latinos in San Diego had better grades and lower dropout rates than fellow public-school students whose parents were not born in the United States.[20]

One alarming indicator is the decreasing but still high dropout rate of Hispanic high school students—in particular, Mexican and Puerto Rican teens (see Table 11.3). These statistics translate into lower incomes and higher poverty rates compared to whites and blacks.

Income

The median family income for Latino families has been traditionally higher than for black families (see Table 11.4). Moreover, the income gap is growing. Despite a strong Hispanic middle class—over 1 in 10 families had incomes of $75,000 or more in 2000 (see Figure 11.4)—more than one in five Hispanic families live in

TABLE 11.3   High School Dropouts by Race and Hispanic Origin: 1970, 1980, 1990, and 1999 (in percentages)

Race and Age	1970	1980	1990	1999
White	10.8	11.3	10.1	9.3
16–17 years	7.3	9.2	6.4	5.3
18–21 years	14.3	14.7	13.1	13.1
22–24 years	16.3	14.0	14.0	12.5
African American	22.2	16.0	10.9	10.8
16–17 years	12.8	6.9	6.9	4.9
18–21 years	30.5	23.0	16.0	16.8
22–24 years	37.8	24.0	13.5	14.8
Hispanic	NA	29.5	26.8	23.9
16–17 years	NA	16.6	12.9	9.5
18–21 years	NA	40.3	32.9	32.1
22–24 years	NA	40.6	42.8	36.1

Source: U.S. Bureau of the Census, *Statistical Abstract of the United States 2001,* (Washington, DC: U.S. Government Printing Office, 2001), Table 258, p. 163.

TABLE 11.4   Median Income of Hispanic, Black, and White Families for Selected Years, 1970-2000

Year	Median Family Income			Hispanic Family Income as Percentage of White Income
	Hispanic	Black	White	
1970	NA	$ 6,279	$10,236	NA
1980	$14,716	$12,674	$21,904	67
1990	$23,431	$21,423	$36,915	64
2000	$33,447	$30,439	$45,904	73

Source: U.S. Bureau of the Census, *Money Income in the United States 2000.* (Washington, DC: U.S. Government Printing Office, 2001), P60-213, September 2001.

TABLE 11.5   Poverty Rate of Hispanic, African American, and White Families for Selected Years, 1975-1999 (in percentages)

| Year | Percentage of Families Below Poverty Level | | | Ratio of Hispanic to White Poverty Rate |
	Hispanic	African American	White	
1975	25.1	27.1	7.7	3.3
1980	23.2	28.9	8.0	2.9
1990	25.0	29.3	8.1	3.1
1999	20.2	21.9	7.3	2.8

Source: U.S. Bureau of the Census, *Statistical Abstract of the United States 2001.* (Washington, DC: U.S. Government Printing Office, 2001), Table 685, p. 445.

poverty. Generally, Hispanics consistently have had a lower percentage of impoverished families than blacks (see Table 11.5). A higher percentage of Puerto Ricans live in poverty than of any other group, including blacks, whereas Central and South Americans are the least likely of all Hispanic subgroups to live in poverty (see Table 11.6). Also, Puerto Ricans have significantly narrowed the poverty gap with other Hispanic groups in just two years, moving from four percentage points of differential with Mexican Americans to just one percentage point.

As with the education data, we must again note the impact of immigration on these income and poverty statistics. New entrants into the U.S. labor force typically earn less than those with longer residence because they lack the education, training, experience, and seniority of other workers. Therefore they tend to take lower-skill jobs at entry-level salaries. Like past European peasant immigrants, they make

TABLE 11.6   Persons Below Poverty Level, 1999 (in percentages)

White Non-Hispanic	7.7
African American	23.6
All Hispanic	22.8
Mexican American	24.1
Puerto Rican	25.8
Cuban American	17.3
Central and South American	16.7
Other Hispanic	21.6

Source: U.S. Bureau of the Census, *Current Population Reports,* Series P20–535, Table 14.1.

economic survival their immediate goal. The United States for them is, as William Bradford described North America for the English Puritans in the early 17th century, a place "where they must learn a new language and get their livings they [know] not how."

Occupation

Occupation provides an important basis for personal esteem, and the occupational distribution of an entire ethnic group thus serves as a comparative measure of its status within the larger society. Table 11.7 addresses this aspect of Hispanic structural assimilation. As might be expected from the educational data, most Hispanic males (except Cubans and Other Hispanics) are heavily underrepresented in managerial and professional occupations; and an unusually high number work in unskilled blue-collar occupations. Mexicans also have a disproportionate amount of their labor force in farming. Reflecting the typical gender occupational distribution in U.S. society, Hispanic females tend to be just as likely to work in technical, sales, and administrative support positions as non-Hispanic females. Hispanic women are less likely than non-Hispanics, however, to occupy managerial and

TABLE 11.7 **Occupational Distribution, 2000**

Males	Non-Hispanic	Mexican	Puerto Rican	Cuban	Central/South American	Other Hispanic
Managerial, professional	30.8	9.1	14.4	21.8	12.8	20.5
Technical, sales, administrative support	20.5	12.8	13.9	25.8	16.4	19.0
Service occupations	9.9	14.7	15.9	11.1	15.2	15.9
Precision production, crafts, repair	17.7	23.5	17.2	18.3	22.6	15.3
Operators, fabricators, laborers	18.2	28.6	27.4	22.0	29.7	26.2
Farming, fishing, forestry	2.9	11.3	1.2	1.1	3.3	3.2
Females						
Managerial, professional	33.5	16.2	19.9	25.8	17.4	23.6
Technical, sales, administrative support	40.4	37.5	46.4	45.2	31.8	40.6
Service occupations	16.9	25.7	20.6	16.8	33.0	23.2
Precision production, crafts, repair	2.1	4.0	2.6	1.3	2.9	1.6
Operators, fabricators, laborers	6.0	13.8	10.4	11.0	14.0	10.4
Farming, fishing, forestry	1.1	2.8	0.1	—	0.8	0.6

Source: U.S. Bureau of the Census, "Hispanic Population in the United States," *Current Population Reports,* March 2000, Series P20–535.

professional positions, although Cuban and Other Hispanic women are more strongly represented in these jobs than are other Hispanic women. All Hispanic women are more likely than non-Hispanics to work in service occupations as well as in unskilled blue-collar positions as operators, fabricators, and laborers.

THE MEXICANS

Most of the 21 million Mexican Americans are concentrated in the southwestern states, and Mexican Americans account for more than three fourths of all Latinos in Arizona, California, Illinois, and Texas, as well more than half of all Latinos in Colorado and New Mexico. The largest population concentrations live in Los Angeles, Chicago, Houston, San Antonio, and Phoenix.[21]

Much diversity exists within this ethnic group in degree of assimilation and socioeconomic status, ranging along a continuum from the most newly nonacculturated arrivals to the *Hispanos* of northern New Mexico and southern Colorado who trace their ancestry in that region to the days of the Spanish conquest of what is now the southwestern United States.

Throughout New Mexico—which, unlike Texas and California, has not had constant contact with Mexico through border crossings—the employment pattern is bright. In fact, Hispanic Americans there are heavily represented in civil-service occupations at the local, state, and federal levels. Like many recent non-Western immigrants, they retain a cultural heritage that includes their diet, child-rearing philosophy, emphasis on the family, and extended family contacts, but they hold economically secure occupational positions.

Second-generation Mexican Americans living in large cities typically display greater structural assimilation as evidenced by separate residences for nuclear families, English-language competency, fewer children, and comparable family values, jobs, and income in border towns or agricultural regions.[22] However, most present-day Mexican Americans, whether they live in an urban setting or a rural area, lag far behind the rest of the U.S. population on every measure of socioeconomic well-being: education, income, and employment status.

Recruiting Mexicans

In the second half of the 19th century, Mexicans from south of the border helped fill U.S. labor needs for the construction of railroad lines and the expansion of cotton, fruit, and vegetable farms. Thereafter, the Chinese Exclusion Act of 1882 curtailed one source of laborers, and later the Immigration Acts of 1921 and 1924 curtailed another. But the demand for labor—especially for agricultural workers—increased, and Mexicans left their poverty-stricken country for the economic opportunities available in the United States.

Despite U.S. government restrictions on immigration, it was easy for Mexicans to cross the largely unpatrolled border and enter the United States illegally; and many did so. The ones who crossed into Texas were known as "wetbacks" because they had crossed the Rio Grande. Some Mexican aliens also entered the United States legally as contract laborers. Under the *bracero* program, Mexican aliens entered the United States on temporary visas, and then returned to Mexico after the harvest. This system provided needed workers without incurring the expenses of educating their children, and of extending welfare and other social services to them during the off-season. The program lasted from 1942 until 1964, when farm mechanization, labor shortages in Mexico, and the protests of native Hispanics in the United States ended it.

Expulsion

Although cheap Mexican labor was a boon to the southwestern economy, Mexicans usually found themselves unwelcome during downturns in the U.S. economy. One such time was the 1930s, when many U.S. citizens were jobless. Some Mexicans returned home voluntarily, and others did so under pressure by local residents. Many who did not leave willingly were rounded up and deported:

> During the depression the U.S. Government and public agencies, in what was called a "repatriation program," deported literally hundreds of thousands of Mexicans and Mexican Americans to cut down on welfare costs. Roundups extended through southern California, to most cities of the Southwest, and as far north as Chicago and Detroit.
>
> In Los Angeles, official trucks would grind into the barrios—the Mexican American neighborhoods—and the occupants would be herded into them. There was little or no determination of national origin. Citizenship or noncitizenship was not considered. Families were divided; the bringing of possessions was not permitted. . . .
>
> "They pushed most of my family into one van," one of the victims, Jorge Acevedo, remembers bitterly. "We drove all day. The driver wouldn't stop for bathroom nor food nor water. Everyone knew by now we had been deported. Nobody knew why, but there was a lot of hatred and anger. . . . We had always known that we were hated. Now we had proof."[23]

During the recession of the mid-1950s, the U.S. Immigration and Naturalization Service launched "Operation Wetback" to find and return all undocumented Mexican aliens. Between 1954 and 1959, concentrating on California and Texas but ranging as far north and east as Spokane, Chicago, Kansas City, and St. Louis, government officials found and expelled 3.8 million Mexicans, only 63,515 of whom ever received a formal hearing. Not all were undocumented aliens. INS agents stopped and questioned many U.S. citizens, if they "looked Mexican." Those unable to prove their legal status on the spot found themselves arrested and sent "home" without any further opportunity to defend themselves.[24]

Violence

One infamous incident in which prejudices against the Mexicans erupted into violence was the Zoot Suit Riot of 1943. The name came from the popularity among

Mexican American youths at that time of wearing long, loose-fitting jackets with wide shoulders; high-waisted, baggy trousers with tight cuffs; and flat-topped hats with broad brims. The gamblers in the original show and the film version of *Guys and Dolls* dressed in this fashion.

On June 3, 1943, two events triggered the riot. Some Mexican boys, returning from a police-sponsored club meeting, were assaulted by a group of non-Mexican hoodlums from the neighborhood in Los Angeles. That same evening, 11 sailors on leave were attacked, and 1 sailor was badly hurt. The sailors said that their assailants were Mexican youths who outnumbered them 3 to 1. When the police, responding late, found no one to arrest in the area, about 200 sailors decided to settle the matter themselves the following evening. Cruising through the Mexican section in a caravan of 20 taxicabs, they savagely beat every Mexican they found. The police did nothing to stop them, and the press gave this event and its aftermath wide publicity:

> The stage was now set for the really serious rioting of June seventh and eighth. Having featured the preliminary rioting as an offensive launched by sailors, soldiers, and marines, the press now whipped public opinion into a frenzy by dire warnings that Mexican zoot-suiters planned a mass retaliation. To ensure a riot, the precise street corners were marked at which retaliatory action was expected and the time of the anticipated action was carefully specified. In effect these stories announced a riot and invited public participation. . . .
>
> On Monday evening, June seventh, thousands of *Angelenos,* in response to twelve hours' advance notice in the press, turned out for a mass lynching. Marching through the streets of downtown Los Angeles, a mob of several thousand soldiers, sailors, and civilians proceeded to beat up every zoot-suiter they could find. Pushing its way into the important motion picture theaters, the mob ordered the management to turn on the house lights and then ranged up and down the aisles dragging Mexicans out of their seats. Street cars were halted while Mexicans, and some Filipinos and Negroes, were jerked out of their seats, pushed into the streets, and beaten with sadistic frenzy. . . .
>
> Here is one of the numerous eyewitness accounts written by Al Waxman, editor of *The Eastside Journal:*

> Four boys came out of a pool hall. They were wearing the zoot-suits that have become the symbols of a fighting flag. Police ordered them into arrest cars. One refused. He asked: "Why am I being arrested?" The police officer answered with three swift blows of the night-stick across the boy's head and he went down. As he sprawled, he was kicked in the face. Police had difficulty loading his body into the vehicle because he was one-legged and wore a wooden limb. . . .
>
> At the next corner a Mexican mother cried out, "Don't take my boy, he did nothing. He's only fifteen years old. Don't take him." She was struck across the jaw with a night-stick and almost dropped the two-and-a-half-year-old baby that was clinging in her arms. . . .
>
> A Negro defense worker, wearing a defense-plant identification badge on his work clothes, was taken from a street car and one of his eyes was gouged out with a knife. Huge half-page photographs, showing Mexican boys, stripped of their clothes, cowering on the pavements, often bleeding profusely, surrounded by jeering mobs of men and women, appeared in all of the Los Angeles newspapers. . . .

Armed with clubs, soldiers, sailors, and civilians roam through the streets of Los Angeles, looking for Mexicans to attack. The three-day rampage in June 1943, dubbed the "zoot suit riot" because of the distinctive clothing favored by Mexican youth that marked them as targets, was similar to other riots in a minor incident triggering excessive violence.
(*Source:* © Bettmann/CORBIS)

When it finally stopped, the Eagle Rock *Advertiser* mournfully editorialized: "It is too bad the servicemen were called off before they were able to complete the job. . . . Most of the citizens of the city have been delighted with what has been going on."[25]

This bloody incident, like the Know-Nothing riots, the anti-Chinese race riots, lynchings, and many other acts of violence, was the result of increasing societal tensions and prejudices against a minority that erupted into aggression far in excess of the triggering incident. Whatever Mexicans thought about Anglo society before this wartime incident, they would long remember this race riot waged against them with official sanction from the police, the newspapers, and city hall.

Urban Life

In some places, such as Los Angeles and New Mexico, Mexican Americans often are better integrated into the mainstream of society than their compatriots elsewhere. There they have higher intermarriage rates, nuclear- instead of extended-family residence patterns, and less patriarchal male roles. They enter more diverse occupations, and many attain middle-class status and move from the barrio to the suburbs and outskirts of the city. Yet in East Los Angeles and in other areas of the Southwest, particularly in smaller cities and towns, Mexican Americans reside in large ethnic enclaves, virtually isolated from participation in Anglo society. Even some

Hispano middle-class individuals whose families have lived in the United States for generations choose to live among their own people and interact mostly with them.

Many Mexican Americans live in substandard housing under crowded conditions. In the southwestern states where most Mexican Americans live, their housing is more crowded than that of nonwhites; in Texas, twice as many Mexicans as blacks live in overcrowded housing. Segregated in the less desirable sections of town, with their children attending schools that warrant the same criticisms as inner-city schools in major cities, they experience many forms of discrimination.

The large influx of Mexican Americans and their residential clustering in urban areas have resulted in a high level of increasingly segregated schools. This trend toward isolation of schoolchildren holds for most urban Hispanics but is particularly pronounced in the Southwest. For example, the percentage of white students in Los Angeles County high schools attended by Mexican American students has dropped from 45 percent to 15 percent since 1970.[26]

Stereotyping

Negative stereotypes of Mexican Americans persist in U.S. society. Such categorizations as their being lazy, unclean, treacherous, sneaky, or thieving once appeared frequently in the mass media. Currently, the two most common stereotypes that Mexican Americans have had to combat involve being undocumented aliens and belonging to youth gangs. "Looking" Mexican often raises suspicions about legal residence or makes prospective employers wary of hiring a possible undocumented alien, even if the individual is a legal U.S. resident. In the poor urban barrios of Los Angeles, San Antonio, and El Paso, youth gangs are an integral subculture within the community. The intergang fights and killings—particularly in East Los Angeles—and the associated drug scene, create a lasting, negative picture of Mexican Americans in the minds of many Anglos.

Sometimes scholarly works inadvertently contribute to the stereotype. Some people used Florence Kluckhohn's study of a remote village in New Mexico as a basis for generalizing about the values of all Mexicans. As a result, such local cultural attributes as present-time orientation, preference for intangible gratification over material rewards, and emphasis on enjoyment rather than on working hard became synonymous with being Mexican.[27] Like blacks and Puerto Ricans, Mexican Americans suffer from culture-of-poverty beliefs held by the dominant society. All too often outsiders blame their low socioeconomic standing on their supposed cultural values.

In reality, Mexican Americans have a participation rate in the labor force comparable to all other groups—white, black, Asian, or other Hispanic.[28] Furthermore, the percentage of Mexican Americans receiving welfare assistance is only about one-sixth that of blacks and of other Hispanic groups, and about one half that of whites. Because Mexican Americans have a large proportion of immigrant workers, the usual pattern of lower wages for the foreign-born wage earners impacts significantly on the median income of all Mexican Americans.

Another reason for their low earnings despite a high rate of labor-force participation is the exploitation of many Mexican Americans. Composing a majority of the workforce in the garment industry in southern California and Texas, they may work 55 to 70 hours a week in sweatshops, often under deplorable working conditions, and perhaps earn only $50 a week.[29] In nonunion meat-packing plants in Chicago and other midwestern areas, Mexican Americans work for low wages in an occupation with an extremely high job-related accident rate.[30]

Chicano Power

Until the 1960s, the term *Chicano* was a derogatory name applied in Mexico to the "lower"-class Mexican Indian people rather than to the Mexican Spanish. Then, as an outgrowth of the civil-rights movement and in direct contradiction to the stereotype of the passive, apathetic Mexican community, the Chicano movement emerged. Seeking to instill pride in the group's *mestizo* heritage (mixed Spanish and Indian ancestry), activists adopted the term in their efforts to promote political activism and demands for economic and educational quality. Prominent leaders emerged—Cesar Chavez and his United Farm Workers Union, Rodolfo Gonzales and his *La Raza Unida* political third-party movement, Reies Lópes Tijerina and his Alianza group seeking to recover land lost or stolen over the years, and David Sanchez and his militant Brown Berets, who modeled themselves after the Black Panthers. These leaders have left center stage now, and a new generation of Chicanos is making its presence known. One significant entity is the Mexican-American Legal Defense and Education Fund (MALDEF). This civil-rights organization effectively uses its influence in the public arena to address such issues as bilingualism, school financing, segregation, employment practices, and immigration reform.[31]

Before this national movement dawned, rapid expansion in Sunbelt cities in the 1950s and 1960s had generated problems and tensions that led to the formation of community groups opposed to urban renewal plans threatening Mexican-American neighborhoods. These organized neighborhood protests were the vanguard of what became known as the Chicano movement. In San Jose, for example, activists of diverse origins and agendas united in opposition not only to the effects of urban development on the barrios, and this city later became a center for the Chicano movement during its time of phenomenal growth.[32]

Older organizations, such as the League of United Latin American Citizens and the American G.I. Forum, focused on assimilation and the Anglo world, with a primary emphasis on social functions. Newer groups—such as *La Raza Unida, Movimiento Estudiantil Chicano de Aztlan*—served as synthesizers, bringing the two cultures together. The newer groups have focused on political issues, such as the farm workers' plight, while promoting a sense of peoplehood.

Turning away from the third-party politics of the past, Chicanos are integrating into the two main political parties. In states where they are heavily concentrated, Chicanos are developing a powerful political base. They are represented mostly by 5,900 locally elected Hispanic public officials, 2,200 of whom are in Texas, 800 in California, 700 in New Mexico, 300 in Arizona, and 200 in Colorado.[33]

Ethnic festivals, such as the Cinco de Mayo Festival in Los Angeles where Hispanics line up to buy food at booths, provide an opportunity to celebrate one's cultural heritage and reaffirm ethnic identity. At the same time such events enable nongroup members to enrich their intercultural experiences by enjoying the foods, music, and crafts that are part of America's diversity.
(*Source:* © David Young-Wolff/PhotoEdit)

Current Patterns

Since 1993, female Mexican immigrants have outnumbered male immigrants, as the percentage of the latter has fallen from 63 in 1992 to 43 in 1998. The median age for all Mexicans arriving in the United States, regardless of gender, dropped from 27 in 1992 to 23, while the female median age was higher, 26.5 years compared to 19.9 years for males.[34]

Illinois is now the third highest state of intended residence among new arrivals. In 1998, 62,113 Mexican immigrants settled in California, 22,956 in Texas, 10,127 in Illinois, and 4,129 in Washington.[35] The 2000 census revealed that over 1.1 million Mexican Americans live in Illinois, making it the fourth highest in Mexican American population behind California, Texas, and Arizona. More than three times as many Mexican Americans live in Illinois as in New Mexico.[36]

Mexican immigration continues into both rural and urban areas, but most immigrants are settling in urban neighborhoods, although not necessarily in inner cities. About 90 percent live in metropolitan areas, but fewer than half reside inside central cities.[37] Many of the central-city residents are of a low socioeconomic status and live in areas where the school dropout rate of Mexican American youth runs as high as 45 percent and where drug use and gang violence are everyday realities.[38]

THE PUERTO RICANS

Puerto Ricans frequently refer to their island as the "true melting pot," unlike the U.S. mainland, which has only claimed to be one. Originally inhabited by the Arawak and Caribe indigenous tribes, Puerto Rico came under Spanish domination in 1493 and remained so for 400 years. When its native population was decimated, black slaves were imported. **Miscegenation** (interracial marriage) was common, resulting in a society that deemphasized race. The high degree of color integration discussed earlier is reflected in words such as *moreno, mulatto, pardo,* and *trigueño,* indicating a broad range of color gradations. Today, structural assimilation in the island's multiracial society extends to housing, social institutions, government policy, and cultural identity.[39] A high degree of intermarriage often means that people classified as being in one racial category have close kin relationships with people in other racial categories, either by bloodline or by adoption:

> The racial scene in Puerto Rico has also been characterized by what I would call a high degree of two-way integration, while in the U.S. one-way integration has been and is the norm. That is, Blacks are usually sent to White schools, not vice-versa. Blacks integrate into White America, not Whites into Black America. . . . In this country it rarely happens that a Black couple adopts a White child. The number of White babies available for adoption and the limited income of many Blacks tend to discourage this action. In most agencies the action is not permitted and the reverse is encouraged. In Puerto Rico, it is a fairly common occurrence to rear other people's children as one's own. These "hijos de crianza" come in all colors. Thus, a "White" couple may rear the darker, orphaned children of a neighbor and vice-versa.[40]

Joseph Fitzpatrick identified several cultural and historical factors that led to the more tolerant racial attitudes found in Puerto Rico (and in other Latin American countries):

1. Spain has had long experience with dark-skinned people (Moors), who often married white women.
2. In the wars of Christians against Moors and Saracens, captured whites also became slaves. Laws were developed to protect certain fundamental rights of all slaves, and this tradition carried over to the Spanish colonies.
3. Upper-class men in the Spanish colonies recognized their illegitimate children by women of color, frequently freeing the babies at their baptism.
4. Through the practice of *compadrazgo,* outstanding white members of a community became the godparents of a child of color at baptism. Even in cases where the child's real father was unknown, the *padrino,* or *compadre,* was well respected and became a significant person in the child's life.

5. A shared sense of community, by rich and poor, white and nonwhite, gave all a sense of place that was expressed in gatherings for fiestas, religious processions, and public events.[41]

Early Relations

The annexation of Puerto Rico by the United States in 1898 (after the Spanish-American War) was followed by an attempt at forced Americanization. U.S. authorities discouraged anything associated with the Spanish tradition and imposed the use of the English language. Presidents appointed governors, usually from the mainland, to rule the territory. The inhabitants received U.S. citizenship in 1917, but otherwise the island remained a virtually ignored, undeveloped, poverty-stricken land. Citizenship brought open migration because it eliminated the need for passports, visas, and quotas; but it did not give the people the right to vote for president or to have a voting representative in Congress. By 1930, approximately 53,000 Puerto Ricans were living on the mainland. During the Depression and the war years, migration effectively stopped, but this period was followed by the mass migration of the post–World War II era.

In the 1940s, several improvements occurred. The *Partido Popular Democratico* emerged as a powerful force on the island. Puerto Rico became a commonwealth, with the people writing their own constitution and electing their own representatives. In addition, the island gained complete freedom in its internal affairs, including the right to maintain its Spanish heritage and abolition of all requirements to use English. Another party, the *Partido Nuevo Progresista*, favors statehood and enjoys substantial public support. Questions in Washington about the retention of Spanish as the official island language and about phasing in federal income taxes have contributed to keeping the statehood issue bottled up so far, despite strong public support in a nonbinding voter referendum in Puerto Rico in December 1998.

To help the island develop economically, the U.S. government launched "Operation Bootstrap" in 1945. U.S. industries received substantial tax advantages if they made capital investments in Puerto Rico. The tax breaks and abundant supply of low-cost labor encouraged businesses to build 300 new factories by 1953 (increasing to 660 by 1960), creating over 48,000 new jobs. As a result, Puerto Rico became the most advanced industrialized land, with the highest per capita income, in the Caribbean and in most of Central and South America.

By the 1980s, however, expiring tax exemptions prompted numerous industries to leave the island in search of cheaper labor and tax exemptions elsewhere, thereby reducing available job opportunities. Puerto Rico's unemployment rate has consistently been twice that of the mainland, rising and falling in response to mainland economic conditions. Following the 1980–1982 recession, the island's unemployment rate peaked at 23 percent in 1983, dropped with improved economic conditions on the mainland, rose again during the 1990–1992 recession, and stood at 12.3 percent in April 2002.[42]

The Push-Pull Factors

Despite the creation of thousands of factory jobs through Operation Bootstrap, the collapse of the Puerto Rican sugar industry in the 1950s triggered the beginning of *La Migracion,* one of the most dramatic voluntary exoduses in world history. One of every six Puerto Ricans—480,000 altogether—migrated to the mainland, driven by the island's stagnant agrarian economy and encouraged by inexpensive plane fares and freedom of entry as U.S. citizens. Many were rural people who settled in metropolitan urban centers, drawn by the promise of jobs. The greatest period of Puerto Rican migration was 1946–1964, when about 615,000 moved to the mainland. Only the Irish migration of the mid-19th century offers a close comparison, but that was forced in part by the Potato Famine (see the accompanying Ethnic Experience box).

After 1964, a significant drop in Puerto Rican migration occurred, aided in part by a revived Puerto Rican sugar industry after a U.S. boycott of all Cuban trade. Many factors contributed to this drop. The pull factor lost its potency, as

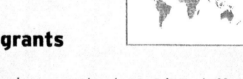

The Ethnic Experience
Harassment Against Early Migrants

"**M**y husband and I bought our own house in Brooklyn after the Second World War, and a few years later we bought other property on Long Island, where we moved to raise our family. In 1956 we were employed by the U.S. Military Academy, West Point, and purchased a lovely home in a so-called exclusive area not too far away. This was a quaint neighborhood where custom-built homes ranged from $40,000 up to $100,000.

"Shortly after we moved in, we went down to Florida on vacation. When we came back, the house was empty. We slept on the floor and the following day our attorney by telephone searched every place high and low until he found our possessions in a warehouse in Nyack. Some of our neighbors had learned we were originally from Puerto Rico, were unhappy to have us as neighbors, and had plotted this against us.

"The harassment continued for a long time. They threw their garbage every night on our lawn. They even sent the police to intimidate us and even tried to buy us out. We told them they couldn't afford the luxury of buying us out. We felt we had all the rights in the world to enjoy all the privileges others had. We were honest, hard-working, respectable citizens, too. So we took legal action and demanded for damages. The judge was fair and ruled for us."

Source: Puerto Rican woman who came to the mainland in 1946 in her 20s.

cities such as New York lost hundreds of thousands of manufacturing jobs and lost its promise as a job market. An island population of less than 2.4 million at that time and a declining fertility rate made sustaining the previous high exodus rate impossible. Furthermore, the earlier exodus relieved pressure on the home job market; increases in U.S. government welfare support, combined with remittances from family members on the mainland, encouraged many to stay on the island. In the 1970s, migration dropped to 65,900, before rising dramatically to 333,000 in the 1980s, prompted in large measure by the high unemployment rates mentioned earlier.

High migration rates and birth rates resulted in a 35 percent increase in the Puerto Rican population living on the mainland—from 2.7 million in 1990 to 3.4 million in 2000.[43] Of all the Puerto Rican people living either on the island or on the mainland, 49 percent were living on the mainland in 2000.

Like members of most ethnic groups, some Puerto Ricans return to their homeland to visit, and others to stay. Close proximity to the island is an obvious inducement, although the reasons for moving back vary. For some, the return migration stems from retirement or the desire for the more family-oriented society without discrimination and violent crime. Researchers investigating the motives for this circular migration also found that economic marginality is an important factor. That is, some migrants fail to succeed economically on the mainland and return to the island. The children of these less successful returning migrants are more likely to be impoverished than the children of migrants who remain on the mainland and the children of natives who never left the island. This outcome could also be caused by migration-related disruptions in employment.[44]

The Family

In Puerto Rico, as in all Latin American countries, an individual's identity, importance, and security depend on family membership. A deep sense of family obligation extends to dating and courtship; family approval is necessary because of the emphasis on marriage as a joining of two families, not just a commitment between two individuals. An indication of family importance is the use of both the father's and mother's surnames, but in reverse order to the U.S. practice. José Garcia Rivera, whose father's last name is Garcia and whose mother's is Rivera, should be called Mr. Garcia, not Mr. Rivera. Fitzpatrick notes that erroneous interpretation of these names in the United States by non-Hispanics is a constant source of embarrassment to Spanish-speaking people.[45] José's wife retains her family name and calls herself Maria Gonzalez de Garcia. On formal occasions, she may use both sets of family names, such as Maria Gonzalez Medina de Garcia Rivera, whereas her husband would write his name José Garcia Diaz y Rivera Colon.[46]

Fitzpatrick identified four common types of families among Puerto Ricans: (1) the extended family residing either in the same household or in separate households with frequent visits and strong bonds; (2) the nuclear family, increasingly common among the middle class; (3) the nuclear family plus other children of different names from previous unions of husband or wife; (4) the female-headed household, with children of one or more men, but with no permanent male in the home.[47] The last type is frequently found among welfare families and is thus the target of much criticism.

Religion

The Catholic Church traditionally played an important role with immigrant groups, assisting in succession the French, Irish, Germans, Italians, Slavs, Poles, Syrians, Lebanese, and others.[48] This pattern did not at first repeat itself with the Puerto Ricans, at least in terms of representation in the church hierarchy, church leadership in the ethnic community, and immigrant involvement in the church. In 1970, Nathan Glazer and Daniel P. Moynihan observed,

> The Puerto Ricans have not created, as others did, national parishes of their own. Thus the capacities of the Church are weak in just those areas in which the needs of the migrants are great—in creating a surrounding, supporting community to replace the extended families, broken by city life, and to supply a social setting for those who feel lost and lonely in the great city. . . .
> Most of the Puerto Ricans in the city are Catholic, but their participation in Catholic life is small.[49]

Several factors contributed to this departure from the usual pattern. Because the island was a colony for so long, first Spanish and then U.S. priests predominated within the church hierarchy on the island. Few Puerto Ricans became priests, and the few who did rarely came to the mainland with the immigrants. The distant and alien nature of the church in Puerto Rico caused Puerto Ricans to internalize the sense of their Catholic identity without formally attending mass and receiving the sacraments. Baptisms, weddings, and funerals all became important as social occasions, and the ceremony itself was of secondary importance. Throughout Latin America, Catholicism means personal relationships with the saints and a community manifestation of faith, not the individual actions and commitments expected in the United States. Another aspect of religious life in Puerto Rico, Brazil, and other parts of Latin America is the widespread belief in spiritualism and superstition. These practices, which undoubtedly constitute remnants of old folk rites, continue to be observed by various cults as well as by many Catholics.[50]

On the mainland, a few other factors weakened any possibility that the Puerto Ricans would develop a strong ethnic church. The movement of various white Catholic ethnics out of the cities left behind clusters of old national churches with few parishioners. Church leaders decided to use these existing churches, schools, and other buildings to accommodate the newcomers. Thus, instead of having their own churches, the Puerto Ricans had the services of one or more Spanish-speaking priests, with special masses and services performed in a basement chapel, school hall, or other area of the parish. Although this practice was cost-effective for the Catholic Church, it prevented the parish from becoming the focal point for a strong, stable community because the group could not identify with it.

As the integrated parishes became more heavily Hispanic over the years, the New York archdiocese added more Spanish-speaking priests. In time, the annual

Fiesta de San Juan each June became a widely observed religious festival in New York City. Religious/civic organizations such as the *Centro Católico Puertorriqueño* in Jersey City and the *Caballeros de San Juan* in Chicago became effective support organizations, further uniting the Puerto Rican community.

For many people in the lowest socioeconomic class, whatever their racial or ethnic background, religion serves as an emotional escape from the harsh realities of everyday life. The **Pentecostal faith,** a form of evangelical Christianity that inspires a sense of belonging through worship participation, thus offers greater attraction for some than Catholicism. Pentecostal churches represent the largest Hispanic Protestant religious movement in Puerto Rico and the U.S. mainland, as well as throughout Latin America. In the United States, storefront churches, with small and intimate congregations of about 60 to 100, offer their largely immigrant members a sense of community they cannot find elsewhere. Second-generation participation falls off sharply, however, and it remains to be seen whether Pentecostalism among Puerto Rican Americans will be more than a first-generation phenomenon of limited duration.[51]

Church estimates reveal that only 6 percent of the Puerto Rican population on the mainland belongs to any Protestant denomination, including Pentecostalism, and only 33 percent are practicing Catholics.[52] It seems unlikely, then, that religious identification will be an important factor in either assimilation or cultural pluralism, as it was for earlier immigrant groups.

Puerto Rican Communities

New York City contains two thirds of all Puerto Ricans living on the mainland. They comprise a larger shore of the city's Hispanic population than any other group (37 percent). They are particularly concentrated in the Bronx and Brooklyn, each of which contains more people of Puerto Rican origin than any other county in the nation. Puerto Ricans live in all 50 states, with the largest concentrations (more than 250,000) living in New York, Florida, New Jersey, and Pennsylvania.[53]

For many years, the continuous **shuttle migration** prevented an organized community life from fully developing. Hometown clubs—voluntary organizations based on one's place of birth—provided a place to celebrate weddings, birthdays, first communions, and confirmations. But because they drew members from scattered New York neighborhoods, they did not serve as community centers; nor did any other social institution. Only the annual Puerto Rican Day Parade, begun in 1958, served to galvanize group identity. By 1977, however, Clara Rodriguez discerned increased ethnic neighborhood organization:

> Note, for example, the growth of what are today Puerto Rican "cuchifrito" stands, social clubs, and after-hour clubs. These and other institutions did not exist years ago or existed in a very different form. Today they are identifying symbols of a Puerto Rican neighborhood. This same phenomena of change is also reflected in the speech of many second generation Puerto Ricans who no longer speak continuous Spanish, but whose English is decidedly "Rican."[54]

A familiar sight in any ethnic neighborhood is stores catering to the needs of the community with familiar products and signs in the residents' native language. This bodega, with its signs and outside wares in a New York City Hispanic neighborhood, also fills the typical additional role of a support system in connecting people with each other and with various service agencies.
(*Source:* © Robert Brenner/PhotoEdit)

As in most ethnic communities, many social institutions have evolved. Some are informal, like the *bodega,* or local grocery store, which serves as more than a source of Hispanic foods. It is a social gathering place where social interaction, gossip, and neighborly community create an "oasis of Latin culture." Here one can obtain advice on finding a home, getting a job, or buying a car.[55] The *bodega* thus functions as an important part of the community's infrastructure.

Other community institutions are civic and social organizations. Some, born out of the War on Poverty and dependent on federal funding, have declined; but others remain strong. Most notable is *Aspira,* founded in 1961. Through guidance, encouragement, and financial assistance, *Aspira* seeks to develop cultural pride and self-confidence in youths and to encourage them to further their education and enter the professions, technical fields, and the arts. Begun in New York City, its grassroots program achieved national fame and expanded to other cities. A more direct community-action group is the New York City–based Puerto Rican Community Development Project, which attempts to promote a sense of identity among Puerto Ricans and to develop community strength. Another organization begun in New York City is the Puerto Rican Family Institute, which provides professional social services to Puerto Rican families. Parent-action groups, athletic leagues, cultural organizations, and social clubs also exist, providing services and fulfilling community needs. Because of their limited political involvement, Puerto Ricans have had less electoral influence than have some other groups. This may be changing, though: In the 1990s, they played decisive roles in local and congressional elections in Illinois, New Jersey, New York, and Pennsylvania.[56]

Socioeconomic Characteristics

Of all the major racial or ethnic groups, Puerto Ricans have the highest poverty rate, although this picture has improved in recent years (see Table 11.6). Most Puerto Ricans on the U.S. mainland live inside central cities in old neighborhoods formerly inhabited by lower-class European immigrants. Unlike their predecessors, however, Puerto Ricans often cannot find work to match their limited job skills and educational background. Manufacturing and other blue-collar employment, most notably in the garment industry, moved from the Snowbelt to the Sunbelt and from the cities to the suburbs.

Intensifying the ill effects of unemployment is the island ethic that women should not work. Among the more recently arrived Puerto Ricans, it is unusual to find women working, whether they live with a spouse or head a household—and 37 percent of all Puerto Rican households are headed by a woman. This percentage is significantly higher than the percentage for all other Hispanic groups but is slightly lower than the percentage for African American families.[57]

Puerto Rican families are more likely than African American families to be poor and on welfare. One reason for this is that African American women participate at a much higher rate in the labor market. Like all groups, Puerto Ricans include people with varying socioeconomic characteristics. By no means do all live in poverty. In 1999, the annual income of 40 percent of Puerto Rican families exceeded $35,000; the annual income of 26 percent exceeded $50,000. In about 57 percent of all Puerto Rican families both parents live together—a figure that is lower than for other Hispanic families.[58]

MEXICANS AND PUERTO RICANS: A COMPARISON

At first glance, the statistics seem contradictory. Compared to Mexican Americans, most Puerto Ricans are less likely to have arrived recently, are better educated, and speak better English. Furthermore, employed Puerto Ricans, on average, earn more than employed Mexicans. However, fewer Mexican Americans live in poverty; and of those who do, far fewer seek government assistance than do the Puerto Rican poor. The labor-force nonparticipation rate—the rate of those who have stopped looking for work—is far higher for Puerto Ricans.[59]

What accounts for this? Employed Puerto Ricans work in highly unionized labor markets that have favorable wages and working conditions. Mexican Americans work in states that are less well organized by unions and where continually arriving newcomers create an extensive labor supply, enabling exploitative practices by employers and depressing the wage scale. Another part of the answer lies in settlement patterns. Because more Puerto Ricans live inside central cities than do Mexican Americans, their economic well-being depends on the highly localized economic conditions there, and central cities have experienced a significant decline in low-skill jobs in recent decades. The Southwest, in contrast, has experienced rapid growth, making job prospects for less-skilled workers better there than in northern cities.[60] Consequently, more Mexican Americans than Puerto Ricans can find work, but for less pay.

Another factor that has an impact on poverty is the difference in the number of families headed by females. In 1999, women headed 37 percent of Puerto Rican families compared to 21 percent of Mexican American families (see Figure 11.5). Cultural values partly explain this phenomenon. Mexicans tend to stress the family unit, whereas rural Puerto Rico, from which many female Puerto Rican immigrants come, has a long tradition of out-of-wedlock childbearing. Also, immigrant Puerto Rican women are more likely than those who remain on the island to have recently gone through the breakup of a marriage or serious relationship. Notably, female-headed Puerto Rican families declined by 4 percent between 1995 and 1999.[61]

THE CUBANS

Although the United States granted Cuba independence after the 1898 war with Spain, it continued to exercise *de facto* control over the island. The United States pressured Cuba to relinquish the large naval base it still operates at Guantánamo

FIGURE 11.5 **Hispanic Married-Couple Families, by Origin, in 1999 (in percentages)**

Origin	Percentage
Hispanic	68.0%
Non-Hispanic	76.6%
Mexican	69.9%
Puerto Rican	56.7%
Cuban	79.2%
Central and South American	66.6%
Other Hispanic	61.7%

Source: U.S. Bureau of the Census.

Bay; and through the Platt Amendment of 1902, it reserved the right to intervene in Cuba if necessary to protect U.S. interests. The Cubans resented these infringements on their newly achieved sovereignty. In the 1930s, Franklin Roosevelt's Good Neighbor Policy helped ease relations between the two countries.

Migration

Because the U.S. government until 1950 did not differentiate Cuban immigrants from others listed as originating in the West Indies, we do not know the exact numbers of Cuban immigrants prior to that time. Almost 500,000 people came to the United States from the West Indies between 1820 and 1950, although the Cubans appear to have had little impact on the U.S. scene during that period. Still, a few legacies persisted, such as the Cuban community in northern New Jersey that dates back to 1850 and attracted many immigrants in the 1960s.

Since 1960, more than 768,000 Cubans—more than came from the entire West Indies over a period of 130 years—have entered the United States. Touched off by Castro's rise to power, Cuban immigration surged in the first years of the Cuban revolution, then ebbed and flowed with shifts in both U.S. and Cuban government policies (see the accompanying Ethnic Experience box). In the 1960s and early 1970s, the first waves of postrevolutionary refugees were "displaced bourgeoisie"—well-educated middle- and upper-class professionals and businesspeople alienated by the new regime.[62] Sympathetically received by the U.S. government as resisters against and refugees from the first communist regime in the western hemisphere, these Cubans began to concentrate in several major cities, notably Miami and New York. Initial concern in those cities that the new immigrants might overburden the educational, welfare, and social-services systems quickly dissipated as the Cubans made rapid economic progress and became a part of the community.

The largest single influx of Cubans occurred in late 1980, when the Mariel boatlift brought 125,000 newcomers to the United States in just a few months. Most were urban working-class and lower-class people, but Castro also included several thousand criminals among them—which triggered an unfavorable U.S. response. By 2000, the Cuban American population exceeded 1.2 million, with about three fourths, identified as first-generation U.S. residents.[63]

Ethnic Communities

In some instances, Cubans at first found themselves treated disparagingly because non-Hispanic residents did not differentiate them from other, poorer Spanish-speaking groups such as the Puerto Ricans and Dominicans. Although the Cubans had previously looked on such other Caribbean peoples with disdain, they found that it was in their own best interests to work cooperatively with other Hispanic groups. In a pattern reminiscent of the Sephardic and Ashkenazic Jews, who first resisted and then were very helpful to the central and eastern European Jewish immigrants, the Cubans sometimes established closer relations with other Hispanic

The Ethnic Experience
Brotherhood in Talk and in Deed

"*I* have to tell you that the Spanish-speaking people are always talking about brotherhood and the brotherhood of the Latin American countries. They say our brother country Mexico and our brother country Venezuela, and every time they mention a Latin American country, they say the brother country. Well, in reality, it is wrong. When we needed an escape from Cuba, we only had America. America was the only country that opened the door. America is the only place where you can go for freedom and where you can live as a human being.

"I love Cuba very much but I can tell you that we never had the freedom that we have here. I can sincerely say that the opportunities in this country—America—are so great and so many, that no matter how bad they say we are as far as economics right now—they're talking about recession and everything—no matter how bad they say, it will never be as bad as it was and it is, actually, in Cuba.

"America took us in and we are grateful to America and to the Americans. And remember, when we came over, we were looking for freedom and liberty. Now we have freedom, we have liberty, and we have the chance to make money. Many Cubans are doing very well, better than me. I make enough to support my family and to live decently. I am very happy and grateful.

"Believe me, I am not only speaking for myself, but for a large group of Cubans who feel the same way I feel. We are happy here. We miss Cuba. Sometimes we get tearful when we think about the old friends and the old neighborhoods, but we are lucky. We are lucky because we still can say what we want to say, and we can move around wherever we want, and be what we want to be."

Source: Cuban refugee who came to the United States in 1960 at age 18.

groups, particularly in New York City. These cooperative efforts helped bring greater stability and visible progress to Hispanic neighborhoods.

Cubans often settled in blighted urban areas, but their motivation, education, and entrepreneurial skills enabled them to bring color, vitality, stability, and improvement to previously declining neighborhoods. Long-time residents of areas heavily populated by Cubans often credit them with restoring or increasing the beauty and vigor of the community.

Miami offers an excellent example. Its climate and nearness to Cuba made it the ideal choice of many exiles, thereby increasing the fears of residents about so large an ethnic group being in their midst. Yet by 1966, one observer commented,

> Though some ill-feeling still persists in Miami, by and large the city has come to count its new Cuban community as its own good fortune. . . . There is even something of a real-estate boom in Miami—one of the few cities in the U.S.

where housing markets are strong—and an estimated 30 percent of the new FHA commitments there are to Cubans. Enterprising Cubans have been credited with bringing a new commercial vigor to much of the downtown area, especially the former commercial center of Flagler Street, which had been rapidly running down. Many of the former Havana cigar manufacturers and their employees have set up nearly a dozen companies in Miami, helping the city to displace Tampa as the hand-rolled-cigar capital of the U.S. At least one cigarette company, Dorsal & Mendes, is thriving; there are also sizable and prosperous Cuban-owned garment companies, shoe manufacturers, import houses, shopping centers, restaurants and night clubs. To the northwest of Miami, Cuban entrepreneurs have set up sugar plantations and mills.[64]

In the early 1980s, however, a series of ethnic-related traumas—labor union restrictions, negative newspaper and public responses to the Marielitos, voter approval of a harsh Dade County antibilingual ordinance, and four days of anti-Cuban rioting by African Americans—prompted a Cuban reaction that quietly reshaped Miami's political, social, professional, and architectural landscape. Alejandro Portes and Alex Stepick point out that Cubans responded to discrimination by forming their own economic enclave and entering local politics. Unlike the classical assimilation model of integration and absorption within the dominant society, this movement toward economic and political empowerment enabled Cubans to assert themselves and *then* enter the societal mainstream. Significantly, studies show that Cuban entry into the labor force did *not* negatively affect the city's black population.[65]

Because two out of every three Cuban Americans live in Florida, the Cuban impact on Miami, now dubbed "Little Havana," has been significant. About 52 percent of all Cuban Americans live in the Miami-Dade County, where Cuban influence has transformed Miami from a resort town to a year-round commercial center with linkages throughout Latin America and has turned it into a leading bilingual cultural center. Over 57 percent of Miami-Dade County is now Hispanic, including 657,000 Cubans, 80,000 Puerto Ricans, 38,000 Mexicans, and 522,000 others from Central and South America.[66]

New Jersey has the second-largest Cuban American concentration, with 6 percent (77,000) of the U.S. total. California contains 6 percent of the Cuban American population (72,000), and New York another 5 percent (63,000). Other Cuban Americans are scattered among the remaining states.[67]

Because Cubans have had a high status throughout the Caribbean for a long time, their presence in Hispanic American neighborhoods has brought a new dimension in intracommunity relations, expectations, and cohesion:

> In the Caribbean, the Dominicans, Puerto Ricans and Jamaicans are all highly regarded as entrepreneurs. However, even they acknowledge, sometimes ruefully, that it is the Cubans who are to the tropics what the Parisians are to France and the Genoans to Italy: People who possess that special admixture of diligence and brashness, making the shrewd and prudently risky decisions that are the difference between high success and just making a living.[68]

Cultural Values

In addition to sharing a commonality of values with other Latinos, Cubans also share certain subcultural values that differ from those of the dominant U.S. culture.[69] Among these are attitudes toward work, personal qualities, and the role of individuals in society.

Dominant-group values in the United States stress hard work as a means of achieving material well-being, whereas the Cuban orientation is that material success should be pursued for personal freedom, not physical comfort. Cubans do not consider work an end in itself, as they believe Anglos do. Instead, they think one should work to enjoy life. Intellectual pursuits are highly valued; idleness is frowned on.

Cubans are fervent believers in generosity, in contrast to the old Anglo Puritan values of thrift and frugality. Common group traits include sharing good fortune, maintaining a warm open-house policy, and reaching out socially to others. Cubans believe that one of the worst sins is to be a *tacaño*, a cheapskate who does not readily show affection and friendship through kindnesses and hospitality.

In Miami's "Little Havana," some older Cuban American men spend the afternoon playing dominoes at an outdoor table in front of a mural. This daily activity is an institutionalized form of ethnic solidarity and social interaction, similar to the card games once found in European clubs and coffeehouses in most U.S. cities. (*Source:* © Robert Holmes/CORBIS)

Individualism is a value best shown through national and personal pride, which Anglos often misperceive as haughtiness. Yet Cubans believe in expressing individualism not so much through self-assertiveness as through attitudes and actions oriented toward a group, sometimes a large number of people. Hostility needs to be directed through *choteo* and *relajo*, the continuous practice of humor, jokes, and wit, and accepted by others in good part. This is because one should avoid being a *pesado*—someone unlikable, disagreeable, and without wit—which is the worst of all cultural sins.

Although they remain the most metropolitan of all Hispanic American groups, Cubans today are as likely to live in such well-groomed suburbs as Coral Gables or Hialeah in Miami-Dade County, Florida—or others in California, New Jersey, or New York—as they are to live in the nearby cities. Cubans have a lower fertility rate, lower unemployment rate, higher median family income, greater education rate, and greater middle-class population composition than other Hispanic groups. As Table 11.7 shows, 22 percent of males and 26 percent of females are in managerial or professional occupations, a significantly higher proportion than for any other Hispanic group.

CARIBBEAN, CENTRAL, AND SOUTH AMERICANS

Several push factors—overpopulation, acute shortage of farmland, economic hardship, and political turmoil—triggered a significant increase in **emigration** from several Latin American countries in recent decades. Central and South Americans now constitute 9 percent of all Hispanic Americans (see Figure 11.6). After Mexico, the largest contingents come from the Dominican Republic, Cuba, Colombia, and Ecuador; they have been joined in recent years by growing numbers of refugees from El Salvador, Nicaragua, and Peru (see Table 11.8). Nearly 1 million Caribbean immigrants arrived in the 1990s, maintaining a steady 14 to 17 percent increase each decade since the 1970s. From over 430,000 Central and South American immigrants in the 1970s, their numbers leaped to about 930,000 in the 1980s, and surpassed that in the 1990s.[70]

The 1980s numbers include undocumented aliens who applied for permanent residence under the amnesty provision in the Immigration and Reform Act of 1986, a category led by El Salvador (143,070) followed by Guatemala (52,544), Colombia (26,363), the Dominican Republic (18,273), and Nicaragua (16,012). The Nicaraguan Adjustment and Central American Relief Act of 1997 eased the situation for subsequent undocumented aliens. It granted permanent resident green cards to 150,000 Nicaraguans and 5,000 Cubans, and allowed more than 250,000 Salvadorans, Guatemalans, and East Europeans to stay and apply for suspension of deportation under more lenient rules.[71]

Over a half million Central Americans live in Los Angeles. Substantial numbers also reside in San Francisco, Houston, Washington, DC, New York, Chicago, New Orleans, and Miami. As the largest Central American group in the United States, Salvadorans usually constitute the majority of Central Americans in most

FIGURE 11.6 **Hispanic Americans by Origin (as a percentage of all Hispanics), in 2000**

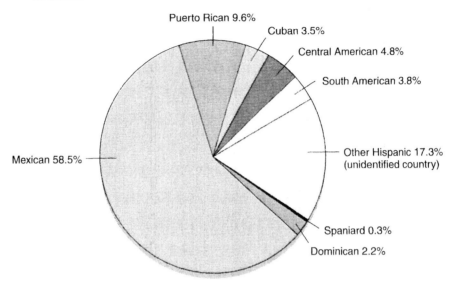

Puerto Rican 9.6%

Cuban 3.5%

Central American 4.8%

South American 3.8%

Mexican 58.5%

Other Hispanic 17.3% (unidentified country)

Spaniard 0.3%

Dominican 2.2%

Source: U.S. Bureau of the Census.

TABLE 11.8 **Number of Western Hemisphere Immigrants from Leading Countries, 1971-1998**

1.	Mexico	4,227,374
2.	Dominican Republic	700,235
3.	Cuba	546,152
4.	Jamaica	484,849
5.	Canada	484,441
6.	El Salvador	427,025
7.	Haiti	335,895
8.	Colombia	304,735
9.	Guyana	207,698
10.	Peru	181,739
11.	Ecuador	166,423
12.	Trinidad and Tobago	153,647

Source: U.S. Immigration and Naturalization Service, *Statistical Yearbook 1998*, (Washington DC: U.S. Government Printing Office, 2000), pp. 22–27.

cities, followed by Guatemalans (see Table 11.9). Nicaraguans predominate in Miami, however, and Hondurans in New Orleans among Central Americans.

The Dominicans

More than 717,000 Dominican immigrants have left their Caribbean homeland for the United States since 1971, over 20,000 annually—which makes the Dominican Republic the second-leading source of Spanish-speaking immigrants to the United States. Two of every three Dominicans live in New York State, for a total of about 500,000, according to the 2000 census. Most live in New York City, particularly in Washington Heights in Manhattan and in the Bronx, where Dominicans are a majority in the borough. Other primary areas of residence are New Jersey (53,000), Florida (34,000), and Massachusetts (30,000).

Dominicans are more likely to live and interact within their own ethnic neighborhoods instead of integrating into mixed Hispanic neighborhoods. A common pattern is to coexist alongside Puerto Ricans, each ethnic group keeping mostly to itself. In the South Bronx, however, where Dominican immigrants are primarily

TABLE 11.9 **Number of Central and South Americans Living in the United States, 2000**

Central Americans	1,686,937
Costa Ricans	68,588
Guatemalans	372,487
Hondurans	217,569
Nicaraguans	177,684
Panamanians	91,723
Salvadorans	655,165
Other Central Americans	103,721
South Americans	1,353,562
Argentineans	100,864
Bolivians	42,068
Chileans	68,849
Colombians	470,684
Ecuadorians	260,559
Paraguayans	8,769
Peruvians	233,926
Uruguayans	18,804
Venezuelans	91,507
Other South Americans	57,532

Source: U.S. Bureau of the Census.

men and the Puerto Rican family is headed predominantly by women, Dominican–Puerto Rican marriages and liaisons are common.[72]

Most Dominicans are people who have fled the poverty of their land. Because many lack specialized skills, they have a high unemployment rate and often live in poor urban neighborhoods, suffering the deprivation and family disruption so common among people with low levels of education and job skills. Racial discrimination further compounds their problems, and some find work as migrant farm laborers, away from urban troubles.

The Salvadorans

Several push factors account for the large-scale Salvadoran emigration to the United States.[73] Agricultural modernization and expansion of property holdings by the landowning oligarchy displaced tens of thousands of rural peasants. Relocating to such urban centers as San Salvador, many of these dispossessed poor could not find work despite the growing industrialization. Conditions deteriorated when the Salvadoran government responded to protests and demonstrations with severe repression. Paramilitary death squads composed of members of the ruling elite, as well as regular security and military forces targeted peasant leaders, union militants, and political activists. Revolutionary movements arose, and guerrilla offensives in the 1980s prompted escalating violence by the security and military forces and the death squads. Large-scale attacks against civilian populations in rural areas occurred, including massacres of entire villages believed to be sympathetic to the guerrillas.

As a stream of undocumented Salvadorans fled into the United States, immigration agents sought to apprehend and return them, denying them refugee status. The Reagan-era State Department argued that, although El Salvador might be a war-torn country, none of those who left could prove that they had been specifically singled out for persecution and thus did not have the necessary "well-founded fear of persecution" to qualify for political amnesty. Out of this conflict was born the sanctuary movement in the United States: Clergy defied the government, hiding Salvadoran refugees in churches and homes. The clergy and members of their congregations provided food, shelter, and clothing and secretly helped the refugees get to safe locations. These refugees were among the 143,070 Salvadoran applicants for amnesty and permanent residence in the United States.

Although the political situation improved in El Salvador in the 1990s, most Salvadorans in the United States have remained, putting down roots and enjoying the support system within their evolving ethnic communities. Through chain migration, other relatives and friends join them, continuing a steady migration flow that ranks El Salvador sixth among western hemisphere countries providing immigrants to the United States (see Table 11.8).

The Nicaraguans

Nicaraguans have entered the United States as immigrants, refugees, asylees, and undocumented aliens. A **refugee** lives outside his or her country, unable or unwilling to return because of persecution or a well-founded fear of persecution. An **asylee** is identical to a refugee, except for being physically in the United States or at a port of entry when requesting refuge.

After the Sandinistas came to power in Nicaragua and the Contras undertook a guerrilla war against the new government, more than 46,000 middle-class refugees entered the United States between 1980 and 1990.[74] Simultaneously, another 79,000 Nicaraguans streamed into Texas, filing asylum applications.[75] Most of this latter group, unlike the refugees, consisted of poor, unskilled, and illiterate *campesinos* from the countryside. Just over 11,000 asylum seekers were granted asylum by 1990.[76] Between 1991 and 1998, more than 22,000 additional refugees and asylees received permanent resident status, while yet another 15,000 asylum cases remained pending.[77]

Drawn by the Latin American population and the already established Nicaraguan communities in Miami and southern California, most refugees chose one of those two destinations. Miami–Dade County schools, for example, experienced almost a quadrupling of their Nicaraguan student enrollment. With no previous educational experience, most of the 13- to 15-year-olds were illiterate and had to be taught the basics of reading and arithmetic.[78] Sweetwater, a western suburb of Miami, became almost completely Nicaraguan, earning the nickname "Little Managua."

When Daniel Ortega's Sandinista regime was voted out of office in February 1990 and the Contra war fizzled out, the 11-year-long exodus of refugees subsided. Some Nicaraguans returned to their homeland, but most chose to stay in the United States.[79] The 2000 census identified about 178,000 Nicaraguans, most of whom were either in Florida or California. Other states with sizable population concentrations include New York, Texas, New Jersey, Maryland, and Virginia.

The Colombians

Among South American countries, Colombia supplies the most immigrants to the United States, more than 314,000 since 1971.[80] Population pressures, the promise of better economic opportunities abroad, and chain-migration networking have increased the annual immigration totals, which now average over 11,000 yearly. Of the 471,000 Colombians tallied in the 2000 census, 80 percent were foreign-born. Most of the remainder were children born to these first-generation Colombian Americans.

Socioeconomically, Colombians are a mixture of educated professionals and low-skilled peasants seeking a better life (see the accompanying Ethnic Experience box). Living mostly in urban neighborhoods near other Hispanics, they form their own social clubs and institutions, attempting to preserve their culture through ethnic folk-dance groups and holiday celebrations. Colombian Americans are mostly concentrated in New York, Florida, New Jersey, and California.

A minute percentage of Colombians are involved in the cocaine trade and in related drug-war killings. The high profile of this small number of criminals unfortunately smears the rest, just as Italian Americans have suffered from nationality stereotype because of the Mafia. In reality, almost all Colombian Americans are decent, law-abiding people who work hard to make a life for themselves in their adopted country.

The Ethnic Experience
Cultural Traits and Adjustment

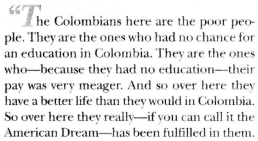

"The Colombians here are the poor people. They are the ones who had no chance for an education in Colombia. They are the ones who—because they had no education—their pay was very meager. And so over here they have a better life than they would in Colombia. So over here they really—if you can call it the American Dream—has been fulfilled in them.

"Emotionally they're very attached to their country. See, this is the thing that is very hard for people to understand. They want them to become American and to forget everything. You can't! The ties—the blood ties—are too strong! You just can't become—as I said, I cannot even become an American. I can't! Even if I wanted to. You would have to make me all over again. And I love this country and I choose to stay in this country.

"Now with these people—take some of them. They have come because of necessity—sheer necessity. We criticize them because they don't love America, but I don't think that is the fact. Also, if you notice the kind of people that come here. For instance, I had students who were the children of my father's workers on the coffee plantation. Now in my country they were tilling the soil. You know, the children of the owner go to school. The children of the

worker go to till the soil. They had no chance of an education. They had huts up in the mountains where they had no running water, no electricity. Now they come here and they have all the conveniences. If they live poorly, Americans criticize them but they don't realize where they were living before. If they're not clean and spotless and they don't keep the shades the right way—but these people have been doing this for a hundred years! The people who just came in never even had a shade to talk about. They never had a venetian blind. They never even had a window to talk about!" (Laughs.)

"I think we have to be careful because we often make the mistake of imposing our way to the people. Now you could say, we're not going to them, they're coming here. But if you accept them in the country, I think you also have to accept a big risk. I think the melting pot idea is not the prevalent idea. It is not a workable idea. Each one has a culture. Each people has a culture and if you want them in America, if you allow them to stay here, you have to work something by which each one is able to live. I don't mean to say that we have independent little countries, but that they are comfortable. Because you cannot remove—those are strong things that you cannot remove from a person."

Source: Colombian immigrant who came to the United States in 1952 at age 16.

HISPANIC AMERICAN ASSIMILATION

As with all immigrant groups, any discussion of assimilation must take into account the cultural diversity among the groups identified as "Hispanic," as well as such other variables as length of residence, place of residence, social class, family structure, and education of parents. Those differing socioeconomic characteristics among the various Latino groups, as discussed in earlier sections, affect integration into the societal mainstream. Because Hispanics can be of any race, we must also consider that variable in any discussion of assimilation. Consequently, Hispanic Americans can be found at all stages along the pluralism–assimilation continuum. Within the broad range of areas of assimilation, the social institutions of education and family provide valuable insights.

Education. One means of interpreting rapid assimilation to the United States is educational enrollment. A 2001 study found that, although the overwhelming majority of high-school-age immigrant youths are as likely as their native-born peers to be enrolled in school, some Hispanic groups have above-average levels of school attrition. The most serious of these is among Mexican teenagers, where almost half of Mexican-born 15- to 17-year-olds are not in school. This nonenrollment pattern, though not to the same level, exists among Central American youth, especially those from El Salvador and Guatemala. However, immigrants from these countries who arrived before the start of their schooling are not more likely than native-born Americans to drop out of high school. National origin and age of entry are therefore significant variables in the effectiveness of education as an agent of assimilation.[81]

Another finding in this study was that below-average rates of high-school enrollment did not change with longer duration in the country for immigrants from Puerto Rico, Cuba, and the Dominican Republic. The pattern is most likely among groups concentrated in central cities and attending schools with a demoralized educational climate. In this setting, longer duration of residence in the United States may lead to greater acculturation to U.S. society, but not necessarily to the middle-class ideal of high educational aspirations among these groups.

Perhaps another study in 2000 gives some insight into this pattern. Ramon Grosfoguel and Chloe Ramon argue that the social position of Latino Caribbean populations in the United States today continues relationships rooted in racial hierarchies produced by centuries of European colonialism. Thus they identify Puerto Ricans as colonial racialized subjects in the "Euro-American imaginary" and Dominicans as transformed into colonial immigrants in the New York Metropolitan Area. They also speak of the disassociation of pre-1980s Cuban middle-class migrants from the "Puerto Ricanization" experienced by the Dominicans. In their view, this legacy of colonialism affects the social acceptance of racially distinct Latino Americans.[82]

Family. As often stated in this book, intermarriage patterns are important indicators of assimilation. Recent studies show high rates of intermarriage with non-Hispanics among Cubans, Mexicans, Central Americans, and South Americans. A notable exception exists among Puerto Ricans and Dominicans, who have exceptionally high rates of intermarriage with each other, lower rates of intermarriage with non-Hispanics, no intergenerational increase in exogamy, and higher rates of nonmixed ancestry among the second generation.[83] Considerable intermarriage also occurs within the Hispanic population among the different national-origin groups, significantly influenced—says Michael Rosenfeld—by a pan-national identity of being "Hispanic" that transcends different national origins.[84]

A related study on family and assimilation examined the relationship between acculturation and maternal teaching behaviors in Dominican and Puerto Rican mothers. One finding was that Puerto Rican mothers tended to be more acculturated than Dominican mothers. Although both groups preferred Caribbean-influenced teaching behaviors that involved giving directives, visual cues, and modeling, Puerto Rican mothers made significantly greater use of American preferences of inquiry and praise, whereas Dominican mothers employed more modeling behaviors.[85]

Without question, cultural pluralism is a everyday reality among many Latinos and Latinas whose ethnic identity is a vibrant dynamic. A steady influx of newcomers and the presence of many first-generation Hispanic Americans means continuance of that pattern. However, it would be a mistake either to conclude that the forces of assimilation are not at work, especially among the second generation, or to ignore the assimilation of many Hispanic Americans because of their length of residence and socioeconomic status.

SOCIOLOGICAL ANALYSIS

Like other immigrant groups before them, the new arrivals from Latin America are changing the face of the United States, making their distinctive contributions to the neighborhoods in which they live. But with their growing numbers, they also are encountering the hostility historically accorded to almost all newly arriving ethnic groups. Applying sociological perspectives can place their current experiences in a comparative context.

The Functionalist View

Rapid population growth has been a mixed blessing for these newcomers. They have been able to develop supportive ethnic subcommunities, providing social institutions and an interactive network that ease adjustment to a new country. Cuban settlement in deteriorated urban neighborhoods has both revitalized those areas and inevitably brought interethnic assistance to other Hispanic groups. Because 86 percent of all Hispanics live in nine states (California, Arizona, Colorado, New Mexico, Texas, Illinois, New York, New Jersey, and Florida), they are quickly realizing their potential political power, enabling them to improve their life situation. Concern exists that their numbers and common language may be dysfunctional, delaying assimilation and creating an "Hispanic Quebec" within the United States.

Immigrants with lower levels of educational attainment often fill the needs of industries on the periphery, such as garment factories, restaurants, and hotels, which depend on low-skilled workers, even undocumented aliens and minors. This segment of the labor market prefers to hire immigrants with less than a high-school education, as discovered by Héctor Cordero-Guzmán and Ramon Grosfoguel in an ongoing study of New York City's immigrant and U.S.-born labor force. They find that immigrants with less than a high-school diploma (except Dominicans, Puerto

Ricans, and Russians) have higher rates of labor-force participation than U.S.-born people in the same category and that they also have slightly higher earnings. These advantages decrease with increased education, suggesting that in the less competitive, lower-status jobs, Latin American immigrants have become the highest earners as they fill manual labor jobs needed by labor-intensive industries.[86]

Rapid social change is the key to functional analysis of existing problems. The influx of large numbers of immigrants in a short period and the changing occupational structure of U.S. society have prevented the social system from absorbing so many low-skilled workers right away. How can we ease Hispanic newcomers into the societal mainstream? We can either take a *laissez-faire* attitude, allowing the passage of time to produce acculturation and economic improvement, or we can seek an interventionist means of resolving the problems. Advocates of the latter approach argue that, through bilingual and other educational programs, job-training programs, and business investment incentives for more job opportunities, we can improve the system to help newcomers realize the American Dream that brought them here.

The Conflict View

Although Robert Blauner first applied the concept of internal colonialism to the black ghetto (see Chapter 2), Chicano activists found the idea appealing because it coincided with the legacy of Anglo takeover and domination of the Southwest in 1848 and continued Anglo control of the barrios in the cities of the region since that date. They readily embraced the concept of the barrio as an internal colony, dependent on Anglo investment and subservient to Anglo domination of municipal government and commerce. They criticized the concentration of the Mexican American working class in poor urban barrios and the exodus of the Anglo and Latino middle class to the suburban fringe. In these economically weakened barrios, Mexican Americans struggled against larger economic and political trends.

Analysts of internal colonialism maintain that the continued residential segregation of Mexican Americans in ghetto areas of many U.S. cities states is unlike the pattern experienced by European immigrants to the United States. In the case of Europeans, the level of segregation declined with length of residence in the United States. But with the newer immigrants, instead of seeing a gradual acculturation or structural assimilation process, these analysts see the persistence of subordination, with Mexican Americans confined to certain areas of rental properties controlled by absentee landlords and restricted to low-paying job opportunities, inferior schools, and many other forms of discrimination.

Economic exploitation is another dimension of conflict analysis. Mexicans, Puerto Ricans, and other Hispanics work as migrant farm laborers in many places under abysmal conditions for meager pay despite repeated exposés. City sweatshops employing thousands of undocumented aliens, refugees, and low-skilled legal immigrants operate in clandestine settings, prospering from the toil of low-wage employees. The rise of an ethnic bourgeoisie—the *padrino* in urban or farm settings, the token elite among the Chicano population, or the small middle class with other Hispanic groups—only helps control the rest and does not signal an economic upgrading and assimilation of the remaining group members.

Resolving the problem of the inferior status of millions of Hispanic Americans, according to this view, will occur only through protest movements, organized resistance to exploitation, and the flexing of political muscle. New citizens need to realize more fully their commonalities, taking a lesson from the Irish and using their ballot power to create the necessary changes to benefit themselves. If they effectively wield their political clout, they will begin to overcome the power differential that exists in the social and economic spheres as well.

The Interactionist View

Anglo–Hispanic relations often are strained by inaccurate perceptions. Members of the dominant group tend to think that there is but one Spanish-speaking public, when actually a variety exists, each preferring different foods, music, and recreation and having different cultural attributes. Too many Anglos view Hispanic ethnic subcommunities, parallel social institutions, and limited command of English as detrimental to the cohesiveness of U.S. society, failing to realize that 83 percent of Hispanics are first-generation Americans repeating a resettlement pattern of earlier European immigrants. Extensive poverty among many Hispanics often invites outsiders to blame the victim or to engage in culture-of-poverty thinking. Instead of confronting the problems of poor education and lack of job skills and job opportunities, some find fault with the group itself, reacting with avoidance, indifference, or paternalistic behavior.

In our earlier discussion about eye contact, physical proximity, the notion of hurrying, and the relevance of time, we identified a few areas of potential cultural misunderstanding. Add to this Anglo impatience with language problems, African American concerns about economic competition, taxpayer resistance to welfare costs, labor-union fears that wages will be undermined by cheap labor, and nativist alarm at the failure of the melting pot to "melt" the Hispanics, and you have further reasons for members of non-Hispanics to stereotype Latinos as an increasing social problem. Because perceptions influence interaction patterns and social policy, the potential for tensions and conflict is strong.

Witnessing extensive Spanish-language usage is no doubt the main "hot button" that triggers nativists' ire more than any other ethnic manifestation by Hispanics. Similar reactions once occurred when German and Italian newcomers concentrated in large clusters and their languages were everyday commonalities. As discussed in Chapter 2, language and culture share an interdependent relationship; each fosters the other, with both usually ebbing through the assimilation process over the generations. In Chapter 14, we examine the issues and concerns involving language retention and English literacy.

For Hispanics, clinging to the old country's culture and ethnic identity is a matter of pride and personal commitment to a rich heritage. Some find it their only solace against discrimination, and even those who achieve economic mobility retain a strong ethnic identification. Washed afresh with new waves of Hispanic immigrants, the ethnic communities retain their vitality, prompting even successful Hispanics to hold onto their ethnic traditions. Interactionists thus point to the resiliency of an ethnic self-definition, which is somewhat at odds with assimilationist views.

RETROSPECT

In many ways, recent Hispanic immigrants repeat the patterns of earlier racial and ethnic groups. Coming in large numbers from impoverished lands, many enter the lowest strata of society, cluster together in substandard housing units, and face the problems of adjustment, deprivation, frustration, and pathology (sickness and crime). Marked as strangers by their language, customs, and physical appearance, they have difficulty being accepted and achieving economic security. The Hispanic poor face the same problems and criticisms as earlier groups. They also are criticized for failing to overcome these problems immediately, even though other groups often took three generations to do so. The dominant–minority response patterns in this case are thus quite similar to those of earlier immigrant peoples.

Particularly significant for the Hispanic immigrants, in comparison to other groups, are the changed structural conditions. The restrictive immigration laws of the 1920s drastically curtailed the great influx of southern, eastern, and central Europeans. Consequently the immigrants already here did not receive continuous cultural reinforcement from new arrivals. But among Hispanics, there is a sizable flow of new arrivals, and rapid and inexpensive communications and transportation encourage return trips to the not-so-far-away homeland. In addition, earlier European immigrants encountered sometimes heavy-handed attempts at Americanization, whereas today's immigrants live in a time when pluralism and ethnic resurgence are common among members of the dominant group.

Another crucial change in structural conditions has taken place in technology and the job market. When the European poor came to the United States, they could find many unskilled and semiskilled jobs. Despite many evils and abuses in industry, an immigrant could secure a little piece of the American Dream through hard physical labor. The immigrant today enters a labor market where technology has eliminated many low-skill jobs and mostly skilled jobs exist. The poor of the western hemisphere are not qualified for these positions; they find they cannot improve their lot through hard physical labor because this labor is no longer to be found.

During the mass European migration, the fledgling labor unions struggled to improve, and eventually did improve, the economic condition of the immigrant workers. Nowadays unions have limited means to help newcomers, and the federal government is less inclined to offer welfare aid than in the 1960s, when the government encouraged individuals to apply for welfare by liberalizing eligibility requirements. With structural unemployment leaving no alternative, the system maneuvers many Hispanics into a marginal existence.

Highly visible because of their numbers, language, culture, and poverty, many Latinos find themselves the objects of resentment, hostility, and overt discrimination from the dominant society. The familiar pattern of blaming the victim results in negative stereotyping, social segregation, and all shades of prejudice and discrimination against the Hispanic and Caribbean poor.

Not all are poor, of course. For those who are not, attaining economic security means a very different life experience. Other positive factors offer some promise of easing the transition to life in the United States: bilingual education, increased public awareness, a greater tolerance for cultural pluralism, and civic and government programs. Serious problems remain for a disproportionate number of Hispanic Americans, however, and it is too soon to tell whether new legislation designed to control the influx of undocumented aliens will have any positive impact on the Hispanic poor.

KEY TERMS

Asylee
Dignidad
Emigration
Machismo

Marianismo
Miscegenation
Pentecostal faith
Refugee

Shuttle migration
Undocumented alien

REVIEW QUESTIONS

1   What cultural value orientations do most Hispanics share to some degree?

2   What changes in structural conditions make upward mobility difficult for many of the newcomers to the United States?

3   How diverse a group are Mexican Americans? What factors influence the continued poverty status among so many of them?

4   What factors distinguish the Puerto Rican experience from that of other Hispanic groups?

5   How do Cubans differ from other Hispanics in cultural values and economic mobility?

6   What other Hispanic peoples currently migrate in significant numbers, and why are they doing so?

SUGGESTED READINGS

Chavez, Leo R. *Shadowed Lives: Undocumented Immigrants in American Society.* Fort Worth, TX: Harcourt Brace Jovanovich, 1992.

Profiles of unskilled and skilled undocumented Mexicans residing in rural and urban America.

De Anda, Roberto M. *Chicanas and Chicanos in Contemporary Society*. Boston: Allyn and Bacon, 1995.

An anthology of essays about the roles and lives of Mexican American women and men in their families, school, and the workplace.

Firmat, Gustavo Perez. *Life on the Hyphen*. Austin: University of Texas Press, 1994.

An examination of Cuban American communities and their culture, including art, food, music, recreation, achievements in business, and their impact on the United States.

Grassmuck, Sherri, and Patricia Pessar. *Between Two Islands: Dominican International Migration*. Berkeley: University of California Press, 1991.

A valuable profile of an often-overlooked immigrant group whose numbers far exceed those of other groups frequently studied.

Knouse, Stephen B.; Paul Rosenfield; and Amy L. Culbertson. *Hispanics in the Workplace*. Newbury Park, CA: Sage, 1992.

An anthology of articles focusing on Latinos and employment, including career mobility, discrimination, and job stress.

Mahler, Sarah J. *Salvadorans in Suburbia: Symbiosis and Conflict*. Boston: Allyn and Bacon, 1995.

An informative, ethnographic study of daily life and challenges faced by Salvadorans living on Long Island.

Perez y Gonzalez, Marie. *Puerto Ricans in the United States*. Westport, CT: Greenwood, 2000.

A thoughtful analysis about Puerto Rican culture, migrant adjustment and adaptation on the mainland, socioeconomic status, intergroup relations, and societal impact.

Pessar, Patricia R. *A Visa for a Dream: Dominicans in the United States*. Boston: Allyn and Bacon, 1995.

A detailed ethnographic profile of Dominicans living in New York, now its single largest immigrant group.

Portés, Alejandro (ed.). *The New Second Generation*. New York: Russell Sage Foundation, 1996.

A sociological profile of the children of immigrants in such locales as New York City, Miami, New Orleans, and Southern California.

Portés, Alejandro, and Alex Stepick. *City on the Edge: The Transformation of Miami*. Berkeley: University of California Press, 1993.

An excellent depiction of the Cuban impact on this resort city, revealing a different model of assimilation not detrimental to the economic welfare of the city's black population.

Rodriguez, Clara E. *Changing Race: Latinos, the Census, and the History of Ethnicity in the United States*. New York: New York University Press, 2000.

Through interviews and census data analysis, an analysis of how Latinos define their own racial and ethnic identity in America's divided racial landscape.

Sonnaborn, Liz. *Immigrants in America: The Cuban-Americans.* Farmington Hills, MI: Lucent Books, 2001.

An account of Cuban emigrants creating a vibrant community in Miami's "Little Havana" and emerging as one of America's most prosperous and politically active immigrant groups.

INTERNET LINKS

Go to *http://www.ablongman.com/parrillo* for numerous links relevant to this chapter under "Internet Readings and Exercises."

CHAPTER

18 The Ever-Changing U.S. Mosaic

As a nation of immigrants, the United States has seen many different groups of strangers arrive and interact with its people. The strangers perceived a different world that the native population took for granted, and their reactions ranged from wonder to bewilderment to dismay, from fulfilled expectations to culture shock. Because their language, appearance, and cultural background often made them conspicuous, the newcomers were categorically identified and judged as a group rather than as individuals. Native-born U.S. residents' responses ranged from receptive to impatient and intolerant, while their actions ranged from indifferent to helpful to exploitative.

Throughout the nation's history, then, varied patterns of majority–minority relations existed. Ethnocentric values prompted the natural development of ingroup loyalty and outgroup hostility among both indigenous and migrant groups. Competition for scarce resources, colonialism, and political dominance by the Anglo-Saxon core groups also provided a basis for conflict. However, the resulting prejudicial attitudes and discriminatory actions varied greatly in intensity. In addition, attitudes and social and economic conditions in this country changed over the years, affecting the newcomers' experiences.

Not all groups came for the same reasons or from the same backgrounds. Because of variations in social class, education, and occupational skills, not all immigrants began at the bottom of the socioeconomic ladder. Some came as sojourners, intending to stay only as long as necessary to earn enough money for a better life back in their homeland. Some came with the desire to become U.S. citizens in every sense of the word; others insisted on retaining their own culture.

Dominant attitudes, as well as sociological analyses, tend to focus on either assimilation or pluralism as the preferred minority adaptation. Which process the public considers more acceptable greatly influences dominant–minority relations. For example, if assimilation is held to be the "proper" goal, then evidence of pluralism will probably draw negative reactions, even though pluralism is a normal manifestation among first- and second-generation Americans. In recent years, the growing presence in U.S. cities and suburbs of Spanish-speaking peoples and of people of color from non-Western cultures has led many other U.S. residents to question the country's immigration policies.

Although race and economics are undoubtedly influencing factors, so too are genuine concerns about widespread pluralism overwhelming the "melting-pot" capabilities of the United States.

Stir in words such as *affirmative action, illegal aliens,* and *multiculturalism,* and the debate reaches "white heat" temperatures. These aspects of intergroup relations suggest to many that the majority group and the dominant culture are seriously threatened. In many quarters, the level of intolerance for any manifestation of pluralism has risen to alarming proportions.

How important is ethnicity today? Are immigration and assimilation concerns justified? What is the future of race and ethnicity in the United States? In this chapter, we attempt to answer these questions as we examine concepts of ethnic consciousness; evolutionary changes in ethnicity; and issues of legal and illegal immigration, bilingual education, and political correctness in a multicultural society.

Ethnic Consciousness

Sociologists have long been interested in the attitudinal and behavioral patterns that emerge when people migrate into a society with a different culture. For example, what factors encourage or discourage ethnic self-awareness or culture preservation? If succeeding generations supposedly identify less with their country of origin, how do we explain the resurgence of ethnicity among White ethnics in recent years? Are there ethnic differences in social mobility, social change, and behavior patterns even among third-generation U.S. citizens? Sociologists frequently raise these questions and offer a number of sociological explanations in an effort to describe scientifically the diversity of ethnic experience.

Country of Origin as a Factor

Mary Sengstock asserted that focusing on the relationship between the migrant and the country of origin will produce a better understanding of the degree of assimilation.[1] She contended that it is incorrect to assume that a migrant group today is affected primarily by factors in the receiving country, although this may have been truer of groups that came to the United States before World War I, when transportation and communication were limited. Furthermore, immigration restrictions in the 1920s sharply curtailed the number of new immigrants, thereby aiding the assimilation process since fewer newcomers arrived to reinforce the language and customs of the old country.

In today's world, however, an immigrant group can maintain contact with the country of origin not only through airmail letters but also (and more importantly) through telecommunications, rapid transportation, and the continued arrival of newcomers. Mexican and West Indian immigrant communities benefit from geographical proximity, and the homeland can exert more influence over its emigrants than in years past. Where greater social contact occurs, cultural transmission is greater too.

That contact with one's country of origin also affects politics. In an analysis of the political activities of Asian Americans, I identified three general and overlapping phases of acculturation in their political activities. These were: (1) the *alien phase,* when the political locus remains with the country of origin; (2) the *reactionary phase,* when immigrants form political organizations to protect their interests and fight discrimination; and (3) the *acceptance phase,* when they display a greater degree of cultural and structural discrimination.[2]

In examining the political activities of immigrants from the Dominican Republic, Haiti, and El Salvador, Jose Itzigsohn found manifestations of that first phase. Immigrants' transnational politics rested heavily on the government structure and political parties in the country of origin. The rise of a pattern of transnational politics, he states, is contingent on the home country's need for a steady flow of remittances, migrant organizations in the country of reception, and consolidation of competitive politics in democratic regimes.[3]

Sheila E. Henry finds a connection between country of origin and recent levels of ethnic and racial inequality in the United States. Focusing on Chinese, Japanese, and African Americans, she suggests that the U.S. stratification system closely reflects global economic stratification systems. Because Japan ranks among the leading capitalist nations, its immigrants enjoy a status of "honorary whites," something she suggests Chinese immigrants may soon enjoy, given their country's current economic boom. However, since no African country is likely to achieve economic global success in the near future, she thinks it is unlikely that the ethnic-group status of African Americans will change.[4]

The degree of stability or social change in the homeland has a profound effect on the migrant community's sociocultural patterns and lifestyle:

> Where the country of origin has experienced a relatively stable or gradually changing culture, the effect on the immigrant community will most likely be to encourage retention of the ethnic culture. This is much the same case as has occurred with Puerto Ricans and Mexican-Americans.
>
> Some societies, however, have experienced drastic changes in recent years. When groups of immigrants from such areas experience constant immigration and other types of contact with the mother country, one might expect such contact to produce profound effects on the immigrant community as well.[5]

To illustrate her position, Sengstock used a study of Chaldean immigrants from Iraq who settled in Detroit both before and after World War II. Iraq, presently occupied by U.S. troops, is nonetheless an independent nation-state, not a colonial land of different tribes all under the control of another nation. It replaced centuries-old tribal rivalries with the unity of nationalism, and these changes reached the Detroit community through visitors and immigrants. Recent immigrants, who have more education and more experience with urban settings and bureaucracies, are more likely to interact with others. Thus, willingness to extend one's social contacts to members of other groups could, according to Sengstock, produce a more assimilable group. The social structure of an immigrant group's country of origin, then, may help explain both nationalistic sentiment and social interaction with others in the adopted country.[6]

The Three-Generation Hypothesis

Historian Marcus Hansen conceptualized a normal pattern of ethnic revival in what he called the "Law of the Return of the Third Generation."[7] The third generation, more secure in its socioeconomic status and U.S. identity, becomes interested in the ethnic heritage that the second generation neglected in its efforts to overcome discrimination and marginality. Simply stated, "What the child wishes to forget, the grandchild wishes to remember." Hansen, who based his conclusions mainly on midwestern Swedish Americans, reaffirmed his position several years later:

> Whenever any immigrant group reaches the third-generation stage in its development a spontaneous and almost irresistible impulse arises which forces the thoughts of many people of different professions, different positions in life and different points of view to interest themselves in that one factor which they have in common: heritage—the heritage of blood.[8]

Hansen suggested a pattern in the fall and rise of ethnic identity in succeeding generations of Americans. His hypothesis generated extensive discussion in the academic community, resulting in studies and commentaries that both supported and criticized his views.

In a study of Irish and Italian Catholics in Providence, Rhode Island, John Goering found that the ideology of both the first and second generations living in the ethnic ghetto was more "American" and more tolerant of U.S. society than that of the third generation living outside the ghetto:

> Ethnicity is not clearly perceived in the ghetto. The boundaries of the ghetto became the boundaries of the real world. The awareness of ethnicity, and its divisiveness, comes with the "children of the uprooted." All forms of ethnic consciousness are not associated with the ethnic ghetto.[9]

These comments follow Hansen's law in that they assume that the second generation perceives its ethnicity as a disadvantage in being accepted in U.S. society. However, Goering perceived growing ethnic awareness among third-generation members not as a progression but as a regression to the "seclusiveness of ethnicity in resentment against unattained promises."[10]

Peter Skerry suggested there are other motives, including a reawakening of one's ethnic identity on college campuses as well as group competition and conflict. In relating the complexities of the assimilation process to Hansen's hypothesis, Skerry states, "However flawed as a precise predictor of generational differences within specific ethnic groups, Hansen's basic insight remains valid:

the process of assimilation is a dialectical one."[11] By this, he means that assimilation is not simply a linear progression but instead is a process that moves back and forth across the generations. Assimilation is not irreversible. Subsequent generations, even those who are the product of intermarriages, may emphasize their ethnic identity and learn the language of their cultural heritage.

In contrast, a study by Neil Sandburg found that Polish Americans in the Los Angeles area tended to become less ethnic over several generations.[12] In a similar study of Italian Americans in two suburbs of Providence, Rhode Island, John P. Roche also found increased assimilation over several generations and lower levels of attitudinal ethnicity.[13]

Studies of more recently arrived groups also find a similar decline in ethnicity among second-generation Asian and Hispanic Americans as they seek to assimilate. In fact, Valentine found a negative relationship between cultural assimilation and Hispanic identity; the acculturation process functioned as a trade-off between traditional Latino tendencies and mainstream Anglo-American practices.[14] Similarly, Portes and MacLeod (1996), in a survey of immigrant children from south Florida and southern California, reported that children who adopt the "Hispanic" label are the least well assimilated; these children had poorer English skills, lower self-esteem, and higher rates of poverty than those who identified themselves as Americans or as hyphenated Americans.[15]

Among Asian Americans, Kibria found a pattern somewhat akin to the one reported by Goering.[16] Second-generation East Asian Americans (those whose ancestry was from China, Japan, or Korea) developed a sense of a shared Asian American culture in their socialization into the Asian values of education, family, hard work, and respect for elders. In this instance, the "backlash" in the construction of a common cultural background was an attempt to distinguish it from the homogeneously conceived White mainstream culture.

Although most Asian and Hispanic Americans are too recently part of U.S. society to apply the three-generation hypothesis, the experience of Japanese Americans, among whom many are third-, fourth-, and even fifth-generation Americans, may offer an insight. With above average educational, occupational, and income levels, as well as high intermarriage rates, they are arguably the most assimilated of all Asian Americans. Still, they retain symbolic vestiges of their heritage and cling to the aforementioned values as part of their sense of self and group identity. Perhaps a similar future awaits our newest groups, although undoubtedly their racial experiences will mediate their identity formation.

Harold Abramson dismissed the three-generation hypothesis, arguing that the many dimensions of ethnic diversity preclude any macrosocial theory about ethnic consciousness.[17] Besides differences in time period—which may have influenced the experience, adjustment, and intergenerational conflict or consensus of ethnic groups—diversity exists within the groups themselves. Possibly, only the better educated among each ethnic group, being in wider contact with the outside world and more ambivalent about their identity, experience an ethnic resurgence, while the majority quietly progress in some steady fashion. In addition, the enormous variability in the U.S. social structure affects what happens to the grandchildren of all ethnic groups:

> Here I am talking about the diversity of region, of social stratification, of urban and rural settlement. In other words, the immigrants of Old and New and continuing migrations, the blacks of the North and of the South, the native American Indians, all experience their encounters with America under vastly different conditions. The French-Canadians in depressed mill towns of New England, the Hungarians and Czechs in company coal towns of Pennsylvania, and the Chicanos in migrant labor fields of California, do not experience the social mobility or social change of the Irish in Boston politics, the Jews in the garment industry of New York, or the Japanese in the professions of Hawaii. Not only are there traditional cultural factors to explain these phenomena, but there are structural reasons of settlement, region, and the local composition of the ethnic mosaic as well.[18]

Furthermore, the responses of different cultural groups to the host society vary. Conservative social scientists such as Thomas Sowell argue that cultural characteristics that either mesh or clash with the dominant cultural values determine a group's upward mobility.[19] Liberal social scientists such as Stephen Steinberg downplay cultural characteristics and emphasize social-structural variables instead. Steinberg maintains that pluralism appeals only to groups that benefit from maintaining ethnic boundaries, while disadvantaged groups willingly compromise their ethnicity to gain economic security and social acceptance.[20] More likely, the interplay of culture and social structure enables groups to achieve economic success or prevents them from doing so.

The Changing Face of Ethnicity

In the 1980s, social scientists shifted from an emphasis on a resurgence of ethnicity in the 1960s and 1970s, to a suggestion that, at least for those of European ancestry, ethnicity was now in its twilight stage. Obviously, for relatively new groups of immigrants, ethnicity is a very real component of their everyday lives and will remain so for some time, much as it once was for first- and second-generation European Americans.

Ethnicity as a Social Process

Ethnicity is a creation of a pluralistic U.S. society. Usually, culture shock and an emerging self-consciousness lead immigrant groups to think of themselves in terms of an ethnic identity and to become part of an ethnic community to gain the social and emotional support they need to begin a new life in their adopted country. That community is revitalized with a continual influx of new arrivals.

Some sociologists have argued that ethnicity should be regarded not as an ascribed attribute, with only the two discrete categories of assimilation and pluralism, but as a continuous variable. In a review of the literature, William L. Yancey, Eugene P. Ericksen, and Richard N. Juliani concluded that ethnic behavior is conditioned by occupation, residence, and institutional affiliation—the structural situations in which groups have found themselves.[21] The old immigrants, migrating before the Industrial Revolution, had a more dispersed residential pattern than did the new immigrants, who were bunched together because of concentrated large-scale urban employment and the need for low-cost housing near their place of employment. Similarly, when the new immigrants arrived, they were drawn to areas of economic expansion, and the migration chains—the subsequent arrival of relatives and friends—continued the concentrated settlement pattern.

> The Germans and Irish, who were earlier immigrants, concentrated in the older cities such as Philadelphia and St. Louis. By contrast, the new immigrants from Poland, Italy and Russia concentrated in Buffalo, Cleveland, Detroit and Milwaukee, as well as in some of the older cities with expanding opportunities. Different migration patterns occurred for immigrants with and without skills. . . . Rewards for skilled occupations were greater, and the skilled immigrant went to the cities where there were opportunities to practice his trade. Less highly skilled workers went to the cities with expanding opportunities. Thus, the Italian concentration in construction and the Polish in steel were related to the expansion of these industries as these groups arrived. The Jewish concentration in the garment industry may have been a function of their previous experience as tailors, but it is also dependent upon the emergence of the mass production of clothing in the late nineteenth century.[22]

The authors conclude that group consciousness arises and crystallizes within the work relationships, common residential areas, interests, and lifestyles of working-class conditions. Moreover, normal communication and participation in ethnic organizations on a cosmopolitan level can reinforce ethnic identity even among residentially dispersed groups.[23]

Ethnicity and Migration Patterns

Stanley Lieberson and Mary C. Waters examined the location of ethnic and racial groups in the United States on the basis of the 1980 census and of patterns of internal migration in 1975–1980. They found that the longer a group had been in the United States, the less geographically concentrated it was. This was hardly a surprising finding, but their analysis of internal migration patterns revealed that ethnicity still affected the changing spatial patterns:

> We have concluded that although current patterns of internal migration are tending to reduce some of the distinctive geographic concentrations in the nation, this will still not fully eliminate distinctive ethnic concentrations. This is because groups differ in their propensity to leave and in their propensity to enter each area in a way that reflects the existing ethnic compositions of the areas.

Thus, even with the massive level of internal migration in the United States, there is no evidence that the ethnic linkage to region is disappearing.[24]

Lieberson and Waters observe that a numerically small group, if highly concentrated in a small number of localities, possesses greater political and social influence than one dispersed more uniformly. Thus, the linkage between demographic size and location will influence visibility, occupational patterns, interaction patterns, intermarriage, and assimilation (Figure 7.1).

A Bureau of the Census analysis of migration patterns between 1995 and 2000 revealed that more than 62 percent of the 5.6 million immigrants who came to the United States entered through just seven states (Figure 7.2). At the same time, three of these gateway states—California, New York, and Texas—had considerable net outmigration of their foreign-born populations to other states. As the leading destination for migrants from abroad, California and New York were also the leaders in this internal migration, sending 237,000 and 205,000, respectively, to other states.[25]

Just as chain migration is an important factor in migration from abroad, so too does it appear to play an important role in this population redistribution of the foreign born to other states. As a result, the ethnic dimension in internal migration patterns that Lieberson and Waters found 20 years earlier is still significant. By far, the greatest numbers of interstate movers were Asians (667,000), followed by Mexicans (472,000) and other Latin Americans (438,000). States where this internal migration had the most dramatic impact on population composition were Nevada, North Carolina, Georgia, Arkansas, Minnesota, Nebraska, and Indiana.[26]

Symbolic Ethnicity

Among first-generation U.S. immigrants, ethnicity is an everyday reality that everyone takes for granted. For most immigrants living within an ethnic community or network, shared communal interactions make ethnic identity a major factor in daily life. Not yet structurally assimilated, these immigrants find that their ethnicity provides the link to virtually everything they say or do, what they join, and whom they befriend or marry.

What happens to the ethnicity of subsequent generations depends on the immediate environment. As Richard D. Alba reaffirmed in a 1990 study in Albany, New York, the presence of ethnic neighborhoods or organizations in the vicinity helps sustain a strong sense of ethnic identity.[27] For most Whites of European origin, living away from visible ethnic links and becoming part of the societal mainstream reduces the importance of their ethnic identity in comparison to their occupational and social identity. At this point, ethnicity rests on acknowledging ancestry through attachment to a few ethnic symbols not pertinent to everyday life.[28]

German

Highest densities: North Dakota 46%, South Dakota 46%, Nebraska 43%, Wisconsin 43%, Minnesota 38%, Iowa 37%, Kansas 33%, Ohio 30%, Indiana 27%.

Irish

Highest densities: Massachusetts 23%, New Hampshire 21%, Rhode Island 20%, Delaware 19%, Connecticut 18%, New Jersey 17%, Missouri 14%, New York 14%, West Virginia 14%.

English

States with the highest densities of English: Utah 30%, Maine 25%, Idaho 22%, New Hampshire 21%, Wyoming 19%, Vermont 18%, Oregon 15%, Delaware 14%.

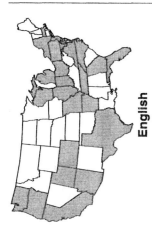

Italian

Highest densities: Rhode Island 20%, Connecticut 20%, New Jersey 18%, New York 15%, Massachusetts 14%, Alabama 11%, New Mexico 8%.

Go west, go east

At first they came to New England, the Carolinas and what are now the mid-Atlantic states. Then they crossed the Appalachians and headed west. Now, the destination for many immigrants is California, and most are reaching it by going east or north—from Asia or Latin America. In 1999, 26 percent of new immigrants settled in California, compared to 15 percent settling in New York, which until 1976 was the first choice of new arrivals.

These maps show the biggest concentration of ethnic groups—500,000 or more in a state—as identified in the 2000 census. California is the top choice for immigrants from China, El Salvador, Guatemala, Hong Kong, India, Iran, Korea, Mexico, the Philippines, and Vietnam. New York has the most from Bangladesh, Colombia, the Dominican Republic, Ecuador, Guyana, Jamaica, Pakistan, and the former Soviet Union.

Captions below the maps show where specific ethnic groups make up the biggest shares of the state's population, such as South Dakota with its large percentage of people of German descent.

☐ States in color are those with at least 500,000 persons of the indicated ethnic groups in the latest census.

FIGURE 7.1 Where We Settled

(continued)

528

French or French Canadian

Highest densities: Vermont 27%, New Hampshire 27%, Maine 25%, Rhode Island 20%, Louisiana 18%, Massachusetts 14%, Connecticut 11%.

Asian

Highest densities: Hawaii 42%, California 11%, New Jersey 6%, New York 6%, Washington 6%, Nevada 5%, Maryland 4%, Massachusetts 4%, Virginia 4%.

African American

Highest densities: Mississippi 36%, Louisiana 33%, South Carolina 30%, Georgia 29%, Alabama 26%, Maryland 25%, North Carolina 22%.

Mexican

Highest densities: California 25%, Texas 24%, Arizona 21%, New Mexico 18%, Nevada 14%, Colorado 11%, Illinois 9%.

Hispanic

Highest densities: New Mexico 42%, California 32%, Texas 32%, Arizona 25%, Colorado 17%, Florida 17%, New York 15%, New Jersey 13%, Illinois 12%.

Polish

Highest densities: Wisconsin 9%, Michigan 9%, Connecticut 8%, Illinois 7%, New Jersey 7%, Pennsylvania 7%, New York 5%.

FIGURE 7.1   Continued

Source: Basic data from U.S. Bureau of the Census

FIGURE 7.2 Reasons for Ethnic Consciousness

Country of Origin

1. Psychological nearness through rapid communication and transportation.
2. Geographic proximity.
3. Degree of stability or social change in the homeland.
4. Social contact with recent immigrants.

Three-Generation Hypothesis

1. Second generation emphasizes U.S. ways and neglects its own heritage.
2. Third generation rediscovers ethnic identity.

Other Explanations

1. Religion is replacing national origin as basis of identity.
2. Ethnicity is less perceived in an ethnic community than in the real world.

3. Outside events heighten ethnic awareness.
4. Only the better educated of a group become ethnically self-conscious.
5. Variations in time and social structure and within ethnic groups encourage different types of responses.

The Changing Face of Ethnicity

1. White ethnic revival is a backlash or affirmation of Hansen's law.
2. Resiliency of ethnic identity even through acculturation.
3. Increased visibility and attention do not constitute an ethnic revival.
4. Ethnicity is a social process affected by and affecting residence.
5. Symbolic ethnicity is now the most common form among European Americans.

Alba speaks of a twilight stage of ethnicity among White ethnics. High intermarriage rates not only have reduced the intergenerational transmission of distinctive cultural traits but also have diversified the ethnic ancestry of third- and fourth-generation European Americans. A coalesced new ethnic group, European Americans, has emerged. Its ethnicity is muted and symbolic, a personal and voluntary identity that finds expression in such activities as "church and synagogue attendance, marching in a St. Patrick's or Columbus Day parade, voting for a political candidate of a similar ethnicity, or supporting a political cause associated with the country of origin, such as the emigration of Russian Jews to Israel or the reunification of Ireland."[29]

Although socially assimilated and integrated into middle-class society, third- and fourth-generation European Americans maintain this quiet link to their origins. As Gans suggests, it can find form in small details, such as objects in the home with an ethnic meaning, occasional participation in an old-country ritual, or a fondness for ethnic cuisine.[30] Individuals may remain interested in the immigrant experience, participate in ethnic political and social activities, or even visit the ancestral homeland. All these private, leisure-time activities help preserve ethnicity in symbolic ways, giving people a special sense of self in the homogenized world of White U.S. culture.

African Americans express symbolic ethnicity through such elements as musical styles, fashion and dress styles (Afros, braids, dreadlocks, tribal symbols cut into the hair, bandanna headbands, Kufi hats, harem pants, African beads), cuisine (soul food), and festivals (such as Kwanzaa, a holiday based on traditional African harvest celebrations). Sometimes called *manifestations of cultural nationalism*—a movement toward African American solidarity based on encouraging African culture and values—these activities resemble those of the descendants of other ethnic groups proudly recalling their heritage.

Current Ethnic Issues

Two highly controversial issues punctuate race and ethnic relations in the United States: immigration and bilingual education. Although the latter is a fairly new issue, arguments against both repeat objections hotly asserted in the late nineteenth and early twentieth centuries. Nativist fears of being overrun by too many "non-American types" and losing societal cohesion as a result of their cultural pluralism are quite similar to concerns raised by dominant-

Symbolic ethnicity is an occasional means for native-born U.S. residents to reaffirm their cultural heritage. Sometimes these activities are carryovers from the old country, but other times they are of U.S. origin, as with Kwanzaa, a fairly recently developed observance based on traditional African harvest celebrations. This three-generation group of African Americans, whose native-born roots predate the Civil War, enjoy this special event together.

(*Source:* Lawrence Migdale/Stock, Boston)

group members of past generations. A third issue is "political correctness." Less controversial than a decade ago, this issue embraces women's and homosexuals' rights as well as the rights of ethnic minorities.

Immigration Fears

The extent to which other countries begin, continue, or cease to send large numbers of immigrants helps determine the cultural impact of these immigrants on U.S. society. Moreover, as different parts of the world become primary sending areas, the interests of the newly naturalized citizens—and in turn, U.S. foreign policy—become increasingly involved in developments in those parts of the world. Table 7.1 shows the leading suppliers of immigrants since 1820 and the past dominance of countries from Europe and the Western hemisphere in total numbers. Table 7.2 shows the shifting patterns since the immigration law changed in 1965, with significant changes among the top fifteen sending countries. Many immigrants still come from European countries, but they now account for less than 18 percent of the overall number annually, due to the large increase in Asian and Hispanic immigrants. Given the ongoing processes of chain migration and family reunification—and contrasting birthrates in Europe as opposed to Asia and Latin America—we can safely assume the continued dominance of developing nations in sending new strangers to these shores.

Almost 9.1 million legal immigrants (including undocumented aliens who were subsequently granted amnesty) came to the United States between

TABLE 7.1   Leading Suppliers of Immigrants to the United States, 1820–2002

1. Germany	7,219,222	9. Philippines	1,630,142
2. Mexico	6,560,312	10. China	1,440,285
3. Italy	5,442,044	11. Sweden	1,263,129
4. United Kingdom	5,309,331	12. Cuba	971,625
5. Ireland	4,785,052	13. India	951,556
6. Canada/New Foundland	4,517,275	14. Dominican Republic	889,117
7. Austria/Hungary*	4,373,998	15. France	833,434
8. Soviet Union†	4,017,143		

*Data for Austria/Hungary were not reported until 1861. Austria and Hungary have been reported separately since 1905. From 1938 to 1945, Austria was included in figures for Germany.

†The Soviet Union is no longer a political entity. Data include immigrants from republics formerly part of the Soviet Union.

Source: Office of Immigration Statistics, *2002 Yearbook of Immigration Statistics* (Washington, D.C.: U.S. Government Printing Office, 2003), table 2.

TABLE 7.2   Major Sources of Newcomers to the United States, 1965 versus 2002

1965		2002	
1. Canada	38,327	1. Mexico	219,380
2. Mexico	37,969	2. India	71,105
3. United Kingdom	27,358	3. China, People's Republic	61,282
4. Germany	24,045	4. Philippines	51,308
5. Cuba	19,760	5. Vietnam	33,627
6. Colombia	10,885	6. El Salvador	31,168
7. Italy	10,821	7. Cuba	28,272
8. Dominican Republic	9,504	8. Bosnia-Herzegovina	25,373
9. Poland	8,465	9. Dominican Republic	22,604
10. Argentina	6,124	10. Ukraine	21,217
11. Ireland	5,463	11. Korea	21,021
12. Ecuador	4,392	12. Russia	20,833
13. China and Taiwan	4,057	13. Haiti	20,268
14. France	4,039	14. Canada	19,519
15. Haiti	3,609	15. Colombia	18,845

Source: Office of Immigration Statistics, *2002 Yearbook of Immigration Statistics Annual Report*, U.S. Government Printing Office, Washington, DC, 2003, table 3.

1991 and 2000, exceeding the previous record set in 1901–1910, when 8.8 million arrived.

Some opposition to current immigration results from concern about the ability of the United States to absorb so many immigrants. Echoing xenophobic fears of earlier generations, immigration opponents worry that U.S. citizens will lose control of the country to foreigners. This time, instead of fears about the religiously different Catholics and Jews or the physically different Mediterranean Whites who were dark-complexioned, the new anti-immigration groups fear the significantly growing presence of religiously and physically different immigrants of color. Visible differences, together with the prevalence of languages other than English, constantly remind multiple-generation U.S. residents about the strangers in their midst, whom some perceive as a threat to U.S. society as they know it. This is especially true for Arab and Muslim Americans, whom anti-immigration advocates point to as illustrating a too-liberal immigration policy that allowed terrorists in our midst. The reality that virtually all Arab and Muslim Americans denounce terrorism does little to assuage public fears.

It is not just the increasing visibility of so many "strangers" in neighborhoods, schools, and workplaces that encourages this backlash. The nation's stable birthrate means that immigrants account for a larger share of population growth than in previous years. According to the Population Reference Bureau, that share is currently 23 percent.[31] Some demographers, such as Leon Bouvier, interpret this as meaning that the racial composition of the United States will change dramatically in the next two generations, a prospect that displeases some people.[32]

Another concern about immigration is economic. The public worries that immigrants take away jobs, drive down wages, and use too many government services at taxpayers' expense. How real are these fears?

Jobs. Despite the popular belief, immigrants do *not* take away jobs from American workers. Experts note that people often blame immigrants for unemployment because they see the jobs immigrants fill but not the new jobs they create through productivity, capital formation, and demand for goods and services.[33]

Wages. According to Rubén Rumbaut, little evidence exists from the many research studies of both legal and undocumented immigrants that they adversely affect the earnings of any group or that they cause unemployment either in the nation as a whole or in areas of high concentration of immigrants.[34]

Services. In a cost–benefit analysis of immigrants who came to the United States between 1970 and 1992, Jeffrey Passel found that, from aggregate incomes of $300 billion (9 percent of all U.S. personal income), immigrants paid a total of over $70 billion in taxes of all kinds. When subtracting from those taxes the estimated costs for all forms of social services used by immigrants and their children, including education expenses disproportionately borne by state and local governments, Passel determined that the immigrants entering the United States between 1970 and 1992 generated a surplus of at least $25 billion to $30 billion.[35]

In 1997, the National Research Council reported similar findings.[36] It found that immigrants may add as much as $10 billion to the economy each year. Immigrant labor allows many goods and services to be produced more cheaply and provides the work force for some businesses that otherwise could not exist. These include U.S. textile and agricultural industries, as well as restaurants and domestic household services. They compete primarily with each other and with U.S. citizens who lack a high school diploma; wages of the latter have dropped by about 5 percent in the past 15 years. In some areas with large concentrations of low-skilled, low-paid immigrants, such as California, taxpayers at both state and local levels pay more on average to support the publicly funded services needed by these immigrants. Still, economists say, immigrants and their children bring long-term benefits for most U.S. taxpayers because—like most U.S. residents—they and their descendants will add more to government coffers than they receive over their lifetimes.

Public Opinion Polls. Statistics notwithstanding, Americans have mixed opinions about immigration, and they did so even before the September 2001 terrorist attacks. In the early 1990s, a majority of Americans held a negative view. For example, a 1992 *BusinessWeek*/Harris poll revealed that 68 percent of all respondents said immigration was bad for the country.[37] As the United States enjoyed a booming economy throughout the rest of the decade, public opinion about immigration completely changed. A June 2001 Gallup poll revealed that 62 percent thought immigration was a good thing for the country, whereas 31 percent thought it was bad. Hispanics thought more favorably about immigration (73 percent) than did Blacks (61 percent) or Whites (62 percent). When contemplating past immigration, Americans are even more positive with 75 percent believing it was a good thing and only 20 percent viewing it as bad for the country. In this regard, Whites were as positive about past immigration as Hispanics (each at 75 percent), while Blacks were much less so (63 percent).[38]

Three months after this poll, vicious acts of terrorism rekindled anti-immigrant sentiments. For some, the focus was narrowly confined to Arabs and Muslims; for others, especially nativists, these acts galvanized them to urge for the curtailment of all immigration. A Fox News opinion poll in November 2001 found that 65 percent of Americans favored stopping all immigration, and a January 2002 Gallup poll reported that 58 percent of Americans thought immigration should be decreased, up from 45 percent a year earlier.[39] Often, elite and mass opinion on immigration differ, as in another 2002 poll in which 55 percent of the public said legal immigration should be reduced compared with 18 percent of opinion leaders.[40]

Undocumented Aliens

Despite recent laws imposing severe sanctions on employers who hire undocumented aliens, a large number of people from foreign lands continue to slip across U.S. borders. Official estimates place the number of undocumented aliens currently living in the United States at 7 million (two-thirds of them are Mexican), a total based on census surveys and immigration service statistics. Slightly more than half of this number first arrived as visitors (tourists, students, or businesspeople) and then simply overstayed their visas. Of nearly 30 million annual visitors, the estimated 11,200 apprehended in 2001 as illegals came from a wide range of countries, with the largest population groups originating from Mexico, Canada, Jamaica, Indonesia, the Dominican Republic, and Pakistan.[41]

Entering the country easily and then disappearing within it, these undocumented aliens usually escape detection by the Immigration and Naturalization Service, which spends millions to patrol the border of the United States. In the Southwest, where the problem draws the greatest amount of public attention, the most apprehension about undocumented aliens occurs (almost 1.1 million in 2002). In 2002, Mexicans dominated the list of those apprehended, at 94 percent of the total. Other major source countries of those

This cartoon, remarkably similar to those preceding immigration legislation in the 1920s, appeared first in the *Miami Herald* in 1984 and was reprinted in both *Time* and *Newsweek*, giving it a widespread national audience. It effectively captures nativist fears of the United States being inundated with a tidal wave of aliens, a response pattern displayed earlier against the Irish and then the southern and eastern Europeans.

(*Source:* © 1984 by The Miami Herald. Reprinted with permission.)

apprehended were El Salvador, Honduras, Guatemala, the Dominican Republic, Canada, Cuba, Brazil, Colombia, and Jamaica.[42]

In the aftermath of the 9/11 attacks, amid concerns about insufficient screening of aliens coming to the United States and the growing presence of undocumented aliens, the government reorganized in March 2003. Services once provided by the much-criticized Immigration and Naturalization Service now occur within the Department of Homeland Security under the Bureau of Citizenship and Immigration Services (BCIS). Immediate priorities "are to promote national security, continue to eliminate immigration adjudication backlogs, and improve the delivery of immigration and citizenship services."[43] With ongoing public and government concern about further acts of terrorism, the national security priority may lead to stronger enforcement against all undocumented aliens, not just those from Muslim countries.

Hostility against undocumented aliens is strong and often carries over to negative reactions toward legal immigrants. The most notable public action thus far against undocumented aliens was California voters' approval of Proposition 187 in 1994. Designed to block publicly funded health and education benefits to undocumented aliens, its implementation was thwarted by an adverse court ruling on constitutional grounds.

Bilingual Education

Offering **bilingual education**—teaching subjects in both English and the student's native language—can take the form of a transitional program (gradually phasing in English completely over several years) or a maintenance program (continued native-language teaching to sustain the students' heritage with a simultaneous but relatively limited emphasis on English proficiency). For the many U.S. residents who assume that English-speaking schools provided the heat for the melting pot, the popularity of bilingual education—particularly maintenance programs—is a sore point. Some see these efforts as counterproductive because they tend to reduce assimilation in and the cohesiveness of U.S. society, while simultaneously isolating ethnic groups from one another. Advocates of bilingual programs emphasize that they are developing **bilingualism**—fluency in both English and the students' native tongue—and that many youngsters are illiterate in both when they begin school.

Public funding for bilingual education began in 1968, when Congress passed the Bilingual Education Act, designed for low-income families only. Two years later, the Department of Health, Education, and Welfare specified that school districts in which any national-origin group constitutes more than 5 percent of the student population had a legal obligation to provide bilingual programs for low-income families. In 1974, two laws significantly expanded bilingual programs. The Bilingual Act eliminated the low-income requirement and urged that children receive various courses that provided appreciation of their cultural heritage. The Equal Opportunity Act identified failure to take "appropriate action" to overcome language barriers impeding equal participation in school as a form of illegal denial of equal educational opportunity. **English as a Second Language (ESL) programs** have since expanded to function in about 125 languages, including 20 Native American languages. With 10 million immigrant children now enrolled in the public schools—both urban and suburban—schools must overcome cultural, language, and literacy barriers to provide for their education.

Types of Programs. What most U.S. citizens fail to realize is that three-fourths of all limited-English-proficient (LEP) students receive English as a Second Language instruction, and only one-fourth have this instruction paired with native-language academic instruction, more commonly known as bilingual programs. Together, the programs enable educators to teach 10

U.S. bilingual education classes continue to stir controversy over cost, effectiveness, and their alleged "threat" to societal cohesiveness, provoking some U.S. citizens to demand that they be eliminated. Some recent studies indicate that immersion programs have success rates comparable to bilingual programs, but contradictory findings in other studies keep the issue in dispute.
(*Source:* © 1986 Susan Lapides/Design Conceptions)

million school-age students in the United States whose first language is not English, as well as 3.4 million other students whose English proficiency is limited.[44] The practical value of ESL programs over native-language instruction is readily apparent from just a few statistics: In just one Los Angeles school 60 different languages are spoken in the homes of students; in Fairfax County, northern Virginia, the corresponding number is 187 different languages; and in New York City, more than 185 different languages are spoken. It is practically impossible to offer native-tongue classes in so many languages. As it is, urban and suburban schools struggle for funds, space, and qualified teachers for their various bilingual programs.[45]

Older naturalized U.S. citizens often cite difficulty with the English language while they were students as one of the most difficult aspects of adjusting to the United States and gaining acceptance. Bilingual proponents argue that their programs ease that adjustment and accelerate the learning process. Since the 1970s, the National Education Association has supported an **English-plus program** to promote the integration of language minority students into the U.S. mainstream and to develop foreign language competence in native-born U.S. students to function in a global economy.[46]

Criticism and Effectiveness. Opponents charge that the programs are too costly, are frequently staffed by **paraprofessionals** who lack fluency in English themselves, or subsidize political activities of vocal minority groups. Furthermore, they complain that the "transitional" bilingual programs are not transitional and that students remain in these classes for many years, learning little English. When a 1985 Massachusetts Board of Education report confirmed that substantial numbers of its Hispanic students remained in bilingual classes for 6 or more years, critics became more vocal.[47] That same year, a national policy change allowed up to 25 percent of federal funds to be used instead for **English immersion programs,** in which students are taught in English with their native language used only as a backup support system. Then, in 1988, a new federal law specified that unless stringent guidelines were met, no student could participate in a federally funded transitional bilingual program for more than 3 years.

How effective is bilingual education in helping children learn English? Christine H. Rossell and Keith Baker examined three hundred studies pursuing this question and found that in only 22 percent of methodologically acceptable studies was transitional bilingual education better than regular classroom instruction when the outcome is reading; for math, it was only 9 percent.[48] A scalding report from the New York City Board of Education in 1995 concluded that new immigrants instructed in English alone performed better than students in bilingual programs. Students who entered this "bilingual prison," as their parents called it, spoke so little English each day that 90 percent of sixth through ninth graders failed to move on to regular classes within the required 3 years.[49]

A 2001 report by the General Accounting Office took a neutral stance about bilingual education versus English immersion programs, stating, "Available research does not definitively indicate the best teaching methods to use or the amount of time support should be provided." It concluded that many variables may influence what is the best approach, such as the percentage of students with limited English proficiency, the number of languages spoken by the students, and students' family backgrounds.[50] A study by the U.S. Department of Education found that bilingual and immersion programs were comparable in their success rates. Students in total immersion, short-term, and long-term bilingual programs learned English at about the same rate in all three groups, and they also improved their verbal and math skills as fast as or faster than did other students in the general population.[51] Since bilingual programs vary so widely in approach and quality, it is difficult to assess their overall effectiveness. However, studies show that students who are given enough time in well-taught bilingual programs to gain English proficiency test better in the eleventh grade than do those with no prior preparation in any bilingual program.[52]

Regardless of what the studies report, the American public heavily favors the immersion of non-English-speaking students in regular classes, not any form of bilingual classes. A May 1998 Gallup poll showed that, by a 63 percent to 33 percent margin, the public chose the immersion option, a result similar to those measured in Gallup polls since 1980.[53] That same year, California voters approved Proposition 227 by a 61 percent to 39 percent margin. This action eliminates bilingual education in the state in favor of programs that provide a year of intensive English instruction followed by transition into regular classrooms. Two years later, Arizona voters approved a similar measure and other states considered following their lead.

Although educators predicted a catastrophe, in 2000 the affected California students improved in reading and other subjects, often significantly, in their standardized test scores. Although some argued that these results proved the superiority of immersion programs, others argued that smaller class sizes and improved teaching techniques were the reasons. And so the debate continues.[54] For its part, New York City offered a revised bilingual program beginning September 2001 that gave parents of children who speak little English the right to move them into a range of new classes that emphasize instruction in English rather than in native languages.[55] We appear to be witnessing the beginning of a widespread change in language programs for immigrant children.

The English-Only Movement

Opponents of bilingual education argue that the program encourages "ethnic tribalism," fostering separation instead of a cohesive society. Their objections come in response to Hispanic leaders in such groups as the National Council of La Raza and the League of United Latin American Citizens (LULAC), who claim that "language rights" entitle Hispanic people to have their language and culture maintained at public expense, both in the schools and in the workplace. The oldest Hispanic civil-rights group still in existence, LULAC was founded in 1929. Ironically, it began as an assimilationist organization, accepting only U.S. citizens as members, conducting its official proceedings in English, and declaring as one of its goals "to foster the acquisition and facile use of the official language of our country."[56]

With hundreds of thousands of Hispanic immigrants entering the United States each year, the extensive use of Spanish alarms many nativists. Of course, many Asian and other non-English-speaking immigrants add to nativists' concerns. The 2000 Census revealed that nearly one in five Americans does not speak English at home. In fact, more than 10.5 million said they speak little or no English, up from 6.5 million in 1990. According to experts, some of the rise is due to the fast growth of the new-immigrant population, which included millions of people who came here illegally. The share of people who speak little English is highest among those in their working years, ages 18 to 64.[57]

In reaction, the nativists have pressed to make English the official language for all public business. The largest national lobbying group, U.S. English, was cofounded by Japanese immigrant S. I. Hayakawa, a former U.S. senator from California and former president of and linguistics professor at San Francisco State University. By 2003, the group claimed 1.7 million members, and its success prompted critics to attack it as being anti-immigrant, racist, divisive, and dangerous.[58] The group's goals are to reduce or eliminate bilingual education, to abolish multilingual ballots, and to prevent state and local expenditures on translating road signs and government documents and translating to assist non–English-speaking patients at public hospitals.

By 2003, twenty-seven states had passed English-only legislation; thirteen other states had rejected similar proposals. New Mexico's legislature went beyond rejecting the proposal; in 1989, it approved "English Plus," stating, "Proficiency in more than one language is to the economic and cultural benefit of our State and Nation." Then, in 1998, the Arizona Supreme Court struck down the state's official English law as unconstitutional. Nevertheless, polls since the mid-1990s consistently show that Americans think English should be the official language.[59] Since 1981, more than 50 bills have been introduced in Congress to make English the nation's official language. Four of these bills passed in one chamber but not in the other.

Although proponents of English-only legislation claim that such action is essential to preserve a common language and provide a necessary bridge across a widening language barrier within the country, numerous polls and studies demonstrate that the action is unnecessary. For example, Rodolfo de la Garza reported that most U.S.-born Latinos and Asians use English as their primary language.[60] Echoing previous newspaper polls taken since the 1980s, a 1996 poll found that more than 80 percent of Hispanic parents want their children taught in English, not in Spanish.[61] That same year, the Center for Equal Opportunity commissioned a survey entitled "The Importance of Learning English." Among its findings was that 63 percent of Hispanic parents believed that Hispanic children should be taught English before they were taught Spanish. Parents interviewed in Spanish were actually more likely to say learning English was most important for their children than those questioned in English.[62]

Speaking against the English-only movement, the American Jewish Committee stated:

> It is not necessary to make English the official language of the United States. . . . English is the principal language used in the United States. Virtually all government agencies conduct their business in English and virtually all public documents are written in English. It is de facto the official language of the U.S. The use of additional languages to meet the needs of language minorities does not pose a threat to America's true common heritage and common bond—the quest for freedom and opportunity.[63]

Despite fears about immigrants not learning English, the Census Bureau reports that, of those U.S. residents aged 18 to 64 who spoke an Asian or Pacific Islander language in 2000, 78 percent also spoke English "very well" or "well." Of the same age cohort who spoke Spanish in 2000, 68 percent also spoke English "very well" or "well."[64] Rubén Rumbaut reports that those who do not yet speak English well or at all are disproportionately the elderly (especially those in dense ethnic enclaves, such as among the Cubans in Miami), the most recently arrived, the undocumented, and the least educated.[65]

Multiculturalism

In its early phase, during the 1970s, **multiculturalism** meant including material in the school curriculum that related the contributions of non-European peoples to U.S. history. Next followed efforts to change all areas of the curriculum in elementary and secondary schools and colleges to reflect the diversity of U.S. society and to develop students' awareness of and appreciation for the impact of non-European civilizations on U.S. culture. The intent of this movement was to promote an expanded U.S. identity that recognized previously excluded groups as integral components of the whole, both in heritage and in present actuality (see the accompanying International Scene box).

Some multiculturalists subsequently moved away from an assimilationist or integrative approach, rejecting a common bond of identity among the distinct minority groups. The new multiculturalists advocate "minority nationalism" and "separatist pluralism," with a goal of specific, separate group identities, not of a collective national identity.[66]

To create a positive group identity, these multiculturalists go beyond advocacy for teaching and maintaining a group's own cultural customs, history, values, and festivals. They also deny the validity of the dominant culture's customs, history, values, and festivals. Two examples are Native Americans who object to Columbus Day parades and Afrocentrists who assert that Western culture was merely derived from Afro-Egyptian culture. Another striking example is the argument that only groups with power can be racist. This view holds that because Whites have power, they are intrinsically racist, whereas people of color lack power and so cannot be racist.[67]

Opponents counter that racism can and does exist within any group, regardless of how much power that group has. John J. Miller, a longtime pro-immigration advocate, argues that multiculturalism undermines the assimilation ethic, and the weaker our assimilation efforts, the fewer immigrants we can accept. His ten-point "Americanization Manifesto" includes ending ethnic-group preferences, bilingual education, and multilingual voting; strengthening the naturalization process; and reducing illegal immigration.[68]

Another battleground for multiculturalists involves offering or eliminating courses in Western civilization. Some institutions, such as Providence College in Rhode Island, expanded such course requirements and made them

The International Scene
Multiculturalism in France

For many generations, the French saw themselves as a seamless population bloc whose culture was directly descended from that of the tribes of ancient Gaul. Those who lived in the provinces—Alsatians, Bretons, Gascons, Provencals, and Savoyards, for example—were trained in school to become "French." Physically punished if they spoke their provincial dialects during recess, all were homogenized into the dominant culture, with the brightest students finishing their education in Paris.

The millions of Italian, Polish, and Spanish immigrants who entered France did not join the mainstream easily, despite their common Catholic faith and European heritage. At the turn of the last century in southern France, for instance, a massacre of Italians occurred. Just before World War II, the French government imposed a ban against the establishment of any organizations by foreigners—a stricture that remained in effect until 1981. Assimilation, or Franco-conformity, was the allowable choice—not pluralism.

By 1998, France had 4 million legal immigrants (6 percent of the total population) and perhaps another million *clandestins* (illegal aliens), most coming from Muslim North Africa. Many French became concerned that their nation was losing its cultural identity because of the large influx of immigrants whose appearance, language, religion, and values were so different. Indeed, after winning a record 15 percent of the vote in 1998, the far right, anti-immigrant National Front Party finished second in the 2002 election, with an 18 percent total. Spearheaded by left-wing parties and human-rights groups, both elections sparked protest demonstrations by tens of thousands of people across France. In the streets of Paris, people chanted, "We're all immigrants."

That public chanting echoed former Prime Minister Michel Rocard's call for a new recognition of French diversity. It also recalled the encouragement of a multiculturalist viewpoint by President François Mitterrand who, several years earlier, had observed: "We are French. Our ancestors are the Gauls, and we are also a little Roman, a little German, a little Jewish, a little Italian, a small bit Spanish, more and more Portuguese, who knows, maybe Polish, too. And I wonder whether we aren't already a bit Arab."

Critical thinking question: How do you think France and the United States compare in public attitudes about immigration and diversity?

---

interdisciplinary; other institutions, such as Stanford University, questioned their inclusion at all. At many institutions, the proposals for curriculum change ranged from making all students take non-Western and women's studies courses as part of their degree requirements to excluding all Western history and culture courses from such requirements.

Regardless of their orientation, most multiculturalists are pluralists waging war with assimilationists. Neither side will vanquish the other, though, for both forces remain integral parts of U.S. society. The United States continues to offer a beacon of hope to immigrants everywhere, keeping the rich tradition of pluralism alive and well. And yet, as has been consistently demonstrated for centuries, assimilationist forces will remain strong, particularly for immigrant children and their descendants. Multiculturalism will no more weaken that process than did the many past manifestations of ethnic ingroup solidarity.

People who cite the Afrocentrist movement as divisive need to consider the reality of separate racial worlds within the United States, from colonial times to the revelations generated by the O. J. Simpson verdict. These separate worlds result not from multiculturalist teachings but from systemic racism. Only by breaking down the remaining racial barriers, eliminating institutional discrimination, and opening up paths to a good education and job opportunities for everyone can society improve racial integration. Afrocentrist schools do not undermine a cohesive U.S. society any more than Catholic schools, yeshivas, or other religious schools do.

Political Correctness

As various groups pursued the liberation of the American mind from its narrow perspective, advocates also looked beyond curricular change. By 1990, various streams of liberation—including those championing peoples of color, feminism, gay rights, and the movement for the interests of individuals with handicaps—coalesced into a movement that became known as **political correctness.**

Advocates sought to create on college campuses an atmosphere intolerant of hostility toward any discrete group of people. Required courses on racism, sexism, and ethnic diversity were only one approach. Through the advocates' lobbying efforts, numerous universities established codes delineating various forms of "forbidden speech" and inappropriate behavior; these codes were designed to protect groups from abuse and exclusion. Some universities focused on abusive or offensive language, including racial and sexual epithets. Other universities imposed more sweeping restrictions; the University of Connecticut at Storrs outlawed "inappropriately directed laughter," and Sarah Lawrence College disciplined a student for inappropriate laughter when his friend shouted "faggot" during an argument with a former roommate.

Critics of political correctness asserted that the movement's advocates were themselves ethnocentric and intolerant of opinions at variance from their own. They argued that Western civilization, with its cosmopolitan nature and absorption of aspects of other cultures, was more tolerant and inclusive than the divisive and exclusive positions of multiculturalists.[69]

Opponents also complained that the course substitutions were watering down the curriculum. They argued that politically correct educators were depriving students of the opportunity to grapple with civilization's greatest thinkers by substituting, in the name of multiculturalism, inferior works by

As the world's leading immigrant-receiving nation, the United States creates a social climate in which ethnic intergroup cooperation often exists in stark contrast to the ethnic hostilities in the same groups' homelands. Although visible in other U.S. settings as well, such scenes are especially commonplace on college campuses, which promote cultural diversity, such as this Washington University in St. Louis student fair.

(*Source:* © Judy S. Gelles, Stock, Boston)

female and minority writers to replace those of "dead white males." Allan Bloom's *The Closing of the American Mind,* Roger Kimball's *Tenured Radicals,* Charles Sykes's *The Hollow Men,* and Dinesh D'Souza's *Illiberal Education: The Politics of Race and Sex on Campus* attacked what they saw as the suppression of intellectual freedom on the nation's campuses.[70]

Advocates of cultural diversity countered that the traditionalists and neoconservatives were posing as defenders of intellectual rigor and the preeminence of the canon of great books merely to preserve their own cultural and political supremacy. And of course, both sides charged that the other was pursuing personal economic advantage in seeking to have its courses declared part of the core curriculum and the other side's courses merely elective.

Political correctness became a controversial term with praiseworthy or derogatory connotations depending on one's perspective. The hottest debates focused on campus speech codes, which opponents maintained violated First Amendment rights of free speech. The issue raised here is similar to the one discussed in Chapter 5 in connection with the concept of justice. At what point do efforts to secure justice for one group (in this case, eliminating biased expression) infringe on the rights of others?

In 1992, the U.S. Supreme Court issued a decision that, according to First Amendment experts, swept away all speech codes at public institutions. The case, *R.A.V. v. City of St. Paul,* involved a hate crime committed by a teenage skinhead who burned a cross on the lawn of the only Black family in a working-class neighborhood. Unanimously, the court overturned that city's ordinance banning behavior that "arouses anger, alarm or resentment in others on the basis of race, color, creed, religion or gender." In the majority opinion, Justice Antonin Scalia made clear that attempting to regulate expression (speech) in any manner that reflects the government's hostility or favoritism to particular messages is unconstitutional. Because most college speech codes rest on a similar laundry list of offense categories, they are presumably in trouble. Since then, many colleges have returned to general student-conduct codes instead of specific ones dealing with speech.

Political correctness may be muted somewhat on college campuses, but it lives on in academia and well as in other public arenas. Often appropriate and at times excessive, it continues to have its admirers and detractors. For example, shortly after the terrorist attacks in New York City and Washington, the Berkeley, California, fire chief banned the display of U.S. flags on city fire trucks so as not to offend anyone in the community, and in an "act of tolerance," the library director at Florida Gulf Coast University ordered her staff not to sport stickers declaring "Proud to Be an American" to avoid offending international students. Howls of protest forced both individuals to issue public apologies and rescind their orders. These are but two instances of overzealous guardians of tolerance undermining the laudatory goals of political correctness by their own intolerance.[71]

Racial and Ethnic Diversity in the Future

The Census Bureau, assuming that present demographic trends will continue, projects a dramatic change in the composition of U.S. society by the mid-twenty-first century. Its estimates include an average of 1 million immigrants and 200,000 undocumented aliens entering the country each year for the next five decades. Fertility rates, currently at 2.1, were adjusted by race and factored into the population projections.[72]

However, the Census Bureau reports that the cumulative effects of immigration will be more important than births to people already living in the United States. By the mid-twenty-first century, it said, 21 percent of the population—an estimated 82 million—will be either immigrants who arrived after 1991 or children of those immigrants.

By 2050, Hispanics will number about 98.2 million, or 24 percent of the total population. The Census Bureau projects that African Americans will then number about 53.5 million, or 13 percent (Figure 7.3). All data reflect midrange projections, not high or low estimates.

The nation's Asian and Pacific Islander population will grow to about 37.6 million, or 9 percent, by 2050. Native Americans will have increased to about 4.4 million by then, slightly more than 1 percent of the total. The number of non-Hispanic Whites will be 213 million by 2050, or 53 percent of the population.

Some observers have reacted to these projections with alarm, using them to argue for immigration restrictions. Others relish the thought of U.S. society becoming more diverse. These projections, however, have some limitations, not the least of which is their assumption that conditions worldwide will remain constant 50 or more years into the future. Certainly, 50 years ago, no one would have predicted the current birth, death, and migration patterns that currently affect the United States. A forecast about the year 2050, then, is anything but certain.

Even more significant is the high probability that these Census Bureau projections will fall victim to the **Dillingham Flaw.** Who is to say that today's group categories will have the same meaning in the mid-twenty-first century? Fifty years ago, Italian, Polish, and Slavic Americans were still members of distinct minority groups that lacked economic, political, and social power. They displayed all the classic characteristics of minority groups: ascribed status, endogamy, unequal treatment, and visibility. Today, they are mostly in the mainstream, displaying traits of civic, marital, and structural assimilation. Like European Americans who intermarried earlier, those whose ancestry is Italian, Polish, and Slavic are now mostly a blend of other nationalities. Fifty

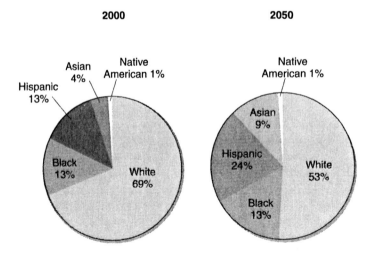

FIGURE 7.3 America's Growing Diversity

Source: U.S. Bureau of the Census middle-range projections.

years from now, the same may be true of other groups, such as Hispanics. Two generations from now, Americans will likely view one another very differently from how we do now.

Indicators of Ethnoreligious Change

Although the demographic patterns of fertility, mortality, and migration are helpful in making projections, other patterns give reason for caution in predicting the future.

Interethnic Marriages. Our expectation that Hispanic Americans will marry outside their ethnic group, as have European Americans, finds support in the process that is already under way. In 2000, more than 1.7 million Hispanic Americans were married to someone of non-Hispanic origin, up 96 percent from 891,000 in 1980.[73] That is approximately 5 percent of the adult Hispanic American population, not an overwhelming proportion but nonetheless a growing one. The children born from these exogamous marriages are obviously of mixed ethnic heritage, which suggests that one day Hispanic American may be no more a separate ethnic category than Italian, Polish, or Slavic now is.

Interracial Marriages. So far, we have not succeeded in eliminating the racial barrier, so in 50 years that barrier may still exist. Nevertheless, one present-day trend suggests that our current simplistic racial categories are already obsolete. In 2000, 2.5 percent of all marriages in the continental United States were interracial, compared to 0.7 percent in 1970. By then, interracially married couples numbered over 1.4 million, more than one-fourth of them (363,000) Black–White couples—nearly six times more than the 65,000 in 1970. Whites married to a non-White spouse of a race other than Black (most often, Asian) grew from 233,000 to 1,051,000. Couples consisting of Blacks married to a non-Black spouse of a race other than White increased from 12,000 to 50,000.[74]

Researchers are developing some interesting findings about interracial relationships. George and Sherelyn Yancey report that biracial relationships seem to form along the same lines as same-race relationships—that race is only an aesthetic factor, similar to others' preference of hair color or eye color.[75] They also suggested that, because interracial dating brings together individuals from different cultures, such relationships may increase appreciation for the partner's culture and promote healthy racial relations through marital assimilation.[76] Richard Lewis, Jr., George Yancey, and Siri S. Bletzer found that persons with a premarital history of biracial dating said cross-racial personal and sexual attractiveness, along with ease of talking, were important spouse selection factors.[77]

Over 3 million biracial children now live in the United States, and many adult Blacks and Whites also claim mixed racial ancestry. If we add to the biracial offspring from these marriages those Latinos, Filipinos, Native

Americans, and Hawaiians with multiracial ancestry, we can readily understand why past Census Bureau single-race classifications were inadequate.
Fortunately, the census in 2000 for the first time enabled people to identify
themselves as members of more than one racial group, allowing the Bureau
to report more accurately the multiracial reality that contributes to U.S. diversity and aiding demographers in making projections in this area. As a result, 6.8 million Americans said they belonged to more than one race in the
2000 census. As Kathleen Korgen reports:

> Biracial Americans today face choices in racial identity never available to pre-
> ceding generations. Now the nation must adjust to their growing resolve to iden-
> tify with both sides of their racial heritage.[78]

Religion and Migration. Earlier immigration waves transformed the United
States from an almost exclusively Protestant country into a land of three major
faiths: Catholic, Jewish, and Protestant. Because religion is often closely intertwined with ethnicity, current migration patterns offer clues about the religious
preferences of future Americans if current trends continue.

Latino and Filipino migration may increase the Catholic population
from the current one-fourth to one-third by 2050. Migration from Africa, Asia,
and the Middle East may increase the Muslim population from 1 percent of
the total to 5 percent. Other projections are that the Jewish population will decline from 2 percent to 1 percent and the Protestant population from 56 percent to 49 percent; the populations of other religions—including Buddhism,
Hinduism, and Sikhism—will increase from 4 percent to 5 percent.[79] Even if
these predictions turn out to be somewhat inaccurate, the future will show
greater religious diversity than the present does.

Caution is needed in accepting these predictions, of course, because the
Dillingham Flaw of oversimplified generalizations and the imposition of
present-day sensibilities may lead to a misreading of the eventual reality. Since
religious intermarriage is now increasing among followers of all faiths, and
since the nonreligious segment of society is also growing, we may find a very
different future with respect to religion than we can accurately project.

Beyond Tomorrow

Diversity is the word that best describes the past, present, and future of the
United States. United by a core culture and shared beliefs in certain ideals, the
nation's peoples have not always understood their common bond or openly accepted one another as equals. As the dual realities of assimilation and pluralism
continue to pull people seemingly in two directions at once, few people recognize that they are witnessing a recurring set of historical patterns. Instead, some
voices cry out again against immigration, brand the newcomers as "unassimilable," and express fear for the character and cohesiveness of society.

Despite some progress, the United States has never fully resolved its race relations problems. As it becomes a more multiracial society than ever before, it may see a worsening of race relations. We've seen some indicators here: Black–Asian and Black–Latino conflicts in addition to Black–White conflicts, as well as polar-opposite perceptions between Blacks and Whites of the O. J. Simpson trial and verdict. Perhaps, though, the situation will improve with deconstruction of the rigid racial categories that presently promote greater social distance and with more sharing of power through the increased presence of non-White Americans in elective offices and other policymaking positions.

As we approach the future, we do so with the educational attainment of all Americans rising. If knowledge is power, perhaps that reality will lead us to greater appreciation and tolerance for one another. This book has been an attempt to enhance that understanding. We need to comprehend the larger context and patterns within which the dynamics of intergroup relations exist. We need to realize that pluralism has always been part of the U.S. experience and does not threaten either the assimilation process or the cohesiveness of society. We need to recognize that race and ethnicity are simply other people's humanity. When we reach that level of understanding, we will be able to acknowledge that diversity is the nation's strength, not its weakness; and when that happens, our society will be even stronger.

KEY TERMS

Bilingual education
Bilingualism
Dillingham Flaw
English as a Second Language
   (ESL) programs

English immersion programs
English-plus programs
Multiculturalism
Paraprofessionals
Political correctness

REVIEW QUESTIONS

1. What are some of the explanations for ethnic consciousness? Which seems most plausible? Why?

2. Discuss ethnicity as a social process, applying the concepts of assimilation and pluralism to your discussion.

3. What do current immigration patterns indicate? Is immigration a problem for native-born U.S. residents? Explain.

4. What are the pros and cons of bilingual education?

5. Describe the varying viewpoints about multiculturalism and political correctness.

6. What is the future of ethnicity in the United States?

SUGGESTED READINGS

Allen, James P., and Turner, Eugene J. *We the People: An Atlas of America's Ethnic Diversity.* New York: Macmillan, 1998.
An effective atlas with 110 maps showing the migration and population distribution of sixty-seven ethnic groups.

Gordon, Milton M. *Assimilation in American Life.* New York: Oxford University Press, 1964.
A highly influential and still pertinent book analyzing the role of race and ethnicity in American life and the different forms assimilation takes.

Hollinger, David A. *Postethnic America: Beyond Multiculturalism,* rev. ed. New York: Basic Books, 2000.
A review of current issues in the multiculturalist–nativist debate from a historical perspective, advocating a middle-ground cosmopolitan approach and suggesting the need to find common ground, not just to tolerate one another.

Lind, Michael. *The Next American Nation: The New Nationalism and the Fourth American Revolution,* reprint ed. New York: Free Press, 1996.
A wide-ranging, thought-provoking proposal for a coherent, unified national identity based on recognition that the forces of nationalism and the ideal of a transracial melting pot need not conflict with one another.

Miller, John J. *The Unmaking of Americans: How Multiculturalism Has Undermined America's Assimilationist Ethic.* New York: Simon & Schuster, 1998.
A history of Americanization from its organized beginnings around 1907 to the current controversy on multiculturalism and a call for renewed Americanization efforts to sustain higher immigration.

Mindel, Charles H., Habenstein, Robert W., and Wright, Roosevelt, Jr. (eds.). *Ethnic Families in America: Patterns and Variations,* 4th ed. New York: Prentice Hall, 1997.
An excellent portrait of U.S. racial and ethnic groups, their family characteristics, and the impact of the feminist movement on ethnic family life.

Novak, Michael. *Unmeltable Ethnics: Politics & Culture in American Life,* 2d. ed. New Brunswick, N.J.: Transaction Publishers, 1966.
A provocative and influential book examining assimilation problems of White ethnics and their reactions to efforts on behalf of contemporaneous identified minorities.

Parrillo, Vincent N. *Diversity in America.* Thousand Oaks, Calif.: Pine Forge Press, 1996.
A brief look at our past, present, and future, with emphasis on immigration, multiculturalism, assimilation versus pluralism, and national identity. Includes a full discussion of the Dillingham Flaw.

Sowell, Thomas. *Ethnic America: A History,* reprint ed. New York: Basic Books, 1983.
A fine comparative analysis of major racial and ethnic groups in the United States, with discussion of reasons for their varying success in U.S. society.

Thernstrom, Stephan (ed.). *Harvard Encyclopedia of American Ethnic Groups.* Cambridge, Mass.: Harvard University Press, 1980.
An outstanding, comprehensive reference book for information about hundreds of U.S. racial and ethnic groups.

Glossary

Abstract typification The generalization of people or things into broad categories.

Acceptance A minority response to prejudice and discrimination; based on powerlessness, fear for personal safety, desire for economic security, or fatalism.

Accommodation (pluralistic) theory A tendency to accept the situation as it exists, without seeking to change it or make others conform; pluralism.

Acculturation The process by which a group changes its distinctive cultural traits to conform with those of the host society.

Action-oriented level of prejudice A positive or negative predisposition to engage in discriminatory behavior toward members of a particular group.

Affirmative action Deliberate efforts to improve minority representation, as well as their economic and educational opportunities.

Afrocentrism A viewpoint emphasizing African culture and its influence on Western civilization and U.S. black behavior.

Amalgamation (melting-pot) theory The biological and cultural blending of two or more groups of people into a distinct new type; the melting-pot theory.

Americanization movement The effort to have ethnic groups quickly give up their cultural traits and adopt those of the dominant U.S. group.

Anglo-conformity A behavioral adherence to the established white Anglo-Saxon Protestant prototype; what many ethnocentric U.S. residents mean by assimilation.

Annihilation The extermination of a specific group of people.

Ascribed status One's socially defined, unchangeable position in a society based on such arbitrary factors as age, sex, race, or family background.

Assimilation (majority-conformity) theory The process by which members of racial or ethnic minorities are able to function within a society without indicating any marked cultural, social, or personal differences from the people of the majority group.

Asylee An alien found in a country or port of entry who is unable or unwilling to return to his or her country of origin, or to seek the protection of that country, because of persecution or a well-founded fear of persecution.

Authoritarian personality A set of distinct personality traits, including conformity, insecurity, and intolerance, said to be common to many prejudiced people.

Avoidance A minority-group response to prejudice and discrimination by migrating or withdrawing to escape further problems; a majority-group attempt to minimize contact with specific minority groups through social or spatial segregation.

Bilingual education Teaching subjects in both English and the student's native language to develop fluency in both.

Bilingualism Fluency in two languages.

Bipolarization Two opposite trends occurring simultaneously.

Black codes Southern state laws enacted during Reconstruction to keep blacks in a condition close to slavery.

Brain drain Emigration of large numbers of skilled workers, professionals, or scientists who are badly needed by their home country.

Categoric knowing A stereotype of others based merely on information obtained visually and perhaps verbally.

Celibacy Refraining from any form of sexual intimacy.

Chain migration A sequential flow of immigrants to a locality previously settled by friends, relatives, or other compatriots.

Child care Supervised, quality care for preschool youngsters while one or both parents work.

Civil religion A shared, nondenominational belief system incorporated into the culture.

Cognitive level of prejudice Beliefs and perceptions about other racial or ethnic groups.

Conflict theory A sociological perspective emphasizing conflict as an important influence and permanent feature of life.

Convergent subculture A subgroup gradually becoming completely integrated into the dominant culture.

Cultural assimilation Changing cultural patterns of behavior to those of the host society; acculturation.

Cultural determinism A theory that a group's culture explains its position in society and its achievements or lack thereof.

Cultural differentiation Differences between cultures that make one group distinguishable from another.

Cultural diffusion The spread of ideas, inventions, and practices from one culture to another.

Cultural drift A gradual change in the values, attitudes, customs, and beliefs of the members of a society.

Cultural nationalism A movement toward black solidarity through encouragement of African culture and values.

Cultural pluralism Two or more culturally distinct groups coexisting in relative harmony.

Cultural transmission The passing on of a society's culture from one generation to another.

Culture The values, attitudes, customs, beliefs, and habits shared by members of a society.

Culture-of-poverty A controversial viewpoint arguing that the disorganization and pathology of lower-class culture is self-perpetuating through cultural transmission.

Culture shock Feelings of disorientation, anxiety, and a sense of being threatened when unpreparedly brought into contact with another culture.

Cumulative causation Gunnar Myrdal's term for the vicious-circle process in which prejudice and discrimination mutually "cause" each other, thereby continuing and intensifying the cycle.

De facto segregation Physical separation of a group that is entrenched in customs and practices.

Defiance A peaceful or violent action to challenge openly what a group considers a discriminatory practice.

De jure segregation Physical separation of a group that is established by law.

Deviance Characteristics or behavior violating social norms and therefore negatively valued by many people in that society.

Dialectical relationship A struggle between two opposing forces.

Dichotomy A division into two, possibility contrasting, parts.

Dignidad Hispanic cultural value that the dignity of all humans entitles them to a measure of respect.

Dillingham Flaw Any inaccurate comparison based on simplistic categorizations and anachronistic judgments.

Discrimination Differential and unequal treatment of other groups of people, usually along racial, religious, or ethnic lines.

Displaced aggression Hostility directed against a powerless group rather than against the more powerful cause of the feelings of hostility.

Dominant group Any culturally or physically distinctive social grouping possessing economic, political, and social power, and discriminating against a subordinate minority group.

Dysfunction A disruption of the equilibrium in a social system or of the functioning of some unit within the system.

Economic determinism A theory that a society's economic base establishes its culture and general characteristics.

Ecumenical movement An effort to find universality among all faiths.

Emigration Act of leaving one's country or region to settle in another.

Emotional level of prejudice The feelings aroused in a group by another racial or ethnic group.

Endogamy The tendency for people to marry only within their own social group.

English-as-a-second-language (ESL) programs Teaching children English competency as one would teach English speakers another language.

English-immersion programs Placing children in English-only classes, where the teacher facilitates their acquisition of the language.

English-plus programs A dual approach under which foreign-language students learn English and native-born U.S. students develop foreign-language competency.

Entrepreneurs People who set about to carry out any enterprise.

Ethclass A social-group classification based on a combination of race, religion, social class, and regional residence.

Ethnic antagonism Various forms of intergroup hostility, including ideologies, beliefs, behavior, and institutionalized practices.

Ethnic consciousness A self-awareness of ethnic identity; the deliberate maintenance of one's culture in another cultural environment.

Ethnic group A group of people who share a common religion, nationality, culture, and/or language.

Ethnic stratification Structured inequality of different groups with different access to social rewards as a result of their status in the social hierarchy.

Ethnic subcultures Ongoing lifestyles and interaction patterns separate from the larger society that are based on religious or other cultural group memberships.

Ethnicity A cultural concept in which a large number of people who share learned or acquired traits and close social interaction regard themselves and are regarded by others as constituting a single group on that basis.

Ethnocentrism A tendency to judge other cultures or subcultures by the standards of one's own culture.

Ethnogenesis A process in which immigrants hold onto some homeland values, adapt others, and adopt some values of the host country.

Ethnophaulism A derogatory word or expression used to describe or refer to a racial or ethnic group.

Ethnoviolence Behavior ranging from verbal harassment and threats to murder against people targeted solely because of their race, religion, ethnicity, or sexual orientation.

Eurocentrism A viewpoint emphasizing Western civilization, history, literature, and other humanities.

Exploitation The selfish use of the labor of others for profit at their expense.

Expulsion The forced removal of a group of people from an area.

Extended family A family unit that includes other kin in addition to parents and children.

Exurbs Newest ring of settlement beyond the old suburbs.

False consciousness Holding attitudes that do not accurately reflect the objective facts of a situation.

Fast track When women delay child-bearing or forgo motherhood entirely to give full commitment to management to earn promotions over other candidates.

Feminization of poverty A term describing female-headed households living in poverty.

First-generation American Someone born in another country who migrated to the United States.

Flex-time An arrangement that allows workers, within predetermined limits, to set their own working hours.

Functional theory A sociological perspective emphasizing societal order and stability, with harmonious interdependent parts.

Gemeinschaft A small, tradition-dominated community characterized by intimate primary relationships and strong feelings of group loyalty.

Gender-role expectations Anticipated behaviors because of one's gender.

Glass ceiling A real but unseen discriminatory policy that limits female upward mobility into top management positions.

Group A collectivity of people closely interacting with one another on the basis of shared expectations about behavior.

Hansen's law A theory that what the child of an immigrant wishes to forget, the grandchild wishes to remember; also called the three-generation hypothesis.

Ideology A generalized set of beliefs that collectively explains and justifies the interests of those who hold them.

Immigration Movement of people into a new country to become permanent residents.

Indigenous Person, plant, or animal in its natural, native habitat.

Ingroup The group to which an individual belongs and feels loyal.

Institutional discrimination Unequal treatment of subordinate groups inherent in the ongoing operations of society's institutions.

Institutionalization Patterns of behavior organized to meet a basic need of a society, such as family, education, religion, economics, or politics.

Institutionalized racism Unequal treatment of a racial group inherent in the ongoing operations of society's institutions.

Interactionist theory A sociological perspective emphasizing the shared interpretations and interaction patterns in everyday life.

Intergenerational mobility The change in social status within a family from one generation to the next.

Internal-colonialism theory A concept explaining the experiences of Blacks, Chicanos, and Native Americans in terms of economic exploitation and rigid stratification.

Invasion–succession The ecological process in which one group displaces another group in a residential area or business activity.

Jigsaw method A teaching technique that creates interdependent cooperative learning groups.

Jim Crow laws Southern-state segregation laws, passed in the 1890s and early 1900s, which covered use of all public facilities, including schools, restaurants, transportation, waiting rooms, rest rooms, drinking fountains, and parks.

Kye A rotating credit fund enabling Korean Americans to start or expand their businesses.

Latent functions Hidden, unexpected results within a social structure.

Linguistic relativity The recognition that different languages dissect and present reality differently.

Machismo Value orientation defining masculinity in varying terms of virility, honor, and providing for one's family.

Manifest functions Obvious and intended results within a social structure.

Marginality The situation of individuals who are the product of one culture but are attempting to live within another, and therefore are not fully a part of either one.

Marianismo Value orientation defining feminine virtue as accepting male dominance and emphasizing family responsibilities.

Marital assimilation (amalgamation) A pattern of intermarriage of minority-group members with dominant-group members.

Material culture All physical objects created by members of a society and the meanings/significance attached to them.

Matrilineal When descent and inheritance pass through the female side of the family.

Matrilocal The custom of married partners settling in or near the household of the wife's family.

Melting-pot theory *See* Amalgamation (melting-pot) theory.

Middleman minority A minority group occupying an intermediate occupational position in trade or commerce between the top and bottom strata.

Migration Movement of people into and out of a specified area, either within a country or from one country to another.

Miscegenation Mixture of races by sexual union.

Minority group A culturally and physically distinctive group that experiences unequal treatment, an ascribed status, a sense of shared identity, and that practices endogamy.

Mommy track When women try to juggle both family and work, which often slows or halts their upward mobility within the company.

Mortality rate Number of deaths per 1,000 people in a given year.

Multiculturalism Ranges from efforts for an all-inclusive curriculum to an emphasis on separatist pluralism.

Nativist One who advocates a policy of protecting the interests of native inhabitants against those of immigrants.

Negative self-image The result of social conditioning, differential treatment, or both, causing people or groups to believe themselves inferior.

"New" immigrants A term used by the Dillingham Commission (1907–1911) to identify immigrants from southern, central, and eastern Europe.

Nondenominational Interchurch; not pertaining to any particular faith.

Nonmaterial culture Abstract human creations and their meanings/significance in life.

Norms The internalized rules of conduct that embody the fundamental expectations of society.

Objectivity Disciplining oneself to examine and interpret reality with the least possible amount of personal bias and distortion.

Occupational mobility Ability to change one's job position with regard to status and economic reward.

"Old" immigrants A term used by the Dillingham Commission (1907–1911) to identify immigrants from northern and western Europe.

Outgroup Any group to which an individual does not belong or feel loyal.

Pan-Indianism Social movement in which tribes not united by kinship join together in a common cause.

Paralinguistic signals Use of sounds but not words to convey distinct meanings.

Parallel social institutions A subcultural replication of institutions of the larger society, such as churches, schools, and organizations.

Paraprofessionals Aides lacking certification, licensing and/or a minimum educational level who work with qualified professionals; one example is a teacher's aide.

Paternalism A condescending treatment of adults, managing and regulating their affairs as a father would handle his children's affairs.

Pentecostal faith A form of evangelical Christianity that inspires a sense of belonging through worship participation.

Persistent subculture A subgroup adhering to its own way of life and resisting absorption into the dominant culture.

Pluralism A state in which minorities can maintain their distinctive subcultures and simultaneously interact with relative equality in the larger society.

Political correctness Movement to create an atmosphere in which abusive or offensive language directed toward any social group is not tolerated. Critics use the term to attack its First Amendment infringements.

Polygyny A form of marriage joining one male with two or more females.

Power-differential theory The theory that intergroup relations depend on the relative power of the migrant group and the indigenous group.

Prejudice A system of negative beliefs, feelings, and action orientations regarding a certain group or groups of people.

Primary group A small number of people who interact with one another in close, personal, and meaningful relationships.

Primary structural assimilation Integration in which dominant- and minority-group members share close, personal interactions in churches, families, social clubs, or gatherings.

Primogeniture Inheritance or succession by the eldest son.

Push–pull factors A combination of negative elements at home and positive inducements elsewhere that encourage migration from one place to another.

Race A categorization in which a large number of people sharing visible physical characteristics regard themselves or are regarded by others as a single group on that basis.

Racial stratification Differences in socioeconomic status within a society that is structured according to race.

Racism False linkage between biology and sociocultural behavior to assert the superiority of one race.

Reciprocal typifications People's categorizations of one another based on their shared experiences.

Redlining Unwillingness of some banks to make loans in lower-income minority neighborhoods.

Reference group A group to which people may or may not belong but to which they refer when evaluating themselves and their behavior.

Refugee Any person outside his/her country of orgin in who is unable or unwilling to return because of persecution or a well-founded fear of persecution.

Relative deprivation A lack of resources or rewards in one's standard of living in comparison with others in the society.

Reputational method A technique for measuring social class by questioning people about others' social standing.

Role Behavior determined by the status the individual occupies.

Role entrapment The culturally defined need to be "feminine" that prevents many women from doing things that would help them achieve success and self-realization.

Scapegoating Placing blame on others for something that is not their fault.

Scientific method A process involving repeated observation, precise measurement, careful description, theory formulation, and gathering further information based on questions that followed from those theories.

Second-generation American A child born in the United States of immigrant parents; can also refer to a child born elsewhere but raised from a young age in the United States by immigrant parents.

Secondary group A collectivity of people who interact on an impersonal or limited emotional basis for some practical or specific purpose.

Secondary structural assimilation Integration in which dominant- and minority-group members share the more impersonal public sphere of civic, school, recreational, or work settings.

Selective perception A tendency to see or accept only information that agrees with one's value orientations or that is consistent with one's attitudes about other groups.

Self-fulfilling prophecy A prediction that so influences behavior that the consequence is a realization of the prediction.

Self-justification A defense mechanism whereby people denigrate another person or group to justify maltreating them.

Separatist pluralism Effort to seek specific, separate group identity rather than a collective U.S. national identity.

Sexism Institutionalized prejudice and discrimination based on gender.

Shunning An Amish social-control practice of complete avoidance, including even eye contact.

Shuttle migration Large-scale movement back and forth between two countries.

Situational ethnicity Ethnic consciousness generated by residence, special events, work relationships, or working-class lifestyle.

Social change Any alteration, whether gradual or swift, in patterns of social behavior or in social structure.

Social class A categorization designating people's places in the stratification hierarchy on the basis of similarities in income, property, power, status, and lifestyle.

Social conditioning A socialization process through which people are molded to fit into the social system.

Social construction of reality The process by which definitions of reality are socially created, objectified, internalized, and then taken for granted.

Social discrimination Exclusion of outgroup members from close relationships with ingroup members.

Social distance The degree of closeness or remoteness one desires in interaction with members of a particular group.

Social hierarchy The stratified levels of status within a group or society.

Social identity theory Holds that ingroup members enhance their self-image by considering their group better than others.

Social interaction The reciprocal process by which people act and react toward one another.

Socialization process The process of social interaction by which people acquire personality and learn the culture or subculture of their group.

Social mobility Change from one status to another in a stratified society.

Social norms Generally shared rules or expectations of what is and is not proper behavior.

Social organization Any grouping formed to provide a means of social interaction among individuals.

Social ostracism Excluding a person or persons from social privileges and interaction.

Social segregation A situation in which participation in social, fraternal, service, and other types of activities is confined to members of the ingroup.

Social status Position one holds in society or other grouping.

Social stratification The hierarchy within a society based on the unequal distribution of resources, power, or prestige.

Social structure The organized patterns of behavior in a social system governing people's interrelationships.

Society A group of individuals who share a common culture and territory.

Socioeconomic status (SES) A social-prestige ranking determined by numerous factors, including occupation, income, educational background, and place of residence.

Sojourners Those who stay temporarily.

Sovereign Having independent power or authority.

Spatial segregation The physical separation of a minority group from the rest of society, such as in housing or education.

Split-labor-market theory A concept explaining ethnic antagonism on the basis of conflict between higher-paid and lower-paid labor.

Status positions Places a person holds in society as determined by class structure, gender, and occupational roles.

Stereotype An oversimplified generalization attributing certain traits or characteristics to any person in a group without regard to individual differences.

Structural assimilation Large-scale entrance of minority-group members into primary-group relationships with the host society in its social organizations and institutions.

Structural differentiation Status distinctions for different racial and ethnic groups entrenched within the social system.

Structural discrimination Differential treatment of groups of people that is entrenched in the institutions of a society.

Structural pluralism Coexistence of racial and ethnic groups in separate subsocieties also divided along social class and regional boundaries.

Subculture A group that shares in the overall culture of a society while retaining its own distinctive traditions and lifestyle.

Subjectivity Observing the world from one's own viewpoint, as shaped by cultural input, personal opinion, emotions, and experiences.

Subordinate Less powerful than another group that possesses political, economic, or technological advantages.

Superordinate Possessing superior political, economic, or technological power.

Symbol Anything that can be understood to signify something else, such as a word or gesture that represents or conveys an attitude or feeling.

Symbolic ethnicity Identifying with one's heritage through ethnic foods, holidays, and political and social activities.

Symbolic interaction The use of symbols—such as signs, gestures, and language—through which people interact with one another.

Third-generation American Someone born in the United States whose grandparents migrated to the United States.

Thomas theorem An observation that if people define situations as real, the situations become real in their consequences.

Three-generation hypothesis *See* Hansen's law.

Triple-melting-pot theory The concept that intermarriage is occurring among various nationalities within the three major religious groupings.

Undocumented alien Illegal immigrant without a green card or visa authorizing entry.

Upward mobility An improvement in one's socioeconomic position.

Value neutrality An ideal state, never fully possible, in which the observer eliminates all personal bias in order to be completely objective.

Values Socially shared conceptions of what is good, desirable, and proper or bad, undesirable, and improper.

Value-stretch approach Adoption of values representing realistic levels of attainment.

Vicious-circle phenomenon Dynamics of intergroup relations where prejudice and discrimination serve as reciprocal stimuli and responses to reinforce one another.

Xenophobia The irrational fear of or contempt for strangers or foreigners.